Major Problems
in the
Civil War and Reconstruction

MAJOR PROBLEMS IN AMERICAN HISTORY SERIES

GENERAL EDITOR
THOMAS G. PATERSON

Major Problems
in the
Civil War and Reconstruction

DOCUMENTS AND ESSAYS

EDITED BY
MICHAEL PERMAN
UNIVERSITY OF ILLINOIS AT CHICAGO

D. C. HEATH AND COMPANY
Lexington, Massachusetts   Toronto

Acquisitions Editor: James Miller
Developmental Editor: Sylvia Mallory
Production Editor: Tina V. Beazer
Designer: Sally Thompson Steele
Production Coordinator: Charles Dutton
Permissions Editor: Margaret Roll

Cover: *Flag of Fort Sumter, October 20, 1863* by Conrad Wise Chapman.
     (The Museum of the Confederacy, Richmond, VA.)
     Photograph by Katherine Wetzel.

Published simultaneously in Canada.

Printed in the United States of America.

International Standard Book Number: 0–669–20148–0

Library of Congress Catalog Card Number: 90–81121

10 9 8 7 6 5 4 3 2 1

Preface

The sectional conflict of the mid-nineteenth century was quite probably the greatest crisis in the history of the United States. Consequently, courses on this momentous episode—usually called Civil War and Reconstruction— have become a staple and necessary feature of the history curriculum in American colleges and universities.

This anthology, a volume in the Major Problems in American History Series, is intended to provide students and instructors with essential, read- able, and provocative documents and essays on the issues of the period. Since the Civil War has probably been written about more than any other event in the nation's history, the amount of literature and documentation about it is simply immense. Deciding what to include therefore involved difficult choices.

The criterion for selecting the essays was their quality as pieces of historical writing and interpretation as well as their contribution to ongoing debates among historians. For the documents, the aim was to choose those that either related to the essays in some way, or conveyed the spirit of the contemporary issues under discussion, or simply were important in their own right. Some of these documents—or primary sources, as historians call them—are very well known and so significant that they could not be excluded. Most of them, however, are less familiar, and several have not been previously published.

Like the other volumes in the series, *Major Problems in the Civil War and Reconstruction* is organized into chapters, each one of which covers a significant topic or aspect of the period. Every chapter opens with a brief introduction that sets the scene and defines the central issues. The docu- ments and essays aim to provide evidence and interpretation that will enable readers to develop their own understanding and assessment of the topic, and even perhaps to formulate their own interpretation. Each chapter closes with a list of books and articles for further reading.

The chapter topics reveal the diversity and richness of the history of the Civil War and Reconstruction. Because the national crisis from roughly 1840 until 1880 centered on questions of government and public policy, it was essentially political in nature. Nevertheless, while politics may have shaped the crisis, social, cultural and economic developments coursed through it. So the anthology includes topics on a variety of aspects of the era—political, social, military, economic, cultural. In this respect, the book attempts to reflect historical reality as a whole, not just one or two facets of it.

In compiling this anthology, I incurred a number of debts and would now like to thank all the people who helped by offering information or comments.

For generously providing specifics about their own Civil War and Reconstruction courses, I am most grateful to Gabor S. Boritt of Gettysburg College; Richard O. Curry of the University of Connecticut at Storrs; David Herbert Donald of Harvard University; George Forgie of the University of Texas at Austin; William E. Gienapp of Harvard University; William Gillette of Rutgers University; William C. Harris of North Carolina State University; Herman M. Hattaway of the University of Missouri at Kansas City; Robert W. Johannsen of the University of Illinois at Urbana; Jacqueline Jones of Wellesley College; William S. McFeely of the University of Georgia; Robert E. May of Purdue University; Roger Ransom of the University of California at Riverside; Richard H. Sewell of the University of Wisconsin at Madison; Mark W. Summers of the University of Kentucky; and Sarah W. Wiggins of the University of Alabama at Tuscaloosa.

At a later stage, the outline and table of contents were evaluated. For their comments and cautions, I want to thank the following very much: Richard H. Abbott of Eastern Michigan University; William L. Barney of the University of North Carolina at Chapel Hill; Richard E. Beringer of the University of North Dakota; Mary A. DeCredico of the U.S. Naval Academy; Paul D. Escott of Wake Forest University; David R. Goldfield of the University of North Carolina at Charlotte; William C. Harris of North Carolina State University; Peter Kolchin of the University of Delaware; Mary Beth Norton of Cornell University; Thomas G. Paterson of the University of Connecticut at Storrs, the general editor of the Major Problems series; Lawrence N. Powell of Tulane University; James L. Roark of Emory University; and Emory M. Thomas of the University of Georgia.

And finally, the staff at D. C. Heath were a pleasure to work with: James Miller, history editor; Margaret Roll, permissions editor; Tina V. Beazer, production editor; and especially Sylvia Mallory, the developmental editor, whose knowledge of American history was almost as impressive as her editorial skill.

M.P.

Contents

C H A P T E R   6

Fighting the War: The Experience of the Soldiers

Page 202

D O C U M E N T S

E S S A Y S

C H A P T E R   7

Behind the Lines: Wartime Politics

Page 237

D O C U M E N T S

CHAPTER 8
Behind the Lines: Disaffection in the Confederacy
Page 278

CHAPTER 9
The Home Front: Women and the War
Page 316

C H A P T E R 10
Emancipation and Its Aftermath
Page 353

C H A P T E R 11
The Republican Party and Reconstruction Policy
Page 400

C H A P T E R   12
Reconstructing the South
Page 441

• C H A P T E R   13
The African-American Experience in the Reconstruction South
Page 474

C H A P T E R 14
The Collapse of Reconstruction
Page 525

CHAPTER 15
Economic Developments After the Civil War
Page 565

*Major Problems
in the
Civil War and Reconstruction*

CHAPTER 1

The Nature and Significance
of the American Civil War

↵

The Civil War is the one event in U.S. history with which most, if not all, Americans are familiar. The military struggle between the armies of the Union and the Confederacy and the towering figure of Abraham Lincoln, America's preeminent statesman and politician, have had immense appeal. This fascination is even shared by foreigners who often know little else about the history of the United States.

The war itself was a major military undertaking. It lasted four years, and has been characterized as the first modern war. Besides the duration and scope of the war itself, the problems that gave rise to it preoccupied the nation politically for a half-century, from 1830, or even earlier, until 1880. In a national history of just two hundred years, this constitutes a large segment of time. Consequently, understanding an episode of such significance should provide considerable insight into the nature and course of American history.

Slavery was, of course, the issue on which the conflict turned. To suggest otherwise is simply foolish. Slavery has, however, existed in many societies in ancient and modern times, yet it did not necessarily endanger their survival. The outbreak of a massive civil war in the United States cannot therefore be explained solely by slavery itself. Rather, there had to have been other factors to account for this particular outcome. Among them are distinctive features of slavery as it existed in America, namely that slavery was confined to a specific geographic location, that it challenged certain widely held values and interests, and that the debate over it occurred within a particular institutional framework. These circumstances gave focus and context to the debate over southern slavery, transforming it into an internecine conflict over the fate of the nation itself.

The exact nature of this conflict has been a continuing source of dispute among historians. Their uncertainty is evident in the variety of terms they have employed to describe the entire episode. In addition to "civil war," it has been referred to as "the war between the states," "the sectional conflict," "the war for southern independence," "the war of secession," "the war of the rebellion," and "the war for the Union." Each of these descriptions has a connotation that offers a different explanation or account of what the struggle was *about. Moreover, on this historical issue, as on all significant problems concerning the interpretation of events and developments in the past, there cannot be a definitive or final "verdict of history."*

D O C U M E N T S

In public addresses throughout the war, the two heads of state, Lincoln and Davis, tried frequently to explain to their citizens what the war was about. In the first selection, President Jefferson Davis presents his government's view of the nature of the coming war in his Message to the Confederate Congress of April 29, 1861, in the aftermath of the Confederacy's firing on Fort Sumter. The second document is President Abraham Lincoln's celebrated address of November 19, 1863, dedicating the battlefield cemetery at Gettysburg, Pennsylvania. Lincoln offers a succinct but profound assessment of the war's meaning and significance.

Confederate President Jefferson Davis on the Issues of the War, April 1861

. . . We feel that our cause is just and holy; we protest solemnly in the face of mankind that we desire peace at any sacrifice save that of honor and independence; we seek no conquest, no aggrandizement, no concession of any kind from the States with which we were lately confederated; all we ask is to be let alone; that those who never held power over us shall not now attempt our subjugation by arms. This we will, this we must, resist to the direst extremity. The moment that this pretension is abandoned the sword will drop from our grasp, and we shall be ready to enter into treaties of amity and commerce that cannot but be mutually beneficial. So long as this pretension is maintained, with a firm reliance on that Divine Power which covers with its protection the just cause, we will continue to struggle for our inherent right to freedom, independence, and self-government. . . .

President Abraham Lincoln on the Meaning of the War: The Gettysburg Address, November 1863

Four score and seven years ago our fathers brought forth on this continent, a new nation, conceived in liberty, and dedicated to the proposition that all men are created equal.

Now we are engaged in a great civil war, testing whether that nation, or any nation so conceived and so dedicated, can long endure. We are met on a great battlefield of that war. We have come to dedicate a portion of that field, as a final resting place for those who here gave their lives that that nation might live. It is altogether fitting and proper that we should do this.

But, in a larger sense, we cannot dedicate—we cannot consecrate— we cannot hallow—this ground. The brave men, living and dead, who struggled here, have consecrated it, far above our poor power to add or detract. The world will little note, nor long remember what we say here, but it can never forget what they did here. It is for us the living, rather, to be dedicated here to the unfinished work which they who fought here have thus far so nobly advanced. It is rather for us to be here dedicated to the great task remaining before us—that from these honored dead we take increased devotion—that we here highly resolve that these dead shall not have died in vain—that this nation, under God, shall have a new birth of freedom—and that government of the people, by the people, for the people, shall not perish from the earth.

⤶ E S S A Y S

Three approaches to discovering the character and impact of the American Civil War are presented here. In the first essay, the late David M. Potter of Stanford University highlights the significance of the conflict by placing it in the context of nineteenth-century European liberalism and nationalism. The second piece is by Arthur Bestor of the University of Washington who argues that the Civil War is best understood as a constitutional crisis, a crisis of such fundamental and far-reaching proportions that it brought into question the foundations of the American system of government. Finally, Eugene D. Genovese and Elizabeth Fox-Genovese place the South's struggle to protect its ''peculiar institution'' in the wider context of slave systems elsewhere in the modern world.

The Civil War in the History
of the Modern World

DAVID M. POTTER

It has been the curious fate of the United States to exert immense influence in the modern world, without itself quite understanding the nature of this influence. Major trends of the modern world—both constructive trends and socially injurious ones—have repeatedly become apparent in the United States before they became evident elsewhere. But though the United States has often been a step ahead in the process of social change, it has frequently been a step behind in its awareness of the meaning of new developments. The shape of things to come often became visible in America earlier than it did elsewhere, but American preconceptions about the frontier, the classless society, and the agrarian basis of democracy prevented Americans from perceiving this shape as realistically as it was perceived by social thinkers in other countries. If Americans have failed effectively to interpret their experience to people in other societies, it is in part because they have not always been able to explain it to themselves. Further, the distinctive qualities of life in America have caused a good many forces which were generically universal to take forms which seemed more restrictively peculiar to the New World than they really were.

Thus in the late eighteenth century, America executed the first democratic political revolution of a democratic age, but American society was already so equalitarian that the revolutionary implication was muted. Without any great social overturn, the American War of Independence seemed conservative when compared with the socially cataclysmic forces released in France a decade later. In the twentieth century the United States developed what was perhaps the first mass society, but the American cult of equality and individualism prevented Americans from analyzing their mass society in realistic terms. Often they treated it as if it were simply an infinite aggregation of Main Streets in Zenith, Ohio. America has witnessed episodes of extreme industrial conflict, but these have not been interpreted in the class terms which a Marxist society would invoke. America has experienced a sweeping revolution in sex behavior, but has not incorporated this change into the system of values by which it explains itself. Ironically, the United States has cherished a belief in its mission to spread a democracy for which it has had difficulty in finding converts, while it has led the world in technological changes which produced social transformations that it had no especial desire to bring about.

The reader need not be astonished, therefore, if the Civil War has been interpreted in terms which disguised its broader meaning. If, as some Americans asserted, its chief importance was in putting an end to chattel slavery, this could hardly be regarded as a leading development in the history of Western civilization; for slavery had disappeared from western Europe, except vestigially, while it still flourished in the Americas, and it had disappeared from most of Latin America, except Cuba and Brazil, while it still persisted in the United States. The American republic was almost destroyed, therefore, in a struggle over an institution which world opinion regarded as an anachronism.

If, on the other hand, the Civil War was, as some other Americans asserted, important chiefly because it preserved the American Union, this statement also was framed in restrictive terms which failed to reveal its broader implications. Beginning with the mystic phrase *E pluribus unum,* the republic had not been able for two generations to resolve the question whether it was, in the last analysis, *pluribus* or *unum.* The Civil War gave *unum* the upper hand, and the importance of this fact became visible in world history in 1917 and again in 1941, when the strength of a consolidated American republic impinged decisively on two world wars. But at the time, in a literal sense, there was not much significance for other nations in the fact that the United States waited for fourscore years and ten to settle a question which other nations settled at their inception. There seemed little universality of significance in a war fought to find, or at least determine, a clear meaning for a cryptic federal system such as no other nation had ever had, and such as was deliberately made ambiguous in the first place in order not to lose the support which it certainly would have lost if its meaning had been clarified.

While the war was in progress, European policy-makers tended to think of it simply in terms of whether it would leave the United States weaker or stronger than before. After it was over, the only people who examined it closely were military historians, looking for the lessons of strategy and tactics that might be derived from the first major conflict in which repeating arms, ironclad vessels, trench warfare, and railroads as supply lines were used on a significant scale.

Thus, while the campaigns of Lee and Grant have fascinated English and European readers, just as the campaigns of Napoleon have fascinated Americans, and while the personality of Lincoln has held an appeal for men everywhere, writers have scarcely asked the question: what was the role of the American Civil War in the history of the modern world? Did it have historical significance for anyone except Americans?

If we are seeking an answer to this question, it may be useful to begin by asking ourselves, simply, what were the prevalent tendencies of the nineteenth century, and what did the Civil War contribute in causing these tendencies to prevail? Historians have neglected the latter part of this question, but have repeatedly given an answer to the first part. They tell us, over and over, that the nineteenth century was an era of liberalism and nationalism. The basis for the generalization is obvious. Nationalism, as we know it in its modern form, scarcely existed before the French Revolution; but by the end of the nineteenth century Britain, France, Germany, Italy, and Japan had become prototypes for modern nationality, sometimes after great travail. Nationalistic forces were fermenting throughout other parts of Europe, and even in the colonial world of Asia and Africa the premonitory stirrings of a latent nationalism could already be detected. The Monroe Doctrine had done its bit to make the Western Hemisphere safe for nationalism, and the Latin Americans had responded by erecting eighteen separate nationalistic republics. Likewise with liberalism. It was scarcely more than an ideology in the minds of British and French rationalists before the French Revolution, but by the beginning of the twentieth century representative government and other liberal institutions prevailed in Britain, France, and Italy, and to some extent even in Germany and Austria-Hungary. The Hapsburgs, the Hohenzollerns, and the Romanoffs were still on their thrones, but they stood on the defensive before the onslaughts of Social Democrats, Social Revolutionaries, and other militant reformers.

All these facts are familiar to the point of triteness and it would be parochial to exaggerate the importance of the American Civil War in connection with them. But if we are to define the place of this war in terms of world history, rather than merely of American history, there are two aspects in which it exercised a crucial effect in shaping the tendencies of world history. These aspects may or may not have served the long-range welfare of human society, and it may be argued that, ultimately, their effect was pernicious. But for good or ill, here are two things which the Civil War did: first, it turned the tide which had been running against nationalism for forty years, or ever since Waterloo; and second, it forged a bond between nationalism and liberalism at a time when it appeared that the two might draw apart and move in opposite directions.

Because of the ultimate triumph of nationalism as a worldwide force by 1900, it is easy to forget how seriously nationalism appeared to have failed at the time when the Civil War occurred. After establishing firm bridgeheads in Britain and France, it had met with disaster after disaster in its efforts to spread into southern and central Europe. Britain had moved successfully to suppress nationalism in Ireland, and Russia had taken the most repressive measures in 1830 to crush it out in Poland. After the galaxy of nationalist revolutions of 1848 the dreams of a united Italy had ended with disaster at Custozza, those of a united Germany with the anticlimax of the Frankfurt Parliament, those of Czechoslovakia with the overthrow of the Pan-Slavic Congress, and those of Hungary with the defeat of Louis Kossuth. Simultaneously, in America, the steadily rising tensions between North and South seemed increasingly likely to destroy the feeling of national unity which had appeared completely triumphant during the first two decades of the century. The forces of nationalism reasserted themselves successfully in the Italian peninsula in the two years preceding the American Civil War, but otherwise nationalism and especially liberal nationalism in Europe seemed a lost cause. Louis Napoleon had made himself emperor of France in 1852, and within another decade was busily planting a Hapsburg imperialist regime in Mexico.

Viewed from the standpoint of appearances only, the forces which opposed nationalism in Europe were entirely unlike those which opposed it in America. In Europe, one might say, the forces which thwarted nationalism were those of universalism—of the Catholic Church and of the Hapsburg and Romanoff empires, for which the nationalist impulse seemed too localizing and disruptive. In America, one might say, the forces which thwarted it were those of localism and of sectionalism, for which the nationalist impulse seemed too consolidating and centralizing. In Europe, imperial forces sought to stamp out nationalism from above; in America, particularistic forces sought to resist it from below. It is perhaps because the opposition was centripetal in Europe and centrifugal in America that historians have tended to overlook the parallel triumphs of national unification, all within a period of twelve short years, in Italy, the United States, and Germany.

But the contrast between universalism and localism, as the forces which opposed nationalism, is perhaps more apparent than real. In both Europe and America, the forces of tradition and privilege tended to be arrayed against nationalism, while the forces of liberalism and democracy tended to support it. In America, the secession of the Southern states has been accurately described as a conservative revolt—a revolution by men who were not revolutionists, and who justified their revolution less by a philosophical defense of the right of the self-determination of peoples than by refined, legalistic arguments upon the intent of the Constitution of 1787. These "Rebels," instead of advocating change, were rebelling against it and were the champions of a traditional, relatively static, hierarchical society. They feared, with some reason, as we may now conclude, the transformations that might be wrought by an industrial society. They feared the destruction of a familiar social order and defended the evil institution of slavery less because they believed in human bondage as such than because they could not conceive of their social order without slavery.

In a certain sense, then, the landed planters of the South who opposed American nationalism were not unlike the landed proprietors in central Europe who opposed German or Polish or Italian or Hungarian or Bohemian nationalism. All of them were traditionalists. All feared that nationalism was linked with a democracy which they distrusted. All feared to release from the bottle the genii of manhood suffrage, of democratic equality, of social mobility, of universal education—and in the South, of emancipation for almost four million slaves. In this sense, European and American conservatism shared much in common, and the issue in the war between North and South carried implications considerably beyond the mere question as to whether the American states should form one republic or two.

The uprising of the North in 1861, and its decision to wage a war to preserve the American Federal Union, coming in the same year in which Victor Emmanuel was crowned king of a united Italy, marked a turning of the tide which had been running against nationalism for the preceding forty-five years. For better or worse, the course was set toward a world of sovereign nation-states, subject to no ultimate control in their conduct toward one another. The process of forging additional nations would reach out, within another century, from Europe and the Americas to Asia and Africa, until by 1966 there would be more than 130. As the number of "nations" increased, the beneficial effects of nationalism became increasingly uncertain, for all too many of the new sovereignties regarded the possession of nuclear destructive power as the crowning sanction of their nationhood.

Nationalism today seems something of a curse because of the paradox that while the people of the earth have been growing more and more functionally interdependent socially and economically, they have also simultaneously grown more and more irresponsibly independent of one another politically. The fragmentation of empires and other forms of supranational political authority has proceeded in ironic parallelism with increases in the cohesion of the peoples whose political relationships are being fragmented. At the same time, nationalism has shown that it can have a hideous side, undreamed of by such idealistic nationalists as Mazzini, and Lamartine, and Daniel Webster. Hitler is the supreme example, but even at the present moment a number of tyrants whose authority would command no more respect than that of a gangster if it were not sanctified by the mystique of national inviolability—a number of such tyrants have given us cause to doubt that the advancement of nationalism is necessarily a contribution to human progress. Suppose Lincoln did save the American Union, did his success in keeping one strong nation where there might have been two weaker ones really entitle him to a claim to greatness? Did it really contribute any constructive values for the modern world?

To answer this question, it may be necessary to recognize not only that Lincoln sought to save American nationalism, but also why he sought to save it. To him, as to other idealistic nationalists, the Union—that is, the nation—was not an end in itself but a means to an end. He might affirm that "my paramount object . . . is to save the Union," and he might wage one of the most deadly wars ever fought up to that time to achieve his object. But he thought of the Union primarily as a context within which freedom might be preserved and extended. Moreover, he thought that survival of a liberal nation in America was vital as a test of the survival capacity of liberal nationalism anywhere. Thus, although personally he was distinctively and uniquely and even restrictively American—the only one of the great Presidents who never went outside the United States—he thought of American democracy in the least restrictive of terms. Many years before his Presidency, he eulogized Henry Clay as one who "loved his country partly because it was his own country but mostly because it was a free country." When the Civil War came, he asserted that it involved "more than the fate of these United States" and was of concern "to the whole family of man." The Union mattered to him not because of the question of authority at Washington, but because of the "necessity that is upon us of proving that popular government is not an absurdity." In his supreme moment at Gettysburg, this American nationalist did not once use the word American, or United States. He spoke, to be sure, of the nation "which our fathers brought forth," but this one nation conceived in liberty and dedicated to equality was linked in his thought with "any other nation so conceived and so dedicated." He wanted the war to result, for his own nation, in a "new birth of freedom," but this goal was not for America alone; it was to assure "men everywhere" that "government of the people, by the people, and for the people shall not perish from the earth."

It has been well said that Lincoln fused the cause of union with the cause of freedom, which is equivalent to saying that he fused the cause of nationalism with the cause of liberalism. A number of idealistic nationalists of the nineteenth century made this same equation, and impressed it upon the public mind so vigorously that, even a century later, when we have had fairly numerous as well as traumatic illustrations of how completely antagonistic liberalism and nationalism can sometimes be, most of us respond affirmatively to claims made in the name of national integrity. We do so because our own thought still moves in the grooves cut by the great liberal nationalists of the nineteenth century.

This equation of liberalism and nationalism is not, of course, without logical foundations. Nationalism and liberalism both share certain common assumptions. Both depend upon the awakening self-consciousness of the individual—in the one case awakening to his membership in the political community, in the other awakening to his rights to participate in the decisions of the community and to enjoy its advantages. But while logic might impel nationalism and liberalism to go hand in hand, history often violates logic, and today we have copious proof that nationalism can flourish in separation from any liberal counterpart. It did so in Fascist Italy and Nazi

Germany. It does so in Red China and in Soviet Russia (though these countries theoretically reject nationalism), and it is doing so in various dictatorships in the "emerging" nations. But if one kind of logic would prove nationalism and liberalism to be twin offspring of the idea of the free individual as patriot and as citizen, there is another logic which declares liberalism and nationalism to be opposites, since liberalism regards the state as existing for the individual and nationalism regards the individual as existing for the state.

This is only to say that the nineteenth-century conjunction of nationalism and liberalism was by no means inevitable. To regard it as inevitable is to lose the larger meaning of the Civil War, for the war was one of the important historic developments contributing to a conjunction which, in other circumstances, might never have occurred. Lincoln's dedication of nationalistic means to liberal ends went far to produce this conjunction in the cosmos of American values. But at the same time when Lincoln was fusing nationalism with liberalism in America, another of the great figures who made the nineteenth century a century of nationalism, Count Otto von Bismarck, was carefully disassociating liberalism from nationalism in Germany. Having watched how the debacle of liberalism wrecked all hopes of German unification at Frankfurt in 1848, Bismarck wedded his nationalism to a concept of power and not to ideas of freedom or popular government. He signalized this position by publicly embracing a policy of "blood and iron" when he came to the head of the Prussian ministry in the year of Lincoln's Emancipation Proclamation. Nine years and three wars later, while President Grant, as the head of an imperfectly reunited nation, was struggling to reconcile the liberal principle of home rule for the South with the liberal principle of citizenship rights for the Negro, Bismarck made his monarch emperor of a Germany which was at last firmly united under authoritarian controls.

Bismarck and Lincoln were, perhaps, the two foremost exponents of nineteenth-century nationalism, after Napoleon. No two exemplars of the same force could have been more dissimilar, and no dramatist could have designed two figures better suited to point up contrasting styles of nationalism. The Gettysburg Address would have been as foreign to Bismarck as a policy of "blood and iron" would have been to Lincoln.

The contrast, perhaps, points the way to what was significant, in world perspective, about the American Civil War. The significance lay not in the fact that it was a triumph for nationalism (though the war forged the North as well as the South into a nation larger than any in western Europe), not in the fact that it was a triumph of liberalism (though Lincoln vindicated government of the people, by the people, and for the people, and proved that democracy, with all its weaknesses, can withstand the shocks of war). The significance lay rather in the fact that the Civil War, more perhaps than any event in Europe, fused the two great forces of the nineteenth century—liberalism and nationalism. It fused them so thoroughly that their potential separateness was lost from view. The fusion gave to nationalism a sanction which, frequently since then, it has failed to deserve, and gave to liberalism a strength which, since then, it has frequently not known how to use.

Meanwhile, Americans remained in confusion as to what their war had signified for the world. Some thought they had proved the strength of democracy, forgetting that the Confederacy which they defeated was also democratic and shared democracy's weaknesses. Others thought that they had vindicated the principle of nationalism, forgetting that the loyalty which Southerners gave to the Confederacy was no less nationalistic than the loyalty which Yankees gave to the Union. Few perceived that one of the most sweeping consequences of the war was to identify with one another these two forces which were not necessarily linked. This partially fictitious identification may, in the final analysis, have done great harm by giving a spurious sanction to modern nationalism, with all its potential dangers for the larger human society. But in a more immediate sense, it was perhaps the most constructive identification made during the nineteenth century, for it gave significant moral purpose to the force of nationalism, which, without such purpose, was always in danger of degenerating into mere group egocentrism or chauvinism. At the same time, it also gave significant institutional support to the principle of freedom, which without such support would have had only the ideals of reformers to sustain it.

The American Civil War as a Constitutional Crisis

ARTHUR BESTOR

Within the span of a single generation—during the thirty-odd years that began with the annexation of Texas in 1845 and ended with the withdrawal of the last Union troops from the South in 1877—the United States underwent a succession of constitutional crises more severe and menacing than any before or since. From 1845 on, for some fifteen years, a constitutional dispute over the expansion of slavery into the western territories grew increasingly tense until a paralysis of normal constitutional functioning set in. Abruptly, in 1860–1861, this particular constitutional crisis was transformed into another: namely, that of secession. Though the new crisis was intimately linked with the old, its constitutional character was fundamentally different. The question of how the Constitution ought to operate as a piece of working machinery was superseded by the question of whether it might and should be dismantled. A showdown had come, and the four-year convulsion of Civil War ensued. Then, when hostilities ended in 1865, there came not the hoped for dawn of peace, but instead a third great constitutional struggle over Reconstruction, which lasted a dozen years and proved as harsh and divisive as any cold war in history. When the nation finally emerged from three decades of corrosive strife, no observer could miss the profound alterations that its institutions had undergone. Into the

From "The Civil War as a Constitutional Crisis" by Arthur Bestor, *American Historical Review*, Vol. 69, No. 2, January 1964, 327–352. Reprinted by permission of the author.

prodigious vortex of crisis and war every current of American life had ultimately been drawn.

So all-devouring was the conflict and so momentous its effects, that to characterize it (as I have done) as a series of constitutional crises will seem to many readers an almost irresponsible use of language, a grotesque belittling of the issues. Powerful economic forces, it will be pointed out, were pitted against one another in the struggle. Profound moral perplexities were generated by the existence of slavery, and the attacks upon it had social and psychological repercussions of incredible complexity. The various questions at issue penetrated into the arena of politics, shattering established parties and making or breaking the public careers of national and local leaders. Ought so massive a conflict be discussed in terms of so rarified an abstraction as constitutional theory?

To ask such a question, however, is to mistake the character of constitutional crises in general. When or why or how should they arise if not in a context of social, economic, and ideological upheaval? A constitution, after all, is nothing other than the aggregate of laws, traditions, and understandings—in other words, the complex of institutions and procedures— by which a nation brings to political and legal decision the substantive conflicts engendered by changes in all the varied aspects of its societal life. In normal times, to be sure, routine and recurrent questions of public policy are not thought of as constitutional questions. Alternative policies are discussed in terms of their wisdom or desirability. Conflicts are resolved by the ordinary operation of familiar constitutional machinery. A decision is reached that is essentially a political decision, measuring, in some rough way, the political strength of the forces that are backing or opposing some particular program of action, a program that both sides concede to be constitutionally possible, though not necessarily prudent or desirable.

When controversies begin to cut deep, however, the constitutional legitimacy of a given course of action is likely to be challenged. Questions of policy give place to questions of power; questions of wisdom to questions of legality. Attention shifts to the Constitution itself, for the fate of each particular policy has come to hinge upon the interpretation given to the fundamental law. In debating these constitutional questions, men are not evading the substantive issues. They are facing them in precisely the manner that the situation now requires. A constitutional dispute has been superadded to the controversies already present.

Should the conflict become so intense as to test the adequacy of existing mechanisms to handle it at all, then it mounts to the level of a constitutional crisis. Indeed the capability of producing a constitutional crisis is an ultimate measure of the intensity of the substantive conflicts themselves. If, in the end, the situation explodes into violence, then the catastrophe is necessarily a constitutional one, for its very essence is the failure and the threatened destruction of the constitutional framework itself.

The secession crisis of 1860–1861 was obviously an event of this kind. It was a constitutional catastrophe in the most direct sense, for it resulted in a civil war that destroyed, albeit temporarily, the fabric of the Union.

There is, however, another sense—subtler, but perhaps more significant—in which the American Civil War may be characterized as a constitutional crisis. To put the matter succinctly, the very form that the conflict
finally took was determined by the pre-existing form of the constitutional
system. The way the opposing forces were arrayed against each other in
war was a consequence of the way the Constitution had operated to array
them in peace. Because the Union could be, and frequently had been,
viewed as no more than a compact among sovereign states, the dissolution
of the compact was a conceivable thing. It was constitutional theorizing,
carried on from the very birth of the Republic, which made secession the
ultimate recourse of any group that considered its vital interests threatened.

Since the American system was a federal one, secession, when it finally
occurred, put the secessionists into immediate possession of fully organized
governments, capable of acting as no *ad hoc* insurrectionary regime could
possibly have acted. Though sometimes described as a "Rebellion" and
sometimes as a "Civil War," the American conflict was, in a strict sense,
neither. It was a war between pre-existing political entities. But it was not
(to use a third description) a "War between the States," for in war the
states did not act severally. Instead, the war was waged between two
federations of these states: one the historic Union, the other a Confederacy
that, though newly created, was shaped by the same constitutional tradition
as its opponent. In short, only the pre-existing structure of the American
Constitution can explain the actual configuration even of the war itself.

The *configurative* role that constitutional issues played is the point of
crucial importance. When discussed in their own terms and for their own
sakes, constitutional questions are admittedly theoretical questions. One
may indeed say (borrowing a phrase that even academicians perfidiously
employ) that they are academic questions. Only by becoming involved with
other (and in a sense more "substantive") issues, do they become highly
charged. But when they do become so involved, constitutional questions
turn out to be momentous ones, for every theoretical premise draws after
it a train of practical consequences. Abstract though constitutional issues
may be, they exert a powerful shaping effect upon the course that events
will in actuality take. They give a particular direction to forces already at
work. They impose upon the conflict as a whole a unique, and an otherwise
inexplicable, pattern or configuration.

To speak of a configuration of forces in history is to rule out, as
essentially meaningless, many kinds of questions that are popularly supposed to be both answerable and important. In particular, it rules out as
futile any effort to decide which one of the various forces at work in a
given historical situation was "*the* most important cause" of the events
that followed, or "*the* decisive factor" in bringing them about, or "*the*
crucial issue" involved. The reason is simple. The steady operation of a
single force, unopposed and uninterrupted, would result in a development
so continuous as to be, in the most literal sense, eventless. To produce an
event, one force must impinge upon at least one other. The event is the

consequence of their interaction. Historical explanation is, of necessity, an explanation of such interactions.

If interaction is the crucial matter, then it is absurd to think of assigning to any factor in history an intrinsic or absolute weight, independent of its context. In the study of history, the context is all-important. Each individual factor derives its significance from the position it occupies in a complex structure of interrelationships. The fundamental historical problem, in short, is not to measure the relative weight of various causal elements, but instead to discover the pattern of their interaction with one another. . . .

No single factor, whatever its nature, can account for the distinctive form that the mid-nineteenth-century American crisis assumed. Several forces converged, producing a unique configuration. Men were debating a variety of issues simultaneously, and their various arguments intertwined. Each conflict tended to intensify the others, and not only to intensify them but also to alter and deflect them in complicated ways. The crisis was born of interaction. . . .

When the historical record is as vast as the one produced by the mid-nineteenth-century American crisis—when arguments were so wearisomely repeated by such multitudes of men—it is sheer fantasy to assume that the issues discussed were not the real issues. The arguments of the period were public ones, addressed to contemporaries and designed to influence their actions. If these had not touched upon genuine issues, they would hardly have been so often reiterated. Had other lines of argument possessed a more compelling force, they would certainly have been employed.

The only tenable assumption, one that would require an overwhelming mass of contrary evidence to rebut, is that men and women knew perfectly well what they were quarreling about. And what do we find? They argued about economic measures—the tariff, the banking system, and the Homestead Act—for the obvious reason that economic interests of their own were at stake. They argued about slavery because they considered the issues it raised to be vital ones—vital to those who adhered to the ideal of a free society and vital to those who feared to disturb the *status quo*. They argued about the territories because they felt a deep concern for the kind of social order that would grow up there. They argued about the Constitution because they accepted its obligations (whatever they considered them to be) as binding.

These are the data with which the historian must reckon. Four issues were mentioned in the preceding paragraph: the issue of economic policy, the issue of slavery, the issue of the territories, and the issue of constitutional interpretation. At the very least, the historian must take all these into account. Other factors there indubitably were. To trace the interaction of these four, however, will perhaps suffice to reveal the underlying pattern of the crisis and to make clear how one of these factors, the constitutional issue, exerted a configurative effect that cannot possibly be ignored.

Conflicts over economic policy are endemic in modern societies. They formed a recurrent element in nineteenth-century American political conflict. To disregard them would be an even greater folly than to assume that they determined, by themselves, the entire course of events. Between a plantation economy dependent upon the sale of staples to a world market and an economy in which commerce, finance, and manufacturing were rapidly advancing, the points of conflict were numerous, real, and important. At issue were such matters as banks and corporations, tariffs, internal improvements, land grants to railroads, and free homesteads to settlers. In a general way, the line of division on matters of economic policy tended, at midcentury, to coincide with the line of division on the question of slavery. To the extent that it did so (and it did so far less clearly than many economic determinists assume), the economic conflict added its weight to the divisive forces at work in 1860–1861.

More significant, perhaps, was another and different sort of relationship between the persistent economic conflict and the rapidly mounting crisis before the Civil War. To put the matter briefly, the constitutional theories that came to be applied with such disruptive effects to the slavery dispute had been developed, in the first instance, largely in connection with strictly economic issues. Thus the doctrine of strict construction was pitted against the doctrine of loose construction as early as 1791, when Alexander Hamilton originated the proposal for a central bank. And the doctrine of nullification was worked out with ingenious thoroughness in 1832 as a weapon against the protective tariff. Whatever crises these doctrines precipitated proved to be relatively minor ones so long as the doctrines were applied to purely economic issues. Within this realm, compromise always turned out to be possible. The explosive force of irreconcilable constitutional theories became apparent only when the latter were brought to bear upon the dispute over slavery.

Inherent in the slavery controversy itself (the second factor with which we must reckon) were certain elements that made compromise and accommodation vastly more difficult than in the realm of economic policy. To be sure, slavery itself had its economic aspect. It was, among other things, a labor system. The economic life of many regions rested upon it. The economic interests that would be affected by any tampering with the institution were powerful interests, and they made their influence felt.

Nevertheless, it was the noneconomic aspect of slavery that made the issues it engendered so inflammatory. As Ulrich B. Phillips puts it, "Slavery was instituted not merely to provide control of labor but also as a system of racial adjustment and social order." The word "adjustment" is an obvious euphemism; elsewhere Phillips speaks frankly of "race control." The effort to maintain that control, he maintains, has been "the central theme of Southern history." The factor that has made the South "a land with a unity despite its diversity," Phillips concludes, is "a common resolve indomitably maintained—that it shall be and remain a white man's country."

It was this indomitable resolve—say rather, this imperious demand—that lay at the heart of the slavery controversy, as it lies at the heart of the struggle over civil rights today. To put the matter bluntly, the demand was that of a master race for a completely free hand to deal as it might choose with its own subject population. The word "sovereignty" was constantly on the lips of southern politicians. The concept they were invoking was one that Blackstone had defined as "supreme, irresistible, absolute, uncontrolled authority." This was the kind of authority that slaveholders exercised over their chattels. What they were insisting on, in the political realm, was that the same species of power should be recognized as belonging to the slaveholding states when dealing with their racial minorities. "State Sovereignty" was, in essence, the slaveowner's authority writ large.

If slavery had been a static system, confined geographically to the areas where the institution was an inheritance from earlier days, then the demand of the slaveholding states for unrestricted, "sovereign" power to deal with it was a demand to which the majority of Americans would probably have reconciled themselves for a long time. In 1861, at any rate, even Lincoln and the Republicans were prepared to support an ironclad guarantee that the Constitution would never be amended in such a way as to interfere with the institution within the slaveholding states. An irrepealable amendment to that effect passed both houses of Congress by the necessary two-thirds vote during the week before Lincoln's inauguration. The incoming President announced that he had "no objection" to the pending amendment, and three states (two of them free) actually gave their ratifications in 1861 and 1862. If the problems created by slavery had actually been, as slaveowners so vehemently maintained, of a sort that the slaveholding states were perfectly capable of handling by themselves, then the security offered by this measure might well have been deemed absolute.

As the historical record shows, however, the proposed amendment never came close to meeting the demands of the proslavery forces. These demands, and the crisis they produced, stemmed directly from the fact that slavery was *not* a static and local institution; it was a prodigiously expanding one. By 1860 the census revealed that more than half the slaves in the nation were held in bondage *outside* the boundaries of the thirteen states that had composed the original Union. The expansion of slavery meant that hundreds of thousands of slaves were being carried beyond the territorial jurisdictions of the states under whose laws they had originally been held in servitude. Even to reach another slaveholding state, they presumably entered that stream of "Commerce . . . among the several States," which the Constitution gave Congress a power "to regulate." If they were carried to United States territories that had not yet been made states, their presence there raised questions about the source and validity of the law that kept them in bondage.

Territorial expansion, the third factor in our catalogue, was thus a crucial element in the pattern of interaction that produced the crisis. The timing of the latter, indeed, indicates clearly the role that expansion played. Slavery had existed in English-speaking America for two centuries without producing any paralyzing convulsion. The institution had been brought to an end in the original states of the East and North by unspectacular exercises of legislative or judicial authority. Federal ordinances barring slavery from the Old Northwest had operated effectually yet inconspicuously since

1787. At many other points federal authority had dealt with slavery, outlawing the foreign slave trade on the one hand and providing for the return of fugitive slaves on the other. Prior to the 1840s constitutional challenges to its authority in these matters had been few and unimportant. Indeed, the one true crisis of the period, that of 1819–1821 over Missouri, was rooted in expansionism, precisely as the later one was to be. The nation was awaking to the fact that slavery had pushed its way northward and westward into the virgin lands of the Louisiana Purchase. Only when limits were drawn for it across the whole national domain did the crisis subside.

Suddenly, in the election of 1844, the question of territorial expansion came to the fore again. Events moved rapidly. Within the space of precisely a decade, between the beginning of 1845 and the end of 1854, four successive annexations added a million and a quarter square miles to the area under undisputed American sovereignty. Expansion itself was explosive; its interaction with the smoldering controversy over slavery made the latter issue explosive also.

The annexation of Texas in 1845, the war with Mexico that followed, and the conquests in the Southwest which that war brought about gave to the campaign against slavery a new and unprecedented urgency. Within living memory the plains along the Gulf of Mexico had been inundated by the westward-moving tide of slavery. Alabama and Mississippi, to say nothing of Arkansas and Missouri, furnished startling proof of how quickly and ineradicably the institution could establish itself throughout great new regions. Particularly telling was the example of Texas. There slavery had been carried by American settlers to nominally free soil beyond the boundaries of the United States; yet in the end the area itself was being incorporated in the Union. To guard against any possible repetition of these developments, antislavery forces reacted to the outbreak of the Mexican War by introducing and supporting the Wilmot Proviso. Originally designed to apply simply to territory that might be acquired from Mexico, it was quickly changed into an all-encompassing prohibition: "That there shall be neither slavery nor involuntary servitude in any territory on the continent of America which shall hereafter be acquired by or annexed to the United States . . . in any . . . manner whatever." The steadfast refusal of the Senate to accept the proviso did not kill it, for the prospect of continuing expansion kept the doctrine alive and made it the rallying point of antislavery sentiment until the Civil War.

This prospect of continuing expansion is sometimes forgotten by historians who regard the issue of slavery in the territories as somehow bafflingly unreal. Since 1854, it is true, no contiguous territory has actually been added to the "continental" United States. No one in the later 1850s, however, could know that this was to be the historic fact. There were ample reasons to expect otherwise. A strong faction had worked for the annexation of the whole of Mexico in 1848. Filibustering expeditions in the Caribbean and Central America were sporadic from 1849 to 1860. As if to spell out the implications of these moves, the notorious Ostend Manifesto of 1854 had announced (over the signatures of three American envoys, including a future President) that the United States could not "permit Cuba to be Africanized" (in plainer language, could not allow the slaves in Cuba to become free of white domination and control), and had defiantly proclaimed that if Spain should refuse to sell the island, "then, by every law, human and divine, we shall be justified in wresting it from Spain if we possess the power." This was "higher law" doctrine with a vengeance. . . .

The issues raised by territorial expansion were, however, not merely prospective ones. Expansion was a present fact, and from 1845 onward its problems were immediate ones. Population was moving so rapidly into various parts of the newly acquired West, most spectacularly into California, that the establishment of civil governments within the region could hardly be postponed. Accordingly, within the single decade already delimited (that is, from the beginning of 1845 until the end of 1854), state or territorial forms of government were actually provided for every remaining part of the national domain, except the relatively small enclave known as the Indian Territory (now Oklahoma). The result was an actual doubling of the area of the United States within which organized civil governments existed. This process of political creation occurred not only in the new acquisitions, but it also covered vast areas, previously acquired, that had been left unorganized, notably the northern part of the old Louisiana Purchase. There, in 1854, the new territories of Kansas and Nebraska suddenly appeared on the map. With equal suddenness these new names appeared in the newspapers, connected with ominous events.

The process of territorial organization brought into the very center of the crisis a fourth factor, the last in our original catalogue, namely, the constitutional one. The organization of new territories and the admission of new states were, after all, elements in a constitution-making process. Territorial expansion drastically changed the character of the dispute over slavery by entangling it with the constitutional problem of devising forms of government for the rapidly settling West. Slavery at last became, in the most direct and immediate sense, a constitutional question, and thus a question capable of disrupting the Union. It did so by assuming the form of a question about the power of Congress to legislate for the territories.

This brings us face to face with the central paradox in the pre–Civil War crisis. Slavery was being attacked in places where it did not, in present actuality, exist. The slaves, close to four million of them, were in the states, yet responsible leaders of the antislavery party pledged themselves not to interfere with them there. In the territories, where the prohibition of slavery was being so intransigently demanded and so belligerently resisted, there had never been more than a handful of slaves during the long period of crisis. Consider the bare statistics. The census of 1860, taken just before the final descent into Civil War, showed far fewer than a hundred slaves in all the territories, despite the abrogation of restrictions by the Kansas-Nebraska Act and the Dred Scott decision. Especially revealing was the situation in Kansas. Though blood had been spilled over the introduction of slavery into that territory, there were actually only 627 colored persons, slave or free, within its boundaries on the eve of its admission to statehood

(January 29, 1861). The same situation obtained throughout the West. In 1846, at the time the Wilmot Proviso was introduced, the Union had comprised twenty-eight states. By the outbreak of the Civil War, more than two and a third million persons were to be found in the western areas beyond the boundaries of these older twenty-eight states, yet among them were only 7,687 Negroes, free or slave. There was much truth in the wry observation of a contemporary: "The whole controversy over the Territories . . . related to an imaginary negro in an impossible place."

The paradox was undeniable, and many historians treat it as evidence of a growing retreat from reality. Thus James G. Randall writes that the "larger phases of the slavery question . . . seemed to recede as the controversies of the fifties developed." In other words, "while the struggle sharpened it also narrowed." The attention of the country was "diverted from the fundamentals of slavery in its moral, economic, and social aspects," and instead "became concentrated upon the collateral problem as to what Congress should do with respect to slavery in the territories." Hence, "it was this narrow phase of the slavery question which became, or seemed, central in the succession of political events which actually produced the Civil War." As Randall sees it, the struggle "centered upon a political issue which lent itself to slogan making rather than to political analysis."

Slogan making, to be sure, is an important adjunct of political propaganda, and slogans can easily blind men to the relatively minor character of the tangible interests actually at stake. Nevertheless, a much more profound force was at work, shaping the crisis in this peculiar way. This configurative force was the constitutional system itself. The indirectness of the attack upon slavery, that is to say, the attack upon it in the territories, where it was merely a future possibility, instead of in the states, where the institution existed in force, was the unmistakable consequence of certain structural features of the American Constitution itself.

A centralized national state could have employed a number of different methods of dealing with the question of slavery. Against most of these, the American Constitution interposed a barrier that was both insuperable and respected. By blocking every form of frontal attack, it compelled the adoption of a strategy so indirect as to appear on the surface almost timid and equivocal. In effect, the strategy adopted was a strategy of "containment." Lincoln traced it to the founding fathers themselves. They had, he asserted, put into effect a twofold policy with respect to slavery: "restricting it from the new Territories where it had not gone, and legislating to cut off its source by the abrogation of the slave trade." Taken together, these amounted to "putting the seal of legislation against its spread." The second part of their policy was still in effect, but the first, said Lincoln, had been irresponsibly set aside. To restore it was his avowed object:

> I believe if we could arrest the spread [of slavery] and place it where Washington, and Jefferson, and Madison placed it, it would be in the course of ultimate extinction, and the public mind would, as for eighty years past,

believe that it was in the course of ultimate extinction. The crisis would be past.

Whether or not slavery could have been brought to an end in this manner is a totally unanswerable question, but it requires no answer. The historical fact is that the defenders of slavery regarded the policy of containment as so dangerous to their interests that they interpreted it as signifying "that a war must be waged against slavery until it shall cease throughout the United States." On the other hand, the opponents of slavery took an uncompromising stand in favor of this particular policy because it was the only one that the Constitution appeared to leave open. To retreat from it would be to accept as inevitable what Lincoln called "the perpetuity and nationalization of slavery." . . .

Of all the ambiguities in the written Constitution the most portentous proved in fact to be the ones that lurked in the clause dealing with territory: "The Congress shall have Power to dispose of and make all needful Rules and Regulations respecting the Territory or other Property belonging to the United States." At first glance the provision seems clear enough, but questions were possible about its meaning. Eventually they were raised, and when raised they turned out to have so direct a bearing upon the problem of slavery that they would not [go] down. What did the Constitution mean by mingling both "Territory" and "other Property," and speaking first of the power "to dispose of" such property? Was Congress in reality given a power to govern, or merely a proprietor's right to make regulations for the orderly management of the real estate he expected eventually to sell? If it were a power to govern, did it extend to all the subjects on which a full-fledged state was authorized to legislate? Did it therefore endow Congress with powers that were not federal powers at all but municipal ones, normally reserved to the states? In particular, did it bestow upon Congress, where the territories were concerned, a police power competent to deal with domestic relations and institutions like slavery? . . .

In whose hands, then, had the Constitution placed the power of decision with respect to slavery in the territories? This was, in the last analysis, the constitutional question that split the Union. To it, three mutually irreconcilable answers were offered.

The first answer was certainly the most straightforward. The territories were part of the "Property belonging to the United States." The Constitution gave Congress power to "make all needful Rules and Regulations" respecting them. Only a definite provision of the Constitution, either limiting this power or specifying exceptions to it, could destroy the comprehensiveness of the grant. No such limitations or exceptions were stated. Therefore, Congress was fully authorized by the Constitution to prohibit slavery in any or all of the territories, or to permit its spread thereto, as that body, in exercise of normal legislative discretion, might decide.

This was the straightforward answer; it was also the traditional answer. The Continental Congress had given that answer in the Ordinance of 1787, and the first Congress under the Constitution had ratified it. For half a century thereafter the precedents accumulated, including the precedent of the Missouri Compromise of 1820. Only in the 1840s were these precedents challenged.

Because this was the traditional answer, it was (by definition, if you like) the conservative answer. When the breaking point was finally reached in 1860–1861 and four identifiable conflicting groups offered four constitutional doctrines, two of them accepted this general answer, but each gave it a peculiar twist.

Among the four political factions of 1860, the least well-organized was the group that can properly be described as the genuine conservatives. Their vehicle in the election of 1860 was the Constitutional Union party, and a rattletrap vehicle it certainly was. In a very real sense, however, they were the heirs of the old Whig party and particularly of the ideas of Henry Clay. Deeply ingrained was the instinct for compromise. They accepted the view just stated, that the power of decision with respect to slavery in a particular territory belonged to Congress. But they insisted that one additional understanding, hallowed by tradition, should likewise be considered constitutionally binding. In actually organizing the earlier territories, Congress had customarily balanced the prohibition of slavery in one area by the erection elsewhere of a territory wherein slaveholding would be permitted. To conservatives, this was more than a precedent; it was a constitutional principle. When, on December 18, 1860, the venerable John J. Crittenden offered to the Senate the resolutions summing up the conservative answer to the crisis, he was not in reality offering a new plan of compromise. He was, in effect, proposing to write into the Constitution itself the understandings that had governed politics in earlier, less crisis-ridden times. The heart of his plan was the re-establishment of the old Missouri Compromise line, dividing free territories from slave. An irrepealable amendment was to change this from a principle of policy into a mandate of constitutional law.

That Congress was empowered to decide the question of slavery for the territories was the view not only of the conservatives, but also of the Republicans. The arguments of the two parties were identical, up to a point; indeed, up to the point just discussed. Though territories in the past had been apportioned between freedom and slavery, the Republicans refused to consider this policy as anything more than a policy, capable of being altered at any time. The Wilmot Proviso of 1846 announced, in effect, that the time had come to abandon the policy. Radical though the proviso may have been in a political sense, it was hardly so in a constitutional sense. The existence of a congressional power is the basic constitutional question. In arguing for the existence of such a power over slavery in the territories, the Republicans took the same ground as the conservatives. In refusing to permit mere precedent to hamper the discretion of Congress in the *use* of that power, they broke with the conservatives. But the distinction they made between power and discretion, that is, between constitutional law and political policy, was neither radical nor unsound.

One innovation did find a place in antislavery, and hence in Republican, constitutional doctrine. Though precedent alone ought not to hamper the discretion of Congress, specific provisions of the Constitution could, and in Republican eyes did, limit and control that discretion. With respect to congressional action on slavery in the territories, so the antislavery forces maintained, the due process clause of the Fifth Amendment constituted such an express limitation. "Our Republican fathers," said the first national platform of the new party in 1856, "ordained that no person shall be deprived of life, liberty, or property, without due process of law." To establish slavery in the territories "by positive legislation" would violate this guarantee. Accordingly the Constitution itself operated to "deny the authority of Congress, of a Territorial Legislation [*sic*], of any individual, or association of individuals, to give legal existence to Slavery in any Territory of the United States." The Free Soil platform of 1848 had summed the argument up in an aphorism: "Congress has no more power to make a SLAVE than to make a KING; no more power to institute or establish SLAVERY, than to institute or establish a MONARCHY." As a doctrine of constitutional law, the result was this: the federal government had full authority over the territories, but so far as slavery was concerned, Congress might exercise this authority in only one way, by prohibiting the institution there.

The conservatives and the Republicans took the constitutional system as it stood, a combination of written text and historical precedent, and evolved their variant doctrines therefrom. By contrast, the two other factions of 1860—the northern Democrats under Stephen A. Douglas, and the southern Democrats whose senatorial leader was Jefferson Davis and whose presidential candidate was John C. Breckinridge—appealed primarily to constitutional theories above and beyond the written document and the precedents. If slogans are meaningfully applied, these two factions (each in its own way) were the ones who, in 1860, appealed to a "higher law."

For Douglas, this higher law was the indefeasible right of every community to decide for itself the social institutions it would accept and establish. "Territorial Sovereignty" (a more precise label than "popular sovereignty") meant that this right of decision on slavery belonged to the settlers in a new territory fully as much as to the people of a full-fledged state. At bottom the argument was one from analogy. The Constitution assigned responsibility for national affairs and interstate relations to the federal government; authority over matters of purely local and domestic concern were reserved to the states. So far as this division of power was concerned, Douglas argued, a territory stood on the same footing as a state. It might not yet have sufficient population to entitle it to a vote in Congress, but its people were entitled to self-government from the moment they were "organized into political communities." Douglas took his stand on what he regarded as a fundamental principle of American political philosophy: "that the people of every separate political community (dependent colonies, Provinces, and Territories as well as sovereign States) have an inalienable right to govern themselves in respect to their internal polity."

Having thus virtually erased the constitutional distinction between a territory and a state—a distinction that was vital (as we shall see) to the state sovereignty interpretation—Douglas proceeded to deal with the argument that since a territorial government was a creation of Congress, the powers it exercised were delegated ones, which Congress itself was free to limit, to overrule, or even to exercise through direct legislation of its own. He met the argument with an ingenious distinction. "Congress," he wrote, "may institute governments for the Territories," and, having done so, may "invest them with powers which Congress does not possess and cannot exercise under the Constitution." He continued: "The powers which Congress may thus *confer* but cannot *exercise,* are such as relate to the domestic affairs and internal polity of the Territory." Their source is not to be sought in any provision of the written Constitution, certainly not in the so-called territorial clause but in the underlying principle of self-government.

Though Douglas insisted that the doctrine of popular sovereignty embodied "the ideas and principles of the fathers of the Revolution," his appeal to history was vitiated by special pleading. In his most elaborate review of the precedents (the article in *Harper's Magazine* from which quotations have already been taken), he passed over in silence the Northwest Ordinance of 1787, with its clear-cut congressional ban on slavery. Douglas chose instead to dwell at length upon the "Jeffersonian Plan of government for the Territories," embodied in the Ordinance of 1784. This plan, it is true, treated the territories as virtually equal with the member states of the Union, and thus supported (as against subsequent enactments) Douglas's plea for the largest measure of local self-government. When, however, Douglas went on to imply that the "Jeffersonian Plan" precluded, in principle, any congressional interference with slavery in the territories, he was guilty of outright misrepresentation. Jefferson's original draft (still extant in his own hand) included a forthright prohibition of slavery in all the territories. The Continental Congress, it is true, refused at the time to adopt this particular provision, a fact that Douglas mentioned, but there is no evidence whatever to show that they believed they lacked the power to do so. Three years later, the same body exercised this very power by unanimous vote of the eight states present.

Disingenuousness reached its peak in Douglas's assertion that the Ordinance of 1784 "stood on the statute book unrepealed and irrepealable . . . when, on the 14th day of May, 1787, the Federal Convention assembled at Philadelphia and proceeded to form the Constitution under which we now live." Unrepealed the ordinance still was, and likewise unimplemented, but irrepealable it was not. Sixty days later, on July 13, 1787, Congress repealed it outright and substituted in its place the Northwest Ordinance, which Douglas chose not to discuss.

Despite these lapses, Douglas was, in truth, basing his doctrine upon one undeniably important element in the historic tradition of American political philosophy. In 1860 he was the only thoroughgoing advocate of local self-determination and local autonomy. He could justly maintain that he was upholding this particular aspect of the constitutional tradition not only against the conservatives and the Republicans, but also (and most emphatically) against the southern wing of his own party, which bitterly repudiated the whole notion of local self-government, when it meant that the people of a territory might exclude slavery from their midst.

This brings us to the fourth of the parties that contested the election of 1860, and to the third and last of the answers that were given to the question of where the Constitution placed the power to deal with slavery in the territories.

At first glance there would appear to be only two possible answers. Either the power of decision lay with the federal government, to which the territories had been ceded or by which they had been acquired; or else the decision rested with the people of the territories, by virtue of some inherent right of self-government. Neither answer, however, was acceptable to the proslavery forces. By the later 1850s they were committed to a third doctrine, state sovereignty.

The theory of state sovereignty takes on a deceptive appearance of simplicity in most historical accounts. This is because it is usually examined only in the context of the secession crisis. In that situation the corollaries drawn from the theory of state sovereignty were, in fact, exceedingly simple. If the Union was simply a compact among states that retained their ultimate sovereignty, then one or more of them could legally and peacefully withdraw from it, for reasons which they, as sovereigns, might judge sufficient. Often overlooked is the fact that secession itself was responsible for reducing the argument over state sovereignty to such simple terms. The right to secede was only one among many corollaries of the complex and intricate doctrine of the sovereignty of the states. In the winter and spring of 1860–1861, this particular corollary, naked and alone, became the issue on which events turned. Earlier applications of the doctrine became irrelevant. As they dropped from view, they were more or less forgotten. The theory of state sovereignty came to be regarded simply as a theory that had to do with the perpetuity of the Union.

The simplicity of the theory is, however, an illusion. The illusion is a consequence of reading history backward. The proslavery constitutional argument with respect to slavery in the territories cannot possibly be understood if the fifteen years of debate prior to 1860 are regarded simply as a dress rehearsal for secession. When applied to the question of slavery, state sovereignty was a positive doctrine, a doctrine of power, specifically, a doctrine designed to place in the hands of the slaveholding states a power sufficient to uphold slavery and promote its expansion *within* the Union. Secession might be an ultimate recourse, but secession offered no answer whatever to the problems of power that were of vital concern to the slaveholding states so long as they remained in the Union and used the Constitution as a piece of working machinery.

As a theory of how the Constitution should operate, as distinguished from a theory of how it might be dismantled, state sovereignty gave its own distinctive answer to the question of where the authority lay to deal with matters involving slavery in the territories. All such authority, the theory insisted, resided in the sovereign states. But how, one may well ask, was such authority to be exercised? The answer was ingenious. The laws that maintained slavery—which were, of course, the laws of the slaveholding states—must be given extraterritorial or extrajurisdictional effect. In other words, the laws that established a property in slaves were to be respected, and if necessary enforced, by the federal government, acting as agent for its principals, the sovereign states of the Union.

At the very beginning of the controversy, on January 15, 1847, five months after the introduction of the Wilmot Proviso, Robert Barnwell Rhett of South Carolina showed how that measure could be countered, and pro-slavery demands supported, by an appeal to the *mystique* of the sovereignty of the several states:

> Their sovereignty, unalienated and unimpaired . . . , exists in all its plen-itude over our territories; as much so, as within the limits of the States themselves. . . . The only effect, and probably the only object of their reserved sovereignty, is, that it secures to each State the right to enter the territories with her citizens, and settle and occupy them with their property—with whatever is recognised as property by each State. The ingress of the citizen, is the ingress of his sovereign, who is bound to protect him in his settlement.

Nine years later the doctrine had become the dominant one in proslavery thinking, and on January 24, 1856, Robert Toombs of Georgia summed it up succinctly: "Congress has no power to limit, restrain, or in any manner to impair slavery: but, on the contrary, it is bound to protect and maintain it in the States where it exists, and wherever its flag floats, and its juris-diction is paramount." In effect, the laws of slavery were to become an integral part of the laws of the Union, so far as the territories were concerned.

Four irreconcilable constitutional doctrines were presented to the Amer-ican people in 1860. There was no consensus, and the stage was set for civil war. The issues in which the long controversy culminated were ab-struse. They concerned a seemingly minor detail of the constitutional sys-tem. The arguments that supported the various positions were intricate and theoretical. But the abstractness of constitutional issues has nothing to do, one way or the other, with the role they may happen to play at a moment of crisis. The sole question is the load that events have laid upon them. Thanks to the structure of the American constitutional system itself, the abstruse issue of slavery in the territories was required to carry the burden of well-nigh all the emotional drives, well-nigh all the political and economic tensions, and well-nigh all the moral perplexities that resulted from the existence in the United States of an archaic system of labor and an intol-erable policy of racial subjection. To change the metaphor, the constitu-tional question of legislative authority over the territories became, so to speak, the narrow channel through which surged the torrent of ideas and interests and anxieties that flooded down from every drenched hillside upon which the storm cloud of slavery discharged its poisoned rain.

The Southern Slaveholders in the Modern World

ELIZABETH FOX-GENOVESE
and EUGENE D. GENOVESE

Americans have, with reason, long brooded over slavery as if it were our own national equivalent of original sin. For slavery rent the world's most noble republic and disgraced the world's most promising democracy; it precipitated a war, often literally though not metaphorically fratricidal, that proved ghastly in itself and terrifying in its implications for the future of humanity; and it left a legacy of racism that has brought mortification and unremitting agony to southerners and northerners, whites and blacks. Yet, the burden of slavery fell not upon our country alone, not upon the slave-holding countries of the Western Hemisphere alone, but upon the world.

An advanced state of economic integration and international struggle for power marked the world of the nineteenth century. During that extraordinary era of bourgeois ascendancy and world conquest, European capitalists and workers, nationalists, liberals, and democrats, imperialists and racists permeated and recast the world at large. The slaveholders of the Old South, like those of the Caribbean and South America and like the residual landholding classes of Europe, deeply influenced the capitalist world in which we still live, much as the resistance of slaves and peasants deeply influenced both that world and the revolutionary societies that have arisen to challenge it.

Slavery burdened not merely the United States but the entire world with the creation of powerful landholding classes based on unfree labor. These classes enormously strengthened opposition to the revolutionary tidal wave of bourgeois liberalism and democracy, although slavery had re-emerged in the modern world largely under bourgeois auspices. The spread of capitalism in Europe had created a mass market for cotton, sugar, to-bacco, and other plantation staples. The growth of a capitalist shipping industry had made possible the magnitude of the slave trade, and other capitalist sectors had provided not only the capital but the commodities necessary to sustain the African connection and service the American plantations. Plantation slavery arose in the Americas as part of the process of international capitalist development.

The specific conditions of plantation life and organization, however, provided fertile ground for the emergence of retrograde ruling classes. And for the moment it makes little difference whether we view these new landed classes as variant capitalist classes, as incipient new aristocracies, as some kind of hybrid, or as social classes of a new type. Clearly, they began by advancing world economic development and ended by threatening to stifle it. Initially, these ruling classes brought millions of Africans and other self-sufficient peoples into commodity production for a world market, provided commodities needed to sustain capitalist expansion in Europe, created new markets for burgeoning European industry, and accumulated capital, some of which spurred European industry directly and more of which indirectly contributed to market formation and commercial expansion.

Yet, in the end they built no technologically advanced, economically progressive, politically and militarily self-reliant nations of their own; much less did they create anything their warmest admirers could recognize as a great culture or civilization. Their initial dynamism became frozen in place. In one country after another, sad decline followed stagnation, at least relative to the progressive capitalist sectors of the world. Retrogression followed an orgy of prosperity: the West Indies became cultural as well as economic wrecks; Brazil lost its chance to become a great power; and the American South became this country's least dynamic and prosperous region—to put it charitably. The great slaveholding countries moved from a central position in the worldwide advance of capitalism, with its unprecedented standards of living even for the masses, to a periphery of misery, poverty, discouragement, and general embarrassment. But, of course, for the slaves whose blood and toil had created the original wealth, those countries had never been anything else.

The underdevelopment and backwardness that still grip most of the old slaveholding countries have provided burden enough for today's world to bear. But much more remains at stake. The slaveholders of the Americas in effect reinforced the political role of the declining landholding classes of Europe, first in opposing the spread of bourgeois liberalism and then, after their own defeat by the bourgeoisie, in opposing the spread of democracy. The influence of the slaveholders and the European landed classes was uniformly reactionary, although by no means uniform in specific content or intensity. In Europe, in Latin America, and, to a lesser extent, even in the United States, these classes significantly retarded the great movements for recognition of autonomy of the individual and the legitimate participation of the masses in political life.

The intervention of these landed classes on the side of reaction came at a fateful moment in the history of Europe and America—at the very moment at which the bourgeoisie itself, faced with threats from the Left, was being forced to recognize the contradiction between its historic commitment to individual freedom and its early, if always uneasy, flirtation with democracy and equality. Jacobinism, after all, was quintessentially a bourgeois movement, but by the middle of the nineteenth century any form of Jacobinism looked like socialism, communism, or anarchy to a bourgeoisie increasingly frightened by mass politics.

Even the most liberal bourgeoisies—those of England, France, and the United States—which continued to adhere to some form of democratic commitment, turned outward in an attempt to solve what they condescendingly called "the social question" at home at the expense of colonial peoples. The legacy of the old colonialism and its ideologically essential racism served their strategy well, as did the remnants of the old landed classes directly. We need not follow Joseph Schumpeter in attributing modern imperialism to the atavistic tendencies of the old landholding elites to recognize the importance of their role.

By 1861 the slaveholders were determined to defend their property and power. In this respect they stood alongside the slaveholding planters of Brazil and Cuba, alongside the Russian lords—elegantly delineated by Pushkin, Turgenev, Dostoevski, and Tolstoi and unforgettably satirized by Gogol—lords who, with the support of such brutal rulers as Catherine the Great, had slowly reduced their serfs to a status close to that of slaves, and who set a high standard of pitiless brutality in the suppression of peasant revolts. And as late as 1861 the southern slaveholders also stood alongside such dying but still deadly landholding classes as those of Poland, Hungary, Italy, and Japan, which commanded unfree or only technically free labor in regimes even then looked upon as barbarous by both the bourgeois and working classes of western Europe.

The southern slaveholders were not transplanted boyars or Junkers or Polish lords or even Brazilian *senhores de engenho* [sugar planters]. Each of these classes had its own traditions, sensibilities, characteristics, notions of civilized life, and peculiar relation to labor; each had its own internal divisions. The slaveholders of Virginia were not quite the same as those of Louisiana, any more than the *senhores de engenho* of the sugar-growing Brazilian Northeast were quite the same as the *fazendeiros* [planters] of the coffee-growing Brazilian South. And yet, they did, in a broad sense, represent variations on one side of a great historical divide.

These classes mounted, in different degrees, stubborn opposition to the emerging forces of the modern world. Some of them were remnants of a world that was steadily being overthrown by the expansion of world capitalism. Others, including the American slaveholders, had their class origins in that very expansion. But all, to the extent that they could create and consolidate their political power, had increasing difficulty in living in a world of emerging cities, industries, mechanization, international finance, and the participation of the masses in politics.

From an economic point of view, these landed classes commanded regimes that, however profitable in the narrow sense, lacked the development possibilities of regimes based on free labor and, therefore, the military possibilities for survival in a world of increasingly competitive nation-states. The Junkers learned that hard lesson during the Napoleonic wars, although not until Bismarck's time did they learn it well enough. The Russian lords learned it, to the extent that they learned it at all, during the Crimean War and the peasant rebellions that came before and after it. The Brazilians had their own national disaster during the Paraguayan War and the unraveling of their social and political structure. And the Japanese suffered the humiliation of the so-called opening by the West. The nineteenth century, in short, demonstrated from one end of the world to the other that the path of safety and survival for old ruling classes as well as for new nations was the path of accommodation to the irresistible advance of nationalism and industrial capitalism. Whether in a death struggle or a reluctant compromise, the great landholders who survived as individuals, as families, or as whole classes did so at the price of surrendering their traditional ways of life as well as their political autonomy, not merely to new men but to a new class based on the property relations of money and markets.

The passing of the great landed classes, however slow, partial, or disguised, marked the final victory and consolidation of a worldwide system of capitalist production and, with it, of a new world view or, rather, a new complex of antagonistic world views. In a sense, the economic struggle between contending economic systems had long ago been settled. The decisive struggles had become political, ideological, and moral. From the sixteenth century onward, the new system of capitalist production, spreading across the world from northwestern Europe, embraced something much more important, something more decisive, than international commerce. International commerce had played an important role in the ancient world and in the great empires of China and India. And it was particularly notable in the magnificent expansion of Islam across the Mediterranean basin into Spain and black Africa and eastward to China, Central Asia, and Indonesia. Without a vigorous and well-organized commercial system, the great Muslim caliphates of the eighth and ninth centuries and beyond, with their brilliant contributions to art, science, philosophy, and law, would have been impossible. Yet none of these commercially developed civilizations succeeded in creating an integrated worldwide system of production and exchange; nor did they even try.

The spread of capitalism in early-modern Europe marked the rise of a new mode of production—that is, of new social relations based on personal freedom and on a revolutionary and apparently self-revolutionizing technology associated with those relations. And it also marked a revolution in human values, the decisive feature of which was precisely the freedom of labor—that is, the transformation of labor-power into a commodity. That freedom liberated human beings to work for themselves and to accumulate wealth; it also forced the laboring poor out of their traditional dependence on the protection, such as it was, of lords and patrons and placed them under the stern whip of marketplace necessity.

This new mode of production gave rise to a new theory of property. The right of the individual to property both in his own person and his labor-power constituted not merely its economic but also its moral foundation. Once that theory of property took root, the very definition of the rights and duties of the individual in relation to the state changed dramatically, and so did the content of race relations.

True, the Christian tradition had long established the principle of equality before God and the responsibility of the individual for his actions. The Christian ethic had long stressed that, while men must render unto Caesar the things that are Caesar's, men must also assume full responsibility for rendering unto God the things that are God's; and God's things included the moral sanctity of individual life and the immortality of the soul. But this great tradition, itself so revolutionary and heroic, did not destroy the principle of property in man, and the specific history of the Catholic Church had actually reinforced and legitimized the principle of class subordination. It is in this sense that David Brion Davis, in his excellent book *The Problem of Slavery in the Age of Revolution,* refers to the new bourgeois idea of freedom, especially in its Hegelian form, as bearing only superficial resemblance to the Christian idea, although the early emergence of the Christian idea of freedom in Western civilization decisively prepared the ground for the emergence of the secular bourgeois idea during the Enlightenment.

The spread of capitalism revolutionized thought as well as material life. Liberalism, in those eighteenth- and nineteenth-century forms which today are usually associated with free-market conservatives, became the dominant ideology of the bourgeoisie. This new ruling class took its stand on the freedom of the individual and on some form of political representation. In time, new bourgeois nation-states, most notably Germany and Japan, would assume a more authoritarian political stance. But even there, industrial capitalism carried with it an expanded commitment to individual freedom and to broadened political participation.

In short, the forward movement of capitalist relations of production required a new definition of the rights and responsibilities of the individual and, as John C. Calhoun, George Fitzhugh, and other leading southerners understood, posed a powerful challenge to all previous ideas of an organic society within which some men assumed major responsibility for the lives and well-being of others. The bourgeoisie and the older landed classes eventually contended over the nature and destiny of human life. For centuries, political leaders deliberately obscured this issue and arranged compromises to deal with its manifestations. In the end, two irreconcilable world views met in combat, sometimes quickly or peacefully resolved and sometimes, as in the United States, resolved by a brutal test of physical strength.

But this struggle was not to be so clean-cut, if only because the wonderful new freedom bestowed upon the laboring classes carried with it a good dose of hunger, neglect, deprivation, misery, and death. The roots of the working-class democratic and socialist movement lay in the attempt of artisans and craftsmen to resist the destruction of their independent way of life and their absorption into the marketplace of labor. But by the middle of the nineteenth century, the struggle of the artisans and craftsmen had irrevocably been lost; its impulses and ideas of equality, fraternity, and democracy had passed into the working-class movement, most militantly into its socialist contingent.

Accordingly, the old landed classes faced ideological and political challenge both from bourgeois liberalism and from a proletarian socialism with origins in bourgeois thought but increasingly independent of it. Recall, therefore, the dire warnings of Calhoun, Fitzhugh, James Hammond, G. F. Holmes, Henry Hughes, and others that the bourgeoisie would rue the day it destroyed the landed classes and with them, a great bulwark against lower-class radicalism. And, in fact, in many countries the bourgeoisies did unite with their old landowning enemies to turn back the challenge from the Left. Still, in this unequal partnership, the bourgeoisie steadily strengthened its position as senior partner, and the landowners steadily surrendered their old way of life to become, in effect, a mere appendage of the capitalist class. The old organic relations among men disappeared, sometimes quickly, sometimes slowly as in the more patriarchal areas of the New South in which paternalism lingered well into the twentieth century, if only as an echo of a bygone era.

Even in such countries as Germany, Japan, and Italy, the upper-class coalition agreed upon the essential bourgeois principles of freedom of labor, at least in the marketplace sense, while it took a hard line against the democratic and egalitarian impulses that had themselves arisen within the earlier bourgeois revolutions.

Thus, even the most admirable and genuinely paternalistic of the old landed classes generally surrendered the best of their traditions, most notably, the organic view of society and the idea that men were responsible for each other, while they retained the worst of their traditions, most notably, their ever deepening arrogance and contempt for the laboring classes and darker races. These vices they offered as a gift to a triumphant bourgeoisie, which had acquired enough of the same already. The postbellum South provided a striking, if qualified, example of this worldwide reactionary tendency. The Calhouns and Fitzhughs might have been startled to learn that the great conservative coalition they had called for could come into being only after the destruction of their beloved plantation-slave regime. But it could not have been other; nor, despite appearances, was it other in Germany or Japan. In every case, the terms of the coalition had to include, as sine qua non, acceptance of bourgeois property relations and the hegemony of the marketplace, albeit qualified by authoritarianism and state regulation of the economy. In the United States the price was relatively low: the postbellum South suffered political reaction and economic stagnation, and the nation as a whole suffered from the strengthening of the conservative elements in its political life. But, on balance, the United States, more than any other country with the possible exception of England, successfully blended the classic bourgeois commitment to individual freedom with the more radical currents of democracy and mass participation in politics; and, in addition, it provided a high standard of material comfort.

To present the southern slaveholders as one of many landed classes arrayed against the progressive currents of the eighteenth and especially nineteenth centuries implies no identity or equation. As a class, the southern slaveholders had their own extraordinary virtues as well as vices and could not escape being American in their inheritance of traditions of freedom and democracy; indeed with justice they claimed to have helped shape those traditions. The constitutions of states like Mississippi ranked among the country's most democratic, and South Carolina's conservatism made it an exception among the slave states. The slave states maintained a degree of freedom of speech, assembly, and the press that might have been the envy of the people of much of Europe, a degree of freedom unheard-of in the rest of the world. Even most of the poorer white men had some access to politics and some effect on the formation of social policy. And if the white literacy rate and general educational standard opened the South to just abolitionist criticism, they still compared favorably with those of most other countries.

Hence, many learned and able historians have stressed the "Americanness" of the Old South and viewed its deviations from national norms as a mere regional variation on a common theme. And let it be conceded that by many useful criteria even the most reactionary elements of the slaveholding class had more in common with northern Americans of all classes than with the Russian boyars or Prussian Junkers.

This interpretation nonetheless loses sight of slavery's overwhelming impact on the South, of the dangerous political role it was playing in American national life, and of the fundamental historical tendency it represented. If world-historical processes of the nineteenth century are viewed as a coherent whole, then that cranky and sometimes insincere reactionary George Fitzhugh was right in seeing the slaveholding South as part of a great international counterrevolutionary movement against the spread of a bourgeois world order. The great problem for the most progressive, liberal, and democratically inclined slaveholders and other proslavery southerners was that the slavery question could not be isolated as a regional peculiarity occasioned by a special problem of racial adjustment.

Consider the basic question of political freedom. Foreign travelers often supported southern claims to being a liberal-spirited and tolerant people. What northern state, for example, was sending Jews to the United States Senate? The only drawback concerned abolitionist propaganda that threatened to unleash anarchy and bloodshed. And here, southern intolerance was neither paranoid nor irrational nor blindly Neanderthal; it represented a local version of the elementary principle of self-preservation. And here, the slaves themselves ruined their masters. No matter that they rose in insurrection rarely and in small numbers. As the medieval scholastics insisted, existence proves possibility. However infrequent and militarily weak the appearance of a Gabriel Prosser, a Denmark Vesey, or a Nat Turner, they and others like them did exist, and so, therefore, did the danger of slave revolt. White southerners would have been mad to teach significant numbers of their slaves to read and write, to permit abolitionist literature to fall into their hands, to take an easy view of politicians, clergymen, and editors who so much as questioned the morality and justice of the very foundation of their social order and domestic peace. The economic, social, and political consequences of slavery ill served the mass of whites too, and agitation of the slavery question threatened to open a class struggle among whites. To that extent the slaveholders' actions were overdetermined.

On national terrain, slave-state politicians fought for the gag rule and thereby threatened the sacred right of petition. They had to advocate tampering with the mails, had to defend a measure of lynch law against people who talked too much, had to proclaim boldly that a free press could not safely be allowed to be too free, and had to offend northern sensibilities by demanding a fugitive-slave law that bluntly doubted the scrupulousness of the vaunted jury system. The slaveholders demonstrated time and time again that, despite their honest protestations of respect for freedom and even democracy, the exigencies of their social system were dragging them irresistibly toward political and social policies flagrantly tyrannical, illiberal, and undemocratic, at least by American standards. No matter how much and how genuinely they tried to stand by their cherished Jeffersonian traditions, they were compelled, step by step, down the road charted by their most extreme theorists, for their commitment to survival as a ruling class as well as a master race left them less and less choice.

It was not necessary for the slaveholders and their supporters to embrace Fitzhugh's extreme doctrines; indeed, it is doubtful that they ever could or would have. Yet, the thoughtful Calhoun tried to reform the federal Constitution to make it safe for slavery, and younger politicians during the 1850s made desperate attempts to bully northern consent to increasingly unpalatable measures. From a northern perspective, slaveholding southerners, drunk with their near-absolute power over human beings, had become tyrannical, intransigent, and incapable of reasoned compromise. From a southern perspective, even friendly and moderate northerners were willing to acquiesce in measures that would threaten southern property and social order and, to make matters worse, were increasingly willing to view slavery as a kind of moral leprosy. Both sides were right in their own terms, for slavery had, as Tocqueville and others had warned, separated two great white American peoples even more deeply in moral perspective than in material interest. And moral separation, quite as readily as material, threatened confrontation and war once made manifest on political terrain.

We end then with the paradox that the southern slaveholders, who might have qualified for inclusion among the world's most liberal and even democratic ruling classes, qualified in the eyes of their northern fellow Americans as a grossly reactionary and undemocratic force, much as the hardened and retrograde landowners of Europe so qualified in the eyes of the liberal bourgeoisie. The southern slaveholders were doing in American terms what the English colonial slaveholders were doing when they threw their weight against parliamentary reform, what the French slaveholders in the colonies and the aristocrats at home were doing when they supported the counterrevolution, what the Prussian Junkers were doing when they demolished the liberal movement of 1848, and what the Russian boyars were doing when they suicidally refused to limit the imperial power. . . .

↘ *F U R T H E R   R E A D I N G*

David Herbert Donald, *Liberty and Union* (1978)
Eric Foner, ''The Causes of the American Civil War: Recent Interpretations and New Directions,'' *Civil War History* 20 (1974), 197–214
Barrington Moore, Jr., ''The American Civil War: The Last Capitalist Revolution,'' in *Origins of Dictatorship and Democracy* (1966), 111–155
Allan Nevins, *Ordeal of the Union*, 4 vols. (1947–1950)
———, ''A Major Result of the War,'' *Civil War History* 5 (1959), 237–250

Frank L. Owsley, "The Fundamental Cause of the Civil War: Egocentric Sectionalism," *Journal of Southern History* 7 (1941), 3–18

Phillip S. Paludan, "The American Civil War: Triumph Through Tragedy," *Civil War History* 21 (1975), 254–260

————, "The American Civil War as a Crisis of Law and Order," *American Historical Review* 77 (1972), 1013–1034

Peter J. Parish, *The American Civil War* (1975)

James G. Randall, "The Blundering Generation," *Mississippi Valley Historical Review* 27 (1940), 3–28

James G. Randall and David H. Donald, *The Civil War and Reconstruction* (1969)

John S. Rosenberg, "The American Civil War and the Problem of 'Presentism,'" *Civil War History* 21 (1975), 242–253

Arthur M. Schlesinger, Jr., "The Causes of the Civil War: A Note on Historical Sentimentalism," *Partisan Review* 16 (1949), 969–981

William G. Shade, " 'Revolutions May Go Backwards': The American Civil War and the Problem of Political Development," *Social Science Quarterly* 55 (1974), 753–767

Kenneth M. Stampp, "The Irrepressible Conflict," in *The Imperiled Union* (1980), 191–245

CHAPTER
2

The North and South Compared

⤴

The conflict in mid-nineteenth-century America was waged by two separate geographical regions. It was therefore significantly different from the internal wars in England in the 1640s and 1650s, known as the English Civil War, and those in France in the late eighteenth century and Russia in the early twentieth century, known as the French and the Russian Revolutions. On the other hand, the attempt by the South to break away and form an independent country was quite similar to the contemporaneous movements within the Austro-Hungarian Empire in the 1860s and 1870s to secede and create the new nations of Germany and Italy.

By withdrawing from the United States, the Confederacy was in effect embarking on a parallel course of nation-making. And the embryonic Confederate States of America seemed to possess all the ingredients of a nation. Its people spoke a common language—English. They practiced a common religion—Protestant Christianity. The majority of them possessed a common ancestry and ethnicity—Scots-Irish and English. And they shared a common political outlook—the profession and practice of republicanism, federalism, representative government, and broad-based electoral participation. Few nations that endured for any length of time have been endowed with so many widely shared features.

Ironically, however, most of these values and characteristics were also true of the United States from which the southerners were trying to distance and separate themselves. Thus the question arises as to why the southern states felt so acutely conscious of their difficulties and distinctiveness that they took the drastic step of seeking their independence. Perhaps there was just a conflict of interests, rather than of basic beliefs and attitudes. If so, why could they not be reconciled? After all, every sovereign state or nation contains within its confines divergent interests, such as antagonistic social classes or competing economic groups and occupational sectors. Yet these differences can usually be accommodated or surmounted.

Perhaps the two regions were different in such a subtle way that points of friction such as these could not be assuaged. Maybe the differences that did exist became exaggerated or blown out of proportion somehow, and then proved impossible to reconcile. Whatever the circumstances, people at the time were apparently convinced that accommodation between the regions was out of reach. But historians have to examine and ponder the reasons for this if they are to explain why war became the final outcome.

🔖 *D O C U M E N T S*

Among contemporaries, the nature and degree of the contrast between the two sections was the subject of a good deal of comment as well as polemic. The selections that follow demonstrate this. The first three are critical of the South, while the last four are forcefully defensive of it.

The first observation comes from Frederick Law Olmsted, a northern journalist and later a famous urban planner, who undertook several tours of the southern states in the 1850s. Here, in a *New York Times* article of January 12, 1854, he points out how sharply divergent were the values and self-images of the South's ruling class. The second selection is from Hinton Rowan Helper's extremely controversial *The Impending Crisis of the South: How to Meet It* (1857), in which the author, a nonslaveowning North Carolinian, claims that slavery had made the South economically backward, and urges his fellow nonslaveholders to acknowledge the problem and do something about it. Olmsted is the author of the third selection, from his book, *The Cotton Kingdom* (1861), in which he emphasizes the rapidity of material change and improvement in the northern states compared with the South.

In the fourth document, an extract from the pamphlet, "The Non-Slaveholders of the South," James D. B. DeBow, a leading southern nationalist, demonstrates why he thinks southerners without an apparent interest in maintaining slavery can be relied upon to support it. The fifth selection is from the first of two public letters written in 1845 by James Henry Hammond, a future governor and U.S. senator from South Carolina, to Thomas Clarkson, a leading English abolitionist. In this extract, Hammond points out his region's cultural superiority in relation to the North. In the sixth selection, this boast is carried to an extreme by George Fitzhugh, the South's most provocative polemicist, in his essay "Slavery Justified" of 1854. The last piece is a combative editorial of January 21, 1861, from the New Orleans *Daily Crescent*, suggesting that the North covets the South's prosperity and economic worth.

Frederick Law Olmsted Observes Southern Lassitude, 1854

. . . The direct influence of Slavery is, I think, to make the Southerner indifferent to small things; in some relations, we should say rightly, *superior* to small things; prodigal, improvident, and ostentatiously generous. His ordinarily uncontrolled authority, (and from infancy the Southerner is more free from control, in all respects, I should judge, than any other person in the world,) leads him to be habitually impulsive, impetuous, and enthusiastic: gives him self-respect and dignity of character, and makes him bold, confident, and true. Yet it has not appeared to me that the Southerner was frank as he is, I believe, commonly thought to be. He seems to me to be very secretive, or at least reserved, on topics which most nearly concern himself. He minds his own business, and lets alone that of others; not in the English way, but in a way peculiarly his own; resulting partly, perhaps, from want of curiosity, in part from habits formed by such constant intercourse as he has with his inferiors, (negroes,) and partly from the caution in conversation which the "rules of honor" are calculated to give. Not, I said, in the English way, because he meets a stranger easily, and without timidity, or thought of how he is himself appearing, and is ready and usually accomplished in conversation. He is much given to vague and careless generalization, and greatly disinclined to exact and careful reasoning. He follows his natural impulses nobly, has nothing to be ashamed of, and is, therefore, habitually truthful; but his carelessness, impulsiveness, vagueness, and want of exactness in everything, make him speak from his mouth that which is in point of fact untrue, rather more often than any one else.

From early intimacy with the negro, (an association fruitful in other respects of evil,) he has acquired much of his ready, artless and superficial benevolence, good nature and geniality. The comparatively solitary nature and somewhat monotonous duties of plantation life, make guests usually exceedingly welcome, while the abundance of servants at command, and other circumstances, make the ordinary duties of hospitality very light. The Southerner, however, is greatly wanting in hospitality of mind, closing his doors to all opinions and schemes to which he has been bred a stranger, with a contempt and bigotry which sometimes seems incompatible with his character as a gentleman. He has a large but unexpansive mind.

The Southerner has no pleasure in labor except with reference to a result. He enjoys life itself. He is content with being. Here is the grand distinction between him and the Northerner; for the Northerner enjoys progress in itself. He finds his happiness in doing. Rest, in itself, is irksome and offensive to him, and however graceful or beatific that rest may be, he values it only with reference to the power of future progress it will bring him. Heaven itself will be dull and stupid to him, if there is no work to be done in it—nothing to struggle for—if he reaches perfection at a jump, and has no chance to make an improvement.

The Southerner cares for the end only; he is impatient of the means. He is passionate, and labors passionately, fitfully, with the energy and strength of anger, rather than of resolute will. He fights rather than works to carry his purpose. He has the intensity of character which belongs to Americans in general, and therefore enjoys excitement and is fond of novelty. But he has much less curiosity than the Northerner; less originating genius, less inventive talent, less patient and persevering energy. And I think this all comes from his want of aptitude for close observation and his dislike for application to small details. And this, I think, may be reasonably supposed to be mainly the result of habitually leaving all matters not either of grand and exciting importance, or of immediate consequence to his comfort, to his slaves, and of being accustomed to see them slighted or neglected as much as he will, in his indolence, allow them to be by them.

Of course, I have been speaking of the general tendencies only of character in the North and the South. There are individuals in both communities in whom these extreme characteristics are reversed, as there are graceful Englishmen and awkward Frenchmen. There are, also, in each, those in whom they are more or less harmoniously blended. Those in whom they are the most enviably so—the happiest and the most useful in the social sphere—are equally common, so far as I know, in both; and the grand distinction remains in the mass—manifesting itself, by strikingly contrasting symptoms, in our religion, politics and social life.

In no way more than this: The South endeavors to close its eyes to every evil the removal of which will require self-denial, labor and skill. If, however, an evil is too glaring to be passed by unnoticed, it is immediately declared to be constitutional, or providential, and its removal is declared to be either treasonable or impious—usually both; and, what is worse, it is improper, impolite, ungentlemanly, unmanlike. And so it is ended at the South. But, at the North this sort of opposition only serves to develop the reform, by ridding it of useless weight and drapery. . . .

Hinton Rowan Helper Exposes Southern Economic Backwardness, 1857

And now that we have come to the very heart and soul of our subject, we feel no disposition to mince matters, but mean to speak plainly, and to the point, without any equivocation, mental reservation, or secret evasion whatever. The son of a venerated parent, who, while he lived, was a considerate and merciful slaveholder, a native of the South, born and bred in North Carolina, of a family whose home has been in the valley of the Yadkin for nearly a century and a half, a Southerner by instinct and by all the influences of thought, habits, and kindred, and with the desire and fixed purpose to reside permanently within the limits of the South, and with the expectation of dying there also—we feel that we have the right to express our opinion, however humble or unimportant it may be, on any and every question that affects the public good; and, so help us God, "sink or swim, live or die, survive or perish," we are determined to exercise that right with manly firmness, and without fear, favor or affection.

And now to the point. In our opinion, an opinion which has been formed from data obtained by assiduous researches, and comparisons, from laborious investigation, logical reasoning, and earnest reflection, the causes which have impeded the progress and prosperity of the South, which have dwindled our commerce, and other similar pursuits, into the most contemptible insignificance; sunk a large majority of our people in galling poverty and ignorance, rendered a small minority conceited and tyrannical, and driven the rest away from their homes; entailed upon us a humiliating dependence on the Free States; disgraced us in the recesses of our own souls, and brought us under reproach in the eyes of all civilized and enlightened nations—may all be traced to one common source, and there find solution in the most hateful and horrible word, that was ever incorporated into the vocabulary of human economy—*Slavery!* . . .

To undeceive the people of the South, to bring them to a knowledge of the inferior and disreputable position which they occupy as a component part of the Union, and to give prominence and popularity to those plans which, if adopted, will elevate us to an equality, socially, morally, intellectually, industrially, politically, and financially, with the most flourishing and refined nation in the world, and, if possible, to place us in the van of even that, is the object of this work. Slaveholders, either from ignorance or from a wilful disposition to propagate error, contend that the South has nothing to be ashamed of, that slavery has proved a blessing to her, and that her superiority over the North in an agricultural point of view makes amends for all her shortcomings in other respects. On the other hand, we contend that many years of continual blushing and severe penance would not suffice to cancel or annul the shame and disgrace that justly attaches to the South in consequence of slavery—the direst evil that e'er befell the land—that the South bears nothing like even a respectable approximation to the North in navigation, commerce, or manufactures, and that, contrary to the opinion entertained by ninety-nine hundredths of her people, she is far behind the free States in the only thing of which she has ever dared to boast—agriculture. We submit the question to the arbitration of figures, which, it is said, do not lie. With regard to the bushel-measure products of the soil, of which we have already taken an inventory, we have seen that there is a balance against the South in favor of the North of *seventeen million four hundred and twenty-three thousand one hundred and fifty-two bushels,* and a difference in the value of the same, also in favor of the North, of *forty-four million seven hundred and eighty-two thousand six hundred and thirty-six dollars.* It is certainly a most novel kind of agricultural superiority that the South claims on that score! . . .

Frederick Law Olmsted Criticizes the South's Lack of Material Progress, 1861

. . . One of the grand errors, out of which this rebellion has grown, came from supposing that whatever nourishes wealth and gives power to an ordinary civilized community must command as much for a slave-holding community. The truth has been overlooked that the accumulation of wealth and the power of a nation are contingent not merely upon the primary value of the surplus of productions of which it has to dispose, but very largely also upon the way in which the income from its surplus is distributed and reinvested. Let a man be absent from almost any part of the North twenty years, and he is struck, on his return, by what we call the "improvements" which have been made. Better buildings, churches, schoolhouses, mills, railroads, etc. In New York city alone, for instance, at least two hundred millions of dollars have been reinvested merely in an improved housing of the people; in labour-saving machinery, waterworks, gasworks, etc., and much more. It is not difficult to see where the profits of our manufacturers and merchants are. Again, go into the country, and there is no end of substantial proof of twenty years of agricultural prosperity, not alone in roads, canals, bridges, dwellings, barns and fences, but in books and furniture, and gardens, and pictures, and in the better dress and evidently higher education of the people. But where will the returning traveller see the accumulated cotton profits of twenty years in Mississippi? Ask the cotton-planter for them, and he will point in reply, not to dwellings, libraries, churches, school-houses, mills, railroads, or anything of the kind; he will point to his negroes—to almost nothing else. Negroes such as stood for five hundred dollars once, now represent a thousand dollars. We must look then in Virginia and those Northern Slave States which have the monopoly of supplying negroes, for the real wealth which the sale of cotton has brought to the South. But where is the evidence of it? where anything to compare with the evidence of accumulated profits to be seen in any Free State? If certain portions of Virginia have been a little improving, others unquestionably have been deteriorating, growing shabbier, more comfortless, less convenient. The total increase in wealth of the population during the last twenty years shows for almost nothing. One year's improvements of a Free State exceed it all. . . .

J. D. B. DeBow Explains Southern Social Harmony, 1860

. . . Having then followed out, step by step, and seen to what amounts the so much paraded competition and conflict between the non-slaveholding and slaveholding interests of the South; I will proceed to present several general considerations which must be found powerful enough to influence the non-slaveholders, if the claims of patriotism were inadequate, to resist any attempt to overthrow the institutions and industry of the section to which they belong.

1. *The non-slaveholder of the South is assured that the remuneration afforded by his labor, over and above the expense of living, is larger than that which is afforded by the same labor in the free States.* To be convinced of this he has only to compare the value of labor in the Southern cities with those of the North, and to take note annually of the large number of laborers who are represented to be out of employment there, and who migrate to our shores, as well as to other sections. No white laborer in return has been forced to leave our midst or remain without employment. Such as have left, have immigrated from States where slavery was less productive. Those who come among us are enabled soon to retire to their homes with a handsome competency. The statement is nearly as true for the agricultural as for other interests, as the statistics will show. . . .

2. *The non-slaveholders, as a class, are not reduced by the necessity of our condition, as is the case in the free States, to find employment in crowded cities and come into competition in close and sickly workshops and factories, with remorseless and untiring machinery.* They have but to compare their condition in this particular with the mining and manufacturing operatives of the North and Europe, to be thankful that God has reserved them for a better fate. Tender women, aged men, delicate children, toil and labor there from early dawn until after candle light, from one year to another, for a miserable pittance, scarcely above the starvation point and without hope of amelioration. The records of British free labor have long

exhibited this and those of our own manufacturing States are rapidly reaching it and would have reached it long ago, but for the excessive bounties which in the way of tariffs have been paid to it, without an equivalent by the slaveholding and non-slaveholding laborer of the South. Let this tariff cease to be paid for a single year and the truth of what is stated will be abundantly shown. . . .

[3.] *The non-slaveholder of the South preserves the status of the white man, and is not regarded as an inferior or a dependent.* He is not told that the Declaration of Independence, when it says that all men are born free and equal, refers to the negro equally with himself. It is not proposed to him that the free negro's vote shall weigh equally with his own at the ballot-box, and that the little children of both colors shall be mixed in the classes and benches of the school-house, and embrace each other filially in its outside sports. It never occurs to him, that a white man could be degraded enough to boast in a public assembly, as was recently done in New York, of having actually slept with a negro. And his patriotic ire would crush with a blow the free negro who would dare, in his presence, as is done in the free States, to characterize the father of the country as a "scoundrel." No white man at the South serves another as a body servant, to clean his boots, wait on his table, and perform the menial services of his household. His blood revolts against this, and his necessities never drive him to it. He is a companion and an equal. When in the employ of the slaveholder, or in intercourse with him, he enters his hall, and has a seat at his table. If a distinction exists, it is only that which education and refinement may give, and this is so courteously exhibited as scarcely to strike attention. The poor white laborer at the North is at the bottom of the social ladder, whilst his brother here has ascended several steps and can look down upon those who are beneath him, at an infinite remove.

[4.] *The non-slaveholder knows that as soon as his savings will admit, he can become a slaveholder, and thus relieve his wife from the necessities of the kitchen and the laundry, and his children from the labors of the field.* This, with ordinary frugality, can, in general, be accomplished in a few years, and is a process continually going on. Perhaps twice the number of poor men at the South own a slave to what owned a slave ten years ago. The universal disposition is to purchase. It is the first use for savings, and the negro purchased is the last possession to be parted with. If a woman, her children become heir-looms and make the nucleus of an estate. It is within my knowledge, that a plantation of fifty or sixty persons has been established, from the descendants of a single female, in the course of the lifetime of the original purchaser.

[5.] *The large slaveholders and proprietors of the South begin life in great part as non-slaveholders.* It is the nature of property to change hands. Luxury, liberality, extravagance, depreciated land, low prices, debt, distribution among children, are continually breaking up estates. All over the new States of the Southwest enormous estates are in the hands of men who began life as overseers or city clerks, traders or merchants. Often the overseer marries the widow. Cheap lands, abundant harvests, high prices, give the poor man soon a negro. His ten bales of cotton bring him another, and second crop increases his purchases, and so he goes on opening land and adding labor until in a few years his draft for $20,000 upon his merchant becomes a very marketable commodity. . . .

[6.] *The sons of the non-slaveholder are and have always been among the leading and ruling spirits of the South; in industry as well as in politics.* Every man's experience in his own neighborhood will evince this. He has but to task his memory. In this class are the McDuffies, Langdon Cheves, Andrew Jacksons, Henry Clays, and Rusks, of the past; the Hammonds, Yanceys, Orrs, Memmingers, Benjamins, Stephens, Soules, Browns of Mississippi, Simms, Porters, Magraths, Aikens, Maunsel Whites, and an innumerable host of the present; and what is to be noted, these men have not been made demagogues for that reason, as in other quarters, but are among the most conservative among us. Nowhere else in the world have intelligence and virtue disconnected from ancestral estates, the same opportunities for advancement, and nowhere else is their triumph more speedy and signal.

[7.] *Without the institution of slavery, the great staple products of the South would cease to be grown, and the immense annual results, which are distributed among every class of the community, and which give life to every branch of industry; would cease.* The world furnishes no instances of these products being grown upon a large scale by free labor. The English now acknowledge their failure in the East Indies. Brazil, whose slave population nearly equals our own, is the only South American State which has prospered. Cuba, by her slave labor, showers wealth upon old Spain, whilst the British West India Colonies have now ceased to be a source of revenue, and from opulence have been, by emancipation, reduced to beggary. St. Domingo shared the same fate, and the poor whites have been massacred equally with the rich. . . .

In conclusion I must apologize to the non-slaveholders of the South, of which class, I was myself until very recently a member, for having deigned to notice at all the infamous libels which the common enemies of the South have circulated against them, and which our everyday experience refutes; but the occasion seemed a fitting one to place them truly and rightly before the world. This I have endeavored faithfully to do. They fully understand the momentous questions which now agitate the land in all their relations. They perceive the inevitable drift of Northern aggression, and know that if necessity impel to it, as I verily believe it does at this moment, the establishment of a Southern confederation will be a sure refuge from the storm. *In such a confederation our rights and possessions would be secure, and the wealth being retained at home, to build up our towns and cities, to extend our railroads, and increase our shipping, which now goes in tariffs or other involuntary or voluntary tributes, to other sections; opulence would be diffused throughout all classes, and we should become the freest, the happiest and the most prosperous and powerful nation upon earth.* . . .

James Henry Hammond Claims
Southern Cultural Superiority, 1845

. . . In a social point of view the abolitionists pronounce Slavery to be a monstrous evil. If it was so, it would be our own peculiar concern, and superfluous benevolence in them to lament over it. Seeing their bitter hostility to us, they might leave us to cope with our own calamities. But they make war upon us out of excess of charity, and attempt to purify by covering us with calumny. You have read and assisted to circulate a great deal about affrays, duels and murders, occurring here, and all attributed to the terrible demoralization of Slavery. Not a single event of this sort takes place among us, but it is caught up by the abolitionists, and paraded over the world, with endless comments, variations and exaggerations. You should not take what reaches you as a mere sample, and infer that there is a vast deal more you never hear. You hear all, and more than all, the truth.

It is true that the point of honor is recognized throughout the slave region, and that disputes of certain classes are frequently referred for adjustment, to the "trial by combat." It would not be appropriate for me to enter, in this letter, into a defence of the practice of duelling, nor to maintain at length, that it does not tarnish the character of a people to acknowledge a standard of honor. Whatever evils may arise from it, however, they cannot be attributed to Slavery, since the same custom prevails both in France and England. . . . Slavery has nothing to do with these things. Stability and peace are the first desires of every slave-holder, and the true tendency of the system. It could not possibly exist amid the eternal anarchy and civil broils of the ancient Spanish dominions in America. And for this very reason, domestic Slavery has ceased there. So far from encouraging strife, such scenes of riot and bloodshed, as have within the last few years disgraced our Northern cities, and as you have lately witnessed in Birmingham and Bristol and Wales, not only never have occurred, but I will venture to say, never will occur in our slave-holding States. The only thing that can create a mob (as you might call it) here, is the appearance of an abolitionist, whom the people assemble to chastise. And this is no more of a mob, than a rally of shepherds to chase a wolf out of their pastures would be one. . . .

It is roundly asserted, that we are not so well educated nor so religious here as elsewhere. I will not go into tedious statistical statements on these subjects. Nor have I, to tell the truth, much confidence in the details of what are commonly set forth as statistics. As to education, you will probably admit that slave-holders should have more leisure for mental culture than most people. And I believe it is charged against them, that they are peculiarly fond of power, and ambitious of honors. If this be so, as all the power and honors of this country are won mainly by intellectual superiority, it might be fairly presumed, that slave-holders would not be neglectful of education. In proof of the accuracy of this presumption, I point you to the facts, that our Presidential chair has been occupied for forty-four out of fifty-six years, by slave-holders; that another has been recently elected to fill it for four more, over an opponent who was a slave-holder also; and that in the Federal Offices and both Houses of Congress, considerably more than a due proportion of those acknowledged to stand in the first rank are from the South. In this arena, the intellects of the free and slave States meet in full and fair competition. Nature must have been unusually bountiful to us, or we have been at least reasonably assiduous in the cultivation of such gifts as she has bestowed—unless indeed you refer our superiority to moral qualities, which I am sure *you* will not. More wealthy we are not; nor would mere wealth avail in such rivalry.

The piety of the South is unobtrusive. We think it proves but little, though it is a confident thing for a man to claim that he stands higher in the estimation of his Creator, and is less a sinner than his neighbor. If vociferation is to carry the question of religion, the North, and probably the Scotch, have it. Our sects are few, harmonious, pretty much united among themselves, and pursue their avocations in humble peace. In fact, our professors of religion seem to think—whether correctly or not—that it is their duty "to do good in secret," and to carry their holy comforts to the heart of each individual, without reference to class *or color,* for his special enjoyment, and not with a view to exhibit their zeal before the world. So far as numbers are concerned, I believe our clergymen, when called on to make a showing, have never had occasion to blush, if comparisons were drawn between the free and slave States. And although our presses do not teem with controversial pamphlets, nor our pulpits shake with excommunicating thunders, the daily walk of our religious communicants furnishes, apparently, as little food for gossip as is to be found in most other regions. It may be regarded as a mark of our want of excitability—though that is a quality accredited to us in an eminent degree—that few of the remarkable religious *Isms* of the present day have taken root among us. We have been so irreverent as to laugh at Mormonism and Millerism, which have created such commotions farther North; and modern prophets have no honor in our country. Shakers, Rappists, Dunkers, Socialists, Fourrierists and the like, keep themselves afar off. Even Puseyism has not yet moved us. You may attribute this to our domestic Slavery if you choose. I believe you would do so justly. There is no material here for such characters to operate upon. . . .

George Fitzhugh Praises Southern Society, 1854

. . . At the slaveholding South all is peace, quiet, plenty and contentment. We have no mobs, no trades unions, no strikes for higher wages, no armed resistance to the law, but little jealousy of the rich by the poor. We have but few in our jails, and fewer in our poor houses. We produce enough of the comforts and necessaries of life for a population three or four times as numerous as ours. We are wholly exempt from the torrent of pauperism, crime, agrarianism, and infidelity which Europe is pouring from her jails and alms houses on the already crowded North. Population increases slowly, wealth rapidly. In the tide water region of Eastern Virginia, as far as our experience extends, the crops have doubled in fifteen years, whilst the population has been almost stationary. In the same period the lands, owing to improvements of the soil and the many fine houses erected in the country, have nearly doubled in value. This ratio of improvement has been approximated or exceeded wherever in the South slaves are numerous. We have enough for the present, and no Malthusian* spectres frightening us for the future. Wealth is more equally distributed than at the North, where a few millionaires own most of the property of the country. (These millionaires are men of cold hearts and weak minds; they know how to make money, but not how to use it, either for the benefit of themselves or of others.) High intellectual and moral attainments, refinement of head and heart, give standing to a man in the South, however poor he may be. Money is, with few exceptions, the only thing that ennobles at the North. We have poor among us, but none who are over-worked and under-fed. We do not crowd cities because lands are abundant and their owners kind, merciful and hospitable. The poor are as hospitable as the rich, the negro as the white man. Nobody dreams of turning a friend, a relative, or a stranger from his door. The very negro who deems it no crime to steal, would scorn to sell his hospitality. We have no loafers, because the poor relative or friend who borrows our horse, or spends a week under our roof, is a welcome guest. The loose economy, the wasteful mode of living at the South, is a blessing when rightly considered; it keeps want, scarcity and famine at a distance, because it leaves room for retrenchment. The nice, accurate economy of France, England and New England, keeps society always on the verge of famine, because it leaves no room to retrench, that is to live on a part only of what they now consume. Our society exhibits no appearance of precocity, no symptoms of decay. A long course of continuing improvement is in prospect before us, with no limits which human foresight can descry. Actual liberty and equality with our white population has been approached much nearer than in the free States. Few of our whites ever work as day laborers, none as cooks, scullions, ostlers, body servants, or in other menial capacities. One free citizen does not lord it over another; hence that feeling of independence and equality that distinguishes us; hence that pride of character, that self-respect, that give us ascendancy when we come in contact with Northerners. It is a distinction to be a Southerner, as it was once to be a Roman citizen. . . .

A New Orleans Editor Boasts of Southern Prosperity, 1861

. . . But, why is there such objection made to the withdrawal of the South? We are told by Abolition orators and organs that the South is a poor, miserable region—that most of the wealth, the enterprise, and the intel-

---

* Reverend Thomas Malthus was a British economic philosopher who, in 1798, argued that there was a tendency in nature for populations to exceed their means of subsistence and resources, resulting in disease, famine, and other suffering.

ligence of the nation is in the North—that the Southern people, as was said by Sumner in the Senate, are identified with, and apologists for, an institution essentially "barbaric"—that our section is unable to support a mail system, and that we are pensioners, to that extent, of the Federal Government—that we are, in short, a semicivilized, God-forsaken people, a long ways behind the "great North" in the arts, in refinement, in education, in enterprise, and in everything else that constitutes what they call "civilization." One would suppose they would be eager to be relieved of association with a people of whom they have so poor an opinion. So far the contrary, however, they are, as we have before said, mortally offended at the bare idea of our dissolving with them our political connection.

There must be a reason for this, as there is for everything else, and the reason is plain enough. All that they say about the South is false, and, what is more, they know it to be false. They know that the South is the main prop and support of the Federal system. They know that it is Southern productions that constitute the surplus wealth of the nation, and enables us to import so largely from foreign countries. They know that it is their import trade that draws from the people's pockets sixty or seventy millions of dollars per annum, in the shape of duties, to be expended mainly in the North, and in the protection and encouragement of Northern interests. They know that it is the export of Southern productions, and the corresponding import of foreign goods, that gives profitable employment to their shipping. They know that the bulk of the duties is paid by the Southern people, though first collected at the North, and that, by the iniquitous operation of the Federal Government, these duties are mainly expended among the Northern people. They know that they can plunder and pillage the South, as long as they are in the same Union with us, by other means, such as fishing bounties, navigation laws, robberies of the public lands, and every other possible mode of injustice and peculation. They know that in the Union they can steal Southern property in slaves, without risking civil war, which would be certain to occur if such a thing were done from the independent South. And, above and beyond all this, is the Puritanic love of mean tyranny and cold-blooded, inexorable oppression, which the Union enables them to cherish and reduce to practice—coupled with the Pharisaical boast of "holier than thou," which they are constantly uttering as a reproach to the South—both of which feelings are innate in the descendants of the Pilgrims, and have become a part of their nature, which they could not get rid of if they wished.

These are the reasons why these people do not wish the South to secede from the Union. They are enraged at the prospect of being despoiled of the rich feast upon which they have so long fed and fattened, and which they were just getting ready to enjoy with still greater *goût* and gusto. They are mad as hornets because the prize slips them just as they are ready to grasp it. Their fruitless wailing and frantic rage only serve to confirm the South in her inflexible determination to break up an alliance which is as unnatural as it is, to us, oppressive and degrading.

↜ E S S A Y S

The evaluations of the differences between the sections that were proffered by contemporaries were, of course, part of a propaganda war. The historian's task is to discover the reality behind the polemics. The first selection reprinted here comes from Edward Pessen of the City University of New York. He finds that a comparison of the social structures, economic systems, and political practices of the two regions reveals that the similarities outweigh the differences. By contrast, James M. McPherson of Princeton University concludes that the South was very different from the rest of the country yet it was more in step with contemporary European societies than were other areas of the United States.

The Similarities Between
the Antebellum North and South

EDWARD PESSEN

How different from each other were the North and South before the Civil War? Recent work by historians of antebellum America throws interesting new light on this old question. Since some of these studies deal with individual communities, others with single themes of antebellum life, they are in a sense Pirandelloan pieces of evidence in search of an overarching synthesis that will relate them to one another and to earlier findings and interpretations. My modest hope is that the discussion that follows will be useful to historians in pursuit of such a synthesis.

The terms "North" and "South" are, of course, figures of speech that distort and oversimplify a complex reality, implying homogeneity in geographical sections that, in fact, were highly variegated. Each section embraced a variety of regions and communities that were dissimilar in climatic, topographical, demographic, and social characteristics. If, as Bennett H. Wall has written, "there never has been the 'one' South described by many historians," neither has there been the one North. Historians who have compared the antebellum South and North without referring to the diversity of each have not necessarily been unaware of this diversity. Their premise, in speaking of the North and South, is that the Mason-Dixon line divided two distinctive civilizations, the basic similarities within each of which transcended its internal differences.

The modern discussion is a continuation of a scholarly controversy that has engaged some of the giants of the American historical profession. Charles A. Beard, Ulrich B. Phillips, Allan Nevins, David M. Potter, C. Vann Woodward, and other scholars of stature have been drawn to the theme because it is inextricably related to perhaps the most fascinating of all questions in American history: the causes of the Civil War. Many historians attribute that "irrepressible conflict" to the fundamental differences

From "How Different from Each Other Were the Antebellum North and South?" by Edward Pessen, *American Historical Review,* Vol. 85, No. 5, December 1980, pp. 1119–1143, 1147–1149. Reprinted by permission of Edward Pessen.

between the two civilizations that were parties to it. Even those scholars who have played down the role of sectional differences in bringing on the war have found themselves unable to avoid comparing the ways of life and thought of the two belligerents.

Unsurprisingly, the discussion has produced a variety of interpretations. Some scholars have emphasized the similarities of the North and South, a much greater number have stressed their dissimilarities, and others have judiciously alluded to their significant likenesses—"commonalities," in Potter's terminology—and unlikenesses. The greater popularity, among scholars and laity alike, of comparisons that emphasize differences is doubtless due, in part, to the fact that the war heightened our perceptions of those supposedly irreconcilable differences and, in part, to the fact that several dissimilarities were so striking, so unarguable, so obviously significant. While much of the scholarly controversy has concerned subtle sectional distinctions, whether in values, ideals, or other complex intangibles that might be read one way or the other, depending on the predilections of the interpreter, other disparities transcend subjectivity, based as they are on hard, quantifiable evidence.

Here were two sections containing roughly equal areas for human settlement. Yet on the eve of the Civil War the population of the North was more than 50 percent greater than that of the South. The most dramatic disparity concerned racial balance: roughly one-quarter of a million Northern blacks comprised slightly more than 1 percent of the Northern population; the more than four million blacks in the South constituted one-third of the Southern population. And almost 95 percent of Southern blacks were slaves. Although the value of agricultural products in the two sections was almost equal, Northern superiority in manufactures, railroad mileage, and commercial profits was overwhelming, far surpassing the Northern advantage in population. Similarly, Northern urban development outdistanced Southern, whether measured by the number of cities or by the size and proportions of the population within them. What did these and other, harder to measure, differences signify? To what extent were they balanced out by important sectional similarities? These are among the questions this essay will consider.

In comparing the great antebellum sections, it is useful to remember that all powerful, complex, and viable contemporaneous societies are likely to converge or be similar in some respects, dissimilar in others. It would be lovely were we able to estimate precisely the relative significance of the various criteria of comparison, the points at which similarities or differences become critical, and the nature of the balance between likenesses and unlikenesses that would justify appraising two societies as "essentially" different or similar. Alas, we cannot. A society or civilization is a complex Gestalt. The subtle reciprocity binding together its elements cannot be understood by mechanically attempting to weigh the significance of each of these elements and then adding up the total. The impossibility of contriving a simplistic calculus for measuring societies does not, of course, mean that a sensible comparison is impossible. It means only that such a comparison will inevitably be subjective and serve, at best, as a point of departure to those who evaluate the evidence differently.

A comprehensive comparison of the two sections would overlook nothing, not even the weather, which, according to Phillips, "has been the chief agency in making the South distinctive." In the space available here I shall focus on what our sociological friends might call three social indicators: (1) the economy, (2) the social structure, and (3) politics and power. In selecting these matters for examination, I do not mean to suggest that they are more important than values, ideals, the life of the mind, or any number of other features of antebellum life. Tangible phenomena may be easier to measure than intangible, but they offer no better clue to the essential character of a place and a people. I emphasize economic, social, and political themes because all of them are clearly important, the evidence on them is substantial, and each has recently been re-examined to interesting effect.

The economic practices of each section—one hesitates to call them economic "systems" in the face of the contradictory and largely planless if not improvisatory nature of these practices—were similarly complex. Northerners and Southerners alike made their living primarily in agriculture. Guided by the unique weather and the unequal length of the growing seasons in their sections, Northern and Southern farmers increasingly specialized, but in dissimilar crops. Tobacco and, above all, rice, sugar, and cotton were largely unknown to the North. Yet in the South, as in the North, farmers—whether large or small—sought and, for the most part achieved, self-sufficiency. They produced more grains and corn than anything else and in both sections raised and kept domestic animals roughly equal in quantity and, it has recently been claimed, comparable in quality. In view of the regularity with which Northern farmers brushed aside the lonely voices in their midst who urged subordination of profits to the "long-range needs of the soil," their money-mindedness in planting wheat (their own great dollar earner) year after year, and their unsentimental readiness to dispose of "family land" so long as the price was right, what Stanley L. Engerman has said about Southern planters seems to apply equally well to Northern agriculturalists: they were certainly not "non-calculating individuals not concerned with money."

The enduring popularity of *Gone with the Wind* suggests that the American popular mind continues to believe that the Old South was a land of large plantations populated by masters both honorable and courtly, cruel and sinful, by Southern belles "beautiful, graceful . . . , bewitching in coquetry, yet strangely steadfast," by loyal, lovable, comic, but sometimes surly Negroes, and by white trash or "po' buckra." American historians have, however, known for at least half a century that the plantation legend "is one of great inaccuracy"—false to the character of Southern society, to the diversity of Southern whites, and to the realities of black life. Great plantations centering on splendid mansions did exist in the Old South but not in very great numbers.

The most distinctive feature of the antebellum Southern economy, as of Southern life as a whole, was, of course, its "peculiar institution." Slavery had not been unknown in the North, flourishing through much of the seventeenth and eighteenth centuries and persisting in New Jersey until 1846. But it had involved relatively few blacks and had had slight effect on Northern life and thought. Northern public opinion, better represented by the authors of the Federal Constitution in 1787 and the Missouri Compromise in 1820 than by the abolitionists of the antebellum decades, accepted slavery, approved of doing business with those who controlled it, abhorred its black victims, and loathed Northern whites who agitated against it. Northern acquiescence in Southern slavery does not erase this most crucial difference between the sections, but it does argue for the complementarity and economic interdependence of North and South.

The profitability and other economic implications of antebellum slavery have become the subjects of intense recent debate, stimulating the development of cliometrics or the new economic history. Since slavery was more than a labor system, historians have also searchingly investigated its non-economic implications for both blacks and whites. A fair reading of the recent evidence and argument is that, while more slaves by far worked as field hands, slaves also performed with great efficiency a great variety of other jobs, many of them skilled, allowing for significant economic differentiation within the slave community. And, as exemplary workers and as costly and valuable properties, skilled slaves were ordinarily spared gratuitous maltreatment or deprivation. Despite the inevitable brutality of the system, slaves appear to have managed to maintain the integrity of their personalities, customs, values, and family ties.

Several trade unionists in the antebellum North agreed with slavery's apologists that not only the working and living conditions but in some respects the "liberty" enjoyed by Northern hirelings compared unfavorably with the situation of slaves. These were patently self-serving arguments, designed to put the lot of the Northern worker in the worst possible light. The fact remains that the economic gap between enslaved black and free white workers in antebellum South and North was narrower than historians once thought. Evidence bearing on the conditions of white Northern as well as black Southern labor demonstrates that during the middle decades of the nineteenth century the real wages of Northern workingmen declined and their living conditions remained bleak, their job security was reduced, their skills were increasingly devalued, and in many respects their lives became more insecure and precarious.

At mid-century industrial workers in the South as in the North worked primarily in small shops and households rather than in factories. Trade unionists in Baltimore, Louisville, St. Louis, and New Orleans were with few exceptions skilled and semi-skilled white artisans, precisely as they were in Philadelphia, New York, Boston, and Pittsburgh. In Southern as in Northern towns and cities, the least skilled and prestigious jobs were those done preponderantly by Catholic immigrants rather than by older Protestant, ethnic groups. Significantly, the South attracted far fewer of the antebellum era's "new immigrants"—that is, Germans and Irish—than did the North. For all of their smaller numbers in the South, European immigrants played an economic and social role there that was not dissimilar to what it was in the North. Diverse measurable evidence indicates that the pattern of immigrant life in the United States was national, rather than distinctly regional, in character. A similar point can be made about Southern urbanism and manufacturing—namely, quantitative distinctiveness (or deficiency), qualitative similarity to the North. Although the value of Southern manufactured products was usually less than one-fifth of the national total during the antebellum decades, the South was hardly a region devoid of industrial production. Articulate Southerners "crusade[d] to bring the cotton mills to the cotton fields," and, whether due to their exhortations or to the play of market forces, the amount of capital the slave states invested in cotton manufacturing doubled between 1840 and 1860, surpassing their rate of population growth. Because the South nevertheless lagged far behind the Northeast in manufacturing, one influential school of historians has described the antebellum economy—and, for that matter, Southern society as a whole—as noncapitalist, prebourgeois, or "seigneurial."

Some historians have criticized Southern deficiencies in commerce, finance, transportation, and manufacturing as manifestations of economic wrongheadedness and irrationality and have attributed to these deficiencies the South's defeat in the Civil War. A number of modern economic historians, cliometricians for the most part, have interpreted the evidence somewhat differently. Invoking the old argument of "comparative advantage," they have noted that heavy investment in cotton, the nation's great dollar earner in international trade, was hardly irrational, since it enabled the South to equal the national rate of profit during the era. Southerners who did invest in Southern factories got a return that compared favorably with industrial profits elsewhere. (Why, ask the critics, didn't they invest more of their capital that way?) If Southern manufacturing was outdistanced by that in the Northeast, it compared favorably with industrial production in the Northwest and, for that matter, in Continental Europe in the mid-nineteenth century. If the South suffered inordinately in the wake of the financial panics of 1837 and 1839, it was, as Reginald C. McGrane noted long ago, precisely because the South had speculated excessively in transportation projects and land acquisition as well as other investments. The South's "unusually favorable system of navigable streams and rivers" has been cited to explain its lag in railroads. Yet in the 1840s Southern railroads "equalled or exceeded the national average capitalization per mile." The views of many scholars are expressed in Gavin Wright's recent observation that "before the War the South was wealthy, prosperous, expanding geographically, and gaining economically at rates that compared favorably to those of the rest of the country."

Antebellum Northern investors, like their counterparts in the South and in Europe, put their money into American products, industrial and agricultural, solid and flimsy, drawn almost entirely by the profit margin likely to result from their investment. Investors in all latitudes appear to have been indifferent to possible long-range consequences of their financial transactions, acting rather on the principle that the "rational" investment was the one likely to pay off. That the railroads, the diversified industry, and the commercial superiority of the North turned out to have important military implications in the 1860s could hardly have been anticipated by earlier profit-seekers. When the commercial magnates known as the Boston Associates invested heavily in factories built in the new suburbs of Boston, they hardly had in mind outfitting Union troops a generation later; they were much more concerned about maintaining close ties with Southern cotton magnates on whose raw materials they were so heavily dependent. There is something bizarre in historians, more than a century after the event, scrutinizing the economic behavior of antebellum capitalists and subjecting that behavior to unrealistic tests of rationality and farsightedness that these men themselves would have found farfetched.

To argue, however, as several historians have, that a substantial Southern lag—whether in railroad mileage or urban growth—is not as great when it is measured in *per capita* rather than absolute terms explains away rather than explains these fundamental sectional differences. For it can reasonably be maintained that the antebellum South's comparatively small white population (which accounted for its high *per capita* rates) was not due to historical accident but to significant features, if not failings, in Southern civilization. That all differences between two communities indubitably have a historical explanation—be it the smaller population, the hotter climate, or the prevalence of enslaved blacks—in no sense detracts from the significance of those differences. The burden of my argument is not that antebellum economic developments in the states south of the Potomac were almost exactly like, let alone a mirror image of, those in the states north of the river but rather that the economies were similar in significant ways that are often taken for granted, as, for example, in the similar operation of the profit motive or the similarity of the laws of inheritance in the two sections. And even where, as in industrial production and labor systems, the South and North differed most glaringly, modern evidence has reduced and placed in a somewhat different perspective the gulf between them. As for the recent suggestion that the South was not capitalistic, I shall defer comment until I have first dealt with social and political matters, since capitalism concerns more than economic arrangements alone.

Historians have long known that a society's social structure offers an important clue to its character. The kind of social classes that exist, the gulf between them, their roles in society, the ease or difficulty of access to higher from lower rungs on the social ladder, and the relationships between the classes tell as much about a civilization as do any other phenomena. What distinguishes modern from earlier historians in their treatment of social class is the extent to which they have borrowed from social scientists both in theorizing about class and in the methodology used for measurement. Employing these new approaches, historians have drastically modified earlier notions of antebellum society.

The ancient belief that the white antebellum South consisted of two classes, wealthy planters at the top and a great mass of poor whites below, may continue to command some popular acceptance. That belief has been so long dead among historians, however, that as early as 1946 Fabian Linden could remark that "the debunking of the 'two class' fallacy" had "become the tedious cliché." For, beginning in 1940 and continuing steadily thereafter, Frank L. Owsley and a group of scholars influenced by his work utilized hitherto neglected primary sources to reveal that the most typical white Southerners by far were small farmers working the modest acreage they owned with few, if any, slaves.

The too neat portrait that the Owsley school drew of the white Southern social structure was quite similar to the picture of *Northern* society accepted by historians less than a generation ago. The white population was ostensibly composed primarily of the great "middling orders," hard-working, proud, and not unprosperous farmers for the most part, whose chance to rise even higher socially matched the opportunities an increasingly democratic society gave them to exert political influence and power. Small groups of rich men—great planters in the one clime and merchants and industrialists in the other—occupied the highest social plateau; professionals who served the rich were slightly above the middle, which was occupied by small business people and independent farmers, skilled artisans, and clerks; and below them stood industrial and landless agricultural laborers. Since class is determined not by bread alone, blacks—whether slave or free and regardless of how much individuals among them had managed to accumulate—were universally relegated to the lowest levels of the social structure, scorned even by white vagrants and frequently unemployed workers, urban and rural, who constituted America's equivalent of a propertyless proletariat.

The achievement of recent research is its transformation of what was a rather blurred image of social groups, whose membership and possessions were both unclear, into a more sharply focused picture. By digging deeper, particularly in nineteenth-century data on wealth and property, historians have come close to knowing the numbers of families belonging to different wealth strata and the amount of wealth these families owned. The beauty of the new evidence on who and how many owned what and how much is that in the antebellum era wealth appears to have been the surest sign of social, as well as of economic, position. Antebellum wealth was almost invariably made in socially acceptable ways. Modern scholars have found that "the social divisions of antebellum America were essentially wealth-holding categories." The upper class did not comprise so much the families who "controlled the means of production" as it did the families who "controlled the vast wealth created largely through the exchange of goods produced." Degree of wealth was the surest sign of the quality of housing, furnishings, and household goods a family could afford, of its style of living and uses of leisure, and of the social circle within which it moved and its

individual members married. Gathering from the manuscript census schedules, probate inventories, and tax assessors' reports statistically valid sam-
ples or, in some cases, evidence on every family in the community under
study, modern scholars have been able to arrange the antebellum Southern
and Northern populations on a wealth-holding scale. While it is close to a
statistical inevitability that the distribution of wealth in the South and North
would not be precisely the same, the most striking feature of the evidence
is how similarly wealth was distributed—or maldistributed—in the two
sections.

On the eve of the Civil War one-half of the free adult males in both
the South and the North held less than 1 percent of the real and personal
property. In contrast, the richest 1 percent owned 27 percent of the wealth.
Turning from the remarkable similarity in sectional patterns of wealth-
holding at the bottom and the very top, the richest 5 to 10 percent of
propertyowners controlled a somewhat greater share of the South's wealth,
while what might be called the upper middle deciles (those below the top
tenth) held a slightly smaller share in the North. The South also came close
to monopolizing wealthy counties, the per capita wealth of which was $4,000
or more and, despite its smaller population, the South, according to the
1860 census, contained almost two-thirds of those persons in the nation
whose worth was at least $110,000. According to Lee Soltow, the leading
student of this evidence, these sectional disparities "could be attributed
almost entirely to slave values. . . . If one could eliminate slave market
value from the distribution of wealth in 1860 . . . , the inequality levels in
the North and South were similar."

In view of the centrality of slavery to the antebellum South, it is idle
to speak of "eliminating the market value" of slaves from the sectional
comparison. Northern free labor, rural and industrial, also represented a
form of "sectional wealth," if a much overlooked form. Although as individual human beings they did not add to their own private wealth or to
the wealth of the employers they served, their labor created wealth for
themselves and for these same capitalists at rates of productivity that, I
believe, even Robert W. Fogel and Stanley L. Engerman would concede
compared favorably with the rates of the most efficient slaves. In other
words, the North had access to a form of wealth, free labor, that was
roughly as valuable per capita as was slave wealth, however absent this
Northern wealth was from the reports prepared by census takers and assessors. Given the known habits of these officials to overlook small property
holdings—precisely the kind of holdings that would have been owned by
Northern working people—and to accept as true the lies people swore to
as their worth, it is likely that the fairly substantial cumulative wealth owned
by small farmers and modest wage earners was almost entirely omitted
from the wealth equation. Such groups were far more numerous in the
North than in the South. Had slaves been treated as part of the potential
property-owning Southern population to which they actually belonged, instead of being treated as property pure and simple, the total wealth of the
antebellum South would have been diminished by several billion dollars:

the product of multiplying the number of slaves by the average market price of almost $1,000 per slave. The addition of nearly four million very poor black people to the number of potential propertyowners in the South would have increased its rate of inequality (and the Gini coefficient of concentration that measures it), although not everywhere to the same extent.

Wealth in both sections was distributed more equally—perhaps the more apt phrase is less unequally—in the countryside than in towns and cities. While the rural North has been less intensively investigated than its Southern counterpart, enough research has been completed to disclose that the North was hardly a haven of egalitarian distribution of property. Rural Wisconsin (which had a Gini coefficient of inequality as high as that of antebellum Texas), the Michigan frontier, and northwestern New York State were centers of inequality and poverty. At mid-century, the proportion of white men who owned land in any amount was substantially lower in the Northwest than in the South. The percentage of free males owning land in the North as a whole was slightly smaller than in the South. Owing to the absence of slaves and to the relative paucity of very large farms, wealth was somewhat less unequally distributed in the rural North than in the South.

In investigating the distribution of wealth in the antebellum rural South, scholars have probed data on different states, counties, and regions. The patterns throughout are remarkably similar, whether for wealth in general, land and real estate, or personal and slave property. Accentuating the maldistribution of landed wealth—whether in Alabama, Mississippi, Louisiana, Texas, the "cotton South," or the agricultural South as a whole—was a fact of life that the Owsley school neglected: the dollar value per acre of large farms owned by slave-owning planters was substantially greater than the value per acre of the small farm. And yet, regardless of the nature of the soil or the proportion of large farms in a given region, the rates of wealth concentration were remarkably similar as well as constant during the decades before the war. Paralleling the recent finding that in antebellum Texas, no matter what the differences were "in climate, soil, and extent of settlement, the most striking fact is . . . the high degree of concentration in wealthholding across all the regions," another recent study reports no great differences in "the degree of inequality" between the cotton South and the other "major agricultural regions" of grain, tobacco, sugar, and rice production in 1860.

The distribution of slave wealth closely followed the pattern of other forms of Southern wealth. During the decade before the war, slaveownership was confined to between 20 and 25 percent of white families, and maldistribution of this form of property was the rule within the slave-owning population. Half of all slaveowners owned five or fewer slaves, with only one-tenth owning the twenty or more slaves that by Ulrich B. Phillip's definition made them "planters." Less than one-half of 1 percent owned one hundred or more slaves. As with other forms of wealth, the concentration of slave wealth increased slightly between 1850 and 1860.

While the South had long lagged behind the North in urban development, recent scholarship has unearthed evidence that Southern cities grew
at a remarkable rate during the antebellum decades. If the Southern rate
of urban expansion still did not match the Northern quantitatively, Southern
cities, old and new, were qualitatively not unlike their Northern counterparts. Antebellum cities in all latitudes were amazingly similar in the roles
they played in the political, administrative, financial, economic, artistic,
and intellectual affairs of their regions. Antebellum cities were also alike
in the types of men who ran them, in the underlying social philosophies
guiding those men, and in their "social configurations." Not the least of
the similarities of cities in both great sections was in their distribution of
wealth.

Three things can be said about the distribution of wealth in the towns
and cities of the Old South. Property ownership was even more concentrated there than in rural areas. Riches became more unequally distributed
with the passage of time, with the proportion of the propertyless increasing
sharply between 1850 and 1860. There was an increase too in the proportion
of urban wealth owned by the largest wealthholders—at least for the dozen
communities measured to date. And the patterns of wealth distribution in
Southern cities were very much like those that obtained in the North.

The pattern of wealth distribution in Providence and Newport (Rhode
Island), Pelham and Ware (Massachusetts), Newark, Pittsburgh, Cleveland,
Milwaukee, the great cities on the Northeastern seaboard, and a dozen
other Northern urban centers was impressively consistent and glaringly
unequal. The sharp maldistribution of the 1820s and 1830s became more
widely skewed with the passage of time (the Gini coefficients of inequality
for 1860 matched those prevalent in the South). On the eve of the Civil
War, the wealth of most cities, while greatly augmented, was "less widely
dispersed than it had been earlier"; the propertyless groups in Stonington
(Connecticut) and Chicago, for example, comprised between two-thirds and
three-fourths of all households by the outbreak of the war.

Nor do sectional rates of vertical mobility appear to have been much
different. In 1856 Cassius M. Clay told an Ohio audience that "the northern
laboring man could, and frequently did, rise above the condition [into]
which he was born to the first rank of society and wealth," but he "never
knew such an instance in the South." Recently unearthed evidence on the
social origins of the men in the "first rank" does not sustain Clay's surmise,
so popular with contemporary yeasayers. In the South, "increasing barriers
to slaveownership resulting from higher slave prices and the growing concentration of wealth" left "lesser planters," not to mention laboring men,
with their "aspiration thwarted." And in the North—whether in Wayne
County (Michigan), Newport, Stonington, small towns in Massachusetts,
Chicago, and Brooklyn, or the great cities of New York, Boston, and
Philadelphia—eminent and rich men of humble birth were a rarity. Evidence
on the more likely movement from a lower social position to an adjacent
one, rather than to the very top, remains in pitifully short supply. In antebellum Philadelphia, small New England counties, and rural Georgia, even

the modest movement from one plebian level to another appears to have seldom occurred.

Throwing important, if indirect, light on the relatively slight opportunities for upward social and economic movement antebellum America offered to poor or economically marginal men is the era's high rate of physical or geographical mobility. In rural as well as urban communities, in large cities and small, and on both sides of the Mason-Dixon line, armies of footloose Americans were on the move, following trails never dreamed of in the Turner thesis. One-half of the residents, primarily the poorer and propertyless, left those communities from one decade to another in their search for a more acceptable living. I have no doubt that future research will yet disclose that, during what was a period of economic expansion in both sections, significant numbers of Americans improved their lot, even if modestly. To date, however, the data reveal equally slight rates of social mobility and high rates of geographical mobility on both sides of the Mason-Dixon line.

Carl Degler has recently observed that Southern society "differed from northern in that the social hierarchy culminated in the planter, not the industrialist. At mid-century, great Northern fortunes, in fact, owed more to commerce and finance than to manufacturing. What is perhaps more important is that a sharply differentiated social hierarchy obtained in both sections. In Degler's phrase, planter status was "the ideal to which other white southerners aspired." A good case can be made for the equally magnetic attraction that exalted merchant status had for Northerners. If the fragmentary evidence on Virginia, Georgia, and the Carolinas, which Jane H. Pease has so effectively exploited, is any indication, then great planters lived less sybaritically and consumed less conspicuously than historians have previously thought. If Philip Hone's marvelous diary—two dozen full-to-the-brim volumes of life among the swells during the antebellum decades—has broader implication, then the Northeastern social and economic elite commanded a lifestyle of an elegance and costliness that, among other things, proved irresistibly attractive to the aristocratic Southerners who graced Hone's table, pursued diversion with other members of Hone's set, and married into its families—the Gardiners, Coolidges, Coldens, Bayards, Gouverneurs, and Kortrights.

That the social structures of the antebellum South and North were in some important respects similar does not, of course, make them carbon copies of one another. In this as in other respects the chief difference between the sections was that one of them harbored a huge class of enslaved blacks. John C. Calhoun, James H. Hammond, George Fitzhugh, and other influential Southern champions of white supremacy never ceased reminding their antebellum audiences, therefore, that in the South "the two great divisions of society [were] not the rich and the poor, but white and black, and all the former, the poor as well as the rich, belong to the upper classes." Several historians have recently agreed that great planters and small white farmers in the South shared common interests, for all the disparity in their condition. The interests of the different social classes will be considered in the discussion of influence and power that follows. Whatever these interests may have been, Southern whites, rural and urban, lived as did Northerners—in a stratified society marked by great inequalities in status, material condition, and opportunity.

Influence, power, and, above all, politics in antebellum America have been the subjects of massive recent research. Most discussions of antebellum politics have stressed differences between the major parties. The literature takes on new meaning peculiarly germane to this discussion when it is recast and its focus shifted to a comparison of politics in the North and South. Politics, as Samuel Johnson once observed, often touches human beings but lightly. A recent study of antebellum North Carolina reports that its political system, which was indifferent to pressing problems, was only saved from "violent explosions" by "its own practical insignificance." That people may be indifferent to the politics of their time, perhaps sensibly so, does not render politics insignificant to the historian. In retreating from history as past politics, some of us appear to have taken up a history of nonpolitics. This is silly. For how the political system works, whether for good or for ill, is as important a clue to the character of a civilization as any other.

By mid-century the American political system was everywhere formally democratic. Notorious exceptions to and limitations on democracy persisted, but they persisted in both North and South and for largely the same reasons. If blacks could not vote in the Old South, with rare exceptions neither could they vote in the Old North, where they were barred by statute, subterfuge, custom, and intimidation. The South initiated the movement to limit the powers and terms of office of the judiciary and substitute popular elections for the appointment of judges. When Fletcher M. Green reminded us a generation ago that antebellum Southern states created new, and modified old, constitutions that were fully as democratic as those in Northern states, he concluded that by this "progressive expansion in the application of the doctrine of political equality . . . , the aristocratic planter class had been shorn of its political power." Power, he claimed, had now been transferred to "the great mass of whites." As Green's critics were quick to point out, popular suffrage and theoretical rights to hold office are not synonymous with popular power. Yet these are not empty or hollow rights. That they have often been made so testifies not to their insignificance but rather to the importance of the larger context in which democratic political gains are registered. It remains neither a small matter nor a small similarity that on the constitutional level the antebellum North and South were similarly democratic and republican.

At least as important as a society's system for selecting political officeholders is the kind of men who are regularly selected and their characteristic performance in office. In collecting evidence on political figures, scholars have sought to measure the measurable—above all, the social and economic characteristics of officeholders and party leaders. I think it safe to assume that historians performing these chores have the wit to know

that an individual of whatever background is perfectly capable of tran-
scending it. Their unspoken working assumption is one that has been known
since before Aristotle: the material and social circumstances of men in
power may throw some light on their motives and behavior, taking on
added significance when these circumstances are uniform or close to uniform. That Charles A. Beard's mechanistic overemphasis of these points
may have given them a bad name does not detract from their usefulness.

Abundant data have been accumulated on the occupations, wealth and
property ownership, church affiliations, education, and other social indicators not only of antebellum officeholders in several dozen cities equally
divided between South and North and in counties in every Southern state
but also of state officials in all of the Southern and most of the Northern
states and of Congressmen from most of the states in the Union. The
resultant picture inevitably is not uniform. Humble county and town officials, for example, were less likely to be drawn from the highest levels of
wealth and from the most prestigious occupations than were men who
occupied more exalted state and federal positions. Aldermen and council-
men usually did not match the mayor either in wealth or in family prestige.
But the relatively slight social and economic differences found between
men at different levels of government or between men nominated by the
parties that dominated American politics from the 1830s to the 1850s were
not differences between the North and South. In the South as in the North,
men similar in their dissimilarity to their constituencies held office and
exercised behind-the-scenes influence. In contrast to the small farmers,
indigents, laborers, artisans, clerks, and shopkeepers—the men of little or
no property who constituted the great majority of the antebellum population—the men who held office and controlled the affairs of the major parties
were everywhere lawyers, merchants, businessmen, and relatively large
property owners. In the South they were inordinately men who owned
slaves and owned them in unusually large numbers. It may well be that a
society that is stratified economically and socially will confer leadership on
those who have what Robert A. Dahl has called substantial material "advantages." It is not clear that this is an iron law. What is clear is that the
Old South and the North awarded leadership to precisely such men.

More important than the social and economic backgrounds of political
leaders are their public behavior and the ideologies or "world views"
underlying this behavior. Not that the thinking or action of powerful men
is totally unaffected by their material circumstances. But, in view of the
complexity of any individual's ideology and of the diverse elements that
help shape it, the effect of these circumstances cannot be assumed and is
likely to vary from one individual to another. Although the political philosophies of men do not lend themselves to quantitative or precise measurement, the burden of recent scholarship is that most Southern and Northern political activists were similarly ambitious for worldly success,
opportunistic, materialistic, and disinclined to disturb their societies' social
arrangements. Men with values such as these were ideally suited to lead
the great pragmatic parties that dominated antebellum politics.

Many parties flashed across the American political horizon during the antebellum decades. That the Antimasonic Party, the Liberty Party, and the Free Soil Party almost entirely bypassed the South is an important difference between the sections. The South was not hospitable to organized political dissent, particularly dissent hostile to the expansion of slavery. These parties were small and ephemeral organizations whose leverage stemmed not so much from any great voting support they were able to command as from the nearly equal strength in both sections of the great major parties, the Democrats and the Whigs. Whoever would evaluate the actions of those who held executive or legislative office in antebellum America must, almost invariably, evaluate Whigs or Democrats—at least until the mid-1850s, when a new party emerged during the great controversy over the extension of slavery in the territories.

The Democrats and Whigs were national parties drawing their leaders and followers from both sections. They could usually count on intersectional support for the national tickets they presented quadrennially to the nation at large. Interestingly, the presidency—whether occupied by Southerners Jackson, Tyler, Polk, and Taylor and the Southern-born Harrison or Northerners Van Buren, Fillmore, Pierce, and Buchanan—was in the 1830s, 1840s, and 1850s in the hands of Whigs and Democrats who displayed great sensitivity toward the political and economic interests of the slave-owning South. In the 1840s Congressmen voted not by region as Northerners or Southerners but primarily as Whigs and Democrats. Party rather than sectional interest prevailed in the roll calls on most issues reaching the national political agenda. In the 1850s, as Thomas B. Alexander has reported, "forces greater than party discipline . . . were evidently at work . . . , forcing party to yield to section on a definable number of issues." Yet, even in the 1850s, "both major parties maintained a high level of cohesion and intersectional comity" with regard to the range of issues not bearing on slavery and its right to expansion.

The great national issues of antebellum politics, culminating as they did in Sumter and the ensuing war, were of transcendant importance to Americans. A good case can nonetheless be made that local and state politics touched the lives of people more often and more directly than did national politics, particularly during an era when the men in the nation's capital were inclined to treat laissez faire as an article of faith. State governments in North and South, by contrast, engaged in vigorous regulation of a wide range of economic activities. Local governments taxed citizens and, if with limited effectiveness, sought to provide for their safety, regulate their markets and many of their business activities, look after the poor, maintain public health, improve local thoroughfares, dispose of waste, pump in water, light up the dark, and furnish some minimal cultural amenities through the exercise of powers that characteristically had been granted by state government. States chartered banks, transportation companies, and other forms of business enterprise, determined the scope of such charters, themselves engaged in business, disposed of land, and regulated local communities. The great question is how did the actual operations of local and state governments in the North and South compare during the antebellum decades.

Antebellum state government was almost invariably controlled by either Whigs or Democrats. The major parties were essentially state parties, bound together in the most loosely organized national confederations. Citizens divided not by geographical section but by party preference within each state. The parties were in all latitudes characteristically controlled by tight groups of insiders that sometimes monopolized power, sometimes shared it with rival factions, in the one case as in the other controlling nominations and conventions, hammering out policy, disseminating and publicizing the party line, organizing the faithful to support it, enforcing strict discipline, and punishing those who dared challenge either the policies or the tactics pursued by the leadership. While party policies could conceivably have been infused with the noble principles proclaimed in party rhetoric, such infusion rarely appears to have been the case. The "Albany Regency," the "Richmond Junto," the "Bourbon Dynasty" of Arkansas, and similar cliques in control elsewhere have been described as realists rather than idealists.

To call attention to the gulf between the pronouncements and the actions of antebellum state political leaders is not to indulge in cynicism but simply to report the facts as historians have recorded and interpreted them. J. Mills Thornton's recent description of antebellum Alabama's political leaders as demagogues who felt a "secret contempt for the voters" they publicly extolled and whose "primary function was to gain as many offices as possible for the party faithful" is not unlike historians' characterizations of other leaders in other states, both in the North and in the South. In New York as in Alabama, in Michigan as in Georgia, in Pennsylvania as in Mississippi, in Illinois as in Missouri, the "compelling aim" of the major parties and the groups that ran them appears to have been "to get control of the existing machinery of government" and to dispense to party loyalists the jobs that attended electoral success. While seemingly preoccupied with patronage and gerrymandering or with keeping from the agenda of state governments issues that posed a "threat to property and the social order or which threatened . . . stability," the major parties did not sidestep altogether economic, social, and cultural issues of some moment. The most germane feature of roll call evidence on such issues is how little there is to choose between legislative voting patterns in the South and the North.

In towns and cities, unlike the states, party counted for little. Candidates for the mayor's office and the local council or board of aldermen did not fail to remind voters of the moral superiority of their own parties. But, as students of antebellum urban politics have noted, it mattered little whether this major party or that won the election or whether the town was located north or south of the Mason-Dixon line. True, the problems faced by cities in Texas, where "Indian fighting was probably the most important municipal activity," were unknown in the Northeast (and, for that matter, the Southeast). The amazing thing is how similar were both the problems taken up by local government everywhere and the measures enacted for coping with them.

Perhaps in no other milieu was governmental policy so permeated with class bias. Whether it was Natchez or Springfield, Charleston or Brooklyn, New Orleans or Boston, the lawyers, merchants, and large propertyowners who occupied city hall ran things in the interests of the "wealthier inhabitants." Tax rates were everywhere minuscule and property flagrantly underassessed, at the insistence of large taxpayers. Valuable lots were leased to rich men at ridiculously low rates, if not sold to them for a song. Funds provided by the niggardly budgets typical of the time were spent most freely to improve or widen streets used by businessmen rather than to clean streets in the neighborhoods of the poor. Improved public facilities for disposing of waste or carrying fresh water into the city were usually introduced first in upper-class residential districts. The "indisputable connection between the policies of the city council and the interests of the wealthier inhabitants" that Richard Wade discerned in Cincinnati early in the era could be found in most other cities.

A contemporary New Yorker attributed to corruption the not atypical favoritism the city showed its propertied elements, observing that "nearly every alderman has in some degree owed his success to the personal efforts and influence of 'backers,' who must be recompensed for their services." In the absence of evidence that local officeholders were so motivated, it is more reasonable to assume that they acted out of an honest conviction that the prosperity of the larger community depended in the first instance on the prosperity of its wealthiest inhabitants. That such beliefs were colored by the material advantages of those who possessed them, as by the conservative social values typically absorbed by men of their standing, seems equally reasonable. In any case, the pattern of uncommonly prosperous propertyowners controlling localities in the interests of men and families similarly situated was not confined to one geographical section.

Power is not, of course, confined to control of government. Control over banks, credit, capital, communications, and voluntary associations, which in an era of laissez faire often exercised more influence than did public authorities over education and culture, crime and punishment, social welfare and poverty, gave to those who had it a power that was barely matched by those who held the reins of government. The burden of recent research is that small social and economic elites exercised a degree of control over the most important institutions in the antebellum North that bears close resemblance to the great power attributed to the great planter-slaveowners by William E. Dodd a half century ago and by Eugene D. Genovese more recently. Influential voluntary associations and financial institutions appear to have been run by similarly atypical sorts on both sides of the Mason-Dixon line.

Shortly after secession, Governor Joseph E. Brown told the Georgia legislature that in the South the "whole social system is one of perfect homogeneity of interest, where every class is interested in sustaining the interest of every other class.'' Numerous Southerners agreed with him, and many scholars concur. In their failure to challenge planter supremacy, small farmers—slaveowners and nonslaveowners alike—ostensibly demonstrated the unique identity of interest that was said to bind all whites together in the antebellum South. The interest of a group is a normative term, known only to God (and perhaps to Rousseau in his capacity as authority on the General Will), in contrast to its perceived interests, as stated in its words and implicit in its actions. There are, therefore, as many interpretations of the ''true interests'' of Southern—or, for that matter, of Northern—small farmers as there are historians writing on the subject. The South's large enslaved black population doubtless affected the perceptions of all Southern whites, if in complex and unmeasurable ways. Recent research indicates that poorer and nonslave-owning Southern whites were, nevertheless, sensitive enough to their own social and economic deprivation to oppose their social superiors on secession and other important matters. Whether the acquiescence of the mass of antebellum Northerners in their inferior social and economic condition was in their own interest will be decided differently by conservative, reformist, and radical historians. Our admittedly insubstantial evidence on the issue suggests that the degree of social harmony coexisting with subtle underlying social tensions was, racial matters apart, not much different in the North and the South. . . .

The striking similarities of the two antebellum sections of the nation neither erase their equally striking dissimilarities nor detract from the significance of these dissimilarities. Whether in climate, diet, work habits, uses of leisure, speech and diction, health and disease, mood, habits, ideals, self-image, or labor systems, profound differences separated the antebellum North and South. One suspects that antebellum Americans regarded these matters as the vital stuff of life. The point need not be labored that a society, one-third of whose members were slaves (and slaves of a distinctive ''race''), is most unlike a society of free men and women. An essay focusing on these rather than on the themes emphasized here would highlight the vital disparities between the antebellum South and North. And yet the striking dissimilarities of the two antebellum sections do not erase their equally striking similarities, nor do they detract from the significance of these similarities.

The antebellum North and South were far more alike than the conventional scholarly wisdom has led us to believe. Beguiled by the charming version of Northern society and politics composed by Tocqueville, the young Marx, and other influential antebellum commentators, historians have until recently believed that the Northern social structure was far more egalitarian and offered far greater opportunity for upward social movement than did its Southern counterpart and that white men of humble position had far more power in the Old North than they did in the Old South. In disclosing that the reality of the antebellum North fell far short of the egalitarian ideal, modern studies of social structure sharply narrow the gulf between the antebellum North and South. Without being replicas of one another, both sections were relatively rich, powerful, aggressive, and assertive communities, socially stratified and governed by equally—and disconcertingly—oligarchic internal arrangements. That they were drawn into the most terrible of all American wars may have been due, as is often the case when great powers fight, as much to their similarities as to their differences. The war owed more, I believe, to the inevitably opposed but similarly selfish interests—or perceived interests—of North and South than to differences in their cultures and institutions.

It is a commonplace in the history of international politics that nations and societies quite similar to one another in their political, social, and economic arrangements have nevertheless gone to war, while nations profoundly different from one another in their laws of property or their fundamental moral and philosophical beliefs have managed to remain at peace. The Peloponnesian War, which, like the American Civil War, was a bitter and protracted struggle between two branches of the same people whose societies were in vital respects dissimilar from one another, appears to have owed little to these differences. In Thucydides' great account, Athens and the Athenians were profoundly unlike Sparta and the Lacedæmonians, whether in "national" character, wealth, economic life, ideals and values, system of justice, attitudes toward freedom, or life-style. But to Thucydides, as to the leading spokesmen for the two sides, these dissimilarities were one thing, the causes of the war quite another. Athens and Sparta fell out primarily because both were great imperial powers. "The real cause of the war," concluded Thucydides, "was formally . . . kept out of sight. The growth of the power of Athens and the alarm which this inspired in Lacedæmon, made war inevitable." None of this is to say that sectional differences had no influence whatever on the actions of those influential men that in April 1861 culminated in the outbreak of the American Civil War. The point rather is that, insofar as the Peloponnesian War throws any light whatever on the matter, wars between strikingly dissimilar antagonists break out not necessarily because of their differences, important as these are, but because of their equally significant similarities.

Late in the Civil War, William King of Cobb County, Georgia, reported that invading Union officers had told him, "We are one people, [with] the same language, habits, and religion, and ought to be one people." The officers might have added that on the spiritual plane Southerners shared with Northerners many ideals and aspirations and had contributed heavily to those historical experiences the memory and symbols of which tie a people together as a nation. For all of their distinctiveness, the Old South and North were complementary elements in an American society that was everywhere primarily rural, capitalistic, materialistic, and socially stratified, racially, ethnically, and religiously heterogeneous, and stridently chauvinistic and expansionist—a society whose practice fell far short of, when it was not totally in conflict with, its lofty theory.

The Differences Between
the Antebellum North and South

JAMES M. McPHERSON

The notion of American Exceptionalism has received quite a drubbing since the heyday of the exceptionalist thesis among the consensus school of historians in the 1950s. Interpreters of the American experience then argued that something special about the American experience—whether it was abundance, free land on the frontier, the absence of a feudal past, exceptional mobility and the relative lack of class conflict, or the pragmatic and consensual liberalism of our politics—set the American people apart from the rest of mankind. Historians writing since the 1950s, by contrast, have demonstrated the existence of class and class conflict, ideological politics, land speculation, and patterns of economic and industrial development similar to those of Western Europe which placed the United States in the mainstream of modern North Atlantic history, not on a special and privileged fringe.

If the theme of American Exceptionalism has suffered heavy and perhaps irreparable damage, the idea of Southern Exceptionalism still flourishes—though also subjected to repeated challenges. In this essay, "Southern Exceptionalism" refers to the belief that the South has "possessed a separate and unique identity . . . which appeared to be out of the mainstream of American experience." Or as Quentin Compson (in William Faulkner's *Absalom, Absalom!*) expressed it in a reply to his Canadian-born college roommate's question about what made Southerners tick: "You can't understand it. You would have to be born there."

The questions of whether the South was indeed out of the mainstream and if so, whether it has recently been swept into it, continue to be vital issues in Southern historiography. The clash of viewpoints can be illustrated by a sampling of titles or subtitles of books that have appeared in recent years. On one side we have: *The Enduring South; The Everlasting South; The Idea of the South; The Lasting South;* and *The Continuity of Southern Distinctiveness*—all arguing, in one way or another, that the South was and continues to be different. On the other side we have: *The Southerner as American; The Americanization of Dixie; Epitaph for Dixie; Southerners and Other Americans; The Vanishing South;* and *Into the Mainstream.* Some of these books insist that "the traditional emphasis on the South's differentness . . . is wrong historically." Others concede that while the South may once have been different, it has ceased to be or is ceasing to be so. There is no unanimity among this latter group of scholars about precisely when or how the South joined the mainstream. Some emphasize the civil rights revolution of the 1960s; others the bulldozer revolution of the 1950s; still others the Chamber of Commerce Babbittry of the 1920s;

James M. McPherson, "Antebellum Southern Exceptionalism: A New Look at an Old Question," *Civil War History*, Volume 29, Number 3, September 1983, pp. 230–244. Reprinted with permission of The Kent State University Press.

and some the New South crusade of the 1880s. As far back as 1869 the Yankee novelist John William De Forest wrote of the South: "We shall do well to study this peculiar people, which will soon lose its peculiarities." As George Tindall has wryly remarked, the Vanishing South has "staged one of the most prolonged disappearing acts since the decline and fall of Rome."

Some historians, however, would quarrel with the concept of a Vanishing South because they believe that the South as a separate, exceptional entity never existed—with of course the ephemeral exception of the Confederacy. But a good many other historians insist that not only did a unique "South" exist before the Civil War, but also that its sense of a separate identity that was being threatened by the North was the underlying cause of secession. A few paired quotations will illustrate these conflicting interpretations.

In 1960 one Southern historian maintained that "no picture of the Old South as a section confident and united in its dedication to a neo-feudal social order, and no explanation of the Civil War as a conflict between 'two civilizations,' can encompass the complexity and pathos of the antebellum reality." But later in the decade another historian insisted that slavery created "a ruling class with economic interests, political ideals, and moral sentiments" that included an "aristocratic, antibourgeois spirit with values and mores emphasizing family and status, a strong code of honor, and aspirations to luxury, ease, and accomplishment" which "set it apart from the mainstream of capitalist development." This ruling class possessed "the political and economic power to impose their values on [Southern] society as a whole." Since submission to the hegemony of Northern free-soilers would have meant "moral and political suicide" for this "special civilization" of the South, a "final struggle [was] so probable that we may safely call it inevitable." The first historian was Charles Sellers; the second, Eugene Genovese.

Or let us examine another pair of quotations, the first published in 1973 by a Southern historian who asserted that the thesis of a "basically divergent and antagonistic" North and South in 1861 is "one of the great myths of American history." Almost as if in reply, a historian wrote a few years later that such an assertion "belies common sense and the nearly universal observation of contemporaries. We submit a single figure that . . . attests to the irrelevance of all [statistical manipulations] purporting to show similarities between North and South. The figure is 600,000—the number of Civil War graves." The first of these quotations is from Grady McWhiney. The second is from—Grady McWhiney.

Finally, let us look at another pair of statements, the first from one of the South's most eminent historians writing in 1958: "The South was American a long time before it was Southern in any self-conscious or distinctive way. It remains more American by far than anything else, and has all along." The second is from an equally eminent historian writing in 1969: "A great slave society . . . had grown up and miraculously flourished in the heart of a thoroughly bourgeois and partly puritanical republic. It had renounced its bourgeois origins and elaborated and painfully rationalized its institutional, legal, metaphysical, and religious defenses. . . . When the crisis came [it] chose to fight. It proved to be the death struggle of a society, which went down in ruins.'' The first historian was C. Vann Woodward; the second—it should come as no surprise by now—was C. Vann Woodward.

If given the opportunity, McWhiney and Woodward might be able to reconcile the apparent inconsistencies in these statements. Or perhaps they really changed their minds. After all, as Ralph Waldo Emerson told us more than a century ago, ''a foolish consistency is the hobgoblin of little minds.'' In any case, the more recent vintage of both McWhiney and Woodward has a fuller, more robust, and truer flavor.

Many antebellum Americans certainly thought that North and South had evolved separate societies with institutions, interests, values, and ideologies so incompatible, so much in deadly conflict that they could no longer live together in the same nation. Traveling through the South in the spring of 1861, London *Times* correspondent William Howard Russell encountered this Conflict of Civilizations theme everywhere he went. ''The tone in which [Southerners] alluded to the whole of the Northern people indicated the clear conviction that trade, commerce, the pursuit of gain, manufacture, and the base mechanical arts, had so degraded the whole race'' that Southerners could no longer tolerate association with them, wrote Russell. ''There is a degree of something like ferocity in the Southern mind [especially] toward New England which exceeds belief.'' A South Carolinian told Russell: ''We are an agricultural people, pursuing our own system, and working out our own destiny, breeding up women and men with some other purpose than to make them vulgar, fanatical, cheating Yankees.'' Louis Wigfall of Texas, a former U.S. senator, told Russell: ''We are a peculiar people, sir! . . . We are an agricultural people. . . . We have no cities—we don't want them. . . . We want no manufactures: we desire no trading, no mechanical or manufacturing classes. . . . As long as we have our rice, our sugar, our tobacco, and our cotton, we can command wealth to purchase all we want. . . . But with the Yankees we will never trade—never. Not one pound of cotton shall ever go from the South to their accursed cities.''

Such opinions were not universal in the South, of course, but in the fevered atmosphere of the late 1850s they were widely shared. ''Free Society!'' exclaimed a Georgia newspaper. ''We sicken at the name. What is it but a conglomeration of greasy mechanics, filthy operatives, small-fisted farmers, and moon-struck theorists . . . hardly fit for association with a southern gentleman's body servant.'' In 1861 the *Southern Literary Messenger* explained to its readers: ''It is not a question of slavery alone that we are called upon to decide. It is free society which we must shun or embrace.'' In the same year Charles Colcock Jones, Jr.—no fire-eater, for after all he had graduated from Princeton and from Harvard Law School— spoke of the development of antagonistic cultures in North and South: ''In this country have arisen two races [i.e., Northerners and Southerners] which, although claiming a common parentage, have been so entirely sep-

arated by climate, by morals, by religion, and by estimates so totally opposite to all that constitutes honor, truth, and manliness, that they cannot
longer exist under the same government.''

Spokesmen for the free-labor ideology—which had become the dominant political force in the North by 1860—reciprocated these sentiments.
The South, said Theodore Parker, was "the foe to Northern Industry—to
our mines, our manufactures, and our commerce. . . . She is the foe to our
institutions—to our democratic politics in the State, our democratic culture
in the school, our democratic work in the community, our democratic
equality in the family.'' Slavery, said William H. Seward, undermined
"intelligence, vigor, and energy" in both blacks and whites. It produced
"an exhausted soil, old and decaying towns, wretchedly neglected roads
. . . an absence of enterprise and improvement.'' Slavery was therefore
"incompatible with all . . . the elements of the security, welfare, and greatness of nations.'' The struggle between free labor and slavery, between
North and South, said Seward in his most famous speech, was "an irrepressible conflict between two opposing and enduring forces.'' The United
States was therefore two nations, but it could not remain forever so: it
"must and will, sooner or later, become either entirely a slaveholding
nation, or entirely a free-labor nation.'' Abraham Lincoln expressed exactly
the same theme in his House Divided speech. Many other Republicans
echoed this argument that the struggle, in the words of an Ohio congressman, was "between systems, between civilizations.''

These sentiments were no more confined to fire-breathing Northern
radicals than were Southern exceptionalist viewpoints confined to fire-
eaters. Lincoln represented the mainstream of his party, which commanded
a majority of votes in the North by 1860. The dominant elements in the
North and in the lower South believed the United States to be composed
of two incompatible civilizations. Southerners believed that survival of their
special civilization could be assured only in a separate nation. The creation
of the Confederacy was merely a political ratification of an irrevocable
separation that had already taken place in the hearts and minds of the
people.

The proponents of an assimilationist rather than exceptionalist interpretation of Southern history might object that this concept of a separate
and unique South existed *only* in hearts and minds. It was a subjective
reality, they might argue, not an objective one. Objectively, they would
insist, North and South were one people. They shared the same language,
the same Constitution, the same legal system, the same commitment to
republican political institutions, an interconnected economy, the same predominantly Protestant religion and British ethnic heritage, the same history,
the same shared memories of a common struggle for nationhood.

Two recent proponents of the objective similarity thesis are Edward
Pessen and the late David Potter. In a long article entitled "How Different
from Each Other Were the Antebellum North and South?" Pessen concludes that they "were far more alike than the conventional scholarly
wisdom has led us to believe.'' His evidence for this conclusion consists

mainly of quantitative measures of the distribution of wealth and of the socioeconomic status of political officeholders in North and South. He finds that wealth was distributed in a similarly unequal fashion in both sections, that voting requirements were similar, and that voters in both sections elected a similarly disproportionate number of men from the upper economic strata to office. The problem with this argument, of course, is that it could be used to prove many obviously different societies to be similar. France and Germany in 1914 and in 1932 had about the same distribution of wealth and similar habits of electing men from the upper strata to the Assembly or the Reichstag. England and France had a comparable distribution of wealth during most of the eighteenth century. Turkey and Russia were not dissimilar in these respects in the nineteenth century. And so on.

David Potter's contention that commonalities of language, religion, law, and political system outweighed differences in other areas is more convincing than the Pessen argument. But the Potter thesis nevertheless begs some important questions. The same similarities prevailed between England and her North American colonies in 1776, but they did not prevent the development of a separate nationalism in the latter. It is not language or law alone that are important, but the uses to which they are put. In the United States of the 1850s, Northerners and Southerners spoke the same language, to be sure, but they were increasingly using this language to revile each other. Language became an instrument of division, not unity. The same was true of the political system. So also of the law: Northern states passed personal liberty laws to defy a national Fugitive Slave Law supported by the South; a Southern-dominated Supreme Court denied the right of Congress to exclude slavery from the territories, a ruling that most Northerners considered an infamous distortion of the Constitution. As for a shared commitment to Protestantism, this too had become a divisive rather than unifying factor, with the two largest denominations—Methodist and Baptist—having split into hostile Southern and Northern churches over the question of slavery, and the third largest—Presbyterian—having split partly along sectional lines and partly on the question of slavery. As for a shared historical commitment to republicanism, by the 1850s this too was more divisive than unifying. Northern Republicans interpreted this commitment in a free-soil context, while most Southerners continued to insist that one of the most cherished tenets of republican liberty was the right of property— including property in slaves.

There is another dimension of the Potter thesis—or perhaps it would be more accurate to call it a separate Potter thesis—that might put us on the right track to solving the puzzle of Southern exceptionalism. After challenging most notions of Southern distinctiveness, Potter concluded that the principal characteristic distinguishing the South from the rest of the country was the persistence of a "folk culture" in the South. This gemeinschaft society, with its emphasis on tradition, rural life, close kinship ties, a hierarchical social structure, ascribed status, patterns of deference, and masculine codes of honor and chivalry, persisted in the South long after the North began moving toward a gesellschaft society with its impersonal, bureaucratic meritocratic, urbanizing, commercial, industrializing, mobile, and rootless characteristics. Above all, the South's folk culture valued tradition and stability and felt threatened by change; the North's modernizing culture enshrined change as progress and condemned the South as backward.

A critic of this gemeinschaft-gesellschaft dichotomy might contend that it was more myth than reality. One might respond to such criticism by pointing out that human behavior is often governed more by myth—that is, by people's perceptions of the world—than by objective reality. Moreover, there *were* real and important differences between North and South by the mid-nineteenth century, differences that might support the gemeinschaft-gesellschaft contrast.

The North was more urban than the South and was urbanizing at a faster rate. In 1820, 10 percent of the free-state residents lived in urban areas compared with 5 percent in the slave states; by 1860 the figures were 26 percent and 10 percent, respectively. Even more striking was the growing contrast between farm and non-farm occupations in the two sections. In 1800, 82 percent of the Southern labor force worked in agriculture compared with 68 percent in the free states. By 1860 the Northern share had dropped to 40 percent while the Southern proportion had actually increased slightly, to 84 percent. Southern agriculture remained traditionally labor-intensive while Northern agriculture became increasingly capital-intensive and mechanized. By 1860 the free states had nearly twice the value of farm machinery per acre and per farm worker as the slave states. And the pace of industrialization in the North far outstripped that in the South. In 1810 the slave states had an estimated 31 percent of the capital invested in manufacturing in the United States; by 1840 this had declined to 20 percent and by 1860 to 16 percent. In 1810 the North had two and a half times the amount per capita invested in manufacturing as the South; by 1860 this had increased to three and a half times as much.

A critic of the inferences drawn from these data might point out that in many respects the differences between the free states east and west of the Appalachians were nearly or virtually as great as those between North and South, yet these differences did not produce a sense of separate nationality in East and West. This point is true—as far as it goes. While the western free states at midcentury did have a higher proportion of workers employed in non-farm occupations than the South, they had about the same percentage of urban population and the same amount per capita invested in manufacturing. But the crucial factor was *the rate of change*. The West was urbanizing and industrializing more rapidly than either the Northeast or the South. Therefore while North and South as a whole were growing relatively farther apart, the eastern and western free states were drawing closer together. This frustrated Southern hopes for an alliance with the Old Northwest on grounds of similarity of agrarian interests. From 1840 to 1860 the rate of urbanization in the West was three times greater than in the Northeast and four times greater than in the South. The amount of capital invested in manufacturing grew twice as fast in the West as in the Northeast and nearly three times as fast as in the South. The same was true of employment in non-farm occupations. The railroad-building boom of the 1850s tied the Northwest to the Northeast with links of iron and shifted the dominant pattern of inland trade from a North-South to an East-West orientation. The remarkable growth of cities like Chicago, Cincinnati, Cleveland, and Detroit with their farm-machinery, food-processing, machine-tool, and railroad-equipment industries foreshadowed the emergence of the industrial Midwest and helped to assure that when the crisis of the Union came in 1861 the West joined the East instead of the South.

According to the most recent study of antebellum Southern industry, the Southern lag in this category of development resulted not from any inherent economic disadvantages—not shortage of capital, nor low rates of return, nor non-adaptability of slave labor—but from the choices of Southerners who had money to invest it in agriculture and slaves rather than in manufacturing. In the 1780s Thomas Jefferson had praised farmers as the "peculiar deposit for substantial and genuine virtue" and warned against the industrial classes in cities as sores on the body politic. In 1860 many Southern leaders still felt the same way; as Louis Wigfall put it in the passage quoted earlier, "we want no manufactures; we desire no trading, no mechanical or manufacturing classes."

Partly as a consequence of this attitude, the South received only a trickle of the great antebellum stream of immigration. Fewer than one-eighth of the immigrants settled in slave states, where the foreign-born percentage of the population was less than a fourth of the North's percentage. The South's white population was ethnically more homogeneous and less cosmopolitan than the North's. The traditional patriarchal family and tight kinship networks typical of gemeinschaft societies, reinforced in the South by a relatively high rate of cousin marriages, also persisted much more strongly in the nineteenth-century South than in the North.

The greater volume of immigration to the free states contributed to the faster rate of population growth there than in the South. Another factor in this differential growth rate was out-migration from the South. During the middle decades of the nineteenth century, twice as many whites left the South for the North as vice versa. These facts did not go unnoticed at the time; indeed, they formed the topic of much public comment. Northerners cited the differential in population growth as evidence for the superiority of the free-labor system; Southerners perceived it with alarm as evidence of their declining minority status in the nation. These perceptions became important factors in the growing sectional self-consciousness that led to secession.

The most crucial demographic difference between North and South, of course, resulted from slavery. Ninety-five percent of the country's black people lived in the slave states, where blacks constituted one-third of the population in contrast to their one percent of the Northern population. The implications of this for the economy and social structure of the two sections, not to mention their ideologies and politics, are obvious and require little elaboration here. Two brief points are worth emphasizing, however. First, historians in recent years have discovered the viability of Afro-American culture under slavery. They have noted that black music, folklore, speech patterns, religion, and other manifestations of this culture influenced white society in the South. Since the Afro-American culture was preeminently a folk culture with an emphasis on oral tradition and other non-literate forms of ritual and communication, it reinforced the persistence of a traditional, gemeinschaft, folk-oriented society in the South.

Second, a number of recent historians have maintained that Northerners were as committed to white supremacy as Southerners. This may have been true, but the scale of concern with this matter in the South was so much greater as to constitute a different order of magnitude and to contribute more than any other factor to the difference between North and South. And of course slavery was more than an institution of racial control. Its centrality to many aspects of life focused Southern politics almost exclusively on defense of the institution—to the point that, in the words of the *Charleston Mercury* in 1858, "on the subject of slavery . . . the North and South . . . are not only two Peoples, but they are rival, hostile Peoples."

The fear that slavery was being hemmed in and threatened with destruction contributed to the defensive-aggressive style of Southern political behavior. This aggressiveness sometimes took physical form. Southern whites were more likely to carry weapons and to use them against other human beings than Northerners were. The homicide rate was higher in the South. The phenomenon of dueling persisted longer there. Bertram Wyatt-Brown attributes this to the unique Southern code of honor based on traditional patriarchal values of courtesy, status, courage, family, and the symbiosis of shame and pride. The enforcement of order through the threat and practice of violence also resulted from the felt need to control a large slave population.

Martial values and practices were more pervasive in the South than in the North. Marcus Cunliffe has argued to the contrary, but the evidence confutes him. Cunliffe's argument is based mainly on two sets of data: the prevalence of militia and volunteer military companies in the free as well as in the slave states; and the proportion of West Pointers and regular army officers from the two sections. Yet the first set of data do not support his thesis, and the second contradicts it. Cunliffe does present evidence on the popularity of military companies in Northern cities, but nowhere does he estimate the comparative numbers of such companies in North and South or the number of men in proportion to population who belonged to them. If such comparative evidence could be assembled, it would probably support the traditional view of a higher concentration of such companies in the South. What Northern city, for example, could compare with Charleston, which had no fewer than twenty-two military companies in the late 1850s— one for every two hundred white men of military age? Another important quasi-military institution in the South with no Northern counterpart escaped Cunliffe's attention—the slave patrol, which gave tens of thousands of Southerners a more practical form of military experience than the often ceremonial functions of volunteer drill companies could do.

As for the West Point alumni and regular army officers it is true, as Cunliffe points out, that about 60 percent of these were from the North and only 40 percent from the South in the late antebellum decades. What he fails to note is that the South had only about 30 percent of the nation's white population during this era, so that on a proportional basis the South was overrepresented in these categories. Moreover, from 1849 to 1861 all of the secretaries of war were Southerners, as were the general in chief of the army, two of the three brigadier generals, all but one commander of the army's geographical departments of the eve of the Civil War, the authors of the two manuals on infantry tactics and of the artillery manual used at West Point, and the professor who taught tactics and strategy at the military academy.

Other evidence supports the thesis of a significant martial tradition in the South contrasted with a concentration in different professions in the North. More than three-fifths of the volunteer soldiers in the Mexican War came from the slave states—on a per capita basis, four times the proportion of free-state volunteers. Seven of the eight military "colleges" (not including West Point and Annapolis) listed in the 1860 census were in the slave states. A study of the occupations of antebellum men chronicled in the *Dictionary of American Biography* found that the military profession claimed twice the percentage of Southerners as of Northerners, while this ratio was reversed for men distinguished in literature, art, medicine, and education. In business the per capita proportion of Yankees was three times as great, and among engineers and inventors it was six times as large. When Southerners labeled themselves a nation of warriors and Yankees a nation of shopkeepers—a common comparison in 1860—or when Jefferson Davis told a London *Times* correspondent in 1861 that "we are a military people," they were not just whistling Dixie.

One final comparison of objective differences is in order—a comparison of education and literacy in North and South. Contemporaries perceived this as a matter of importance. The South's alleged backwardness in schooling and its large numbers of illiterates framed one of the principal free-soil indictments of slavery. This was one area in which a good many Southerners admitted inferiority and tried to do something about it. But in 1860, after a decade of school reform in the South, the slave states still had only half the North's proportion of white children enrolled in public and private schools, and the length of the annual school term in the South was only a little more than half as long as in the North. Of course education did not take place solely in school. But other forms of education—in the home, at church, through lyceums and public lectures, by apprenticeship, and so on—were also more active in North than South. According to the census of 1860, per capita newspaper circulation was three times greater in the North, and the number of library volumes per white person was nearly twice as large.

The proportion of illiterate white people was three times greater in the South than in the North; if the black population is included, as indeed it should be, the percentage of illiterates was seven or eight times as high in the South. In the free states, what two recent historians have termed an "ideology of literacy" prevailed—a commitment to education as an instrument of social mobility, economic prosperity, progress, and freedom. While this ideology also existed in the South, especially in the 1850s, it was much weaker there and made slow headway against the inertia of a rural folk culture. "The Creator did not intend that every individual human being should be highly cultivated," wrote William Harper of South Carolina. "It is better that a part should be fully and highly educated and the rest utterly ignorant." Commenting on a demand by Northern workingmen for universal public education, the *Southern Review* asked: "Is this the way to produce producers? To make every child in the state a literary character would not be a good qualification for those who must live by manual labor."

The ideology of literacy in the North was part of a larger ferment which produced an astonishing number of reform movements that aroused both contempt and fear in the South. Southern whites viewed the most dynamic of these movements—abolitionism—as a threat to their very existence. Southerners came to distrust the whole concept of "progress" as it seemed to be understood in the North. *DeBow's Review* declared in 1851: "Southern life, habits, thoughts, and aims, are so essentially different from those of the North, that here a different character of books . . . and training is required." A Richmond newspaper warned in 1855 that Southerners must stop reading Northern newspapers and books and stop sending their sons to colleges in the North, where "every village has its press and its lecture room, and each lecturer and editor, unchecked by a healthy public opinion, opens up for discussion all the received dogmas of faith," where unwary youth are "exposed to the danger of imbibing doctrines subversive of all old institutions." Young men should be educated instead in the South "where their training would be moral, religious, and conservative, and they would never learn, or read a word in school or out of school, inconsistent with orthodox Christianity, pure morality, the right of property, and sacredness of marriage."

In all of the areas discussed above—urbanization, industrialization, labor force, demographic structure, violence and martial values, education, and attitudes toward change—contemporaries accurately perceived significant differences between North and South, differences that in most respects were increasing over time. The question remains: were these differences crucial enough to make the South an exception to generalizations about antebellum America?

This essay concludes by suggesting a tentative answer to the question: perhaps it was the *North* that was "different," the North that departed from the mainstream of historical development; and perhaps therefore we should speak not of Southern exceptionalism but of Northern exceptionalism. This idea is borrowed shamelessly from C. Vann Woodward, who applied it, however, to the post–Civil War United States. In essays written during the 1950s on "The Irony of Southern History" and "The Search for Southern Identity," Woodward suggested that, unlike other Americans but like most people in the rest of the world, Southerners had experienced poverty, failure, defeat, and had a skepticism about "progress" that grows out of such experiences. The South thus shared a bond with the rest of humankind that other Americans did not share. This theme of Northern exceptionalism might well be applied also to the antebellum United States— not for Woodward's categories of defeat, poverty, and failure, but for the categories of a persistent folk culture discussed in this essay.

At the beginning of the republic the North and South were less different in most of these categories than they became later. Nearly all Northern states had slavery in 1776, and the institution persisted in some of them for decades thereafter. The ethnic homogeneity of Northern and Southern whites was quite similar before 1830. The proportion of urban dwellers was similarly small and the percentage of the labor force employed in agriculture similarly large in 1800. The Northern predominance in commerce and man- ufacturing was not so great as it later became. Nor was the contrast in education and literacy as great as it subsequently became. A belief in progress and commitments to reform or radicalism were no more prevalent in the North than in the South in 1800—indeed, they may have been less so. In 1776, in 1800, even as late as 1820, similarity in values and institutions was the salient fact. Within the next generation, difference and conflict became prominent. This happened primarily because of developments in the North. The South changed relatively little, and because so many North- ern changes seemed threatening, the South developed a defensive ideology that resisted change.

In most of these respects the South resembled a majority of the societies in the world more than the changing North did. Despite the abolition of legal slavery or serfdom throughout much of the western hemisphere and western Europe, much of the world—like the South—had an unfree or quasi-free labor force. Most societies in the world remained predominantly rural, agricultural, and labor-intensive; most, including even several Eu- ropean countries, had illiteracy rates as high or higher than the South's 45 percent; most like the South remained bound by traditional values and networks of family, kinship, hierarchy, and patriarchy. The North—along with a few countries in northwestern Europe—hurtled forward eagerly toward a future that many Southerners found distasteful if not frightening; the South remained proudly and even defiantly rooted in the past.

Thus when secessionists protested in 1861 that they were acting to preserve traditional rights and values, they were correct. They fought to protect their constitutional liberties against the perceived Northern threat to overthrow them. The South's concept of republicanism had not changed in three-quarters of a century; the North's had. With complete sincerity the South fought to preserve its version of the republic of the founding fathers—a government of limited powers that protected the rights of prop- erty and whose constituency comprised an independent gentry and yeo- manry of the white race undisturbed by large cities, heartless factories, restless free workers, and class conflict. The accession to power of the Republican party, with its ideology of competitive, egalitarian, free-labor capitalism, was a signal to the South that the Northern majority had turned irrevocably toward this frightening, revolutionary future. Indeed, the Black Republican party appeared to the eyes of many Southerners as "essentially a revolutionary party" composed of "a motley throng of Sans culottes . . . Infidels and freelovers, interspersed by Bloomer women, fugitive slaves, and amalgamationists." Therefore secession was a preemptive counterrevolution to prevent the Black Republican revolution from engulfing the South. "*We* are not revolutionists," insisted James D. B. DeBow and Jefferson Davis during the Civil War. "We are resisting revolution. . . . We are not engaged in a Quixotic fight for the rights of man; our struggle is for inherited rights. . . . We are upholding the true doctrines of the Federal Constitution. We are conservative."

Union victory in the war destroyed the Southern vision of America and insured that the Northern vision would become the American vision. Until 1861, however, it was the North that was out of the mainstream, not the South. Of course the Northern states, along with Britain and a few countries in northwestern Europe, were cutting a new channel in world history that would doubtless have become the mainstream even if the American Civil War had not happened. But it did happen, and for Americans it marked the turning point. A Louisiana planter who returned home sadly after the war wrote in 1865: "Society has been completely changed by the war. The [French] revolution of '89 did not produce a greater change in the 'Ancien Regime' than has this in our social life." And four years later George Ticknor, a retired Harvard professor, concluded that the Civil War had created a "great gulf between what happened before in our century and what has happened since, or what is likely to happen hereafter. It does not seem to me as if I were living in the country in which I was born." From the war sprang the great flood that wrenched the stream of American history into a new channel and transferred the burden of exceptionalism from North to South.

FURTHER READING

Clement Eaton, *The Growth of Southern Civilization, 1790–1861* (1961)
Robert W. Fogel and Stanley L. Engerman, *Time on the Cross: The Economics of American Negro Slavery* (1974), chaps. 1–3
Eugene D. Genovese, *The Political Economy of Slavery* (1965)
———, *The World the Slaveholders Made* (1969)
Fletcher M. Green, "Democracy in the Old South," *Journal of Southern History* 12 (1946), 3–23
Peter Kolchin, *Unfree Labor: American Slavery and Russian Serfdom* (1987)
Leon Litwack, *North of Slavery: The Negro in the Free States, 1790–1860* (1961)
Douglass C. North, *The Economic Growth of the United States, 1790–1860* (1961)
James Oakes, *The Ruling Race: A History of American Slaveholders* (1982)
Rollin Osterweiss, *Romanticism and Nationalism in the Old South* (1949)
Frank L. Owsley and Harriet C. Owsley, "The Economic Basis of Society in the Late Ante-bellum South," *Journal of Southern History* 6 (1940), 24–45
David M. Potter, "The Historian's Use of Nationalism and Vice Versa," in *The South and the Sectional Conflict* (1968), 34–83

————, "The Nature of Southern Separatism," in *The Impending Crisis, 1848–1861* (1976)

Charles G. Sellers, Jr., "The Travail of Slavery," in Sellers, ed., *The Southerner As American* (1960), 40–71

Charles S. Sydnor, "The Southerner and the Laws," *Journal of Southern History* 6 (1940), 3–23

Bertram Wyatt-Brown, *Southern Honor: Ethics and Behavior in the Old South* (1982)

CHAPTER
3

Sectional Politics

in the 1850s

A small cadre of activists advocating the immediate and unconditional abolition of slavery emerged in the 1830s. From the start, they encountered massive opposition. Not only were they resisted vigorously by the southern slaveholding interest, but they also encountered northerners' fears that agitation to end slavery would almost certainly destabilize the fragile Union and could result in the liberation of millions of black slaves who would then migrate northward. Also, the abolitionists soon faced the reality that the federal government could not legally intervene in the internal affairs of member states and so could not abolish slavery outright.

For the next fifteen years or so, the abolitionists labored, with some success, to change public opinion and to pressure public officials and governments to take antislavery stands. But in the late 1840s and early 1850s, the debate over slavery changed course when the United States acquired immense tracts of western land as a result of the war against Mexico from 1846–1847. The annexation of Texas had caused some strain between the sections earlier in the decade, but now the southwest region that encompassed what was later to become the states of California, Utah, New Mexico, and Arizona was added, and the status of the new territories as either slave or free would soon have to be decided. Would the nation allow slavery to go into these vast areas, or simply exclude it? An issue that had been somewhat theoretical had now become practical and immediate, since decisions about slavery's legitimacy as an American institution could no longer be postponed. On the other hand, it was also true that the question of slavery's status in the new territories diluted, even diverted, the campaign for abolishing it. Because the territorial issue focused on slavery's restriction, it left the institution untouched where it already existed.

The test case for determining the status of slavery in the unorganized territories was the sparsely settled area of Kansas. Although located to the east of the Mexican Cession, Kansas was not yet ready for statehood. From 1854, when the Kansas-Nebraska bill was introduced, until 1858, when the proslavery Lecompton constitution was defeated, Kansas was the focus of national politics, with each section resolved to control the emergent state. Why did southerners stake so *much on a contest they could not expect to win? And why were northerners so fearful of losing Kansas? Were both sides perhaps overreacting? Whatever one might conclude, examination of this issue as seen by each of the protagonists reveals much about the priorities and concerns of both sides as well as about the state of political feeling in the nation by the mid–1850s.*

DOCUMENTS

Sectional dissension had quieted down somewhat after the Compromise of 1850, but it was rekindled by Senator Stephen Douglas's Kansas-Nebraska proposal and would intensify during the remainder of the decade. The first document reprinted here, the Appeal of the Independent Democrats of January 19, 1854, is an angry response to Douglas's initiative on the part of leading antislavery Democrats, among them Salmon P. Chase and Charles Sumner. Sumner's inflammatory speech on "Bleeding Kansas," delivered in the Senate on May 20, 1856, is the second document. In this extract, he attacks the reputation of Andrew P. Butler, the veteran senator from South Carolina, whose kinsman, Congressman Preston Brooks, took it upon himself to avenge this insult by physically assaulting Sumner in return. The third selection is from a speech in the House on July 11, 1856, by Thomas S. Bocock of Virginia, defending Brooks's act.

The fourth document is from the famous speech of Senator William Henry Seward of New York, given in Rochester, New York, on October 25, 1858. Seward described the sectional dispute as an "irrepressible conflict," a phrase that haunted him in his campaign for the Republican nomination in 1860 and has haunted historians ever since. But in the fifth selection, Seward's depiction of the crisis as irrepressible is refuted by Senator Andrew Johnson of Tennessee, whose speech in the Senate on December 12, 1859, was intended to keep alive the prospects of maintaining the Union. The sixth and final piece is from a speech in the Senate on December 19, 1859, by Albert G. Brown of Mississippi, indicating how southern slaveholders felt about restrictions on their rights.

Independent Democrats Protest the Kansas-Nebraska Act, January 1854

As Senators and Representatives in the Congress of the United States it is our duty to warn our constituents, whenever imminent danger menaces the freedom of our institutions or the permanency of the Union.

Such danger, as we firmly believe, now impends, and we earnestly solicit your prompt attention to it.

At the last session of Congress a bill for the organization of the Territory of Nebraska passed the House of Representatives by an overwhelming majority. That bill was based on the principle of excluding slavery from the new Territory. It was not taken up for consideration in the Senate and consequently failed to become a law.

At the present session a new Nebraska bill has been reported by the Senate Committee on Territories, which, should it unhappily receive the sanction of Congress, will open all the unorganized Territories of the Union to the ingress of slavery.

We arraign this bill as a gross violation of a sacred pledge; as a criminal betrayal of precious rights; as part and parcel of an atrocious plot to exclude from a vast unoccupied region immigrants from the Old World and free laborers from our own States, and convert it into a dreary region of despotism, inhabited by masters and slaves.

Take your maps, fellow citizens, we entreat you, and see what country it is which this bill gratuitously and recklessly proposes to open to slavery. . . .

This immense region, occupying the very heart of the North American Continent, and larger, by thirty-three thousand square miles, than all the existing free States—including California . . . this immense region the bill now before the Senate, without reason and without excuse, but in flagrant disregard of sound policy and sacred faith, purposes to open to slavery. . . .

Nothing is more certain in history than the fact that Missouri could not have been admitted as a slave State had not certain members from the free States been reconciled to the measure by the incorporation of this prohibition [the Missouri Compromise of 1820] into the act of admission. Nothing is more certain than that this prohibition has been regarded and accepted by the whole country as a solemn compact against the extension of slavery into any part of the territory acquired from France [under the Louisiana Purchase] lying north of 36° 30', and not included in the new State of Missouri. The same act—let it be ever remembered—which authorized the formation of a constitution by the State, without a clause forbidding slavery, consecrated, beyond question and beyond honest recall, the whole remainder of the Territory to freedom and free institutions forever. For more than thirty years—during more than half our national existence under our present Constitution—this compact has been universally regarded and acted upon as inviolable American law. In conformity with it, Iowa was admitted as a free State and Minnesota has been organized as a free Territory.

It is a strange and ominous fact, well calculated to awaken the worst apprehensions and the most fearful forebodings of future calamities, that it is now deliberately proposed to repeal this prohibition, by implication or directly—the latter certainly the manlier way—and thus to subvert the compact, and allow slavery in all the yet unorganized territory.

We cannot, in this address, review the various pretenses under which it is attempted to cloak this monstrous wrong, but we must not altogether omit to notice one.

It is said that Nebraska sustains the same relations to slavery as did the territory acquired from Mexico prior to 1850, and that the pro-slavery clauses of the bill are necessary to carry into effect the compromise of that year.

No assertion could be more groundless. . . .

The statesmen whose powerful support carried the Utah and New

Mexico acts never dreamed that their provisions would be ever applied to Nebraska. . . .

Here is proof beyond controversy that the principle of the Missouri act prohibiting slavery north of 36° 30′, far from being abrogated by the Compromise Acts, is expressly affirmed; and that the proposed repeal of this prohibition, instead of being an affirmation of the Compromise Acts, is a repeal of a very prominent provision of the most important act of the series. It is solemnly declared in the very Compromise Acts *"that nothing herein contained shall be construed to impair or qualify"* the prohibition of slavery north of 36° 30′; and yet in the face of this declaration, that sacred prohibition is said to be overthrown. Can presumption further go? To all who, in any way, lean upon these compromises, we commend this exposition.

The pretenses, therefore, that the territory covered by the positive prohibition of 1820, sustains a similar relation to slavery with that acquired from Mexico, covered by no prohibition except that of disputed constitutional or Mexican law, and that the Compromises of 1850 require the incorporation of the pro-slavery clauses of the Utah and New Mexico Bill in the Nebraska act, are mere inventions, designed to cover up from public reprehension meditated bad faith. Were he living now, no one would be more forward, more eloquent, or more indignant in his denunciation of that bad faith, than Henry Clay, the foremost champion of both compromises. . . .

We appeal to the people. We warn you that the dearest interests of freedom and the Union are in imminent peril. Demagogues may tell you that the Union can be maintained only by submitting to the demands of slavery. We tell you that the Union can only be maintained by the full recognition of the just claims of freedom and man. The Union was formed to establish justice and secure the blessings of liberty. When it fails to accomplish these ends it will be worthless, and when it becomes worthless it cannot long endure.

We entreat you to be mindful of that fundamental maxim of Democracy—EQUAL RIGHTS AND EXACT JUSTICE FOR ALL MEN. Do not submit to become agents in extending legalized oppression and systematized injustice over a vast territory yet exempt from these terrible evils.

We implore Christians and Christian ministers to interpose. Their divine religion requires them to behold in every man a brother, and to labor for the advancement and regeneration of the human race.

Whatever apologies may be offered for the toleration of slavery in the States, none can be offered for its extension into Territories where it does not exist, and where that extension involves the repeal of ancient law and the violation of solemn compact. Let all protest, earnestly and emphatically, by correspondence, through the press, by memorials, by resolutions of public meetings and legislative bodies, and in whatever other mode may seem expedient, against this enormous crime.

For ourselves, we shall resist it by speech and vote, and with all the abilities which God has given us. Even if overcome in the impending struggle, we shall not submit. We shall go home to our constituents, erect anew the standard of freedom, and call on the people to come to the rescue of the country from the domination of slavery. We will not despair; for the cause of human freedom is the cause of God.

S. P. Chase
Charles Sumner
J. R. Giddings
Edward Wade
Gerritt Smith
Alexander De Witt

January 19, 1854

Senator Charles Sumner of Massachusetts Ridicules the Southern Gentry, May 1856

My task will be divided under three different heads: *first*, THE CRIME AGAINST KANSAS, in its origin and extent; *secondly*, THE APOLOGIES FOR THE CRIME; and, *thirdly*, THE TRUE REMEDY.

Before entering upon the argument, I must say something of a general character, particularly in response to what has fallen from Senators who have raised themselves to eminence on this floor in championship of human wrong: I mean the Senator from South Carolina [Mr. BUTLER] and the Senator from Illinois [Mr. DOUGLAS], who, though unlike as Don Quixote and Sancho Panza, yet, like this couple, sally forth together in the same adventure. I regret much to miss the elder Senator from his seat; but the cause against which he has run a tilt, with such ebullition of animosity, demands that the opportunity of exposing him should not be lost; and it is for the cause that I speak. The Senator from South Carolina has read many books of chivalry, and believes himself a chivalrous knight, with sentiments of honor and courage. Of course he has chosen a mistress to whom he has made his vows, and who, though ugly to others, is always lovely to him,— though polluted in the sight of the world, is chaste in his sight: I mean the harlot Slavery. For her his tongue is always profuse in words. Let her be impeached in character, or any proposition be made to shut her out from the extension of her wantonness, and no extravagance of manner or hardi- hood of assertion is then too great for this Senator. The frenzy of Don Quixote in behalf of his wench Dulcinea del Toboso is all surpassed. The asserted rights of Slavery, which shock equality of all kinds, are cloaked by a fantastic claim of equality. If the Slave States cannot enjoy what, in mockery of the great fathers of the Republic, he misnames Equality under the Constitution,—in other words, the full power in the National Territories to compel fellow-men to unpaid toil, to separate husband and wife, and to sell little children at the auction-block,—then, Sir, the chivalric Senator will conduct the State of South Carolina out of the Union! Heroic knight! Exalted Senator! A second Moses come for a second exodus!

Not content with this poor menace, which we have been twice told was "measured," the Senator, in the unrestrained chivalry of his nature, has undertaken to apply opprobrious words to those who differ from him on this floor. He calls them "sectional and fanatical"; and resistance to the Usurpation of Kansas he denounces as "an uncalculating fanaticism." To be sure, these charges lack all grace of originality and all sentiment of truth; but the adventurous Senator does not hesitate. He is the uncompromising, unblushing representative on this floor of a flagrant *sectionalism,* now domineering over the Republic,—and yet, with a ludicrous ignorance of his own position, unable to see himself as others see him, or with an effrontery which even his white head ought not to protect from rebuke, he applies to those here who resist his *sectionalism* the very epithet which designates himself. The men who strive to bring back the Government to its original policy, when Freedom and not Slavery was national, while Slavery and not Freedom was sectional, he arraigns as *sectional.* This will not do. It involves too great a perversion of terms. I tell that Senator that it is to himself, and to the "organization" of which he is the "committed advocate," that this epithet belongs. I now fasten it upon them. For myself, I care little for names; but, since the question is raised here, I affirm that the Republican party of the Union is in no just sense *sectional,* but, more than any other party, *national,*—and that it now goes forth to dislodge from the high places that tyrannical sectionalism of which the Senator from South Carolina is one of the maddest zealots. . . .

A Virginia Congressman Defends
Preston Brooks, July 1856

. . . Thus far have I considered it as a question of law. I come now to investigate it as a question of right and justice. Because we happen to be members of Congress, will it be pretended that we are at liberty to rise in our places, and, with absolute impunity, abuse, malign, and slander each other, or any other person we may choose? The doctrine is absolutely monstrous. Nor is its meanness diminished by saying that a majority in framing their rules must properly restrict debate. We know too well that rules are often broken now-a-days. How many of the speeches delivered on this question have conformed to our rule, which requires the debate to relate strictly to the subject under consideration? Scarcely one.

Besides, the gentlemen of the North are largely in the majority on this floor. Sectional feeling runs high. It may be agreeable to them to abuse the southern members—their constituents, their institutions, their families, &c. Shall we be required to submit to it all, and be utterly without redress? Surely not; it is impossible. We have no such right, and could not enjoy it, if it were given. Say by express law, if you choose, that members of Congress shall enjoy perfect freedom of debate, and may abuse, and traduce, and malign whomsoever they choose. The right will be worth but little. There can be no royal prerogative of slander in this country. You may draw around it the strongest muniments of legal defense; you may make the sheriff and his *posse* the warders on the tower; you may make instruments of punishment to bristle on the walls, still the immunity will not be perfect. When it begins to throw its venom fiercely around, injured sensibility will revolt, and aroused manhood will still occasionally break over and inflict condign punishment. A broken head will still pay the penalty for a foul tongue.

Think, sir, of American character, how sensitive, yet how brave; how easily wounded, yet how quick to avenge the injury! Better death than disgrace! Can you, then, by legislation make American gentlemen submit to traduction with composure? Never! never, sir! You must first tame our high hearts, and teach them the low beat of servility; you must make our Anglo-Saxon blood run milk and water in our veins; you must tear from the records of history the pages which tell the deeds of our heroic ancestry, and persuade us that we have descended of drabs and shrews. When you have done that, and changed Billingsgate into rhetoric, and railing into eloquence, you may then convert the Senate and the House of Representatives into two great Schools for scandal, in which your Backbites and your Crabtrees may strut their "*hour*" on the stage and feel happy. Then, too, you may build up your great doctrine of woman's rights; for whereever your Backbites and your Crabtrees are the prominent actors, the Lady Sneerwells and Mrs. Candors should take their parts to make the play complete. If this is your doctrine, gentlemen, bring on your Theodore Parkers, and your Ward Beechers [two leading abolitionists], and your strong-minded women, and have a good time of it here and in the Senate. *Gentlemen* will retire voluntarily from both without the process of expulsion.

Slander never can, (in this country,) under any guise, in any form of authority, enjoy perfect immunity, and have

> "As large a character as the wind,
> To blow on whom it pleases."

Surely there has been no disposition or intention to give it such immunity or liberty heretofore; and any such construction is in the teeth of law and in the face of justice.

This, then, being the doctrine of law and justice, let me apply it to the case in hand.

I believe that Mr. SUMNER's speech was made "*contra morem parliamentarium*"; that under guise of debating the Kansas bill, he sought occasion to pour out his private resentments, and vent his personal malice. In thus stepping beyond his parliamentary right, he lost his constitutional protection, and became liable as any other citizen would be. The assault and battery committed on him occupies, in this regard, the same ground, not lower, not higher, than the same assault and battery upon any other person.

It has been asked, if Mr. SUMNER was liable to an action of libel, why not pursue him in the courts of justice? That question may as well be asked in any other case of assault and battery. If a man insults you in a public crowd, or traduces your wife or daughter, and you knock him down, it may be asked, why not sue him? That, surely, is the legal course. But there are offenses of such a nature, that men cannot always wait for redress on the slow and uncertain course of legal proceedings. The courts are then to inquire how much is to be pardoned to the weakness of human nature under the circumstances?

This is the great case of "the violation of the freedom of speech" in the person of Mr. SUMNER. He wantonly gave an insult, and was punished, rashly perhaps, for it. Why, then, Mr. Speaker, should Massachusetts become so much excited on the subject? Will she adopt the quarrels and take up the fights of her sons wherever they go? Freedom of speech is a right of the private man as well as of the public man. Whenever a son of hers gives an insult and gets a knock, is she to rush forth and cry out "that the freedom of speech has been violated?" I have known parents who identified themselves with their children in all their quarrels and broils with their schoolfellows and playmates; and the consequence in such cases always is, that the parent gets the more ill-will, and the children the more ill-treatment. . . .

Senator William Henry Seward of New York Warns of an Irrepressible Conflict, October 1858

. . . The slave system is one of constant danger, distrust, suspicion, and watchfulness. It debases those whose toil alone can produce wealth and resources for defense, to the lowest degree of which human nature is capable, to guard against mutiny and insurrection, and thus wastes energies which otherwise might be employed in national development and aggrandizement.

The free-labor system educates all alike, and by opening all the fields of industrial employment, and all the departments of authority, to the unchecked and equal rivalry of all classes of men, at once secures universal contentment, and brings into the highest possible activity all the physical, moral and social energies of the whole state. In states where the slave system prevails, the masters, directly or indirectly, secure all political power, and constitute a ruling aristocracy. In states where the free-labor system prevails, universal suffrage necessarily obtains, and the state inevitably becomes, sooner or later, a republic or democracy.

Russia yet maintains slavery, and is a despotism. Most of the other European states have abolished slavery, and adopted the system of free labor. It was the antagonistic political tendencies of the two systems which the first Napoleon was contemplating when he predicted that Europe would ultimately be either all Cossack or all republican. Never did human sagacity utter a more pregnant truth. The two systems are at once perceived to be incongruous. But they are more than incongruous—they are incompatible. They never have permanently existed together in one country, and they never can. It would be easy to demonstrate this impossibility, from the irreconcilable contrast between their great principles and characteristics. But the experience of mankind has conclusively established it. Slavery, as I have already intimated, existed in every state in Europe. Free labor has supplanted it everywhere except in Russia and Turkey. State necessities developed in modern times, are now obliging even those two nations to encourage and employ free labor; and already, despotic as they are, we find them engaged in abolishing slavery. In the United States, slavery came into collision with free labor at the close of the last century, and fell before it in New England, New York, New Jersey and Pennsylvania, but triumphed over it effectually, and excluded it for a period yet undetermined, from Virginia, the Carolinas and Georgia. Indeed, so incompatible are the two systems, that every new state which is organized within our ever extending domain makes its first political act a choice of the one and the exclusion of the other, even at the cost of civil war, if necessary. The slave states, without law, at the last national election, successfully forbade, within their own limits, even the casting of votes for a candidate for president of the United States supposed to be favorable to the establishment of the free-labor system in new states.

Hitherto, the two systems have existed in different states, but side by side within the American Union. This has happened because the Union is a confederation of states. But in another aspect the United States constitute only one nation. Increase of population, which is filling the states out to their very borders, together with a new and extended net-work of railroads and other avenues, and an internal commerce which daily becomes more intimate, is rapidly bringing the states into a higher and more perfect social unity or consolidation. Thus, these antagonistic systems are continually coming into closer contact, and collision results.

Shall I tell you what this collision means? They who think that it is accidental, unnecessary, the work of interested or fanatical agitators, and therefore ephemeral, mistake the case altogether. It is an irrepressible conflict between opposing and enduring forces, and it means that the United States must and will, sooner or later, become either entirely a slaveholding nation, or entirely a free-labor nation. Either the cotton and rice-fields of South Carolina and the sugar plantations of Louisiana will ultimately be tilled by free labor, and Charleston and New Orleans become marts for legitimate merchandise alone, or else the rye-fields and wheat-fields of Massachusetts and New York must again be surrendered by their farmers to slave culture and to the production of slaves, and Boston and New York become once more markets for trade in the bodies and souls of men. It is the failure to apprehend this great truth that induces so many unsuccessful attempts at final compromise between the slave and free states, and it is the existence of this great fact that renders all such pretended compromises, when made, vain and ephemeral. Startling as this saying may appear to you, fellow citizens, it is by no means an original or even a moderate one. Our forefathers knew it to be true, and unanimously acted upon it when they framed the constitution of the United States. They regarded the existence of the servile system in so many of the states with sorrow and shame, which they openly confessed, and they looked upon the collision between them, which was then just revealing itself, and which we are now accustomed to deplore, with favor and hope. They knew that either the one or the other system must exclusively prevail. . . .

Senator Andrew Johnson of Tennessee Argues
for an Irrepressible Conflict
Between Capital and Labor, December 1859

. . . The doctrine here proclaimed is, that there is an irrepressible conflict between slave labor and free labor. I hope the Senate will pardon me if I digress again from the line of my argument, to combat what, as I conceive, is a false proposition, which has no foundation in truth. The premises of the Senator are wholly incorrect; but, as long as the conclusions drawn from them are not combated, they have the same strength as if the premises were correct. Now, sir, is there, in fact, a conflict between slave labor and free labor? If I know myself, I want to be fair and honest on this subject; and as humble as I conceive myself to be, and as poor an estimate as I put on any argument of mine, I wish to God that I might to-day speak to the citizens of every free State in this Confederacy, and could get them, with unprejudiced minds, to look at this proposition as it is. What, sir; a conflict, an irrepressible conflict between free and slave labor! It is untrue. It is a mistaken application of an old principle to an improper case. There is a conflict always going on between capital and labor; but there is not a conflict between two kinds of labor. By sophistry and ingenuity, a principle which is conceded by all, is applied to a wrong case. There is a war always going on between capital and labor; but there is a material difference between two descriptions of labor, and a conflict between labor in the aggregate on the one hand and capital on the other.

Where is the conflict? We know that as far as labor and capital are concerned, labor is always trying to get as much capital for labor as it can; on the other hand capital is always trying to get as much labor for capital as it can. Hence there is an eternal warfare going on between capital and labor, labor wanting to absorb capital and capital wanting to absorb labor. Does that make a conflict between two kinds of labor? Not at all. Where is the conflict in the United States between slave labor and free labor? Is the slave who is cultivating the rice fields in South Carolina, is the slave who is following the plow in the rich and fertile plains of Mississippi, in competition with the man who is making boots and shoes in New York and Massachusetts? Is there any conflict between their labor? Is there any conflict between the man who is growing mules and hogs and horses in the State of Ohio, and the man in the South who is raising cotton, rice, and tobacco with his slaves? The assumption is false, and upon these false premises a conclusion has been drawn which has deluded thousands of honest men in the country.

Instead of there being a conflict, an irrepressible conflict, between slave labor and free labor, I say the argument is clear and conclusive that the one mutually benefits the other; that slave labor is a great help and aid to free labor, as well as free labor to slave labor. Where does the northern man go, to a very great extent, with his manufactured articles? He goes to the South for a market, or the southern merchant goes to the North and buys them. With what does he buy them? Does he buy them with the product of labor that is in conflict with his labor? No. What then? He buys them with the product of cotton, of rice, of tobacco, and of sugar. Is that conflict? The fact that he can produce these articles with slave labor, enables him to get the means, and sometimes a superabundance of means, by which he can pay higher prices for articles raised in the North.

Again, when a man raises mules and hogs in the West and Southwest, and another man raises cotton in the South, by means of his slaves, is there, as I before inquired, any competition, any irrepressible conflict between them? None. It is not entitled, in point of fact, to be dignified with the appellation of an argument; it is sophistry, the product of ingenuity, calculated, if not intended, to deceive thousands of honest laboring minds. Sir, I had been vain enough to think that I could satisfy a northern man, strip him of his prejudices, that the southern man who has his capital invested in slave labor, is his best friend. Let us analyze this a little more, and see where it will carry us to. You talk about a slave aristocracy. If it is an aristocracy, it is an aristocracy of labor. What kind of aristocracy have you in the North? Capital and money. Which is the most odious in its operations—an aristocracy of money or an aristocracy of labor? Which is the most unyielding? Which is the most exacting? Every man has the answer in his own mind.

But to illustrate still further. The southern man puts his capital into labor. He commences the production of cotton, or any other product peculiar to slave labor. Is he not interested in obtaining the highest price for slave labor? His capital is in slave labor. His talent, his mind, and his influence are employed to make slave labor productive, and, at the same time, to make it yield the greatest amount in dollars and cents; and just in proportion as he can find new markets, devise more ways and means for consumption, and thereby increase the price, in the very same proportion he increases his means—to do what? Whenever you see cotton and the other great staple of the South run up in price, does not everything increase in price, does not every article manufactured at the North run up correspondingly? Thus the southern man, in obtaining the highest price for the product of his capital invested in labor, gets the means by which he pays the highest price for labor. He is interested in getting the highest price for his products, and by doing so he becomes enabled to pay the highest price for free labor, and he is the most reliable advocate and the best friend of the laboring man at the North. Who can contradict the proposition? He is interested in obtaining the highest prices, and he pays corresponding prices for everything that he consumes. Who gets the benefit of it?

As I said just now, there is a conflict going on between capital and labor. Do we not know that a man who has his thousand dollars invested in a slave producing cotton, is interested in the product of that labor, while the man who has his thousand dollars invested in money is interested in reducing the price of labor. Capital at the North is the oppressor of the laboring man. There is where the oppression is; there is where the irrepressible conflict exists. It is between the dollars and cents of the North and the free labor of the North, not between slave labor and free labor. . . .

Senator Albert G. Brown of Mississippi Explains the South's Position, December 1859

. . . All we ask—and, in asking that, we shall never cease—is, that our property, under the common Government, be put upon the same footing with other people's property; that this Government of ours shall be allowed to draw no insulting discrimination between slave property and any other kind of property; that wherever the authority of the Government extends, it shall be given to us in an equal degree with anybody else; and, by that, I say again, I mean given to the extent of affording us adequate and sufficient protection. Who does not know that, in the last two or three years, emigrant trains were robbed in Utah by the Mormons; not robbed of slaves, but robbed of other kinds of property. What was done? An army was promptly sent to repair the injury, at an expense, I dare say, when we shall sum up the bill and pay it, of $20,000,000. Who believes that if the property had been our slaves, any reparation would have been insisted upon? Is the Government so prompt to send armies to protect us against the underground process? No. Twenty millions of property may be stolen from us, and the Government stands by and contents itself with simply remonstrating, with giving gentle hints that it is all wrong. When I say this is done by the Government, I do not mean the government of James Buchanan, or Franklin Pierce, or Millard Fillmore; but I mean the Government in whosoever hands it happened to rest. Justice has never been done us; our property has never been treated like the property of other people; has never received the same sort of protection, the same kind of security. While the Government has been ready to protect other people's property on the high seas and in the Territories; while it has been ready to make war at home and declare war against foreign countries for the protection of other people's property, we have received no such guarantees from it. I demand them. I demand to be treated as an equal. If you will insist upon taxing me as an equal, I do not feel disposed to come up and pay my taxes, simply to know the Government through its power to make exactions on me. I do not choose to perform military service, and spill my blood and risk my life and lay down the lives of my people for the common protection, in defense of a Government which only knows me through its powers to tax me. I claim the same right to protection on the part of my people as I concede to you. Wherever your property is on the face of God's habitable globe, on the sea or on the land, I claim that the arms and power of this Government must go to protect and defend it. For that was the great object of creating the Government; and when it falls short of that object, it fails in its great mission, the great purpose for which it was created.

I know of no mission which this Government has to perform except to protect the citizen in his life, his liberty, and his property. When it fails in these great essentials, it has failed in everything; and I stand even in this august presence to say, as I have said in the more august presence of my immediate constituents, the Legislature of my State—and if they choose to repudiate me for saying it, I am willing to be repudiated—that whenever the Government fails, I do not ask it to refuse, but when it fails to protect me and my people in our lives, our liberties, and our property, upon the high seas or upon the land, it ought to be abolished. If that be treason, gentlemen, make the most of it. That is all I have said; and by that proposition living or dying, sinking or swimming, surviving or perishing, I mean to stand here and elsewhere.

Those who have served with me in this House and in the other House of Congress, know, or ought to know, that I am deeply and earnestly and at heart devoted to the Democratic party. I am devoted to it, because I have always regarded it as a party that dispensed equal and exact justice to every part of the country. I am a Democrat because I have always felt that this Government would dispense to Massachusetts the same measure of justice that it gave to Mississippi; that it would give to Pennsylvania no more than it gave to Virginia; and I should be as ready to despise it if I thought it would give more to my State than to any other State in the Confederacy. While I say this, I am equally free to say, that I would, if it were in my power, rend it into ten thousand fragments, if it exacted of me to do that for Massachusetts which the Senator from Massachusetts would not do for Mississippi. If I have asked, in all this, anything more for my country, for my State, or for my section, than I would give to any other State or section, show me in what, and I am ready to submit. I ask nothing for my section that I am not willing to yield to any other.

Now, Mr. President, thanking the Republican benches for the patient and polite attention which they have given me, I take my seat. [Laughter, every seat on the Republican side being vacant.] . . .

↵ *E S S A Y S*

The issues of "Bleeding Kansas" and "Bleeding Sumner" were interrelated, and they contributed significantly to the climax of the sectional crisis in the late 1850s. In the first essay, William E. Gienapp of Harvard University points out how Brooks's caning of Sumner was a decisive incident that hardened northerners' distaste and hostility toward the South and its values. The accompanying piece, by Don E. Fehrenbacher of Stanford University, is an analysis of the Kansas episode and how it confirmed southerners' fears that the North did not respect their rights and interests.

The Caning of Charles Sumner and the Rise of the Republican Party

WILLIAM E. GIENAPP

When the Republican party elected its first President, Abraham Lincoln, in 1860, only six years had elapsed since its formation, and only four years

William E. Gienapp, "The Crime Against Sumner: The Caning of Charles Sumner and the Rise of the Republican Party," *Civil War History*, Vol. 25, No. 3, September 1979, pp. 218–245. Reprinted with permission of The Kent State University Press.

since the creation of its national organization. Despite this remarkable achievement, the party had a precarious early existence, and emerged as the principal opposition to the Democrats only after a severe and difficult struggle with the rival American or Know Nothing party. It certainly was anything but clear initially that the Republicans would become a permanent fixture in the two party system. In fact, the 1855 state elections were a serious setback for the fledgling party. With only one year remaining until the 1856 presidential election, the Know Nothings were the Democrats' most formidable opponent. Indeed, in several Northern states the Know Nothings were so strong the Republican party did not even exist.

In late November 1855, as he surveyed the political disorder of the previous two years, former New York Governor Washington Hunt expressed strong doubts about the permanence of the Republican party. He remained hopeful that the Whig party could be revived. Still, he admitted that he was uneasy. With an eye to the convening of a new Congress, now less than two weeks away, he predicted that the Republicans, hoping for new outrages in Kansas and in Washington to bolster their party's sagging fortunes, would try to provoke Southerners with insults and bravado. "We must be prepared for high words and stormy scenes," he warned, "but we will hope that there will be sense and moderation enough to prevent any desperate deeds, or any violent action in Congress." Hunt's fears were as well taken as his optimism misplaced. The most dramatic event of the session was the caning of Senator Charles Sumner of Massachusetts by Representative Preston S. Brooks of South Carolina. This was precisely the kind of event Hunt had feared: it inflamed popular emotions in both the North and the South, intensified sectional animosity, and destroyed the cherished hopes of men such as himself for the preservation of a national conservative party.

Most historians, in seeking to explain the rise of the Republican party, have emphasized, sometimes almost without qualification, the Kansas issue. There is no doubt that the repeal of the Missouri Compromise and the ensuing troubles in the Kansas Territory were critical to the party's increasing strength. Nevertheless, if this issue were primarily responsible for the party's growth, one must ask why, despite the persistence of the Kansas crisis and the vigorous efforts of Republicans to capitalize on it, the party had remained so weak. Why did the party's spectacular growth occur in the late spring and summer of 1856, and not earlier? This is a complex question, but one reason that has not received the emphasis it deserves is Brooks' attack on Sumner.

When Congress convened in December, 1855, observers quickly noticed an intensified animosity between antislavery men and Southerners. The continuing troubles in Kansas, where free-state men had established their own government in opposition to the recognized territorial authorities, greatly contributed to this hardening of feeling. "We have before us a long session of excitement, & ribald debate," Sumner commented when debate over Kansas opened in the Senate. A staunch antislavery man, Sumner immediately began preparing to speak on affairs in Kansas. On May 19 and 20, 1856 he delivered a carefully rehearsed speech on "The Crime Against Kansas," in which he severely lashed the Administration, the South, and the proslavery men in Kansas. The Republican leader also made scathing personal attacks on several prominent Democrats, including Senator Andrew P. Butler of South Carolina, then absent from the Senate. Sumner's attack on the sixty year old Butler, a kindly man of charm and grace who was widely admired and respected in Washington, produced considerable resentment.

No one was more angered by Sumner's comments than Preston S. Brooks. A distant relative of Butler's, Brooks was a proud, aristocratic South Carolina congressman now serving his second term. He considered Sumner's speech an insult to his aged relative and his state, for which he decided to chastise the Massachusetts senator, as a Southern gentleman would any inferior. When the Senate adjourned on May 22, Brooks entered the Senate Chamber. Sumner was seated at his desk, writing letters and franking copies of his speech. When the Chamber was clear of ladies, Brooks walked up to Sumner's desk and, pronouncing the speech a libel on South Carolina and on Butler, began to strike the Senator over the head with a gutta percha cane. In his excitement Brooks forgot his original intention merely to flog Sumner, and began to hit him with all his strength. Sumner, stunned and blinded by blood, vainly tried to ward off the blows to his head. Brooks continued the attack, even after his cane had shattered, until he was seized by a Northern congressman who had rushed to the scene of the attack. Brooks' friends then quietly led him away. Sumner lay on the floor, unconscious and bleeding profusely. The following day Brooks informed his brother that he gave Sumner "about 30 first rate stripes" with the cane. "Every lick went where I intended," he wrote triumphantly. It was four years before Sumner returned to his seat in the Senate.

At the insistence of the Republican members, the Senate established a special committee of investigation. Lacking a single Republican member, it met and promptly decided that it had no jurisdiction over the matter. Attention thus turned to the Republican dominated House of Representatives. Although the House voted to appoint a committee of investigation, only two Southern members, both border state men, supported the majority. Speaker Nathaniel P. Banks of Massachusetts appointed a committee which recommended by a straight party vote to expel Brooks. After a heated debate the House voted for expulsion by 121 to 95, but as it required a two-thirds vote, the motion failed. Only one Southern congressman voted against Brooks. Following the vote, Brooks made a defiant speech in defense of his action and resigned, confident that his constituents would support him. Unanimously re-elected, he triumphantly returned to the session. Ultimately the only punishment Brooks received was a $300 fine for assault levied by a Washington court.

Though the focus of this essay is on the Northern reaction to the caning, it is necessary to examine briefly the Southern response, for the former can be understood fully only against the background of the latter. Some Southerners privately expressed disapproval of Brooks' action. A handful even wrote letters of sympathy to Sumner. Other Southerners, while not disapproving of the caning, criticized Brooks for assaulting Sumner on the floor of the Senate. Senator James Mason of Virginia, despite his belief that Sumner "did not get a lick amiss," added that "for appearances it would have been better, had it lighted on him outside the Chamber." Public criticism, however, was rare. The general Southern response was one of strong approval. A virtual unknown before the incident, Brooks returned home a hero and a celebrity. Resolutions endorsing the assault were passed at meetings in the South and a number of souvenir canes were ostentatiously presented to him. "Every Southern man sustains me," Brooks boasted after the caning. "The fragments of the stick are begged for as *sacred relicts*."

Meanwhile, Southern editors vied with each other in the enthusiasm of their endorsements of Brooks. This praise was not confined to South Carolina, where the press was unanimous in its approval. The influential Richmond *Enquirer* declared:

> We consider the act good in conception, better in execution, and best of all in consequence. The vulgar Abolitionists in the Senate are getting above themselves. . . . They have grown saucy, and dare to be impudent to gentlemen! . . . The truth is, they have been suffered to run too long without collars. They must be lashed into submission.

It went on to suggest that Republican Senators Henry Wilson and John P. Hale would benefit from a similar beating. In another issue it demanded that the Republicans in Congress be silenced if the Union were to survive. The rival Richmond *Whig* hailed the assault as "A Good Deed," and suggested that William H. Seward, another prominent Republican Senator, "should catch it next," while the Richmond *Examiner* maintained that Brooks' example should be followed by other Southern gentlemen whose feelings were outraged. With the reckless bravado that increasingly characterized Southern politics in this decade, the Southern press deliberately taunted Northerners by their endorsements of Brooks, phrasing them in a manner best designed to humiliate Northern sensibilities.

Even before the Southern reaction was known, news of the attack on Sumner electrified the North. Statements of shock and outrage poured in to the stricken Senator from sympathizers. A Boston clergyman declared, "I have experienced more moral misery in thinking on the assault than any other event ever excited in me," while a prominent German leader in Chicago testified that news of the attack "perfectly overwhelmed me with indignation and rage." Horace Mann, the famous educator, eloquently expressed Northern sentiment when he wrote Sumner: "We are all not only shocked at the outrage committed upon you, but we are wounded in your wounds, & bleed in your bleeding." Richard Henry Dana, Jr., perhaps best described the impact of the assault when he told Sumner, "When Brooks brought his cane in contact with your head, he completed the circuit of electricity to 30 millions!''

The depth of feeling and the level of excitement in the North surpassed anything observers had witnessed. A western correspondent assured Sumner that he had never seen men so aroused before; William H. Furness, the prominent clergyman, observed the same response in Philadelphia. A New York man told Banks that no event in the history of Congress had produced so much excitement. The greatest indignation naturally was felt in Massachusetts, where conservatives were badly shaken by the depth of the sectional animosity they observed. "You can have little idea of the depth & intensity of the feeling which has been excited in New England," Robert C. Winthrop warned Senator John J. Crittenden of Kentucky after the assault. Edward Everett, a sober, level-headed observer, affirmed that "when the intelligence of the assault on Mr. Sumner . . . reached Boston, it produced an excitement in the public mind deeper and more dangerous than I have ever witnessed. It was the opinion of some persons that if a leader daring & reckless enough had presented himself, he might have raised any number of men to march on Washington."

Public indignation over the Sumner-Brooks affair inevitably increased when news arrived that the town of Lawrence, Kansas, headquarters of the free-state movement, had been "sacked" by a proslavery army the day before the attack on Sumner. Historians now know that the reports of the attack on Lawrence were grossly exaggerated. Still, as the first accounts arrived, Republican newspapers shrilly proclaimed that yet another pro-slavery outrage had occurred. The coincidental timing of these two events served to magnify northern indignation. Winthrop reported with alarm that the "concurrence of the Kansas horrors" with the Sumner caning "has wrought up the masses to a state of fearful exasperation." Winthrop's fellow conservative Bostonian, Amos A. Lawrence, noted that the invasion of Lawrence and the assault on Sumner had excited the people of the country more than he had ever seen.

During the initial outcry over the caning, a handful of Republicans believed that the Kansas outrages were more important. This view, however, was decidedly the exception among seasoned political observers. Despite the attack on Lawrence, most politicians in the North agreed that, at least during the first weeks immediately following these two events, the Sumner assault was more important in producing northern indignation. Meetings to protest the caning dwarfed Kansas meetings in size, they attracted many more non-Republicans, both in the audience and as participants, and revealed more widespread excitement and deeply felt anger. There are several reasons why this was the case. Unlike accounts of the Sumner-Brooks incident, the news from Kansas was invariably fragmentary, uncertain, and contradictory; the deliberate attack on a senator for words spoken in debate seemed an attack on the Constitution, and as such it was much more ominous and threatening than events in a distant, sparsely settled territory. "The Kansas murders are on the border and border men are always represented and known to be often desperate but to see a senator assaulted in the Senate Chamber no one can find any excuse for it," one Northerner explained. Not only did Brooks' act undermine the basic principles of the American political system, but Northerners were keenly aware of the deliberately insulting nature of the caning. "We all or *nearly* all felt that we had been personally maltreated & insulted," a Boston man told Sumner afterwards. Men who had listened for over a year to stories of Kansas outrages without feeling that drastic action was necessary were suddenly shaken from their complacency by the Sumner affair. "The Northern blood is boiling at the outrage upon you," a New York Republican wrote Sumner. "It really sinks Kansas out of sight."

Nothing better demonstrated the almost universal extent of the outrage over the assault than the indignation meetings held in the North in late May and early June. Countless meetings, in small towns as well as large cities, in the West as well as the East, protested the caning. The two most significant meetings were held in New York City and Boston.

In New York [for example] a large group assembled at the Broadway Tabernacle to condemn the assault. The impulse for the meeting came largely from conservatives. Aware of the harmful consequences of making the meeting a partisan gathering, Republicans quietly encouraged its organization but shrewdly left its direction to others. The Tabernacle was jammed to overflowing, with perhaps as many as 5,000 people inside, and thousands more outside, unable to gain entrance. The conservative influence at the meeting was readily apparent. George Griswold, one of the city's most respected merchants, presided. Vice presidents included such notable conservatives as Luther Bradish, William Kent, James A. Hamilton, and William F. Havemeyer. Among the speakers were Daniel Lord, a leading member of the bar; Samuel B. Ruggles, a prominent Know Nothing and former Whig; John A. Stevens, President of the Bank of Commerce; and Charles King, President of Columbia College. The crowd cheered as Lord defended free speech and denounced the Senate for failing to uphold its privileges; as King declared that the time had come for the North to act as well as talk; as Stevens called for "union at the ballot box" to stop these outrages; and as Ruggles asserted that if Congress would not maintain its dignity, then "force must be met by force." At the end of the meeting, the audience roared its approval of the moderately worded resolutions. Yet observers noted that the crowd was prepared for even stronger language.

Describing this meeting as "the most remarkable & significant assembly I ever attended," publisher George Putnam asserted that "no public demonstration has ever equalled this denunciation of the alarming crime. . . . The feeling was *deep,* calm, but resolute." Another observer noted that the vast multitude was "earnest, unanimous, and made up of people who don't often attend political gatherings." It was led by men "not given to fits of enthusiasm or generous sympathy, unlike[ly] to be prominent in anything wherein the general voice of the community does not sustain them."

Commentators immediately recognized the significance of the meeting. Antislavery sentiment had never been strong in New York City, where conservatives had persistently sought grounds of political accommodation with the South. In the aftermath of the assault on Sumner—a man for whom they had no political sympathy—they suddenly found themselves using language which previously they would have thought inflammatory. The New York *Tribune* was struck by this change in public sentiment. Men who had always been "conservative and cotton loving to the last degree," it noted, were now denouncing the Slave Power: "At no period since the formation of the Constitution has the public mind of this city been wrought to such a pitch of feeling and indignation as at the present moment." Putnam excitedly proclaimed that "a *new era* is inaugurated. . . . Never in my life have I felt anything like the stirring excitement & earnest determination which has been roused up by the blows of that bludgeon." . . .

In the wake of these indignation meetings, many men described the North as united in condemnation of Brooks. [Richard Henry Dana, Jr.], for example, reported that "it looks . . . as though the North was going all one way." Yet this appearance of unanimity was misleading. A few Northerners openly approved of Brooks' course, and more expressed such sentiments privately. Several prominent newspapers tempered their criticism of the assault with the assertion that Sumner had provoked it by his speech. Although in a more limited way than in the South, Northern public opinion on the caning was coercive, a situation Republicans used to pressure reluctant conservatives to cooperate with the party. A full month after the assault Everett, who had good reason to know, commented that the caning of Sumner "threw the entire north . . . into a frenzy of excitement . . . & no one dares speak aloud on the subject except to echo the popular voice." Former Governor Emory Washburne of Massachusetts made a similar complaint about Republican pressure after the assault: "It is not enough that you agree with them. You must say your creed in their words with their intonation and just when they bid you or they hang or burn you as a heretic." Some observers, especially conservatives frightened by the increasing sectionalism of American politics, vainly argued that the assault was purely a personal affair between Brooks and Sumner. But the enthusiastic and widespread support of Brooks in the South, and the ardent championing of Sumner in the North, necessarily made it a sectional incident. "That which hitherto has been an issue between the Southern Senators and Mr. Sumner," the New York *Tribune* asserted, "they have now made an issue between them and the great body of the people of the North. . . ."

Although Northern indignation meetings were non-partisan, "Bleeding Sumner" inevitably became a Republican issue. It was an ideal issue in several respects. Freedom of speech had always been a sacred American principle. Northerners, after years of abolitionist agitation, were keenly aware that, at least on the slavery issue, freedom of speech had long ago ceased in the South. Now it seemed directly under attack in Congress. The fact that the Constitution specifically protected congressional freedom of debate made the assault more startling. A conservative Republican organ, the *Illinois State Journal,* which was not given to exaggeration, characterized the assault as "the most direct blow to freedom of speech ever made in this country." "The great thing before the free states is the fact that freedom of debate is practically destroyed in Congress," one Massachusetts Republican solemnly proclaimed: "The inmost essence of the Constitution, that which gives it life and meaning, has been struck at, and grievously wounded, if not killed." This attack on free speech, and the subsequent failure of the Senate to defend its privileges, was the theme of Lord's widely reprinted speech at the New York meeting. Republicans lost no time in linking this issue with the assault, and the defense of free speech with their party. Free Soil, Free Labor, Free Men, Free Speech, and Frémont, chanted the party faithful in 1856.

According to Republicans, Brooks' attack was ominous because it was part of a conspiracy to destroy free speech and liberty everywhere. In explaining why the Sumner assault had aroused "a deeper feeling in the public heart of the North than any other event of the past ten years," the staid New York *Times* commented:

> The great body of the people, without distinction of party, feel that *their* rights have been assailed in a vital point,—that the blow struck at SUMNER takes effect upon Freedom of Speech in that spot where, without freedom of speech, there can be no freedom of any kind. . . .

This issue could be linked effectively to the Kansas outrages for, according to Republicans, free-state men in Kansas had been murdered and terrorized, and free-state newspapers destroyed, because they opposed slavery. The infamous code of laws enacted by the proslavery territorial legislature had even made it a crime to assert that slavery did not legally exist in Kansas. Both in Kansas and in the nation's capital, men seemed to be attacked for what they said. Slavery propagandists, the Cincinnati *Gazette* asserted, "cannot tolerate free speech anywhere, and would stifle it in Washington with the bludgeon and the bowie-knife, as they are now trying to stifle it in Kansas by massacre, rapine and murder." Other Republican newspapers echoed this theme. Nor was this threat to liberty confined to Washington and Kansas. "It seems that the Missouri Kansas Statutes, with additions, are to be established throughout the Union," one Indiana man wrote to Sumner. Henry Ward Beecher concisely brought these themes together in a powerful article on the caning entitled "Silence Must be Nationalized." Such events were part of a "long-formed, deeply-laid plan, of destroying free speech in the Republic, and making SILENCE NATIONAL!," he argued. Brooks "was the arm, but the whole South was the body!"

This linking of the Sumner and Kansas outrages was an extremely important aspect of the Republicans' use of the caning as a campaign issue. Republicans, far from viewing the Sumner assault as competing with the Kansas crisis for public attention, viewed them as mutually reinforcing. Historians have recognized that Bleeding Sumner and Bleeding Kansas were very powerful Republican symbols in the 1856 campaign. However, the manner in which the Sumner outrage gave credence to Bleeding Kansas has not been sufficiently emphasized. "It may seem hard to think but still it is true that the north needed in order to *see* the slave aggression, one of its best men Butchered in Congress, or something else as wicked which could be brought home to them. Had it not been for your poor head, the Kansas outrage would not have been felt at the North . . . ," one supporter consoled Sumner. Despite a year of agitation by the Republican press over the situation in Kansas, many Northerners, especially conservative former Whigs, remained skeptical of Republican claims. Such men were naturally suspicious of agitation and abolitionism anyway, and it was difficult to decide what was the truth about Kansas. This changed with the Sumner assault. Men were now more easily convinced that Southern aggression was a fact, that the South was capable of any atrocity to maintain its national power. "Soon men will be convinced Kansas difficulties are real, not stories circulated without foundation, for mere political capital," a correspondent assured Congressman Edwin B. Morgan after the caning. A Vermont Republican agreed: "*Brooks* has knocked the scales from the eyes of the blind, and they now *see!*"

At the same time, the Sumner assault gave the Republican party another means of increasing anti-Southern sentiment in the North. This was consistent with the party's primary goal, which was more to check the political power and arrogance of the South than to attack slavery. When confronted with united Southern opinion, it was only a short step from condemning Brooks to condemning the South. The Republican view of the South as a backward, degraded, barbaric society built on brutality and depravity, gained increased credibility as Southerners rallied to the defense of Brooks, the symbol of everything that Northerners despised in Southern chivalry. Brooks, in Republican rhetoric, became the inevitable product of a slave society. The North was the symbol of civilization, the South of barbarism. "The symbol of the North is the pen; the symbol of the South is the bludgeon," Beecher thundered at the New York meeting to tremendous cheering. A prominent New York conservative, earlier sympathetic to the South, now denied that Southerners were the cultivated aristocrats so often pictured: "they are, in fact, a race of lazy, ignorant, coarse, sensual, swaggering, sordid, beggarly barbarians, bullying white men and breeding little niggers for sale." This had been a common abolitionist theme, but Northerners generally had resisted endorsing it. Now it did not appear so extreme. . . .

The ideological significance of the Sumner caning was not the new ideas it developed, but the way it strengthened the persuasiveness of already existing Republican themes. Republicans used the Sumner assault and the incidents in Kansas to support their basic contention that the South, or more accurately, the Slave Power, had united in a design to stamp out all liberties of Northern white men. This became one of the most important and persuasive themes in the Republican campaign of 1856. Northern liberties, Northern manhood, Northern equality were all under assault by the Slave Power, party spokesmen argued. By such rhetoric, Republicans made the threat posed by the Slave Power seem much more real and personal. They used the symbol of slavery, the essence of everything Northerners feared and hated, to express this threat. Thus the New York *Evening Post* asked after the caning:

> Has it come to this, that we must speak with bated breath in the presence of our Southern masters . . . ? If we venture to laugh at them, or to question their logic, or dispute their facts, are we to be chastised as they chastise their slaves? Are we too, slaves, slaves for life, a target for their brutal blows, when we do not comport ourselves to please them?

Brooks' blows were directed at every Northern freeman and must be resisted, contended a conservative New York minister after attending the meeting at the Tabernacle. "If the South appeal to the rod of the slave for argument with the North," he sternly insisted, "no way is left for the North, but to strike back, or be slaves." The Slave Power, arrogant and domineering, was determined to rule the country at all costs, the New York *Times* declared. The Sumner assault helped confirm the impression that "it will stop at no extremity of violence in order to subdue the people of the Free States and force them into a tame subserviency of its own domination."

To the modern reader, these Republican claims seem grossly exaggerated. Yet they struck a responsive chord in the minds of countless Northerners. Historians have not given sufficient attention to the manner in which Republicans utilized the civil liberties issue in the 1850s. Most Northerners had no sympathy for a crusade to abolish slavery in the South. But from their perspective the South, not the North, was acting aggressively, and Northern rights, not Southern, were under attack. After the Civil War a Republican journalist argued, with some justice, that the slavery issue would not have been so precipitated "but for the fatuity of the slaveholders, exhibited in their persistent demand that there should be no discussion." Avery Craven is only partially correct when he says that the sectional conflict "assumed the form of a conflict between *right* and *rights*." For Republicans, as well as Southerners, the issue was one of rights.

Some Democrats, such as the distinguished Pennsylvania jurist Jeremiah S. Black, charged the Republicans with hypocrisy on this issue. Such criticism was not totally without foundation. The fact that it was a leading Republican Senator who had been struck down, rather than someone else, influenced the response of *both* parties, Republican *and* Democratic. No doubt Republicans exploited the assault for political advantage, and such agitation did nothing to improve understanding between sections. Still their protests cannot be dismissed as mere party rhetoric. If these outrages had been isolated incidents, it would have been impossible to convince Northern public opinion that a real threat existed. What made the Republican view compelling was the fact that these latest outrages were part of a long series of what were perceived as assaults on Northern civil liberties, beginning with the gag rule in the 1830s. This cumulative effect, coupled with the particularly dramatic nature of the assault on Sumner and the sack of Lawrence, convinced many Northerners that these charges were more than political propaganda. After explaining that he had paid little attention to political matters in the past, one of Seward's correspondents confessed that the Sumner and Kansas outrages "startled me as tho a thunderbolt has fallen at my feet." The assault on Sumner was "not merely an *incident, but a demonstration,*" Hannibal Hamlin's father-in-law asserted. Citing the repeal of the Missouri Compromise, the invasions of Kansas, the behavior of Southern congressmen, the policy of the Administration, and all the acts of violence of the period, he concluded:

> bring all the proofs together & do as they not furnish a clear demonstration of a settled purpose to annihilate freedom. . . . It seems to me the demonstration is as certain as any demonstration in mathematics. Incidents are no longer incidents—they are links in the chain of demonstration, infallible, plain, conclusive.

Republican strategists were acutely aware that concern for the welfare of blacks, free or slave, had never been a strong sentiment in the free states, and that appeals based on the immorality of slavery were not calculated to bring political success. The symbols of Bleeding Sumner and Bleeding Kansas allowed Republicans to attack the South without attacking slavery. By appropriating the great abolitionist symbol of the Slave Power, and linking it to the threat to Northern rights, Republicans made a much more powerful appeal to Northern sensibilities than they could have otherwise. As John Van Buren warned James Buchanan during the campaign, this appeal was especially strong among old Jacksonian Democrats. Such men coupled an intense hatred of the slave with a bitter animosity against slaveholders. The acrimonious struggle between the Van Buren Democrats and Southern political leaders in the previous decade had made them especially sensitive to charges of Southern arrogance and dictation. They were quite willing to enter a movement to check the political power of the South, but not to strike at slavery. One rank-and-file Democrat who joined the Republican party after the Sumner caning denied that he had any sympathy for abolitionism, or that his views on the social position of blacks had changed. But he was no longer willing to tolerate the aggressions of the Slave Power in Congress, in Kansas, and in the country generally: "Had the Slave power been less *insolently aggressive,* I would have been content to see it extend . . . but when it seeks to extend its sway by fire & sword . . . I am ready to say hold enough!" "Reserve no place for me," he told a long-time Democratic associate, "*I shall not come back.*" . . .

Republicans were incalculably aided by the South's foolish course in endorsing Brooks' action. Had the South repudiated Brooks, it would have helped retard (at least temporarily) the growth of anti-Southern sentiment in the North. Immediately after the caning, some leading conservatives confidently predicted that Southerners, both at home and in Congress, would not sustain Brooks. Events mocked their prediction and destroyed their influence. Conservatives vainly implored Southern congressmen not to endorse Brooks. A prominent Southern banker in New York City warned Howell Cobb, the leading Southern member of the House investigating committee, that the assault was unjustifiable and any attempt by the South to sustain it "will prove disastrous in the extreme." The Southern defense of Brooks came as a great shock to many calm, responsible Northerners. "It was not the act itself (horrible as that was) that excited me," a prominent New York conservative told Hamilton Fish, "but the tone of the Southern Press, & the approbation, apparently, of the whole Southern People." Similarly, Daniel Lord wrote after the Senate report on the assault: "On this subject our Southern friends have a folly rising to madness. Instead of cutting from it as a miserable indiscretion and meeting it as such, they tie themselves to it and it will sink them." The New York *Times,* in an editorial titled "Stupidity of the South," spoke of "the fatuous blindness" of Southerners in approving Brooks' conduct:

> There never was so good an opportunity offered to the South, before, to make capital for itself, as in this case of the ruffian BROOKS; but, true to their instincts, and blinded by the madness that must lead to their utter defeat, they have chosen to defend the outrageous scoundrelism of their self-appointed champion and have thus made themselves responsible for his acts.

When Sumner returned to the Senate four years later, the Boston *Evening Transcript* declared that Southerners had only themselves to blame for his increased influence.

Confronted with Southern unity, Republicans argued that Northern unity was the only defense against aggression. The time for compromise had passed. The South's only hope was in Northern division. In making this appeal, Republicans sought to accomplish two objectives. First, by emphasizing sectional issues, they portrayed the American party, which sought to avoid them, as irrelevant in the present crisis. The contest was strictly between Republicans and Democrats. Second, they identified Northern Democrats with the unpopular policies and actions of their Southern allies. "Old party names must be forgotten, old party ties surrendered, organizations based upon secondary issues abandoned," Samuel Bowles' Springfield *Republican* proclaimed after the Sumner assault. The solution was for the people to unite and vote out of office those men who upheld these outrages, and this could be done only by supporting the Republican party. . . .

Confronted with Northern outrage, Democrats in the free states were decidedly on the defensive after the Sumner assault. Democratic newspapers, recognizing the difficulty of defending Brooks, quickly sought simply to ignore the caning. This course proved impossible in Congress. There, concern for party harmony forced Northern Democrats to support Brooks by their votes and published avowals, while privately expressing disapproval. Democratic hopes that the issue would soon subside proved delusive. Unable to disarm Republican agitation, Democrats ultimately emphasized the charge that Sumner was shamming. Despite Republican denials, the accusation persisted, and party leaders were aware of the damage it was causing in the North. To counteract this, [Henry] Wilson [the other senator from Massachusetts] collected and published affidavits from Sumner's doctors attesting to the Senator's serious injuries. The effort Republicans made to contradict it indicates that this charge had some influence among the voters; nevertheless, the fundamental problem confronting Northern Democrats was that they had no adequate response to Republican exploitation of the caning. Sumner's continued absence from the Senate kept the issue alive, to which the Democrats had no effective reply. "Your empty chair can make a more fervent appeal than even you," [the abolitionist Wendell] Phillips perceptively assured Sumner as his disability continued.

Some historians, drawing on the findings of political scientists, have questioned the importance of specific issues in determining American political behavior. Recent studies of the modern electorate, however, have sharply demonstrated that at certain times voters display a strong cognizance of issues. In periods of political realignment, when large numbers of voters form new party identities, specific issues assume a critical importance. It is precisely in such periods as the 1850s that voters are most issue conscious. Nor was greater political sophistication necessary to understand the issues raised by Republicans over the Sumner assault. The Republican interpretation of this incident, whatever it lacked in accuracy, was simple and straightforward. Contemporaries of all parties widely acknowledged the issue's powerful impact. As the election approached, one of Sumner's friends assured him that the issue of the caning "has sunk deep in many minds, whom political tracts and politicians never reach."

Although the political realignment in the 1850s has not yet been fully analyzed, it is evident that the Republican party gained great accessions between its first national organizing convention in Pittsburgh in February, 1856, and the election in November. The Sumner caning was an important cause of the party's new strength. In the existing political uncertainty many Northerners, especially former Whigs and anti-Nebraska Democrats, were politically adrift, uncertain where they would go. The attack on Sumner occurred just before the Democratic and Republican nominating conventions were to assemble, when numerous uncommitted voters were beginning to form new (or reaffirm old) party identities. Contemporaries recognized the party's rapid growth as events unfolded in 1856. Edwin D. Morgan, Chairman of the Republican National Committee, observed after the Sumner protest meeting in New York City that "the changes *now taking place* in our city, are very great." Republican hopes for victory, weak and limited before the events of late May, soared in the aftermath of the beating of Sumner. One journalist told John McLean, an aspirant for the party's nomination, that the Sumner and Kansas outrages had made an issue which "properly directed, might carry the election by storm." Democratic leaders initially believed that they faced an easy contest in 1856. By the summer, however, confronted with unexpected reports of Republican strength, they recognized that it would be a difficult campaign.

Just as the Sumner assault allowed Republicans to moderate and broaden their appeal, so it proved a powerful stimulus in driving moderates and conservatives into the Republican party. What made the Sumner caning of vital importance was not its effect on committed antislavery men, who had already gone into the Republican party, but its impact on moderates and conservatives, who had previously held aloof from the party out of fear that it was too radical and threatened to disrupt the Union. For many of these men, the Sumner assault was critical in their decision to join the Republican party. From New York Morgan reported after the Sumner protest meeting: "The Straight Whigs and conservatives are fast finding their places. . . . The doubtful and hesitating men are more excited now— than those who took the right ground early." Observers in other areas noted the same phenomenon: conservatives were most aroused by the assault, and they were now vehement in their denunciations of the South. . . .

No single event or issue can account for the remarkable Republican vote in the 1856 presidential election. Still, by helping to bring Whigs, Democrats, and Know Nothings into the Republican party, the Sumner assault was critical to the party's vote. Reflecting on the repeal of the Missouri Compromise, the attempt to subjugate Kansas, and the assault on Sumner, one Northerner concluded that Southerners were mad: in all their ingenuity they could not have devised a better means of uniting the North against them than this series of outrages. Democrats were badly shaken by the defections to the Republican party that they observed. Brooks' attack was doing the party "vast injury," a prominent New York Democrat warned Stephen A. Douglas. "You can scarcely imagine how much steam they are getting up on the subject." Democrats and Republicans alike concurred that the caning caused many antislavery Democrats to break finally with their party and go over to the Republicans. The Pennsylvania Republican wheelhorse Alexander McClure maintained that the party's most effective issue with such Democrats was Brooks and his bludgeon. Secretary of the Treasury James Guthrie agreed. From Washington he warned John C. Breckinridge, the Democratic Vice Presidential nominee: "This nomination of Freemont & Sumner excitement will give the free States against us with few exceptions . . . N[ew] York is gone in the opinion of many of our best Politicians here and the Sumner Beating has done it in this early stage of the Game." William L. Marcy, a shrewd observer of Northern public opinion, predicted that the Sumner-Brooks affair would cost the Democratic party 200,000 votes in the fall election. Guthrie believed that such losses were even greater.

The impact of the Sumner caning on the [Millard] Fillmore movement was devastating. By bringing conservatives into the Republican party— men whose support Fillmore [presidential nominee of the American, or Know Nothing, party] absolutely needed if he were to have any hope of election—the Sumner assault, along with the Kansas outrages, destroyed Fillmore's chances of carrying a single Northern state. This was the most important political consequence of the caning. Fillmore's weakness in the North, in the wake of these events, severely crippled his strength in the South, as many of his supporters, believing that the election was now reduced to a contest between Buchanan and Frémont, deserted Fillmore to vote for Buchanan. At the same time, these events caused countless Northern antislavery Know Nothings to join the Republican party. Fillmore's supporters became despondent as they saw his strength eroded by events. As he helplessly watched these developments, Winthrop insisted that "Brooks & Douglas deserve Statues from the Free Soil [Republican] party. The cane of the former & the Kansas bill of the latter . . . have secured a success to the Agitators which they never could have accomplished without them." Fillmore himself reinforced this feeling. "Brooks' attack upon Sumner has done more for Freemont than any 20 of his warmest friends North have been able to accomplish," he complained during the campaign. "If Freemont is elected, he will owe his election entirely to the troubles in Kansas, and the martyrdom of Sumner . . . the Republicans ought to pension Brooks for life. . . ."

After the election, a Northern Democrat sought to explain the reasons for the remarkable strength of the Republican party. The flood which swept over the North, he declared, arose from feeling rather than judgment. Northerners had become alarmed by the arrogant demands of the slaveholders; they felt that their own rights were in danger; they were disgusted by the brutality which applauded the bludgeon in the Senate; and they were indignant at the events in Kansas. Everywhere one heard nothing but recitals of Kansas outrages and Brooks' assault, "and certain it is, that the Club which broke Mr. Sumner's head, has . . . turned more votes than all other causes that were at work. It admitted neither defence nor palliation . . . and so the feeling grew stronger and stronger until it reached the result we have seen."

Despite the caning of Sumner and the Kansas violence, Frémont was defeated in November, as Fillmore polled enough votes nationally to give Buchanan a plurality and victory. The Republican party was unable to overcome the handicaps under which it commenced the campaign. Yet even in defeat, Republicans expressed optimism about the future. What was remarkable in the election results was not that Frémont lost, but that he did so well. From the beginning of the campaign the most prescient Republican leaders had believed that there was little chance of victory in their party's first national contest. The Republican party lacked an efficient national organization; in several Northern states the party had not even existed prior to 1856; Fillmore's candidacy would divide the opposition vote; the Democrats were well organized and well financed. Faced with these problems, Republican leaders had hoped to establish a sound national organization and, by crushing the American party, emerge as the only significant opposition party to the Democrats. In view of these difficulties, the Republican performance in the 1856 election was astounding. With a vote in the free states which exceeded that of either opponent, Frémont managed to carry all but five Northern states. Moreover, the American party had been destroyed as a viable national organization. It was clear in the aftermath of the 1856 election that the Republican party constituted the major opposition to the Democracy. Far from being discouraged, most Republicans were heartened by the results. With four years to strengthen their party organization and clarify their program, they were confident of victory in 1860. . . .

Throughout the summer and fall of 1856, as the presidential campaign rolled on and his disability continued, Sumner impatiently chafed at his incapacity to campaign for Frémont. He wrote letter after letter bemoaning his inability to speak now, when so much was at stake. More sagacious friends tried to console him. The old Jacksonian editor Francis P. Blair, now a prominent Republican manager, urged Sumner not to exert himself until he was fully recovered. "You have . . . done more to gain the victory than any other," he comforted the Senator with his sharp eye for the currents of popular feeling. Other Republicans provided similar testimony of his unique service to the party. Sumner did more for his party by his suffering than he ever had done by his speeches. The Brooks assault was of critical importance in transforming the struggling Republican party into a major political force. "By great odds the most effective deliverance made by any man to advance the Republican party was made by the bludgeon of Preston S. Brooks," McClure acutely concluded in retrospect. The caning of Charles Sumner was a major landmark on the road to civil war.

Kansas, Republicanism, and the Crisis
of the Union

DON E. FEHRENBACHER

"All Christendom is leagued against the South upon this question of domestic slavery," said James Buchanan on the Senate floor in 1842. "They have no other allies to sustain their constitutional rights, except the Democracy of the North. . . . In my own State, we inscribe upon our banners hostility to abolition. It is there one of the cardinal principles of the Democratic party."

The crisis of 1850 once again confirmed the crucial importance of northern Democrats in the southern strategy of defense, and it also revealed the extent to which that defense might be breached by an unsympathetic president. The South accordingly appears to have benefited more from the political consequences of the Compromise of 1850 than from any of its specific provisions. For a reunited Democratic party, pledging faithful adherence to the Compromise, swept to victory in the presidential election of 1852 and also won a two-thirds majority in the House of Representatives.

During the next eight years, under Franklin Pierce and his successor, James Buchanan, southern influence dominated the executive branch of the federal government through the agency of northern doughfaces [Northern politicians sympathetic to the South] like Caleb Cushing and Jeremiah S. Black, as well as southerners like Jefferson Davis and Howell Cobb.

"Kansas, Republicanism, and the Crisis of the Union," reprinted by permission of Louisiana State University Press from *The South and the Sectional Crisis*, pp. 46–65 by Don E. Fehrenbacher. Copyright © 1980 by Louisiana State University Press.

Throughout the period, the Senate remained safely Democratic and therefore safely prosouthern on slavery questions. In the House of Representatives, three of the five speakers serving between 1850 and 1860 were Democrats from Georgia, Kentucky, and South Carolina. Seven of the nine members of the Supreme Court were Democrats; and in 1857, six of them declared the Missouri Compromise restriction unconstitutional on the ground that Congress had no power to prohibit slavery in the territories.

Of course, these were things that southerners had come to expect. In 1861, Alexander H. Stephens reminded his fellow Georgians: "We have had a majority of the Presidents chosen from the South; as well as the control and management of most of those chosen from the North." Then he went on to name other offices in which southerners had outnumbered northerners: Supreme Court justices, 18 to 11; speakers of the House, 23 to 12; presidents pro tem of the Senate, 24 to 11; attorneys general, 14 to 5; foreign ministers, 86 to 54; and in the appointment of some 3,000 clerks, auditors, and controllers, better than a two-to-one advantage.

The extraordinary power traditionally exercised by southerners in national affairs constituted one of the principal deterrents to disunion; for as long as it endured, the South had better reason to remain in the Union than to leave. It was the loss of a substantial part of that power in 1860 that drove the seven states of the Lower South into secession, and the critical element in the loss was the weakened condition of the South's only ally in Christendom—the northern Democracy.

The structure of southern power in national politics during the 1850s was a kind of holding-company arrangement in which the South held majority control of the Democratic party, and the Democrats were the majority party in the nation. The same pattern had prevailed during much of the preceding half century, and the recent experience with Zachary Taylor had revealed that the Whig party could *not* be brought under southern control—not even when it was headed by a southern slaveholder. In any case, the distress of the Whig party soon left the Democrats as the only national party organization through which the South could exercise national power.

Nothing, then, was more vital to southern security within the Union than maintaining the majority status of the Democratic party. And in this respect, the Democratic victory in 1852 was not as overwhelming as it appeared on the surface, especially in the North. Although Pierce carried fourteen out of the sixteen free states, he did so with only a plurality of their popular vote. The structure of southern political power therefore resembled a bridge that rested at one end on an insecure foundation. To be sure, Democratic mastery seemed firm enough in 1853, with the presidency recaptured and the party controlling both houses of the incoming Congress by huge majorities. But this flush of prosperity proved to be ominous, in a way, and also treacherous—ominous because of what it signified about the condition of the Whig party, and treacherous because it encouraged the disastrous blunder of the Kansas-Nebraska Act.

The disintegration of the Whig party, and thus of the second American party system, began with the alienation of southern Whigs from Taylor in

1849–1850 and was largely completed by 1855. Historians continue to ponder the question of why the Whig party perished in the 1850s while the Democratic party, though presumably subject to the same disruptive pressures, managed to survive. It may be, simply, that the Whigs lacked the symbolic appeal, the tradition of victory, and the degree of cohesion necessary for survival in the 1850s. Another explanation is that Whiggery was in a sense absorbed by the burgeoning nativist movement, which then failed in *its* efforts to become a major, bisectional party. But in addition, it appears that differences of sectional balance *within* the two parties may account for the greater vulnerability of the Whigs. Since the South was much more united than the North on the issue of slavery, it was accordingly easier for many northern Democrats to remain within a party increasingly dominated by proslavery southerners than it was for southern Whigs to remain within a party increasingly dominated by antislavery northerners. That is probably why the disruption of the second American party system started with the collapse of Whiggery in several states of the Lower South.

Why the Whig organization did not at least survive in the North as a major antislavery party, instead of giving way to the Republicans, is another question and need not be answered here. The point is that the death of the Whig party as a national organization proved harmful to the health of the Democratic party and thus to the structure of southern political power. For the Democrats, during the later 1850s, were opposed in both the North and the South by sectional or local parties that did not have to make any concessions to intersectional accommodation within their organizations. The cross-pressures of party and section upon northern Democrats became much more severe when the Whigs were replaced by a more aggressively antislavery party that stood to profit organizationally from continued agitation of the slavery issue. The challenge of Republicanism compelled men like Stephen A. Douglas, in the interest of political survival, to show more independence of southern influence where slavery was concerned, and this necessity could not fail to place heavy strains upon party unity.

And even in the South, where the Democrats themselves were supposedly the radical party on sectional issues, they came under cross-pressure from the post-Whig opposition parties, which, as a matter of political strategy, often tried to outdo them in proslavery extremism. It was the southern opposition press, for instance, that started the attacks on Buchanan's Kansas policy in the summer of 1857, and it was the southern opposition press that set up the loudest clamor for a territorial slave code two years later. As John V. Mering has pointed out, "Only in Tennessee among southern states that had elections for governor in 1859 did the Opposition refrain from taking a stronger stand on behalf of slavery in the territories than the Democrats."

But the first baneful consequence of the Whig decline was passage of the Kansas-Nebraska bill, which never could have been accomplished if the Democrats had not held such large majorities in both houses of Congress. The bill received the support of nearly nine-tenths of all southern members casting votes and nearly three-fourths of all Democrats. It was an official party measure, endorsed and vigorously promoted by the Pierce administration, but its disruptive influence is strikingly illustrated by the fact that in the House of Representatives, northern Democrats were divided, 44 in favor and 44 against. The political aftermath turned into a Democratic nightmare, with waves of popular indignation sweeping through the free states, 66 out of 91 House seats held by northern Democrats lost in the midterm elections, and the emergence of a broad anti-Nebraska coalition that would soon crystallize into the Republican party.

The struggle over the Kansas-Nebraska bill was the most egregious of several instances in which southerners, during the 1850s, traded some of their power advantage for empty sectional victories. Although its momentous consequences are plain to see, the struggle is of interest not only because of what it did *to* the South, but also because of what it revealed *about* the South.

Historians differ about the degree to which southerners of the 1850s were committed to the further expansion of slavery. The South delineated by William L. Barney, for instance, was a society in constant need of more room for its growing slave population and of new land to replace its easily depleted soils. "The continual maturation of slavery within a fixed geographical area," he writes, "created class and racial stresses that could be relieved only through expansion." Furthermore, "as long as the option of adding slave territory was kept open, Southerners could delude themselves with the comforting belief that eventually slavery and its terrible racial dilemma could vanish slowly and painlessly, by a diffusion of all the blacks out of the American South into the tropics of Central and South America."

On the other hand, there are historians disposed to believe that the sectional controversy of the 1850s had less to do with the further expansion of slavery than with the future of slavery in modern America. In their view, the pernicious and seemingly useless quarrel over the territories was primarily a symbolic struggle laden with implication—or, as has been said, "merely the skirmish line of a larger and more fundamental conflict."

No doubt there is room enough for both interpretations in any comprehensive explanation of the coming of the Civil War, but southern expansionism hardly seems to have been the animating spirit of the Kansas-Nebraska Act. The measure, by repealing the 36° 30′ restriction of the Missouri Compromise, admitted slavery into an area unsuited for it and in no way facilitated the expansion of slavery southward into areas that *were* suited for it.

It is true that some southerners cherished the hope of making Kansas the sixteenth slave state, but even if they had succeeded, it would have been a nominal and temporary triumph gained at excessive cost. Proslavery imperialism became an absurdity in Kansas, and, as far as southern political power was concerned, it would have been much better strategy to settle for the admission of Kansas as a free but *Democratic* state, like the three states actually admitted in the 1850s—California, Minnesota, and Oregon.

That was precisely the strategy adopted by Robert J. Walker as governor of Kansas in 1857, but the South rose up in revolt against it and saw Kansas admitted just a few years later as a Republican state instead.

The bitterest irony in the Kansas-Nebraska Act was that its sponsors justified it as a logical and reconciliatory extension of the Compromise of 1850. They insisted, erroneously, that the old dividing-line policy had been replaced with a new, uniform national policy of nonintervention [Douglas's theory of popular sovereignty, whereby the voters of a territory rather than Congress would determine whether slavery should be admitted] and that, accordingly, to retain the slavery restriction north of 36° 30' in the organization of new territories would violate the letter and spirit of the recent Compromise. Actually, however, the popularity of the Compromise of 1850 resulted largely from its general pacificatory effect, not from any principles that could be inferred from its specific provisions. In short, the clearest violation of the spirit of the Compromise would be *any* legislative action that revived the slavery controversy. And the political power of the South, depending as it did upon the strength and unity of the Democratic party, likewise stood to suffer grievously from any renewal of slavery agitation. Southerners must have realized as well as Douglas that repeal of the Missouri Compromise restriction would, in his words, "raise a hell of a storm." Why, then, did they risk so much for so little to be gained?

For one thing, it appears that the southern members of Congress more or less drifted into the Kansas-Nebraska struggle without giving it much thought beforehand. Certainly there was no strong pressure on them from home to secure the repeal at that time, and it is notable that members from the Lower South were not prominent in the early stages of the affair. In fact, the senator who initiated the move to make the repeal explicit was a Kentucky Whig—the successor of Henry Clay.

Southern press support for the Kansas-Nebraska bill was relatively restrained, as Avery O. Craven has shown. "It is difficult for us to comprehend, or credit the excitement . . . in the North on account of the Nebraska question," wrote an Alabaman in the summer of 1854. "Here," he continued, "there is no excitement, no fever, on the subject. It is seldom alluded to in private or public and so far as the introduction of slavery [into Kansas and Nebraska] is concerned, such a consummation is hardly hoped for." But the savage northern denunciation of the measure encouraged southern members to close ranks on the issue, and they supplied more than 60 percent of the votes cast for passage. With sectional violence thereafter erupting and becoming chronic on the prairies of Kansas, the South's emotional investment in the proslavery cause in Kansas grew to enormous proportions, even while the chances of gaining anything of practical importance were steadily dwindling.

Southern attitudes throughout the Kansas controversy demonstrate the intensely reactive nature of southern sectionalism. That is, the South did not so much respond to the Kansas-Nebraska issue itself as react to the northern response to the issue; and much the same thing happened four years later in the struggle over the Lecompton constitution. Similarly, what angered southerners most about John Brown's raid on Harpers Ferry was the amount of applause it received in the North.

The language of antislavery denunciation had a cumulative effect by the 1850s, and southern skin, far from toughening under attack, had become increasingly sensitive. According to Senator Judah P. Benjamin of Louisiana, the heart of the matter was not so much what the abolitionists and Republicans had *done* or might *do* to the South, as it was "the things they *said*" about the South—and the moral arrogance with which they said them. Southerners, though often emphatically denying it, in fact cared deeply about northern opinion of the South and its people. They wanted, above all, an end to being treated as moral inferiors, and thus an end to the fear of eventually *accepting* the badge of inferiority. The result, says Charles G. Sellers, was a "series of constantly mounting demands for symbolic acts by which the North would say that slavery was all right."

The most conspicuous badge of sectional inferiority was overt federal prohibition of slavery in the territories. For many southerners by the 1850s, such exclusion had become a moral reproach of unbearable weight. When Douglas offered them the opportunity to erase a large part of the stigma by repealing the Missouri Compromise restriction, they could scarcely do otherwise than grasp it.

The symbolic victory thus achieved in the Kansas-Nebraska Act was not really expected to bring any tangible benefits. But the course of events in Kansas did conspire to offer the South a chance in 1858 to win another victory of the same kind—that is, the admission of Kansas as a nominal slaveholding state under the Lecompton constitution. Once again, and in an even more dubious cause, southern members of Congress closed ranks. Knowing that the constitution did not represent the will of the territorial population, knowing that Kansas was destined to be a free state whatever the formal terms of her admission might be, and knowing that the issue would surely cause havoc among the northern Democracy, they nevertheless voted almost unanimously for the Lecompton bill.

Again there appeared to be an important principal at stake. For here was an opportunity to test one of the items in the Georgia platform of 1850—namely, whether a slave state could ever again be admitted to the Union, now that an antislavery party had become predominant in the North. There had *been* no such admission, after all, since that of Texas twelve years earlier. The test came, moreover, in the aftermath of the Dred Scott decision, when southerners were again reacting to a northern reaction and also discarding the notion that the Constitution, of its own force, gave them any protection against antislavery attack.

As it became increasingly clear that the Lecompton bill, with half of the northern Democrats opposing it, could not command a majority in the House, another secession crisis developed. The ultimatum "Lecompton or disunion" reverberated in the halls of Congress, in the southern press, and in southern legislatures. With Alabama leading the way, contingent steps toward secession were officially taken by several states. "Upon the action of this Congress, must depend the union or disunion of this great Confederacy," a Georgia congressman warned. The people of the South were determined, he said, "to have equality in this Union or independence out of it . . . you must admit Kansas . . . with the Lecompton constitution." "The equilibrium in the balance of power is already lost," declared a member from Mississippi. "Reject Kansas and the cordon is then completed. . . . Against this final act of degradation I believe the South will resist—resist with arms." "Save the Union, if you can," wrote a South Carolinian to Senator James H. Hammond. "But rather than have Kansas refused admission under the Lecompton Constitution, let it perish in blood and fire."

The symbolic importance of the issue was not diminished but rather was enhanced by the fact that the South had nothing material to gain from the admission. As Buchanan's pro-Lecompton message to Congress perceptively argued: "In considering this question, it should never be forgotten that in proportion to its insignificance . . . the rejection of the constitution will be so much the more keenly felt by the people of . . . the States of this Union, where slavery is recognized." So, paradoxically, the very futility of the proslavery cause in Kansas made the Lecompton question more clearly a "point of honor" and a meaningful test of how *little* could be expected from the North in the way of concessions. In the words of one South Carolinian, it would have been "dirt cheap" for the free states to yield.

Once again, however, a legislative crisis ended in a legislative compromise—or rather, in this case, a pseudocompromise that did not conceal the reality of southern defeat. The critical question was whether the Lecompton bill should be passed as it was or be amended to allow resubmission of the constitution to the voters of Kansas, which would surely mean rejection. With the House of Representatives this time standing its ground, southern members of Congress ended by accepting the so-called "English compromise," which provided for an indirect resubmission of the constitution and thus allowed them to save face a little with their constituents.

For this miserable achievement the South paid dearly. The Democratic party, split by an anti-Lecompton revolt with Douglas at its head, suffered another election defeat in 1858 and became the minority party in virtually every northern state. From that point on, the odds favored election of a Republican president in 1860. Moreover, the English compromise was so obviously a southern backdown from the threat of disunion that it encouraged Republicans to regard later secession threats as mere resumption of a game of bluff.

The compromise nevertheless satisfied many southerners, even some aiming at disunion, because it enabled them to retreat from a shaky limb. The Lecompton constitution, for a number of reasons, provided a very dubious basis for a sectional ultimatum. Governor Joseph E. Brown of Georgia, who was ready at the time to inaugurate a secession movement, later acknowledged that an outright defeat of the Lecompton bill would have caused "great confusion," and that "the democratic party of the state would have been divided and distracted." It appears, then, that in 1858 there was some possibility of an *unsuccessful* secession movement that might have thrown secessionism generally into disrepute and thus, like a small earthquake, taken off some of the underlying stress.

The Lecompton affair proved to be the last full-dress legislative crisis and compromise in the tradition of 1819–1821, 1832–1833, and 1846–1850. Reflecting upon the pattern of events from the introduction of the Tallmadge proviso [a House amendment to the bill of 1819 to admit Missouri to statehood, which, if enacted, would have prohibited further introduction of slaves into Missouri] to the hollow triumph of the English compromise, one is disposed to doubt that legislative crisis was ever the proper fuse for setting off a civil war in the United States. A crisis arising in Congress could usually be controlled by Congress. The greatest danger in 1850, for instance, had been that presidential intervention might take matters out of congressional hands.

The end of the Lecompton controversy in fact marked the end of the territorial issue as a serious threat to the Union. Kansas ceased to be disputed ground and was admitted quietly as a free state in 1861. There was no other sectional issue with which Congress seemed likely, in the near future, to create another legislative crisis. Certainly not the agitation for a reopening of the African slave trade; for that had only minority support even in the Lower South. And certainly not the issue of a slave code for the territories, which provoked so much congressional debate in 1859 and 1860. That was not a southern demand upon Congress for legislation, but rather a southern Democratic demand upon Douglas for renunciation of his apostasy or withdrawal from the approaching presidential race.

James Buchanan had entered the presidency in 1857 determined to end the conflict in Kansas and thereby restore sectional peace. He hoped that "geographical parties," as he phrased it in his inaugural, would then "speedily become extinct." His efforts ended in a curious mixture of success and failure; for the resolution of the Kansas problem, by the very manner in which it was accomplished, substantially increased the strength of the Republican party. . . .

The disintegration of the Whig party, and hence the breakup of the second American party system, had begun before 1854, but it was the Kansas-Nebraska Act, more than anything else, that determined the character of the third party system in its early years. If the sectional truce of 1850 had remained more or less in effect, the Whig party might well have been succeeded by the Native American or Know-Nothing party. Instead, with the slavery controversy reopened to the point of violence, the anti-Nebraska coalition of 1854 swiftly converted itself into the nation's first major party organized on antislavery principles. Suddenly, the South faced a new menace and a new potential cause for secession—the possibility that a Republican might be elected to the presidency.

The causes for secession listed in the Georgia platform of 1850 [a list of six eventualities drawn up by a Georgia state convention, any one of which would be sufficient cause for disunion] had all been legislative acts that might be passed by Congress. The sectional crises of 1820, 1833, 1850, and 1858 had all been precipitated by such legislation, enacted or proposed. But, beginning in 1856, the election of a Republican president became a more probable occasion for disunion than any legislative proposal likely to receive serious consideration in Congress. Beginning in 1856, a different finger was on the trigger mechanism. Control passed from the professional politician to the ordinary voter, particularly the northern voter. And if worse should come to worst, how did one go about compromising the results of a presidential election?

It was difficult for the people of the South to view Republicans as merely a political opposition. "If they should succeed in this contest," said a North Carolina newspaper in September 1856, "the result will be a separation of the States. No human power can prevent it. . . . They would create insurrection and servile war in the South—they would put the torch to our dwellings and the knife to our throats. They are, therefore, our enemies."

We should perhaps pay more attention to the fact that 1856 was a year of genuine secession crisis, mitigated only by the general belief that the Republicans had but an outside chance of capturing the presidency. For southerners, the outcome of the election spelled temporary relief but very little reassurance. The Democrats did elect James Buchanan to succeed Franklin Pierce, and they did recapture control of the House of Representatives. Buchanan triumphed by sweeping the South, except for Maryland, and by carrying also the five free states of New Jersey, Pennsylvania, Indiana, Illinois, and California. But only two of those five states gave him popular majorities—Indiana, 50.4 percent, and his own Pennsylvania, 50.1 percent. The Democratic share of the free-state vote fell from 50.7 percent in 1852 to 41.4 percent in 1856. John C. Frémont, the Republican candidate, outpolled Buchanan in the North by more than a hundred thousand votes. Frémont and Millard Fillmore, the American party candidate, together outpolled him by more than a half million votes in the North. There was little difficulty visualizing what would happen to the Democratic party in the free states if its divided opposition should become united. The party had, in fact, hung on to the presidency with its fingertips; and the loss of that precarious hold, even many conservative southerners agreed, would mean a prompt disruption of the Union.

In these circumstances, the all-out drive to make Kansas a slave state under the Lecompton constitution was plain political folly. And the midterm congressional elections of 1858 accordingly proved disastrous for the Democrats because of what happened in those same northern states that Buchanan had carried two years earlier. The Republicans increased their share of the total vote in New Jersey, Pennsylvania, Indiana, and Illinois from 35 percent in 1856 to 52 percent in 1858. The most stunning reversal came in Pennsylvania. There, just the year before, the Democrats had elected a governor by more than forty thousand votes, but in 1858 they lost nearly all of their congressional seats and were outpolled by twenty-five thousand votes. "We have met the enemy in Pennsylvania," said Buchanan, "and we are theirs."

From the Lecompton struggle onward, all the signs of the times pointed to a Republican victory in 1860 and to some kind of secession movement as a consequence. Yet the Democratic party, instead of reuniting to meet the danger, became increasingly a house divided against itself. The quarrel between Douglas and the South, aside from its strong influence on the shape of the final crisis, deserves attention because of what it reveals about the psychological escalation of the sectional conflict.

Douglas in 1856 had been the favorite presidential nominee of the South, and especially of the Lower South, which gave him thirty-eight of its forty-seven votes at the Cincinnati convention. Four years later at Charleston, however, delegates from the Lower South walked out of the convention rather than accept his leadership of the party. In the interval, Douglas made his fight against the Lecompton constitution, opposing even the English compromise; he issued the Freeport doctrine [that slavery could not exist anywhere without the support of local police regulations] during the debates with Lincoln as a means of salvaging the principle of popular sovereignty while at the same time endorsing the Dred Scott decision [that slavery had to be permitted in the territories]; and, presumably as a consequence of those actions, he managed to win reelection to the Senate against the Republican tide that swept so many northern Democrats out of office in 1858.

It was success at the polls that the South needed most from its northern allies, but what southern Democratic leaders proceeded to insist upon instead was party orthodoxy, as they defined it. Ignoring the plain fact that for Douglas, opposition to the Lecompton constitution had been a matter, not only of principle, but also of political survival, they branded him a traitor. And ignoring the fact that the Freeport doctrine was actually of southern origin, they branded him a heretic. As punishment, the Senate Democratic leadership in December 1858 stripped him of his chairmanship of the committee on territories, a position that he had held continuously for more than ten years.

Douglas responded with his usual vigor and combativeness. The southern Democrats, in turn, set out to make approval of a territorial slave code the supreme test of party loyalty. That was the ostensible issue that eventually disrupted the party at Charleston, but the real issue was Douglas, and the purpose of the slave-code agitation was to destroy him as a presidential candidate.

Of course, the South never approached unanimity in such matters, and the Little Giant continued to have supporters in every southern state right down to 1860. Even the Lower South gave him 11 percent of its total popular vote for president that year. One is nevertheless struck by the volume and intensity of southern hatred for Douglas in the period 1858–1860. He was with us, the indictment ran, "until the time of trial came; then he deceived and betrayed us." He "placed himself at the head of the Black column and gave the word of command," thereby becoming "stained with the dishonor of treachery without a parallel in the political history of the country." And now, covered with the "odium of . . . detestable heresies" and the "filth of his defiant recreancy," he would receive what southern patriots had always given northern enemies—"war to the knife." Then, "away with him to the tomb which he is digging for his political corpse."

In retrospect, it appears that the only hope of preventing a Republican presidential victory lay in uniting the Democratic party behind Douglas. Yet, by 1860, southern hostility toward Douglas had taken on a life of its own and become implacable. The motives of southern leaders at this point are not easily fathomed or summarized. Perhaps as many as a score of them harbored serious presidential aspirations and so had personal reasons for wanting Douglas out of the way. There were also committed secessionists working openly to disrupt the Democratic party and welcoming the likelihood of a Republican presidential victory as the best means of achieving disunion. Covertly or subconsciously allied with them was a larger group of southerners (including Jefferson Davis, for example) who continued to call secession a "last resort," while conducting themselves in a way that tended to eliminate other choices. Their "conditional Unionism" with impossible conditions amounted to secessionism in the end.

But in addition to all the purposes visible in southern attitudes toward Douglas, his defection had an important symbolic meaning that weighed heavily on the southern spirit. The theme of betrayal and fear of betrayal runs prominently through much of the southern rhetoric of alienation. The South had been betrayed, in a sense, by its own ancestors who first accepted the role of slaveholder. It felt betrayed by New England, whose abolitionist zealots now made war on an institution introduced into the country by New England slave traders. It felt betrayed by Taylor as president and by Walker as territorial governor of Kansas. Southerners also feared treachery from their slaves and free blacks. They distrusted the sectional loyalty of nonslaveholding southern whites, and in the Lower South there was strong doubt that the border states could be depended upon in a crisis.

In such a context, the defection of Douglas was an especially painful blow. Perhaps no single event contributed so much to the southern sense of being isolated in a hostile world. "[It] has done more than all else," wrote a South Carolinian, "to shake my confidence in Northern men on the slavery issue, for I have long regarded him as one of our . . . most reliable friends." A correspondent of the Charleston *Mercury* put it more tersely: "If he proved false, whom can you trust?" To despair of Douglas was virtually to despair of the Union itself. At the Charleston convention in the spring of 1860, the states of the Lower South withdrew from the Democratic party organization rather than submit to the nomination of Douglas. Who could then doubt that those same states would withdraw from the Union rather than submit to the election of a Republican president? In this respect, the dramatic walkout of delegates at Charleston was a dress rehearsal for secession.

The final crisis of the Union is commonly thought of as starting with the election of Lincoln in November 1860, but the entire presidential campaign had taken place in an atmosphere of crisis that extended back into the preceding year. When the Thirty-sixth Congress convened on December 5, 1859, John Brown was just three days in his grave, and the storm of emotion caused by his adventure at Harpers Ferry had not yet begun to abate. The House of Representatives plunged immediately into a two-month-long speakership contest of such bitterness that many members of Congress armed themselves for protection against assault. One senator, with grim hyperbole, said that the only persons not carrying a revolver and a knife were those carrying two revolvers.

Then, after an angry renewal of the slave-code debate in the Senate, there came the splitting of the Democratic party at Charleston. By mid-summer, many southerners recognized that the odds strongly favored a Republican victory, and they began, in their minds, at least, to prepare for it. October elections for state offices in Pennsylvania and Indiana turned probability almost into certainty, and still there was another month left for preparation.

Meanwhile, with the apprehension aroused by John Brown still keenly felt, a new wave of fear swept through the South. There were reports of slaves in revolt, of conspiracies uncovered just in time, of mass poisonings attempted, of whole towns burned, and of abolitionist agents caught and hung. And the full terror, presumably, still lay ahead. "If such things come upon us," said a Georgia newspaper, "with only the *prospect* of an Abolition ruler, what will be our condition when he is *actually in power?*" The very vagueness of the prospect made it all the more ominous. Fear of Republican rule was to no small degree a fear of the unknown. Chief Justice Roger B. Taney was not alone in believing that the news of Lincoln's election might be the signal for a general slave uprising. But other prophets of doom, like the editors of the Richmond *Enquirer,* pictured Republican purposes working out in more insidious ways:

> Upon the accession of Lincoln to power, we would apprehend no direct act of violence against negro property, but by the use of federal office, contracts, power and patronage, the building up in every Southern State of a Black Republican party, the ally and stipendiary of Northern fanaticism, to become in a few short years the open advocates of abolition. . . . No act of violence may ever be committed, no servile war waged, and yet the ruin and degradation of Virginia will be as fully and fatally accomplished, as though bloodshed and rapine ravished the land.

One wonders how often in history rebellions and other cataclysmic events have not occurred, even in the presence of adequate causes, simply because there was no practical point of impulse where feeling and belief could be translated into action. For southerners, the presidential election of 1860 was just such a point of impulse—its date fixed on the calendar, its outcome predictable and not subject to compromise, its expected consequences vague but terrible. All the passion of the sectional conflict became concentrated, like the sun's rays by a magnifying glass, on one moment of decision that could come only once in history—that is, the *first* election of a Republican president. If secessionists had not seized the moment but instead had somehow been persuaded to let it pass, such a clear signal for action might never again have sounded.

Yet, even under these optimum conditions created by Lincoln's election, the southern will to act was but partly energized. The South, though long united in defense of slavery, had never been close to unity on the subject of secession. And so, in the end, the best fuse available set off only half of the accumulated charge. Just the seven states of the Lower South broke away from the Union in the winter of 1860–1861, although their very number, as I have already suggested, probably had a critical influence on the subsequent course of events.

But if only the Lower South seceded, the entire Slaveholding South had contributed heavily to the event that activated the secession movement—that is, to the Republican capture of the presidency. In 1852, the Free Soil Candidate for president received only 7 percent of the popular vote in the free states and did not come close to winning a single electoral vote. Just eight years later, Lincoln won 55 percent of the popular vote in the free states and 98 percent of their electoral vote. It is difficult to believe that a political revolution of such magnitude would have occurred if southerners had not chosen to pursue the will-o'-the-wisp of Kansas, sacrificing the realities of power to an inner need for reassurance of their equal status and moral respectability in the face of antislavery censure.

The Charleston *Mercury,* commenting on the Dred Scott decision in 1857, said that it was "a victory more fatal, perhaps, than defeat," because the antislavery forces always rose up stronger after each sectional confrontation and, in fact, seemed to feed on adversity. Pursuing the same theme more than a century later, David M. Potter wrote:

> For ten years the Union had witnessed a constant succession of crises; always these ended in some kind of "victory" for the South, each of which left the South with an empty prize and left the Union in a weaker condition than before. . . . Not one of [the victories] added anything to the area, the strength, the influence, or even the security of the southern system. Yet each had cost the South a high price, both in alienating the public opinion of the nation and in weakening . . . the Democratic party, which alone stood between the South and sectional domination by the Republicans.

Yet the victories of the South, though useless, were not meaningless. Important values seemed to be at stake—values associated, above all, with regional and personal self-respect. More than one southern political leader insisted that the fight for the Lecompton constitution had to be made because it was a "point of honor." With the same sensitivity about honor and the same disregard for possible consequences, many a southerner had faced his opponent on the dueling ground.

In the spring of 1861, with secession accomplished and the Confederate States of America a functioning reality, there remained still another point of honor to be settled, another empty prize to be won at exorbitant cost.

It appears now that the Confederacy's best hope of survival may have been to avoid war and consolidate its independent status as long as possible, rather than trying to win a war against a stronger enemy. But the stars and stripes still flying on a fortified island in Charleston Harbor had become an infuriating symbol of southern independence unrecognized and thus another instance of southern honor degraded. So, in the early morning of April 12, 1861, southerners once again did what they had to do. They opened fire on Fort Sumter and this time gained a military victory more disastrous, perhaps, than any of their later military defeats.

FURTHER READING

William L. Barney, *The Road to Secession: A New Perspective on the Old South* (1972)

William J. Cooper, Jr., *The South and the Politics of Slavery, 1828–1856* (1978)

David Donald, *Charles Sumner and the Coming of the Civil War* (1960)

Don E. Fehrenbacher, *Prelude to Greatness: Lincoln in the 1850s* (1962)

———, *The Dred Scott Case: Its Significance in American Law and Politics* (1978)

Eric Foner, *Free Soil, Free Labor, Free Men: The Ideology of the Republican Party Before the Civil War* (1970), 77–93

———, "Racial Attitudes of the New York Free Soilers," in *Politics and Ideology in the Age of the Civil War* (1980)

William E. Gienapp, *The Origins of the Republican Party, 1852–1856* (1987)

Michael F. Holt, *The Political Crisis of the 1850s* (1978)

Harry V. Jaffa, *Crisis of the House Divided: An Interpretation of the Lincoln-Douglas Debates* (1959)

Robert W. Johannsen, ed., *The Lincoln-Douglas Debates of 1858* (1965)

———, *Stephen A. Douglas* (1973)

John McCardell, *The Idea of a Southern Nation: Southern Nationalists and Southern Nationalism, 1830–1860* (1979)

David M. Potter, *The Impending Crisis, 1848–1861* (1976)

James A. Rawley, *Race and Politics: "Bleeding Kansas" and the Coming of the Civil War* (1969)

Thomas Schott, *Alexander H. Stephens: A Biography* (1988)

Richard H. Sewell, *Ballots for Freedom: Antislavery Politics in the United States, 1837–1860* (1976)

J. Mills Thornton, III, *Politics and Power in a Slave Society: Alabama, 1800–1860* (1978)

CHAPTER
4

The Secession Crisis

ॐ

As President-elect Abraham Lincoln journeyed from Springfield, Illinois, to Washington in February 1861, negotiations and conferences were still taking place in the capital to stall and reverse the movement for southern secession. Even if they failed, war was not the only possible outcome. So the situation remained quite fluid, or was that just an illusion? Perhaps too much had already transpired, not only in the few months following Lincoln's election but in the previous quarter-century of sectional wrangling, for the momentum to be stopped.

Secession had been urged for roughly a decade by a group of southern politicians who recognized that there was no permanent security within the Union for the South's way of life, based as it was on its "peculiar institution." So they had maneuvered and organized to prepare the South for the break that had now arrived as a result of the disintegration of the Democratic party and the attainment of the presidency by the antislavery Republicans. But most southern voters were not convinced. Secession was closely contested in Texas as well as in Alabama and Georgia, with many in those states feeling that withdrawal was completely ill advised, or else that it was premature until Lincoln demonstrated hostile intentions with an overt act.

Meanwhile, in the Upper South—Virginia, Tennessee, North Carolina, and Arkansas—secession had been voted down or not even put to a vote at all. These Upper South states were less committed to slavery than the Deep South, while they also had valuable economic ties to the North. Their inhabitants concluded that secession was not only a risky undertaking but it might also jeopardize their own interests.

When Lincoln took office, only the seven lower South states had seceded. A conciliatory approach might therefore have confined the Confederacy to a remnant that was not likely to survive as an independent nation. But what could the president offer without undermining his party and betraying the voters who had elected him? Historians continue to debate whether an opportunity was lost during the secession crisis or whether the die had already been cast.

↘ *D O C U M E N T S*

With the Deep South states in the process of seceding, the new Republican administration, headed by Abraham Lincoln, deliberated over the course it should pursue. The documents reprinted here represent the options that were considered. In the first selection, Henry Adams (the future historian and novelist who was in Washington with his father, Charles Francis Adams, Lincoln's designated ambassador to London) describes the competing approaches of Secretary of State William H. Seward and President Lincoln to the secession crisis. Like his father, the young Adams preferred Seward's policy, a position evident in the extract from his essay entitled "The Great Secession Winter of 1860–61," written just after the war began. The second document is President-elect Lincoln's firm statement to Senator Lyman Trumbull of Illinois on December 10, 1860, that he would not back down from his party's campaign position on slavery in the territories.

While the Upper South states were deciding whether or not to secede, Congressman John A. Gilmer of North Carolina became an important spokesman for the Unionists there. Lincoln's reply of December 15, 1860, to an inquiry from Gilmer about the incoming president's likely policy toward the Upper South appears here as the third document. The fourth is Gilmer's letter to Seward of March 8, 1861, imploring that a strategy of delay and conciliation be pursued to keep the remaining states, particularly Virginia, from seceding. And the final selection is from Seward's memorandum of March 15, 1861, to Lincoln on the resupply of Fort Sumter; the president had asked the entire cabinet for their written advice, and Seward still urged avoidance of confrontation.

Henry Adams Later Describes
the Policy Options, 1861

. . . Rather through the faults and mistakes of their opponents than through their own skill, the Republicans managed to maintain their ground tolerably well. Their first fear had been that the North would again yield to some compromise by which the old state of things would be brought back and a new struggle become necessary. Probably their fears would have been justified if the southern States had not, by withdrawing, thrown the whole power into the hands of the firmer anti-slavery men. But when it became evident that the danger did not now lie on this side, but was rather lest all the slave States should be dragged out and thus involve the whole country in a common ruin, a difference of opinion, as to the policy to be pursued, soon showed itself. One wing of the party declared for a strong policy by which the seceding States should be compelled to submit to the laws. Many of these really underrated the danger and difficulty, or, if they saw it, yet could not conscientiously take any steps to avoid it. Others confounded the conspirators with the slave-holders, placing all on the same footing, which was exactly what the disunionists were straining every nerve to bring about. Thus these practically played into the hands of the traitors by doing all in their power to combine the southern States. Others were perhaps conscientiously not unwilling that all the slave States should secede, believing that to be the shortest and surest way of obtaining the destruction of the slave power, as it was certainly a very sure way of obtaining the destruction of their own, if their policy should lead to civil war and a revulsion of feeling in the North. On the other hand, an influential portion of the party urged temporizing till the height of the fever was over, and were in favor of shaping their policy in such a way as to secure the border States and prevent bloodshed. Mr. Seward declared himself very early in the winter a favorer of conciliation in this way. He felt that something must be done, not only to resist disunion in the South, where it was every day acquiring more strength, but to sustain himself and his party in the North, where they were not strong enough to sustain the odium of a dissolution and civil war. For it is a fact, and it is right that it should be so, that with the people the question of the nation's existence will in the end override all party issues, no matter what they may be, and Mr. Seward foresaw that if the new administration was to prove a success it must shape its course so as to avoid the responsibility of the convulsion, and obtain the confidence of a large majority of the people. . . .

Mr. Lincoln arrived in Washington and took up the reins of control. It soon became very evident that, so far as the Republican party is concerned, secession if properly managed is rather a benefit than a misfortune. Anti-slavery was the only ground on which it could act with anything like unanimity. In ordinary times the tariff bill would have broken it down, and even under the tremendous pressure of disunion, the struggle over the Cabinet shook it to its very centre. On all questions except that of slavery it can never act together with any reliable degree of concert, made up as it is of incongruous elements freshly and roughly joined together. Under these circumstances the task of Mr. Lincoln was one which might well have filled with alarm the greatest statesman that ever lived. He had to deal with men and measures that would have taxed the patience of Washington and required the genius of Napoleon. It was therefore not to be expected, nor indeed wished, that on his arrival he would instantly throw himself into the arms of either set of his friends before judging for himself the merits of the case; nor was it possible that all the dangers and pressing necessities of the time should be wholly apparent to him. The matter of the passage of the Corwin measures [essentially, an amendment protecting slavery in the states] became one of secondary interest, the result of those measures depending as they did on the influence which was to prevail in the Cabinet. This influence became now the great feature of the day, and the struggle was vehement between the two wings of the party. The mere fact that the Cabinet had not yet been agreed upon was sufficient to prove that Mr. Lincoln, while placing Mr. Seward in the chief place in his councils, did not intend to allow his influence to rule it, and the result of the contest between the friends of Mr. [Henry] Winter Davis and Mr. [Montgomery] Blair soon decided this question beyond a doubt. Mr. Seward's policy had been to go outside of the party in selecting members of the Cabinet from southern States, and to choose men whose influence would have strengthened the administration. The fact that Mr. Blair, a strict Republican, was preferred over any other man to represent Maryland and Virginia in the Cabinet, was decisive of the policy of Mr. Seward.

When once this question was settled it was of little consequence what became of the proposed measures of conciliation, which were worth nothing, except as one weak link in the chain by which the border States were to be held to the Union. . . .

President-Elect Lincoln Explains
What Is at Stake, December 1860

I.

Private, & confidential

Springfield, Ills. Dec. 10, 1860

Hon. L. Trumbull.

My dear Sir: Let there be no compromise on the question of *extending* slavery. If there be, all our labor is lost, and, ere long, must be done again. The dangerous ground—that into which some of our friends have a hankering to run—is Pop. Sov. Have none of it. Stand firm. The tug has to come, & better now, than any time hereafter. Yours as ever,

A. Lincoln

II.

Strictly confidential.

Springfield, Ill. Dec 15, 1860.

Hon. John A. Gilmer:

My dear Sir—Yours of the 10th is received. I am greatly disinclined to write a letter on the subject embraced in yours; and I would not do so, even privately as I do, were it not that I fear you might misconstrue my silence. Is it desired that I shall shift the ground upon which I have been elected? I cannot do it. You need only to acquaint yourself with that ground, and press it on the attention of the South. It is all in print and easy of access. May I be pardoned if I ask whether even you have ever attempted to procure the reading of the Republican platform, or my speeches, by the Southern people? If not, what reason have I to expect that any additional production of mine would meet a better fate? It would make me appear as if I repented for the crime of having been elected, and was anxious to apologize and beg forgiveness. To so represent me, would be the principal use made of any letter I might now thrust upon the public. My old record cannot be so used; and that is precisely the reason that some new declaration is so much sought.

Now, my dear sir, be assured, that I am not questioning *your* candor;

I am only pointing out, that, while a new letter would hurt the cause which I think a just one, you can quite as well effect every patriotic object with the old record. Carefully read pages 18, 19, 74, 75, 88, 89, & 267 of the volume of Joint Debates between Senator Douglas and myself, with the Republican Platform adopted at Chicago, and all your questions will be substantially answered. I have no thought of recommending the abolition of slavery in the District of Columbia, nor the slave trade among the slave states, even on the conditions indicated; and if I were to make such recommendation, it is quite clear Congress would not follow it.

As to employing slaves in Arsenals and Dockyards, it is a thing I never thought of in my life, to my recollection, till I saw your letter; and I may say of it, precisely as I have said of the two points above.

As to the use of patronage in the slave states, where there are few or no Republicans, I do not expect to inquire for the politics of the appointee, or whether he does or not own slaves. I intend in that matter to accommodate the people in the several localities, if they themselves will allow me to accommodate them. In one word, I never have been, am not now, and probably never shall be, in a mood of harassing the people, either North or South.

On the territorial question, I am inflexible, as you see my position in the book. On that, there is a difference between you and us; and it is the only substantial difference. You think slavery is right and ought to be extended; we think it is wrong and ought to be restricted. For this, neither has any just occasion to be angry with the other.

As to the state laws, mentioned in your sixth question, I really know very little of them. I never have read one. If any of them are in conflict with the fugitive slave clause, or any other part of the constitution, I certainly should be glad of their repeal; but I could hardly be justified, as a citizen of Illinois, or as President of the United States, to recommend the repeal of a statute of Vermont, or South Carolina.

With the assurance of my highest regards I subscribe myself

Your obt. Servt.,

A. Lincoln

A North Carolina Unionist Urges Delay and Conciliation, March 1861

Confidential.

Greensboro, N.C., March 8th

Since the defeat of the secessionists on the 28th in this state they have become furious. Our Governor went down to Wilmington on last Saturday among his fellow disunionists, was called, and made a speech to a large crowd of disunionists. He was bold, and defiant. He said that circumstances would soon occur, which would induce N.C. to retrace her steps, and that she would be out of the Union soon.

The only hope of the secessionists now is that some sort of collision will be brought about between federal and state forces in one of the seceding states. I have full confidence that you in some way wiser and better than I can devise or suggest can prevent this.

If you can do this, I believe I can say that Virginia can be kept from secession. You can do much to quiet Virginia. If the Virginia convention can adjourn without harm to the peace of the country, a great point will be gained. If the border states can be retained, Mississippi, Louisiana and Texas will soon be back. If the others never come back, there will be no great loss. But I believe Georgia and Alabama will also soon want to return.

If for any decent excuse the Govt. could withdraw the troops from all the southern fortifications, the moment this is known N.C., Va., Md., Del., Ky., Tenn., Md. and I believe Arkansas are certainly retained. The only thing now that gives the secessionists the advantage of the conservatives is the cry of coercion—that the whipping of a slave state, is the whipping of slavery.

When these states come back as many of them will they will come with the fortifications. If they do not find it to their interest to return let them keep their plunder—or if any whipping is to be done let it be after the other slave states have certainly determined to remain.

The present excitement should be allowed to pass away as soon as possible without fighting.

Secretary of State Seward Advises Restraint, March 1861

. . . The policy of the time, therefore, has seemed to me to consist in conciliation, which should deny to disunionists any new provocation or apparent offence, while it would enable the Unionists in the slave states to maintain with truth and with effect that the alarms and apprehensions put forth by the disunionists are groundless and false.

I have not been ignorant of the objections that the administration was elected through the activity of the Republican party; that it must continue to deserve and retain the confidence of that party; while conciliation toward the slave states tends to demoralize the Republican party itself, on which party the main responsibility of maintaining the Union must rest.

But it has seemed to me a sufficient answer—first, that the administration could not demoralize the Republican party without making some sacrifice of its essential principles, while no such sacrifice is necessary, or is anywhere authoritatively proposed; and secondly, if it be indeed true that pacification is necessary to prevent dismemberment of the Union and civil war, or either of them, no patriot and lover of humanity could hesitate to surrender party for the higher interests of country and humanity.

Partly by design, partly by chance, this policy has been hitherto pursued by the late administration of the Federal government, and by the Republican party in its corporate action. It is by this policy, thus pursued, I think, that the progress of dismemberment has been arrested after the seven Gulf states had seceded, and the border states yet remain, although they do so uneasily, in the Union.

It is to a perseverance in this policy for a short time longer that I look as the only peaceful means of assuring the continuance of Virginia, Maryland, North Carolina, Kentucky, Tennessee, Missouri, and Arkansas, or most of those states in the Union. It is through their good and patriotic offices that I look to see the Union sentiment revived and brought once more into activity in the seceding states, and through this agency those states themselves returning into the Union. . . .

The fact, then, is that while the people of the border states desire to be loyal, they are at the same time sadly, though temporarily, demoralized by a sympathy for the slave states, which makes them forget their loyalty whenever there are any grounds for apprehending that the Federal government will resort to military coercion against the seceding states, even though such coercion should be necessary to maintain the authority, or even the integrity, of the Union. This sympathy is unreasonable, unwise, and dangerous, and therefore cannot, if left undisturbed, be permanent. It can be banished, however, only in one way, and that is by giving time for it to wear out, and for reason to resume its sway. Time will do this, if it be not hindered by new alarms and provocations. . . .

The question submitted to us, then, practically is: Supposing it to be possible to reinforce and supply Fort Sumter, is it wise now to attempt it, instead of withdrawing the garrison?

The most that could be done by any means now in our hands would be to throw two hundred and fifty to four hundred men into the garrison, with provisions for supplying it five or six months. In this active and enlightened country, in this season of excitement, with a daily press, daily mails, and an incessantly operating telegraph, the design to reinforce and supply the garrison must become known to the opposite party at Charleston as soon at least as preparation for it should begin. The garrison would then almost certainly fall by assault before the expedition could reach the harbor of Charleston. But supposing the secret kept, the expedition must engage in conflict on entering the harbor of Charleston; suppose it to be overpowered and destroyed, is that new outrage to be avenged, or are we then to return to our attitude of immobility? Should we be allowed to do so? Moreover, in that event, what becomes of the garrison?

I suppose the expedition successful. We have then a garrison in Fort Sumter that can defy assault for six months. What is it to do then? Is it to make war by opening its batteries and attempting to demolish the defences of the Carolinians? Can it demolish them if it tries? If it cannot, what is the advantage we shall have gained? If it can, how will it serve to check or prevent disunion?

In either case, it seems to me that we will have inaugurated a civil war by our own act, without an adequate object, after which reunion will be hopeless, at least under this administration, or in any other way than by a popular disavowal both of the war and of the administration which unnecessarily commenced it. Fraternity is the element of union; war is the very element of disunion. Fraternity, if practised by this administration, will rescue the Union from all its dangers. If this administration, on the other hand, take up the sword, then an opposite party will offer the olive branch, and will, as it ought, profit by the restoration of peace and union. . . .

↯ *E S S A Y S*

Believing that no stone should be left unturned in determining whether war could have been avoided, historians have written extensively about the secession crisis and Lincoln's role in it. In the first essay, Kenneth M. Stampp of the University of California at Berkeley explains Lincoln's policy and outlines why it was justified. Disagreeing with this sympathetic treatment of Lincoln's course, the author of the second essay, Daniel W. Crofts of Trenton State College, argues that Seward's policy was based on an accurate appraisal of Unionist strength in the Upper South and therefore should have been given more careful consideration. Each of these essays is a distillation of a longer study—Stampp's *And the War Came* (1950) and Crofts's *Reluctant Confederates* (1988).

Lincoln and the Secession Crisis

KENNETH M. STAMPP

"Lincoln never poured out his soul to any mortal creature at any time. . . . He was the most secretive—reticent—shut-mouthed man that ever existed." This, the studied opinion of his former law partner, William H. Herndon, defined the perplexing quality in the character of Abraham Lincoln that caused both contemporaries and historians to view him as something of an enigma. This is why his acts frequently permit antithetical explanations; perhaps, too, why forthright motives sometimes appear devious. Because we tend to assume that "shut-mouthed" men are necessarily complex, his reticence always seemed to belie his self-professed simplicity.

As President-elect during the months of the secession crisis, Lincoln kept his own counsel even more rigidly than usual. The confessions of close associates such as Herndon and Judge David Davis that they knew nothing of his plans verified the remark of a newspaper correspondent that "Mr. Lincoln keeps all people, his friends included, in the dark. . . . Mr. Lincoln promises nothing, but only listens." This may help to explain why the available evidence has led some historians to conclude that Lincoln deliberately provoked hostilities at Fort Sumter, while others contended that the Sumter episode was precisely what he had hoped to avoid.

The debate over Lincoln's intentions began during the war itself, but

Charles W. Ramsdell introduced it to modern scholarship in 1937 with an article that accused Lincoln of cynically maneuvering the Confederates into firing on Fort Sumter. His action, according to Ramsdell, resulted from a belief that a war was necessary to save not only the Union but his administration and the Republican party. Three years later, James G. Randall replied to Ramsdell in an article claiming that Lincoln's policy was at all times peaceful and that his Sumter strategy was designed to minimize the danger of war. David M. Potter, in a book-length study of the Republican party during the secession crisis, amplified Randall's thesis. Lincoln's policy, Potter argued, was based on a common northern belief that Unionism was still strong in the South and that a pro-Union reaction was bound to come. His aim, therefore, was to avoid further irritation of the South and thus to provide both time and the best possible conditions for southern Unionists to regain control. Potter, like Randall, believed that Lincoln was still trying to maintain the peace at the time of the crisis at Fort Sumter, that he considered evacuation under certain circumstances, and that ultimately he tried to relieve the fort in the manner least likely to provoke a hostile Confederate response. Therefore, Potter concluded, the Confederate attack on Sumter was a defeat, not a victory for Lincoln's policy. However, the same scanty evidence suggests still another possible interpretation.

Fortunately, the President-elect left the record unmistakably clear on two points. First, there can be no doubt that he was an intense nationalist and that he regarded the Union as indestructible. Lincoln was an old Whig, an admirer of Webster and Clay, and he repeatedly expressed pride in his political origins and scoffed at the dogmas of the state-rights school. In his first inaugural address, he took pains to prove that "the Union of these States is perpetual." While he added little to the classical nationalist argument, he showed that the thought of acquiescing in disunion never entered his mind:

> It follows from these views that no State, upon its own mere motion, can lawfully get out of the Union,—that *resolves* and *ordinances* to that effect are legally void; and that acts of violence, within any State or States, against the authority of the United States, are insurrectionary or revolutionary, according to circumstances.
>
> I therefore consider that, in view of the Constitution and the laws, the Union is unbroken. . . .

Second, through private and confidential letters to political friends in Congress, Lincoln expressed firm opposition to any compromise on the issue of slavery expansion. His past speeches, he contended, provided sufficient evidence that he assumed no right to interfere with slavery in the states where it already existed, that he had no desire to menace the rights of the South, and that he would enforce the fugitive slave law. He would tolerate slavery in the District of Columbia and the interstate slave trade— "whatever springs of necessity from the fact that the institution is among us"—and he might even agree to the admission of New Mexico as a slave state. But he was "inflexible" on the territorial question, and he cautioned his friends to "hold firm as with a chain of steel."

Any explanation of Lincoln's opposition to compromise must be speculative, for his words are sometimes ambiguous and subject to varying interpretations. He objected to the restoration of the Missouri Compromise line on the grounds that it would settle nothing, that it would simply stimulate "filibustering for all South of us, and making slave states of it. . . ." He also expressed a distaste for the personal humiliation involved in proposals to "buy or beg a peaceful inauguration" through concessions, thus indicating that considerations of prestige and "face-saving" were involved. He seemed to be no less concerned about the prestige of the federal government itself: "I should regard any concession in the face of menace the destruction of the government . . . and a consent on all hands that our system shall be brought down to a level with the disorganized state of affairs in Mexico." In addition, Lincoln apparently had decided that this was an appropriate time for a final settlement of the questions of secession and slavery expansion. If concessions were made, he warned, Southerners "will repeat the experiment upon us *ad libitum*. A year will not pass, till we shall have to take Cuba, as a condition upon which they will stay in the Union." Hence, he advised, "Stand firm. The tug has to come, and better now, than any time hereafter." Many Republican politicians and editors shared his determination to resolve the sectional crisis this time, whatever the cost. "If we must have civil war," wrote the conservative Edward Bates, "perhaps it is better now than at a future date." A western Republican paper asserted that "we are heartily tired of having this [secession] threat stare us in the face evermore. . . . We never have been better prepared for such a crisis than now. We most ardently desire that it may come." Throughout the secession crisis it is remarkable how often Lincoln shared, or merely reflected, popular Republican views.

In his private advice against compromise the President-elect made some rather vague remarks to the effect that as soon as a compromise was adopted "they have us under again; all our labor is lost, and sooner or later must be done over." Compromise "would lose us everything we gained by the election," he wrote, adding that it would be "the end of us." These apprehensions might indicate deep concern for the well-being of the Republican party and a fear that compromise would spell its ruin. Most of Lincoln's political friends and advisers were acutely aware that concessions to the South would threaten their organization and that the radical wing might bolt the new administration. They remembered the fate of the Whig party, which, one Republican insisted, had "died of compromises." Thurlow Weed, on a visit to Washington, found the Republicans overwhelmed by this fear. Open the territories to slavery, warned one of the faithful, and "Republicanism is a 'dead dog.' "

Yet there was little in Lincoln's remarks on compromise to invalidate the possibility that, in opposing it, he was thinking less of party than of what he regarded as the best interests of the North, perhaps of the whole nation. More than likely the two concerns were fused in his mind. Politicians have a happy facility for identifying personal and party interests with broad national interests, and Lincoln may have believed sincerely that what was good for the Republican party was good for everyone.

Having flatly rejected both compromise and acquiescence in disunion, Lincoln could have hoped to deal with the secession crisis in only two other ways. Either he could encourage loyal Southerners to overthrow the secessionists, voluntarily renew their allegiance to the federal government, and thus achieve a peaceful reconstruction of the Union, or he could resort to whatever force might be necessary to collect federal revenues and to recover or maintain possession of federal property. To that extent, in other words, he could have coerced the secessionists, defining coercion broadly as any attempt to enforce federal laws against the wishes of state authorities or large bodies of disaffected citizens.

In all probability Lincoln regarded neither the device of peaceful reconstruction nor coercion as a basic policy. These were merely tactical alternatives to be used according to circumstances. From the traditional viewpoint of practical statesmanship the preservation of peace and the launching of war are never the supreme objects of policy. They are potential means to some desirable end; the more fundamental goal is to preserve, defend, or advance primary national interests. These interests are guarded by peaceful means when possible, but the use of force is never ruled out as a last resort. "National interest" is a loose concept easily abused, but it has ever been a prime concern of governments.

When Lincoln's problem is placed in this context, his words and acts during the secession crisis appear to be rational, realistic, and remarkably consistent. Because he opposed compromise and peaceful secession it does not follow that his basic purpose was to resort to force any more than it was to risk everything on a policy of peace. Rather, his chief concern was the maintenance of the Union, a national interest which he regarded as vital enough to take precedence over all other considerations. And the integrity of the Union continued to be his paramount objective throughout the ensuing conflict—even his Emancipation Proclamation was conceived and justified with that goal in mind. There is no reason to doubt that Lincoln would have accepted peaceful and voluntary reconstruction as a satisfactory solution within the time limits fixed by political realities, especially northern public opinion. But there is abundant evidence that the possible necessity of coercion entered his calculations as soon as he understood the seriousness of the crisis. Lincoln was not a pacifist, and as both a practical statesman and a mystical believer in an American mission to the world, he looked upon disunion as a sufficient threat to justify resistance by military force if necessary. . . .

The fact that Lincoln intimated the possible use of force does not necessarily imply that he visualized, as an inevitable consequence, a long civil war, or the need for any war at all. Like many others, he may have thought that "a little show of force," entailing a minimum of bloodshed, would suffice to crush the southern rebellion. Better still, a sufficient demonstration of federal power might result in the immediate collapse of the

Confederacy without so much as a skirmish. However, the consequence of coercive measures was really out of the President's hands. It would depend upon the secessionists. And from this critical fact Lincoln formulated his basic strategy.

From the outset the new President, in dealing with the disunion crisis, had three clear advantages. First, the northern people, with few exceptions, agreed with him that the states did not have a constitutional right to secede. However many may have favored compromise and hoped to avoid the use of military force, the masses of Republicans and Democrats alike shared the belief that the Union was perpetual. It was not difficult, or even necessary, to convince them that the preservation of the Union was both a moral obligation and a vital national interest. Second, the burden of direct action rested upon the seceding states, which, after all, were seeking to disturb the political *status quo*. In order to make their independence a reality, they thought it essential to seize government forts and other property, and to destroy the symbols of federal authority. As a result, the Union government could easily claim that it would avoid aggressive action and merely assume a defensive posture. In other words, the exigencies of the situation would almost certainly suggest to a wise and practical political leader a strategy of defense—of throwing the initiative to the South.

This is where Lincoln's third important advantage made itself evident. Given the general northern belief that, in spite of southern ordinances of secession, the Union was not and could not be dissolved, the government was entitled to make a number of "defensive" moves. These presumably nonaggressive acts might include such things as collecting the revenues, holding federal property, perhaps even reinforcing the forts or recovering those that had been seized. Action of this kind, most Northerners believed, would be far different from marching a hostile army into the South to overawe and coerce it. "There is no form in which coercion . . . can be applied," wrote a northern editor. "The general government can do no more than see that its laws are carried out." Of course, secessionists, who regarded the dissolution of the Union as an accomplished fact, brushed aside these fine distinctions and branded any federal intervention in the South as coercion. Perhaps abstract logic was on their side, but to Lincoln that was irrelevant. Always holding the preservation of the Union above peace, he exploited his three strategic advantages in order to cast coercion in the mold of defense and to shift responsibility for any resulting violence to his "dissatisfied fellow-countrymen."

This defensive concept was in no sense an original idea of Lincoln's. Soon after the election of 1860 the Republican press began to propose the strategy with remarkable spontaneity. "The Republican policy," predicted the Springfield (Massachusetts) *Republican,* "will be to make no war upon the seceding states, to reject all propositions for secession, to hold them to the discharge of their constitutional duties, to collect the revenues as usual in southern ports, and calmly await the results. There can be no war unless the seceders make war upon the general government." The New York *Evening Post* suggested that if South Carolina should make it impossible to collect duties at Charleston, Congress could simply close it as a port of entry. "Here then we have a peaceful antidote for that 'peaceful remedy' which is called secession. It is no act of war, nor hostility, to revoke the permission given to any town to be opened as a port of entry; but when that permission is revoked it would be an act of hostility . . . to disregard the injunction." A northern clergyman summed up the strategy precisely in advising the South: "Secede on paper as much as you please. We will not make war upon you for that. But we will maintain the supremacy of the constitution and laws. If you make war on the Union, we will defend it at all costs, and the guilt of blood be on your heads." Thus the strategy, occasionally defined as one of "masterly inactivity," had been outlined in advance; Lincoln had only to read the newspapers to discover its value.

From the time the President-elect left Springfield in February until the firing on Fort Sumter, the central theme of his public utterances was the further development and clarification of a strategy of defense. Holding inflexibly to the conviction that his fundamental purpose must be the preservation of the Union, he chose his words carefully and shrewdly to protect himself from any charge of aggression. Appreciating the possibility that hostilities might ensue, Lincoln seemed preoccupied with an intense desire to leave the record clear, to make it evident to the northern people that war, if it came, would be started by the South. His words were not those of a man confused about the true situation, about what his policy should be, or about possible consequences. The coercive intimations were nearly always of a sort that would be perceived as such only by southern secessionists, seldom by northern Unionists.

During his first stop, at Indianapolis, Lincoln began at once to expound his defensive strategy. In a speech from the balcony of the Bates House he denied any intention to invade the South with a hostile army and made it clear that the government would only defend itself and its property. On February 21, he assured the New Jersey General Assembly that he would do everything possible to secure a peaceful settlement. "The man does not live who is more devoted to peace than I am." The next day, before the Pennsylvania legislature, he expressed regret "that a necessity may arise in this country for the use of the military arm. . . . I promise that, (in so far as I may have wisdom to direct,) if so painful a result shall in any wise be brought about, it shall be through no fault of mine." On the same day, in Philadelphia, Lincoln spoke with unusual clarity: "Now, in my view of the present aspect of affairs, there is no need of bloodshed and war. There is no necessity for it. I am not in favor of such a course, and I may say in advance, there will be no blood shed unless it is forced upon the Government. The Government will not use force unless force is used against it." . . .

Having already outlined his defensive strategy on several occasions, Lincoln's inaugural address contained no surprises on that score—only a final clear exposition of his nonaggressive intentions. Once more he insisted that in upholding the authority of the government "there needs be no bloodshed or violence; and there shall be none, unless it be forced upon the national authority." He would refrain from doing many things which he had a right to do, but which could be forgone without injury to the prestige of the government. However, though he desired a peaceful solution, the matter was beyond his control: "In *your* hands, my dissatisfied fellow-countrymen, and not in *mine,* is the momentous issue of civil war. The government will not assail *you.* You can have no conflict, without being yourselves the aggressors. *You* have no oath registered in Heaven to destroy the government, while *I* shall have the most solemn one to 'preserve, protect and defend it.' "

Thus, by the time of his inauguration, Lincoln had firmly established his intention to preserve the Union by measures that Unionists would accept as purely defensive. With consummate skill he had at once hamstrung the South, satisfied the great majority of Northerners that he contemplated no aggression, and yet conveyed his determination to defend the authority of the federal government. The Republican press glowed with appreciation. "No party can be formed against the administration on the issue presented by the inaugural," observed one friendly editor. Another noted that "the fiat of peace or war is in the hands of Mr. Davis rather than of Mr. Lincoln." Samuel Bowles of the Springfield *Republican* believed that the inaugural had put "the secession conspirators manifestly in the wrong, and hedges them in so that they cannot take a single step without making treasonable war upon the government, which will only defend itself." By the fourth of March, Lincoln had already cornered the disunionists.

It should be evident, then, that Lincoln's reaction to the problem of supplying Fort Sumter, which confronted him immediately after his inauguration, was in perfect harmony with the strategy he had already conceived. His decision to sustain the Sumter garrison involved no change of plans—no reluctant abandonment of a policy of voluntary reunion, no sudden determination to provoke a war. It was a logical consequence of the President's fixed determination to defend the Union even at the risk of hostilities. Had the Sumter crisis not arisen, or had Lincoln been convinced ultimately that military necessity dictated evacuation, his strategy almost certainly would have led to a similar violent confrontation somewhere else. In fact, while he was exploring the possibility of sending supplies to Major Robert Anderson, he was also searching for other means of developing his defensive policy. For example, he instructed General Scott "to exercise all possible vigilance for the maintenance of all the places within the military department of the United States, and to promptly call upon all the departments of the government for the means necessary to that end." In addition, he offered the deposed Unionist governor of Texas, Sam Houston, military and naval support if Houston would put himself at the head of a Union party; and he considered the collection of duties from naval vessels off southern ports, or even a blockade of the Confederacy. . . .

Even before Lincoln's inauguration there were abundant signs that the general uncertainty was becoming intolerable. More and more it appeared that time was not on the side of the Union, that the secession movement was actually gaining in strength. After March 4, Republican leaders bombarded Lincoln with advice favoring decisive action, and with warnings that the people would not tolerate the abandonment of Sumter. Meanwhile, the differences between Union and Confederate tariff schedules frightened many conservative merchants into a mood for drastic remedies. By the end of March numerous businessmen had reached the point where they felt that anything—even war—was better than the existing indecision which was so fatal to trade. "It is a singular fact," wrote one observer, "that merchants who, two months ago, were fiercely shouting 'no coercion,' now ask for anything rather than *inaction*." Even anti-Republican and anti-coercion papers could bear the suspense no longer and urged that something be done. Lincoln might well have hoped for a little more time to organize his administration before dealing with the secessionists; but the general unrest in the North, as well as the Sumter crisis, forced his hand at once. The time for delay had passed.

Such was the atmosphere in which Lincoln dispatched a relief expedition to Fort Sumter. Every circumstance combined to make this a satisfactory culmination of his defensive strategy. Popular attention had long been focused on the small federal garrison in Charleston harbor. A southern attack was almost certain to consolidate northern opinion behind the new administration, while permitting the garrison to receive supplies would seriously damage Confederate prestige. Having authorized [Secretary of State William H.] Seward to promise the Confederate Commissioners in Washington that relief would not be sent without due notice, the President could be doubly sure that this step, one way or another, would be decisive. Equally important, the fact that he could force the issue merely by sending supplies served to underscore the defensive nature of his move. He instructed his messenger, Robert S. Chew, to notify Governor Francis W. Pickens of South Carolina that "an attempt will be made to supply Fort-Sumpter [*sic*] with provisions only; and that, if such attempt be not resisted, no effort to throw in men, arms, or ammunition, will be made, without further notice, or in case of an attack upon the Fort." After that, whether the Confederates attacked or submitted, Lincoln would triumph.

The President himself pointed to the Sumter expedition as the fulfillment of the policy he had outlined in the past. He did so first in his reply to Seward's memorandum of April 1, in which the Secretary of State proposed, for all practical purposes, Lincoln's own strategy, except that he favored the evacuation of Sumter. Professing surprise at this, Lincoln reminded Seward that his inaugural embraced "the exact domestic policy you now urge," except that he would not give up Fort Sumter. Even more emphatic was his response, on April 13, to a delegation sent by the Virginia convention to inquire about his policy. "Not having, as yet, seen occasion to change," he said, "it is now my purpose to pursue the course marked out in the inaugural address." He would hold federal property in the South. However, if it proved true that "an unprovoked assault" had been made on Sumter, he would feel free "to re-possess . . . like places which have been seized before the Government was devolved upon me." It was at this point, more clearly than ever before, that Lincoln expressed his unqualified decision in favor of coercion. Yet, he still insisted that his policy was altogether defensive, for he added that he would simply "repel force by force."

The Confederate attack upon Fort Sumter was, in effect, a striking victory for Lincoln's defensive strategy. Just as Republican editors had first suggested the formula, their appreciation of its success was immediate and spontaneous. In one great chorus they denounced the Confederates as the aggressors. "It was," wrote one, "an audacious and insulting aggression upon the authority of the Republic, without provocation or excuse." A Boston editor piously described the event as one furnishing "precisely the stimulus which . . . a good Providence sends to arouse the latent patriotism of the people." "*Let it be remembered,*" cried the Providence *Journal,* "*that the Southern government has put itself wholly in the wrong, and is the aggressor.* On its head must be the responsibility for the consequences." These were accurate expressions of the feelings of an indignant northern people. . . .

That Lincoln understood the probability of Confederate resistance at Charleston is beyond a reasonable doubt, for the messengers he sent there in March informed him of the state of opinion in South Carolina. During the period of preparation the President strove to organize the defenses of Washington and urged Governor Curtin of Pennsylvania to prepare for an emergency. Lincoln's secretaries, John G. Nicolay and John Hay, believed that it was "reasonably certain" that he expected hostilities to ensue, and they observed that when the news arrived of the attack upon Sumter he was neither surprised nor excited. Indeed, if he had believed that Sumter could be supplied peacefully, there was no reason why he should ever have considered evacuation as a possible military necessity. During the weeks when members of the Cabinet and military officers discussed the Sumter crisis, they simply took for granted that a federal relief expedition would result in a Confederate attack.

There is no evidence that Lincoln regarded the result of his strategy with anything but satisfaction. Having derived his policy from his deter-mination to preserve the Union at all costs, he had reason to congratulate himself, for with a united North behind him he was likely to succeed. "You and I both anticipated," he wrote Captain Fox [Gustavus Vasa Fox, who commanded the Sumter relief expedition], "that the cause of the country would be advanced by making the attempt to provision Fort-Sumpter [*sic*], even if it should fail; and it is no small consolation now to feel that our anticipation is justified by the result." A few months later, after Lincoln had gained greater perspective, he told Senator Orville H. Browning of Illinois that he had "conceived the idea" of sending supplies without re-inforcements and of notifying the governor of South Carolina in advance. According to Browning, Lincoln added: "The plan succeeded. They at-tacked Sumter—it fell, and thus did more service than it otherwise could." . . .

The crucial point about the Sumter crisis was that, except for the important consideration of northern public opinion, it mattered little whether Lincoln attempted to supply Sumter in the least provocative or the most provocative way, because, as he had reason to know, *any* attempt was bound to open hostilities. Moreover, it is possible to argue that Lincoln's Sumter policy was not in fact the least provocative course he might have followed. For example, he might have done what he subsequently claimed that he had hoped to do—that is, evacuate Fort Sumter and reinforce Fort Pickens, as Seward suggested. The reinforcement of Pickens was accomplished with ease, and the federal position there was so strong that the fort was never lost to the Confederates. As to Sumter, before sending a relief expedition, Lincoln might have directed Major Anderson to try to obtain the needed supplies in Charleston. South Carolina authorities might well have refused such a request (though they permitted Anderson to purchase fresh meats and vegetables in the Charleston market), but the request was never made. Finally, although Lincoln assured the governor of South Carolina that the relief expedition would land provisions only, he also hinted that an attempt (with notice) to land "men, arms, or ammunition" might be made at some future time. A Sumter policy designed to minimize provocation would hardly have suggested such a possibility at that crucial juncture. Yet, it is not to accuse Lincoln of deliberately starting a war to conclude that the Confederate attack on Sumter was a triumph, not a defeat, for his policy.

With the fall of Sumter Lincoln's defensive policy had served its purpose, and instantly he changed his ground. In his proclamation of April 15, calling for 75,000 volunteers, he did not propose merely to "hold" or "possess" federal property and to collect the revenues. Instead, he summoned the militia to suppress an insurrection, "to re-possess the forts, places, and property which have been seized," "to cause the laws to be duly executed," to preserve the Union, and "to redress wrongs already long enough endured." A few days later, when addressing the Frontier Guard in Washington, Lincoln gave additional evidence that he had always preferred coercion to disunion. While professing peaceful intentions, he predicted that "if the alternative is presented, whether the Union is to be broken in fragments . . . or blood be shed, you will probably make the choice, with which I shall not be dissatisfied."

Although Lincoln accepted the possibility of war, which, in retrospect, was the almost certain consequence of his defensive strategy, the indictment—if such it be—can be softened considerably by surrounding circumstances. It was a burden that he shared with many others, for his standards of statesmanship and his concept of the national interest were those common to his age—and, for that matter, to ours as well. The Union was a thing worth fighting for! If Lincoln was no pacifist, neither were his contemporaries. The growing impatience in the North and the widespread demand for action no doubt helped to shape his final decision. And it is still a moot question whether politicians in a democracy are morally bound to yield to popular pressures or to resist them. Moreover, without quibbling over who was guilty of the first act of aggression, the case would be distorted if one overlooked the fact that southern leaders shared with Lincoln the responsibility for a resort to force. . . .

It may well have been true, as [Charles W.] Ramsdell claimed, that the outbreak of war saved the Republican party from disintegration and that a practical politician such as Lincoln could not have ignored the political consequences of his action. But the Machiavellian implication of that hypothesis is based on sheer speculation. We cannot read Lincoln's mind; and the available evidence makes equally valid the counter-hypothesis that he considered only the country's best interests. Or, again, he may have had a comprehensive understanding of what both the country and political expediency demanded. Perhaps it was simply Lincoln's good fortune that personal, party, and national interests could be served with such favorable coincidence as they were by his strategy of defense.

William Henry Seward and the Decision for War

DANIEL W. CROFTS

Very few citizens of New York State have had a more significant political career than William Henry Seward. Born in 1801 in Orange County, he was graduated from Union College in 1821, and then established his law practice and his home in Auburn. For three decades, first as governor of New York (1839–1842), then as United States senator (1849–1861), and finally as secretary of state under Presidents Abraham Lincoln and Andrew Johnson (1861–1869), Seward was one of the most prominent figures in the political life of New York and the nation. He is probably best remembered for events in which he took part as secretary of state—for the purchase of Alaska in 1867, and for his stand in the secession crisis of 1861.

Though the acquisition of Alaska, originally criticized, has long been accepted as extraordinarily farsighted, Seward's activities in the uncertain opening weeks of the Lincoln presidency are quite another matter. His role in the secession crisis is at once superficially well known and yet poorly understood. No textbook would be complete without the story of the presumptuous would-be premier, a meddling busybody who exuded confidence that the troubles facing the country could be overcome—and that he alone knew how to do it. For months oblivious to the true seriousness of the crisis, this Seward belatedly awoke to make the rash and foolish proposal about starting a foreign war rather than fighting the Confederacy. The true story is, of course, complex and multidimensional, as serious Seward biographers and historians of the secession period have all discovered. Perhaps because an accurate record is not easily established, the stereotype lingers. . . .

Daniel W. Crofts, "Secession Winter: William Henry Seward and the Decision for War," *New York History*, Volume 65, Number 3, July 1984, pp. 229–230, 237–256. Reprinted by permission of the author. Also see *Reluctant Confederates: Upper South Unionists in the Secession Crisis* by Daniel W. Crofts (Chapel Hill: University of North Carolina Press, 1989).

For Seward as for almost all other Republicans, the extent and seriousness of the secession crisis came as a rude shock. Republicans had persuaded themselves that Southern threats to sever the Union in the event of Lincoln's election were just that—threats designed simply to bluff and intimidate Northern voters. Unlike most other Republicans, however, Seward quickly realized his miscalculation. Within two weeks after the election, while most of his party still imagined that the troubles would blow over, Seward travelled to Albany to consult about the crisis with his political manager and alter ego, Thurlow Weed, editor of the Albany *Evening Journal*.

Through Weed, Seward initiated discussion of the idea that Republicans might need to modify the key tenet of party orthodoxy—the restriction of slavery from all federal territories. Their hope was to deflate a favorite secessionist argument: that because Republicans would not respect Southern rights or equality in the territories, Republicans would in fact endanger slavery in the states where it already existed. Weed's public position, echoed ambiguously by Seward, was that Republican victory in the presidential election assured that the territories would be administered so that they would become free. Thus, there was no longer any reason to insist on specific legislation toward that end. Weed himself went even further: he was ready to allow Southerners the right to take slaves to territories south of 36° 30'—though he regarded this right as abstract and barren because the climate in the Southwest was entirely unsuited for plantation slavery.

Weed's proposed "compromise" of party "principle" provoked an outburst of Republican disagreement. Seward found it necessary to disavow Weed's heresies in order to maintain his influence within the party. But there can be no doubt that the editor did speak for the Senator. Frederic Bancroft [Seward's first biographer] has written persuasively that "Weed and Seward were never in closer communication than during these months . . . he and Seward were working together like the two hands of one man." Even though Seward found it expedient to assign Weed the responsibility for taking a more explicit procompromise position, that should not obscure the fact that "Seward's whole argument about slavery in the territories was similar to that of the Northern Whig compromisers of 1850, and was entirely inconsistent with what he had been saying for the past twelve years."

Seward interpreted his position as requiring that he appear "hopeful, calm, conciliatory." His demeanor was thus in sharp contrast to many other public men during the secession winter. Passion, anxiety, bewilderment, and despair were the order of the day in Washington. Too many historians have interpreted Seward's conscious effort to appear otherwise as evidence that he underestimated the seriousness of the crisis. The opposite was more nearly true: Seward believed that Republicans generally were blind to impending disaster, and he took it upon himself to develop conciliatory strategy that would arrest the secession movement and hold the upper South in the Union. But to maintain his power within the party, Seward concealed his forebodings.

Seward already had an unusually wide range of contacts among men of all parties and all sections. During the secession winter his circle grew further still. He reached out discreetly to Southern Unionists to show that he was sympathetic to their plight. Consequently, he came to view himself as uniquely well informed and indispensable to the peaceful resolution of the crisis. At no point, perhaps, did Seward's sense of self-importance blaze forth so prominently as in a dramatic letter he wrote to Lincoln on February 24:

> I, my dear sir, have devoted myself singly to the study of the case here—with advantages of access and free communication with all parties of all sections. . . . You must, therefore, allow me to speak frankly and candidly. . . . I know the tenacity of party friends, and I honor and respect it. It has not been their duty to study it, as it has been mine. Only the soothing words which I have spoken have saved us and carried us along thus far. Every loyal man, and, indeed, every disloyal man in the South, will tell you this.

The general reaction among historians has been, as David Potter has noted, to indulge "in polite smiles at the self-importance which Seward exhibited during the winter of 1860–1861." Yet the historians best qualified to make such a judgment broadly acknowledged the validity of Seward's claim. Bancroft wrote that "Great as his egotism appears, it was not out of proportion to his superiority and responsibility at the time." And Potter himself likewise concluded that Seward's apparent vanity was "not without cause." Potter quoted with approval the conclusion of young Henry Adams that Seward had "fought, during these three months of chaos, a fight which might go down in history as one of the wonders of statesmanship."

Seward's most basic hope was to prevent the spread of secession beyond the states of the deep South. He believed that if secession were confined there its novelty would eventually wear off and the Union could be peacefully restored. For Seward, therefore, the immediate goal was to strengthen Unionism in the upper South, especially in Virginia. Throughout the secession winter he devoted his best energies to building a network of secret allies in the upper South.

Southern Unionists insisted that their position was hopeless unless Republicans embraced the Crittenden Compromise, sponsored by Kentucky Senator John J. Crittenden, which would have protected slavery in territories south of 36° 30′ and seemingly invited the conquest of new slave territory in Central America and the Caribbean. Although it would also have prohibited territorial slavery north of 36° 30′, Crittenden's formulation was entirely unacceptable to Republicans. Only a minority of Republicans would even consider restoring the Missouri Compromise line, which had prohibited slavery north of 36° 30′ while only by implication allowing it in existing territory south of that line. Thurlow Weed visited Lincoln in Springfield in mid-December to urge restoration of the Missouri line. But Lincoln emphatically opposed any territorial compromise.

Lincoln's stance made the task of conciliating the Southern Unionists a stern challenge to Seward. He necessarily devised a complex and, at times, misleading strategy. On a number of different occasions he privately avowed that he would work for something "substantially" along the lines of the Crittenden Compromise, though he could not yet afford to say as much in public. At the same time, Seward also reassured hard-line Republicans such as Massachusetts Senator Charles Sumner that his apparent willingness to compromise was a tactical gesture, designed for effect, and that he had "no idea" of having Congress actually enact such measures.

Knowing that hardly any Republican could countenance the Crittenden Compromise, Seward devised a package of less drastic proposals to relieve Southern anxieties. Most important, perhaps, was the agreement he and Weed won from Lincoln to offer a position in the cabinet to Congressman John A. Gilmer, a prominent North Carolina Unionist. Seward also supported the idea of a Constitutional amendment to guarantee the safety of slavery in the states, a proposal formally sponsored by his ally, Charles Francis Adams. Seward likewise worked behind the scenes in favor of two alternative territorial formulas. New Mexico statehood, sponsored by Adams and Maryland Congressman Henry Winter Davis, contemplated admission into the Union forthwith of the remaining federal territory south of 36° 30', the region covered by the Crittenden Compromise. The so-called Border State plan would have forbidden either Congress or a territorial legislature from passing any law for or against slavery south of 36° 30', thereby modifying what Republicans considered the most objectional features of the Crittenden Compromise. Lincoln, however, opposed the Border State plan just as adamantly as he had the Crittenden Compromise, while Southern Unionists thought the Constitutional amendment an insufficient concession, and suspected that New Mexico statehood would simply add another free state to the Union.

Events by mid-January, 1861, intersected to leave Seward tense and irritable, despite his best efforts to maintain a cheerful, unruffled facade. None of the conciliatory alternatives to the Crittenden Compromise were materializing. The Border State plan, the New Mexico statehood scheme, Southerner in the cabinet, a Constitutional amendment to guarantee the safety of slavery in the states—none could attract the essential combination of support from both Lincoln and Southern Unionists. Meanwhile the secession of states in the lower South continued unabated, while many upper South moderates talked as if their Union-saving efforts would be doomed without prompt Republican acceptance of the Crittenden Compromise. It increasingly appeared that there was no common policy which could unite conciliatory Republicans and Southern Unionists. . . .

The first state in the upper South to put the secession issue to a popular vote was Virginia. The Virginia voting on February 4 dramatically repudiated Southern nationalists. Of the 152 delegates elected to the convention, no more than 30 favored immediate secession. A provision to require a popular referendum on any convention action—a proposal favored by Unionists, who wanted some control over a runaway secession convention

—carried by a margin of more than two to one. Conservative Unionists wrote to warn Seward that the triumph would be illusory if Republicans did not "come forward promptly with liberal concessions," and make it possible for the peace convention to "rally all the conservative influences North and South." Before the Virginia vote Seward had apparently encouraged Unionists there to believe that he would "substantially" support the Crittenden Compromise, but in the aftermath of the election, he became confident that "we could trust the Union sentiment in Virginia to an indefinite extent." Seward was heard to boast: "I have already whipped Mason and Hunter in their own state. I must crush out Davis and Toombs and their colleagues in sedition in their respective states. Saving the border states to the Union by moderation and justice, the people of the cotton states, unwillingly led into secession, will rebel against their leaders, and reconstruction will follow."

During the week after the Virginia vote, Seward felt more optimistic than at any time since the secession crisis began. No sooner had his efforts to hold Virginia in the Union succeeded than Tennessee, on February 9, made an even more unqualified Unionist affirmation. Voters there refused by popular referendum even to call a convention. "The ancient Seward is in high spirits and chuckles himself hoarse with stories," reported Henry Adams. "He says it's all right. We shall keep the border states, and in three months or thereabouts, if we hold off, the Unionists and Disunionists will have their hands on each other's throats in the cotton states." The senior Adams, Charles Francis, Seward's close ally in Congress, reflected the hopeful spirit generated by the Virginia and Tennessee voting: "In my opinion the chances are now that the epidemic has reached its limits," he wrote to a friend. Adams, like Seward, looked forward to "a reaction that will terminate this difficulty in the course of a couple years."

But then on February 11, Lincoln departed for Washington by train from Springfield. That same evening, speaking in Indianapolis, Lincoln asserted the right to retake forts, enforce laws, and collect duties in the seceded states, and he denied that such action would constitute "coercion." The tone of his remarks, there and elsewhere en route, suggested that he would be unlikely even to make conciliatory gestures toward Southern Unionists.

All at once, Seward's Union-saving schemes began to crumble. His supposed influence in the new administration appeared barren, since Lincoln's speeches gave the impression that Seward's policy would not be implemented. In two revealing letters, Charles Francis Adams, Jr., reported that his father and Seward were "more depressed" than at any previous time. Lincoln's speeches, he continued, had left Virginia Unionists in despair. If Lincoln's policy was indeed as he stated it at Indianapolis, then Virginia would secede and every slave state would follow. Seward would refuse to serve in the cabinet, and war would break out within a month. But if Lincoln gave his full support to Seward's conciliatory policy, Virginia would remain in the Union, and the country would weather the crisis.

Young Adams summarized what he had learned from his father and his brother Henry: "Within ten days they tell me the question will be decided and they look blue as they say so."

Seward girded for the struggle just ahead. A few glimpses reveal what lay behind his "cool and calm" facade. "I have had to feel my own way in the dark and amid the tempest," he wrote irritably to James Watson Webb. Seward refused to make any promises of patronage because he wanted to give himself the best chance of winning the confidence of Lincoln "on whom all depends." After talking to Lincoln en route to Washington, Thurlow Weed sent a letter to warn Seward about the coming "ordeal." His conversation with Lincoln, Weed wrote, did not diminish his concern for the nation. "You have a delicate duty before you."

As Seward restlessly awaited Lincoln's appearance in Washington, he braced himself for a maximum effort to bend the mind of the president-elect. His rivals had made plans to install Lincoln in a private home until inauguration day; Seward thwarted that scheme and arranged for Lincoln to stay at Willard's Hotel. When General Winfield Scott warned Seward about possible dangers facing Lincoln in Baltimore, Seward dispatched his son, Frederick, to bring Lincoln secretly to Washington from Harrisburg, Pennsylvania. As soon as Lincoln arrived in Washington early on the morning of Saturday, February 23, there began a virtuoso performance that effectively monopolized most of the president-elect's first two days at the capital. Seward met Lincoln at the train station, accompanied him to the hotel, conducted him on an escorted tour for introductory meetings with President James Buchanan, his cabinet, and General Scott. . . . The next day Seward accompanied Lincoln to church and then entertained him at home until late afternoon. At some point on Saturday or Sunday, Seward also scrutinized Lincoln's projected inaugural address, and suggested numerous line-by-line modifications to give the document a more conciliatory tone.

Three paramount issues dominated Lincoln's agenda during this first frantic week in Washington—the choice of a cabinet, the text of his inaugural address, and the possible adoption of conciliatory legislation by Congress during its final few days in session. On all three matters, Lincoln's mind was basically determined, but Seward hoped to bend him in a more conciliatory direction.

Seward and Weed had been attempting since December to award most cabinet posts to conciliatory minded ex-Whigs, including Southern Unionists from outside the Republican party. Lincoln had agreed to offer an appointment to one such individual, John A. Gilmer of North Carolina, but Gilmer hesitated to take the position in view of the uncertainty about Lincoln's Southern policy. Only the appointment of other conservative cabinet members plus Lincoln's avowed support for conciliation and peace seemed likely to win over the reluctant North Carolinian. The reassurances Gilmer sought were not forthcoming. Instead, Lincoln had decided to include in his cabinet the symbolic leader of the no-compromise Republicans, Salmon P. Chase of Ohio. Furthermore, Lincoln's choice to represent the upper South, in the absence of Gilmer, was a fierce Republican coercionist, Montgomery Blair. The latter's appointment constituted "the death-blow to the policy of Mr. Seward," according to Henry Adams.

Lincoln had arrived in Washington with a draft of a hard-line inaugural address, which supported none of the conciliatory overtures currently under discussion, refused to take any action inconsistent with the Republican platform, indicated an intention to retake federal property in Confederate hands, and closed with an ominous threat to defend the Union by force if necessary. Lincoln did give Seward a copy to consider, and the latter promptly reported that it would drive Maryland and Virginia out of the Union. He proposed, in a letter dated Sunday evening, February 24, and already partially quoted above, that Lincoln make an extensive and more conciliatory rewriting of the document. By the end of the week, Seward had no reason to believe that his suggestions had been heeded. Uncompromising Republicans who had seen advance drafts of the inaugural address were jubilant. A reading of the same document had, by contrast, helped to persuade Gilmer that he could not serve in Lincoln's cabinet.

Lincoln's week in Washington before his inauguration coincided with the ending of the Congressional term. Legislative proposals to alleviate the crisis had remained in limbo during February. . . . Finally, however, a fragile coalition of Southerners, Northern Democrats, and conciliatory Republicans secured Congressional approval of one conciliatory measure— Charles Francis Adams's Constitutional amendment protecting slavery in the states. The Senate vote did not come until long after midnight on the morning of March 4, inauguration day.

Two days before the adoption of the Adams amendment, Seward made his boldest gamble of the secession winter. His Union-saving program apparently in ruins, Seward sent a brief letter to Lincoln, declining to serve as secretary of state. Seward obviously hoped that Lincoln would be unwilling to accept an open breach with the leading conciliatory Republican, and that some accommodation on Southern policy might yet be arranged.

The bluff worked, though Seward did not find out until he heard Lincoln's inaugural address. In that all-important statement of his intended policies, Lincoln deleted both his earlier defense of Republican territorial orthodoxy, and his threat to try to recapture federal property in secessionist hands. Instead, Lincoln endorsed the just-passed Constitutional amendment, and also declared his willingness to have a Constitutional Convention meet to consider further guarantees of Southern rights—a palliative Seward had long favored. At a number of other points, most notably in the concluding paragraph of the address, Lincoln adopted many of the conciliatory revisions suggested by Seward. That afternoon, Lincoln and Seward met at the White House, and the latter countermanded his still-secret resignation.

The evidence is overwhelming that Seward received substantial reassurances from Lincoln that Southern policy would be conducted in such a way as to strengthen the Unionists of the upper South. Their primary concern had been, for several months, to secure some kind of territorial compromise. But by early March, the Unionists began to realize that the immediate priority was to avoid an armed clash between the federal government and the Confederacy. They believed that so long as peace continued, they could thwart secession in their own states and deprive the Confederacy of support that its founders had counted upon.

Virginia was the state which had demanded the greatest amount of attention from Seward. Its Unionist-dominated convention had commenced in mid-February and remained in session in March, hoping to develop a statement of common policy that might win the approval of the other states in the upper South. Virginia Unionists were looking ahead to the scheduled state Congressional elections in May, when they hoped to sweep from power the many secession-tainted incumbents. Seward regarded the success of the Virginia Unionists in the May elections as "the decisive point" that would vindicate his conciliatory policies, and establish the basis for peaceable reunion.

The great horror in the upper South was "coercion"—war waged by the federal government against the seceding states. Indeed, one reason the Virginia Convention remained in session was, in effect, to watch Lincoln and make sure that no "coercion" was attempted. Most Virginia Unionists had indicated that they would stand with the South in a war between the Confederacy and the federal government.

Under the circumstances, the great object for Seward and other promoters of peaceable reunion was to prevent any fighting. Their concern focused especially on the two remaining outposts in the seceded states that remained in federal hands—Fort Pickens, off-shore the harbor of Pensacola, Florida, and Fort Sumter, within the harbor of Charleston, South Carolina. Of the two, Sumter was by far the most visible and important. Sitting in the harbor of the city that could well consider itself the cradle of the Confederacy, Sumter had been in the public eye ever since late December, when a contingent of federal troops, led by Major Robert Anderson, had fled there from the mainland. Sumter was also increasingly vulnerable to assault. Confederate batteries at the mouth of the harbor had the fort within easy range and also effectively blocked any relief or support from federal ships in the Atlantic. Pickens, by contrast, was far enough offshore, on the ocean side of Santa Rosa Island, so that it remained safely in federal hands throughout the war.

Seward exerted his best efforts during March to arguing for the abandonment of Fort Sumter. The basis for his thinking was straightforward: holding the fort meant war; war would, at least at present, drive the upper South into the arms of the Confederacy and make reunion impossible. For a period of several weeks in March, Seward believed that Lincoln agreed that the fort must be abandoned. He so informed Unionist leaders in Virginia who reacted with great enthusiasm.

Only at the very end of March did Lincoln decide to try to retain Sumter. This decision threw Seward into one last frenzy of activity to save his program of peaceable reunion. Seward had favored abandonment of Pickens as well as Sumter in order to minimize the chance of any "collision." But upon learning that Lincoln intended to hold Sumter, Seward urged the president to divert the federal relief force, instead, to Pickens. Preservation of federal control over Fort Pickens would preserve a symbol of federal authority in the seceded states, and a refusal to acquiesce in permanent separation. That policy would, however, be vindicated at a location where the federal position was relatively invulnerable to hostile military activity. A "collision"—especially a humiliating one in which the Confederates defeated the federal government—was far less likely at Pickens than at Sumter. The holding of Pickens rather than Sumter would, furthermore, allow Seward to fulfill the promises he had made to Unionist leaders in Virginia.

Seward also put a Virginia Unionist leader into direct contact with Lincoln, in hopes that the president could be persuaded to reverse his plan to hold Sumter. The Virginian, John B. Baldwin, who visited the White House on April 4, made an eloquent case for abandoning Sumter and avoiding any "collision." But Lincoln responded to Baldwin in a noncommittal manner about Sumter and instead suggested that he would be glad to see the Virginia convention adjourned. The interview proved fruitless.

Seen in the context of Lincoln's recently revealed determination to hold Sumter, Seward's April 1 "Thoughts for the President's Consideration" becomes readily comprehensible. The famous memorandum was written three days after Lincoln ordered the preparation of a fleet to sail to Sumter, and the same day that Seward summoned the Virginia Unionists to send a representative to meet with the president. Seward's purpose in threatening war against France and Spain was to bluff the European powers out of any recognition of or commercial treaty with the Confederate states. He wanted to make sure that European nations would not interpret abandonment of Sumter—if Lincoln could still be persuaded to change his mind—as a de facto recognition of Confederate independence. Beyond this, Seward hoped for a patriotic or nationalistic revival in the upper South. Abandoning Sumter was meant to show Southern Unionists that federal policy was designed neither to benefit the Republican party nor to interfere with slavery. Reunion was to be sought in a manner that could command broadest support. Seward's "Thoughts" have traditionally received low marks even from relatively sympathetic historians. Potter, for example, describes Seward's proposal as "fantastic" and "wild"—a "slap-dash improvisation" that showed "Seward was at the end of his tether." But Kinley J. Brauer's sensible reassessment of the memorandum concludes that Seward had no intention of starting a foreign war. His plan, instead, contemplated "the maintenance of peace both at home and abroad." Lincoln, of course, brushed Seward's objections aside and proceeded to try to resupply Fort Sumter—with results that are well known.

What overall assessment should be made of Seward's secession crisis policy? To say that it did not work obscures the fact that it was never implemented. Less than a month after agreeing to give the conciliatory approach a fair trial, Lincoln decided to risk a confrontation with the Confederates over Fort Sumter. Seward's policy was based on the assumption that it was not yet necessary or desirable to make a stark choice between disunion and forcible reunion. He assumed that peaceful reunion still remained possible, and therefore opposed any action that might lead to war. He believed that the use of force to achieve reunion could not be considered until the growth of more unconditional Unionism in the upper South. The elapse of time would, Seward calculated, either bring peaceable reunion, or so isolate the deep South Confederacy as to make the use of force feasible.

Seward has most frequently been criticized for underestimating the strength of the secession movement, and for placing excessive reliance upon and misconceiving the basic character of Southern Unionism. These accusations do not stand up well under careful scrutiny. A strong case can indeed be made that Unionism in early 1861 was all but extinguished in the seceded states. But it was Seward who recognized sooner than most other Republicans that secession would not just go away. His efforts to devise a policy to meet the threat of secession were most strongly criticized by inflexible Republicans who argued that the threat was illusory or contrived. Seward knew that the states of the lower South were, for the present, estranged. But if lower South secession could be prevented from spreading to the upper South, Seward believed that circumstances would work so as to draw the seceded states back into the Union. That a seven-state Confederacy would either grow or perish was an idea widely shared by knowledgeable observers both in Washington and Montgomery.

Even less tenable is the accusation that Seward both misunderstood and placed excessive reliance upon Southern Unionism. Through personal contacts and an aggressive search for accurate information, Seward had developed by far the best knowledge about Virginia and the upper South of any official close to Lincoln. Seward realized, as many Republicans did not, that even though the states of the upper South had so far been kept out of the Confederate orbit, it would take time to make upper South Unionism reliable and unconditional. His memo to Lincoln of March 15 pointed out that "while the people of the border states desire to be loyal, they are at the same time sadly, though temporarily, demoralized by a sympathy for the slave states. . . . This sympathy is unreasonable, unwise, and dangerous, and therefore cannot, if left undisturbed, be permanent. It can be banished, however, only in one way, and that is by giving time for it to wear out, and for reason to resume its sway. Time will do this, if it be not hindered by new alarms and provocations."

Seward therefore did his best to demonstrate the folly of militaristic Republicans such as Montgomery Blair and his father, Francis Preston Blair, who believed that secession was a minority coup, and that loyal Southerners would rally to the Union cause as soon as federal armies appeared to crush the conspirators. Seward realized that the initiation of hostilities between the federal government and the Confederacy would, under existing conditions, transform nearly the entire South into a hostile armed camp.

Seward also realized, however, that the popular vote against secession had potentially transformed the political landscape of states such as Virginia, North Carolina, and Tennessee. He knew that the division between Unionists and secessionists had triggered a major political realignment, which promised to make a new Union party the dominant political force throughout the upper South. He was in close touch with many of the national Whigs who had gravitated toward positions of leadership in the Union party. Virginia, as noted earlier, was to have been the case in point. Her Congressional elections in May would have indicated whether Seward's approach was working.

Seward was extremely pessimistic about the likelihood of forcible reunion. Keenly aware that war would tend to unite the South, he suspected that war would, by contrast, divide the North. If the administration were "to take up the sword," he predicted, then "an opposite party" would "offer the olive branch." What Seward perhaps did not allow himself to see was that the passions generated by the firing on Fort Sumter and the Proclamation for 75,000 troops would produce an outburst of patriotic unanimity in the North as well as in the South, such as to make forcible reunion possible, though at a ghastly price in blood and treasure. Seward's policy required no use of force unless and until the upper South could be counted upon to sustain the Union. Confronted by a united North and upper South, a seven-state Confederacy would have been entirely unable to effect serious resistance.

Lincoln by contrast, appears to have judged that the eclipse of Unionism in the deep South made peaceful reunion impossible. It is not known how he expected the outbreak of war to affect the upper South. He may have underestimated the latent pro-Confederate sympathies of states which had only recently rejected secession. Or he may have concluded that a fight against an enlarged Confederacy was inevitable, if the Union was to be restored, and better to fight sooner than later. What may especially have motivated Lincoln was the undoubted political and diplomatic danger resulting from a hands-off policy towards the Confederacy. Restlessness within his own party would have burst into open revolt if Lincoln had abandoned Fort Sumter. And foreign encouragement or recognition of the Confederacy was a greater threat so long as the administration appeared unwilling to challenge secession. It may well have been that Lincoln decided to try to resupply Fort Sumter in order to avoid the likely and, to him, unacceptable consequences of continued inaction, but without fully knowing what would result from sending the resupply fleet.

Writing in late April 1861, Henry Adams first asked: "what would have been the end of the matter if Mr. Seward had then carried his point, and the conciliatory policy had become the policy of the Government." Only rarely since has the question been seriously considered. Pro-Northern historians, both early and modern, have generally applauded Lincoln and dismissed the efforts of those who opposed a military confrontation with the Confederacy in April 1861. The policy Lincoln followed of course brought eventual reunion, but at a price that still startles—more American lives lost than in all other American warfare from the Revolution to the present. It would be hard to imagine a more costly alternative. . . . [T]he epitaph on Seward's policy written by Henry Adams in 1861 is still pertinent:

> Like all such attempts at wisdom and moderation in times of heated passions and threatening war, it was swallowed up and crushed under the weight of brute force, that final tribunal to which human nature is subjected or subjects herself without appeal. Yet it is right to make the effort even if overruled.

⚓ F U R T H E R   R E A D I N G

William L. Barney, *The Secessionist Impulse: Alabama and Mississippi in 1860* (1974)

Steven A. Channing, *Crisis of Fear: Secession in South Carolina* (1970)

Daniel W. Crofts, *Reluctant Confederates: Upper South Unionists in the Secession Crisis* (1989)

Richard N. Current, *Lincoln and the First Shot* (1963)

———, "The Confederates and the First Shot," *Civil War History* 7 (1961), 357–369

Michael P. Johnson, *Toward a Patriarchal Republic: The Secession of Georgia* (1977)

George H. Knoles, ed., *The Crisis of the Union, 1860–1861* (1965)

Roy F. Nichols, *The Disruption of American Democracy* (1948)

Stephen B. Oates, *With Malice Toward None: The Life of Abraham Lincoln* (1977)

Phillip S. Paludan, "The Civil War as a Crisis of Law and Order," *American Historical Review* 77 (1972), 1013–1034

David M. Potter, *Lincoln and His Party in the Secession Crisis* (1942)

———, *The Impending Crisis, 1848–1861* (1976)

Charles W. Ramsdell, "Lincoln and Fort Sumter," *Journal of Southern History* 3 (1937), 259–288

Kenneth M. Stampp, *And the War Came: The North and the Secession Crisis, 1860–1861* (1950)

CHAPTER
5

Fighting the War:
The Strategy of the Generals

Did the North win the Civil War because its armies were better led? It is often said so, and there is some truth in the claim. After all, the task of the Union armies was considerably more difficult. While the Confederacy was engaged in a struggle to maintain its independence and therefore had simply to defend its territory and repel northern attacks, the Federals had to assume the offensive, move their troops great distances into the South, seize strategic locations, defeat enemy armies, and then occupy Confederate terrain and subjugate the population. Yet the northern generals and their armies were ultimately victorious.

Offsetting these disadvantages, however, was the superiority of the North in the resources with which to wage a war, particularly if it lasted a long time. The Federal side could draw upon a greater reserve of manpower, since its population was three times the size of the South's if the slaves were excluded. Furthermore, the North had a preponderance of physical assets in the form of railroads and raw materials as well as a more diverse and self-sufficient economy. And, as the war dragged on, its superiority actually increased in relation to the South.

It must also be acknowledged that it took the North a long time to develop a strategy to win the war and find the generals capable of carrying it out. Lincoln may have understood what was necessary, but Generals George McClellan and Joseph Hooker and their subordinates proved stubborn and unadaptable. Meanwhile, Generals Robert E. Lee, T. J. ("Stonewall") Jackson, and Joseph E. Johnston managed to defend Confederate territory and keep the Federals at bay. Moreover, the southerners were neither as unaware of the novel features of this war and its technology nor as incapable of adjusting to them as their numerous critics have maintained. Unfortunately, the Confederates did not have the time or opportunity that their opponents had to experiment with alternative strategies and objectives. Nevertheless, much of the evaluation of the Civil War generals has turned on this question of their relative ability to adapt and innovate.

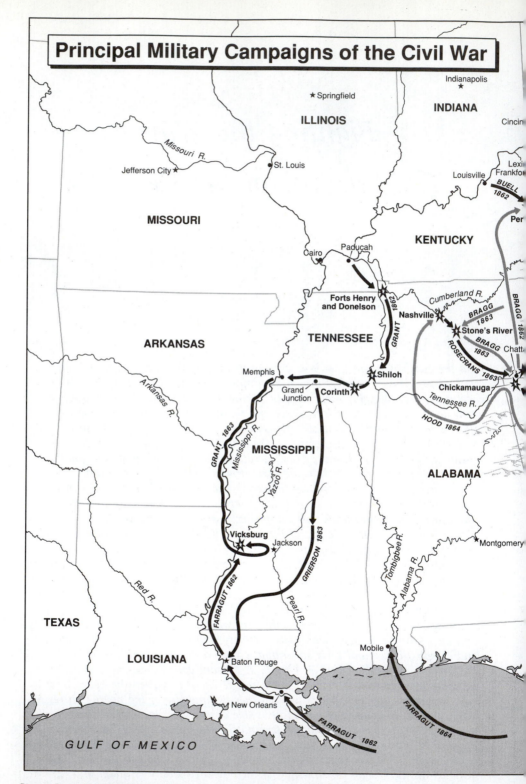

Principal Military Campaigns of the Civil War

Springfield

ILLINOIS

INDIANA

Indianapolis

Cincin

Missouri R.

Jefferson City

St. Louis

Louisville

Lexi
Frankfo

BUELL
1862

MISSOURI

KENTUCKY

Per

Cairo

Paducah

GRANT 1862

Forts Henry
and Donelson

Nashville

Cumberland R.

BRAGG
1863

BRAGG 1862

ARKANSAS

TENNESSEE

Stone's River

BRAGG
1863

Chatt

ROSECRANS 1863

Memphis

Grand
Junction

Corinth

Shiloh

Chickamauga

Arkansas R.

Tennessee R.

HOOD 1864

GRANT 1863

Mississippi R.

MISSISSIPPI

Yazoo R.

ALABAMA

Montgomery

Vicksburg

Jackson

GRIERSON 1863

Tombigbee R.

Alabama R.

FARRAGUT 1862

Pearl R.

Red R.

TEXAS

LOUISIANA

Baton Rouge

Mobile

FARRAGUT 1864

New Orleans

FARRAGUT 1862

GULF OF MEXICO

Source: James M. McPherson, *Ordeal by Fire* (New York: Knopf, 1982), inside front cover. By permission
of the publisher.

148

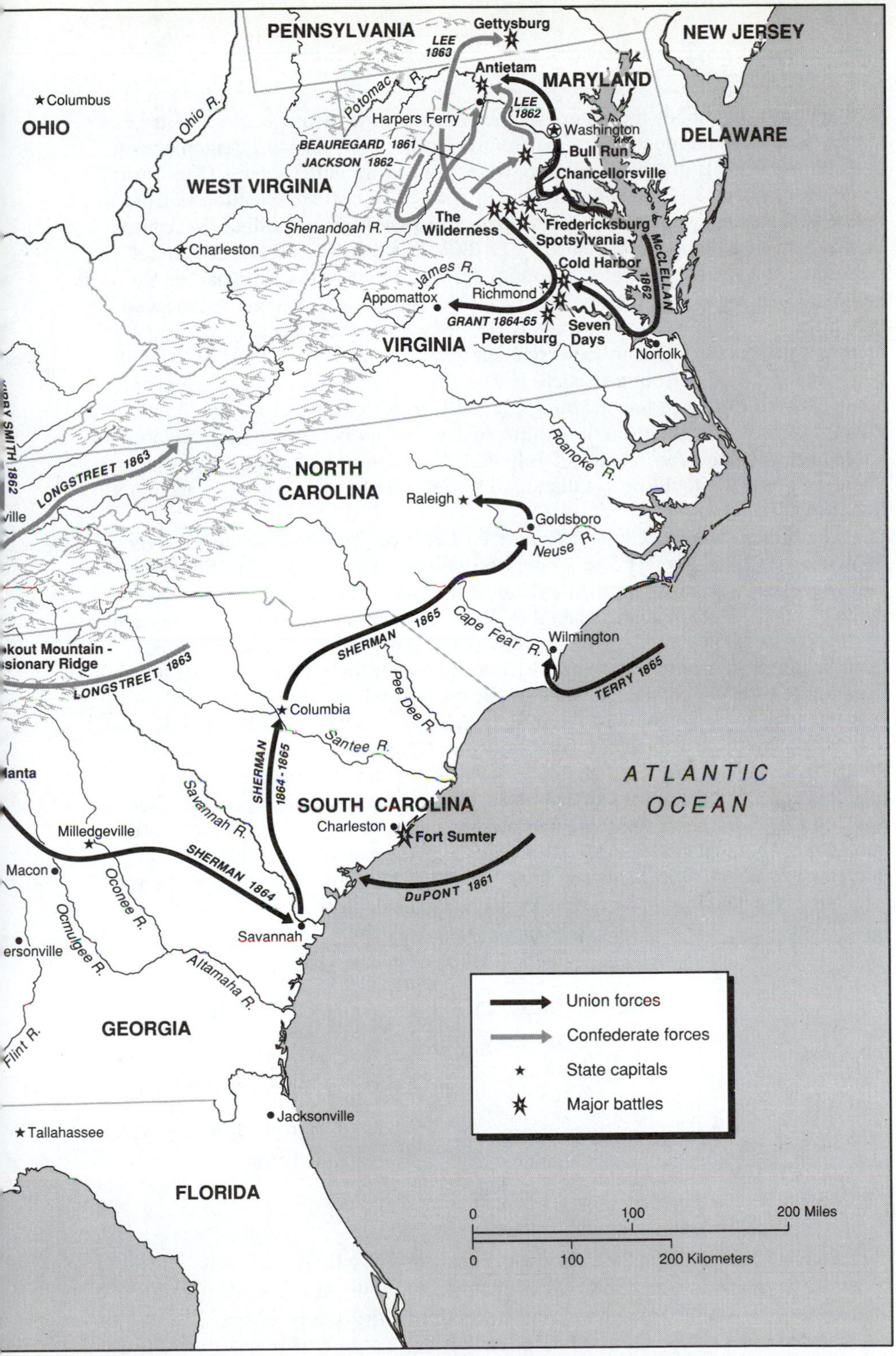
PENNSYLVANIA
Gettysburg
LEE 1863
NEW JERSEY
Antietam
MARYLAND
Columbus
OHIO
Potomac R.
Ohio R.
LEE 1862
Harpers Ferry
Washington
DELAWARE
BEAUREGARD 1861
Bull Run
JACKSON 1862
WEST VIRGINIA
Chancellorsville
The Wilderness
Fredericksburg
Shenandoah R.
Spotsylvania
Charleston
McCLELLAN 1862
Cold Harbor
James R.
Appomattox
Richmond
GRANT 1864-65
Seven Days
Petersburg
VIRGINIA
Norfolk
Roanoke R.
NORTH CAROLINA
LONGSTREET 1863
Raleigh
Goldsboro
Neuse R.
Cape Fear R.
SHERMAN 1865
Wilmington
Lookout Mountain - Missionary Ridge
LONGSTREET 1863
TERRY 1865
Columbia
Pee Dee R.
Santee R.
SHERMAN 1864-1865
ATLANTIC OCEAN
Savannah R.
SOUTH CAROLINA
Charleston
Fort Sumter
Milledgeville
SHERMAN 1864
Macon
DuPONT 1861
Oconee R.
Ocmulgee R.
Savannah
Altamaha R.
GEORGIA
Flint R.
Union forces
Confederate forces
State capitals
Major battles
Jacksonville
Tallahassee
FLORIDA
0
100
200 Miles
0
100
200 Kilometers

↘ *D O C U M E N T S*

Strategic thinking about the nature of the war and how to prosecute it is the subject matter of the documents that follow. In the first, Lincoln demonstrates early in the war his grasp of military strategy when he tells General Don Carlos Buell on January 13, 1862, what he has in mind. The second selection is from a report to Lincoln by George B. McClellan, the general commanding the United States Armies, submitted on January 31, 1862, in which the confident general assesses the two available strategic options for the Army of the Potomac in Virginia and concludes that the approach Lincoln prefers is less likely to succeed. While the Civil War was being fought, Karl Marx reported on it for several German newspapers. In the third selection, he offers insightful analyses of the military situation; one is from an article in *Die Presse* on March 27, 1862, and the other is taken from a letter of March 27, 1862, to his collaborator, Frederick Engels. General McClellan is the author of the fourth document, a confidential letter to his commander-in-chief of July 7, 1862, informing him what the war is about and how it should be conducted. This letter is known as "the Harrison's Landing letter."

The fifth document, General Robert E. Lee's dispatch to President Davis of September 3, 1863, reveals Lee's intention of embarking on a risky, but in his view necessary, offensive into Maryland, a dramatic example of the "offensive defense" that he advocated. General William T. Sherman's analysis of the nature of the war as it appeared to him by 1864 is the sixth selection, and it is taken from his angry response to a request from the mayor and council of Atlanta for leniency toward the civilian population. In the seventh document, General Joseph E. Johnston complains to General Dabney H. Maury on September 1, 1864, that his policy of disengagement in the face of Sherman's forces was wise and did not warrant his removal from command. In the next selection, an extract from his report of operations of February 15, 1865, Johnston's successor, General John B. Hood, explains why he believed that a change of tactics had been necessary. The final document presents General Ulysses S. Grant's report to Secretary of War Edwin M. Stanton of July 22, 1865, on his conduct of the war as general-in-chief from spring 1864 to the surrender a year later.

President Lincoln Discerns the Military Issues, January 1862

Executive Mansion,

Washington, Jan. 13, 1862.

Brig. Genl. Buell.

My dear Sir:

Your despatch of yesterday is received, in which you say "I have received your letter and Gen. McClellan's; and will, at once, devote all my efforts to your views, and his." In the midst of my many cares, I have not seen, or asked to see, Gen. McClellan's letter to you. For my own views, I have not offered, and do not now offer them as orders; and while I am glad to have them respectfully considered, I would blame you to follow them contrary to your own clear judgment—unless I should put them in the form of orders. As to Gen. McClellan's views, you understand your duty in regard to them better than I do. With this preliminary, I state my general idea of this war to be that we have the *greater* numbers, and the enemy has the *greater* facility of concentrating forces upon points of collision; that we must fail, unless we can find some way of making *our* advantage an overmatch for *his;* and that this can only be done by menacing him with superior forces at *different* points, at the *same* time; so that we can safely attack, one, or both, if he makes no change; and if he *weakens* one to *strengthen* the other, forbear to attack the strengthened one, but seize, and hold the weakened one, gaining so much. To illustrate, suppose last summer, when Winchester ran away to re-inforce Manassas, we had forborne to attack Manassas, but had seized and held Winchester. I mention this to illustrate, and not to criticise. I did not lose confidence in McDowell, and I think less harshly of Patterson than some others seem to.[1] In application of the general rule I am suggesting, every particular case will have its modifying circumstances, among which the most constantly present, and most difficult to meet, will be the want of perfect knowledge of the enemies' movements. This had it's part in the Bull-Run case; but worse, in that case, was the expiration of the terms of the three months men. Applying the principle to your case, my idea is that Halleck shall menace Columbus, and "down river" generally; while you menace Bowling-Green, and East Tennessee. If the enemy shall concentrate at Bowling-Green, do not retire from his front; yet do not fight him there, either, but seize Columbus and East Tennessee, one or both, left exposed by the concentration at Bowling Green. It is a matter of no small anxiety to me and one which I am sure you will not over-look, that the East Tennessee line, is so long, and over so bad a road.

Yours very truly

A. Lincoln

General George B. McClellan Submits His Plan for the Peninsula Campaign, February 1862

Head Quarters of the Army

Washington January 31st [February 3] 1862

Hon E M Stanton
Secty of War
Sir:

I ask your indulgence for the following paper, rendered necessary by circumstances. . . .

---

[1] Lincoln is here referring to events in July 1861, which culminated in the battle of Manassas, or Bull Run. In this campaign Irvin McDowell commanded the army which fought at Manassas and Robert Patterson commanded forces around Winchester in the Shenandoah Valley. The Confederates in the Valley eluded Patterson and joined the main army at Manassas.

When I was placed in command of the Armies of the U.S. I immediately turned my attention to the whole field of operations—regarding the Army of the Potomac as only *one,* while the most important, of the masses under my command.

I confess that I did not then appreciate the absence of a general plan which had before existed, nor did I know that utter disorganization & want of preparation pervaded the western armies. I took it for granted that they were nearly, if not quite, in condition to move towards the fulfillment of my plans—I acknowledge that I made a great mistake.

I sent at once, with the approval of the Executive, officers I considered competent to command in Kentucky & Missouri—their instructions looked to prompt movements. I soon found that the labor of creation & organization had to be performed there—transportation, arms, clothing, artillery, discipline—all were wanting; these things required time to procure them; the Generals in command have done their work most creditably—but we are still delayed. I had hoped that a general advance could be made during the good weather of December—I was mistaken.

My wish was to gain possession of the Eastern Tennessee Railroads as a preliminary movement,—then to follow it up immediately by an attack on Nashville & Richmond as nearly at the same time as possible.

I have ever regarded our true policy as being that of fully preparing ourselves & then seeking for the most decisive results;—I do not wish to waste life in useless battles, but prefer to strike at the heart.

Two bases of operations seem to present themselves for the advance of the Army of the Potomac.—

I. That of Washington—its present position—involving a direct attack upon the enemy's entrenched positions at Centreville, Manassas etc., or else a movement to turn one or both flanks of those positions, or a combination of the two plans. . . .

[This first plan was proposed by Lincoln. McClellan proceeds to describe the plan at length, and then turns to "II," his own proposal.]

II. The second base of operations available for the Army of the Potomac is that of the lower Chesapeake Bay, which affords the shortest possible land routes to Richmond, & strikes directly at the heart of the enemy's power in the East.

The roads in that region are passable at all seasons of the year.

The country now alluded to is much more favorable for offensive operations than that in front of Washington (which is *very* unfavorable)—much more level—more cleared land—the woods less dense—soil more sandy—the spring some two or three weeks earlier.

A movement in force on that line obliges the enemy to abandon his entrenched position at Manassas, in order to hasten to cover Richmond & Norfolk.

He *must* do this, for should he permit us to occupy Richmond his destruction can be averted only by entirely defeating us in a battle in which he must be the assailant.

This movement if successful gives us the Capital, the communications, the supplies of the rebels; Norfolk would fall; all the waters of the Chesapeake would be ours; all Virginia would be in our power; & the enemy forced to abandon Tennessee & North Carolina.

The alternatives presented to the enemy would be to beat us in a position selected by ourselves; disperse;—or pass beneath the Caudine Forks. Should we be beaten in a battle, we have a perfectly secure retreat down the Peninsula upon Fort Monroe, with our flanks perfectly secured by the fleet. During the whole movement our left flank is covered by the water, our right is secure for the reason that the enemy is too distant to reach us in time—he can only oppose us in front; we bring our fleet into full play.

After a successful battle our position would be—Burnside forming our left, Norfolk held securely, our centre connecting Burnside with Buell, both by Raleigh & Lynchburg, Buell in Eastern Tennessee & Northern Alabama, Halleck at Nashville & Memphis.

The next movement would be to connect with Sherman on the left, by reducing Wilmington & Charleston; to advance our centre into South Carolina & Georgia; to push Buell either towards Montgomery, or to unite with the main army in Georgia; to throw Halleck southward to meet the Naval Expedition at New Orleans.

We should then be in a condition to reduce at our leisure all the southern seaports; to occupy all the avenues of communication; to use the great outlet of the Mississippi; to reestablish our Govt & arms in Arkansas, Louisiana & Texas; to force the slaves to labor for our subsistence instead of that of the rebels;—to bid defiance to all foreign interference.

Such is the object I have ever had in view; this is the general plan which I have hoped to accomplish. For many long months I have labored to prepare the Army of the Potomac to play its part in the programme; from the day when I was placed in command of all our armies, I have exerted myself to place all the other armies in such a condition that they too could perform their allotted duties. Should it be determined to operate from the lower Chesapeake, the point of landing which promises the most brilliant results is Urbana on the lower Rappahannock.

This point is easily reached by vessels of heavy draught, it is neither occupied nor observed by the enemy; it is but one long march from West Point, the key to that region, & thence but two marches to Richmond.

A rapid movement from Urbana would probably cut off Magruder in the *Peninsula,* & enable us to occupy Richmond before it could be strongly reinforced. Should we fail in that we could, with the cooperation of the Navy, cross the James & throw ourselves in rear of Richmond, thus forcing the enemy to come out & attack us—for his position would be untenable, with us on the southern bank of the river.

Should circumstances render it not advisable to land at Urbana we can use Mob Jack Bay,—or—the worst coming to the worst—we can take

Fort Monroe as a base, & operate with complete security, altho' with less celerity & brilliancy of results, up the Peninsula.

To reach whatever point may be selected as the base, a large amount of cheap water transportation must be collected—consisting mainly of canal boats, barges, wood boats, schooners etc. towed by small steamers—all of a very different character from those required for all previous expeditions. This can certainly be accomplished within 30 days from the time the order is given.

I propose, as the best possible plan that can, in my judgment, be adopted, to select Urbana as the landing place of the first detachments. To transport by water four (4) Divisions of Infantry, with their batteries, the Regular Infty, a few wagons, one bridge train & a few squadrons of Cavalry—making the vicinity of Hooker's position the place of embarkation for as many as possible. To move the Regular Cavalry, & Reserve Artillery, the remaining bridge trains, & wagons to a point somewhere near Cape Lookout, then ferry them over the river by means of North River ferry boats, march them over to the Rappahannock (covering the movement by an Infantry force placed near Heathsville), cross the Rappahannock in a similar way.

The expense & difficulty of the movement will thus be much diminished (a saving of transportation of about 10,000 horses!), & the result none the less certain.

The concentration of the Cavalry etc. in the lower counties of Maryland can be effected without exciting suspicion, & the movement made without delay from that cause.

This movement, if adopted, will not at all expose the city of Washington to danger.

The total force to be thrown upon the new line would be (according to circumstances) from 110,000 to 140,000. I hope to use the latter number, by bringing fresh troops into Washington, & still leaving it quite safe.

I fully realize that, in all projects offered, time is probably the most valuable consideration—it is my decided opinion that in that point of view the 2nd plan should be adopted. It is possible, nay highly probable, that the weather & state of the roads may be such as to delay the direct movement from Washington, with its unsatisfactory results & great risks, far beyond the time required to complete the second plan. *In the first case,* we can fix no definite time for an advance—the roads have gone from bad to worse—nothing like their present condition has ever been known here before—they are impassable at present, we are entirely at the mercy of the weather. In the second plan, we can calculate almost to a day, & with but little regard to the season.

If at the expense of 30 days delay we can gain a decisive victory which will probably end the war, it is far cheaper than to gain a battle tomorrow that produces no final results, & may require years of warfare & expenditure to follow up.

Such, I think, is precisely the difference between the two plans discussed in this long letter. A battle gained at Manassas will result merely in the possession of the field of combat—at best we can follow it up but slowly, unless we do what I now propose, viz:—change the line of operations.

On the Manassas line the rebels can, if well enough disciplined (& we have every reason to suppose that to be the case) dispute our advance, over bad roads, from position to position.

When we have gained the battle, if we do gain it, the question will at once arise—"What are we to do next?"—

It is by no means certain that we can beat them at Manassas.

On the other line I regard success as certain by all the chances of war.

We demoralize the enemy, by forcing him to abandon his prepared position for one which we have chosen, in which all is in our favor, & where success must produce immense results. My judgment as a General is clearly in favor of this project.

Nothing is *certain* in war—but all the chances are in favor of this movement.

So much am I in favor of the southern line of operations, that I would prefer the move from Fort Monroe as a base, as a certain, tho' less brilliant movement than that from Urbana, to an attack on Manassas.

I know that his Excellency the President, you & I all agree in our wishes—& that our desire is to bring this war to as prompt a close as the means in our possession will permit. I believe that the mass of the people have entire confidence in us—I am sure of it—let us then look only to the great result to be accomplished, & disregard everything else.

In conclusion I would respectfully, but firmly, advise that I may be authorized to undertake at once the movement by Urbana.

I believe that it can be carried into execution so nearly simultaneously with the final advance of Buell & Halleck that the columns will support each other.

I will stake my life, my reputation on the result—more than that, I will stake upon it the success of our cause.

I hope but little from the attack on Manassas;—my judgment is against it. Foreign complications may entirely change the state of affairs, & render very different plans necessary. In that event I will be ready to submit them.

I am very respectfully your obedient servant

Geo B McClellan
Maj Genl Comdg USA

Karl Marx Discusses Grand Strategy, 1862

I.

Up to the capture of Nashville no concerted strategy between the army of Kentucky and the army on the Potomac was possible. They were too far apart from one another. They stood in the same front line, but their lines of operation were entirely different. Only with the victorious advance into Tennessee did the movements of the army of Kentucky become important for the entire theater of war.

The American papers influenced by McClellan are going great guns with the "anaconda" envelopment theory. According to this an immense line of armies is to wind round the rebellion, gradually constrict its coils and finally strangle the enemy. This is sheer childishness. It is a rehash of the so-called *"cordon system"* devised in Austria about 1770, which was employed against the French from 1792 to 1797 with such great obstinacy and with such constant failure. At Jemappes, Fleurus and, more especially, at Moutenotte, Millesimo, Dego, Castiglione and Rivoli, the knock-out blow was dealt to this system. The French cut the "anaconda" in two by attacking at a point where they had concentrated superior forces. Then the coils of the "anaconda" were cut to pieces seriatim.

In well populated and more or less centralized states there is always a center, with the occupation of which by the foe the national resistance would be broken. Paris is a shining example. The slave states, however, possess no such center. They are thinly populated, with few large towns and all these on the seacoast. The question therefore arises: Does a military center of gravity nevertheless exist, with the capture of which the backbone of their resistance breaks, or are they, as Russia still was in 1812, not to be conquered without occupying every village and every plot of land, in a word, the entire periphery? Cast a glance at the geographical formation of *Secessia,* with its long stretch of coast on the Atlantic Ocean and its long stretch of coast on the Gulf of Mexico. So long as the Confederates held Kentucky and Tennessee, the whole formed a great compact mass. The loss of both these states drives an immense wedge into their territory, separating the states on the North Atlantic Ocean from the states on the Gulf of Mexico. The direct route from Virginia and the two Carolinas to Texas, Louisiana, Mississippi and even, in part, to Alabama leads through Tennessee, which is now occupied by the Unionists. The *sole* route that, after the complete conquest of Tennessee by the Union, connects the two sections of the slave states goes through Georgia. This proves that *Georgia is the key to Secessia*. With the loss of Georgia the Confederacy would be cut into two sections which would have lost all connection with one another. A reconquest of Georgia by the Secessionists, however, would be almost unthinkable, for the Unionist fighting forces would be concentrated in a center position, while their adversaries, divided into two camps, would have scarcely sufficient forces to summon to a united attack.

Would the conquest of all Georgia, with the seacoast of Florida, be requisite for such an operation? By no means. In a land where communication, particularly between distant points, depends more on railways than on highways, the seizure of the railways is sufficient. The southernmost railway line between the states on the Gulf of Mexico and the Atlantic coast goes through Macon and Gordon near Milledgeville.

The occupation of these two points would accordingly cut *Secessia* in two and enable the Unionists to beat one part after another. At the same time, one gathers from the above that no Southern republic is capable of living without the possession of Tennessee. Without Tennessee, Georgia's vital spot lies only eight or ten days' march from the frontier; the North would constantly have its hand at the throat of the South, and on the slightest pressure the South would have to yield or fight for its life anew, under circumstances in which a single defeat would cut off every prospect of success.

From the foregoing considerations it follows:

The Potomac is *not* the most important position of the war theater. The taking of Richmond and the advance of the Potomac army further South—difficult on account of the many streams that cut across the line of march—could produce a tremendous moral effect. From a purely military standpoint, they would decide *nothing*.

The decision of the campaign belongs to the Kentucky army, now in Tennessee. On the one hand, this army is nearest the decisive points; on the other hand, it occupies a territory without which Secession is incapable of living. This army would accordingly have to be strengthened at the expense of all the rest and the sacrifice of all minor operations. Its next points of attack would be Chattanooga and Dalton on the Upper Tennessee, the most important railway centers of the entire South. After their occupation the connection between the eastern and western states of *Secessia* would be limited to the connecting lines in Georgia. The further question would then arise of cutting off another railway line with Atlanta and Georgia, and finally of destroying the last connection between the two sections by the capture of Macon and Gordon.

On the contrary, should the "anaconda" plan be followed, then despite all successes in particular cases and even on the Potomac, the war may be prolonged indefinitely, while the financial difficulties together with diplomatic complications acquire fresh scope.

Die Presse, [Vienna] March 27, 1862.

II. Marx to Engels

August 7, 1862

I do not altogether share your views on the American Civil War. I do not think that all is up. The Northerners have been dominated from the first by the representatives of the border slave states, who also pushed McClellan, that old partisan of Breckinridge, to the top. The Southerners, on the other hand, acted as one man from the beginning. The North itself has turned the slaves into a military force on the side of the Southerners, instead of turning it against them. The South leaves productive labor to the slaves and could therefore put its whole fighting strength in the field without disturbance. The South had unified military leadership, the North had not. That no strategic plan existed was already obvious from all the maneuvers of the Kentucky army after the conquest of Tennessee. In my opinion all this will take another turn. In the end the North will make war seriously, adopt revolutionary methods and throw over the domination of the border slave statesmen. A single Negro regiment would have a remarkable effect on Southern nerves.

The difficulty of getting the 300,000 men seems to me purely political. The Northwest and New England wish to and will force the government to give up the diplomatic method of conducting war which it has used hitherto, and they are now making terms on which the 300,000 men shall come forth. If Lincoln does not give way (which he will do, however), there will be a revolution.

As to the lack of military talent, the method which has prevailed up till now of selecting generals purely from considerations of diplomacy and party intrigue is scarcely designed to bring talent to the front. General Pope seems to me to be a man of energy, however.

With regard to the financial measures, they are clumsy, as they are bound to be in a country where up to now no taxes (for the whole state) have in fact existed; but they are not nearly so idiotic as the measures taken by Pitt and Co. The present depreciation of money is due, I think, not to economic but to purely political reasons—distrust. It will therefore change with a different policy.

The long and short of the business seems to me to be that a war of this kind must be conducted on revolutionary lines, while the Yankees have so far been trying to conduct it constitutionally.

General McClellan Gives a Lesson
in Grand Strategy, July 1862

Head Quarters, Army of the Potomac
Camp near Harrison's Landing, Va. July 7th 1862

(Confidential)

Mr President

You have been fully informed, that the Rebel army is in our front, with the purpose of overwhelming us by attacking our positions or reducing us by blocking our river communications. I can not but regard our condition as critical and I earnestly desire, in view of possible contingencies, to lay before your Excellency, for your private consideration, my general views concerning the existing state of the rebellion; although they do not strictly relate to the situation of this Army or strictly come within the scope of my official duties. These views amount to convictions and are deeply impressed upon my mind and heart.

Our cause must never be abandoned; it is the cause of free institutions and self government. The Constitution and the Union must be preserved, whatever may be the cost in time, treasure and blood. If secession is successful, other dissolutions are clearly to be seen in the future. Let neither military disaster, political faction or foreign war shake your settled purpose to enforce the equal operation of the laws of the United States upon the people of every state.

The time has come when the Government must determine upon a civil and military policy, covering the whole ground of our national trouble. The responsibility of determining, declaring and supporting such civil and military policy and of directing the whole course of national affairs in regard to the rebellion, must now be assumed and exercised by you or our cause will be lost. The Constitution gives you power sufficient even for the present terrible exigency.

This rebellion has assumed the character of a War; as such it should be regarded; and it should be conducted upon the highest principles known to Christian Civilization. It should not be a War looking to the subjugation of the people of any state, in any event. It should not be, at all, a War upon population; but against armed forces and political organizations. Neither confiscation of property, political executions of persons, territorial organization of states or forcible abolition of slavery should be contemplated for a moment. In prosecuting the War, all private property and unarmed persons should be strictly protected; subject only to the necessities of military operations. All private property taken for military use should be paid or receipted for; pillage and waste should be treated as high crimes; all unnecessary trespass sternly prohibited; and offensive demeanor by the military towards citizens promptly rebuked. Military arrests should not be tolerated, except in places where active hostilities exist; and oaths not required by enactments—Constitutionally made—should be neither demanded nor received. Military government should be confined to the preservation of public order and the protection of political rights.

Military power should not be allowed to interfere with the relations of servitude, either by supporting or impairing the authority of the master; except for repressing disorder as in other cases. Slaves contraband under the Act of Congress, seeking military protection, should receive it. The right of the Government to appropriate permanently to its own service claims to slave labor should be asserted and the right of the owner to compensation therefore should be recognized. This principle might be extended upon grounds of military necessity and security to all the slaves within a particular state; thus working manumission in such state—and in Missouri, perhaps in Western Virginia also and possibly even in Maryland the expediency of such a military measure is only a question of time. A system of policy thus constitutional and conservative, and pervaded by the influences of Christianity and freedom, would receive the support of almost all truly loyal men, would deeply impress the rebel masses and all foreign nations, and it might be humbly hoped that it would commend itself to the favor of the Almighty. Unless the principles governing the further conduct of our struggle shall be made known and approved, the effort to obtain requisite forces will be almost hopeless. A declaration of radical views, especially upon slavery, will rapidly disintegrate our present Armies.

The policy of the Government must be supported by concentrations of military power. The national forces should not be dispersed in expeditions, posts of occupation and numerous Armies; but should be mainly collected into masses and brought to bear upon the Armies of the Confederate States;

those Armies thoroughly defeated, the political structure which they support would soon cease to exist.

In carrying out any system of policy which you may form, you will require a Commander in Chief of the Army; one who possesses your confidence, understands your views and who is competent to execute your orders by directing the military forces of the Nation to the accomplishment of the objects by you proposed. I do not ask that place for myself. I am willing to serve you in such position as you may assign me and I will do so as faithfully as ever subordinate served superior.

I may be on the brink of eternity and as I hope forgiveness from my maker I have written this letter with sincerity towards you and from love for my country.

Very respectfully your obdt svt

Geo B McClellan
Maj Genl Comdg

His Excellency A Lincoln
Presdt U.S.

General Robert E. Lee Takes the Offensive, September 1862

Headquarters, Alexandria & Leesburg Road
Near Dranesville, September 3, 1862

Mr. President:

The present seems to be the most propitious time since the commencement of the war for the Confederate Army to enter Maryland. The two grand armies of the United States that have been operating in Virginia, though now united, are much weakened and demoralized. Their new levies, of which I understand sixty thousand men have already been posted in Washington, are not yet organized, and will take some time to prepare for the field. If it is ever desired to give material aid to Maryland and afford her an opportunity of throwing off the oppression to which she is now subject, this would seem the most favorable. After the enemy had disappeared from the vicinity of Fairfax Court House and taken the road to Alexandria & Washington, I did not think it would be advantageous to follow him farther. I had no intention of attacking him in his fortifications, and am not prepared to invest them. If I possessed the necessary munitions, I should be unable to supply provisions for the troops. I therefore determined while threatening the approaches to Washington, to draw the troops into Loudoun, where forage and some provisions can be obtained, menace their possession of the Shenandoah Valley, and if found practicable, to cross into Maryland.

The purpose, if discovered, will have the effect of carrying the enemy north of the Potomac, and if prevented, will not result in much evil. The army is not properly equipped for an invasion of an enemy's territory. It lacks much of the material of war, is feeble in transportation, the animals being much reduced, and the men are poorly provided with clothes, and in thousands of instances are destitute of shoes. Still we cannot afford to be idle, and though weaker than our opponents in men and military equipments, must endeavor to harass, if we cannot destroy them. I am aware that the movement is attended with much risk, yet I do not consider success impossible, and shall endeavor to guard it from loss. As long as the army of the enemy are employed on this frontier I have no fears for the safety of Richmond, yet I earnestly recommend that advantage be taken of this period of comparative safety to place its defence, both by land and water, in the most perfect condition. A respectable force can be collected to defend its approaches by land, and the steamer *Richmond* I hope is now ready to clear the river of hostile vessels. Should Genl [Braxton] Bragg find it impracticable to operate to advantage on his present frontier, his army, after leaving sufficient garrisons, could be advantageously employed in opposing the overwhelming numbers which it seems to be the intention of the enemy now to concentrate in Virginia. I have already been told by prisoners that some of [General Don Carlos] Buell's cavalry have been joined to Genl Pope's army, and have reason to believe that the whole of McClellan's, the larger portions of Burnside's & Cox's and a portion of [General David] Hunter's, are united to it. What occasions me most concern is the fear of getting out of ammunition. I beg you will instruct the Ordnance Department to spare no pains in manufacturing a sufficient amount of the best kind, & to be particular in preparing that for the artillery, to provide three times as much of the long range ammunition as of that for smooth bore or short range guns.

The points to which I desire the ammunition to be forwarded will be made known to the Department in time. If the Quartermaster Department can furnish any shoes, it would be the greatest relief.

We have entered upon September, and the nights are becoming cool.

> I have the honor to be with high respect, your ob't servant
>
> R. E. Lee
> *Genl*

General William T. Sherman Explains How the War Has Changed, September 1864

> Headquarters Military Division of the Mississippi,
> in the Field, Atlanta, Georgia, September 12, 1864.

JAMES M. CALHOUN, Mayor, E. E. RAWSON and S. C. WELLS, representing City Council of Atlanta.

Gentlemen: I have your letter of the 11th, in the nature of a petition to revoke my orders removing all the inhabitants from Atlanta. I have read it carefully, and give full credit to your statements of the distress that will be occasioned, and yet shall not revoke my orders, because they were not designed to meet the humanities of the case, but to prepare for the future struggles in which millions of good people outside of Atlanta have a deep interest. We must have peace, not only at Atlanta, but in all America. To secure this, we must stop the war that now desolates our once happy and favored country. To stop war, we must defeat the rebel armies which are arrayed against the laws and Constitution that all must respect and obey. To defeat those armies, we must prepare the way to reach them in their recesses, provided with the arms and instruments which enable us to accomplish our purpose. Now, I know the vindictive nature of our enemy, that we may have many years of military operations from this quarter; and, therefore, deem it wise and prudent to prepare in time. The use of Atlanta for warlike purposes is inconsistent with its character as a home for families. There will be no manufactures, commerce, or agriculture here, for the maintenance of families, and sooner or later want will compel the inhabitants to go. Why not go now, when all the arrangements are completed for the transfer, instead of waiting till the plunging shot of contending armies will renew the scenes of the past month? Of course, I do not apprehend any such thing at this moment, but you do not suppose this army will be here until the war is over. I cannot discuss this subject with you fairly, because I cannot impart to you what we propose to do, but I assert that our military plans make it necessary for the inhabitants to go away, and I can only renew my offer of services to make their exodus in any direction as easy and comfortable as possible.

You cannot qualify war in harsher terms than I will. War is cruelty, and you cannot refine it; and those who brought war into our country deserve all the curses and maledictions a people can pour out. I know I had no hand in making this war, and I know I will make more sacrifices to-day than any of you to secure peace. But you cannot have peace and a division of our country. If the United States submits to a division now, it will not stop, but will go on until we reap the fate of Mexico, which is eternal war. The United States does and must assert its authority, wherever it once had power; for, if it relaxes one bit to pressure, it is gone, and I believe that such is the national feeling. This feeling assumes various shapes, but always comes back to that of Union. Once admit the Union, once more acknowledge the authority of the national Government, and, instead of devoting your houses and streets and roads to the dread uses of war, I and this army become at once your protectors and supporters, shielding you from danger, let it come from what quarter it may. I know that a few individuals cannot resist a torrent of error and passion, such as swept the South into rebellion, but you can point out, so that we may know those who desire a government, and those who insist on war and its desolation.

You might as well appeal against the thunder-storm as against these terrible hardships of war. They are inevitable, and the only way the people of Atlanta can hope once more to live in peace and quiet at home, is to stop the war, which can only be done by admitting that it began in error and is perpetuated in pride.

We don't want your negroes, or your horses, or your houses, or your lands, or any thing you have, but we do want and will have a just obedience to the laws of the United States. That we will have, and, if it involves the destruction of your improvements, we cannot help it.

You have heretofore read public sentiment in your newspapers, that live by falsehood and excitement; and the quicker you seek for truth in other quarters, the better. I repeat then that, by the original compact of Government, the United States had certain rights in Georgia, which have never been relinquished and never will be; that the South began war by seizing forts, arsenals, mints, custom-houses, etc., etc., long before Mr. Lincoln was installed, and before the South had one jot or tittle of provocation. I myself have seen in Missouri, Kentucky, Tennessee, and Mississippi, hundreds and thousands of women and children fleeing from your armies and desperadoes, hungry and with bleeding feet. In Memphis, Vicksburg, and Mississippi, we fed thousands upon thousands of the families of rebel soldiers left on our hands, and whom we could not see starve. Now that war comes home to you, you feel very different. You deprecate its horrors, but did not feel them when you sent car-loads of soldiers and ammunition, and moulded shells and shot, to carry war into Kentucky and Tennessee, to desolate the homes of hundreds and thousands of good people who only asked to live in peace at their old homes, and under the Government of their inheritance. But these comparisons are idle. I want peace, and believe it can only be reached through union and war, and I will ever conduct war with a view to perfect and early success.

But, my dear sirs, when peace does come, you may call on me for any thing. Then will I share with you the last cracker, and watch with you to shield your homes and families against danger from every quarter.

Now you must go, and take with you the old and feeble, feed and nurse them, and build for them, in more quiet places, proper habitations to shield them against the weather until the mad passions of men cool down, and allow the Union and peace once more to settle over your old homes at Atlanta. Yours in haste,

W. T. Sherman, *Major-General commanding*.

General Joseph E. Johnston Defends His Strategy
of Disengagement, September 1864

Macon, Ga., September 1st, 1864

My Dear Maury:

I have been intending ever since my arrival at this place to pay a part of the epistolary debt I owe you. But you know how lazy it makes one to have nothing to do, and so with the hot weather we have been enduring here, I have absolutely devoted myself to idleness. I have been disposed to write more particularly of what concerns myself—to explain to you, as far as practicable, the operations for which I was laid on the shelf, for you are one of the last whose unfavorable opinion I would be willing to incur.

You know that the army I commanded was that which, under General Bragg, was routed at Missionary Ridge. Sherman's army was that which routed it, reinforced by the Sixteenth and Twenty-third Corps. I am censured for not taking the offensive at Dalton—where the enemy, if beaten, had a secure refuge behind the fortified gap at Ringgold, or in the fortress of Chattanooga, and where the odds against us were almost ten to four. At Resaca he received five brigades, near Kingston three, and about 3500 cavalry; at New Hope Church one; in all about 14,000 infantry and artillery. The enemy received the Seventeenth Corps and a number of garrisons and bridge guards from Tennessee and Kentucky that had been relieved by "hundred-day men."

I am blamed for not fighting. Operations commenced about the 6th of May; I was relieved on the 18th of July. In that time we fought daily, always under circumstances so favorable to us as to make it certain that the sum of the enemy's losses was five times ours, which was 10,000 men. Northern papers represented theirs up to about the end of June at 45,000. Sherman's progress was at the rate of a mile and a quarter a day. Had this style of fighting been allowed to continue, it is not clear that we would soon have been able to give battle with abundant chances of victory, and that the enemy, beaten on this side of the Chattahoochee, would have been destroyed? It is certain that Sherman's army was stronger, compared with that of Tennessee, than Grant's, compared with that of Northern Virginia. General Bragg asserts that Sherman's was absolutely stronger than Grant's. It is well known that the army of Virginia was much superior to that of Tennessee.

Why, then, should I be condemned for the defensive while General Lee was adding to his great fame by the same course? General Bragg seems to have earned at Missionary Ridge his present high position. People report at Columbus and Montgomery that General Bragg said that my losses had been frightful; that I had disregarded the wishes and instructions of the President; that he had in vain implored me to change my course, by which I suppose is meant assume the offensive.

As these things are utterly untrue, it is not to be supposed that they were said by General Bragg. The President gave me no instructions and expressed no wishes except just before we reached the Chattahoochee, warning me not to fight with the river behind us and against crossing it, and previously he urged me not to allow Sherman to detach to Grant's aid. General Bragg passed some ten hours with me just before I was relieved, and gave me the impression that his visit to the army was casual, he being on his way further west to endeavor to get us reinforcements from Kirby Smith and Lee. I thought him satisfied with the state of things, but not so with that in Virginia. He assured me that he had always maintained in Richmond that Sherman's army was stronger than Grant's. He said nothing of the intention to relieve me, but talked with General Hood on the subject, as I learned after my removal. It is clear that his expedition had no other object than my removal and the giving proper direction to public opinion on the subject. He could have had no other object in going to Montgomery. A man of honor in his place would have communicated with me as well as with Hood on the subject. Being expected to assume the offensive, he attacked on the 20th, 22d, and 28th of July, disastrously, losing more men than I had done in seventy-two days. Since then his defensive has been at least as quiet as mine was.

Very truly yours,

J. E. Johnston

Major-General Maury

General John B. Hood Criticizes Johnston's Strategy, February 1865

Report of General John B. Hood, C. S. Army, commanding Army of Tennessee, of operations July 18–September 6.

Richmond, Va., February 15, 1865.

General: I have the honor to submit the following report of the operations of the Army of Tennessee while commanded by me, from July 18, 1864, to January 23, 1865:

The results of a campaign do not always show how the general in command has discharged his duty. The inquiry should be not what he has done, but what he should have accomplished with the means under his control. To appreciate the operations of the Army of Tennessee it is necessary to look at its history during the three months which preceded the day on which I was ordered to its command. To do this it is necessary either to state in this report all the facts which illustrate the entire operations of the Army of Tennessee in the recent campaign, or to write a supplemental or accompanying report. I deem the former more appropriate, and will, therefore, submit in a single paper all the information which seems to me should be communicated to the Government.

On the 6th of May, 1864, the army lay at and near Dalton awaiting the advance of the enemy. Never had so large a Confederate army assembled in the West. Seventy thousand effective men were in the easy direction of a single commander, whose good fortune it was to be able to give successful battle and redeem the losses of the past. Extraordinary efforts had been used to secure easy victory. The South had been denuded of troops to fill the strength of the Army of Tennessee. Mississippi and Alabama were without military support, and looked for protection in decisive battle in the mountains of Georgia. The vast forces of the enemy were accumulating in the East, and to retard their advance or confuse their plans, much was expected by a counter-movement by us in the West. The desires of the Government expressed to the Confederate commander in the West were to assume the offensive. Nearly all the men and resources of the West and South were placed at his disposal for the purpose. The men amounted to the number already stated, and the resources for their support were equal to the demand. The re-enforcements were within supporting distance. The troops felt strong in their increased numbers, saw the means and arrangements to move forward and recover (not abandon) our own territory, and believed that victory might be achieved. In such condition was that splendid army when the active campaign fairly opened. The enemy, but little superior in numbers, none in organization and discipline, inferior in spirit and confidence, commenced his advance. The Confederate forces, whose faces and hopes were to the North, almost simultaneously commenced to retreat. They soon reached positions favorable for resistance. Great ranges of mountains running across the line of march and deep rivers are stands from which a well-directed army is not easily driven or turned. At each advance of the enemy the Confederate army, without serious resistance, fell back to the next range or river in the rear. This habit to retreat soon became a routine of the army, and was substituted for the hope and confidence with which the campaign opened. The enemy soon perceived this. With perfect security he divided his forces, using one column to menace in front and one to threaten in rear. The usual order to retreat, not strike in detail, was issued and obeyed. These retreats were always at night; the day was consumed in hard labor. Daily temporary works were thrown up, behind which it was never intended to fight. The men became travelers by night and laborers by day. They were ceasing to be soldiers by the disuse of military duty. Thus for seventy-four days and nights that noble army—if ordered to resist, no force that the enemy could assemble could dislodge from a battle-field—continued to abandon their country, to see their strength departing, and their flag waving only in retreat or in partial engagements. At the end of that time, after descending from the mountains when the last advantage of position was abandoned, and camping without fortifications on the open plains of Georgia, the army had lost 22,750 of its best soldiers. Nearly one-third was gone, no general battle fought, much of our State abandoned, two others uncovered, and the organization and efficiency of every command, by loss of officers, men, and tone, seriously diminished. These things were the inevitable result of the strategy adopted. It is impossible for a large army to retreat in the face of a pursuing enemy without such a fate. In a retreat the losses are constant and permanent. Stragglers are overtaken, the fatigued fall by the wayside, and are gathered by the advancing enemy. Every position by the rear guard, if taken, yields its wounded to the victors. The soldiers, always awaked from rest at night to continue the retreat, leave many of their comrades asleep in trenches. The losses of a single day are not large. Those of seventy-four days will embrace the strength of an army. If a battle be fought and the field held at the close, however great the slaughter, the loss will be less than to retreat in the face of an enemy. There will be no stragglers. Desertions are in retreat; rarely, if ever, on the field of battle. The wounded are gathered to the rear and soon recover, and in a few weeks the entire loss consists only of the killed and permanently disabled, which is not one-fifth of the apparent loss on the night of the battle. The enemy is checked, his plans deranged, territory saved, the campaign suspended or won. If a retreat still be necessary it can then be done with no enemy pressing and no loss following. The advancing party loses nothing but its killed and permanently disabled. Neither straggler nor deserter thins its ranks. It reaches the end of its march stronger for battle than when it started. The army commanded by General Sherman and that commanded by General Johnston, not greatly unequal at the commencement of the campaign, illustrate what I have written. General Sherman in his official report states that his forces, when they entered Atlanta, were nearly the same in number as when they left Dalton. The Army of Tennessee lost 22,750 men, nearly one-third of its strength. I have nothing to say of the statement of losses made by General Johnston in his official report, except to state that by his own figures he understates his loss some thousands; that he excludes the idea of any prisoners, although his previous official returns show more than 7,000 under the head "absent without leave," and that the returns of the army while he was in command, corrected and increased by the records of the army, which has not been fully reported to the Government, and the return signed by me, but made up under him as soon as I assumed command, show the losses of the Army of Tennessee to be what I have stated, and a careful examination of the returns with the army will show the losses to be more than stated. . . .

General Ulysses S. Grant Reports His Assignment Accomplished, July 1865

Report of Lieutenant-General U. S. Grant,
of the United States Armies—1864–'65

Headquarters Armies of the United States,
Washington, D. C., July 22, 1865.

Hon. E. M. Stanton, Secretary of War.

Sir:—I have the honor to submit the following report of the operations of the Armies of the United States from the date of my appointment to command the same.

From an early period in the rebellion I had been impressed with the idea that active and continuous operations of all the troops that could be brought into the field, regardless of season and weather, were necessary to a speedy termination of the war. The resources of the enemy and his numerical strength were far inferior to ours; but as an offset to this, we had a vast territory, with a population hostile to the government, to garrison, and long lines of river and railroad communications to protect, to enable us to supply the operating armies.

The armies in the East and West acted independently and without concert, like a balky team, no two ever pulling together, enabling the enemy to use to great advantage his interior lines of communication for transporting troops from East to West, reinforcing the army most vigorously pressed, and to furlough large numbers, during seasons of inactivity on our part, to go to their homes and do the work of producing, for the support of their armies. It was a question whether our numerical strength and resources were not more than balanced by these disadvantages and the enemy's superior position.

From the first, I was firm in the conviction that no peace could be had that would be stable and conducive to the happiness of the people, both North and South, until the military power of the rebellion was entirely broken.

I therefore determined, first, to use the greatest number of troops practicable against the armed force of the enemy; preventing him from using the same force at different seasons against first one and then another of our armies, and the possibility of repose for refitting and producing necessary supplies for carrying on resistance. Second, to hammer continuously against the armed force of the enemy and his resources, until by mere attrition, if in no other way, there should be nothing left to him but an equal submission with the loyal section of our common country to the constitution and laws of the land.

These views have been kept constantly in mind, and orders given and campaigns made to carry them out. Whether they might have been better in conception and execution is for the people, who mourn the loss of friends fallen, and who have to pay the pecuniary cost, to say. All I can say is, that what I have done has been done conscientiously, to the best of my ability, and in what I conceived to be for the best interests of the whole country. . . .

ESSAYS

An examination of the two leading generals can yield an appreciation of the way each side fought the Civil War. In the first essay, Russell F. Weigley of Temple University offers a critical analysis of Robert E. Lee's abilities as strategist and commander. The second selection, by the late Bruce Catton, is a defense of Ulysses S. Grant against his detractors, who have claimed that he lacked strategic insight and simply slogged his way to victory.

Robert E. Lee: Napoleon of the Confederacy

RUSSELL F. WEIGLEY

On March 2, 1862, Davis called Lee back to Richmond to resume his place of the previous summer, as confidential military adviser at the President's side. The strategy of mere defense had crumbled in the Mississippi Valley during the previous month, when the Federals broke through the defensive line of the Ohio River and went far toward detaching Tennessee as well as Kentucky from the Confederacy by utilizing their naval power again, this time to steam up the Tennessee and Cumberland rivers and in conjunction with the Union Army to capture Forts Henry and Donelson which guarded the routes into the state of Tennessee. When Lee arrived in Richmond, no fewer than four separate Federal forces were forming to threaten Virginia and the Confederate capital, from Washington, from Fort Monroe at the tip of the Peninsula between the James and York rivers, from Winchester in the Shenandoah Valley, and from the western counties beyond the Allegheny Mountains. By dividing the Southern forces to try to confront each of these Federal groupings, the Confederacy with its inferior numbers merely made each detachment so thin that each was threatened with engulfment.

In these circumstances, Lee concluded that the only salvation for the Confederacy was to concentrate its forces and attack. "It is only by concentration of our troops," he was to say, "that we can hope to win any decisive advantage." ". . . we must decide between the positive loss of inactivity and the risk of action."

The risk of action: the Confederacy, Lee believed, must go from a defensive strategy to an offensive-defensive, attacking at some chosen point or points and causing the war to focus there in order to prevent the enemy from attacking everywhere. In Virginia's peril against multiple Federal threats in the spring of 1862, and as Federal activity on the Peninsula between the York and the James took shape as the principal threat, his solution in part was to urge a junction of as many as possible of the troops facing western Virginia and on the Rappahannock line opposite Washington with the force in the Shenandoah Valley, so that the latter might mount an offensive. This course involved the risk of action—the risk that the enemy would take advantage of a concentration in the Shenandoah to move on one of the weakened points. To offset the risk, Lee would have the Confederacy depend on swiftness of action and the paralyzing effect of an unanticipated offensive stroke.

Lee's office as adviser to President Davis gave him power to do little more than persuade, for the troops to be employed were mainly subject to

---

"Napoleonic Strategy: R. E. Lee and the Confederacy," in Russell Weigley, *The American Way of War*, pp. 101–127. Reprinted with permission of Macmillan Publishing Company. Copyright © 1973 by Russell F. Weigley.

the orders of General Joseph E. Johnston, who was taking position on the Peninsula to meet the Federal threat there. But Lee found an eager coadjutor in the commander of the Shenandoah Valley army, Major General Thomas Jonathan Jackson, known since his brigade's stand at Manassas as "Stonewall." "I have hoped," Lee wrote Jackson, "in the present divided condition of the enemy's forces that a successful blow may be dealt them by a rapid combination of our troops before they can be strengthened themselves either in position or by reinforcements." Out of Lee's recommendations and urgings and Jackson's brilliant application of them came the Valley Campaign of April–May, 1862, in which Jackson first sent the Federals in the Valley fleeing north of the Potomac, and then drew upon himself an aggregation of Federals from their Valley army, from western Virginia, and from the Rappahannock.

Lee's perception of the uses of concentration was not the simplistic kind represented by Halleck's criticism of Lincoln. He recognized that the kind of concentration that serves a defensive strategy best is that which causes the enemy to draw strength away from the vital points or leads him to disperse his forces. Lee saw the object of the Valley Campaign as fulfilled when the Federal concentration against Jackson kept reinforcements away from the main Union force on the Peninsula. Thereupon Lee turned his attention to the Peninsula, and obeying his theory of concentration, he hurried Jackson's Army of the Valley southeastward to join the direct fight against those Federals whom Jackson's indirect action had just weakened.

By now Lee could order Jackson, not merely recommend. In the battle of Seven Pines on the Peninsula on May 31, General Johnston fell wounded, and President Davis put Lee in Johnston's place at the head of the Confederate force which Lee now designated the Army of Northern Virginia. For all the success of Jackson's Valley Campaign in diverting Federal troops away from the Richmond area, this army and the Confederate capital remained in a dangerous situation. Reinforced by 18,500 men under Jackson, Lee could hope to muster somewhat over 80,000 men in his army; but he faced a Federal force, the Army of the Potomac under Major General George B. McClellan, estimated to approach 150,000 despite Jackson's diversions. (McClellan actually had 117,000.) When Lee took command, McClellan's army already stood within sound of the church bells of Richmond, the Confederates paying the penalty for having placed their capital in so exposed a state as Virginia and almost within reach of Union sea power on the tidal estuaries. McClellan's approach march up the Peninsula had been ponderous, but Lee believed that unless the Confederates grasped the initiative from him, he would eventually push his way into Richmond through sheer weight. If he should clamp Richmond into a siege, in time the city would fall. Therefore Lee again resolved upon the risk of action, determining to attack McClellan despite his inferiority in numbers.

He also displayed again his mastery of the strategic uses of concentration. Both the opposing armies outside Richmond were divided by the

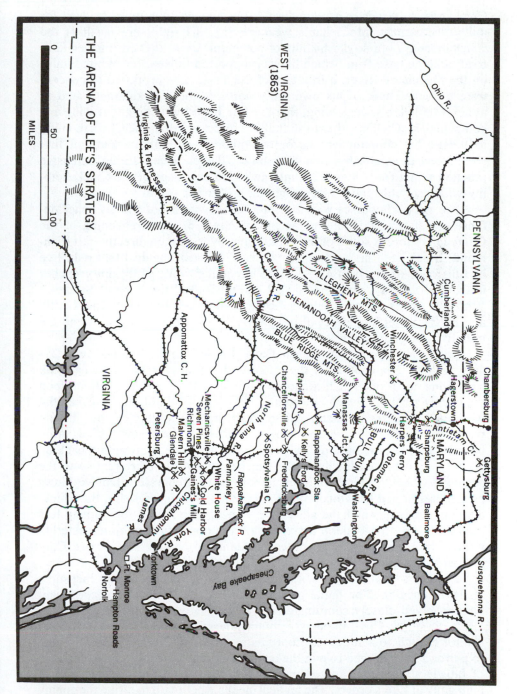

Source: Reprinted, by permission of the publisher, from Harold Woodman, *King Cotton and His Retainers* (Lexington: University Press of Kentucky, 1968), inside back cover. Copyright © 1968 by the University Press of Kentucky.

Chickahominy River, a stream formidable enough to require bridges for military crossings. McClellan's weaker wing, his right, lay north of the Chickahominy, but so did his line of communication, the York River Railroad, and the base from which he was supported by sea, the White House on the Pamunkey River, a tributary of the York. Lee proposed to concentrate the great bulk of his own army north of the Chickahominy and to attack McClellan's weak wing, thereby Lee hoped wrecking that wing and compelling McClellan either to shift all his forces north of the Chickahominy to defend his communications or to withdraw everything south of that stream and to establish a new base on the James River. Either defensive reaction would force McClellan into awkward crossings of the Chickahominy which should render him vulnerable to further offensive strokes.

The risk, of course, was that McClellan would not merely react defensively, but would take advantage of Lee's drastic weakening of the Confederate forces south of the Chickahominy to plunge directly into Richmond, which itself lay south of the stream. To guard against that risk, Lee had his men strain themselves in the unpopular work of digging trenches in front of the city, until they called him unkindly "the King of Spades." While the strong trenches helped, Lee again had to count on striking swiftly and on the unsettling effect of his blow to assure that once he seized the initiative, he could keep it.

Lee's plan opened the Seven Days' Battles for Richmond, June 25–July 1, 1862. His capture of the initiative by attacking McClellan's weak right wing north of the Chickahominy did have the paralyzing effect upon the enemy's will on which he counted. McClellan did not move against the weakened defenses of Richmond south of the Chickahominy, but instead went over to the defensive and tried to reestablish the security of his army by setting up a new base on the James. In the process of pulling back all his forces to the south side of the Chickahominy and of retreating to the James, McClellan opened himself to further Confederate offensive blows as Lee had hoped he would. While McClellan was entangled in the Chickahominy crossings and the adjacent swamps, Lee hoped for nothing less than to destroy the Federal army: to find the opportunity for an Austerlitz battle which would effect a strategy of annihilation. He had carried Confederate strategy a long way from President Davis's defensive.

But Lee's plan did not work out so neatly as had Stonewall Jackson's Valley Campaign. The initial onslaught to ruin McClellan's exposed right wing involved closely coordinated converging movements by a number of Lee's divisions. The Confederate commanders and staffs proved as yet not skillful enough to achieve the coordination desired. Jackson himself failed to perform his assigned role in the opening action, probably in part because of fatigue after a long forced march from the Valley, in part because of ambiguity in Lee's orders. The tactical means wherewith to strike the enemy had to be the close-order infantry assault; no other method of attack permitted adequate communication among the attacking troops or could hope to muster enough weight to break the enemy's lines and achieve Napoleonic results. But the war was beginning to reveal that rifled weapons extracted horrendous losses from the makers of such attacks. One of Lee's division commanders, Major General A. P. Hill, impatiently began the assault upon McClellan's right before Jackson was on hand to join in. Although A. P. Hill eventually received support from James Longstreet's and D. H. Hill's divisions, his close-ordered attacks suffered a bloody repulse, known as the battle of Mechanicsville, on June 26.

Mechanicsville removed the element of surprise from Lee's intentions against McClellan's right wing, and the next day the Federal right was strongly placed in a new position, still north of the Chickahominy, along Boatswain's Swamp near Gaines's Mill, the place which gave its name to the June 27 battle. Lee persisted in the attack. He did so partly because poor intelligence work by his staff and cavalry, and poor maps, misled him about the location of the Federal position and the direction of Federal retreat, so that he thought he enjoyed opportunities to outflank and cut off the Federal right which in fact did not exist. More than that, Lee persisted in the attack because his belief in the offensive-defensive as the only strategy which could save the Confederacy compelled it. He believed that if he did not retain the initiative he had grasped, Richmond and in time the Confederacy would fall. He believed he must hold on to the initiative, though Gaines's Mill became a battle of Confederate frontal assaults, still poorly coordinated, which at length drove the Federal right wing from its position, but at a cost of some 8,000 Confederate dead and wounded against lesser Federal losses.

By that time McClellan was ready to give up the position anyway, as he prepared to shift his base from the York River southward to the James. Through the next several days Lee continued to assault the rear and the western flank of the retreating Federal army, hoping that while it was strung out along the roads to the James and hindered by another watercourse, White Oak Swamp, he could deal it a mortal blow. A major action developed on June 30 at Glendale, or Frayser's Farm, where Longstreet and A. P. Hill attempted to break the Federal army in two while Jackson was to fall upon its rear. Longstreet and Hill fought hard, but again other divisions failed to coordinate their actions properly, and again Jackson failed to display the vigor expected of him. Glendale was Lee's last chance to inflict major damage before McClellan's army consolidated itself on the James. The next day, July 1, the Federals stood fast in an excellent defensive position on Malvern Hill. Frustrated by the repulse of his previous attacks, again as at Gaines's Mill not altogether informed about the Federal position or that of his own troops, with his staff again dispensing ambiguous orders, Lee allowed another series of frontal assaults to take place. At a cost of 5,500 casualties, they hardly shook the Federals.

To the government and people of the Confederacy, the main result of the Seven Days' Battles was that the Federal grip on Richmond was broken. The months since Manassas had brought the Confederacy so many reverses, McClellan had approached so close to the capital, and the Federal army had seemed so strong, that this result appeared almost miraculous. Lee, so recently in eclipse after his western Virginia campaign, became the hero of the Confederacy to remain so forever, and already the new name he had given his army, "the Army of Northern Virginia," became charged with evocative magic.

It was a great achievement indeed, but the price was 20,141 casualties out of somewhat over 80,000 men with whom Lee had opened the contest: 3,286 dead, 15,909 wounded, 946 missing. A humane and Christian gentleman, Lee grieved over the casualties; but as a soldier, he was troubled less by them than by his conviction that "Under ordinary circumstances the Federal army should have been destroyed." What he meant by "ordinary circumstances" was a professional command and staff which would not have been guilty of the lapses he suffered during the campaign. He resolved to improve the organization of his army before the next campaign.

Clearly, lapses had occurred. Clearly, the commanding general of the Army of Northern Virginia had to coordinate too many separate "commands" and divisions without intermediate corps headquarters, and too many of the division commanders were not up to snuff. Staff work, intelligence gathering, even at this stage of the war the reconnaissance work of Jeb Stuart's cavalry, all required improvement. But was it realistic of Lee to hope that even the best army conceivably available to him could have achieved what he sought, not merely McClellan's withdrawal from Richmond but the destruction of the Army of the Potomac? Was not the very idea of the destruction of so mighty a host in a single campaign an illusion now that the defense had rifled weapons, but an illusion still fostered by the Napoleonic legend and the Napoleonic concept of the climactic battle? Yet Lee's thoughts dwelt upon his failure to destroy the Army of the Potomac, a state of mind which implied another similar attempt in similar battle on some future day.

"My desire has been to avoid a general engagement, being the weaker force, and by maneuvering to relieve the portion of the country referred to." George Washington might have written that, but it was Lee reporting to President Davis on the morning of August 30, 1862, the second day of the Army of Northern Virginia's next great battle, Second Manassas. The Federal government had responded to Lee's checking of McClellan's offensive on the Peninsula by forming a new army of invasion in northern Virginia, under Major General John Pope. To Pope the Federals dispatched drafts from McClellan's army, on an accelerating schedule. Against Pope, Lee then directed his own attention, sending first Jackson's command to watch him and eventually following with the bulk of his army. The quotation indicates that Lee was surely not unmindful of the risks and losses of a general battle. His strategic conceptions, however, drove him into the very general engagement he professed to want to avoid and which formed the ironic setting for his dispatch to the President; for when he moved north from Richmond his avowed purpose was again to destroy the enemy army before him, first hoping to catch Pope in the cul-de-sac formed by the junction of the Rappahannock and Rapidan rivers, then, failing his first opportunity, seeking to ruin Pope by falling on his line of communication around Manassas before Pope's reinforcement by McClellan could be complete.

At Second Manassas, Lee succeeded better than in the Seven Days, fixing the Federal army with Jackson's troops and then routing them with a flank attack by Longstreet's troops that would have done credit to Napoleon himself. Lee's losses this time fell short of the Federals': 9,197 Confederate casualties of all types to 16,054 Federal. Lee's intelligence system functioned superbly well, the movements of his army were swift and well coordinated, and by dividing the army into two wings under Longstreet and Jackson he found the basis of an adequate system of command. He outgeneraled Pope so decisively that the Federals retreated into the defenses of Washington, where the rest of McClellan's men joined them. On the 25th of June, the United States Army had looked upon the spires of Richmond; by the end of August, Virginia east of the Allegheny Mountains was almost cleared of Federal soldiers, and it was Washington, not Richmond, that seemed threatened.

Against such achievements, Lee's mastery of the offensive-defensive mode of war he had elected to practice can scarcely be gainsaid. His Second Manassas campaign was a showpiece of Napoleonic warfare, a campaign of maneuver which drew the enemy into a disadvantageous position and then stunned him in a climactic battle. But nemesis lay in this very mode of war. Even having caught Pope in a disadvantageous position, to pursue his objective of the destruction of the enemy army Lee finally had to attack, and his losses in killed and wounded at Manassas amounted to 19 percent of his force, as against Federal losses in those categories of 13 percent. As in the Seven Days, the Federal army was not destroyed; the Confederate advantage was mainly moral and psychological. The Army of Northern Virginia could not so much as follow up its triumph with a vigorous pursuit. Its triumph left it too exhausted; its own losses were too large. And the logic of an offensive-defensive strategy which so much emphasized the offensive that it aimed at the destruction of the enemy army still beckoned Lee to court further losses of similar proportions.

For as soon as his army caught its breath and gathered itself together, Lee decided to invade the North, to carry the offensive into Maryland and if possible Pennsylvania. Brilliant though his achievements had been, he knew there was a hollowness about them. Not only had they failed to destroy McClellan's and Pope's armies; they had failed to weaken visibly the resolve of the North to restore the Union, and they had not halted Northern advances elsewhere into the Confederacy, especially in the Mississippi Valley. Lee could not assault the defenses of Washington; they were too rich in strongpoints and artillery. He believed he could not go over passively to the defensive. His men were hungry, and it would aid both the army and the Confederate economy to subsist his army during the harvest season in the Northern states. More than that, merely to rest now, shielding Virginia against new invasion, would have violated Lee's philosophy of war. So he saw the invasion of Maryland as the only acceptable course open to him.

Again as on the morning of August 30 at Manassas, he professed to hope he could avoid a costly general engagement. His intent, he said, was to wage a campaign of maneuver north of the Potomac, which he hoped might persuade slaveholding Maryland to join the Confederacy and so discourage the North that overtures from Richmond for the recognition of Confederate independence might bring positive results. But he could not hope that the Federal armies would allow him to maneuver in Maryland and Pennsylvania without challenging him to battle, and when the challenge in fact came, as usual he welcomed it.

Lincoln placed McClellan in command of the combined forces of his own army and Pope's. McClellan marched northwestward from Washington into Maryland to try to halt Lee's progress. The lucky finding of a copy of Lee's orders to his division commanders outlining his plan of campaign permitted McClellan to move against Lee with uncharacteristic swiftness and assurance. As the campaign approached its climax, Lee faced McClellan with the Army of Northern Virginia divided into five widely spaced detachments in order to try to capture Harpers Ferry, and a real prospect that the Federals' unexpectedly rapid advances might compel the detachments to fight while still dispersed. In Lee's situation, a general of even moderate caution would have pulled his forces back across the Potomac into Virginia. The strain imposed by prolonged campaigning and a weak supply system, along with a certain aversion among the Confederate rank and file to a campaign of invasion when the Confederacy claimed to be defending itself, produced unprecedented straggling in Lee's army; and at best, if he could get all his troops reunited, Lee could hope to confront McClellan with only about 50,000 men to 75,000 or more. There could be no prospect on this occasion of a battle that would destroy the Federal army.

Yet Lee had already demonstrated a strain of stubbornness in his nature, pushing him beyond even the demands of his offensive strategy to offer battle once he found himself in the presence of the enemy—the stubbornness which persisted in driving the frontal attacks forward at Gaines's Mill, and which allowed the sacrifices of Malvern Hill to occur. When McClellan now closed in on him, Lee did not retreat across the Potomac. He drew in his scattered forces and, though his brigades could not all be reassembled if McClellan attacked with the most minimal promptness, he stood to fight along Antietam Creek around the village of Sharpsburg. There was no prospect of destroying the Federal army; there was a much more likely prospect of the destruction of Lee's own army, if it should be mauled by McClellan's superior numbers with the barrier of the Potomac behind it. There was only Lee's unwillingness to abandon the invasion of Maryland without a fight, the consideration of the moral loss to be suffered by throwing away the hopes with which the invasion had begun by fleeing from a Federal challenge.

For the Confederacy, in quest of foreign recognition, such a loss could not have been taken lightly. But neither could the casualties of the battle of Antietam. On September 17 McClellan attacked, and in giving battle the Army of Northern Virginia lost some 13,724 men, against 12,410 Federal casualties. Lee's army was not destroyed, but on several occasions in the course of the battle its fate hung by a thread, as reinforcements reached threatened points at the last possible moment. After the battle Lee had to retreat into Virginia anyway, and Antietam consequently looked enough like a Federal victory to embolden Lincoln to issue the Emancipation Proclamation and thus to snuff out whatever prospects of foreign intervention might have existed. On Lee's behalf it must be noted that in the course of the campaign he had captured the Union garrison at Harpers Ferry, about 11,000 men, together with seventy-three guns and 13,000 small arms. Accordingly, total Federal losses in the campaign, including prisoners, were about double Lee's total casualties; and some 11,000 Federal prisoners were eventually exchanged to retrieve Confederates. Nevertheless, there is much to be said for the view that counts the Maryland campaign and the battle of Antietam as the turning point of the war—in favor of the Union.

Still, in the months that followed, Lee refused to abandon the reasoning that had led him to attempt the invasion. When he first assumed command of the Army of Northern Virginia in front of Richmond, he had not thoroughly probed the question of how to achieve the ultimate purpose of winning the war; for the moment it was all he could do to liberate Richmond from McClellan's grasp and hope to destroy the enemy army immediately before him. By the time he drove Pope from Virginia, his thoughts could run beyond immediate crises to the problem of bringing the Union government to make peace with an independent Confederacy. This purpose, Lee then began to conclude, could be achieved only by moving beyond an offensive-defensive strategy, even beyond one which sought the annihilation of enemy armies as the object of its offensives, to a still more thoroughly offensive strategy that would produce victories on Northern soil. To win recognition of the Confederacy, the Northern will to pursue the war must be broken. To that end, Lee believed victories in Virginia would not suffice even if they were more complete than those he had already won. Despite his own victories, the Union continued to conquer Confederate territory in the Mississippi Valley, and the coils of the blockade continued to tighten. To convince the Union government that the war was futile, and to do so before Union successes in theaters other than his own became irreversible, Lee came to believe that he must defeat Union armies *in the North,* and perhaps march into one of the great northeastern cities, Philadelphia or Baltimore or Washington itself. Less than a week after his retreat into Virginia from Antietam, Lee was writing to Davis:

> In a military point of view, the best move, in my opinion, the army could make would be to advance upon Hagerstown and endeavor to defeat the enemy at that point. I would not hesitate to make it even with our diminished numbers, did the army exhibit its former temper and condition; but as far as I am able to judge, the hazard would be great and a reverse disastrous. I am, therefore, led to pause.

But he remained impatient for the day when he would no longer need to pause, but could march northward again. Lee had never felt much hope for foreign intervention to rescue the Confederacy. He always believed the

Confederacy would have to win Northern recognition through its own strength. The Confederacy must conquer peace for itself. But to win peace, to break the will of the North, the Confederacy must do more than defend its capital at Richmond, more even than to smash enemy armies in Virginia. The Confederacy must *conquer;* it must win victories on Northern ground.

In the Piedmont and the Shenandoah Valley of northern Virginia in the autumn of 1862, Lee recruited and refitted his army after the losses and the strains of the summer, but he also looked forward to the time when he might resume the invasion of the North. To him, and to Stonewall Jackson at his side, the Fredericksburg campaign of the late fall and early winter was painfully frustrating. A new commander of the Federal Army of the Potomac, Major General Ambrose E. Burnside, replaced McClellan and returned to the invasion of Virginia before either Lee's preparations or the season could encourage a second Confederate invasion of the North. The route which Burnside chose brought Lee's army to face him at the crossings of the Rappahannock at Fredericksburg. There on December 13 Lee repulsed Burnside's attacks in an almost purely defensive battle. The terrain afforded no opportunity for Confederate maneuver or counterattack. Merely receiving the enemy's assaults, the Confederates suffered only 5,300 casualties to 12,700 Federal losses. But Lee was sure that static victories such as this one, on Virginia soil, could not break the Northern will and win the war.

Early in 1863, Lee felt obliged to detach Longstreet with two divisions of what was now his First Army Corps to southeastern Virginia, with a third division going to North Carolina, to guard against a possible Federal amphibious threat to the railroad connections between Richmond and North Carolina. If it had not been for this development, Lee might well have begun a new invasion march northward in the spring of 1863 before the Federals opened another drive against Richmond.

As it was, the Army of the Potomac under yet another new commander, Major General Joseph Hooker, crossed the Rappahannock southward again at the end of April. Hooker chose to avoid Lee's defenses around Fredericksburg by staging his main thrust farther westward, in a wooded area called the Wilderness around Chancellorsville. By doing so, however, Hooker gave Lee an opportunity to seize the initiative by means of a flanking maneuver, conceived and conducted by Lee and Jackson still more brilliantly than their Second Manassas campaign. Jackson's Second Army Corps descended upon Hooker's exposed right flank, rolled it up, and so panicked Hooker that, although his men fought hard and reestablished a tenable position, on May 5–6 the Federal army retreated across the Rappahannock. In the absence of three of his divisions, Lee fought this battle of Chancellorsville with at most 60,000 men, against the Army of the Potomac in one of its most powerful phases, numbering perhaps as many as 134,000. The Confederates extracted over 17,000 casualties from the Federals, while suffering fewer than 13,000 themselves.

Yet Chancellorsville cost Lee the irreplaceable loss of Stonewall Jackson, shot down by his own men in the course of a reconnaissance; and even if it had not brought that disaster, Lee would have been dissatisfied with the battle. He would have preferred using Jackson at the height of his abilities, and having the absent Longstreet with him too, to win a Chancellorsville victory on northern soil. Convinced that only victories in the North could win the war, Lee turned toward another invasion immediately after Chancellorsville, despite the death of Jackson. He recalled Longstreet to the main army, and on June 3 the Army of Northern Virginia began breaking its camps on the Rappahannock to march once more to the Potomac.

Lee's battlefield victories from the Seven Days to Chancellorsville had of course immensely enhanced President Davis's confidence in him, and Davis continued to consult Lee as a general military adviser though Lee had to give his attention principally to the Army of Northern Virginia. Despite his confidence in Lee, however, the President still inclined to favor a more purely defensive strategy, and he felt doubts especially about Lee's moving from an offensive-defensive to a candidly offensive strategy. Before Chancellorsville, Davis suggested to Lee the possibility of reinforcing the western Confederacy from Lee's army, and this idea still appealed to Davis as an alternative to an offensive north of the Potomac. Along the Mississippi, U. S. Grant's Federal army was moving toward the investment of Vicksburg at the time when the idea of Lee's new invasion of the North was germinating, and Grant's siege of Vicksburg had begun by the time Lee's army began moving northward. Between Virginia and Vicksburg, rival armies in middle Tennessee were quiescent, and their strength was balanced closely enough so that an increment to the Confederates might allow advantageous operations. Davis wondered whether the Confederacy should not exert every effort to prevent being sundered by Federal control of the entire Mississippi River, and whether exerting every effort did not imply reinforcement of the western armies, if not directly around Vicksburg, then in middle Tennessee to permit diversionary actions there which might draw some Federals away from Vicksburg.

Lee's response was that he could offer no reinforcements sufficient to turn the western balance, certainly not without incapacitating himself before the Army of the Potomac. In truth, Lee seems to have been less than fully responsive to the problems of the West, partly out of Virginia parochialism—he always regarded his sword as serving first his state of Virginia—and partly in adherence to his military philosophy. The vast expanses of the Mississippi Valley did not afford opportunity for the limited manpower of the Confederate armies to mount an offensive which could hope for decisive effects.

Lee began his new offensive with skillful maneuver, placing the protective shelter of the Blue Ridge between himself and Hooker's Army of the Potomac before Hooker was certain of the nature of his movements. A head start in the march northward combined with the Blue Ridge to permit the Army of Northern Virginia to cross the Potomac and enter Maryland and south-central Pennsylvania unmolested by any Federals except small detachments and emergency levies of militia. Yet to succeed, the campaign could not remain one of maneuver; the fulfillment of Lee's design demanded a climactic, Napoleonic battle. On June 28, Lee learned at Chambersburg, Pennsylvania, that the Army of the Potomac had crossed from Virginia into Maryland and that he must concentrate his army to meet it. Such news was bound to have come. To approach the Susquehanna and move upon Washington, Baltimore, or Philadelphia, Lee had to leave the sheltering Blue Ridge behind him. His head start had never been long enough to permit his reaching one of the great Northern cities before the Army of the Potomac interposed itself. The North could not yield any of these cities without a battle; winning a decisive victory in battle was the essence of Lee's own design.

Lee counted on the prowess his troops had displayed so often in Virginia to win that battle, and with it perhaps the war; but as the Antietam campaign might have warned, the conditions of battle were not likely to be so favorable north of the Potomac as in Virginia. On this invasion Lee managed to avoid the costly straggling which had plagued him in Maryland the year before. Also, his troops were able to subsist comfortably off the rich farmlands of Pennsylvania. For replenishment of ammunition, however, he was dependent on uncertain wagon shipments over the long route through the Shenandoah Valley from the Virginia Central Railroad. This dependence meant that there would be severe risks in prolonged battle, lest his ammunition, especially his artillery ammunition, be exhausted. It also meant that his capacity to maneuver would be limited by the necessity to maintain a connection with the Shenandoah Valley route. Longstreet, already concerned by the attrition which Lee's offensive battles had imposed on the Army of Northern Virginia, had urged that if an offensive into Pennsylvania were attempted, it should be combined with a tactical defensive. The Federals should be forced to attack, in order to drive the Confederate army from their soil. But when Union and Confederate detachments collided at Gettysburg on July 1 and the whole of both armies was drawn into battle there, the perils of maneuver with a limited ammunition supply militated against such a course. So did the Confederates' relative unfamiliarity with the terrain. So did Lee's confidence in his troops, and his belief that he must stake the results of the invasion upon a climactic battle. Because his army was living off the country, Lee could not remain long in one place inviting attack. Lee himself attacked, and attacked again, through three days of battle.

In this campaign Lee again was sometimes served less than well by his corps, division, and brigade commanders. After the war he said of the campaign: "If I had had Stonewall Jackson with me, so far as man can see, I should have won the battle of Gettysburg." The attrition suffered by the command structure of the Army of Northern Virginia by the time of the battle of Gettysburg, which D. S. Freeman blames for much of the failure there, was itself, however, largely a product of the casualties and strains that Lee's strategy imposed upon the army. If Stonewall Jackson had been at Gettysburg, or if his successor in the Second Corps, Lieutenant General Richard S. Ewell, had moved against Cemetery Hill on the evening of July 1, or if Longstreet had attacked the Union left as promptly as possible on July 2, it still remains highly uncertain—indeed, utterly unlikely—that Lee could have won the kind of overwhelming battlefield victory he wanted. His friends have always tended to exaggerate Union weaknesses both on Cemetery Hill, at the time on the evening of July 1 when they say Ewell should have been attacking, and on the Union left, where Union strength was already heavy at the earliest hour Longstreet could conceivably have been ready to attack on July 2. The new commander who took over the Army of the Potomac on the eve of Gettysburg, Major General George G. Meade, gave the Confederates no opening for a *manoeuvre sur les derrières* [flanking maneuver] like Jackson's against Hooker at Chancellorsville. If Lee had won at Gettysburg, his ammunition would have been nearly exhausted in victory, while Federal logistics would have improved as the Army of the Potomac fell back toward the eastern cities. Lee had to stake the whole campaign on one battle; the Federals did not.

Lee's efforts to roll up both Federal flanks on July 2 resolved themselves into costly frontal assaults, as they almost certainly would have done no matter how early in the day they had been launched. They strained Lee's army at least as much as they strained the enemy, and they gave little reason to hope that renewed attacks on the following day would do better. Nevertheless, the importance with which his whole strategy had invested this battle, and the stubbornness which had driven him on at Gaines's Mill, Malvern Hill, and Antietam, impelled Lee to try still another major attack on July 3. When disagreements and reluctance among his lieutenants changed the concept of the July 3 attack from another effort against the Federal left flank to the most unsubtle of frontal assaults, Lee's stubborn pugnacity still pushed the attack forward, until three divisions totalling about 15,000 men suffered wreckage beyond recovery in the failure of Pickett's Charge. Those 15,000 Confederates who followed their red battleflags through solid shot, canister, grape shot, and minnie balls from Seminary to Cemetery Ridge on the humid afternoon of July 3, 1863, deserve all the romantic rhapsodizing they have received, for soldiers never fought more bravely to rescue so mistaken a strategic design. Much the same thing might be said for the whole tragic career of the Army of Northern Virginia.

The problem of the frontal assault against rifled weapons was not simply one of inability to penetrate the enemy lines. If it had been that alone, if strong positions could never be penetrated at all, generals such as Lee might have abandoned the frontal assault as futile more quickly than they did. Despite the costs, the assailants sometimes got inside the defender's position, as George Pickett's gallant battalions did break into the Union lines near the famous copse of trees on Cemetery Ridge. The greater problem was how to stay there and exploit the advantage once the enemy's line was pierced. Almost invariably, by that time the attacker had lost so heavily, and his reserves were so distant, that he could not hold on against a counterattack by the defending army's nearby reserves. So it was with Pickett's Charge; the men of Armistead's, Kemper's, and Garnett's brigades who entered the Federal lines were too few to stay, let alone make further headway, when reserves from the whole Union center converged against them.

With that, the renewed offensive into the North of which Lee had dreamed since Antietam was dead. The Gettysburg campaign cost Lee about 23,000 casualties, and with such losses and all that had gone before, the offensive capacity of the Army of Northern Virginia was also virtually dead. Lee kept the war in Virginia stalemated in a campaign of maneuver through the autumn of 1863. He could do so because Meade proved a cautious adversary who would not permit a bloody, full-scale battle unless he was sure he could win, and Lee remained too skillful to give him such an opening. On the other hand, a bungled Confederate attack at Bristoe Station, and a Federal coup which snuffed out two Confederate bridgeheads and inflicted 2,023 casualties at a cost of 419 at Rappahannock Station and Kelly's Ford showed that the fighting edge of the Army of Northern Virginia was no longer what it had been.

When the Army of the Potomac crossed the Rappahannock southward once again in the spring of 1864, with the aggressive U. S. Grant directing it, the Army of Northern Virginia for two days essayed counteroffensives in the Chancellorsville manner, on May 5 and 6 in the Wilderness. These counterattacks achieved local, tactical success, but they failed to stop Grant's southward advance. Thereafter, the Army of Northern Virginia dug into entrenchments, never again to fight a campaign of offensive maneuver and general counterattack. It had bled so much that against the Army of the Potomac its offensive power was gone.

For a belligerent with the limited manpower resources of the Confederacy, General Lee's dedication to an offensive strategy was at best questionable. To be able to come to no decision between an offensive strategy such as Lee's and a strategy of defense such as Jefferson Davis favored and to waver between the two was still worse. Yet the course of indecision was the one followed by the Confederacy in the West. Indecision, as usual, offered the worst of both worlds; it produced casualties comparable to Lee's, combined with territorial and logistical losses which began to stagger the Confederacy before the dust had settled from the first campaign. . . .

[There follows a discussion of Confederate military failure in the West—Kentucky and Tennessee as well as Georgia—from 1862 to early 1864.]

To all these [developments] in the West, Lee remained remarkably indifferent, despite President Davis's continuing to call upon him as a military adviser. He persistently underrated the strength and importance of Federal offensives in the West. As late as the spring of 1864, when Sherman faced Johnston with a larger numerical advantage than Grant's over Lee, Lee argued that "the great effort of the enemy in this campaign will be made in Virginia," and accordingly urged Johnston to take the offensive. Lee persistently neglected also the logistical implications of the western campaigns, the loss of the granary of the Confederacy when most of Tennessee fell to Union arms so early, the threat to the Confederacy's most important iron mines and to one of the South's two main munitions centers (Richmond being the other) in Sherman's campaigning southward from Chattanooga into the Georgia-Alabama mining, industrial, and transportation complex. The only occasion when Lee consented to a major reinforcement of the West, Longstreet's trip to Bragg for the Chickamauga campaign, occurred after Gettysburg had left Lee's own offensive strategy in ruin. The West probably would have benefited from Lee's application of his strategic perceptions to it; almost any consistent strategy would have been better than vacillation between a dispersed defensive and hasty, belated counteroffensives. Thinking consistently about the West might also have encouraged greater realism in Lee's own mind.

In the spring of 1864 Lee remarked to Major General Jubal Early: "We must destroy this army of Grant's before he gets to James River. If he gets there, it will become a siege, and then it will be a mere question of time." Still, as on the day of Seven Pines when he first commanded the Army of Northern Virginia, at this late date Lee's hope and aim continued to be the destruction of the Federal army. But by the time he spoke to Early, his pursuit of that aim had already exhausted his army far beyond any capacity to accomplish such a purpose. He spoke to Early about the time when he repulsed Grant's attacks at Cold Harbor; by then, the siege warfare which made the outcome a mere question of time had already begun. The Army of Northern Virginia could no longer maneuver or mount a general offensive against its major adversary. It could hope only to hold off superior numbers from behind strong entrenchments and to make occasional diversionary sallies against exposed places and detachments.

Forced to confine himself to this type of warfare, Lee waged it with a skill at least comparable to Johnston's in Georgia. He had shown himself exceptionally talented in the use of field fortifications since those early days of his command when his men called him "the King of Spades"; and he had acknowledged the effects of rifled firepower enough to fight increasingly from trenches whenever his strategy permitted it from Chancellorsville onward. He and the lieutenants trained in his and Stonewall Jackson's school of war could still achieve spectacular diversionary effects with minimal numbers, as when Early made the city of Washington tremble in the summer of 1864 with a new campaign down Jackson's old Shenandoah Valley route, and then across the Potomac into Maryland. But as soon as substantial Federal armed strength confronted a diversion such as Early's, the Confederates had to retreat; and attempting battle outside entrenchments during the autumn, Early was crushed.

No feasible diversion could effect more than a momentary interruption in the now inexorable course of the war toward Confederate defeat. The siege warfare which Lee had always feared began as early as May, at Spotsylvania Court House. Confederate and Federal armies both fought from trenches, with the Federals constantly shifting toward their left, first from Spotsylvania toward the North Anna and the James rivers, then across the James and southward beyond Richmond toward Petersburg, and on toward the railroads which served Richmond and Petersburg from the south. Unable to maneuver or attack, Lee could merely reach out with his own right flank in response, until at last in the trenches around Richmond and Petersburg he stretched his army to the breaking point. Then the enemy both broke into his trenches and cut the indispensable railroads.

In the spring of 1865 Lee's army had to march out of its trenches to undertake a war of motion once more—but the effort sapped its last strength and killed it. Johnston's war of flexible defense failed in Georgia because the Confederacy no longer had enough space for the necessary maneuver; Lee's attempt at a flexible defense in 1864–65 ran out of space and also out of men and commanders able to maneuver enough to make such a defense successful.

Of many of the arts of war, R. E. Lee was a consummate master. He organized his army to extract the best possible efforts from his men and his lieutenants. Within his immediate theater of war, his logistical management was excellent. His famous victories rightly made him the Southern commander most feared by his enemies. In one of them, Second Manassas, he came as close as any general since Napoleon to duplicating the Napoleonic system of battlefield victory by fixing the enemy in position with a detachment, bringing the rest of the army onto his flank and rear, and then routing him front and flank. But Lee was too Napoleonic. Like Napoleon himself, with his passion for the strategy of annihilation and the climactic, decisive battle as its expression, he destroyed in the end not the enemy armies, but his own.

The Generalship of Ulysses S. Grant Defended

BRUCE CATTON

The American Civil War confronted the professional soldier with a vexing series of problems which went far beyond anything he could possibly have been expected to learn at West Point.

West Point gave its graduates a first-rate training, but it told them very little about some of the things that would be required of them in the 1860s. It had trained them for a different sort of war altogether—for a war of professionals, with set rules, established values and recognized limits— and the very fact that it had trained them well and thoroughly meant that they were apt to find themselves bewildered once the nation thrust them into a war which made up its own rules as it went along, groped blindly toward values which had never been defined, and came in the end to recognize no limits whatsoever.

For the Civil War resembled war as set forth in the textbooks only to

Bruce Catton, "The Generalship of Ulysses S. Grant," from *Grant, Lee, Lincoln and the Radicals: Essays on Civil War Leadership,* Grady McWhiney, editor, 1973, pp. 3–29. Reprinted by permission of Northwestern University Press.

an extent. It was, to begin with, what its traditional name says it was—a civil war, not a war with some foreign nation—and it contained elements West Point had never dreamed of. It had to be fought by citizen-soldiers drawn from a land which might be exceedingly pugnacious but which had an immense impatience with restraints and formalities. Problems of politics and of economics were woven through every part of its fabric. The techniques of a newly mechanized age had to be taken into account. On top of everything, it was on both sides a war of the people, whose imperious and often impatient desires exerted a constant pressure which no general could ignore.

To appraise the generalship of any of the great soldiers in that war, therefore, it is necessary to understand first just what it was that the Civil War required of them. It required straight military competence, to be sure, and those indefinable qualities of leadership which professional training may develop but cannot implant; but it also called for a great adaptability, a readiness to find unorthodox solutions for unorthodox problems, an understanding of just what it was that the American people were trying to do in that terrible war they were waging with themselves.

Now the first thing to take into consideration here is that the American Civil War was—or became, not long after it had begun—an all-out war; which means that it was essentially quite unlike the kind of war professional soldiers of the mid-nineteenth century usually had in mind.

Each side was fighting for an absolute; to compromise was to lose. The South was fighting for independence, the North for reunion. Inextricably interwoven with these opposing causes was the matter of chattel slavery. The men of each side, in other words, came at an early stage to believe passionately that they were fighting both for national survival and for human freedom—the Southerner, for his own personal freedom, the Northerner, for freedom in the abstract, but both for freedom. Each side, accordingly, believed that it was fighting for a high and holy cause and that final victory was worth any conceivable sacrifice. Victory was more important than anything else. What it cost did not matter, and what it would finally mean could be settled later on; while the war lasted victory would be pursued with immense singleness of purpose. And to drive for absolute victory is of course to wage all-out war in the modern manner.

Now this was not what most professional soldiers of that era had in mind at all. They had been brought up in a doctrine that came down from the eighteenth century. Wars were usually fought for limited objectives, and they were fought in a limited way; they were primarily matters for the armies, and they were conducted up to the point where they began to cost more than they were likely to be worth, at which point they were brought to an end. The settlement that finally ended a war was of course a matter for governments to determine, not for generals; what the generals had to remember was that sooner or later there would be some sort of settlement, and that until the settlement was made it was wise to conduct affairs without causing too much breakage.

This meant that wars had to a certain extent become formalized. They were in a way like immense chess games, performed with intricate maneuvers that followed the book; going by the book, a good general always knew when he was licked, and behaved accordingly. One of the most cerebral and highly educated of Northern soldiers, General Don Carlos Buell, told the court of inquiry which considered his case after he had been removed from the command of the Army of the Cumberland that it ought to be quite possible to conduct an entire campaign successfully without fighting a single battle. Make the right moves and you will win: you do not need to be especially combative, but you must be very careful, leaving as little as possible to chance, never moving until everything is ready, making those maneuvers and occupying those strategic points which will finally persuade your opponent that he has been beaten.

This attitude formed part of the mental background of a great many of the professional soldiers who were given important assignments in the early part of the Civil War, and it was precisely this attitude which kept some of them from being successful. This, to repeat, was a different kind of war. The two sides which were involved were not going to quit until somebody made them quit. Victories would go, not to the man who followed the book faithfully, but to the man who was willing and able to get in close and slug until something broke. He would, to be sure, need a good deal of professional ability to get in close and to slug effectively after he got there, but his ultimate objective was, quite simply, the enemy's will and ability to resist. Until he broke that he accomplished nothing.

This requirement rested with particular weight on the Federal generals. The Southerner had one thing working for him: it was always conceivable that even if he did not actually win he could compel the Northerner to give up the fight from sheer war weariness. The Northerner had no similar reliance. He would get no final victory unless Confederate strength was utterly destroyed. He had to be aggressive, because a stalemate would work in favor of his opponent. Whether he realized the fact or not, the Federal soldier was fighting to enforce an unconditional surrender. It was his task, not merely to compel his foe to come to terms, but to obliterate a nation.

It was not easy for the average professional soldier to grasp this point, and a number of good men never got an inkling of it. It is perhaps significant that the three Federal generals who most often were called "brilliant" by their Old Army associates—Buell, McClellan, and Halleck—were men who failed utterly to see this requirement and who accordingly never measured up to the high expectations which had been made regarding them. These men had studied the science of war with great care, and they brought keen intelligence to the task. Their trouble was that the Civil War called on them for qualities which their studies had never revealed to them. In his statement that it should be possible to win a campaign without actually fighting a battle, Buell was entirely correct—by the book. But the book did not apply in his case, because his assignment in Kentucky and Tennessee could not be discharged as long as the Confederate Army of Tennessee remained in existence. It was not enough for him to put it at a disadvantage. He had to take it apart, and he could not conceivably do that without compelling it to fight until it could fight no more.

In the same way, Halleck completely missed his opportunity after the battle of Shiloh and the fall of Corinth in the spring of 1862. He had assembled an army of perhaps 125,000 men in northern Mississippi, and to oppose him Beauregard had substantially fewer than half that many men. With the light of after-knowledge it is easy to see that Halleck ought to have pressed his advantage to the utmost, driving his foe on relentlessly and compelling him at last to fight a battle that could only result in annihilation. Instead, Halleck went by the book. He undertook to occupy territory, dividing his army into detachments, leisurely setting to work to consolidate his advantages; he saw the map, and the things which a strategist ought to do on it, rather than the men in arms who carried the opposing nation on the points of their bayonets. Behaving thus, he gave the Confederacy a breathing spell in which it assembled new levies, dug in to resist a new Federal offensive, and in the end took the initiative away from him and marched north almost to the Ohio River. The war went on for two more years.

Another responsibility rested on men in the Federal high command. The Federal government had almost overwhelming advantages in the Civil War, from the beginning to the end. In manpower, in money, in raw materials and manufacturing capacity, in access to world markets, in the ability to raise, feed, equip, and transport armies—in all of the things that go to make up military capacity in time of war—the resources of the North so far overshadowed those of the South that one is compelled at times to wonder what ever made the leaders of the Confederacy think that they could possibly win. This enormous advantage was bound to bring victory, in the end, if it could just be applied steadily, remorselessly and without a break, and it was above all other things up to the Federal generals to see this and to govern themselves accordingly. They had, in other words, the ability to apply and maintain a pressure which the Confederacy could not hope to resist. They could afford mistakes, they could afford wastage, they could afford almost anything except the failure to make constant use of the power that was available to them.

It was just here, perhaps, that the reality of the Civil War departed most completely from the orthodox military tradition. Two very different economic and social systems were struggling for survival. One of them was fitted to win such a struggle if it went to the limit, and the other, the weaker system, was not. In effect, a Confederate leader had his own army to rely on and nothing more; the Federal leader had not only his own army but the infinite war-potential of a rich, populous, highly organized industrial state. "Brilliance" in the purely military field was the reliance of the Southern soldier—possibly his only reliance—as Robert E. Lee abundantly demonstrated; the Northerner's reliance was something quite different, calling not so much for an understanding of the rules of war as for an understanding of the ways by which a great nation enforces its will.

Along with everything else this required the Northern general to give a certain amount of thought to the institution of chattel slavery, simply because the slave system was one of the main props—perhaps the most important one of all—for the Southern economy which was the ultimate support of Southern armies. This prop, while important, was exceedingly fragile. One of the facts that had driven slave-state leaders to secession in the first place had been the dawning realization that the peculiar institution could continue to exist only if it were carefully protected against all outside interference. A general who took a hostile army into slave territory was providing such interference, whether he meant to or not. Regardless of his own feelings in respect to slavery, the peculiar institution became of necessity one of his military objectives. He was fighting, to repeat, a total war, and in a total war the enemy's economy is to be undermined in any way possible. Slavery was the southern economy's most vulnerable spot, and a Northern general could not be neutral in respect to it. Every time one of his soldiers extracted a plantation hand from bondage—every time the mere presence of his army disorganized the slave-labor system in its area and caused a blind exodus of men and women from the huddled slave cabins—he was helping to disarm the Confederacy.

It must be confessed that the Northern general was under certain handicaps during the first year and one-half of the struggle. Up to the fall of 1862, it was official government policy that the war was being fought solely to restore the Union, and generals were instructed not to campaign against slavery. This, to be sure, was a vain hope, but generals were supposed to follow top policy even when it was impossible; and this policy could not be followed, simply because the private soldiers took things into their own hands. The soldiers quickly came to equate the possession of slaves with opposition to the Union. In places like Kentucky this often led them to despoil the property of men who were stoutly Unionist in their leanings, but there was no help for it. Regardless of what the generals might say, the private Federal soldier was predominantly an emancipationist whenever he got south, not because he himself had any especial feelings against slavery but simply because he realized that slavery supported the nation he was fighting against.

Slavery, indeed, was the one institution which could not possibly survive an all-out war. A Union general might deplore this fact, but he was obliged to take it into account. Here, in short, was one more extremely important field in which the professional soldier's training and traditions were of no use to him. He had to understand what made his country tick, and in the long run what he did had to be done in the light of that understanding. There was nothing in the textbooks to help him. Like the men he commanded, the general had to have a good deal of the citizen-soldier in him.

It is sometimes said, indeed, that the most successful generals in the Civil War were men who had left the army in the prewar years and had had experience in the civilian world. This is only partly true. It applies to such men as Grant and Sherman, to be sure, but it does not apply at all to men like Lee, Joseph E. Johnston, Stonewall Jackson, and George

Thomas, who had never been or wanted to be anything but professional soldiers; and one of the men who most faithfully tried to make war by the old tradition was a man who had left the army and had had a highly successful career in business—George B. McClellan. Yet one is bound to feel that particularly on the Northern side a man who had had some experience outside of the army might have gained something from it. The war had strong non-professional aspects, and an officer who had something of a non-professional viewpoint—who had learned, by first-hand experience, something about the way the American people go about their business and try to make their will felt—could derive an advantage from that fact.

I suggest that it is only against this background that we can intelligently evaluate the generalship of the man under whom the Federal armies finally won the Civil War—Ulysses S. Grant.

Grant first came on the wartime stage in the fall of 1861, at Cairo, Illinois, where he commanded a body of troops which would presently be used in the attempt to open the Mississippi Valley. It is possible to see, even before this first campaign got under way, some of his essential qualities: an uncomplicated belief in direct action, a realization of the things that could be done with raw troops, and a constant desire to strike for complete victory rather than for the attainment of a minor advantage.

In September, 1861, Grant commanded approximately 15,000 men. All of his men—like all of the other men in Union and Confederate armies at that time—were poorly trained and poorly armed, but he wanted to use them at once. He told his chief of staff, John A. Rawlins, that when two unprepared armies faced one another, the commander of one of those armies would gain very little by waiting until his troops were thoroughly prepared. This, said Grant, simply meant that his opponent would have time to do the same thing, and in the end the relative strengths of the opposing armies would be about what they had been at the start. It might be noted that in expressing this opinion Grant was departing from military orthodoxy. The professional soldier had a natural distaste for trying to make a campaign with an army whose training, discipline, and equipment were deficient, and the shambling assemblages of newly uniformed young men who made up the armies in the fall of 1861 had deficiencies too obvious to overlook. The disaster at Bull Run simply underlined the point. In his ability to see that the other side was equally handicapped, Grant was being definitely unprofessional. His attitude here was much more the attitude of the civilian than of the trained soldier; he was quite willing to use an imperfect instrument, provided that his opponent's instrument was equally imperfect.

And so Grant, that fall, wanted to attack the Confederate stronghold at Columbus, on the Mississippi River. He knew that his troops were by no means ready to confront a trained, tightly organized army, but he knew also that they were not going to have to confront anything of the kind. The army they would fight was in no better shape than themselves. Under the circumstances, Grant wanted to fight as soon as possible.

There is of course another side to this argument, and Grant doubtless got a certain amount of enlightenment from his first battle, the sharp engagement fought at Belmont, across the river from Columbus. Here Grant attacked a Confederate force and drove it from the field in temporary rout, which was just what he had expected to do. What he had not anticipated was the fact that his unready troops fell into complete disorder because they had won a victory. They got out of hand, wandered about looting the Confederate camp, listening to spread-eagle speeches by their colonels, and in general acting as if the battle was over. The Confederates across the river sent over fresh troops, and Grant's men in turn were driven off in rout, escaping final disaster only because Grant managed at last to get them back to their transports and take them up the river to safety. Because they were so imperfectly disciplined and organized, they had lost a victory which they had won.

Grant's original idea, in other words, needed to be toned down slightly. But it did have some merit, and it went hand in hand with another notion, equally repugnant to military orthodoxy. Not long after Belmont, it was suggested to Grant that by proper maneuvering he could compel the Confederates to evacuate that stronghold at Columbus. Grant dissented vigorously. There was (he insisted) very little point in merely compelling the enemy's army to retreat; sooner or later that army would have to be fought, when it was fought it would have to be destroyed outright—dispersed in open combat, or hemmed in and captured lock, stock and barrel—and this might as well be done at once. Making the enemy retreat simply postponed the showdown that had to come eventually.

The big business, in short, was to fight, to fight all-out, and to win the most decisive victory imaginable. There was no point in a campaign for limited objectives. Any battle which left the opposing army on its feet and breathing struck General Grant as imperfect.

It is a little surprising to find a Federal general feeling this way in the fall of 1861. The war then was still young, and the Northern government was still trying, with much fumbling and inefficiency, to get its strength organized. The lesson taught by Bull Run—that it was folly to try to make a campaign with an unprepared army—was still fresh in every man's mind. Autumn of 1861 was a time to get ready. Decisive action would have to come later.

But it is just possible, in spite of Belmont, that the Bull Run lesson had been learned a little too well. In Missouri, both Sterling Price and Nathaniel Lyon had demonstrated that great things could be done with the most grotesquely unready armies if the man in charge insisted on it. The Bull Run lesson needed to be interpreted in the light of two additional facts, which were not readily recognizable to the average professional. First, every Federal army, no matter how much it lacked in the way of training and equipment, was at least as well off in those respects as the army it was going to have to fight. Second, the Federal side did have an immense advantage in numbers, in war material, and in the capacity to make its losses good. That advantage was just as genuine an asset in the fall of 1861 as it was in the spring of 1864. It needed to be used.

It was used, presently, beginning in January, 1862, and what happened thereafter is instructive.

Albert Sidney Johnston, who commanded for the Confederates in the western theater, did not have nearly enough men to defend the long line that ran from the Mississippi River to the Cumberland Plateau, and he had held his ground throughout the fall simply by a skillful bluff which made his strength look much greater than it was. When Grant and his naval coadjutor, Flag Officer Andrew Foote, insisted that this line be attacked at the earliest possible date they were simply reacting to a subconscious knowledge of that fact, and between the two of them they apparently persuaded the authorities to open an offensive a little ahead of time. So Foote's gunboats promptly knocked off Fort Henry, on the Tennessee— and Johnston's whole line immediately collapsed. (For the record, of course, it should be noted that George H. Thomas had already broken the eastern anchor of the line by winning the battle of Mill Springs, or Logan's Cross Roads, in Kentucky.) Grant drove on to capture Fort Donelson, and Johnston could do nothing but order an immediate retreat and try to regroup in northern Mississippi.

Note that the driving force in this whole campaign came from Grant. His superior officer, General Halleck, was obviously drawn into the campaign before he was quite ready; and General Buell, who commanded for the Federals east of the Tennessee River, went into action with even greater reluctance, protesting that the thing had not been properly prepared for and complaining bitterly because Grant forced the occupation of Nashville before Buell was ready for it. It was Grant, also, who believed that this victory ought to be followed up with speed. Halleck restrained him—we must pause in order to get everything arranged properly, there must be due thought for reinforcements and lines of supply, it would be most risky to go plunging on before everybody is ready—and, as a result, the advance up the defenseless Tennessee was made with much caution. In the end Johnston was given seven weeks, which he did not really need to be given, in order to bring his scattered forces together at Corinth. Johnston used the time to good advantage, and at Shiloh he struck a blow which nearly redressed the balance.

Admittedly, Shiloh does not show Grant at his best. He displayed here the defects of his qualities. Eager to press the advantage and overwhelm a beaten enemy, he thought so much about the delayed offensive that he apparently overlooked the fact that his enemy might launch a counter-offensive. When at last he was allowed to advance he advanced incautiously, and Johnston's massive counterstroke hit him before he was quite ready. The near-debacle at Pittsburg Landing needs to be interpreted in the light of the fact that if Grant had had his way the Federal army would have been ready to move forward from that bleak highland three weeks before the battle actually took place, at which time Johnston would have been in no shape to make an effective defense.

One more point needs to be made about Shiloh, and it highlights one more of Grant's characteristic traits. In the first day's fight, Grant's army unquestionably was defeated: but Grant himself was not defeated at all. Unforgettable, to any student of the battle, is General Sherman's account of meeting Grant at midnight, in the rain, after the first day's fight had ended. Grant was standing under a tree, keeping as dry as he could, puffing a cigar; Sherman came up to him, believing that the only possible course was to order a retreat the next morning, and said something to the effect that the day had been very tough and had gone badly. Grant nodded, bit his cigar, drew on it briefly, and then said: "Yes. Beat 'em in the morning, though." Grant, in other words, hung on, waited for Buell and Wallace to reinforce him, refused to think of withdrawal, made his counterattack on the second day, and in the end won one of the most significant Union victories of the entire war. After Shiloh, the Confederates in the west were doomed to a losing defensive.

Shiloh's gains, once more, were partly nullified by Halleck's caution. Halleck came on the scene a few days after the battle. He brought heavy reinforcements, so that before long the Federal army in northern Mississippi totaled approximately 125,000 men: Beauregard, commanding for the Confederates after Albert Sidney Johnston's battle death, had a scant 50,000. Halleck's army could have gone anywhere it chose. The heart of the South was open, and Beauregard could not conceivably have made a stand-up fight in opposition. But Halleck was a cautious, careful professional, a man who knew war by the book rather than by reality. He knew that Shiloh had almost been a disaster because the Federals had been incautious and had not had their defenses ready. In his advance, Halleck would not make that mistake.

He edged forward with painstaking care, taking upward of a month to make a 30-mile advance, and when Beauregard at last evacuated Corinth and retreated—there was nothing else Beauregard could possibly have done—Halleck split his forces into segments, devoting himself to the occupation of "strategic points," to the protection and repair of railroad lines, to the consolidation of his position. The great opportunity was missed. The Confederates were even able before the summer was out to put on a counteroffensive, which saw a Confederate army go nearly to the Ohio River; to this day no one knows quite what that stroke might have accomplished if it had been commanded by anyone other than Braxton Bragg. The driving offensive spirit which Grant gave his army evaporated once Halleck got on the scene, and in consequence the Federal move to open the Mississippi could not be resumed until nearly the end of 1862.

Grant's Mississippi campaign, from its unhappy beginning at Holly Spring to the final surrender of Pemberton's army at Vicksburg on July 4, 1863, was of course one of the decisive strokes of the war—and one of the most brilliant. It is interesting here simply because it shows Grant in a somewhat unfamiliar guise. His movement downstream from Milliken's Bend, his crossing of the river, his lightning campaign to Jackson and back via Champion Hill to Vicksburg, his ability to herd Pemberton into the isolated fortress and to keep the Confederate relieving column under Joe

Johnston at arm's length until Pemberton at last had to give up—this was one of the most dazzling campaigns of the entire war. It is interesting to note that in its beginning, at least, Grant did not have an advantage in numbers. When he crossed the river, cut loose from his base and marched into the interior, there were actually more Confederates than Unionists in Mississippi. The hoary assertion that Grant won victories simply because the odds were always heavily in his favor collapses here. This was a campaign in the Stonewall Jackson manner—great daring, fast and deceptive movement, hard blows struck at fragments of the opposing forces, ending in a victory which went far to determine the outcome of the entire war.

Whatever else it may have been, this campaign was not the campaign of a dull, unimaginative man who was a simple slugger and nothing more. Military genius was at work here. The Grant of the Vicksburg campaign was one of the great captains.

To midsummer of 1863, in other words, Grant's record is in the main excellent. He has carried out his assignments, learning his grim trade as he goes along, guided always by the offensive spirit, discovering along the way (at a high cost, admittedly) that the offensive needs to be leavened with a certain amount of caution; he has swallowed two opposing armies whole, he has opened the Mississippi Valley to the Union, and he has abundantly justified his belief that a Union general needs to apply the pressure to the Union's foes without a letup. It has worked. The war, as far as the Union is concerned, is over the peak.

The Chattanooga campaign, interesting as it is, must be recognized as more or less incidental. At Chattanooga Grant was called on to do little more than pick up the pieces which had been dropped at the disastrous battle of Chickamauga. Grant took charge at Chattanooga at a time when the Union army had escaped the immediate threat of capture, which loomed so large immediately after the retreat from Chickamauga. All that was needed was a cool, unhurried, business-like grasp of the situation and a determination to break out of the besieging ring as soon as everything was ready. This much Grant provided; it is extremely probable that George H. Thomas, left to himself, would have provided it equally well, and although at the time Grant's victory at Chattanooga struck Northerners as a superlative achievement, the victory must be written down simply as one which any competent Northern commander would have won under similar circumstances. Probably Grant's matter-of-fact, common-sense coolness was his chief asset here.

After Chattanooga, Grant's elevation to supreme command was inevitable. The step came early in the spring of 1864, when Grant was commissioned lieutenant-general and was entrusted with the conduct of the nation's whole military effort. All that had gone before was preparation; now came the great challenge, the unlimited responsibility, the final time of testing. Any appraisal of Grant's qualities as a soldier must finally rest on what he did after the supreme command was given to him.

What Grant did, beginning in the spring of 1864, was by no means confined to Virginia. He stayed in Virginia, to be sure, and the army that fought against Robert E. Lee was known—against logic, and against military reality—as "Grant's Army"; but the whole war was Grant's, and what happened in Tennessee and in Georgia, and elsewhere, was Grant's responsibility. And critiques of Grant's military capacity can grow a little foggy here, because the critic runs the danger of succumbing to one of two oversimplifications.

The first one can be stated thus: Grant was responsible for the grand strategy of the final year, the war was at last won, and Grant therefore is a great soldier.

The other goes off in the opposite direction: Grant fought against Lee with an overwhelming advantage in numbers, took frightful losses, was never able to beat Lee in the open field, won at last because he did have that advantage in numbers, and hence was simply a slugger who came at last to victory because under the circumstances he could hardly have come to anything else.

There is an element of truth in each oversimplification. Neither one offers a proper evaluation of Grant's capacity. Each one needs to be examined closely, and the two finally need to be blended together.

It is entirely true that the grand strategy of the final year, which worked, was Grant's. The war was not simply Virginia; the western theater was part of it, too. Sherman's armies moved remorselessly into the deep South, disemboweling the Confederacy, making it incapable of firm resistance, reducing that tragically beset nation to nothing more than the territory between Richmond, Virginia, and Raleigh, North Carolina, while still other armies mopped up the outlying territories. This concept was Grant's, and the responsibility was his. (If Sherman's bold march from Atlanta to the sea had gone sour and had resulted in a lost army and a fatal setback to the Union cause, the man who would have had to shoulder the blame was Grant.) When 1864 began, the Confederacy lived because of two armies— the Army of Northern Virginia under Lee, and the Army of Tennessee, under Johnston. (There were other, lesser armies elsewhere, but they were peripheral.) As long as these two armies lived, the Confederacy would live; when they were destroyed the Confederacy would die. It was Grant who made those two armies the principal objectives for the Federal war effort; it was Grant who saw to it that the force needed to destroy those armies was mustered, supported, and relentlessly applied. If the grand strategy of the war's final year worked, Grant is the man who is entitled to take the bow. He had the authority to do these things, and he used it up to the hilt. The result was victory.

At the same time, Grant's conduct of the campaign in Virginia is extremely relevant to any appraisal of his abilities, and it is clear that this campaign did not go quite as Grant had hoped that it would go. His real aim when he planned the campaign was neither to capture Richmond nor to force the Confederate army into retreat; it was simply to destroy that army, and he hoped that he would be able to do it fairly quickly. Grant suspected, when he came east, that the Federal Army of the Potomac had somehow never been made to fight all-out. It had capacities, he believed, that had not quite been called on; he would call on them to the limit, and by unremitting aggressiveness would compel Lee to make a stand-up fight in which the superior Federal advantages in manpower and materiel would quickly win a decisive victory.

This, of course, did not happen. The campaign lasted very nearly a year, it was enormously costly to the Union army, and in the end it succeeded largely because the North could endure a long process of attrition better than the South could. Grant did not do what he set out to do; what he had been able to do against other Confederate commanders in the west he was not able to do against Lee. The long series of wearing, hideously expensive battles which in a few months almost destroyed the old fighting capacity of the Army of the Potomac lend some weight to the charge that Grant was an unimaginative bruiser who won, in the end, simply because he had overpowering numbers and used them remorselessly and without finesse.

So the Virginia campaign, which began when the Army of the Potomac crossed the Rapidan early in May, 1864, needs close examination.

One or two points need to be made clear at the beginning.

In the first place it is quite inaccurate to argue that no other Federal general ever enjoyed the over-all authority that was given to Grant when he became general-in-chief. McClellan had that authority, beginning in the fall of 1861 and running through the winter of 1862. Like Grant, he blocked out a comprehensive campaign covering all the important theaters of the war; the difference was that he could not make anything happen the way he wanted it to happen. He could not compel Halleck and Buell to work together, in the west. He could not make Buell drive into East Tennessee, although he repeatedly warned the man that his own strategy in Virginia depended on an aggressive advance by Buell's army. He could not even make his own army move according to his own timetable. If he was presently removed from over-all command of the Federal armies, the reason obviously was that he had not been able to exercise that over-all command effectively.

Halleck became general-in-chief early in the summer of 1862, and there is no question that President Lincoln hoped that he would be a vigorous commander. Halleck simply did not try to become one. The full authority Grant was finally given was Halleck's, when Halleck first came to Washington; but Halleck refused to reach out, seize it, and exercise it, and in a remarkably short time he had reduced himself to a sort of high-level adviser, a paper-shuffler who neither laid down nor enforced a comprehensive strategy for the war as a whole. President Lincoln rendered his own verdict on the man not long after the battle of Fredericksburg, when General Burnside wanted to renew the offensive and his principal subordinates disagreed violently. The army was immobilized as a result, and Lincoln wrote Halleck suggesting that he, as general-in-chief, go down to Fredericksburg, examine the situation, and then either tell Burnside to go ahead, with full support from the top, or call the whole business off and devise something else. "In this difficulty, if you do not help me," Lincoln wrote to Halleck, "you fail me precisely in the point for which I sought your assistance."

This hurt Halleck's feelings, so that he offered to resign, and in the War Department files Lincoln's original letter presently got an addition, in the President's handwriting: "Withdrawn, because considered harsh by General Halleck." As commanding general, Halleck simply refused to function, and the overriding authority that had been given to him withered on the vine because he was incapable of using it. The point to remember, however, is that the authority was there for him to use if he had had the force to exert it.

In addition, the authority which was at last given to Grant was not really as all-inclusive as it is usually supposed to have been, a fact which had a profound effect on the course of military operations.

Grant did not have the full control which he is assumed to have had. He was not, for instance, able to cancel General Nathaniel Banks's ill-advised and desperately unlucky offensive along the Red River—an eccentric thrust which was political rather than military in its conception, which would not have accomplished a great deal even if it had succeeded, and which used men, ships, and materiel that might have been applied elsewhere to much better advantage. Grant had no use for this movement, but not until Banks ran into outright disaster was he able to get it withdrawn.

More important, Grant was not able to select the commanders for two very important subsidiary movements in Virginia: movements which were well conceived and which, if they had been handled skillfully, would almost certainly have enabled Grant to win over Lee the kind of victory he had counted on winning.

One Union army was ordered to proceed up the Shenandoah Valley, depriving the Army of Northern Virginia of the bountiful supplies which it got from that area and, eventually, threatening Richmond from the west. Another army was ordered to advance toward Richmond along the south bank of the James River. The movements of these two armies were as much a part of Grant's Virginia campaign as the movements of the Army of the Potomac itself. If they had gone as scheduled—as they might very well have done if they had been efficiently led—the job which had to be done by the Army of the Potomac would have been ever so much easier. Taken all together, the triple-headed campaign would have been something the Confederacy probably could not have met.

But Grant was not able to get men of his own choice to command either of these subsidiary offensives.

The army which moved up the Shenandoah was put under General Franz Sigel, who was about as completely incompetent a commander as the Union army possessed. Sigel got his job solely because his name had, or was thought to have, political value with the German-born population. The year 1864 was an election year, and Washington decided that it was necessary to give Sigel prominence. And Sigel's Shenandoah campaign collapsed almost before it had got started. Sigel was dismally routed at

New Market, and his army instead of helping the operations of the Army of the Potomac became a source of weakness.

It was the same with the advance up the James. This advance was entrusted to General Ben Butler, of whom it must be said that he was probably Sigel's equal in military incompetence; and Butler most certainly would not have been in command if Grant had had anything to say about it. Butler had the strength to drive right to the outskirts of Richmond, and if he had done this Lee would have been compelled to retreat, or to make ruinously expensive detachments of force, just when the Army of the Potomac was pressing him most severely. As it worked out, however, Butler completely missed his opportunity, and before long permitted himself to be penned up in defensive works at Bermuda Hundred. Lee did not have to detach troops to oppose Butler; on the contrary, Lee was presently reinforced by some of the troops whom Butler should have been keeping busy.

In other words, Grant's Virginia campaign did not go as he had planned it partly because the two subsidiary moves which were essential to the whole design were commanded by inept soldiers who would never have been allowed within miles of the field of operations if Grant had had his way. No appraisal of what Grant did in Virginia is complete if the abysmal failure of these two offensives is not taken into account.

Grant's authority, in other words, was not really as unadulterated as is generally supposed. If the armies in the Shenandoah and along the James had been commanded by real soldiers—by such men, for instance, as John Sedgwick (whom Meade originally proposed for the Shenandoah command) and W. F. Smith—it is obvious that the job which had to be done by Meade's army would have been much easier and, presumably, would have gone much more smoothly. Grant was handicapped by Washington's interference here precisely as McClellan was handicapped when he launched his own offensive in the spring of 1862.

In any case, Grant as general-in-chief made his headquarters with the Army of the Potomac and took that Army across the Rapidan and into the Wilderness on May 4, 1864.

We badly need a detailed examination of the command arrangements which resulted. The army of course was under General George Meade's immediate command. (In the beginning, Burnside's corps, which accompanied the army, was not under Meade's control, but this was rectified before much time had passed.) Grant was present at all times, his own headquarters staff and apparatus being camped, usually, within a short distance of Meade's. The situation undoubtedly was difficult for both commanders: in effect, the army had two heads, Meade was under constant supervision, and on a good many occasions Grant and his staff issued battle orders direct to Meade's subordinates. Both Meade and Grant did their best to make this cumbrous system work, but it unquestionably led to many difficulties.

These difficulties, in addition, were complicated by the fact that the

Army of the Potomac was clique-ridden. Its officer corps contained many men who still felt that only McClellan was a really good commander. They tended to resent the arrival of Grant, the westerner, to question his ability on the ground that the successes he had won in the west had been won against second-raters, and to express open skepticism about his ability to accomplish anything against a soldier of Lee's caliber. (One of the interesting things about the men who enjoyed important commands in the Army of the Potomac was that they seem to have had more respect for Lee than for any of their own superiors.) It seems possible at times to detect a certain sluggishness in army movements arising from this fact. At the very least it must be said that the dual command arrangement was a handicap.

Whether for this reason or for some other, control of the army at corps and divisional level seems to have been defective. The kind of quick, decisive moment which characterized the movements of Grant's army in the Vicksburg campaign, for example, was not in evidence. Cold Harbor was very poorly managed, and the whole attempt to seize Petersburg following the crossing of the James was hopelessly bungled; it is hardly too much to say that during the two or three crucial days in which that key point should have been occupied by Union forces the army as an army was hardly commanded at all. (Indeed, Meade himself said virtually as much, almost in so many words. On June 18, when he had his last chance to drive into Petersburg before Lee's army arrived, he found it utterly impossible to get a co-ordinated advance, and at last he burst out with the revealing telegram to his subordinates: "I find it useless to appoint an hour to effect co-operation . . . what additional orders to attack you require I cannot imagine. . . . Finding it impossible to effect co-operation by appointing an hour for attack, I have sent an order to each corps commander to attack at all hazards, and without reference to each other." The attack failed, naturally enough, and the Confederates held Petersburg for nine more months. It might be noted, in this connection, that the soldiers in the Army of the Potomac fought well enough here; the war weariness which is supposed to have resulted from Cold Harbor, and from the wearing campaign which had preceded it, had not yet set in. It was the army commander's failure to control the battle that was the trouble here.

The army commander, to repeat, was Meade: but Grant was the general-in-chief, he was with the army at the time, and as the man who would have gained the credit if a great victory had been won he can probably be given blame for the failure. It is hard to escape the conclusion that it was the dual command arrangement that was largely at fault . . . hard, also, to avoid the feeling that if a Sheridan or a Thomas had been in Meade's place during those first few days at Petersburg the story would have been different.

However all of that may have been, one more complaint about Grant's generalship in the Virginia campaign must be examined: the charge that he had too much faith in the virtues of a head-on offensive and failed to recognize the immense preponderance of the defensive in frontal assaults like the ones at Spotsylvania and Cold Harbor.

It is undoubtedly true that Grant underestimated the defensive strength of good troops, well entrenched, using rifled muskets. He shared this failing with most of the other Civil War generals, including Lee himself. Weapons used in the Civil War, even though they look extremely primitive today, were in fact much more modern than anything warfare had seen before. A revolution in tactics was taking place, and it took the generals a long time to realize it. One is tempted to speculate that the success of Thomas' great assault at Chattanooga, where a massed army corps captured the Missionary Ridge position which should have been completely invulnerable to any frontal attack, may have stuck too long in the back of Grant's mind. What-ever the reason, it must be said that it took Grant a long time to see that the all-along-the-line attack after the old manner was out of date. A great many men died because of this.

Summing up the criticisms of the Virginia campaign of 1864, then, one must say: (1) that the subsidiary campaigns which should have insured the success of the advance of the Army of the Potomac failed miserably because Grant was unable to control the appointment of the men who led them; (2) that the command arrangement which grew out of his insistence on ac-companying Meade's army was most defective and probably was at least partly responsible for a number of costly setbacks; and (3) that Grant himself showed too much fondness for old-fashioned offensive combat when the conditions under which that kind of combat could have succeeded had disappeared.

Against these criticisms, balance Grant's achievements. They are more solid than is apparent at first glance.

First of all, and perhaps most important of all, Grant was the one Federal general, from first to last, who kept the initiative in the Virginia theater.

Each one of his predecessors had moved South in a great "Forward to Richmond" campaign, and each one of them had found before long that he had lost the ball and was on the defensive; instead of forcing Lee to keep step with him, the Federal general was always trying to keep step with Lee, usually without great success. McClellan, Pope, Burnside, Hooker, even Meade—each one went south to defeat a strongly outnum-bered opponent and before long found either that he was in full retreat or that he was fighting desperately for survival. Here was the fact that had given the generals in the Army of the Potomac such vast respect for Lee's military ability. No matter how a campaign began, it usually ended with Lee calling the shots.

The second achievement grows out of the first.

By keeping the initiative, Grant compelled Lee to fight the kind of war which Lee could not win. Lee's conduct of the campaign which began in the Wilderness and ended at last in front of Petersburg was masterly, enormously costly in Northern lives, almost ruinous to home-front morale— the profound wave of war weariness which swept the North in the summer of 1864 came largely because the Virginia campaign was so dreadfully expensive and seemed to be accomplishing so little—but it did end with

Lee locked up in a fortress where effective offensive movements were impossible for him. Not long after the Wilderness campaign began, Lee remarked that if he were ever forced back into the Richmond lines and compelled to stand on the defensive there the end would be only a matter of time. He was, in spite of his best efforts, forced back into those lines; in spite of his magnificent tactical successes, the process took only a little more than six weeks; and after that it was, as Lee himself had predicted, just a question of time.

The campaign did, to be sure, reduce the fighting capacity of the valiant Army of the Potomac to a low level. Such excellent combat units as Hancock's II Corps, for example, late in the summer became almost impotent; at Reams Station this corps was routed by a Confederate counterattack which the same corps would have beaten off with ease six months earlier. But this grim process of attrition worked both ways. The Army of Northern Virginia was worn down also, so that it likewise became unable to do things which in earlier years it would have done smoothly. The Federal cause could endure this attrition and the Southern cause could not.

Yet it was not actually just a campaign of attrition. The significant thing is that Lee was deprived of the opportunity to maneuver, to seize the openings created by his opponent's mistakes, to make full use of the dazzling ability to combine swift movements and hard blows which had served him so well in former campaigns. Against Grant, Lee was not able to do the things he had done before. He had to fight the sort of fight he could not win.

Finally, even though Grant's original hope was to bring Lee to battle in the open and destroy his army, he was really conducting an immense holding operation, and what happened in Virginia means nothing unless it is examined in the light of what was happening elsewhere. Sherman was advancing in and through Georgia. Unless the Confederacy could intervene against him, Sherman would eventually provide the winning maneuver. Grant held Lee down so effectively that intervention against Sherman became impossible; holding Lee, Grant insured Sherman's victory. When Sherman won, the war was won. Lee, to be sure, held out to the bitter end, but the end came because the Confederacy behind Lee had shrunk to a helpless fragment.

It gets back, in other words, to the grand strategy, the concept of the war as a whole in which the movements of all of the Federal armies were interrelated. What Grant did in Virginia enabled the grand strategy to work. Viewed in that light, the Virginia campaign was a success: costly, agonizing, all but unendurably grueling in its demands on soldiers and on the people back home, but still a success.

Grant, in short, was able to use the immense advantage in numbers, in military resources, and in money which the Federal side possessed from the start. Those advantages had always been there, and what the Northern war effort had always needed was a soldier who, assuming the top command, would see to it that they were applied steadily, remorselessly and without a break, all across the board. The complaint that Grant succeeded only because he had superior numbers is pointless. The superior numbers were part of the equation all along. It was Grant who took advantage of them and used them to apply a pressure which the weaker side could not possibly stand.

This was a most substantial achievement. Achieving it, Grant merits very high ranking as a soldier. He used the means at hand to discharge the obligation which had been put upon him. The war was won thereby, and it is not easy to see how it would have been won without Grant.

FURTHER READING

Michael C. Adams, *Our Masters the Rebels: A Speculation on Union Military Failure in the East, 1861–1865* (1978)

Richard E. Beringer, Herman Hattaway, Archer Jones, and William N. Still, Jr., *Why the South Lost the Civil War* (1986)

Bruce Catton, *Army of the Potomac*, 3 vols. (1951–1953)

————, *U. S. Grant and the American Military Tradition* (1954)

————, *The Centennial History of the Civil War*, 3 vols. (1961–1965)

Thomas L. Connelly, "R. E. Lee and the Western Confederacy," *Civil War History*, 15 (1969), 116–132

———— and Archer Jones, *The Politics of Command: Factions and Ideas in Confederate Strategy* (1973)

David Donald, ed., *Why the North Won the Civil War* (1960)

Michael Fellman, *Inside War: The Guerrilla Conflict in Missouri During the Civil War* (1989)

Douglas S. Freeman, *Lee's Lieutenants: A Study in Command*, 3 vols. (1942–1944)

Edward Hagerman, *The American Civil War and the Origins of Modern Warfare* (1988)

Herman Hattaway and Archer Jones, "Lincoln as Military Strategist," *Civil War History* 26 (1980), 293–303

———— and Archer Jones, *How the North Won: A Military History of the Civil War* (1983)

Ludwell H. Johnson, "Abraham Lincoln and Jefferson Davis as War Presidents: Nothing Succeeds Like Success," *Civil War History* 27 (1981), 49–63

William S. McFeely, *Grant: A Biography* (1981)

James M. McPherson, *Battle Cry of Freedom: The Civil War Era* (1988)

Grady McWhiney, "Who Whipped Whom? Confederate Defeat Reexamined," *Civil War History* 11 (1965), 5–26

————, "Jefferson Davis as Military Strategist," *Civil War History* 21 (1975), 101–112

———— and Perry D. Jamieson, *Attack and Die: Civil War Military Tactics and the Southern Heritage* (1982)

Allan Nevins, *The War for the Union*, 4 vols. (1959–1971)

Stephen W. Sears, *George B. McClellan: The Young Napoleon* (1988)

Russell Weigley, "A Strategy of Annihilation: U. S. Grant and the Union," *The American Way of War: A History of United States Military Strategy and Policy* (1973), 128–152

T. Harry Williams, *Lincoln and His Generals* (1952)

————, *The History of American Wars from 1745 to 1918* (1981)

CHAPTER 6

Fighting the War:
The Experience of the Soldiers

In recent years, the field of history has been transformed by an awareness of and concern about the doings of ordinary people, rather than the leaders and the powerful. Military history has also been affected by this interest in the masses, or "history from the bottom up," instead of "from the top down." Beginning perhaps with John Keegan, in his Face of Battle (1976), which explored the experience of combat by British soldiers in three major battles—Agincourt in 1415, Waterloo in 1815, and the Somme in 1916—many military historians have become social historians of battles and wars. This kind of attention is also being directed toward American military history, especially the Civil War. Studies of how battles were fought from the ground up are appearing, as are analyses of the combat experience of the rank and file.

The sources for this kind of account and analysis are particularly rich for the American Civil War, because the participants left an immense array of memoirs and recollections, and a large number of them were published. This unusual outpouring of accounts by ordinary soldiers occurred for several reasons besides the high level of literacy among the combatants. First, there was a great deal of interest among the civilian populations in a war that was fought on their own soil rather than in a foreign land. And second, those who fought were greeted with respect, even awe, when they returned home since both sides, even the Confederates who were defeated, regarded the struggle as worthy and heroic. So there was an audience eager to read the reminiscences of Civil War soldiers.

The existence of such a valuable resource will undoubtedly facilitate the writing of the military history of the Civil War from the bottom up. But it will have to be used with care, since the writers of most of these memoirs either stressed the adventure and bravery in the experience, or else narrated in great detail what happened without revealing their own feelings and emotions while under fire or in the hospitals and camps. The historian's task of discovering the inner thoughts and experiences of common soldiers is therefore likely to be more difficult than it first seemed, and it will require considerable insight and imagination. Moreover, the outcome of these kinds of studies will almost certainly be

*a greater awareness of the seamy side of this war—its horror, drudgery, and
incompetence. From the foot soldier's point of view, a war that has been treated
almost with reverence by subsequent generations may begin to look rather less
grand.*

DOCUMENTS

The experience of combat is the main focus of the documents that follow, but
other aspects, particularly religion, are also illustrated. The first selection presents two songs from among the many that were composed during the war and
sung by the soldiers. Both are northern, but one is religious and sentimental,
while the other is worldly and impudent. A letter to his father written by Eugene
Blackford of the 5th Alabama Volunteer Infantry Regiment on July 22, 1861, recounting his first battlefield experience, is the second document. The third selection offers a rather different view of courage in combat; it is from a book of
wartime memoirs published by John Dooley, an Irish infantryman in the Confederate Army of Northern Virginia who went into battle on numerous occasions.

The fourth selection captures the frustration, and often anger, that soldiers
felt about the war. In it, Frank Wilkeson, a northern private, approves of his
colleagues' unwillingness to fight at one point during the siege at Petersburg,
Virginia, in June 1864. Similarly, the fifth extract, which is from the letters of
Tully McCrea, an officer in the Army of the Potomac, to his wife, reveals how
commanders' actions were often ridiculed by their soldiers, usually with good
reason, as was the case in this incident before Chancellorsville in January 1863.
The grisly horrors of combat are depicted vividly in the sixth selection, an account by General Carl Schurz of what he witnessed in the Federal field hospitals
after Gettysburg in July 1863.

The last two documents illustrate the role of religion in the Confederacy.
Jefferson Davis's Proclamation of October 26, 1864, calling for a Day of Prayer,
is one instance of many official invocations of God's aid, indicating how much
the Confederate cause was imbued with religious sentiment. And the eighth and
last selection is a postwar account of the religious revivals in the 19th Alabama
Regiment from its chaplain, Reverend Dr. John J. D. Renfroe. This description
is just one of a host of eyewitness reports collected by John William Jones in his
Christ in the Camp; or, Religion in Lee's Army (1887).

Songs the Soldiers Sang—Sentimental and Secular

Just Before the Battle, Mother

> Just before the battle, mother,
> I am thinking most of you;
> While upon the field we are watching,
> With the enemy in view.
> Comrades brave are 'round me lying,
> Filled with thoughts of home and God;
> For well they know upon the morrow
> Some will sleep beneath the sod.

Chorus: Farewell, mother, you may never
Press me to your heart again;
But, oh, you'll not forget me, mother,
If I'm numbered with the slain.

Oh! I long to see you, mother,
And the loving ones at home;
But I'll never leave our banner
'Till in honor I can come.
Tell the enemy around you
That their cruel words, we know,
In every battle kill our soldiers
By the help they give the foe.—*Chorus*

—George F. Root

We Are the Boys of Potomac's Ranks

We are the boys of Potomac's ranks,
    Hurrah! Hurrah!
We are the boys of Potomac's ranks,
We ran with McDowell, retreated with Banks,
And we'll all drink stone blind—
Johnny, fill up the bowl.

We fought with McClellan, the Rebs, shakes, and fever,
    Hurrah! Hurrah!
We fought with McClellan, the Rebs, shakes, and fever,
But Mac joined the navy on reaching James River,
And we'll all drink stone blind—
Johnny, fill up the bowl.

They gave us John Pope, our patience to tax,
    Hurrah! Hurrah!
They gave us John Pope, our patience to tax,
Who said that out West he'd seen naught but *gray backs,*
And we'll all drink stone blind—
Johnny, fill up the bowl.

He said his headquarters were in the saddle,
    Hurrah! Hurrah!
He said his headquarters were in the saddle,
But Stonewall Jackson made him skedaddle—
And we'll all drink stone blind—
Johnny, fill up the bowl.

Then Mac was recalled, but after Antietam,
    Hurrah! Hurrah!
Then Mac was recalled, but after Antietam
Abe gave him a rest, he was too slow to beat 'em,
And we'll all drink stone blind—
Johnny, fill up the bowl.

Oh, Burnside, then he tried his luck,
    Hurrah! Hurrah!

Oh, Burnside, then he tried his luck,
But in the mud so fast got stuck,
And we'll all drink stone blind—
Johnny, fill up the bowl.

Then Hooker was taken to fill the bill,
   Hurrah! Hurrah!
Then Hooker was taken to fill the bill,
But he got a black eye at Chancellorsville,
And we'll all drink stone blind—
Johnny, fill up the bowl.

Next came General Meade, a slow old plug,
   Hurrah! Hurrah!
Next came General Meade, a slow old plug,
For he let them get away at Gettysburg,
And we'll all drink stone blind—
Johnny, fill up the bowl.

—Authur Unknown

A Federal Soldier Deals with Combat, July 1861

Bivouac Camp of the Advanced Guard,
on the railroad near Union Mills
Above Manassas

22nd July, 1861

My Dear Father:

We are very much fatigued and jaded by our late movements. I must relieve your anxiety by letting you know that I am alive and well. I was in the great battle of yesterday, tho our regt. arrived too late to take any considerable part in the action. But I will go back and let you know what I have been doing since this day a week.

Last Monday the enemy advanced their lines considerably and caused our pickets to fall back some two miles. We were up all Tuesday night expecting to march down to the battery to defend it. At 8 o'clock Wednesday, the advance guard of the enemy appeared, and we went out to give battle. We all took our positions behind our entrenchments, and remained there some time while parties of our men were skirmishing in front.

At last they were driven in, and the firing commenced upon our line. The enemy, having minie muskets, could fire upon us long before we could think of returning the compliment, and so we had to take it coolly. No wound was sustained by our men (in my company) except one pretty badly wounded. The balls make a very loud singing noise when they pass near you, and at first caused me to duck my head, but I soon became used to it. I never expected to be alarmed or excited in battle, but really it is a very different affair from what I thought it. I never was cooler in my life, and have ever since been very much pleased therefore, as I shall have no trouble hereafter.

Just as we were about to make our fire general, news was brought that the [Illinois] had retreated from Fairfax Court House and thus had exposed our flank. Of course there was nothing to be done but to retreat. This we barely had time to do, the enemy was almost in sight of the crossroads when we passed at double quick. Had we been twenty minutes later, we would have been cut off utterly. As I said before, we marched quick time for twenty miles to this place, my company being deployed as skirmishers on the side next to the enemy. The part was one of honor and implied trust, but it was at a great cost, as the country was awfully rough, and we suffered very much. . . .

We then came right about and set off to reinforce our men in the great battle (not yet named) about ten miles from us. This distance we marched at double time and came on the field about five o'clock, too late as I said to do much service, but early enough to smell a little gunpowder and receive a little of the enemy's fire. We went over the battlefield several miles in extent. T'was truly awful, an immense cloud of smoke and dust hung over the whole country, and the flashing of the artillery was incessant tho none of the balls struck my company. One bomb burst a little above me, and killed and wounded several. This was our only loss. Had we been an hour earlier, many would not have lived to tell of it.

I shan't attempt to describe the appearance of the field, literally covered with bodies, and for five miles before reaching it I saw men limping off, more or less wounded. We met wagon loads of bodies coming off to Manassas, where they are now piled in heaps. While we were looking over the field, an order came for us to go back to our batteries ten miles off, and defend them from the enemy who were advancing upon them, so we had to go back, tired as we were, to our holes, where we arrived half dead at twelve o'clock last night, having marched twenty-six miles heavily loaded. We have no protection against the rain, which has been falling all day. I have no blanket, not having seen my baggage since leaving Fairfax; I never was so dirty before in my life and besides I have scurvy in my mouth, not having anything but hard bread and intensely salty meat to eat, and not enough of that.

I do not however complain, nor do my men, tho I never thought that such hardships were to be endured. We have our meat in the blaze, and eat it on our bread. A continual firing is now going on around us.

Your affectionate son,

Eugene Blackford

A Confederate Soldier Acknowledges Fear, (Undated)

The Psychology of Soldiers' Fear

We know how straight into the very jaws of destruction and death leads this road of Gettysburg; and none of us are yet aware that a battle is before us; still there pervades our ranks a solemn feeling, as if some unforeseen danger was ever dropping darksome shadows over the road we unshrinkingly trcad.

For myself, I must confess that the terrors of the battlefield grew not less as we advanced in the war, for I felt far less fear in the second battle of Manassas than at South Mountain or even at Fredericksburg; and I believe that soldiers generally do not fear death less because of their repeated escape from its jaws. For, in every battle they see so many new forms of death, see so many frightful and novel kinds of mutilation, see such varying fortunes in the tide of strife, and appreciate so highly their deliverance from destruction, that their dread of incurring the like fearful perils unnerves them for each succeeding conflict, quite as much as their confidence in their oft tried courage sustains them and stimulates them to gain new laurels at the cannon's mouth.

An Officer Laments the Inadequacy of Northern Generals, January 1863

. . . Tomorrow the army is going to cross the river again and attack the enemy. The attack this time is going to be made upon their right, instead of the center. This movement has been in contemplation for a week past and everyone has been praying for a rain or a snow to stop it. No one seems to have any confidence in what we attempt to do. The movement began today. The left and center Grand Divisions commanded by Generals Franklin and Hooker moved up the river today, ready to commence the crossing in the morning. General Sumner's Grand Division, which is the right, is to act as reserve. General Sumner is as mad as he can be because he could not have the advance. Whenever there is a fight he wants to be in the thickest of it, which accounts for his old corps (the Second) being now reduced so low by the severe losses that they have sustained. He never spares himself either, but rides wherever the bullets are thickest and takes his whole staff with him. It did not rain in time to prevent the movement, but now that the movement has begun, it has commenced to rain. . . . About eighty thousand men are now marching or standing shivering in the rain. On the Rebel side I suppose that they are equally busy, for no doubt they are by this time fully informed where the attack is to be made and are preparing to meet it. (January 20, 1863.)

. . . General Sumner was today relieved from command and his splendid staff, with nearly all of whom I was acquainted and intimate, is broken up. Two of them were just here. One is going home on a leave of absence, the other, MacKenzie, is going to Acquia Creek tomorrow to lay fortifications and will not be back for some time. I am not the only one who feels blue. A feeling of despondency hangs over this whole army. Burnside was liked, although none had much confidence in his ability to command this large army. General Franklin, who is regarded as the most able of the generals with the army, has been ordered to Washington like General Sumner, and Joe Hooker takes command. Dear me! This army is fast going to ruin. It is hard indeed after all the hardships, gallant fighting, and long service that it has seen that it should at last be disgraced, all for no fault of its own, but merely through the meddling of the officials at Washington. (January 26, 1863.)

A Federal Private Applauds a Refusal to Fight, June 1864

. . . In the morning I saw that there had been some advance of the line. The Second Corps had gained a little ground at great cost, and we heard that Burnside had also gained ground and captured a redoubt. The dead soldiers of the Second Corps lay thickly in front of us, placed in long trenches by their comrades.

That afternoon the battery quartermaster-sergeant, goaded to desperation by the taunts of the artillery privates, nerved himself with whiskey and came to the battery to display his courage. The Confederate sharp-shooters had attacked us about noon, and our works were hot. I, snugly seated under the earthworks, looked at this representative of the staff with all the intense dislike privates have for the gold-laced officers. I was wicked enough to wish that he would get shot. He swaggered up and down behind the guns, talking loudly, and ignorant of the danger. I, with high-beating heart, looked eagerly at him, hungrily waiting for him to jump and howl. I was disappointed. A sharp-shooter's bullet struck him on the throat. It crashed through his spine at the base of the brain, and he neither jumped nor howled—simply fell on his back dead.

Early on the morning of June 18th, some of our pickets brought word to the battery that the Confederates had abandoned their front line during the night, and that they had moved back to their interior line, which was shorter and stronger and more easily defended. The infantry soldiers moved forward, and occupied the works they had been unable to capture. My battery moved to another position, and again the guns opened on the Confederate line, and again they husbanded their ammunition. But their sharp-shooters fairly made us howl with anguish. I heartily wished that Lee had not abandoned his front line. Our infantry moved to and fro, getting ready to assault the new line of intrenchments. The soldiers were thoroughly discouraged. They had no heart for the assault. It was evident that they had determined not to fight staunchly, not to attempt to accomplish the impossible. At about four o'clock in the afternoon the infantry was sent to the slaughter, and the Confederates promptly killed a sufficient number of them to satisfy our generals that the works could not be taken by assaults delivered by exhausted and discouraged troops. In many places our battle line did not advance to the line of rifle-pits held by the Confederate pickets. We had lost about 12,000 men in the attempts to capture Petersburg. The Second Corps could have taken the city on the night of June 15th without losing more than 500 men. This fact disheartened the enlisted men of the Army of the Potomac. They were supremely disgusted with the display of military stupidity our generals had made.

We marched somewhere at night. The road was lined with sleeping infantry. I was hungry. As I look back at those bloody days it seems to me that I was always hungry. Men to the right of us, to the left of us, lay as though dead—they slept so soundly; but their haversacks were not in sight. They were veterans who knew enough to hide their haversacks when they slept on roads. We came to a heavy double line of men, who looked as if they had opened ranks and then fallen over asleep. Soon we light-artillery men recognized them as 100-day men from Ohio. Their haversacks stood at their heads. Wickedly we all went to plundering the 100-day men as they slept. We exchanged our empty haversacks for full ones, and every man of us had a spare haversack filled with food hanging on the guns or caissons. At the time I thought it a capital joke on the Ohio men; but I now think that some of those men were very hungry before they got any thing to eat. They must have bitter recollections of the night march of some of the Second Corps' artillery. . . .

General Carl Schurz Describes the Horror of the Field Hospitals after Gettysburg, July 1863

. . . There were more harrowing experiences in store for me that day. To look after the wounded of my command, I visited the places where the surgeons were at work. At Bull Run, I had seen only on a very small scale what I was now to behold. At Gettysburg the wounded—many thousands of them—were carried to the farmsteads behind our lines. The houses, the barns, the sheds, and the open barnyards were crowded with moaning and wailing human beings, and still an unceasing procession of stretchers and ambulances was coming in from all sides to augment the number of the sufferers. A heavy rain set in during the day—the usual rain after a battle—and large numbers had to remain unprotected in the open, there being no room left under roof. I saw long rows of men lying under the eaves of the buildings, the water pouring down upon their bodies in streams. Most of the operating tables were placed in the open where the light was best, some of them partially protected against the rain by tarpaulins or blankets stretched upon poles. There stood the surgeons, their sleeves rolled up to the elbows, their bare arms as well as their linen aprons smeared with blood, their knives not seldom held between their teeth, while they were helping a patient on or off the table, or had their hands otherwise occupied; around them pools of blood and amputated arms or legs in heaps, sometimes more than man-high. Antiseptic methods were still unknown at that time. As a wounded man was lifted on the table, often shrieking with pain as the attendants handled him, the surgeon quickly examined the wound and resolved upon cutting off the injured limb. Some ether was administered and the body put in position in a moment. The surgeon snatched his knife from between his teeth, where it had been while his hands were busy, wiped it rapidly once or twice across his blood-stained apron, and the cutting began. The operation accomplished, the surgeon would look around with a deep sigh, and then—"Next!"

And so it went on, hour after hour, while the number of expectant patients seemed hardly to diminish. Now and then one of the wounded men would call attention to the fact that his neighbor lying on the ground had given up the ghost while waiting for his turn, and the dead body was then quietly removed. Or a surgeon, having been long at work, would put down his knife, exclaiming that his hand had grown unsteady, and that this was too much for human endurance—not seldom hysterical tears streaming down his face. Many of the wounded men suffered with silent fortitude, fierce determination in the knitting of their brows and the steady gaze of their bloodshot eyes. Some would even force themselves to a grim jest about their situation or about the "skedaddling of the rebels." But there were, too, heart-rending groans and shrill cries of pain piercing the air, and despairing exclamations, "Oh, Lord! Oh, Lord!" or "Let me die!" or softer murmurings in which the words "mother" or "father" or "home" were often heard. I saw many of my command among the sufferers, whose faces I well remembered, and who greeted me with a look or even a painful smile of recognition, and usually with the question what I thought of their chances of life, or whether I could do anything for them, sometimes, also, whether I thought the enemy were well beaten. I was sadly conscious that many of the words of cheer and encouragement I gave them were mere hollow sound, but they might be at least some solace for the moment.

There are people who speak lightly of war as a mere heroic sport. They would hardly find it in their hearts to do so, had they ever witnessed scenes like these, and thought of the untold miseries connected with them that were spread all over the land. He must be an inhuman brute or a slave of wild, unscrupulous ambition, who, having seen the horrors of war, will not admit that war brought on without the most absolute necessity, is the greatest and most unpardonable of crimes.

President Davis Seeks God's Aid and Mercy, October 1864

A Proclamation

It is meet that the people of the Confederate States should, from time to time, assemble to acknowledge their dependence on Almighty God, to render devout thanks to his holy name, to bend in prayer at his footstool, and to accept, with fervent submission, the chastening of his all-wise and all-merciful providence.

Let us, then, in temples and in the field, unite our voices in recognizing, with adoring gratitude, the manifestations of his protecting care in the many signal victories with which our arms have been crowned; in the fruitfulness with which our land has been blessed, and in the unimpaired energy and fortitude with which he has inspired our hearts and strengthened our arms in resistance to the iniquitous designs of our enemies.

And let us not forget that, while graciously vouchsafing to us his protection, our sins have merited and received grievous chastisement; that many of our best and bravest have fallen in battle; that many others are still held in foreign prisons; that large districts of our country have been devastated with savage ferocity, the peaceful homes destroyed, and helpless women and children driven away in destitution; and that with fiendish malignity the passions of a servile race have been excited by our foes into the commission of atrocities from which death is a welcome escape.

Now, therefore, I, Jefferson Davis, President of the Confederate States of America, do issue this my proclamation, setting apart Wednesday, the 16th day of November next, as a day to be specially devoted to the worship of Almighty God; and I do invite and invoke all the people of these Confederate States to assemble on the day aforesaid, in their respective places of public worship, there to unite in prayer to our Heavenly Father that he bestow his favor upon us; that he extend over us the protection of his almighty arm; that he sanctify his chastisement to our improvement, so that we may turn away from evil paths and walk righteously in his sight; and that he may restore peace to our beloved country, healing its bleeding wounds, and securing to us the continued enjoyment of our own right to self-government and independence, and that he will graciously hearken to us while we ascribe to him the power and glory of our independence.

Given under my hand and the seal of the Confederate States at Richmond, this 26th day of October, in the year of our Lord 1864.

Jefferson Davis.

By the President:

J. P. Benjamin, *Secretary of State.*

A Confederate Chaplain Recounts His Experience of the Revivals (1863–1864), January 1867

[From Rev. Dr. Renfroe, Baptist, Chaplain Tenth Alabama Regiment.]

Talladega, Alabama, January 31, 1867.

Dear Brother Jones: In attempting to give you some account of the religious character of Wilcox's old brigade, in the army of Northern Virginia, I find that I am entirely dependent upon my memory. I loaned my "notes" of events to a brother, who now informs me that he cannot lay his hand on them, having mislaid them.

The Tenth Alabama was the regiment of which I was chaplain. The brigade was composed of the Eighth, Ninth, Tenth, Eleventh and Fourteenth Alabama Regiments. I reckon this brigade comprised as noble a body of men as ever served in any army. I reached my post of duty while the army was in winter-quarters at Fredericksburg, in the early part of the year 1863. There were then three other chaplains in that brigade, but they were all then absent but one. Very little preaching had been done in the brigade up to that time. Many Christian soldiers and other good-disposed men told me that I could do no good in preaching to soldiers, but all seemed glad to welcome me among them. I was acquainted with a large number of the regiment before the war. The first Sabbath after I got there I preached twice, and from that time until I left them, I had a large attendance upon worship, and as good order in my congregations as I ever had at home. About that time the Rev. Mr. Bell, of Greenville, Alabama, visited the Eighth, which had no chaplain. He and I preached daily for two weeks. He baptized a Mr. Lee, of Marion, Alabama, the first profession that I saw in the army; though there were many men in the brigade who were Christians before they went to the army, and who maintained their religion. The chaplains of the brigade soon returned. We built arbors, and preached regularly to large and attentive congregations—on through the spring this continued—only interrupted by the battle of Chancellorsville. Then came the campaign to Gettysburg. I preached thirteen sermons on that campaign, but not more than half of them to our own brigade. I preached several sermons in line of battle. After we returned to the south side of the Potomac, at Bunker's Hill, we had several sermons in the brigade. Two of the chaplains (Mr. Rains, of the Fourteenth, and Mr. Whitten, of the Ninth) remained at Gettysburg with the wounded. Up to this time I saw but few signs of the good work—I saw no evidences of revival—I heard of no conversions in our brigade. Then we fell back to Orange Court House. There we at once established arbors—one in the Fourteenth, one in the Tenth, and began to preach. Rev. Mr. Johnson, chaplain of the Eleventh, and Mr. Cumbie, Lieutenant in the Fourteenth, did the preaching at the Fourteenth's preaching place. Their labors were blessed, and many were converted. At the preaching place of the Tenth I did the preaching for the most part. This lasted for about six weeks, in which time I was visited and aided by Rev. A. E. Dickinson, of Richmond, who preached for me a week; then by Rev. J. B. F. Mays, of Alabama, who preached nearly a week for me. God greatly blessed our efforts. I have stood at that place at night and on Sabbaths and preached, as it seemed to me, to a solid acre of men. I think I have seen as many as five or six hundred men, in one way and another, manifest at one time a desire to be prayed for. I have never seen such a time before or since. There were as many evidences of genuine penitence as I ever noticed at home—yes, more. Almost every day there would be a dozen conversions, and there were in the six weeks in the brigade, not less than five hundred who professed conversion. Not all of our brigade, for there was a battalion of artillery camped near us, and other brigades, who attended our preaching, many of whom professed religion. We estimated the conversions then at five hundred and fifty. I baptized about one hundred, Brother Cumbie about fifty, and most of the others joined the Methodists. This work, as you know, prevailed nearly all through the army. But it was partially interrupted by the fall campaign, when we drove Meade back to Bull Run. But the army returned from that campaign to Orange, went into winter-quarters and spent the winter there. Part of this winter I was at home on furlough. But prayer-meetings, Bible-classes and preaching were successfully kept up through the winter. And the revival also, in a less degree, continued. The Young Men's Christian Association was largely attended, many went to exhorting, and a great many prayed in public, some of whom were greatly gifted. A most interesting feature was the large number who would retire after the evening "roll-call" in groups, to pray. Walk out from camp at that hour in any direction and you would find them, two, three, half-dozen and a dozen, in a place, all bowed in the dark, earnestly praying for themselves and the conversion of their comrades; they nearly always took some unconverted ones with them.

Through the awful campaign of 1864 there were very limited opportunities to preach to this brigade. It was almost constantly under fire or on the march. From the Wilderness to Petersburg and around Petersburg, this was the case. Though I preached to them as often as I could, yet most of my preaching was to other commands. I have several times preached when shot and shell were flying over our heads, and also several times I had minnie-balls to strike in my congregation while preaching. We often had prayer-meetings in the trenches, where God did greatly bless and comfort our hearts. In the winter-quarters at Petersburg there was much faithful preaching, and regular prayer-meetings kept up in this brigade.

1. I believe that the conversions were genuine. There were exceptions of course. But I received candidates for baptism just as I do at home, *i. e.,* I assembled the Baptists of the regiment, heard a relation of the applicants' Christian experience, took the vote, etc. All other Baptist ministers, I think, did the same. And their statements of the work of grace were clear and satisfactory.

2. So far as my knowledge extended, these converts maintained their professions with astonishing faithfulness. Up to the time that I left them, I knew of but two or three exceptions.

3. The character of the brigade was decidedly moral and religious, compared with what it was before this good work began. The worship of God became a fixed part of the regular duties of the brigade. The religious element was as well defined, as well organized and as constant, as in any congregation to whom I have preached. Christians were recognized as such, ministers were respected and kindly treated and loved. I have never had a congregation at home that seemed to esteem me more, and certainly I never loved a congregation so much. I never was treated disrespectfully by a soldier or officer while I was in the army—not in one instance. They preserved a tender regard for my feelings. None of them ever gambled or swore in my immediate presence; if any did swear in my immediate presence in a moment of unguarded levity or haste or passion, they always followed it with a becoming apology. Card-playing and the like ceased to be public in this brigade, except among the Irish Catholics, of whom there were three companies, who seemed "neither to fear God nor regard man"; only they were very good soldiers.

4. The officers of my regiment, to a man, were respectful to me and to my position. They always attended preaching. There was no exception. Some of them were good Christians, while all believed that there was no

officer in the regiment worth more to it than a good chaplain, and no part of their daily duties of so much importance as that of religious services. The men who commanded the regiment for the most part of the time that I was with them, were: Colonel W. H. Forney, Episcopalian; Lieutenant-Colonel Shelley, Methodist inclined; Major Joseph Truss, Baptist; Captain Brewster, of seemingly no fixed denominational preference. There never was a time that any one of these noble spirits would not do any and every thing that I desired to further the interests of public worship, preaching, prayer-meetings, etc. They did not allow anything that they could control to interfere with our hours of worship. And Colonel Shelley, who commanded most of the time (Colonel Forney being a prisoner), often said that the work of the chaplain was essential to the welfare of the regiment, essential to its efficiency, etc. The officers of the brigade, nearly all of them, were similar in conduct and disposition to those of my own regiment. And so I found the officers throughout the army, so far as I had opportunity to test the matter. No one of any rank ever treated me other than respectfully and kindly.

5. There were some very efficient Christians in the brigade. Lieutenant Cumbie, of the Fourteenth Regiment, was a most useful man. He was pious, devoted and active, a very good preacher, a brave soldier and an efficient officer. Privates E. B. Hardie, of the Tenth, and Jacob Nelson, of the same regiment, were both most excellent young men, faithful and zealous in the service of the Lord, and brave soldiers. Both of them were young ministers. These three men were Baptists, and are pastors at home now, and successful. There were many others who were not preachers, that were in every way faithful and true.

6. So far as I have been able to observe, those who professed religion in the army and lived to get home, are as faithful, constant and zealous now, as any other part of the religious community. I am pastor of several of them, and I know many others. Some of them are splendid church-members; but some have made shipwreck of the faith, or never had any faith. Yet I think three-fourths are maintaining a good profession, and proving that they were truly converted.

7. I believe it was generally conclusive that religious men made the best soldiers. And I know that officers frequently expressed themselves as believing thus. Religious soldiers complained less at army regulations, hard service and short rations. They did their duty more generally and more willingly, and I never knew one of them to disgrace himself in battle. Many of them died at their posts. They straggled less on marches, and committed fewer depredations on the rights of citizens.

8. The religious *status* of this brigade remained firm and decided to the surrender of the army.

Brother Jones, I am aware that this letter is a very poor and indifferent account of the religious standing of my old brigade. Maybe, however, that you can get something out of it. I baptized about two hundred while I was in the army, two years, but nearly half of them were men of other brigades than my own, and converted under the ministry of other men. The Lord bless you in your good work,

Yours fraternally,

J. J. D. Renfroe

⤴ E S S A Y S

The two essays reprinted here probe the impact of the war, particularly its psychological and spiritual effects, on those who fought it. The first, by Gerald F. Linderman of the University of Michigan at Ann Arbor, shows how an initial admiration for courage in battle changed as it became apparent to the combatants that the war itself was turning out to be rather different from what they had imagined. The companion piece, by Drew Gilpin Faust of the University of Pennsylvania, discusses a neglected aspect of the soldier's experience—his spiritual life—and focuses on the extraordinary religious revivals that occurred in the Confederate military, especially the Army of Northern Virginia, during the last years of the war.

Courage and Its Unraveling

GERALD F. LINDERMAN

As Civil War battles revealed by degrees that bravery was no guarantor of victory, that rifled muskets and defensive works could thwart the most spirited charge, soldiers sensed the insufficiency of courage and began to move away from many of their initial convictions.

One of the first tenets to be discarded was the one holding that exceptional combat courage deserved special protection, even to the point of suspending efforts to kill the bravest of the enemy. Indeed, certain commanders had opposed such deference almost from the outset. Stonewall Jackson always urged special attention of another sort to the enemy's most courageous soldiers:

> At the battle of Port Republic [June 9, 1862] an officer commanding a regiment of Federal soldiers and riding a snowwhite horse was very conspicuous for his gallantry. He frequently exposed himself to the fire of our men in the most reckless way. So splendid was this man's courage that General Ewell, one of the most chivalrous gentlemen . . . at some risk to his own life, rode down the line and called to his men not to shoot the man on the white horse. After a while, however, the officer and the white horse went down. A day or two after, when General Jackson learned of the incident, he sent for General Ewell and told him not to do such a thing again; that this was no ordinary war, and the brave and gallant Federal

officers were the very kind that must be killed. "Shoot the brave officers and the cowards will run away and take the men with them."

While Ewell continued to uphold courage as the primary virtue wherever demonstrated, Jackson focused on the way courage bonded enemies, and he wanted no part of anything that might vitiate the combativeness of his troops. He also comprehended, as few did so early in the war, that to obliterate the most courageous of the foe was to demoralize those whose discipline drew on their example.

Other officers, without Jackson's relentless certainty in the matter, moved in his direction as the war went on. An example was the commander of the 8th Alabama at Antietam.

> One incident occurred here which I have always thought was an exhibition of bravery that surpassed even the gallant Frenchman who has been immortalized by Victor Hugo, in the vivid picture he draws in *Les Misérables,* of the destruction of the old guard at Waterloo. When the enemy were scurrying back . . . over the hill which was to give them protection, they were completely demoralized; very few used their muskets as they retreated, but there was one man who never marched out of common-time. He marched as deliberately as if on drill . . . loading while going eight or ten steps, then turning and firing. Again and again he fired as he went up the hill and when he got to the top, all his comrades being out of sight . . . he fired for the last time, and then, turning[,] he slapped his hand on his posterior, to indicate the contempt in which he had us. I am sorry to say I did not at the moment appreciate, as sentiment suggests I should have done, the gallantry of this man. While he was walking up that hillside alone, firing at us and his balls were whistling close by, I shouted to my men, "I will give the man a furlough that will shoot that rascal!" At that time I meant business. The bravest of the enemy were the men I wanted to kill—they set bad examples, and that was no time for sentiment.

That logic soon made targets of the enemy's color-bearers, soldiers whose courage had won them positions of honor as carriers of the regimental standards around which men might be inspired to charge or to rally. By the time of Fredericksburg, a Confederate officer was ordering his men, "Now, shoot down the colors," and by 1865 it had become acceptable practice to direct fire upon color-bearers even as they lay on the ground. ("And how we did keep pouring the bullets into them, the flags for a mark! . . . The flags continued to tumble and rise.") Often every member of the color guard, ordinarily one corporal from each of the regiment's ten companies, was shot down before the battle was over. Early in the war soldiers had coveted such positions. By 1863, though by then additional incentives were offered—in the 20th New York, exemption from guard and picket, company drills and roll call; duty of no more than three hours a day—few any longer volunteered. In such brusque ways, soldiers discovered that a war of attrition left less and less room for concessions to the enemy's courage.

A related casualty was the conviction that courageous behavior imparted battlefield protection. Experience taught the opposite: The cowards either remained at home or found ways to avoid battle; the bravest "went farthest and stand longest under fire"; the best died. In January 1863 General Frank Paxton of the Stonewall Brigade complained: "Out of the fifteen field officers elected last spring, five have been killed and six wounded. . . . In these losses are many whom we were always accustomed to regard as our best men." Three months later he again found it "sad, indeed, to think how many good men we have lost. Those upon whom we all looked as distinguished for purity of character as men, and for gallantry as soldiers, seem to have been the first victims." After thirty days of Wilderness combat, Colonel Theodore Lyman of Meade's staff deplored Grant's strategy: "[T]here has been too much assaulting, this campaign! . . . The best officers and men are liable, by their greater gallantry, to be first disabled."

Those in the ranks noted the phenomenon principally by its result: a decline in the quality of their leadership. John Haskell, an artillery commander in Lee's army, was bitter that those who took such care to protect their own lives, "the dodgers," by virtue of their seniority had been promoted to replace dead or disabled officers who had "taken no pains" to preserve their lives. By such routes soldiers moved far from their original conceptions of ostentatious courage as protection and assurance of victory to the realization that it was instead an invitation to death. A few might attempt to find a new virtue in that reality—Charles Russell Lowell, contemplating the death in battle of Robert Gould Shaw, decided that the best colonel of the best black regiment *had to die,* for "it was a sacrifice we owed"—but most simply felt its demoralization.

Godliness as a protective mantle shared the same decline. For every story in the war's first months about a pocket Bible that had stopped an otherwise fatal bullet, there was in later years a matching tale of the opposite implication—that, for example, of the Union colonel who told his men that the replica Virgin Mary around his neck would protect him, and minutes later was mortally wounded. [Alexander] Hunter said of the Confederate rank-and-file in 1864–65: "The soldiers naturally distrusted the efficacy of prayer when they found that the most devout Christians were as liable to be shot as the most hardened sinner, and that a deck of cards would stop a bullet as effectively as a prayer book.

As convictions about the potency and protectiveness of courage yielded to the suspicion that special courage had become the mark of death, another of the war's original precepts—that the courageous death was the good death; that it had about it some nobler quality reflected, for example, in the smiles of courageous dead and withheld from frowning cowardly dead—also failed the test of observation. As [Frank] Wilkeson's experiences in the Army of the Potomac taught him, "Almost every death on the battlefield is different." He knew a soldier who had died quickly and whose face had only then become "horribly distorted," suggesting to passers-by a long agony that he had never experienced. The countenances of other dead had been "wreathed in smiles," allowing survivors to assure themselves that their comrades had died happy, but "I do not believe that the face of a dead soldier, lying on a battle-field, ever truthfully indicates the mental or physical anguish, or peacefulness of mind, which he suffered or enjoyed before his death. . . . It goes for nothing. One death was as painless as the other.'' Despondency sprang from that phrase "It goes for nothing," for the experience of war was teaching him, and so many others, that the rewards of courage were far less significant and the costs far higher than they had imagined and that the individual's powers of control were far feebler than they had supposed.

Doubt that the original equations were still valid sometimes arose in mundane fashion. A Massachusetts soldier noticed that those who persevered to complete arduous marches with the column were often "rewarded" by being placed on guard duty before the stragglers reached camp. [William W.] Blackford, who like other Confederate cavalrymen was required to furnish his own mount, realized that if one were forthrightly courageous in battle, one's horse was more likely to be killed. From month to month replacements became more and more difficult and expensive to procure, and failure to find one resulted in reassignment to the infantry. "Such a penalty for gallantry was terribly demoralizing."

Though disconcerting, such challenges to the notion that courage permitted the soldier to control his life and death were pinpricks set beside the challenges presented by the failed charge. The rapidity with which great numbers of men were killed at Antietam and the ease with which they were cut down at Fredericksburg and Gettysburg produced gloomy reflection as soldiers contemplated a war that had inexplicably recast its actors as victims. Minds groped to comprehend why courage had failed to secure victory and in the face of such disastrous results began, hesitantly and diversely, to move away from conventional thought and language.

Lieutenant William Wood of the 19th Virginia was one of the 15,000 who made Pickett's charge [at Gettysburg]. Prior to the attack he and his men were ordered to lie down, exposed both to a boiling sun and to the fire of Federal artillery batteries. (A Napoleon cannon could hurl a 12-pound ball a mile.) When they were brought to attention to begin the attack, some of the men immediately dropped of "seeming sunstroke," but for the charge itself Wood had only praise. It was a "splendid array" and a "beautiful line of battle." But it failed: "Down! down! go the boys." As he reached that spot of ground beyond which no Confederate could go, he suffered a sense of personal shame: "Stopping at the fence, I looked to the right and left and felt we were disgraced." The assault's failure bluntly told him that he and his comrades had not done enough, and yet he knew that they had done everything they had earlier been sure would carry the victory. The result was a paralyzing disbelief: "With one single exception I witnessed no cowardice, and yet we had not a skirmish line [still standing]." Courage should have conquered!

John Dooley also charged that day, with the 1st Virginia, but his reactions carried him beyond Wood. Those around him who survived the Union shelling, feeling the special impotence that comes to infantry who have no way to respond to a harrowing fire, were "frightened out of our wits." And then the charge: To Dooley it became simply that which opened the "work of death." "Volley after volley of crashing musket balls sweep through the line and mow us down like wheat before the scythe." Only thirty-five of his regiment's 155 men escaped bullets and shells, and Dooley, with his shattered thighs, was not one of them. "I tell you, there is no romance in making one of these charges," he concluded; "the enthusiasm of ardent breasts in many cases *ain't there*." He realized that the spirit of heroism no longer possessed the men; he mildly regretted its departure, but he had lost confidence that its presence would have reversed the outcome. He had not yet developed any clear vision of why failure came to such charges, but what emerged was a sense of his loss of control. His thoughts had turned from his performance to his survival: "Oh, if I could just come out of this charge safely how thankful *would I be!*" By such rough stages did soldier thought evolve.

Even before the assault at Cold Harbor, soldiers entering their fourth year of war understood perfectly what the result would be. They knew that the Confederates had had thirty-six hours in which to prepare their positions and that by that stage of the war *any* attack under such circumstances was doomed. Charles Wainwright thought it absurd that Grant should simply repeat here the order "which has been given at all such times on this campaign, viz: 'to attack along the whole line.'" On the eve of battle, Union soldiers who had glimpsed some part of the Southern defenses or heard them described by the "news-gatherers" were, Wilkeson reported, depressed: "Some of the men were sad, some indifferent; some so tired of the strain on their nerves that they wished they were dead and their troubles over . . . and though they had resolved to do their best, there was no eagerness for the fray, and the impression among the intelligent soldiers was that the task cut out for them was more than men could accomplish." Indeed, numbers of soldiers wrote their names on small pieces of paper and pinned them to their coats, in a hope, signaling hopelessness, that their bodies would not go unidentified. On June 15, 1864, when Grant's army finally reached the James at a cost of 60,000 casualties, a number equivalent to the size of Lee's army at the outset of the campaign, the Union regular Augustus Meyers felt the "gloomy and depressing effect" of such "awful sacrifices without any advantages." Ira Dodd became convinced that following its attacks in the Wilderness and at Cold Harbor, the Army of the Potomac was never again the same.

Not all soldiers felt compelled to abandon or even to modify early-war views. George Stevens of the 77th New York was one who remained steadfast: "Never was heroic valor exhibited on a grander scale than had been manifested by the Army of the Potomac throughout this long struggle, in which every man's life seemed doomed. [T]heir illustrious valor and never failing courage must sooner or later meet with their reward." But change was afoot. Northern civilians might invoke the courage of the attackers at Cold Harbor as if it continued to constitute a substitute for victory, but soldiers contemplating the deaths of friends, their own narrow escapes, and the seeming uselessness of such charges began to speak of "futile courage" and said no more of "sublime courage."

Swelling conviction of courage's insufficiency bred new doubts about commanders whose virtues encompassed but did not extend beyond bravery. James Nisbet was unhappy when Hood replaced Johnston, for he considered Hood "simply a brave, hard fighter." Thus, in courage's depreciating currency, the ultimate accolade had fallen to faint praise. Hood might possess "a Lion's Heart," but it came to count more that he had "a Wooden Head." On the other side that summer, Theodore Lyman, too, noted changing attitudes toward those diminishing numbers of officers whose impulse was to "dash in": "You hear people say, 'Oh, everyone is brave enough; it is the head that is needed.'"

No longer was courage strong enough to stand alone and thus to serve as its own reward. At the outset both sides had considered medals unnecessary. That notion was akin to the view of some Southern gentlemen and respectable organizers of Union regiments that their own willingness to remain "humble" privates constituted the highest expression of self-effacing patriotism. External signs of virtue or achievement were unimportant, and medals were in any case the insignia of an effete and vain-glorious European militarism. But as the war evolved and the centrality of courageous behavior began to erode, agitations arose in both armies for the formal recognition of bravery.

In November 1862 the Confederate Congress authorized the President to bestow medals and badges of distinction on soldiers who had demonstrated special battle courage. Officers were to be cited for individual acts, while the men of each company were to select one of their number for a decoration. Little was done, however. Jefferson Davis was uninterested, and in any case medals were difficult to fabricate in a Confederacy whose resources were being stretched thinner every day. As a substitute of sorts, names were to be inscribed on a Roll of Honor to be read at dress parades, but, given the accelerating tempo of combat, few regiments were able to make time for such a ritual. Fighters increasingly grew to regret that the political leadership seemed simply to assume the Southern soldier's courage and made so little effort to reward extraordinary instances of it. William Owen dined at a Richmond restaurant with English friends, including a Captain Hewitt of the Royal Navy who had won a Victoria Cross at Inkerman. After hearing Hewitt's story, the Confederate complained, "What a pity our boys have no V.C.'s to look forward to! They are doing things every day that deserve decorations."

Regret became vexation in the case of another device that some wished to employ to recognize special courage: promotions for valor. Apparently neither Davis nor Lee permitted them, a stance that raised some anger among the rank-and-file. John Haskell told of two Confederate soldiers who had performed on the battlefield with great bravery. Both had suffered wounds. Their superiors granted them sick leave but sent them off with no word of commendation. When they reached their homes on a stretch of North Carolina coast occupied by Union forces, both took the oath of loyalty and remained out of the war, a loss, Haskell was sure, to be counted against a stingily unappreciative high command.

The situation on the Union side was different but, from the men's perspective, hardly more favorable. Medals and promotions came much more frequently than in the Confederate service—too often for many observers. When the 27th Maine's tour of duty was about to expire just prior to the battle of Gettysburg, President Abraham Lincoln authorized the award of the Medal of Honor to each soldier who would reenlist. Three hundred agreed to remain on duty as "emergency troops," but medals were issued in error to all 864 members of the regiment. The 27th Maine had seen no battle before Gettysburg; its remnant played no role at Gettysburg. Similarly, so many brevet (i.e., honorary) promotions were awarded, Augustus Meyers complained, that they "seemed to lose dignity" and became objects of ridicule. His friends in the ranks began to refer to mules as "brevet horses" and to camp followers as "brevet soldiers." Such awards, moreover, seemed seldom to recognize battlefield bravery. *Field* promotions were almost as rare as in the Confederate Army.

Joshua Chamberlain must rank as one of the Civil War's most stalwart warriors. He fought in at least twenty battles and was wounded six times. On his "day of glory," the bayonet charge into which he propelled his Maine soldiers, their ammunition exhausted, saved Gettysburg's Little Round Top from capture by fiercely fighting Alabamians. General Charles Griffin of the regular army called it a "magnificent sight" to watch him in battle, dashing from one flank to the other, leading assault after assault. Chamberlain's superiors frequently cited his actions in their battle reports and recommended him for promotion to general officer's rank. Yet such recognition did not come until he suffered his fifth wound at Petersburg. In the belief that he was dying and, apparently, that his reputation as a brave soldier required official reinforcement, he asked to be promoted, not for himself but "for the gratification of his family and friends." Grant conferred a battlefield promotion, one of two times he agreed to do so.

Chamberlain was convinced that he had remained unpromoted for so long because he lacked influential friends in Washington, and many others complained that political connections were as nefarious an influence on Union promotions as Southerners thought seniority on their own. The letters of Brigadier General Alpheus Williams reveal graphically the tensions developing between older notions of self-sustaining courage and new desires that others formally acknowledge one's courage. In the Shenandoah Valley campaign of 1862, he remained self-contained: "I court nobody—reporters nor commanders—but try to do my whole duty and trust it will all come out right." He soon began to worry, however, that his accomplishment might require advertisement. He lamented that had he not left the area the day before, he would have been the Union commander during the first battle of Winchester. "I think I could have captured all Jackson's guns and been a major general!"—a selfish thought, he conceded, but the kind prominent in the minds of many around him. Other generals cared little for the common cause. Staff generals "gobble up all the glory." Washington bestowed commands only on its political favorites.

Williams took occasional satisfaction from the tributes paid him from below. When the officers of one of his brigades presented him with a sword, belt, and sash and the enlisted men, hearing of it, offered a gift of their own ("not a usual thing"), he was moved. "You can hardly realize how attached I have become to many of these officers who have been with me through so many trials, privations, and dangers.'' The love of the men, he professed, ''is my chief support and encouragement,'' to be preferred far above the favors of the government.

Still, he could not renounce his hope of favor. When he was denied promotion, the respect of the men counted for little; in the face of such disappointment, he did not know, he said, whether he could ''hold out.'' He began sending his own battle reports *sub rosa* to friendly editors of hometown Detroit newspapers. He encouraged his officers' efforts to memorialize the President in his behalf. He vowed ''a paper war'' on Meade until the general finally amended his Gettysburg report to mention Williams's name. (''We . . . lost more men on the morning of July 3rd than the 2nd Division to which he gives the whole credit.'') He seemed perpetually angry at correspondents and unable to decide whether they slighted him because they were congenital liars or because other generals had bought them. He grew bitter that another brigadier also passed over for promotion but of lesser military accomplishment than Williams should have been able to resign (''in face of the enemy and within sound of his guns''), go to Washington, play politics, and come away with major general's stars. ''I stay and am never thought of.''

He was upset too that civilians did not realize that the war was being waged not for [the] Union but to make heroes of ''charlatans and braggarts,'' to the neglect of the truly meritorious.

> People at home can't see why a man's pride and spirit [are] wounded and diminished. Let them work and toil long months under every exposure, doing, in the written judgment of their superiors, their full duty in all respects, and then let them see dozens of sneaks and drivellers put over their heads.

He threatened to resign, professedly because he suspected that ''the discouragement and depression the government has put upon me is . . . unfitting me for that zealous and ambitious discharge of duty which is properly due from every man holding the responsible position I do.'' Finally, Sherman recommended his promotion—but to no avail. Williams blamed those at home and in the Michigan Congressional delegation (Senator Zachariah Chandler in particular), who had done him ''greater injustice and personal dishonor'' by failing to advance his promotion, and in the end he was compelled to settle for a brevet major generalship.

Alpheus Williams had detested the ''low grovelling lick-spittle subserving and pandering'' to the press and government necessary to win promotion, but while never ceasing to denounce such tactics, he had himself employed many of them, at high cost to his pride, his self-respect, and his sense of solidarity with his officers and men. The initial context of his war, that of the individual testing himself, had proved inadequate; courage and duty, he had concluded, could be validated only by formal recognition within both military and civilian spheres.

Another consequence of the new complexity of combat experience following the displacement of the simple courage of 1861–62 was that it allowed distinctions impermissible earlier. With the awareness that the peripheries of battle could be just as trying as combat itself and that the moral nature of the individual determined far less than supposed, those strict definitions of the courageous and cowardly began to blur and to merge. In early September 1862, at the outset of Lee's first invasion of the North, Alexander Hunter recorded that there was still "no sign of our commissary wagons and not a mouthful of food had the men that day. Some of our best soldiers were left [behind] on account of sickness, and many began to straggle from ranks to seek in farm-houses along the route something to allay their gnawing hunger. . . . [E]ach one was a serious loss, for we never saw any of them until after the campaign." Soldiers without shoes also fell out, and other straggling could be traced to the weakness of the body—diarrhea, fever, anemia—rather than the weakness of the will. Those remaining in the ranks, all of whom had at least brushed with illness and hunger, thus came to temper their views of those who dropped out. Courage was not always at issue. Men could be lost for reasons reflecting no cowardice.

From the shared sense that the rigors of war were broader and the terrors of combat sharper than expected, a readiness to narrow the definition of cowardice arose. [Robert J.] Burdette reported that a private in the 47th Illinois was a good soldier in every way but one: Despite all his efforts to "play the man," he ran from every battle! When he later returned, each time with an excuse no one believed, many in the regiment were angry at first, but they came to realize that he measured well against those who feigned illness or exhaustion, stopped to tie shoes during the charge, arranged hospital details, or in other ways avoided or moved themselves beyond the range of charges of cowardice. He marched into every battle. He was brave until blood appeared, and then he fled. "He was beaten in every fight but he went in" every time. "This man was a coward," but "a good coward." Burdette realized that such a formulation begged questions each day growing more difficult: "But who are the cowards? And how do we distinguish them from the heroes? How does God tell?" Uncertain, he agreed that the man should not be punished, joining others whose anger dissipated as they concluded that "God never intended that man should kill anybody." Angered by a soldier who faltered several times during a charge at Fredericksburg, Abner Small pulled him to his feet and called him a coward, but when the man in obvious agony explained that "his legs would not obey him," Small apologized. Soldiers, he concluded, "were heroes or cowards in spite of themselves." Long Bill Blevins of the 21st Georgia knew that his captain was authorized to detail one man as company cook, and he asked for the job: "Captain, I can't stand the shooting, and I'm afraid I might run,—and disgrace my name." The incident was reported without censure. Perhaps soldiers were coming to feel the disdain of one unable to master his fear less than the relief that another had confessed, in actions or words, to the fear that all shared.

By 1864 the new tolerance for men whose behavior would earlier have brought condemnation had achieved informal incorporation in the military justice system. Colonel Rufus Dawes of the 6th Wisconsin was summoned to head the Fifth Corps's examining board. There "cowards met no mercy. They were dismissed and their names published throughout the land, a fate more terrible than death to a proud spirited soldier." But the board broke with the past in acknowledging that the war was now one in which brave men could be overcome by fear for their lives: The "unexampled [Wilderness] campaign of sixty continuous days, the excitement, exhaustion, hard work and loss of sleep broke down great numbers of men who had received no wounds in battle. Some who began the campaign with zealous and eager bravery, ended it with nervous and feverish apprehension of danger in the ascendancy. Brave men were shielded if their records on other occasions justified another [chance], which ordinarily resulted well." Cowards would continue to meet no mercy, but when did a man become a coward? When he faltered a second time? A third time?

Experience that altered soldier definitions of cowardice perforce modified definitions of courage. The most dramatic example was the final dissolution of the previously vital linkage between courage and the charge.

On November 26, 1863, General George Gordon Meade launched an offensive against Lee's Army of Northern Virginia. The Union commander was outmaneuvered, however, and his Army of the Potomac quickly ran up against the Confederates strongly posted in the small valley of Mine Run, Virginia. On November 28, Meade probed Lee's position and prepared a large-scale assault. Meanwhile, Federal rank-and-file had an opportunity to judge for themselves the strength of the defenses. "All felt that it would be madness to assault," Robert Carter of the 22nd Massachusetts said; "I felt death in my very bones all day." George Bicknell of the 5th Maine wrote that there was not "a man in our command who did not realize his position. Not one who . . . did not see the letters [of] death before his vision. . . . [N]ever before nor since had such an *universal* fate seemed to hang over a command." Fortunately, one who agreed was Gouverneur Warren, the commander of the Second Corps; completing a reconnaissance, he reported to Meade that, contrary to his earlier judgment, he considered an attack hopeless. Some members of Meade's staff, thinking perhaps that so much of their planning was going for nothing, insisted that the Confederate works could be carried, but Meade canceled the assault and on December 1 ordered his army back across the Rapidan, a retreat into winter quarters.

Observers quickly characterized Meade's brief campaign as failed, maladroit, and weak-willed, but the Union ranks celebrated their commander's decision as if it were a great victory. "The enemy is too strong! We shall not charge!" "Oh," [George W.] Bicknell sighed, "such a sense of relief as overspread those men, cannot even be imagined." Lyman praised his superior's courage in ordering withdrawal: Meade had only to "snap his fingers" and there would have been "ten thousand wretched, mangled creatures" lying on the valley's slopes—and praise of Meade for having "tried hard." Earlier in the war audacity in attack had caught much of what men thought important in that word "courage"; now at the close of 1863, to some, courage, turned on its head, had become the will to renounce the charge.

Christian Soldiers: Revivalism in the Confederate Army

DREW GILPIN FAUST

From the fall of 1862 until the last days of the Civil War, religious revivalism swept through Confederate forces with an intensity that led one southerner to declare the armies had been "nearly converted into churches." A remarkable phenomenon in the eyes of contemporary observers, these mass conversions have been largely ignored by modern scholars. The attention recent historians have devoted to other manifestations of nineteenth-century Evangelicalism makes this neglect of Civil War religion seem all the more curious, for scholarly findings about the relationship between revivalism and the processes of social and cultural transformation suggest that an exploration of army Evangelicalism should yield important insights into the meaning of the South's experience in an era of profound dislocation and change.

The centrality of religion within antebellum southern culture gave sacred language and perception a prominent place in the region's response to war. The South had not only embraced evangelical Protestantism with a uniformity and enthusiasm unmatched in the rest of the nation but had also used religion as a crucial weapon in the sectional propaganda battle. Defining itself as more godly than the North, the South turned to the Scriptures to justify its peculiar institution and its social order more generally. With its declaration of nationhood and the subsequent outbreak of war, the Confederacy identified its independence and success as God's will. Their cause, southerners insisted until the very last days of the conflict, was God's cause; the South's war of defense against invasion was unquestionably a just war.

The prominence of such sentiments in public discourse—in the Confederate Constitution itself, in Jefferson Davis's proclamations of fast days, in generals' announcements of military victory, not to mention in church sermons and denominational publications—established religion as the fundamental idiom of national and personal identity; southerners' responses to the unanticipated horrors of the first modern, total war were almost necessarily articulated within a religious framework and in religious language. But if religion was central to the Confederacy as a whole, it was perhaps of greatest importance to the common southern soldier, whose life was most dramatically altered—if not actually ended—by war's demands.

Drew Gilpin Faust, "Christian Soldiers: The Meaning of Revivalism in the Confederate Army," *Journal of Southern History,* 53, (February 1987), pp. 63–65, 67–69, 71–76, 80–86, 88, 89–90. Copyright 1987 by the Southern Historical Association. Reprinted by permission of the Managing Editor.

The widespread army revivals directly reflected the stresses of the soldier's life and death situation: the strains of life in the ranks of a mass army; the pressures of daily confrontation with death—and with a rate of mortality unmatched in any American war before or since.

Although the southern religious press reported scattered conversions of soldiers from the time fighting broke out, Confederates did not begin to identify what one Evangelical called a "genuine and mighty work of grace" until the fall of 1862. At first confined to the Army of Northern Virginia, and always strongest there, significant religious awakenings spread to the Army of Tennessee and to the Trans-Mississippi forces in 1863 and 1864. One observer later calculated that as many as 150,000 soldiers were "born again" during the war, but even if far fewer actually converted, thousands more participated in the revival without themselves undergoing the dramatic personal experience of grace.

For large numbers of men the struggle against the Yankees on the field had its parallel in the battle against Satan in the camp. Soldiers' diaries and letters make clear how widely the phenomenon extended. As one participant expressed it, "'We sometimes feel more as if we were in a camp-meeting than in the army expecting to meet an enemy'." A less sympathetic observer found he could not even write a peaceful letter to his wife. "It seems to me that whereever [*sic*] I go I can never get rid of the 'P-salm-'singers—they are in full blast with a Prayer meeting a few rods off . . . ." To many of those neither directly involved nor firmly opposed, the pattern of Evangelicalism and conversion became simply a part of army routine. One captain wrote indifferently yet revealingly in his diary in mid-1863, "Today is Sunday. Nothing unusual. . . . -preaching in the afternoon and evening. Many joined the church." . . .

Curiously, the evangelical fervor of the Confederate troops was not paralleled by enthusiasm at home, and, as self-righteous southerners loved to charge, "nothing like this occurred in the Yankee army." Despite the widespread perception of the conflict as a holy war, southern civilians, even church members, were not experiencing God's grace in substantial numbers. The coldness of established congregations throughout the war years troubled southern clergy, who attributed their failures to the pre-occupation of their flocks with the secular realities of politics and economic survival. But surely the Confederacy's soldier-converts were even more concerned with the actualities of war. For them, perhaps, the ever-present threat of death gave battle a transcendent, rather than primarily worldly, significance, or possibly the enthusiasm within the army reflected Evangelicals' concerted efforts with the troops.

The comparison with soldiers' experiences in the northern army is more problematic, for revivals did occur with some frequency among Yankee troops. Most nineteenth-century observers, as well as twentieth-century scholars, have remarked, however, upon significant differences in the scale and in the intensity of army religion North and South. Abraham Lincoln himself worried that "rebel soldiers are praying with a great deal more earnestness . . . than our own troops . . . ." A number of explanations for this contrast seem plausible. The greater homogeneity of religious outlook within the overwhelmingly evangelical and Protestant southern army was certainly significant. The more profound stresses on southern soldiers, who because of shortages of manpower and materiel served for longer periods of time, with fewer furloughs, and with greater physical deprivation, undoubtedly played a role as well, for it was as the war increased in duration and intensity that revivalism began to spread.

Men donning the Confederate uniform did not at first demonstrate unusual piety. At the outset the devoted found themselves very much on the defensive, for religious leaders felt obliged to combat a widespread view that godliness would undermine military effectiveness. There "is nothing in the demands of a just and defensive warfare at variance with the spirit and duties of Christianity," an oft-reprinted tract urged. "Piety will not make you effeminate or cowardly." Godly southerners at first feared that the influences might work in just the opposite direction: that battle would prove an impediment to piety. "War is the hotbed of iniquity of every kind," wrote the Reverend Charles Colcock Jones. The army had in all ages been "the greatest school of vice." History showed that men removed from the restraining, "softening" moral influences of womanhood and hearth easily succumbed to the temptations of camp life. One tract drawing soldiers' attention to the grave yawning open before them pointedly summarized the dilemma. "Men, by associating in large masses, as in camps and cities, improve their talents, but impair their virtues." The South, happily free of significant urban centers, must not now abandon her comforting moral advantage.

The initial experience of camp life seemed to bear out these dire expectations. "I think the majority of the men of our Regt. are becoming very wild & contracting many bad habits," a private wrote home from Virginia in November 1861. The Sabbath brought "no preaching, no service" to counteract Satan's growing influence. "The religious destitution of the Army," a soldier confided to his diary, "is awful . . . ." By far the largest portion of the troops appeared to one tract agent as entirely godless. Of the three hundred men in three companies that he visited in the summer of 1861, only seven were "professors of religion." The army presented a moral picture that was "dark indeed." . . .

The mobilization of the southern clergy to confront the wartime challenge paralleled the mobilization of Confederate military resources. Identifying both the hazards and the opportunities that war offered the church, ministers worked to devise a strategy for conquering army camps, and, not incidentally, for making religion—and its preachers—a central force in the creation of the new nation. With the successes of the church among the troops, a chaplain declared to a gathering of his colleagues, "the foundation for a wide religious power over the country is now lain. . . . We, then, here and now, stand at the fountain head of the nation's destiny. We lay our hands upon its throbbing heart. Never again shall we come so near having the destiny of a great nation in our own hands." . . .

In the fall of 1862 these religious labors began to bear fruit, as circumstances came to the aid of the southern churches. The timing of evangelical successes during the war offers important clues to the meaning of the conversion experience. By late 1862 many initial illusions had begun to disappear; after more than a year of "hard service," as one chaplain explained, "the romance of the soldier's life wore off, a more sober and serious mood seemed to prevail in the camps." Conscription had begun the previous spring, and by fall soldiers without the romantic zeal and optimism of the original volunteers had joined the ranks. Perhaps most significantly, however, revivals first broke out among troops retreating from Maryland after the Confederate loss at Antietam, which represented not only the first major southern defeat in the eastern theater but the bloodiest single battle day of American history as well. The experiences of slaughter and military failure surely had their impact in encouraging the "serious reflection and solemn resolve" that preceded evangelical commitment. There was great "eloquence" in the "din" and "carnage" of the field. "We are so much exposed," one soldier observed, as he explained why he had quit "light trashy novels" for the Bible, "we are likely to be called off at any moment."

During the rest of the war the most dramatic outbursts of religious enthusiasm followed fierce and bloody battles—especially losses. The "great revival along the Rapidan" in the late summer and fall of 1863 swept through troops encamped for the first time since their retreat from Gettysburg. The pattern was clear to contemporary observers. As one army correspondent explained in 1863 to the *Confederate Baptist,* "There have been always among us, some pious men, but until that time nothing like a general revival or even seriousness. The regiment had just returned from the disastrous Pennsylvania expedition, and a few days before had the closest and most desperate encounter with the enemy that they had ever had. The minds of the men were fresh from scenes of danger and bloodshed and were forced thereby to contemplate eternity, and in many cases, to feel the necessity of preparation." In the West, Vicksburg and Chattanooga had a similar effect. Individual experiences of grace were closely connected to the wider search for God's favor implicit in the divine gift of military victory. As one recently converted soldier wrote in a letter home, he hoped the revival in his camp would bring "a great blessing nationally as well as Spiritually."

Religion thrived, however, not just on growing personal and national insecurity, not just on individual and collective fear of the Yankees, but on anxieties related to social realities within the Confederate army itself. Chaplains, missionaries, and colporteurs had begun to make clear that rather than hinder military effectiveness, they could do a great deal to enhance it. Officers previously indifferent, if not openly hostile, to religion in the camps came to encourage piety and to provide spaces and occasions for the evangelization of their troops. "It is an interesting fact," observed Baptist preacher J. J. D. Renfroe in November 1863, "that most of our officers have undergone some change on the subject of chaplains. . . . when they first started out it made no difference with them what sort of man they had for chaplain, or whether they had any at all; but now you will not talk with an officer ten minutes about it until you will discover that he does not want a chaplain simply to 'hold service,' but he wants a man who will promote the religious good of his regiment. I have had irreligious officers to tell me that a good chaplain is worth more for the government of troops than any officer in a regiment." Colonel David Lang communicated his satisfaction that his chaplain's efforts in the fall of 1863 were "making good soldiers of some very trifling material."

Despite the notable and inspiring exceptions of Robert E. Lee, Stonewall Jackson, and other pious commanders, army evangelism had its greatest impact among the common soldiers. Missionaries, chaplains, and even Jackson himself complained repeatedly of the religious indifference of the officers. The rhetoric of the Confederate revival, the themes of its sermons and its tracts, suggest one obvious explanation of why so many southern leaders encouraged piety among their troops while they remained largely aloof. "Irreligious colonels," the *Religious Herald* explained, "seek the cooperation of a good chaplain in their desire to render their regiment as efficient as possible." Religion promised significant assistance in the thorny problem of governing the frequently intractable Confederate troops.

From the outset the Confederate army experienced great difficulties with discipline, for the southern soldier was most often a rural youth who had every expectation of becoming—if he was not already—an independent landholding farmer. Despite the uneven distribution of wealth and particularly of slaveownership in the prewar South, the common man ordinarily had no direct experience with political or social oppression, for he lived in a democratic political and social order where decentralization minimized perceptions of sharp stratification between planters and plain folk. The prevalent ideology of republicanism had encouraged rich and poor whites alike to cherish their "independence" and autonomy, emphasizing a sharp contrast between their status and that of enslaved blacks. But the army was to demand a hierarchy and a discipline that the prewar situation had not, even if practices such as election of officers might seem to symbolize the soldier's willing contractual surrender of control over his own life. Previously masterless men were compelled in the army to accept subordination for the first time, and many recruits complained bitterly about this change in expectations and circumstances. As one young soldier wrote home in the summer of 1861, "we are not lowd to go to the Shops without a permit and we are not lowd to miss a drill without a furlo sickness or permit, we are under tite rules you dont no how tite they are I wish I coul see you and then I could tell you what I thought of campt life it is very tite rules and confinen."

Religion promised considerable assistance in easing this difficult transition. Élie Halévy, E. P. Thompson, and others have described the role of Methodism in the transformation of English workers into an industrial proletariat, and more recently Anthony F. C. Wallace has explored the influence of evangelical Protestantism upon laborers in nineteenth-century Pennsylvania textile mills. In the South of the 1860s the role of religion was somewhat different, for young rural Confederates were going to war, not to the factories. But the requirements of industrialized work and industrialized warfare are alike in important ways—in their demand for new levels of discipline, regularity, and subordination. Daniel T. Rodgers has described a process of "labor commitment—. . . by which new industrial employees adjusted deeply set rural loyalties and work habits to the disrupting demands of factory labor." In their identity shift from farmers to soldiers, young southerners needed to make analogous changes in internal values and expectations. A soldier "must be trained," insisted the *Religious Herald,* "and willing to submit to thorough training . . . . There is a *moral* requirement as important as the material one—an inward man as indispensable as the outward one. . . ." Religious conversion and commitment could serve as the vehicle accelerating and facilitating this necessary personal transformation. Both southern military and religious leaders recognized that Evangelicalism could contribute to internalizing discipline and enhancing the efficiency of the Confederate soldier; the church could help to mold disorganized recruits into an effective fighting force. "A spirit of subordination and a faithful discharge of duty," the *Biblical Recorder* summarized, "are [as] essential to the good soldier" as they are to the good Christian.

The term "efficiency" appeared again and again in evangelical rhetoric. The Christian soldier would be an efficient soldier because he would not be afraid to die; he would be obedient and well disciplined because he would understand the divine origin of earthly duty. One army chaplain offered a striking illustration of the "*military power of religion*. In a brigade of five regiments, where there has recently been a glorious revival, two of the regiments, which had not shared in the revival, broke, while the three which had been thus blessed stood firm . . . ." A missionary of the Army of Tennessee made an even more dramatic claim. "Preaching," he asserted, had "corrected" one of "the greatest evils of our army, in a military point of view . . .—that of straggling." The servant of God, he explained, learned that he must execute all earthly as well as all spiritual obligations "conscientiously," and that meant keeping up with your regiment even if you were ill or had no shoes. A colonel of the South Carolina Volunteers emphasized the point when he congratulated a colporteur on the usefulness of his tracts, which he found "of incalculable service in encouraging the soldier to a continuation of his hard duties, and making him feel contented with his lot." The Reverend R. N. Sledd no doubt won similar approval from Confederate military leaders when he insisted to a congregation of common soldiers about to depart for war that "it is . . . not only wise, but necessary to your efficiency, that for the time you surrender your will to that of your officers, . . . This lesson of submission to control is a difficult one for many to learn; but until you have completely mastered it, . . . you are not prepared to behave yourself the most valiantly and the most efficiently in the field of conflict." Significantly, religious leaders stressed the profitable management of time as well as the adoption of regular personal habits, and often chose the bourgeois language of commerce and the marketplace to emphasize the productive uses of religion. A correspondent to the *Religious Herald* suggested in 1863 that chaplains on the field make themselves easily identifiable by wearing badges emblazoned with the epigraph, "Godliness is profitable unto all." Another article reported an imaginary dialogue between an officer and a recently converted private who assured his superior, "'I used to neglect your business; now I perform it diligently'." . . .

In writing of World War I, Eric J. Leed has argued that there occurred a "militarized proletarianization" of European soldiers. Certainly no such dramatic transformation took place in the Confederate South, for this first modern war fell far short of the 1914 conflict in its demands for hierarchy, routine, and control. Nevertheless, Leed's observation, combined with the rhetoric of Confederate army religion, cannot help but draw attention to the new work patterns warfare imposed and to the loss of autonomy and independence it implied for the average southerner. As one Virginia private tellingly observed, "A soldier in the ranks is like a piece of machinery— he moves and acts as commanded." Even though his salary was often not even paid, the Confederate soldier was in most cases undergoing his first experience as a wage laborer subordinate to the direction of his employer. When at the end of the war the *Nation* called for the North to "turn the slothful, shiftless Southern world upside down," little would editor E. L. Godkin have guessed that the leaders of the Confederate army and churches had already been acting as his unwitting allies. For four years they had struggled—albeit with uncertain success—to teach the southern soldier the very same values of training, regularity, and industry that Godkin hoped northern victory might now impose.

Yet such a view of the role of Confederate religion—as manipulative and hegemonic—is partial and one-dimensional. Recent scholarly work has justly insisted that monolithic emphasis on the aspects of social control within evangelicalism must not distort its larger meaning or impugn the authenticity of revivalists' piety and sacred commitment by casting them simply as conspirators seeking to enhance their own social power. Most advocates of the order and discipline central to the revivalistic impulse sincerely believed that their goals were above all to fulfill God's design and only secondarily to serve the needs of men. The perceptions of the common Confederate soldiers who were the targets of army revivalists' efforts is less clear. Certainly the impact of the evangelical message among the troops was profound, as the large number of conversions attests. And many of these converts readily accepted the notion of a regenerate life as one of discipline and self-control, for soldiers frequently wrote home that revivals had made it impossible to find a cardplayer or a profane swearer in the regiment. It seems likely, however, that the cynicism of some reductionist twentieth-century social control historians may have been shared by at least some nineteenth-century soldiers. The suspicion and hostility toward evangelical hegemony expressed by the plain folk who participated in the antimission movement in the prewar South had not, in all probability, entirely disappeared, even though there is scant surviving evidence of its existence in the Confederate army. The revivals could not in any case have completely succeeded in transforming southern soldiers into a tightly disciplined fighting force, for complaints about insubordination continued throughout the war and even increased as the desertion rate rose dramatically in 1864 and 1865.

Common soldiers may well have ignored much of the rhetoric of control in tracts and sermons to appropriate from the evangelical message truths that they found more meaningful. The notion of a disciplined and deferential Christian soldier undoubtedly had a greater appeal to religious and military leaders than to the common fighting man instructed that it was his "business . . . to die." Yet Evangelicalism met important needs for the soldiers themselves as well as for their military masters. Like religion among black slaves or working-class Methodists, army evangelism did what E. P. Thompson has described as a "double service," appealing in different ways both to the powerful and to the powerless. In the Old South the Christianity preached by masters to their bondsmen was quite different from that embraced by the slaves.

Similarly, common Confederate soldiers used religion in their own ways, focusing on the promise of salvation from death as well as upon the reality of an evangelical community that recreated some of the ideals of a lost prewar world. The experience of conversion served as the basis for a shared equality of believers and an Arminian notion of ultimate self-determination that in profound ways replicated the antebellum republican order that military hierarchy and command had obliterated. There was, as the *Religious Herald* observed in 1863, a sense of real "homogeneity and fellow-feeling" within the brotherhood of believers. The comradeship of the regenerate encouraged as well the group solidarity that modern military analysts have identified as critical to the maintenance of morale. Converts formed Christian Associations within their brigades and regiments to assume communal responsibility for evangelical discipline, and, in the words of the constitution of one such organization, "to throw as many strengthening influences around the weak . . . as it is possible to do . . . ." The associations ran Bible and reading classes, established camp libraries of tracts and religious newspapers, but, perhaps most significantly, confronted the fear of death—and of dying abandoned and alone—that haunted so many soldiers. The believers of the Seventh Virginia Infantry covenanted, for example, to "care specially for each other in all bodily or mental suffering, to show each other respect in case of death. . . ." In practice this usually meant that association members would try to identify comrades disabled on the field of battle in order to provide them either with medical care or with Christian burial.

On a more individual level, evangelical religion provided psychological reassurance to southern soldiers struggling with the daily threat of personal annihilation. In its Christian promise of salvation and eternal life, conversion offered a special sort of consolation to the embattled Confederate. In striking ways accounts of camp conversions parallel descriptions of what in World Wars I and II was first known as "shell shock," then as "combat exhaustion" or "combat stress." Shaking, loss of speech, paralysis of limbs, uncontrolled weeping, and severe emotional outbursts often appeared among twentieth-century soldiers when they reached safety after military action. Similar behavior characterized many Confederate converts who found Christ in the emotion-filled revival meetings held in the intervals between Civil War battles. The fiercest encounters brought the largest harvests of souls, just as the most desperate fighting of World Wars I and II yielded the highest incidence of combat stress. These similarities in nineteenth- and twentieth-century soldiers' responses suggest that analogous psychological processes might well have been involved.

Twentieth-century scholars have often commented on the seeming failure of the Civil War soldier to grapple with the emotional significance of his experience. "Much in the Civil War was to be forgotten," Marcus Cunliffe has observed. "Involvement in it was intense yet oddly superficial." Unlike World War I, which yielded its Wilfred Owen, its Siegfried Sassoon, its Ernest Hemingway, the Civil War remained in a real sense unwritten, its horrors, if not unnoticed, at least denied. Yet in their own way and in their own particular idiom, Confederate soldiers were just as expressive as their World War I counterparts. Southerners were very articulate, for example, about their *inability* to portray what they had witnessed. After his first battle in 1861 one infantryman wrote home, "I have not power to describe the scene. It beggars all description." Kate Cumming, working as a nurse in a military hospital, commented even more tellingly on the inability of all those around her to communicate their experiences: "Nothing that I had ever heard or read had given me the faintest idea of the horrors witnessed here. I do not think that words are in our vocabulary expressive enough to present to the mind the realities of that sad scene."

The language of post-Freudian self-scrutiny used by World War I participants was not available to Civil War soldiers. But their silences are eloquent. Their speechlessness was part of a process of numbing, of the denial that is a widespread human response to stress. "We hurry," one soldier wrote, "through the dreadful task apparently unconscious of its demoralizing influences and destructive effects." The war, another confirmed, "is calculated to harden the softest heart." The majority came to act as "unconcerned as if it were hogs dying around them." A correspondent writing to the *Religious Herald* in 1862 understood well, however, "the true fountain" of this apparent indifference. Soldiers' unconcern, he explained, was "the result of an effort to *banish,* not to *master,* the fear of death. . . . the expedient of the ostrich [who acts] . . . as though refusing to look on a peril were to escape from it."

Modern-day analysts of combat stress point out, however, that such denial has its limits, that numbness and indifference can only be retained for so long. Eventually extreme stress results in the appearance of symptoms in virtually everyone. Often denial begins to be interrupted by what psychiatrists call "intrusions," nightmares or irrepressible and unwelcome daytime visions of stress-producing events. One Confederate soldier who had previously told his wife that he had found the battle of Shiloh indescribable wrote again several weeks later, "I've had great and exciting times at night with my dreams since the battle; some of them are tragedies and frighten me more than ever the fight did when I was awake . . . ." Another soldier was obviously more profoundly affected, for, as a friend described him, he began reliving battles in his everyday life. "He became more and more alarmed, and, at last, became so powerfully excited—to use his own words—he felt as if some one was after him with a bayonet, and soon found himself almost in a run, as he moved backwards and forwards in his beat."

Many psychiatrists believe that reliving stress-producing experiences in this way serves to work through and eventually to resolve material repressed in the denial phase. The appearance of intrusions, therefore, signals the emergence of overt conflict that, even though profoundly disruptive, may ultimately enable an individual to cope with and to transcend a traumatic experience. Revivals often explicitly encouraged such intrusions and exacerbated internal tension in the effort to induce the religious conversion that would dissolve all stress in the promise of divine salvation. In order to shake soldiers' personal defenses, preachers and tracts insisted, "Death stares you in the face. The next battle may be your last." The soldier, one revivalist explained, had to be "forced to feel how frail and uncertain is life." The crisis was unavoidable; numbness and denial could be no real or lasting protection. In "the GREAT CONSCRIPTION there is no discharge . . . . Are you ready to take your place with them who will have the victory? . . . Or will your place be in that vast division of death's army, which shall assemble only to be defeated, accursed and pulished forever?"

Significantly, the rhetoric of camp sermons was often designed to encourage a metaphorical reliving of battlefield experiences by casting religion as the equivalent of military conflict. Exhorters focused overwhelmingly on the issue of salvation and its frightening alternative, thus calling forth the feelings associated with the life-and-death struggle that soldiers actually confronted each day. Preachers manipulated already existing fear, stressing the nearness of death and its terrors for the unconverted. But at the same time that revivalists exacerbated the tension and helplessness soldiers felt in the face of battle, they emphasized that the men did retain a dimension of choice; even amidst the barrage of bullets, they could decide for God. As one tract demanded of those who had not yet exercised this option, *Why Will You Die?* Death, its author implied, was a matter of personal will and could be consciously rejected in favor of eternal life. Just as the common soldier concerned about social issues of mastery and subordination within army life could have the symbolic comfort of electing his own captain, so he might psychologically escape from his sense of victimization by choosing Christ as the "Captain of [his] . . . salvation." He might transcend the ultimate and profound loss of control over his destiny that battle involved by making an existential commitment, by enlisting as a Christian soldier under the "banner of the Cross." The decision for Christ restored the illusion of free will. And with the return of a sense of control often comes, as contemporary psychiatrists have observed, the ability once again to cope. . . .

Students of comparative psychiatry have emphasized that anxiety is interpreted and treated in markedly different ways in different cultural settings. What appears as an intense and debilitating conviction of sin in one era may in a more secular and rationalistic age become a case of "shell shock" or "combat exhaustion" that responds to medical treatment. Within southern culture of the 1860s, religion was the obvious cultural resource for explaining and relieving such deeply felt distress. For the common soldier, therefore, Evangelicalism offered a vehicle of personal reintegration and a means of dealing with the physical and psychological assaults of war upon his individual humanity—and even his continued existence. As one private reported to a sympathetic evangelist, "But for the comfort of religion, he thinks he would have lost his mind." The clergy, in turn, found for themselves in war a role of enhanced secular usefulness and importance as well as authentic spiritual fulfillment in the saving of so many souls. For military leaders, revivalism promised a means of inculcating a necessary spirit of discipline and subordination in southerners not previously required to possess such virtues; it was also a way of ensuring the continued favor of the God of Battles.

But the significance of Confederate revivals transcends their meaning for the specific groups involved. Evangelical enthusiasm reflected not just religious but widespread social and cultural tensions that found expression in an evangelical idiom, a discourse that points to the wartime emergence of frictions that were to persist and to grow in the postwar South. Although religion had been at the center of traditional southern identity, it ironically and necessarily became in the army the vehicle and symbol of broader cultural innovation and change. It was religious language that demanded soldiers' adoption of values and behavior representing sharp departures from their accustomed way of life; it was religious exhortation that sought to resolve the social conflicts disrupting Confederate camps by imposing discipline on hitherto "independent" farmers. . . .

The broader significance of army religion may thus be the way in which it points to the importance of the experience of war itself in establishing a framework for the social and political conflicts of a New South. In the Confederate army, as in the South of the postwar years, the protean nature of the evangelical message permitted its adherents to appropriate it to satisfy very different purposes and needs. Revivalism served at once as an idiom of social strife and a context for social unity in an age of unsettling transition; it became a vehicle both for expression and resolution of conflict about fundamental transformations in the southern social order.

The identity crisis of the Confederate soldier adjusting to distressing new patterns of life and labor was but a microcosm of the wartime crisis of a South in the throes of change. Military service inaugurated for many southerners a new era characterized by a loss of autonomy and self-determination that even peace would not restore. In the postwar years a southerner was far more likely to be a tenant and far less likely to be economically self-sufficient than he had been in the antebellum period. He might even follow his experience of military wage labor with that of factory

employment, as the cotton mill campaign drew thousands of white southerners into industry.

But perhaps the most profound transformation for many Confederate
soldiers was deeply personal. In the past decade we have been made sharply
aware of the lingering effects of another lost war upon its veterans' years
after their return to civilian life. Irrational outbursts of violence and debilitating depression are but two characteristic symptoms of what psychiatrists have come to see as a definable "post-Vietnam" syndrome. Southerners deeply scarred by their experiences of horror in the world's first
total war may have been affected in similar ways. Perhaps part of the
explanation for the widespread violence of the postwar South should be
psychological; Klan activity, whitecapping, and lynching may have been a
legacy of soldiers' wartime stresses as well as a political response to new
and displeasing social realities.

In the clues that it offers to the profound impact of battle and to the
social origins of a new South, revivalism is central to the Confederate
experience. The Civil War challenged both the South and her fighting men
to be "born again."

FURTHER   READING

Michael Barton, *Goodmen: The Character of Civil War Soldiers* (1981)
Bruce Catton, "Hayfoot-Strawfoot!" *American Heritage* 8 (1957), 30–37
Henry Steele Commager, ed., *The Blue and the Gray,* 2 vols. (1950)
David Donald, "The Confederate as a Fighting Man," *Journal of Southern History*
    25 (1959), 178–193
William B. Hesseltine, *Civil War Prisons: A Study in War Psychology* (1930)
Reid Mitchell, *Civil War Soldiers* (1988)
Eugene C. Murdock, *One Million Men: The Civil War Draft in the North* (1971)
Stephen W. Sears, *Landscape Turned Red: The Battle of Antietam* (1983)
Paul E. Steiner, *Disease in the Civil War* (1968)
Bell I. Wiley, *The Life of Johnny Reb* (1943)
———, *The Life of Billy Yank* (1952)

CHAPTER
7

Behind the Lines:

Wartime Politics

⌇

On the eve of the Civil War, political parties in the United States were in a state of turmoil. Between 1852 and 1854, the Whig party collapsed. In its place there emerged, for a brief moment, the American, or Know-Nothing, party, which was organized around fear of immigrants and Catholics. The Know-Nothings in turn gave way to the Republicans, a sectional antislavery party that by 1856 had become the rival political organization to the Democrats. In the South, however, no replacement to the Whigs arose, leaving an assortment of political groups as the uncoordinated opposition to the secessionist Democrats. Thus the national two-party system that had arisen in the Jacksonian era disintegrated as the sectional crisis came to a head.

At an even earlier stage in American history, during the Revolution and Early Republic, political parties had been decried as sources of discord and division. A similar repudiation of party politics seemed likely after the Civil War broke out, as the pressures for loyalty and unity increased in each section. Under these circumstances, division into antagonistic parties could be a source of weakness and an unaffordable luxury, especially if the opposition party challenged the war itself and the method of conducting it adopted by the governing party.

In the Confederacy, the opponents of secession did not rally together and form an enduring party organization; but then neither did the victorious secessionists. In fact, the South eschewed organized parties because of a fear that they would jeopardize the cause by fostering disunity. In the North, on the other hand, the Democrats revived after their disastrous division in the presidential election of 1860, and they opposed the Republican administration vigorously. Simultaneously, Lincoln encountered an equally vehement opposition from within his own party, from the radicals who wanted the war to be prosecuted more forcefully.

The problem posed by these divergent wartime party experiences is whether or not the presence of parties aided the North, while their absence harmed the Confederates. In a more general sense, the issue is: what role can or should political parties play when a democratic society is at war?

⤹ D O C U M E N T S

The constitutional systems of the United States and the Confederate States were virtually interchangeable, yet the wartime governments of each seemed to function quite differently, and with contrasting results. The first selection is from the speech of Howell Cobb, the president of the Confederate Provisional Congress, adjourning that body on February 17, 1862, and commending it for its conservatism and its rejection of political parties. A similar antiparty sentiment is expressed in the second document, an editorial of September 25, 1861, from the *North Carolina Standard*. The third selection comes from a major speech on January 14, 1863, in the United States House of Representatives by Clement L. Vallandigham of Ohio, the leading antiwar, or Copperhead, Democrat. Denouncing Lincoln's conduct of the war, Vallandigham calls for its cessation. The fourth document presents a vigorous attack on the Lincoln administration from the opposite end of the political spectrum; it is an excerpt from a derisive speech, called "The Cabinet," given by the abolitionist orator Wendell Phillips, at Abington, Massachusetts, on August 1, 1862.

The fifth document is a letter from Lincoln to Senator Carl Schurz of Missouri on November 10, 1862, explaining the source of, and reasons for, opposition to his administration in the congressional elections of that year. The final extract is from a brief speech Lincoln gave in response to a serenade from supporters at the White House on November 10, 1864 after he had won reelection. He stressed the significance of holding divisive elections in time of war.

Some of the documents in Chapter 8, particularly those of Alexander H. Stephens (the Cornerstone Speech) and Joseph E. Brown, have relevance to the topic of dealing with political opposition.

Howell Cobb Congratulates the Provisional Confederate Congress and Warns Against Party Spirit, February 1862

. . . In truth, gentlemen, I must refer to one remarkable characteristic of this revolution which distinguishes it from all others recorded in history. It can not be too prominently set forth, or too often considered—I mean its conservatism. Usually revolutions are the result of the excited passions of the people whose patience is exhausted, and hence their popular tendencies have too frequently degraded them into anarchy and discord. But here the people at the ballot box deliberately vote a revolution to escape from the very anarchy which they see impending and to preserve those conservative principles of the fathers of the Republic, which were fast being overwhelmed by popular fanaticism. Every step in the drama has been marked by the same tendency. The changes in the Federal Constitution were suggested and adopted with the same views, and every page of the history of this war will show that we, without the checks of government, have imposed upon ourselves the most conservative principles, while our enemies, having the organized government, have trampled under foot every constitutional limitation, and disregarded all public and private rights. That this springs from the people themselves and is not due alone to the wisdom of their rulers, is manifest from the fact, that in more than one of the [Confederate] States, the very occasion of revolution has been used to reform their own Constitution; and to improve it by impressing this same conservatism upon the fundamental law of the State.

Gentlemen, I have perhaps detained you too long. I can not close without commending to those who follow us in government, one element of success to which I may perhaps attribute too much. I refer to the generous confidence which each department of the Provisional Government has exhibited toward all others. In our common danger there should be no divisions. The spirit of party has never shown itself for an instant in your deliberations, and I would that it should be the good fortune of each successive presiding officer in the closing scene of every Congress to be able to bear the testimony I now publicly give to the honor of this body. . . .

A North Carolina Editor Warns Against Partisanship, September 1861

Party! Party! !

Why is it that in the midst of a bloody war waged for the very existence of the State . . . that many of our best and wisest men are rigidly and constantly excluded from the councils of the State and nation, and by our State authorities from the public service?

Mr. Branch and Mr. Davis and others—men surfeited with office, it seems are very proper persons to be sent to confer with the Confederate government at Richmond, or to fill other important positions—pet-men, sometimes filling two or more offices of trust and profit at the same time, but the State, now in imminent hazard, stands in no need of the services of such men as Ruffin or Badger, Brown or Graham, Reid or Morehead . . . and a host of others! Indeed the tried men of the State—men whose ability, wise fore-caste and great prudence, have secured them the confidence of the people, like the above named . . . are put under the ban, to give place to others—*faster* men we suppose, mere politicians or rampant original secessionists of far less weight—who are to sit in the high scale of the synagogue. . . .

What is the reason for all this? We will tell you, fellow-citizens. *It is party!* Party! when war is upon us, and when our brave men of all parties and all positions are suffering and dying for their country. Yes, the depraved oracle of the destructives in this city, clamors for the spoils—must have *all* the fat offices for the original secessionists—indeed yawns and growls like a dog with a sore head, if the original Yancey men [after William Lowndes Yancey of Alabama, the South's most controversial secessionist], the *democratic secessionists don't get them all.* Yes, the men who were unwilling to break up the old government until every effort was made to restore and preserve it—those who in February and April preferred peace to war, but who rose in their might as one man to resist the first indications of coercion and tyranny, as promulgated in Lincoln's proclamation, they are the men who may pay their money to support the war and shoulder their muskets to drive the invader from our soil, but as a general rule, there are no offices for *them*. And forsooth, if *we* dare complain of the corrupting, damaging course of the destructives, because of its manifest injustice and impolicy during the war, we are charged with personal or partizan venom.

The *principle* upon which this miserable policy is based, is rotten to the core—when put in action, it is damaging to the peace and the harmony and the efficiency of the State in this war; and this is the sole ground of our complaint. . . . We contend that North Carolina at this juncture, needs her purest, wisest, ablest, more reliable men, no matter what their politics are or have been. We want the office to fit the man and the man to fit the office—let him have been a whig or democrat, a Union man or a secessionist, we care not a groat. But when we see original secessionists planning and scheming and plotting to fill every office, military or civil, with original Yancey men, we are alarmed for the safety and perpetuity of the new government, and for the prosperity and success of the South in this war. And why, not because we doubt the personal integrity of all of them.—Certainly not. But because their action is based upon a principle which is destructive to the perpetuity of Constitutions, and law, and order, and a permanent government. . . .

Let us say to those who thus carry on, the day is coming when the people will take vengeance for all this.

Raleigh *Standard*, 25 Sept. 1861.

The Leading Copperhead Condemns the Northern War Effort, January 1863

. . . Money and credit, then, you have had in prodigal profusion. And were men wanted? More than a million rushed to arms! Seventy-five thousand first, (and the country stood aghast at the multitude,) then eight-three thousand more were demanded; and three hundred and ten thousand responded to the call. The President next asked for four hundred thousand, and Congress, in their generous confidence, gave him five hundred thousand; and, not to be outdone, he took six hundred and thirty-seven thousand. Half of these melted away in their first campaign; and the President demanded three hundred thousand more for the war, and then drafted yet another three hundred thousand for nine months. The fabled hosts of Xerxes have been out-numbered. And yet victory, strangely, follows the standard of the foe. From Great Bethel to Vicksburg, the battle has not been to the strong. Yet every disaster, except the last, has been followed by a call for more troops, and every time, so far, they have been promptly furnished. From the beginning the war has been conducted like a political campaign, and it has been the folly of the party in power that they have assumed, that numbers alone would win the field in a contest not with ballots but with musket and sword. But numbers, you have had almost without number—

the largest, best appointed, best armed, fed, and clad host of brave men, well organized and well disciplined, ever marshaled. A Navy, too, not the most formidable perhaps, but the most numerous and gallant, and the costliest in the world, and against a foe, almost without a navy at all. Thus, with twenty millions of people, and every element of strength and force at command—power, patronage, influence, unanimity, enthusiasm, confidence, credit, money, men, an Army and a Navy the largest and the noblest ever set in the field, or afloat upon the sea; with the support, almost servile, of every State, county, and municipality in the North and West, with a Congress swift to do the bidding of the Executive; without opposition anywhere at home; and with an arbitrary power which neither the Czar of Russia, nor the Emperor of Austria dare exercise; yet after nearly two years of more vigorous prosecution of war than ever recorded in history; after more skirmishes, combats and battles than Alexander, Cæsar, or the first Napoleon ever fought in any five years of their military career, you have utterly, signally, disastrously—I will not say ignominiously—failed to subdue ten millions of "rebels," whom you had taught the people of the North and West not only to hate, but to despise. Rebels, did I say? Yes, your fathers were rebels, or your grandfathers. He, who now before me on canvas looks down so sadly upon us, the false, degenerate, and imbecile guardians of the great Republic which he founded, was a rebel. And yet we, cradled ourselves in rebellion, and who have fostered and fraternized with every insurrection in the nineteenth century everywhere throughout the globe, would now, forsooth, make the word "rebel" a reproach. Rebels certainly they are; but all the persistent and stupendous efforts of the most gigantic warfare of modern times have, through your incompetency and folly, availed nothing to crush them out, cut off though they have been, by your blockade, from all the world, and dependent only upon their own courage and resources. And yet, they were to be utterly conquered and subdued in six weeks, or three months! Sir, my judgment was made up, and expressed from the first. I learned it from Chatham: "My lords, you can not conquer America." And you have not conquered the South. You never will. It is not in the nature of things possible; much less under your auspices. But money you have expended without limit, and blood poured out like water. Defeat, debt, taxation, sepulchers, these are your trophies. In vain, the people gave you treasure; and the soldier yielded up his life. "Fight, tax, emancipate, let these," said the gentleman from Maine, [Mr. Pike,] at the last session, "be the trinity of our salvation." Sir, they have become the trinity of your deep damnation. The war for the Union is, in your hands, a most bloody and costly failure. The President confessed it on the 22d of September [with the promulgation of the Preliminary Emancipation Proclamation], solemnly, officially, and under the broad seal of the United States. And he has now repeated the confession. The priests and rabbis of abolition taught him that God would not prosper such a cause. War for the Union was abandoned; war for the negro openly begun, and with stronger battalions than before. With what success? Let the dead at Fredericksburg and Vicksburg answer. . . .

But ought this war to continue? I answer, no—not a day, not an hour.

Wendell Phillips Criticizes Lincoln's War Policy, August 1862

I quite agree with the view which my friend (Rev. M. D. Conway [another abolitionist who criticized the administration for its caution on slavery]) takes of the present situation of the country, and of our future. I have no hope, as he has not, that the intelligent purpose of our government will ever find us a way out of this war. I think, if we find any way out of it, we are to stumble out of it by the gradual education of the people, making their own way on, a great mass, without leaders. I do not think that anything which we can call the *government* has any *purpose* to get rid of slavery. On the contrary, I think the present purpose of the government, so far as it has now a purpose, is to end the war and save slavery. I believe Mr. Lincoln is conducting this war, at present, with the purpose of saving slavery. That is his present line of policy, so far as trustworthy indications of any policy reach us. The Abolitionists are charged with a desire to make this a political war. All civil wars are necessarily political wars,—they can hardly be anything else. Mr. Lincoln is intentionally waging a *political* war. He knows as well as we do at this moment, as well as every man this side of a lunatic hospital knows, that, if he wants to save lives and money, the way to end this war is to strike at slavery. I do not believe that McClellan himself is mad or idiotic enough to have avoided that idea, even if he has tried to do so. But General McClellan is waging a political war; so is Mr. Lincoln. . . . When Mr. Lincoln, by an equivocal declaration, nullifies General Hunter [who ordered all slaves in his department to be considered free, May 1862], he does not do it because he doubts either the justice or the efficiency of Hunter's proclamation; he does it because he is afraid of [slaveholders of] Kentucky on the right hand, and the Daily Advertiser [a conservative Republican paper published in Boston] on the left. [*Laughter.*] He has not taken one step since he entered the Presidency that has been a purely military step, and he could not. A civil war can hardly be anything but a political war. That is, all civil wars are a struggle between opposite ideas, and armies are but the tools. If Mr. Lincoln believed in the North and in Liberty, he would let our army act on the principles of Liberty. He does not. . . .

If we go to the bottom, it will be because we have, in the providence of God, richly deserved it. It is the pro-slavery North that is her own greatest enemy. Lincoln would act, if he believed the North wanted him to. The North, by an overwhelming majority, is ready to have him act, will indorse and support anything he does, yes, hopes he will go forward. True, it is not yet ripe enough to demand; but it is fully willing, indeed waits, for action. With chronic Whig distrust and ignorance of the people, Lincoln halts and fears. Our friend Conway has fairly painted him. He is not a genius; he is not a man like [John C.] Fremont, to stamp the lava mass of the nation with an idea; he is not a man like Hunter, to coin his experience into ideas. I will tell you what he is. He is a first-rate *second-rate* man. [*Laughter.*] He is one of the best specimens of a second-rate man, and he is honestly waiting, like any other servant, for the people to come and send him on any errand they wish. In ordinary times, when the seas are calm, you can sail without a pilot,—almost any one can avoid a sunken ledge that the sun shows him on his right hand, and the reef that juts out on his left; but it is when the waves smite heaven, and the thunder-cloud makes the waters ink, that you need a pilot; and to-day the nation's bark scuds, under the tempest, lee-shore and maelstrom on each side, needing no holiday captain, but a pilot, to weather the storm. Mr. Conway thinks we are to ride on a couple of years, and get one. I doubt it. Democracy is poisoning its fangs. It is making its way among the ballot-boxes of the nation. I doubt whether our next Congress will be as good as the last. That is not saying much. . . .

President Lincoln Examines the Causes of Dissatisfaction with His Administration, November 1862

"Private & Confidential"

Executive Mansion,
Washington, Nov. 10, 1862.

Gen. Schurz.

My dear Sir:

Yours of the 8th. was, to-day, read to me by Mrs. S[churz]. We have lost the elections; and it is natural that each of us will believe, and say, it has been because his peculiar views was not made sufficiently prominent. I think I know what it was, but I may be mistaken. Three main causes told the whole story. 1. The democrats were left in a majority by our friends going to the war. 2. The democrats observed this & determined to re-instate themselves in power, and 3. Our newspaper's, by vilifying and disparaging the administration, furnished them all the weapons to do it with. Certainly, the ill-success of the war had much to do with this.

You give a different set of reasons. If you had not made the following statements, I should not have suspected them to be true. "The defeat of the administration is the administrations own fault." (opinion) "It admitted its professed opponents to its counsels" (Asserted as a fact) "It placed the Army, now a great power in this Republic, into the hands of its' enemys" (Asserted as a fact) "In all personal questions, to be hostile to the party of the Government, seemed, to be a title to consideration." (Asserted as a fact) "If to forget the great rule, that if you are true to your friends, your friends will be true to you, and that you make your enemies stronger by placing them upon an equality with your friends." "Is it surprising that the opponents of the administration should have got into their hands the government of the principal states, after they have had for a long time the principal management of the war, the great business of the national government.''

I can not dispute about the matter of opinion. On the the [*sic*] three matters (stated as facts) I shall be glad to have your evidence upon them when I shall meet you. The plain facts, as they appear to me, are these. The administration came into power, very largely in a minority of the popular vote. Notwithstanding this, it distributed to it's party friends as nearly all the civil patronage as any administration ever did. The war came. The administration could not even start in this, without assistance outside of it's party. It was mere nonsense to suppose a minority could put down a majority in rebellion. Mr. Schurz (now Gen. Schurz) was about here then & I do not recollect that he then considered all who were not republicans, were enemies of the government, and that none of them must be appointed to to [*sic*] military positions. He will correct me if I am mistaken. It so happened that very few of our friends had a military education or were of the profession of arms. It would have been a question whether the war should be conducted on military knowledge, or on political affinity, only that our own friends (I think Mr. Schurz included) seemed to think that such a question was inadmissable. Accordingly I have scarcely appointed a democrat to a command, who was not urged by many republicans and opposed by none. It was so as to McClellan. He was first brought forward by the Republican Governor of Ohio, & claimed, and contended for at the same time by the Republican Governor of Pennsylvania. I received recommendations from the republican delegations in congress, and I believe every one of them recommended a majority of democrats. But, after all many Republicans were appointed; and I mean no disparagement to them when I say I do not see that their superiority of success has been so marked as to throw great suspicion on the good faith of those who are not Republicans. Yours truly,

A. Lincoln

President Lincoln Stresses the Importance of Elections, November 1864

November 10, 1864

It has long been a grave question whether any government, not *too* strong for the liberties of its people, can be strong *enough* to maintain its own existence, in great emergencies.

On this point the present rebellion brought our republic to a severe test; and a presidential election occurring in regular course during the rebellion added not a little to the strain. If the loyal people, *united*, were put to the utmost of their strength by the rebellion, must they not fail when *divided*, and partially paralyzed, by a political war among themselves?

But the election was a necessity.

We cannot have free government without elections; and if the rebellion could force us to forgo, or postpone a national election, it might fairly claim to have already conquered and ruined us. The strife of the election is but human nature practically applied to the facts of the case. What has occurred in this case, must ever recur in similar cases. Human nature will not change. In any future great national trial, compared with the men of this, we shall have as weak, and as strong; as silly and as wise; as bad and good. Let us, therefore, study the incidents of this, as philosophy to learn wisdom from, and none of them as wrongs to be revenged.

But the election, along with its incidental, and undesirable strife, has done good too. It has demonstrated that a people's government can sustain a national election, in the midst of a great civil war. Until now it has not been known to the world that this was a possibility. It shows also how *sound,* and how *strong* we still are. It shows that, even among candidates of the same party, he who is most devoted to the Union, and most opposed to treason, can receive most of the people's votes. It shows also, to the extent yet known, that we have more men now, than we had when the war began. Gold is good in its place; but living, brave, patriotic men, are better than gold.

But the rebellion continues; and now that the election is over, may not all, having a common interest, reunite in a common effort, to save our common country? For my own part I have striven, and shall strive to avoid placing any obstacle in the way. So long as I have been here I have not willingly planted a thorn in any man's bosom.

While I am deeply sensible to the high compliment of a reelection; and duly grateful, as I trust, to Almighty God for having directed my countrymen to a right conclusion, as I think, for their own good, it adds nothing to my satisfaction that any other man may be disappointed or pained by the result. . . .

❧ E S S A Y S

The manner in which Lincoln, his administration, and his party ran the Federal government is the subject matter of these two essays, though a comparison with Davis and the Confederacy is also at issue. In the first piece, by Eric L. McKitrick of Columbia University, the author explains how effective, compared with the Confederate leadership, was the Lincoln administration's handling of governmental institutions and political parties. The second essay, by Michael F. Holt of the University of Virginia, offers a rejoinder by suggesting that Lincoln also tried to be above party and did not act much differently from Davis. This discussion revolves around the question of whether it was the qualities of the two presidents or the political culture and institutions of the two governments that account for the Confederate government's apparent ineffectiveness.

Party Politics in Wartime: The Union and the Confederacy Compared

ERIC L. McKITRICK

The Civil War has always lent itself naturally and logically to the comparative method. Comparing the resources of the Union and the Confederacy in everything conceivable—manpower, brainpower, firepower—has been highly productive in helping us to understand the process whereby the North ultimately overwhelmed the South. But it is in the realm of government, where the process of historical comparison normally begins, that the results are on the whole least conclusive and least satisfying. The two sets of institutions exhibit a series of uncanny similarities. We may think we can detect in the Southern body politic a certain pallor, a lack of muscle tone that is in some contrast to the apparent resiliency of the North. But this is only a suspicion. We have not been very certain about how to get at such a subjective matter as the health of a metaphorical organism.

The Union and Confederate governments, as set down on paper, were almost identical. The Confederacy deliberately adopted the federal Constitution with very few changes, some of which might have been improvements had they been carried fully into effect. Cabinet members might sit in Congress, though few did; the executive had an itemized veto on appropriation bills, though it was a power he did not use; and bills for departmental appropriations had to be initiated with an estimate from the department concerned. The general welfare clause was dropped, but the "necessary and proper" clause—so useful for expanding national power— was kept. The states were "sovereign" but had no power to make treaties, which meant that they were in fact not sovereign. Nothing was said about the right of secession, and it was not as though no one had thought of it. The relations of the states to the central government would, in the course of things, reveal some crucial differences, but it is hard to find much evidence for this in the organic law of the two governments. A trend toward centralized power was perfectly possible within either of the two constitutions, and it could proceed just as far under the one as under the other. The co-ordinate branches of government were constitutionally the same, though in the election and term of office of the executive there were certain differences. As for the judiciary, the Confederacy too was to have had a Supreme Court, though it never actually got around to establishing one. In the Confederacy judicial review (with generous citations from *The Federalist,* as well as from the opinions of Marshall and Story) occurred in the states. How much difference this made may be debated, though historians have not in general made an issue of it. In any case, of the three branches of government on either side, the judiciary seems to have made the least

---

Eric L. McKitrick, "Party Politics and the Union and Confederate War Efforts." Excerpted from *The American Party Systems,* edited by William Nisbet Chambers and Walter Dean Burnham. Copyright © Oxford University Press, Inc. 1967. Footnotes omitted. Reprinted by permission.

impact on the waging of war. With regard to the two Congresses, the practices and procedures were strikingly similar. It might be said that even their membership overlapped, since a number of men had served in both.

The same executive departments were established in both governments, and with one exception the positions in each president's cabinet were the same. There has been some debate on the competence of the men who filled those positions. It is generally supposed that Lincoln's cabinet was the "better" one, though there is little clear agreement as to the reasons. One authority emphasizes the over-all deficiencies of the Confederate cabinet; another calls attention to its many merits. It is at least clear that both cabinets contained a mixed lot. Each had its good administrators, and on both sides there was incompetence. Leroy Pope Walker may have made a very poor Secretary of War, but the Union had to fight the first nine months of the war with Simon Cameron [of Pennsylvania as Walker's counterpart]. Comparisons on this level, in short, are certainly enlightening, but they take one just so far. So much has been said about executive leadership that this almost constitutes a separate literature. It seems apparent that the leadership of Abraham Lincoln was superior to that of Jefferson Davis, though the fact of Northern victory is naturally quite helpful in making the case. Lincoln was "flexible," Davis "rigid." And yet conditions may have been such, above and beyond the two men's personal characteristics, as to make Lincoln's flexibility and Davis's rigidity unavoidable political responses to the requirements of war as experienced in their respective sections.

But what were those conditions? What was the nature of the political setting, beyond the actual structure of government, within which the two leaders had to operate? Was it—a subject that has never been systematically investigated—affected by the presence or absence of political parties?

I.

. . . In an essay published in 1960, David Potter suggested "the possibility that the Confederacy may have suffered real and direct damage from the fact that its political organization lacked a two-party system." This, with its implications, constitutes in my opinion the most original single idea to emerge from the mass of writing that has been done on the Civil War in many years. It implicitly challenges two of our most formidable and consistently held assumptions regarding political life of the time, assumptions which until recently have gone unquestioned. One is that Lincoln's leadership of the Union war effort was severely and dangerously hampered by political partisanship—that is, by obstructions put in his path by Democrats on the one hand and, on the other, by extremists within his own Republican party. The other assumption is that Davis and the Confederate government, by deliberately setting aside partisanship, avoided this difficulty. There were no parties in the Confederacy, and thus the South, in this respect at least, had the advantage.

In order to show these notions as fallacies, following Potter's cue, it

should not be necessary to claim that the South "ought" to have encouraged
the establishment of a party system. Even had such a system been seen
as a positive value—which it was not, by either North or South—there
was probably a variety of reasons why an effort of that sort on the eve of
war would have been out of the question. Such things must in any case
grow naturally or they do not grow at all. Indeed it might better be wondered
why the South did not put itself in an avowedly revolutionary posture and
run its government as a kind of Committee of Public Safety, a procedure
which could have given it maximum maneuverability for achieving what
was in fact a set of revolutionary objectives. And yet this course was in
reality even less thinkable; the mentality needed for it simply did not exist.
The Confederates again and again insisted that they were not in rebellion,
that it was not a civil war, that they were not truly engaged in a revolution.
The South's ideological strategy was to declare, in effect, to the people of
the United States: our constitutional title to exist is legally purer than yours.
We are in fact the "true" United States; we are more faithful than you to
the spirit of the Founders; it is you, not we, who have departed from it;
it is you who are the rebels. The Confederates, in short, put an unusual
amount of effort simply into behaving as a fully constituted nation, and
they seemed to feel an almost obsessive need to clothe their government
with as many of the symbols and minutiae of legitimacy as they could.
They imagined themselves engaged not nearly so much in a revolutionary
struggle for liberation as in a fully mounted war between two sovereign
powers.

It is only necessary, then, to take the Confederates for the time being
on their own terms: as a government possessing all the formal incidents of
constitutional legitimacy, but lacking at least one of the informal ones—a
system of political parties—possessed by their opponents. This discrep-
ancy, it is here suggested, has much to tell us about the vigor of the
respective war efforts. It is further suggested that the persistence of party
contention in the North all through the war was on the whole salutary for
Lincoln's government and the Union cause. The war was, of course, in
addition to all else, one long political headache, tying up much of the
executive's valuable time and attention. Obstacles of opposition were bound
up again and again with the most annoying kind of partisan politics. Nobody
at the time, so far as is known, ever explicitly thanked the Almighty for
parties. But by the same token, it was partisan politics that provided the
very framework within which these same obstacles could be contained and
overcome. To Jefferson Davis's government such a framework was not
available. Everything, to be sure, has its price; there were functions and
dysfunctions. But it may well be that on balance the functions outweighed
the dysfunctions, and that the price was worth paying.

II.

The functions of party in the formation of a government seem to involve,
on the face of it, something fairly direct and straightforward. But the process
has its subtleties, which become apparent where there are two governments

being formed at the same time, under comparable circumstances and by men sharing many of the same political traditions, but where, in one of the cases, the principle of party is not a factor.

The rapid growth of the Republican party in the brief span of five or six years prior to 1860 had generated certain by-products. It had certainly dissipated the malaise of the early 1850s in which the expanding antislavery and free-soil sentiment of the North had been, for a time, without any clear vehicle for political organization. There were, moreover, established public men who had come to be identified with this sentiment, and whose careers could no longer be promoted without stultification amid the dissolution of the Whig party and the conservatism of the regular Democrats. Such men, of whom William H. Seward and Salmon P. Chase were conspicuous examples, now found in the Republican party a welcome field for their talents and leadership. In addition, the very effort required in organizing the new party in state after state brought to the fore hundreds of new men within the same short space of time. The very marching clubs which sprang up everywhere—the so-called "Wide Awakes"—amounted to much more than a freakish social phenomenon. They represented the "progressive" element of the community. That the Republicans by 1860 had elected governors in every Northern state, to say nothing of capturing the national government, is evidence of a vitality going far beyond the ordinary. The period was one of mounting public crisis; what has been less noticed is that precisely at this time public life began to present an expanding field for younger men of talent, ambition, and energy.

By the time the Confederacy was being established, politics was not attracting the South's best men to anywhere near this degree. An obvious immediate reason, of course, was that the war crisis naturally brought many of the Southern elite into the army, and many writers have commented on this. But antecedent factors were more pervasive. The chief mechanism for managing political talent and bringing it forward—party organizations—had in effect disintegrated in the South by the time the war began. The organizational stability of both the Whig and Democratic parties at local and state levels all over the country, ever since the emergence of such organizations in the 1830s, had depended on their maintaining some sort of national orientation and national interests. In the South, the growth of a sectional, state-centered ideology in defense of slavery had steadily undermined such interests, and with them, whatever stability such organizations had once had. Thus the collapse in the South of the existing parties—the Whigs in the early 1850s and the Democrats in 1860—had created a setting in which the only real political issue came down to that of whether a man did or did not support secession. "Opposition" implied disloyalty, unless it could be based on state particularism—which was exactly the form opposition would in fact take. There was thus no national (that is, all-Confederate) basis on which a system of parties might be re-fashioned. Meanwhile those organizations which do so much to define political skill and political success, and to measure the satisfactions of politics for all from the humble to the high, had in most respects simply vanished.

How, then, would this affect the standards—of duty and commitment, as well as ability—to be used in the forming of a government?

The vice-presidency might be taken as a minor, though interesting example. The significance of Hannibal Hamlin has never inspired the historian; as with many a Vice-President of the nineteenth century, Hamlin does not even have a modern biographer. Yet in 1860 the man played a role whose specifications were clearly understood by all, especially by those most responsible for placing him in it. He represented an interest within the Republican party which might "balance" a national ticket, broaden its support, and thus help it to win an election. He had already served in Congress as a Democratic representative and senator, and he had been one of the chief organizers of the Republican party in the state of Maine. He could speak for the antislavery element of New England, having strong sympathies with abolition. As Vice-President, Hamlin hardly made a ripple on the surface of events, which is to say he played with unassuming perfection the role marked out for him. His one chance for fame—the presidency itself, which would have fallen to him upon Lincoln's death—was snatched away in 1864 when it was decided that the ticket of that year might be better balanced, in yet a different manner, by someone else, Andrew Johnson, a former Democrat from Tennessee. But in certain small ways Hamlin made himself useful from the first—for example, in the diplomacy of cabinet-making, in the choosing of officers for Negro regiments, and in testing the weather on emancipation. Despite his disappointment, he made no complaint at being superseded in 1864, supported the new ticket, and was eventually compensated in good party fashion with the Collectorship of Boston.

Had any such standards of choice governed the Confederate delegates at Montgomery, the last man they would have picked as Vice-President would have been the distinguished Alexander Stephens. The principal criterion in this case seems to have been the delegates' feeling that something was needed to placate the state of Georgia for having failed to elect a Georgian as President. Yet Stephens had strongly opposed secession, did not really believe in the Confederacy and hardly even pretended to, and had no inclination whatever to stay in Richmond and preside over the Confederate Senate. He spent most of his time at home in Georgia grumbling against his own government and actually attacking it in venomous letters and speeches for usurping the rights of citizens. Few men did more to undermine Davis's administration than his own Vice-President. Perhaps Stephens's one positive act, if such it may be called, was going to meet Lincoln on an unsuccessful peace mission. Davis himself once offered to resign, his one condition being the resignation of Alexander Stephens.

The choice in the one case had been a party matter; in the other, it had been made on a regional, "popular-front" basis. Hamlin's career was tied to the Republican party, and therefore to the success of the Lincoln administration; Stephens had been placed in the Confederate government mainly as a gesture toward the state of Georgia and to the former members of a political party (the Whigs) that no longer existed. He and his friends thus had no direct vested interest in the day-to-day success of the Davis administration. . . .

A further contrast between the Federal and Confederate governments . . . might consist in the standards whereby the cabinets as a whole were organized. For Davis, the chief concern was that each state had to be represented. For Lincoln also, geography counted as a strong consideration; but for him, both merit and geography as factors in choice had to operate within the limits of another criterion, which gave the problem a certain focus and required a certain precision. His cabinet had to be primarily a party alliance, which was its true functioning character, and its character as a coalition of state interests was thus quite secondary. He wanted every shade of commitment within the party, from border-state conservative to antislavery radical—and the influence they commanded—represented in his cabinet and, as it were, under his eye. A further nicety was that, owing to the comparative newness of the party, considerations of present and future support required that a man's antecedents also be weighed: there should be some balance between former Whigs and former Democrats. On the other hand, Davis had no choice but to follow the principle of state representation, and had he not done so he would undoubtedly have suffered even more general dissension and public attacks on his cabinet than he did. But judging both from this and from the cabinet's own instability, the political symbolism of a coalition of states, just in itself, as a focus for loyalty was somehow abstract, lacking in sharpness, and not very compelling. In the Union cabinet such men as Seward, Chase, Gideon Welles, Edward Bates, and Montgomery Blair represented the most powerful elements that made up the party alliance, which was exactly how they were seen both in the party councils and in the country at large. It was understood that the state of the cabinet reflected the state of the party. Thus the chronic tug-of-war which ensued over the relative standing of Seward, Chase, and Blair should be read not primarily as a matter of individuals and their capacities, as such cases would tend to be in the Confederacy. The struggle was over the party influence those individuals represented in the administration, and how, or whether, the balance ought to be altered. Correspondingly, the changes Lincoln made, as well as the ones he refused to make, were on the whole governed not by the official's performance of his duties but by what the result would reflect in the way of party unity. Except in the case of Simon Cameron, which involved both incompetence and corruption, Lincoln's major moves in the management of his cabinet were made for studied party reasons. . . .

The whole corps of federal officeholders may be understood in much the same light. We have no full study of Jefferson Davis's patronage policies, which is probably symptomatic; there may never be much of a basis for generalizing about them. But there certainly was one striking, self-evident difference between Lincoln's and his, which was clarity of standards. Davis wanted merit, zeal, and loyalty. (As one writer puts it, he "favored civil service reform.") Lincoln also, naturally, wanted merit, zeal, and loyalty. But he also had some very straightforward criteria for determining in a hurry what those qualities actually meant and how they were to be found. The appointee had to be a Republican—which was at least helpful in narrowing a swarming field by roughly half—and the most dependable general standard for assessing loyalty and zeal was services to the party. It was within this category that he made his choices on "merit." The rules of procedure were also quite precise. For example:

> The appointments of postmasters, with salaries less than $1000 per annum, will be made upon the recommendations of the [Republican] members of Congress in the different districts. Applications addressed to them will receive attention earlier than if sent to the Department, and save much delay and trouble.

Lincoln was, moreover, very meticulous about "senatorial courtesy."

Though Davis, as might naturally be supposed, accepted the recommendations of others, he does not seem to have felt bound by any given rule in acting upon them. For example, by insisting on having his own way over the postmastership of Montgomery, Davis deeply alienated both the senators from Alabama. Wrote Senator Clement Clay to the equally outraged Senator Yancey: "He did not recognize the duty to respect the wishes of the Senators and Representatives, even when the office was in the town of a Senator and a Representative." And Davis loftily declared: "I am not aware of the existence of any such usage. . . . I must add that the Senate is no part of the *nominating* power, and that according, as I do, the highest respect to the opinions of Senators when they recommend applicants, I decline to yield to any dictation from them on the subject of nominations."

Patronage is a care and a worry; it is also a cherished prerogative, with gratifications for those who give as well as those who receive. They are all part of the same sensitive network. The responsiveness and *esprit* of such a network thus require that both the giving and the receiving be widely shared, and on some understood basis. We have no way of measuring the energy with which the men who made up these two patronage systems supported their respective administrations and worked to carry out their purposes. But we do know that one administration had an intricate set of standards for appraising energy and rewarding it—in addition always, of course, to standards of patriotism—which was not available to the other.

III.

The field of comparison in which contrasts between the two governments are perhaps most grossly striking is that of state-federal relations. In both cases there was a set of natural fault-lines, inherent in a federal structure, between the state and national governments. In the Confederacy, these cracks opened ever more widely as the war went on. Toward the end, indeed, some states were in a condition of virtual rebellion against the Confederate government. In the North, the very opposite occurred. The

states and the federal government came to be bound more and more closely
in the course of the four years, such that by the end of that time the
profoundest change had been effected in the character of their relations.
In the course of things, moreover, the people themselves would come to
be more closely bound to their national government. But the mechanisms
are by no means self-evident. It cannot be taken for granted that in the
nature of things such a process was bound to occur.

For the Confederacy, one very good way to tell this story is in terms
of states' rights. The late Frank Owsley made a seminal contribution to
historical thought on just these lines when he published his *State Rights
in the Confederacy* over forty years ago. With a number of impressive
examples, Owsley asserted that it was the mystique of state sovereignty,
the inability of the South to overcome the states' rights mentality in order
to operate as a nation, that ultimately did in the Confederacy. Most subsequent writers, including the present one, agree that the argument is essentially sound. For comparative purposes, however, something more is
required. There was, after all, considerable states' rights sentiment in the
North as well. Yet there, states' rights pressure came to be counterbalanced
over time by other pressures. What kind? What was the process? How did
it work?

There are two areas in which this may be observed most aptly. One
is that of control and recruitment of troops; the other, of dealing with
disaffection and disloyalty.

For the Confederacy, the great problem in raising and organizing armies
was far less a matter of insufficient manpower than it was of divided authority. The various efforts of the Confederate government to get full access
to and control over military manpower in the states were successfully
obstructed throughout the war by the state governors. The patriotic ardor
of the governors for mobilizing troops need not in itself be doubted. The
perpetual question was rather how it ought to be managed and how troops
were to be used; state resistance to Confederate policy always came down
to one of two principles: local defense, or the dangers of a centralized
military despotism. Referring to Confederate recruiting in his state, one of
the most co-operative of the governors, John Milton of Florida, wrote
angrily to Davis in December, 1861: "These troops have been raised by
authority of the War Department in disrespect to State authority . . . and
I do most solemnly protest, the tendency of the assumption and exercise
of such power by the Confederate Government is to sap the very foundation
of the rights of the States and . . . to [promote] consolidation."

The organization of the army in the spring and summer of 1861 was
held up by shortages not of men but of arms, substantial amounts of which
were in possession of the state governments. They were held back partly
for what were seen as local needs, and partly in pique at the War Department's receiving of volunteers raised without the intermediary of the
governor. Efforts of the states to control the appointment of field officers
led them either to hold back regiments until they were fully formed—instead

of sending them forward by companies—or else by tendering "skeleton regiments" with a full complement of state-commissioned officers and only a few privates. Their insistence on controlling the clothing and supply of their own state troops in Confederate service led to consequences that were almost disastrous. Resources being not only unequal but at the very best limited, the maximum co-ordination of both purchasing and distribution was imperative. Yet as it was, Confederate purchasing agents had to engage everywhere in the most ruinous competition with agents from the states for sources of supply at home and abroad, while at the same time the output of state-controlled factories was kept consistently out of general reach. Governor Zebulon B. Vance of North Carolina actually boasted that, at the time of Robert E. Lee's surrender (of a tattered and starving army), he himself had huge stores of uniforms, blankets, cloth, leather, overcoats, and bacon in his state warehouses.

Conscription was adopted in the Confederacy in April 1862, a full year before the same step was taken in the North. One of the objects was to reorganize the twelve-months' volunteers whose terms were then running out; the other was to get control of the aggregations of militia which had been built up during the previous year and held in the states for local defense. This latter purpose was never properly achieved. State guards were once again built up, the condition of whose discipline and training made them worthless for almost any purpose so long as they were withheld from general service; and conscription itself, especially after the Act of February 1864, was resisted by the governors in a variety of ways. The chief device was that of exemptions, wherein wide categories of persons were sweepingly redefined as "state officers." . . .

In the North, the story of the recruitment and control of the army was, at least by comparison, relatively straightforward. The raising of troops was at the outset fully in the hands of the state governors, and so in a nominal sense it remained throughout. And yet by a series of steps the actual initiative tended to pass increasingly to the national government. By calling for three-year volunteer enlistments during the first month of hostilities and enlarging the regular army without the authority of law before the assembling of Congress, Lincoln took clear control of the national forces. Through most of the first year the recruiting activities of the governors proceeded with the utmost energy. The first major shift in initiative occurred after the failure of the Peninsula Campaign, when patriotic fervor began wearing thin and volunteers became increasingly harder to find. At this point Secretary Seward persuaded all the governors to unite in memorializing the President to call for 150,000 more volunteers, whereupon Lincoln promptly called for twice that many, together with 300,000 nine-months' militia. Both calls were more than met. Under the threat of a militia draft, the governors threw themselves with renewed zeal into a very aggressive campaign of recruiting. After the Emancipation Proclamation, the administration agreed to the enrolling of Negro troops. Aside from the raising of a few independent regiments, this recruiting was done directly by field commanders, entirely outside the control of any state government, and approximately 186,000 men were thus added to the national army. A further step was the adoption of conscription with the National Enrollment Act of March 1863, which gave the President full power to raise and support armies without state assistance. The unpopular Act was not fully exploited, and conscription as such accounted for no more than about 6 percent of the total Union forces. It was successfully used, however, from 1863 to the end of the war, as a device for filling deficiencies in state volunteer quotas and for encouraging the governors to see that such deficiencies did not occur. In the mobilization of military manpower the state governors on the whole performed their function with exceptional vigor, even while becoming—as one writer somewhat extravagantly puts it—"mere agents" of the national government.

The energy of the Union government may be seen with even greater clarity in its actions against disaffection and disloyalty. Without any special legislation, Lincoln immediately assumed executive authority to suspend the writ of habeas corpus and make summary arrests in areas particularly endangered by disloyal activities; and in handling such cases the government made very little use of the courts. A blanket proclamation of September 24, 1862 (previous ones had designated specific localities), made "all persons discouraging volunteer enlistments, resisting militia drafts, or guilty of any disloyal practice . . . subject to martial law and liable to trial and punishment by Courts Martial or Military Commission," anywhere in the country and at any time "during the existing insurrection." Congress made some effort to define the President's powers in the Habeas Corpus Act of March 3, 1863, but whether the Act intended to grant these powers for the first time or to recognize powers he had exercised all along was not clear, and in any event executive policy and practice proceeded unaltered. For such activities as aiding desertion, circulating disloyal literature, bushwhacking, bridge-burning, forming and promoting disloyal secret societies, and so on, the State and War Departments with their network of provost-marshals and other agents made thousands of arrests throughout the war. The exact number will never be known. The chief voices of opposition to these policies came from the Democratic party; the chief supporters were the Republican governors, especially in the Midwest.

No such freedom or directness of action was ever permitted to Jefferson Davis. He could make no summary moves against practices whose effect was to obstruct the war effort until the badly unsettled conditions of early 1862 finally persuaded the Confederate Congress that something needed to be done. The Act passed on February 27 thereupon permitted the executive to suspend habeas corpus and apply martial law to places threatened by invasion. But though Davis used his power in a very restricted way, the resulting hostility to martial law as imposed on Richmond and certain other places was such that Congress in April felt constrained to put further limits on the executive and to amend the law by giving it a fixed date of expiration. A second Act was also limited to a fixed term—it was passed on October

13, 1862, and expired five months later—and did not authorize trials of civilians by military courts. During this time, the writ of habeas corpus was suspended in fewer places than before. But despite Davis's urgings the law was allowed to lapse, and for a year nothing was enacted to take its place. A third Act, in force from the middle of February to the end of July 1864, contained many limits on executive discretion, and after that time the most desperate pleas by the Confederate President could not induce his Congress to pass another. The reason which the Congress gave for its refusal was the opposition of the states. That opposition had, indeed, been so bitter that Confederate law was in many places rendered practically unenforceable. Governor [Joseph E.] Brown insisted that the people of Georgia had "more to apprehend from military despotism than from subjugation by the enemy," and when Alexander Stephens harangued the Georgia legislature in March 1864 on the government's "despotic" suspension of habeas corpus, Brown had the speech printed and mailed to the company officers of every Georgia regiment and to every county clerk and county sheriff in Confederate territory. The legislature of North Carolina passed an Act making it compulsory for state judges to issue the writ, in effect nullifying Confederate law. A meeting of governors in October 1864 adopted a resolution "virtually condemning" the suspension of habeas corpus.

One result was a serious weakening of the South's military system. State judges in Virginia, Texas, North Carolina, and elsewhere issued writs of habeas corpus indiscriminately to persons accused of desertion or evading military service, and Governor Vance used his militia to enforce them. Robert E. Lee complained to the Secretary of War that the drain on the army thus caused by the use of habeas corpus was "more than it can bear." Moreover, the deterioration of civil government in many areas made a wide field for lawless bands, disloyal secret societies, and trading with the enemy. Persons arrested for such activities were again and again freed by habeas corpus on grounds of insufficient evidence. All this despite Davis's plea that "the suspension of the writ is not simply advisable and expedient, but almost indispensable to the successful conduct of the war."

The chief mechanism that prevented such centrifugal tendencies from developing in the Northern states, as William B. Hesseltine pointed out some years ago, was the Republican party. It was the energy of the Republican party that established the potential structure with which the North began the war, and through which the war was prosecuted to the end. More specifically, the governors of every Northern state in 1861 had been put there through the efforts of that party, and these men represented both the state organizations and the national coalition responsible for bringing a Republican administration to Washington. They were politically committed from the very first to positive measures for suppressing disunion. With remarkable unanimity they invited Lincoln at the outset to take steps—indeed, they insisted he take them—which could only draw more and more power into his hands, leaving them with less and less initiative.

As with the raising of armies, there was something cumulative about this process; it came to take on a life of its own.

In turn, the various state administrations—especially after the resurgence of the Democratic party with the reverses of 1862—came more and more, despite their traditions of particularism, to realize their growing dependence on the federal government for political support. There are numerous examples of this. One is the famous case of Governor Oliver Morton of Indiana, whom the elections of 1862 had confronted with a Democratic legislature. These Democrats, denouncing Morton, Lincoln, conscription, emancipation, and arbitrary arrests, tried to remove the state's military affairs from Morton's control and successfully held up appropriation bills until the session expired, leaving the governor without money to run the state. The distraught Morton, not wanting to call a special session and at the same time convinced that treasonable Copperhead conspiracies were about to engulf the entire Northwest, appealed in his extremity to the President, who was no more anxious than he to have Indiana's Democrats crippling the state's war effort. Funds were found in the War Department, which, together with private subscriptions, enabled Morton to steer through a critical period without state appropriations. . . .

In the broadest sense the dependence of the state and national administrations was mutual, and was mutually acknowledged; but in any case the binding agency and energizing force was the Republican party. And this in turn was maintained—indeed, made possible—through the continued existence of the Democrats.

IV.

There is certainly no need here to discuss the beneficial functions of a "loyal opposition." But something might be said about the functions of an opposition which is under constant suspicion of being only partly loyal. The Northern Democratic party during the Civil War stood in precisely this relation to the Union war effort, and its function in this case was of a double nature. On the one hand, its legitimacy as a quasi-formal institution would remain in the last analysis unchallenged, so long as it kept its antiwar wing within some sort of bounds. But by the same token there was the rough and ready principle that "every Democrat may not be a traitor, but every traitor is a Democrat."

Thus, the very existence of the Democratic party provided the authorities (who badly needed some standard) with a ready-made device for making the first rough approximation in the identification of actual disloyalty. It also provided a kind of built-in guarantee against irrevocable personal damage should the guess turn out to be wrong. When in doubt they could always round up the local Democrats, as many a time they did, and in case of error there was always a formula for saving face all around: it was "just politics." There was, in short, a kind of middle way, an intermediate standard that had its lighter side and alleviated such extremes in security policy as, on the one hand, the paralysis and frustration of doing nothing, and, on the other, the perversions of power that accompany political blood-baths. For example, elections in the doubtful border states were always accompanied by rioting, skulduggery, and various kinds of dirty work; a familiar technique for preventing this was to make wholesale arrests of Democrats just beforehand. Or, in the case of Clement L. Vallandigham, the man was arrested in 1863 by order of General Ambrose Burnside, convicted by military commission, and lodged in a Cincinnati military prison for expressing sympathy with the enemy and speaking with intent to hinder the war effort. Vallandigham's prominence in the Democratic party of Ohio both created a dilemma and provided for its solution. On the one hand, it would hardly seem safe to have such a man in high public office; on the other hand a shade might be established somewhere between "treason" and "mere politics." Lincoln's solution, without exactly repudiating General Burnside's, was to commute Vallandigham's sentence to deportation through the Confederate lines.

Two state governments, those of New York and New Jersey, actually did fall into Democratic hands for a time during the war. But despite much talk of states' rights and arbitrary central authority, neither of these administrations did anything that materially hindered the war effort. Both, in fact, did much to promote it, and it was not as though either state was lacking in Democrats ready for almost any measure which might tie up the federal government. But a strong stimulus to the Democratic governors, as well as to the state Democratic organizations, for keeping such elements in check was the existence in each state of a formidable Republican organization which was watching their every move.

Meanwhile Jefferson Davis also had opposition, in his Congress as well as in the states, and it grew ever larger. But it was not "an" opposition in any truly organized sense. It was far more toxic, an undifferentiated bickering resistance, an unspecified something that seeped in from everywhere to soften the very will of the Confederacy. Davis could not move against this; he had no real way of getting at it. He had no way, for example, without either an organized opposition party or an organized administration party, of dealing with a man like Joseph E. Brown. Had there been such organizations, and had Brown himself been at the head of either the one or the other of them in the state of Georgia, the administration forces would have had some sort of check on him. As it was, Brown could claim expansively and with the fullest justice that he simply represented the whole people of Georgia; and had Davis directly challenged Brown's loyalty he would have challenged the good faith of an entire state. Not being held to the administration and the other states by party ties, Brown and others like him were without any continuing mode of instruction in the requirements and interests of the Confederacy as a whole. His supreme parochialism and reluctance to co-operate need not be seen as a matter of mere spite. The world's history is full of political elites—such as the Polish nobles of the eighteenth century, unwilling to give up their *liberum veto* to a king to achieve a strong Polish state—that literally did not know their own best interests. Although Brown could not see beyond the borders of Georgia, it ought to be said for him that what he did see he saw very clearly. His whole sense and image of power was tied up in the relation between himself and the population of his state. Thus to him, Davis's efforts to mobilize the total resources of the Confederacy were as great a threat as was the Union army—Brown as much as said so—and they intruded, in any case, an element of uncertainty into his own political world so gross as to be intolerable. Unlike the Northern governors, Brown had no informal national structure with a clear set of organizational interests, and on which his own power depended, to persuade him otherwise. . . .

A further note on "opposition" might involve the relations of Lincoln with the "Radical" faction of his own party. This question has produced some strong debate among historians, though the principal issues appear by now to have been largely settled. One side of it was opened by the publication in 1941 of T. Harry Williams's *Lincoln and the Radicals,* which represented the President's greatest political burdens as having been heaped on him not so much by the Democrats as by extremists within the Republican ranks. This determined phalanx of "Radicals," or "Jacobins" as John Hay first called them, hounded Lincoln without mercy. Their Committee on the Conduct of the War, with its investigations into military policy and its eternal pressure for changes of generals, was a serious hindrance to the administration. Their insistence on emancipation, Negro troops, and confiscation of rebel property embarrassed Lincoln in his policy of moderation toward the border states during the early stage of the war. They tried to refashion his cabinet; they tried to force his hand on reconstruction; they even tried to replace him as the Republican candidate in 1864 with someone more forceful. On every issue but the last, the Radicals "conquered" Lincoln. Nor was Williams seeing mirages. It may be, indeed, that he saw things in much the way Lincoln himself must at times have seen them. There *were* Radicals; they did harass him constantly; more than once they drove him virtually to despair. It might even be said that in the end they "won." But whether this should mean that Lincoln "lost" is another question. How fundamental, really, was the "struggle"? Williams was eventually challenged on just this ground by David Donald in 1956, and as a result the entire tone of the matter has since become much altered. Donald pointed out that "presidents are always criticized by members of their own parties," but that this is hardly the same as out-and-out warfare. The Radicals were not in fact a very cohesive or disciplined group; they were far from agreed among themselves on a great many things; and they were certainly not inveterate enemies of the President. He wanted their support, and at the most critical points he did not fail to get it. Personal relations were always reasonably good; with one of the leaders, Charles Sumner, they were excellent. As Donald says, "to picture Lincoln at swords' points with the Radical leaders of his own party, then, is an error."

The one point which may need further emphasis is that these Radicals, whatever may have been their many differences, represented the most articulate, most energetic, most militant wing of the Republican party. The one thing that did unite such men as Trumbull, Wade, Greeley, Chandler, Fessenden, Julian, and the rest was their implacable insistence that the war be prosecuted with ever more vigor, and that the President use the national power to the utmost in doing it. There is every evidence that in this over-all objective they and the President were at one, inasmuch as the war was, in the end, so prosecuted. Whether Lincoln welcomed his tormentors is doubtful. But whether he or anyone else would have moved as decisively without them is equally doubtful, and what the Union war effort as a whole would have been without the energy they represented is more doubtful still. The tensions and conflicts of the Lincoln administration—such as those having to do with emancipation, the use of Negro troops, and the complexion of the government that was to stand for re-election in 1864— were, as we know, considerable. But without a party apparatus to harness and direct them, they would surely have been unmanageable.

In any event, we might imagine Jefferson Davis as being quite willing to exchange this sort of ''opposition'' for the one he had. In the Confederate Congress there seem to have been some who pressed for greater vigor than Davis's in fighting the war; a much larger number inclined to measures that would have resulted in less. But perhaps more fundamental was that these men were all mixed in together. There was no recognized way of segregating or defining them, no basis of expectations, no clear principle for predicting what they might do. ''There were no political organizations seeking un-divided loyalty,'' as the historian of that Congress puts it, ''nor was there consistent pressure from the electorate. Conditions changed, opinions changed, consequently administration sympathies changed.'' This lack of sharpness seems to have been accompanied by a certain lack of initiative which is quite noticeable when contrasted with the wartime federal Con-gress, and it is apparent that lack of party responsibility had much to do with it. Davis's Congress for the most part was not violently obstructive, in the sense that groups within it confronted him with formidable alter-natives in policy to which he had to adjust. Much of his legislation, indeed, was rather passively enacted, which is to say that at best he could drag his Congress along. At the worst, however, it ended by being a drag on him. Perhaps his snappishness and rigidity were, after all, only appropriate to the circumstances. Professor Yearns mildly concludes:

> He despaired at Congress's amendments, delays, and occasional rejections. Only subservience satisfied him, and, as his influence with Congress was based primarily on an agreement of ideas, not on party discipline, he ultimately lost some of this influence.

Certainly Davis had no counterpart of Lincoln's ''Radicals'' to spur him on. Could the rabid secessionists of the 1850s, the so-called Southern ''fire-eaters,'' the Robert Barnwell Rhetts, the William Lowndes Yanceys, the Edmund Ruffins, have made such a counterpart? There is little evidence that they could, or would. Such men are quite absent from the roll of the Confederacy's leading statesmen. The most dynamic ''fire-eaters'' who came into their own in the war years were two obstructionist state governors, already mentioned, Zebulon Vance and Joseph E. Brown.

V.

It has been asserted throughout this essay that the Republican party, in the presence of an organized party of opposition, performed a variety of functions in mobilizing and managing the energies needed for sustaining the Union war effort. These were carried on both inside and outside the formal structure of government, and by men active in party affairs whether they held office or not. The absence of such a system in the Confederacy seems to have had more than a casual bearing on the process whereby Southern energies, over and beyond the course of military events, became diffused and dissipated. National commitments in the North were given form and direction by an additional set of commitments, those of party. This hardly means that the Republican party is to be given sole credit for the success of the war effort, which was in fact supported by overwhelming numbers of Democrats. But it does mean, among other things, that there were political sanctions against the Democrats' *not* supporting it, sanctions which did not exist in the Confederacy. When Democratic leaders were inclined to behave irresponsibly they could not, like Brown and Vance, play the role of state patriots. A hint of Democratic disloyalty anywhere tightened the Republican organization everywhere.

The emphasis hitherto has been upon leadership, upon how the process of politics affected the workings of government, but a final word should be said about how that process affected the body of citizenry. What may have been the function of a party system as a vehicle of communication? What did it do toward making popular elections a mode whereby the people were in effect called upon to define and reaffirm their own commitment to the national cause? In 1862, 1863, and 1864, through a series of elections which made the heaviest psychological demands on the entire country, the North had annually to come to terms with the war effort. The Republicans, with varying degrees of success, everywhere made attempts to broaden their coalition by bringing as many Union Democrats into it as possible, and naturally tried to attract as many Democratic voters to it as they could. The national party even changed its name in 1864, calling itself the "Union" party to dramatize the breadth of its appeal. And yet the result was in no true sense an all-party front or bipartisan coalition; rather it was a highly successful device for detaching Democrats from their regular party loyalties. The distinction is of some importance. The initiative for this effort remained throughout in Republican hands, and the Democrats everywhere maintained their regular organizations. The structure of parties was therefore such that every election became, in a very direct way, a test of loyalty to the national government. . . .

The people of the Confederacy, of course, continued to hold elections. Yet we know surprisingly little—indeed, almost nothing—about these elections. No study has ever been made of them, which is some measure of how comparatively little importance was attached to them at the time. The people were asked in November 1861 to choose Davis and Stephens as heads of the "permanent" government. The election "was marked, however, by general apathy." The first elections to Congress, according to Professor [Wilfred B.] Yearns, "went off quietly." There was virtually no campaigning, and "balloting everywhere was light, as is usual when issues are absent." The elections of 1863, from what little glimpse we have of them, seem aggressive only by contrast. The increased activity at that time was principally a product of increased dissatisfaction with Davis's government. Yet even here the opposition was unorganized and unfocused, and candidates "failed to offer any clear substitute for policies they denigrated." "Mixed with rodomontade was the familiar state rights ingredient which gave much criticism a respectable flavor. All of the strong war measures were condemned as evidence of centralized despotism which was abusing the states."

The sluggishness of communication in the Confederacy has often been commented on, and yet here the contrast with the North is one which the disparity in technology does not quite fully account for. There was no counterpart in the South of the resonance which party elections provided for the Northern cause. The historian of Confederate propaganda asserts that official efforts in this direction were very deficient, which is not surprising when it is recalled how preponderantly such efforts in the North were handled through party agencies. We have a description of how such activities were carried on in Washington with the heartiest co-operation of the national government during the fall of 1864:

> The National Republican Committee have taken full possession of all the Capitol buildings, and the committee rooms of the Senate and House of Representatives are filled with clerks, busy in mailing Lincoln documents all over the loyal States. . . .
> The Post Office Department, of course, is attending to the lion's share of this work. Eighty bags of mail matter, all containing Lincoln documents, are daily sent to Sherman's army.

Not long after this time, a measure was timidly offered in the Confederate Congress whereby the government frank might be used for mailing newspapers to soldiers in the field. The Confederate Postmaster-General was distressed. His department was required by law to be self-supporting, and he was very proud of its being the only one to show a surplus, which he had achieved by doing away with all but the bare minimum services. He spoke to the President about this new bill, and the latter solemnly vetoed it as being unconstitutional.

Whether Northern wartime elections served to give refinement and precision to the issues is perhaps less important than that they served to simplify and consolidate them. When the people of Indiana were urged in 1863 to vote for Republicans in their local elections, they were really being asked to do more than elect a few county officers. And by the same token the candidate for such an office accepted, along with his nomination, a whole train of extraordinary responsibilities: Governor Morton, President Lincoln, emancipation, arbitrary arrests, and war to the end. There was no separating them; under the circumstances of war, the voter who took the Republican candidate took them all. And the candidate, if successful in his debates with his Democratic opponent, would have enacted something akin to the principle of the self-fulfilling prophecy. He defined his position, he defended the administration, he persuaded his audience, and in the process he repersuaded and recommitted himself. It may be quite proper to say that it was, after all, the Union's military success that made political success possible. The fall of Atlanta in September 1864, for example, certainly rescued Lincoln's chances for re-election. But conceivably it was not that simple, and short-term correlations may be deceiving. How was the Northern will sustained for the three and a half years that were needed before it could reap successes of any kind in late 1864? A continual affirmation and reaffirmation of purpose was built into the very currents of political life in the Northern states. It is altogether probable that the North's political energies and its military will were, all along, parts of the same process.

Every election, moreover, was a step in nationalizing the war. The extension of local and state loyalties into national loyalties during this period was something of a revolution, and it did not occur easily. This profound change cannot be taken for granted, nor is it best understood simply by examining the formal federal structure through which it began. It is revealed rather through the far less formal political process whereby the national government in the Civil War was able to communicate its purposes, to persuade, and to exercise its will directly upon individuals in state, city, town, and local countryside.

Abraham Lincoln and the Republican Party During the Civil War

MICHAEL F. HOLT

One of the most stimulating analyses of Civil War politics ever written is a brilliant essay by Eric McKitrick called "Party Politics and the Union and Confederate War Efforts." In it, McKitrick argues that the North had a decisive advantage over the South because it continued to have two-party rivalry during the war while the Confederacy did not. The presence of the Democratic party forced Republicans of all kinds to rally behind the policies of the Republican government to win elections. As a result, the North remained more united during the long ordeal than the division-plagued Confederacy.

According to McKitrick, party politics also made Abraham Lincoln a more effective presidential leader than his Confederate counterpart, Jef-

Michael F. Holt, "Abraham Lincoln and the Politics of Union," from *Abraham Lincoln and the American Political Tradition*, John L. Thomas, ed., pp. 111–137 (Amherst: University of Massachusetts Press, 1968), copyright © 1986 by The University of Massachusetts Press.

ferson Davis. The organization and partisan needs of the Republican party provided Lincoln with guidelines, first to select and then to reshuffle his cabinet, with ways to ensure the loyalty of his vice presidents, with incentives to gain the cooperation of state governors, and with sanctions to punish political opponents both inside and outside his own party. In contrast, the hapless Davis lacked party lines to separate friends from foes and to generate institutional loyalty to his administration. Hence he could not control his cabinet, Vice President Alexander Stephens, obstreperous governors like Joe Brown of Georgia and Zeb Vance of North Carolina, or political opponents in Congress and the electorate. McKitrick concludes that it was because of the presence of a two-party system that Lincoln was able to hold the North together long enough to win the war. Without the glue that parties provided, Davis could not prevent centrifugal forces from tearing the Confederacy apart.

Despite the stunning originality of McKitrick's argument, it leaves several crucial questions unanswered. Most important, it slights the critical matter of Lincoln's relationship with the Republican majority in Congress. If the presence of the Democratic opposition pressured Republicans to pull together, how can one explain the well-known hostility of many Republicans to Lincoln, the effort of Republican senators to purge his favorite William Henry Seward from the cabinet, or the palpable conflict between Lincoln and the congressional wing of his party over emancipation, the arming of blacks, reconstruction, and other wartime policies?

Once it was fashionable to blame these clashes on a cabal of vindictive radicals who frustrated the benevolent plans of the magnanimous president. Now we know that such a melodramatic interpretation is misleading. Although there were indeed radical and moderate factions in the Republican party during the war, virtually all congressional Republicans, not just the radicals, blamed Lincoln for failing to prosecute the war vigorously enough and to move against slavery rapidly enough, and virtually all voted for the measures that set Congress's policy apart from Lincoln's. Nor is it satisfactory to contend, as some historians have, that Lincoln and congressional Republicans had the same fundamental goals, that they were traveling the same road at different rates, and that Lincoln was really happy to have the more radical congressmen blaze the trail. Timing is almost everything in politics, and that line of argument fails to explain why Lincoln and Congress wanted to move at different speeds while it simultaneously minimizes the seriousness of the disputes between them. Finally, it is not terribly convincing to assert that the pragmatic and sagacious Lincoln, alone among the Republican politicians in Washington, recognized the need to keep the border slave states and northern Democrats behind the war effort and therefore resisted congressional demands concerning emancipation and the use of black troops that might alienate them. Lincoln had no monopoly on political wisdom or common sense. Congressional Republicans must have recognized the potential political impact of the policies they advocated. Nonetheless, they vigorously demanded them, often against Lincoln's wishes. Why?

This essay suggests that the continuation of the two-party system, which McKitrick sees as the cause of Republican unity during the war, was in fact the source of the division between Lincoln and Congress over wartime policy. Because Lincoln and congressional Republicans adopted different political strategies in response to the challenge posed by the Democratic party, they also pursued different paths to fight the war they both wanted to win. The result of Congress going one way and Lincoln another, however, was a more successful war effort than the North would have achieved had it followed either course alone. McKitrick may not be correct about the precise way in which a two-party system helped the northern war effort, but he is correct about the result. It significantly contributed to northern victory.

To understand Civil War politics it is necessary to remember three facts of political life. First, the Democratic party remained a potent challenger to Republicans in the North. Though divided between two candidates and forced to defend one of the most unpopular and corrupt administrations in American history, the Democrats still won almost 44 percent of the popular vote in the free states in 1860. As the war progressed, moreover, controversial Republican policies like emancipation, conscription, and the suspension of *habeas corpus* gave them golden issues to campaign on. The menace of a Democratic comeback, in sum, was no chimera.

Second, the Republican party had no base of any consequence in any slave state. In 1860 Lincoln's support in the border states that remained in the Union ranged from 24 percent in tiny Delaware to a pitiful 1 percent in his native Kentucky. In the slave states that seceded Lincoln received a handful of votes only in Virginia; no Republican tickets had even been distributed in the other ten states that joined the Confederacy. It may strike some as odd to include Confederate states in a discussion of the political situation that shaped the clash between Lincoln and congressional Republicans, but one must remember that the fundamental northern purpose in the war was to restore those states to the Union. Certainly Lincoln hoped they would be voting again in the congressional and presidential elections of 1864, if not earlier, and they seemed likely to vote against Lincoln and other Republican candidates unless support were developed within them.

Third, and most important, Lincoln and congressional Republicans had different constituencies. Lincoln faced a national electorate, not a local one, and he had won less than 40 percent of the popular vote in 1860. To achieve reelection he had to worry about winning statewide pluralities both in the free states, where the race had often been close even in 1860 when the opposition divided among three candidates, and in the border and Confederate slave states, where he had virtually no organizational or popular support. There is no need to question Lincoln's desire for reelection. Virtually everyone who knew him commented on his insatiable political ambition. Like most politicians, moreover, Lincoln convinced himself that his reelection was in the best interest of the nation and that the political strategy he pursued to achieve it was the best way to restore the Union.

Unlike Lincoln, congressional Republicans did not have to consider areas of existing or potential Democratic strength in their own political calculations. By definition the vast majority of them came from districts where the Republican party was strongest and most secure from the Democratic challenge. Most of them, that is, received a larger proportion of the vote in their local congressional districts than Lincoln did of the statewide vote in their states, especially in the hotly contested battlegrounds of Illinois, Indiana, Ohio, and New York. . . . To such men the campaign formula that had brought Republicans to power in the late 1850s seemed perfectly capable of keeping them in power in the 1860s. That strategy was to denounce southern political power as unfair and dangerous, to expose a supposed Slave Power conspiracy against northern liberties, to arraign northern Democrats for complicity in that southern plot, and to promise to eradicate that southern threat once Republicans achieved power. In short, Republican congressmen believed that they had won office in the past and could win again in the future by running as an antisouthern party. . . .

Nor, so long as Republicans maintained majorities in Congress and northern state legislatures, were congressional Republicans concerned that their policies might strengthen Democrats outside their own strongholds. After all, they personally did not have to run in such areas. On the other hand, they would brook no serious threat to their own hold on state and national governments. They bitterly protested the appointment of Democrats as civilian or military leaders of the war effort. They also tried to deny power to or strip effective power from offices and jurisdictions that Democrats controlled. In January 1862, for example, Republicans expelled the Indiana Democrat Jesse Bright from the Senate on the flimsiest of pretexts. Similarly, when Democrats captured a number of northern legislatures and the governorship of New York and New Jersey in the fall of 1862, Republicans rushed the most nationalistic legislation of the war through Congress between December 1862 and March 1863. The explicit purpose of the National Banking Act, the draft, and the Habeas Corpus-Indemnity-Removal Act was to shift control of banking, manpower, and legal suits against federal officials from state governments which Democrats now controlled to the national government which Republicans still dominated.

This same unwillingness to see Democrats exercise power, finally, explains the Republicans' hostility to a rapid readmission of Confederate states to political rights. Those states seemed sure to aid the Democrats whatever the nominal partisan affiliation of the men they sent to Congress. "What!" an Illinois Republican protested in February 1862, "Bring back the rebel States into full fellowship as members of the union, with their full delegations in both Houses of Congress. They, with the pro-slavery conservatives of the Border States and the Democrats of the Northern states, will control Congress. Republicans and Republican principles will be in the minority. . . ." As early as January 1863, therefore, the Republican caucus in the House determined not to seat men elected from occupied Confederate states. So too they fought Lincoln's ten percent plan, attempted to substitute the more rigorous Wade-Davis bill that would delay restoration, and resisted the readmission of Louisiana until after Lincoln died.

Congressional Republicans, in sum, approached the military conflict with the Confederacy and the political conflict with the Democracy in exactly the same way. In neither would they make concessions to induce cooperation; in neither did they seek compromise or accommodation. In both they demanded war to the hilt.

Lincoln's responses to the Democratic and Confederate challenges were dramatically different. Consolidating the Republican party in its existing strongholds by baiting Democrats and humiliating the South did little to improve his personal prospects for reelection. He could not afford to alienate non-Republicans in the northern, border-state, and Confederate areas outside of those established bastions. His solution was not to confront Democrats with distinctively Republican policies or to deny Democratic areas the power they deserved. Instead he attempted to build a new coalition under his leadership that included proslavery conservatives from the border states, northern Democrats, and former rebels from the Confederacy, just the groups congressional Republicans feared would put Republican principles in the minority. This was *not* simply a matter of broadening the base of the Republican party as some historians have maintained. Rather it was an attempt to replace the Republican party with a new bisectional organization to be called the Union party.

To state the argument most boldly, Lincoln almost from the moment he was elected set out to destroy the Republican party as it existed in 1860, that is, as an exclusively northern party whose sole basis of cohesion was hostility toward the South and the Democratic party. Instead, Lincoln wanted to create a new national coalition with support in both sections, a party built around the issue of restoring the Union, rather than the issue of crushing the Slave Power or abolishing slavery as congressional Republicans wanted. To achieve his own political goal, in short, Lincoln had to jettison the antisouthern platform that congressional Republicans insisted on retaining. . . .

Lincoln clearly hoped to enhance his chances for reelection by forging a new party that would broaden support for him in the North and marshal it in the South. But personal political expediency alone did not dictate his course. Lincoln's lifelong beliefs about the nature of the American republic also impelled him toward the same solution. Perhaps no politician has ever articulated so elegantly and succinctly as Lincoln the fundamental premise of American republicanism, that ours is a government of the people, by the people, and for the people. And the people exercised self-government, he believed, through the votes they cast at elections. As he argued in his message to Congress in July 1861, for example, the purpose of the war was to demonstrate "that ballots are the rightful, and peaceful, successors of bullets; and that when ballots have fairly, and constitutionally, decided, there can be no successful appeal back to bullets; that there can be no successful appeal, except to ballots themselves, at succeeding elections."

For Lincoln, then, the restoration of the Confederate states to the Union was preeminently a political process, a matter of the people of those states going to the polls and voting to return to the Union. Almost as soon as Yankee armies secured various parts of the South, therefore, Lincoln pressed his military governors to hold elections. "If we could somehow, get a vote of the people of Tennessee and have it result properly," he wrote Andrew Johnson on July 3, 1862, "it would be worth more to us than a battle gained." Throughout the war, indeed, Lincoln wheedled, cajoled, and threatened Southerners in attempts to induce them to vote themselves back into the Union. The major purpose of Lincoln's preliminary emancipation proclamation in September 1862, for example, was not to appease congressional Republicans or European governments or even to prepare the way for actual abolition. Rather it was to pressure Confederates to hold elections before January 1, 1863, in order to avoid emancipation. Lincoln made his purpose clear when he ordered his military governors in Louisiana, Tennessee, Arkansas, and North Carolina to arrange elections before that date to demonstrate the fidelity to the Union of those occupied areas. . . . In short, while congressional Republicans wanted to subdue the Confederacy with bullets, Lincoln wanted to redeem it with ballots cast by Southerners themselves.

Lincoln realized, moreover, that for elections in occupied areas to "result properly," Southerners needed something more tangible to vote for than the mere idea of reunion. They had to elect politicians who would establish loyal state governments. For those politicians to be able to retain political control of their states against pro-Confederate elements within them, in turn, voter support had to be institutionalized. Since those pro-Confederate elements were overwhelmingly Democratic, finally, Lincoln had to establish a new anti-Democratic political party in the South in order to achieve reconstruction through the political process as he desired.

Such a party, however, could not be called or even allied with the Republican party as long as the congressional Republicans pursued the harsh antisouthern policies they favored. Events in the South after the collapse of the Whig party in the mid-1850s had demonstrated that no matter how much southern voters and politicians disliked Democrats, they would not and could not support a palpably antisouthern party like the Republicans. Instead they had been compelled to join southern Democrats in denouncing the Republicans while simultaneously attempting to rally opposition to the Democrats through a series of ephemeral non-Republican, anti-Democratic organizations, the most recent of which had been the Constitutional Union party which supported John Bell for president in 1860.

Yet as long as anti-Democratic voters in the South were organized in a different party than Lincoln's own, they would not enhance his chances for reelection against the Democrats once Confederate states returned to the Union. Nor could such a party secure the permanent restoration of the South that Lincoln sought. The course of political history in the antebellum South had demonstrated that no party could survive in the region unless it was an authentic national party with a northern wing, a party with a genuine chance to win the presidency and control Congress. To build a successful anti-Confederate, pro-reunion party in the Confederate states, in short, Lincoln also had to replace the Republicans with a more palatable anti-Democratic party in the North, one that could serve as the northern wing of the party he needed in the South—at least as long as the southern electorate was confined to whites. Both to further his own chances for reelection in 1864 and to effect reunion, therefore, Lincoln attempted to jettison the name and the antisouthern program of the Republicans and to build a new Union party attractive to non-Republicans in both sections.

To understand why Lincoln believed he could accomplish this feat, one must appreciate that few people in the 1850s and 1860s anticipated that the Republicans would remain the permanent successors to the Whigs as the major anti-Democratic party in American politics. Accustomed to twenty years of bisectional interparty competition between Democrats and Whigs, many regarded the exclusively northern Republican party as a temporary aberration. As a result, proposals for displacing the Republicans with other anti-Democratic parties that eschewed sectionally oriented attacks on the South had abounded in the late 1850s. For example, it had required a terrific struggle for Republicans to overcome the Know-Nothing challenge to their credentials as the new anti-Democratic party in 1855–56, and they had been forced to beat back another attempt to launch a conservative, bisectional anti-Democratic party in 1858–59. Although John Bell's Constitutional Union candidacy had fared poorly against Lincoln in the free states in 1860, his virtual monopoly of the anti-Democratic vote in the slave states reaffirmed the potential that a different, non-Republican opposition party might have if it could secure that southern support. . . .

Even before the culmination of secession, [however,] many Republicans protested against any abandonment of Republican principles, "the party issues of the *past*" as the *Times* reporter had called them, to appease the South or any attempt to attract Southerners and northern Democrats to the party through patronage appointments. Thus a dismayed Indiana Republican asked his congressman in January 1861, "Is there not a movement . . . to build a 'union party' in the north which shall absorb Americans and Douglas men and Conservative Republicans; done for the purpose of killing what they term the Abolition element in the Republican party, aimed at men of our Stamp? The movement cannot amount to anything unless it should be the disruption of the Republican party."

The completion of secession and outbreak of warfare widened Republican opposition to changing the party. Secession manifestly meant that attempts to deter it by wooing Southerners had failed. More important, the withdrawal of Southerners meant that Republicans could dominate Congress without southern support. War against the Confederacy, finally, offered an opportunity to build a platform of concrete antisouthern actions, actions they could not have taken against the Slave Power without the excuse the war provided. However amenable some Republicans had been to changing the image and broadening the constituency of the party in the winter of 1860–61, therefore, few remained so six months later. Instead of worrying about extending the party to the South, they focused throughout the war on consolidating its power in the North, a project that seemed to require no change in the party's image or constituency whatsoever.

Nonetheless, as is well known, during the war Lincoln's party did exchange the Republican name for the Union label, first at the state level in 1861, 1862, and 1863 and then at the party's national convention in 1864. Most historians, echoing contemporary Democrats, have regarded this action as a transparently cosmetic attempt by cynical Republicans to lure gullible Democrats and Unionists into supporting Republican candidates and Republican policies, not a genuine transformation of the party's constituency and principles. We in fact know very little about where the impetus for this change came from or what the reaction of regular Republicans to it was. Evidence from several northern states like Illinois, Ohio, Massachusetts, and California, however, suggests that some Republicans resented even changing the party's name. Many more vehemently opposed the steps Lincoln took to give that change real substance—sharing offices with Democrats and Unionists and trying to scuttle the antisouthern policies congressional Republicans demanded.

There is, alas, no "smoking gun" in the form of a letter in which Lincoln explains his purpose or urges state Republican politicians to start Union organizations. Therefore one cannot prove that Lincoln initiated the creation of Union parties which began to appear in the North in the fall of 1861. Nevertheless, one can infer Lincoln's intentions from his behavior, especially when that behavior is correlated chronologically with efforts to start Union parties and help them win elections in various states. Specifically, his attempt to build a new bisectional Union party can be seen in his dispensation of federal patronage, his use of the presidential pulpit to define the purpose of the war as restoration of the Union rather than abolition or social revolution in the South, and his attempts to shape wartime policies toward the South, toward slavery, and toward blacks.

Contrary to the McKitrick thesis, for example, building the Union party rather than balancing factions within the existing Republican party determined Lincoln's cabinet selections throughout his presidency. For the most important post, secretary of state, he chose Seward who, he had been warned, favored the "abandonment" of the Republican party and "the early formation of new combinations, under the name of a 'Union party', or something of that kind." No Republican, indeed, had been more sympathetic than Seward to the Union party movement in the upper South during the secession crisis, and no Republican knew so well what was needed to gain the Union party's support for the Lincoln administration. Thus the purpose of Seward's notorious memorandum to Lincoln (April 1, 1861) was contained in its emphatic insistence that "we must *Change the question before the Public from one upon Slavery, or about Slavery* for a question upon *Union* or *Disunion*." Although Lincoln disregarded the accompanying advice in this note to start a foreign war and to abandon Fort Sumter to prevent a collision with the Confederacy, he was in perfect agreement with Seward about changing the issue from slavery to union.

Indeed, Seward remained Lincoln's primary coadjutor in the Union party scheme throughout the war. Hence it is no coincidence that at precisely the time in September 1862 that Gideon Welles was complaining in his diary that Seward was always closeted with Lincoln, "inculcating his political party notions," Salmon P. Chase was protesting in *his* diary that Lincoln "has already separated himself from the great body of the party which elected him." Nor is it a coincidence that Seward was the chief target in the cabinet of angry congressional Republicans. They knew that Seward's and Lincoln's hopes of a bisectional Union party directly conflicted with their own hope of preserving the Republicans as an exclusively northern and vigorously antisouthern, anti-Democratic organization.

Lincoln also expected that his appointees as secretary of war would further the development of the new party, if only by attracting northern Democrats to it. One of the things that finally persuaded Lincoln to appoint the unsavory Simon Cameron was that he had been assured that "there are thousands of influential democrats in Pennsylvania, who would feel disposed to sustain an administration, of which he should be a member." Cameron lost his value as a lure to Democratic defectors, however, when he endorsed the recruitment of black troops in December 1861. So Lincoln exiled Cameron about as far away from negrophobic northern Democrats as he could—to Russia—and replaced him with another Pennsylvania Democrat, Edwin Stanton. Unlike Cameron, indeed, Stanton had never joined the Republican party, and he had even served briefly in Buchanan's cabinet. Thus an Ohioan gushed to the new secretary, "The great democracy of the West feel especially grateful that the administration has at last called into its councils so thorough and pure a Democrat as Edwin M. Stanton." That gratitude, Lincoln hoped, would be translated into Union votes in upcoming northern elections.

Lincoln's selections from the border states even more clearly illustrate his intentions to replace the Republican party. The tiny Republican organizations there denounced Bell supporters and former Know-Nothings as "our enemies" and demanded posts in the cabinet for pure antislavery Republicans such as the Kentucky abolitionist Cassius M. Clay or Judge William Marshall of Maryland. Maryland Republicans specifically warned Lincoln that the appointment of Montgomery Blair would destroy the Republican organization in that state because Blair favored "a *de*-republicanizing of the party, and a coalition administration," "a sort of 'Union' party to take the place of the Republicans." Precisely because Lincoln sought the same kind of party reorganization, he ignored the pleas of Republicans and selected Blair as well as Edward Bates, another favorite of the proslavery conservatives who were the political enemies of border-state Republicans. For the same reason, despite the anguished protests of Republicans, he divided the lesser federal posts in the border states among Republicans, Bell men, and Democrats who supported the new Union parties.

As the war dragged on, both Bates and Blair, like Seward, drew fire from angry congressional Republicans for delaying the harsh antisouthern, antislavery measures they demanded. Thus Lincoln's decision to replace both men in 1864 is usually interpreted as a concession to radical elements in the Republican party, an attempt to balance the dismissal of the radical Chase from the cabinet or a quid pro quo for John C. Frémont's withdrawal as an independent radical Republican candidate from the presidential campaign that year. Yet equally important in shaping Lincoln's decision was his awareness that the Union parties in both Missouri and Maryland had undergone fundamental transformations. By 1864 radical elements committed to immediate, uncompensated emancipation and the use of black troops had taken them over. Hence conservatives like Bates and Blair no longer served as adequate bridges to the Union parties whose support Lincoln sought. For him to retain their backing, Blair and Bates had to go.

Lincoln also manipulated other federal appointments to build the Union party, especially in 1861 and 1862 when his attention was focused primarily on the North and the border states. It is true that outside of the border states the vast majority of civilian positions went to regular Republicans recommended by Republican congressmen. Nonetheless, Lincoln carefully placed Democrats in highly visible posts in order to woo Democratic backing for new Union organizations in the North. Not only the fact but the timing of these appointments reveals his purpose. The most conspicuous examples were the military commands he showered on Democratic favorites like John McClernand, Don Carlos Buell, and George B. McClellan, appointments that Seward heartily favored and that congressional Republicans increasingly denounced by 1862. Despite this growing protest, Lincoln retained them in command as long as they might lure Democratic votes to the Union parties in northern states—and only that long. Buell was dismissed on October 24, 1862, after the October congressional elections in Illinois, Indiana, Ohio, and Pennsylvania. McClellan received the axe on November 5, 1862, the day after elections in New York and New Jersey. . . .

A closer look at the chronology of conventions and elections involving the Union party in the North and border states also helps explain Lincoln's attempts to delay or frustrate congressional and military initiatives toward abolition and the arming of blacks. One reason for Lincoln's cautious movement on these matters surely was his concern about keeping proslavery Southerners and negrophobic northern Democrats behind the war effort. Arming blacks, he declared in August 1862, could "turn 50,000 bayonets from the loyal Border States against us that were for us." Yet Lincoln was equally worried about turning ballots against his cherished Union party.

Take, for example, his rapid reaction to Frémont's emancipation decree of August 30, 1861. That edict not only menaced Kentucky's future loyalty to the Union, but it also could, in the words of Kentucky's James Speed, "crush out every vistage [sic] of a union party in the state." Although the Kentucky Union party had already won congressional elections in June and the state's legislative elections in August, before Frémont's actions, the legislature itself was due to meet on September 2. More important, state conventions to organize Union parties that would combine Democrats and Republicans were scheduled to meet in September in both Ohio and New York, conventions that could easily fizzle unless Frémont were rebuked.

Thus Lincoln requested Frémont to revoke his order on September 2 and commanded him to on September 11, much to the displeasure of congressional Republicans. Nor was it coincidental that Lincoln first sent the orders to remove Frémont from command on October 24, orders that were finally implemented on November 2. Though firing Frémont angered Republicans, it helped the broad-based Union parties score decisive triumphs in New York and Maryland on November 6. . . .

It's true that Lincoln seemed to contradict these efforts to reassure negrophobic northern Democrats and proslavery border-state Union men when he issued his preliminary Emancipation Proclamation on September 22. But he tried to make even that palatable to the groups he was wooing. For one thing, the emancipation provisions of Congress's confiscation act of July 17 theoretically went into effect in September, so Lincoln's postponement of emancipation until January 1, 1863, seemed to delay actual implementation of abolition by government forces until after the fall elections of 1862. Moreover, by exempting loyal slave states and indicating that Confederate states that returned to the Union before that date would escape abolition, he made it clear that he viewed emancipation as an effort to hasten the restoration of the Union, not to punish Southerners. Thus the measure was compatible with his insistence the previous December that "the integrity of the Union" was "the primary object of the contest" and that he wanted to prevent the war from degenerating "into a violent and remorseless revolutionary struggle."

Equally important, Lincoln took steps to balance whatever losses the proclamation might cost the Union parties in the North and border states by reducing the Democratic vote. On September 24, 1862, he suspended *habeas corpus* throughout the nation for the duration of the war and ordered the military arrest of "all persons . . . guilty of any disloyal practice." Almost by definition such persons would not be supporters of the Union party; instead they would be potential voters against it. Thus the thousands of arrests made in 1862, 1863, and 1864, often immediately before elections took place, kept foes of the Union parties away from the polls.

None of Lincoln's efforts, however, prevented a stunning Democratic comeback in the elections of 1862 in New York, New Jersey, Pennsylvania, Ohio, Indiana, and Illinois. The divergent responses of Lincoln and congressional Republicans to this Democratic resurgence illustrate well how their contrasting political strategies led to conflict between the two branches. Both correctly recognized that the Republicans or Union party had lost primarily because they had suffered significantly more drop-off in their vote since 1860 than the Democrats, but they differed in their explanation of that erosion. Lincoln attributed it to the absence of potential Union voters in the army. Most Republicans instead blamed it on abstention by disgusted Northerners who wanted much harsher policies toward the South and slavery, the kinds of policies Republicans thought Lincoln had thwarted. Congressional Republicans, in other words, believed that former Republican voters had abandoned the party when it in turn seemed to abandon its antisouthern platform.

Equally revealing, angry Republicans bluntly pointed to Lincoln's attempt to include Democrats and Southerners in a new Union party as the chief cause of the debacle. "The Republican organization was voluntarily abandoned by the president and his leading followers, and a no-party Union was formed," fumed Ohio Senator John Sherman. If the Republicans "have the wisdom to throw overboard the old debris that joined them in the Union movement, they will succeed. If not, they are doomed." "Fear of offending the Democracy has been at the bottom of all our disasters," echoed Maine's William Pitt Fessenden. Chicago's Republican editor Joseph Medill also castigated Lincoln's courtship of Democrats. "It is enough to make the strongest men weep tears of blood. The President has allowed the Democratic party to shape the policy of the war and furnish the Generals to conduct it, while the Republicans have furnished the men and the money." What galled these Republicans, it bears repeating, was not simply sharing leadership positions with Democrats and border state Unionists. It was that courting such men precluded or at least obfuscated the punitive actions against the Slave Power like confiscation, abolition, and the arming of former slaves that Republicans thought their constituents wanted. By watering down the Republicans' antisouthern principles in favor of the diluted Union platform, Ohio's Joshua Giddings complained, Lincoln had condemned Republican candidates to enter the elections "without doctrines, principles, or character." The Democratic comeback of 1862, in sum, reinforced the conviction among congressional Republicans that they could defeat Democrats in the North only by retaining the Republican party's exclusively northern, antisouthern, anti-Democratic identity.

That hardening of Republican opposition to the Union party strategy made further clashes with Lincoln inevitable, for the president viewed the Democratic comeback in the North as an even greater reason to press ahead with his plans before the 1864 presidential contest. The palpable failure of substantial numbers of northern Democrats to join the Union coalition probably made them less important in his calculations after 1862. We know he sacked Buell and McClellan immediately after the elections ended, and in January 1863 he went ahead with emancipation and the concomitant enrollment of black troops, policies he had tried to delay earlier. It's also clear that in 1863 and 1864 he relied less on inducements to Democrats than on the soldier vote he thought had been absent in 1862 to carry northern elections. On the other hand, after the 1862 debacle, he sought frantically to shore up Union organizations in the border states and to build them in the Confederate states in order to offset the renewed strength of the Democracy in the North with new support for himself in the South. . . .

Almost as soon as the 1862 returns came in from the North, Lincoln bombarded his military governors in the occupied South with instructions to hold congressional elections, but Republicans in Congress refused to seat the few men who were chosen. These Republicans were even more upset by the lenient terms of Lincoln's amnesty proclamation and ten percent plan, which, with the exception of a small group of Confederate civilian and military officials, restored political and property rights to those who took an oath of future allegiance and encouraged such men to establish and control civil governments that would replace the military regimes in their states. In contrast, congressional Republicans regarded former Confederates as traitors who did not deserve to vote, hold office, or be represented in Congress.

Lincoln's reconstruction policy of December 1863 was in fact a classic example of his attempt to find a middle road for his new Union party between the positions staked out by Democrats and congressional Republicans. Because Lincoln required Confederates who sought amnesty to swear that they and their new state governments would abide by his Emancipation Proclamation, Democrats who objected to any conditions being imposed on southern states as a price of restoration denounced the plan as too harsh. Besides, Democrats regarded the ten percent provisions as evidence that Lincoln was creating rotten boroughs to support him in 1864. Republicans, on the other hand, regarded the plan as far too lenient toward the Slave Power and therefore inimical to their attempt to run on an antisouthern platform in the North. For one thing, they wanted to require Confederate states to revise their constitutions to abolish slavery *before* they elected new state governments and sought readmission. Lincoln said nothing about this requirement in his proclamation, and he seemed prepared to ignore it when he allowed the Union party in Louisiana to elect new state officials in early 1864 before holding a constitutional convention. The difference was one of substance and not just procedure, for the area of Louisiana and Tennessee where Lincoln first tried to apply his policy had been exempted from emancipation by his proclamation. Lincoln's policy, in short, seemed far less certain than their own plan to eradicate slavery permanently, at least until the Thirteenth Amendment passed Congress and was ratified by the states. In addition, congressional Republicans wanted to force southern states to repudiate the Confederate debt as a price of readmission, a matter on which Lincoln's plan was silent. Finally, they wanted to limit the period during which Confederates could apply for pardon and to exclude many more former Confederates from the political process than Lincoln's plan seemed to. For all these reasons, Republicans in July 1864 passed the more stringent Wade-Davis bill as a congressional alternative to Lincoln's plan of reconstruction.

While genuine differences of opinion over the proper policy as well as a jurisdictional conflict over control of reconstruction separated Lincoln from congressional Republicans, their contrasting political strategies also divided them. Lincoln clearly hoped to restore Confederate states to the Union as rapidly as possible, not only because he wanted their votes in 1864 but also because he wanted to prevent Congress from imposing radical changes on the South that might alienate white Southerners from the Union party. Congressional Republicans, in contrast, believed that Lincoln's efforts to lure such men to the Union party through generous policies repeated the mistake of 1862 that had produced Democratic victories in the North. As Herman Belz had ably demonstrated, congressional Republicans wanted to go before the northern electorate in 1864 with a concrete antislavery, antisouthern record. Thus, when the Thirteenth Amendment failed to pass Congress that year, they frantically framed the Wade-Davis bill and begged Lincoln to sign it so they could trumpet their anti–Slave Power credentials to their constituents. Yet precisely because the bill would postpone indefinitely the return of Confederate states to political participation and drive Southerners from the Union party Lincoln had worked so hard to build, he vetoed it. That veto, in turn, provoked a storm of protest from Republican leaders in Congress who refused to count the electoral votes cast by those Union parties in 1864 or to admit their chosen representatives to Congress after the election.

Perhaps no document reveals so plainly the differences between Lincoln and congressional Republicans, indeed, as does the extraordinary Wade-Davis Manifesto of August 1864 in which the Republican leadership spelled out for the northern public why the congressional plan was superior to the president's. Their own bill "exacted" as the price of readmission the "exclusion of dangerous enemies from power and the relief of the nation from the rebel debt, and the prohibition of slavery forever." In contrast, "the President is resolved that people shall not *by law* take *any* securities from the rebel States against a renewal of the rebellion, before restoring their power to govern us." Furious that Lincoln's veto and his own policy would undercut their preferred campaign strategy, congressional Republicans thus publicly repudiated the plan of their presidential candidate in order to reaffirm their own antisouthern credentials with the northern electorate. . . .

Given this intensification of antisouthern sentiment in the North, Lincoln's hope of creating a permanent new anti-Democratic Union party that could incorporate white Southerners in its ranks was doomed. Whatever the reasons for men from the border and Confederate states joining the Union party, they were not antisouthern. Hence the interests of northern and southern opponents of the Democrats were as much at odds as they had been in 1860. The inevitable failure of the Union party became evident when Lincoln's successor, Johnson, who continued Lincoln's efforts to include northern Democrats and anti-Democratic white Southerners in a national Union party, broke with congressional Republicans in 1866. By the fall of that year, those congressmen were campaigning once again as Republicans in open hostility to Johnson's—and Lincoln's—Union party. By the end of 1866, therefore, all hope of substituting a bisectional Union party for the Republicans as the major anti-Democratic party in American political life was gone.

The purpose of this essay, however, has not been to focus on the success or failure of the Union party. Rather it has been to suggest that Lincoln's attempt to build a Union party in response to the Democratic challenge and the determination of congressional Republicans to take a different tack to defeat Democrats was the chief source of the disagreements between Lincoln and Congress during the war. Furthermore, one can argue that their very divisions helped the North win the war. For where Lincoln took the lead, as in the use of arbitrary arrests and military intervention to bulwark Union parties in the border states or of amnesty and the ten percent plan to extend them to the Confederate South, or where Congress took the lead, as in the push for emancipation and the arming of black troops or with the nationalistic legislation passed to remove power from Democratic jurisdictions, the central tendency was toward a stronger war effort or greater weakening of the South. Put differently, Lincoln in effect used a carrot to induce Southerners to renounce the Confederacy and join a Union party that was not based on unremitting hostility to them, as the prewar Republican party had been. Congressional Republicans, in contrast, wanted to use a stick to beat Southerners into submission and thus please their northern constituents. The combination of the carrot and the stick, I suggest, was more successful than either would have been alone.

FURTHER READING

Thomas B. Alexander, and Richard E. Beringer, *The Anatomy of the Confederate Congress* (1972)

Donald P. Crook, *The North, the South and the Powers, 1861–1865* (1974)

Richard N. Current, *The Lincoln Nobody Knows* (1958)

David Donald, *Charles Sumner and the Rights of Man* (1970)

William B. Hesseltine, *Lincoln and the War Governors* (1948)

Harold M. Hyman, *A More Perfect Union: The Impact of the Civil War on the Constitution* (1973)

Frank W. Klement, *The Copperheads of the Middle West* (1960)

———, *The Limits of Dissent: Clement L. Vallandigham and the Civil War* (1970)

Mark W. Kruman, *Parties and Politics in North Carolina, 1836–1865* (1983)

Phillip S. Paludan, *"The People's Contest": The Union and Civil War, 1861–1865* (1988)

Rembert W. Patrick, *Jefferson Davis and His Cabinet* (1944)

Joel Silbey, *A Respectable Minority: The Democratic Party in the Civil War Era* (1977)

Hans Trefousse, *The Radical Republicans: Lincoln's Vanguard for Racial Justice* (1969)

T. Harry Williams, *Lincoln and the Radicals* (1941)

Wilfred B. Yearns, *The Confederate Congress* (1960)

CHAPTER 8

Behind the Lines: Disaffection

in the Confederacy

↶

Because the Confederacy lost the war, it is tempting for historians to focus their attention on the reasons for its defeat and to overlook the South's assets and strengths, which might have contributed to a rather different result. Among the South's advantages were its less demanding military objective of defending its territory rather than having to invade and conquer its adversary, as was incumbent on the North. Also, the Confederate cause was more immediate and compelling than the North's because the inhabitants of the South were protecting their homes and hearths from invasion. Besides, the South had been battling defensively as a besieged minority for over a generation before the war broke out, and so perhaps its people had developed a greater sense of collective destiny than their opponents.

In trying to account for Confederate defeat, historians have also pointed out how great were the demands and burdens placed on southerners and therefore how likely they were to lose heart or dissent. Yet there are two necessary qualifications to this kind of explanation. In the first place, the Confederates experienced a loss of morale only toward the end of the long struggle, when the prospects of success were diminishing rapidly. Second, the rising demands made by the Confederate government on the citizenry were also being imposed by their Federal counterpart. The introduction of a compulsory military draft; the imposition of taxes and impressment; the inflation of the currency and therefore of prices; the declaration of martial law, with the resultant arbitrary arrest of dissenters—all of these were unfamiliar and disagreeable measures, but they were inflicted on northerners as well. Moreover, northerners also objected to them, often vehemently.

Wartime disaffection was not confined therefore to the Confederate side, but it did become more rampant and insidious there than in the North. Why was this so? Was there something about the nature or source of this dissension that made it more serious? An examination of this feature of the Confederate experience may uncover fundamental realities about southern society during its bid for independence as well as about the reasons for the Confederacy's lack of success.

↘ *D O C U M E N T S*

Dissent seems to have been extensive in the Confederacy and must have contributed considerably to the collapse of its war effort. The first three documents offer several contemporary statements of what the Confederates were fighting for, while the last four represent the various kinds of opposition and dissent that surfaced.

The first selection is from a letter of February 20, 1864, to his wife from Colonel Frederick Bartleson of the 100th Illinois Volunteer Infantry. Bartleson was a prisoner in Libby Prison when he believed he had discovered what drove the Confederates to fight so hard. Another explanation is presented in Vice-President Alexander H. Stephens's controversial "Cornerstone Speech" of March 21, 1861, delivered in Savannah, Georgia; according to Stephens, white supremacy, not just slavery, was the foundation of the Confederacy. A third account, depicting vividly what was at stake, is offered by President Jefferson Davis in a speech of December 26, 1862, to the Mississippi legislature.

The remaining documents reveal the sources of dissent. In the fourth selection, Governor Joseph E. Brown of Georgia tells his like-minded friend, Alexander Stephens, in a letter of September 1, 1862, why and how the Confederate government headed by Davis has to be challenged. A confidential communication from Alexander Stephens himself to his superior, President Davis, written on January 22, 1864, shows how fundamentally the two men differed over how best to run the war. In the sixth selection, a group calling themselves "Common People" write a plaintive letter of February 18, 1863, to Governor Zebulon B. Vance of North Carolina, describing the severe hardship they are suffering. And finally, the seventh selection is a private letter of October 13, 1864, to a friend, Nathan Land, from Confederate Congressman Warren Akin of Georgia, who discusses political prospects and complains about the slaveholders' unwillingness to sacrifice for a cause in which they have a greater stake than most.

A Federal Prisoner Discovers Why Southerners Fight, February 1864

. . . Being confined in a building, with insufficient exercise, is very irksome. But there is nothing which does not become systematic, and Libby has its life and its routine and its characters. I wish Dickens could paint and describe it. When I first came here, there was a newspaper edited by a chaplain and published weekly. It contained some good articles occasionally. Then for a long time there were French classes and German classes, and some soldiers improved the time very well.

Now, in regard to the relative treatment of prisoners by respective Governments, I have a word to say. No man can say that prisoners are as well treated there as they are here. There are two reasons against it; one is, they haven't got the means to treat them as well, and another is, they haven't got the disposition. They are fighting from different motives from us. We are fighting for the Union, a sentiment, a high and noble sentiment, but after all a sentiment. They are fighting for independence and are animated by passion and hatred against invaders.

When men fight for independence, it makes no difference whether the cause is just or not. You can get up an amount of enthusiasm that nothing else will excite. And while we feed our prisoners well, and it is our policy to do it, and while public sentiment would not justify any other course, they feed theirs they are not particular how. Public sentiment there will justify almost any treatment of the Yankees.

Confederate Vice-President Alexander H. Stephens Identifies "The Cornerstone of the Confederacy," March 1861

. . . *The prevailing ideas entertained by* [Jefferson] *and most of the leading statesmen at the time of the formation of the old Constitution were, that the enslavement of the African was in violation of the laws of nature; that it was wrong in principle, socially, morally and politically.* It was an evil they knew not well how to deal with; but the general opinion of the men of that day was, that, somehow or other, in the order of Providence, the institution would be evanescent and pass away. This idea, though not incorporated in the Constitution, was the prevailing idea at the time. The Constitution, it is true, secured every essential guarantee to the institution while it should last, and hence no argument can be justly used against the constitutional guarantees thus secured, because of the common sentiment of the day. *Those ideas, however, were fundamentally wrong. They rested upon the assumption of the equality of races. This was an error.* It was a sandy foundation, and the idea of a Government built upon it—when the "storm came and the wind blew, it *fell.*"

Our new Government is founded upon exactly the opposite idea; its foundations are laid, its cornerstone rests, upon the great truth that the negro is not equal to the white man; that slavery, subordination to the superior race, is his natural and moral condition. [Applause.] *This, our new Government, is the first, in the history of the world, based upon this great physical, philosophical, and moral truth.* This truth has been slow in the process of its development, like all other truths in the various departments of science. It is so even amongst us. Many who hear me, perhaps, can recollect well that this truth was not generally admitted, even within their day. The errors of the past generation still clung to many as late as twenty years ago. Those at the North who still cling to these errors with a zeal above knowledge, we justly denominate fanatics. All fanaticism springs from an aberration of the mind; from a defect in reasoning. It is a species of insanity. One of the most striking characteristics of insanity, in many instances, is, forming correct conclusions from fancied or erroneous premises; so with the *anti-slavery* fanatics: their conclusions are right if their premises are. They assume that the negro is equal, and hence conclude that he is entitled to equal privileges and rights, with the white man. If their premises were correct, their conclusions would be logical and just; but their premises being wrong, their whole argument fails. . . .

But to return to the question of the future. What is to be the result of this revolution?

Will every thing, commenced so well, continue as it has begun? In reply to this anxious inquiry I can only say, it all depends upon ourselves. A young man starting out in life on his majority, with health, talent, and ability, under a favoring Providence, may be said to be the architect of his own fortunes. His destinies are in his own hands. He may make for himself a name of honor or dishonor, according to his own acts. If he plants himself upon truth, integrity, honor, and uprightness, with industry, patience, and energy, he cannot fail of success. So it is with us: we are a young Republic, just entering upon the arena of nations; we will be the architect of our own fortunes. Our destiny, under Providence, is in our own hands. With wisdom, prudence, and statesmanship on the part of our public men, and intelligence, virtue, and patriotism on the part of the people, success, to the full measure of our most sanguine hopes, may be looked for. But if we become divided— if schisms arise—if dissensions spring up—if factions are engendered—if party spirit, nourished by unholy personal ambition, shall rear its hydra head, I have no good to prophesy for you. Without intelligence, virtue, integrity, and patriotism on the part of the people, no Republic or representative government can be durable or stable. . . .

President Davis Explains the Confederate Cause, December 1862

. . . The issue before us is one of no ordinary character. We are not engaged in a conflict for conquest or for aggrandizement, or for the settlement of a point of international law. The question for you to decide is: "Will you be slaves or will you be independent?" Will you transmit to your children the freedom and equality which your fathers transmitted to you, or will you bow down in adoration before an idol baser than ever was worshipped by Eastern idolators? Nothing more is necessary than the mere statement of this issue. Whatever may be the personal sacrifices involved, I am surprised that you will shrink from them whenever the question comes before you. Those men who now assail us, who have been associated with us in a common union, who have inherited a government which they claim to be the best the world ever saw—these men, when left to themselves, have shown that they are incapable of preserving their own personal liberty. They have destroyed the freedom of the press; they have seized upon and imprisoned members of State Legislatures and of municipal councils, who were suspected of sympathy with the South; men have been carried off into captivity in distant States without indictment, without a knowledge of the accusations brought against them, in utter defiance of all rights guaranteed by the institutions under which they live. These people, when separated from the South and left entirely to themselves, have, in six months, demonstrated their utter incapacity for self-government. And yet, these are the people who claim to be your masters. These are the people who have determined to divide out the South among their Federal troops. Mississippi they have devoted to the direst vengeance of all. "But vengeance is the Lord's," and beneath his banner you will meet and hurl back these worse than vandal hordes.

The great end and aim of the government is to make our struggle successful. The men who stand highest in this contest would fall the first sacrifice to the vengeance of the enemy in case we should be unsuccessful. You may rest assured, then, for that reason, if for no other, that whatever capacity they possess will be devoted to securing the independence of the country. Our government is not like the monarchies of the Old World, resting for support upon armies and navies. It sprang from the people, and the confidence of the people is necessary for its success. When misrepresentations of the government have been circulated, when accusations have been brought against it of weakness and inefficiency, often have I felt in my heart the struggle between the desire for justice and the duty not to give information to the enemy—because at such time the correction of error would have been injurious to the safety of the cause. Thus, that great and good man, General A. S. Johnston, was contented to rest beneath contumely and to be pointed at by the finger of scorn, because he did not advance from Bowling Green with the little army under his command. But month after month he maintained his post, keeping the enemy ignorant of the paucity of his numbers, and thus holding the invaders in check. I take this case as one instance; it is not the only one by far.

The issue then being: will you be slaves; will you consent to be robbed of your property; will you renounce the exercise of those rights with which you were born and which were transmitted to you by your fathers? I feel that in addressing Mississippians the answer will be that their interests, even life itself, should be willingly laid down upon the altar of their country. . . .

Governor Joseph E. Brown of Georgia Denounces Confederate Policy, September 1862

(Private.)

Canton, [Ga.], Sept. 1st, 1862.

Dear Sir: I have the pleasure to acknowledge the receipt of your letter of the 26th ult. and am gratified that you take the view which you have expressed about the action of Genl. Bragg in his declaration of martial law over Atlanta and his appoint[ment], as the newspapers say, of a civil governor with aids, etc.

I have viewed this proceeding as I have others of our military authorities of late with painful apprehensiveness for the future. It seems military men are assuming the whole powers of government to themselves and setting at defiance constitutions, laws, state rights, state sovereignty, and every other principle of civil liberty, and that our people engrossed in the struggle with the enemy are disposed to submit to these bold usurpations tending to military despotism without murmur, much less resistance. I should have called this proceeding into question before this time but I was hopeful from the indications which I had noted that Congress would take such action as would check these dangerous usurpations of power, and for the further reasons that I have already come almost into conflict with the Confederate authorities in vindication of what I have considered the rights of the State and people of Georgia, and I was fearful, as no other governor seems to raise these questions, that I might be considered by good and true men in and out of Congress too refractory for the times. I had therefore concluded to take no notice of this matter till the meeting of the legislature when I expect to ask the representatives of the people to define the bounds to which they desire the Governor to go in the defense of the rights and sovereignty of the state. I confess I have apprehensions that our present General Assembly does not properly reflect the sentiments of our people upon this great question, but if the Executive goes beyond the bounds where he is sustained by the representatives of the people he exposes himself to censure without the moral power to do service to the great principles involved. I fear we have much more to apprehend from military despotism than from subjugation by the enemy. I trust our generals will improve well their time while we have the advantage and the enemy are organizing another army. Hoping that your health is good and begging that you will write me when your important duties are not too pressing to permit it, I am very truly your friend.

Vice-President Stephens Recommends an Alternative Confederate Strategy, January 1864

Crawfordville, Ga

22 Jan 1864

Private

His Excellency Jefferson Davis

Dear Sir

. . . I feel great interest in what is doing in Congress and shall go on as soon as I feel able—One thing I would say to you. Great apprehension is beginning to be felt amongst the people here that Congress will pass an act suspending the writ of habeas corpus and putting the country under Martial Law. Such an act would in my judgment be exceedingly unwise & impolitic as well as unconstitutional—and I trust if it should pass it will never receive the Executive approval. I am aware of the difficulties and embarrassments on all sides. But there is nothing more important than preserving the entire confidence and cordial support of the great mass of the people in their Government. They have looked upon it from the beginning as a struggle for Constitutional liberty—and as long as this view is kept before them they will give an enthusiastic support of the cause under the greatest trials deprivations and sacrifices. Our greatest, surest last hope is in the willing hearts of the people. This should never be lost sight of. I do not take the same view of our present situation that many do. There is in it really nothing to discourage if prudent & wise counsels prevail. Our strength does not lie in an attempt to match the enemy in the size of our armies—or number of men in the field. This we can not do—and by an attempt to approximate this equality of force we only weaken ourselves. No people can put and keep all its arms bearing population in the field for a long time. A large portion of them must be retained to supply subsistence, munitions of war etc. My opinion respectfully submitted is that we should not attempt to increase our present force in the field. We have got as many as we can maintain in view of the probable continuance of the war. The enemy doubtless looks forward to the coming summer campaign as a decisive one. With this view they will put forth their greatest efforts. Should these premeditated blows be parried or avoided or repelled by energy and skill on our part as they may be, quite a different aspect will rest upon the state of affairs next fall. Their armies may penetrate farther in the interior of the country than they have ever yet done but this will not bring the war any nearer to a conclusion than it was at the beginning if the hearts of our people are kept right. There is such a thing in wars, long wars especially, as whipping the fight without fighting it. In the great inequality of numbers existing between us & our enemy we must rely upon and use our advantages. We must preserve and keep our essential resources active. We must not collapse for want of subsistence. On this point great care prudence and system—real business system—is necessary . . . [there follows a calculation of the provisions now available to the Confederacy].

My opinion is with proper system & management the Govt has nearly enough food to support the army this year without purchasing any more except meat—And how much of this will have to be bought would be very soon ascertained. I call your attention to this because over here when tythes [taxes in kind on farm produce] are lying ready to be sent off, officers are going through the country buying & impressing—this is all wrong & for the want of a proper system and business management. In this connection I will also state that I deem it *essential* that the producing capacity & energy of the country should not be weakened this year. To keep them at the point they were last year two things are essential. First plantations must not be deprived of overseers and managers—and secondly—fair market prices— or in other words just compensation for all articles of subsistence the Govt shall be compelled to buy. The greatest stimulant to production is gain or the hope of it—It is an unalterable law of nature. Please excuse this rambling letter. I am too weak & feeble to continue it. . . .

Plain Folk Protest the Burden of the War, February 1863

february The 18th 1863

M. Z. vance Govener of NC

Sir we take the privilege of writing you a fiew lines to inform you of a fiew things that is mooving at this time in the State of N C the time has come that we the common people has to hav bread or blood & we are bound boath men & women to hav it or die in the attempt some of us has bin travling for the last month with the money in our pockets to buy corn & tryed men that had a plenty & has been unable to buy a bushel holding on for a better price we are willing to gave & obligate two Dollars a bushel but no more for the idea is that the slave oner has the plantations & the hands to rais the brad stufs & the common people is drove of in the ware to fight for the big mans negro & he at home making nearly all the corn that is made & then becaus he has the play in his own fingers he puts the price on his corn so as to take all the solders wages for a fiew bushels & then them that has worked hard & was in living circumstances with perhaps a good little homestid & other thing convenient for there well being perhaps will be credited until the debt will about take there land & every thing they hav & then they will stop all & if not they will hav to Rent there lands of there lords sir we hoos sons brothers & husbands is now fighting for the big mans negros are determd to have bredd out of these barns & that at a price that we can pay or we will slaughter as we go—if this is the way we common people is to be treated in the confedercy we hope that you & your friends will be as smart as govener Elis & his friends was take us out with out the voice of the people & let us try to maniage & defend our own State we hope sir that you will duly consider the a bove mentioned items & if it is in your power to Remedy the present evils do it speedly it is not our desiar to organise and commence operations for if the precedent is laid it will be unanimous but if ther is not steps taken soon nessesity will drive us into measurs that may prove awful we dont ask meet on fair terms for we can live on bread perhaps it would be better for you to isue your proclamation that no man should sell in the State at more than $2 pr bushel you no best &c if you cant remedy Extosan on the staff of life we will & we as your subjects will make Examples of all who Refuse to open there barn Doors & appoint other men over there farms who per haps will hav better Harts we no that this is unlawful at a common time but we are shut up we cant trade with no body only Just those in the confedersy & they can perish all those that has not and it seems that all harts is turned to gizards—Sir consider this matter over & pleas send us a privat letter of instruction direct it to bryant Swamp post office Bladen county N C & to R.L. as our company will be called Regulators

[no signatures]

A Confederate Congressman Discusses Policy and Problems, October 1864

. . . As to calling out the negro men and placing them in the army, with the promise that they shall be free at the end of the war, I can only say it is a question of fearful magnitude. Can we prevent subjugation, confiscation, degradation and slavery without it[?] If not, will our condition or that of the negro, be any worse by calling them into service[?]

On the other hand: Can we feed our soldiers and their families if the negro men are taken from the plantations? Will our soldiers submit to having our negroes along side them in the ditches, or in line of battle? When the negro is taught the use of arms and the art of war, can we live in safety with them afterwards? Or if it be contemplated to send them off to another country, when peace is made, will it be right to force them to a new, distant and strange land, after they have fought for and won the independence of this? Would they go without having another war? Involving, perhaps a general insurrection of all the negroes? To call forth the negroes into the army, with the promise of freedom, will it not be giving up the great question involved by doing the very thing Lincoln is now doing? The Confederate States may take private property for public use, by paying for it; but can we ever pay for 300,000 negro men at present prices, in addition to our other indebtedness? The Confederate Government may buy the private negro property of the Citizens, but can it set them free among us, to corrupt our slaves, and place in peril our existence? These are some of the thoughts that have passed th[r]ough my mind on the subject. But I can not say that I have a definite and fixed opinion. If I were convinced that we will be subjugated, with the long train of horrors that will follow it, unless the negroes be placed in the army, I would not hesitate to enrol our slaves and put them to fighting. Subjugation will give us free negroes in abundance—enemies at that—while white slaves will be more numerous than free negroes. We and our children will be slaves, while our freed negroes will lord it over us. It is impossible for the evils resulting from placing our slaves in the army to be greater than those that will follow subjugation. We may (if necessary) put our slaves in the army, win our independence, and have liberty and homes for ourselves and children. But subjugation will deprive us of our homes, houses, property, liberty, honor, and every thing worth living for, leaving for us and our posterity only the chains of slavery, tenfold more galling and degrading than that now felt by our negroes. But I will not enlarge, I have made suggestions merely for your reflection.

Have you ever noticed the strange conduct of our people during this war? They give up their sons, husbands, brothers & friends, and often without murmuring, to the army; but let one of their negroes be taken, and what a houl you will hear. The love of money has been the greatest difficulty in our way to independence,—it is now our chief obstacle. "For the love of money is the root of all evil; which while some coveted after they have erred from the faith, and pierced themselves through with many sorrows."

What a fearful realizing of this truth many will feel after this war. Their hearts will be "pierced through with many sorrows." . . .

≤ *E S S A Y S*

Three explanations for disaffection in the Confederacy are offered here. The first, by Emory M. Thomas of the University of Georgia at Athens points to the far-reaching governmental and political changes introduced by the Confederacy as a major source of dissatisfaction. The second essay comes from Paul D. Escott of Wake Forest University, who shows how deep and how justified were the grievances of the small farmers, or yeomen, against the Confederacy. And, finally, Kenneth M. Stampp of the University of California at Berkeley questions the degree of southerners' commitment to a war for the preservation of slavery.

The Political Revolution in the Confederacy

EMORY M. THOMAS

In a clever spoof of Civil War buffs, *Will Success Spoil Jeff Davis?*, author Thomas L. Connelly has composed a list of ten requirements for amateur standing as a neo-Confederate. To qualify you must do things like "cry during *Gone with the Wind*" and "have a great-grandmother who buried silver under the smokehouse." The final and most interesting requirement for "Confederatesmanship" is that you "hate Jefferson Davis."

Beneath Connelly's humor is an issue central to this chapter. Southerners during and since the Confederate period have hated Jefferson Davis. Some of Davis' critics have accused "King Jeff I" of despotism and tyranny in his management of Southern statecraft. Other critics have accused Davis of the opposite tendencies—executive weakness and unwillingness to marshal effectively the South's resources for war. Real Davis-haters have leveled both charges simultaneously. Actually the issue is larger than Jefferson Davis; it involves the response of the Confederate government to the demands of total war.

The Confederate government, albeit unwittingly, transformed the South from a state rights confederation into a centralized, national state. In so doing the government, or more usually Jefferson Davis as leader and symbol of the civilian Confederacy, incurred the displeasure of those who felt the government had gone too far and of those who thought it had not gone far enough. Within the limits of its ability the Davis administration dragged Southerners kicking and screaming into the nineteenth century. . . .

The temptation of both critics and friends of Jefferson Davis has been to blame or applaud the Confederate president alone for nearly everything the Confederacy did or failed to do. It is true that Davis as wartime president of a new nation had unprecedented political power. It is also true that Davis

Emory M. Thomas, "The Political Revolution," in Emory M. Thomas, *The Confederacy as a Revolutionary Experience,* 1971, pp. 58–78. Reprinted by permission of Prentice-Hall, Inc., Englewood Cliffs, New Jersey.

exercised his power and influence fully, often arbitrarily. But no one could accuse Davis of being a great politician. Nor could anyone picture other Southern politicians, with their strong heritage of individualism and their habit of asserting their will in national councils, meekly acquiescing to the dictates of any democratic leader, great politician or no. It would seem that the obvious but often overlooked truth was that Davis led the Southern nation in the directions in which the nation grudgingly agreed it had to go. Not everyone liked Davis' policies. The Confederacy never spawned an opposition political party per se. Those who fought the administration often coalesced, but never became a "loyal opposition." The Confederate president feuded with generals, governors, cabinet members, congressmen, senators, and even his vice-president. He sadly lacked the charismatic appeal to the mass of people possessed by his Northern rival Abraham Lincoln. Still when Davis asked his Congress for drastic measures, he got them. The Confederate Congress never really denied the Davis administration what it asked. Moreover Davis used his veto no less than thirty-nine times and only saw one of his vetoes overridden. Thus while we discuss the actions of Davis and those around him, we must realize that the Davis administration retained the support (if not the unquestioning confidence) of Southerners throughout the Confederate period. And to that extent the Richmond government represented the popular will.

With this in mind, let us examine the activities of the Confederate government in (1) raising its army, (2) controlling its citizens, and (3) managing its economy. Then let us sample some state and local actions in the same areas. For the radical departure from state rights and individualism was not restricted to the general government; the drive toward centralization affected every strata of the Confederate polity.

Until 1861 Americans fought wars with a small regular army augmented by volunteer units tendered by the governors of the states. The Civil War changed all this. Under the influence of Napoleonic military thinking, American generals accepted the need for mass and employed armies much larger than ever before. Short-term volunteers, commanded ultimately by governors of the individual states, might prove adequate for adventures in Mexico, but military men on both sides of the Potomac realized that if the war continued long, they must have armies which were more than mere amalgams of state militia units.

It was not surprising that Jefferson Davis grasped the new military reality—the need for a large, national army responsible to the central government. What was surprising was what the Davis administration did about the situation. On March 6, 1861, more than a month before the firing on Fort Sumter, the Confederate Congress authorized the administration to accept militia units tendered in the traditional manner by state governors. Davis, however, as far as possible adopted the practice of accepting militia units from the states and then mustering the men into the Confederate States army. Thus the troops were bound by oath to the national service instead of to the state which sent them. The Confederate War Department adopted the same policy toward state materiel as toward state troops.

Cannon and munitions belonged to the national army, not the state militia. In raising and equipping her army the Confederacy often encountered resistance from state governors. Significantly, however, when a state ordnance officer and a Confederate ordnance officer laid claim to the same cannon, the Confederate officer usually won.

Volunteers alone fought the young Confederacy's battles during the first year of the war. In the spring of 1862, though, the need for larger armies outstripped the volunteering enthusiasm. Too, many of the original volunteers' one-year enlistments were expiring, and the South faced the campaigning season of 1862 with a critical shortage of manpower. At this juncture on April 16, 1862, the Confederate Congress invoked the first military conscription on the North American continent.

The Confederate draft law enrolled all white males between the ages of eighteen and thirty-five and provided categories of exemption for various occupations and situations. Congress revised the system several times during the course of the war to lengthen finally the military age to between seventeen and fifty and to rectify some of the inequities inherent in the exemption classifications.

Predictably conscription was not popular in the Confederate South. Loopholes such as allowing potential draftees to hire substitutes and exempting those who oversaw the work of twenty, and then later fifteen, slaves caused resentment among the less affluent. Despite these problems the draft not only provided badly needed men to fill the gray ranks, but also served to stimulate volunteering among those who wished to avoid the stigma of "conscript." In addition the exemption status, as interpreted and enforced by the War Department, offered the Confederate government the chance to regulate the direction of the Southern economy.

Both the creation of a truly national army and the draft were affronts to the state rights doctrine so dear to the Confederacy's founders. Southerners justified these measures by asserting that their war for independence demanded them. Yet we must ask, now and later, how much erosion a political doctrine can sustain and still be a viable war aim.

The draft raised significant questions about the relation of the individual Southerner to his government. Even more basic to this subject, however, was the act passed by Congress on February 27, 1862, authorizing the president to suspend the writ of habeas corpus, thus invoking martial law. The Confederate legislators did restrict the circumstances under which the president could take such extreme action, but these restrictions were broad enough and vague enough to allow Davis considerable latitude.

In accord with the Habeas Corpus Act and in the face of Union general George B. McClellan's peninsula campaign to capture Richmond, Davis invoked martial law in his capital and surrounding area on March 1, 1862. The operation of martial law in Richmond offers a clear case study of how far the Confederacy was willing to depart from state rights individualism. Command of the city passed from civilian hands to those of General John H. Winder (who later commanded the infamous Andersonville prison). Winder issued general orders forbidding the sale of liquor and requiring all citizens to surrender their firearms to the Confederate Ordnance Department. He initiated a passport system to control entrance and exit to and from the city. Railroad companies and hotels had to submit to the provost marshal daily lists of passengers and guests. Winder's political police made thirty arbitrary arrests during the first two weeks of their reign. One of those arrested for suspected disloyalty was John Minor Botts, a former two-term United States congressman. After two months' confinement in a political prison, the sixty-year-old Botts secured his release by promising to live outside of any urban area and to say nothing against the Confederacy or its government. Winder even experimented with price-fixing in Richmond's food marketplaces. He published a schedule of maximum prices and confiscated any commodities offered for sale at prices above the maximum. The War Department finally ordered Winder to abandon his scheme, not because it interfered with laissez faire economics, but because the system did not work. Farmers simply refused to bring produce into the city if they had to sell at less than free market value.

Many of Winder's restrictions, such as the passport system, remained in force in Richmond throughout the war, and martial law reigned elsewhere in the Confederacy as well. The irony of a state rights confederation turning its capital into a police state requires no comment. One resident of Richmond described the rule of General Winder as a "reign of terror." But apparently most Richmond Confederates accepted arbitrary rule with a docility which only deepens the irony. Richmond's most widely circulated newspaper, no government "organ," stated that "the consequences [of martial law] are peace, serenity, security, respect for life and property, and a thorough revival of patriotism and enthusiasm."

General Winder's abortive experiment at controlling food prices in Richmond markets was but one example of the Confederacy's attempts to manage segments of the nation's economy. Indeed the national government all but nationalized the Confederate economy.

One of the first actions taken by the Davis administration was to place an embargo on Southern cotton. The motive was diplomatic. The president and others hoped to pressure England and France into recognizing and/or assisting the Confederacy by withholding the cotton. If England and France wished to reopen the cotton trade, they would have to comply with the Confederacy's conditions. The naïve scheme did not work, but it was not the only instance in which the Confederate government tried to use private property for the national good.

Cotton proved to be the South's major commodity of any real value in foreign trade. As the Union blockade of Southern ports tightened during the war, the Davis administration perceived that the needs of the government for the war effort should have the highest priority in the Confederacy's ever-declining trade. Accordingly, the administration instituted a Cotton Bureau to impress cotton, pay a uniform price for it, and carry on the trade. Government cotton also backed the Confederacy's one substantial foreign loan made with the French banking house of Erlanger. Finally on February 6, 1864, Congress authorized the administration to control all blockade-running and thus monopolize foreign trade. By this time the federal navy had almost shut off foreign commerce, but some ships slipped through, and for the entire last year of the war the Confederacy embraced the doctrine of State Socialism. In fact one scholar has termed this Confederate economic expedient, "the most successful demonstration of State Socialism to be found up to the time in modern civilization."

When the need arose, the Confederate government did not limit its impressment activity to cotton. Beginning in late 1862 army commanders found it necessary to seize any available food and forage from nearby farms for their troops and horses. The army ordinarily gave the farmers the government's promise to pay a fair price, but the War Department and the farmers seldom agreed on what constituted a fair price. In March 1863 the Confederate Congress regularized the practice in law. The Act to Regulate Impressments required the War Department to establish a schedule of prices to be paid for impressed goods. Even though the department tried to keep its price schedule on a par with the open market, it usually lagged about two jumps behind. One War Department official summarized the dilemma at its worst:

> Farmers are making preparations for only so much corn as will suffice for their own use. They resent the Secretary's schedule prices which are often 50 percent below the market or neighborhood price. The instant impressment of flour, corn and meat, as soon as they are brought to any of the inland towns to be put in market, is causing universal withholding of surplus—secreting and non-production. The army will be starved, and famine will ensue in the cities unless the Secretary changes his policy and buys in the market for the best price.

Similar problems ensued when the government impressed slaves. As with impressment of food, Congress regularized an existing practice when in March 1863 it authorized the military to impress black labor for constructing fortifications and like tasks. The government offered small compensation to the slaves' owners, and slaveholders complained that the government mistreated their chattels, thus reducing their value.

Southerners resented impressment of any kind, whether of cotton, food crops, or slaves. Undoubtedly the Confederacy's impressment policies alienated many and weakened the national morale. Still the stark facts were that the Congress authorized the practice, the courts upheld it, and the people endured it. When the free market economy proved insufficient to sustain the war effort, government seizure took up the slack.

During the first two years of war the Confederacy attempted to finance the effort by issues of loans and bonds and by simply printing money. Predictably an inflationary spiral set in. In 1863, the government finally resorted to taxation in an attempt to finance the war more efficiently and to curb inflation. The Confederate Congress enacted a graduated income tax on April 24, 1863. And on the same day the Congress provided for a "tax-in-kind" on agricultural produce. This tax called for producers to tithe 10 percent of their harvests to the government. In practice the percentages often became muddled when the TIK (tax-in-kind) men swooped down upon unsuspecting farms to collect the tithe. Collection of the income tax and tax-in-kind was often inefficient, but no one in the path of the TIK men could accuse the Confederate government of a lack of energy. Such high-handed methods enabled the Southern nation to carry on for four years with no more than $27 million in "hard" money.

The most systematic and far-reaching of all the Confederate government's economic tentacles emanated from the War Department. We have already seen how the department impressed needed food, forage, and labor. Southern armies, however, required more than this. They required manufactured items, from cannon to belt buckles. Because the South had little in the way of a manufacturing base to convert to war production, the Confederate War Department had to stimulate and subsidize Southern war industry. In so doing the department made a substantial contribution toward the creation of a centralized Confederate state.

The War Department affected the Confederate economy by becoming a part of it. Clothing and shoe factories, mines, arsenals, ordnance plants, powder works, and other industries opened up throughout the South. Great was the effect of these government-run establishments on the Southern economy. Not only did the state provide jobs, from piecework for ladies in uniform factories to full-time employment for skilled machinists, but also the needs of these government industries spurred activity in the private sector of the South's fledgling, industrial economy. And government operated mines led to virtual monopolies in the production of some raw materials.

The War Department did more than erect its own ordnance plants and copper mines. It eventually held considerable regulatory power over all manufacturing activity, public and private. The War Department influenced the markets of Southern industry by dispensing government contracts. Through the use of contracts the department was able to subsidize vital industries at the expense of those not so vital. The War Department also controlled the Southern labor supply by its manipulation of draft exemptions. While important or favored manufacturers had draft-exempt workers, other manufacturers watched their workers march off the job and into the army. Congress increased the War Department's strangle hold on labor still further in February 1864 by enacting a revised draft law which abolished industrial exemptions. The department then mustered workers into the army and detailed back to employers those workers necessary for war production.

The conscription acts also provided the government with control over private profits. By law the War Department was to exempt workers only for those firms whose profits were a set percentage above production costs. In 1862 no firm making more than 75 percent profit over the cost of production was authorized to have draft-exempt labor. Later Congress reduced the allowable rate of profit to $33\frac{1}{3}$ percent.

Beyond its influence on markets and labor, the War Department had authority over transportation through its control of Southern railroads. The Confederacy never nationalized the railroads, and not until late February

1865 did the Congress grant the secretary of war absolute control of the roads. Still the War Department was the railroad's biggest customer during the Confederacy's life span, and to a large extent the department's transportation priorities became the railroads' priorities. If government contracts and patriotism were not enough to insure the cooperation of Southern railroad companies, then the War Department could use the leverage available in its control of draft exemptions. As a result the railroads remained in private hands, but generally served the public good, as defined by military necessity. Rail transportation was assured only to those industrial operations deemed necessary by the War Department. The railroads served the nonessential firms when and if they had an opportunity.

This partnership arrangement among the Davis administration, manufacturers, and railroads allowed the government to manage substantial segments of the wartime economy and make long strides toward national economic planning. Only time, the want of efficiency inherent in any bureaucracy, and the laissez faire heritage of the Southern leadership restrained the Richmond government from going farther. As it was, however, the Confederate States moved faster toward economic nationalism than did the United States.

Still some historians have criticized the Davis administration for not going farther, for not nationalizing the railroads, impressing all the slaves, and other such ambitious undertakings. Had the Confederacy done these things, the fact of an internal revolution within the wartime South would be so obvious as to make this book unnecessary. In truth the Confederate government did centralize and nationalize the Southern economy to the very limits of that government's prudence and efficiency. And in fact late in the war at least one major private manufacturer, Joseph R. Anderson of the Tredegar Iron Works, requested the government to assume direct control of his establishment. The Tredegar firm had been the only iron works worthy of the name in the Confederacy in 1861. Tredegar continued in importance and grew in size during the course of the war. Yet, when Anderson offered the works to the government in 1865, the Davis administration rejected the offer. The Confederate government had found regulation ambitious enough. Nationalization might have solved some problems, but would have cost precious time, many miles of bureaucratic red tape, and the good will of a laissez faire public. Nationalization of the railroads, for example, would have opened the way for standardizing the gauges of track and rolling stock, an elementary but desperate need. But the Confederacy lived a short time. Establishing even temporary national operation of the railroads would have cost some of this time, and even so obvious a reform as standardizing track and axle gauges would have interrupted service and required materials, facilities, and skills desperately needed elsewhere. In the reality of Confederate statecraft, the policies of the Davis government were quite radical and desperate enough. Only in the abstract world of hindsight could we suggest that the Davis government might have mobilized its resources more effectively through nationalization.

Law and legal precedent alone were not sufficient to carry out the

Confederacy's policies of centralization. The hallmark of a centralized, national state is and was the bureaucracy which implements the government's policies. Bureaucrats had been scarce in the antebellum South, which adhered to the maxim "the government which governs least governs best." Nevertheless by 1863 Confederate civil servants were 70,000 strong. Ironically the Richmond government employed more civil servants than its counterpart in Washington. The Davis administration even initiated a rude form of civil service examination. In more than one case the Treasury Department's arithmetic test frustrated the genteel, unschooled ladies who for the first time sought employment to supplement their husbands' incomes.

Taken as a whole the activities of the Davis administration constituted a genuine revolution in Southern politics. During the few harried years of its lifespan the Confederate government raised and sustained a national army and initiated conscription a full year before its enemy began the practice. The Davis administration suspended habeas corpus and used martial law to create police states in some localities. The government directly and indirectly managed broad segments of the Southern economy and engaged in income and confiscatory taxation. In doing these things the Richmond government raised a veritable army of bureaucrats to work the national will in every corner of the South. The ultimate witness to the revolution in Southern government came about as a result of an acute shortage of copper during the last two years of the war. In the summer of 1863 the Federals captured the copper mines near Ducktown, Tennessee, and thus shut off the Confederacy's major source of the vital metal. From this point the Confederate Ordnance Bureau supplied its arsenals with copper by impressing the "worms" (copper coils) from stills in the mountains of North Carolina. Surely a government rude enough to mess with mountaineers' apple brandy–making had reached the limits of centralized authority. . . .

The Opposition

To measure the depth and strength of the revolution in the Southern polity we need to survey opposition to the dominant trend of Confederate thought and action. Naturally many Southerners did not approve of the policies of the Davis government. Even if they recognized the need for centralization and nationalization, they felt that a victory gained by "Yankee methods" would indeed be hollow. Some Confederate senators and congressmen, long accustomed to obstructing the work of the federal Congress, simply took up their familiar roles in the Southern Congress. Some resented the fact that other men held power and attacked the personnel of the Davis government by attacking its measures. Some of the opposition voices to the Davis government were those of sincere state-rightists who abhorred the government's high-handedness. Whatever their motive the opposition generally cloaked their resentment in state rights jargon.

The highest placed Davis-hater in the Confederacy was Vice-President Alexander H. Stephens. The frail but brilliant Georgian was a legalist who opposed the principal measures of the Davis government on state rights grounds. He eventually abandoned even going to Richmond because he felt that his voice was not heard in the government. Stephens' voice and pen spoke loudly in the Confederate hinterland where he denounced Davis as a military despot.

Stephens' charges echoed, too, in the Confederate Congress where the vocal opposition minority obstructed the administration's policies whenever and however it could. Louis T. Wigfall, senator from Texas, remained true to his antebellum fire-eating principles. The most exemplary comment on his relations with the Davis administration was recorded in Mary Boykin Chesnut's diary. Mrs. Chesnut, who has served historians as keeper of Confederate court gossip, wrote after a social gathering, "Wigfall was here last night. He began by wanting to hang Jeff Davis." Robert Toombs of Georgia, who served briefly in the Confederate Senate, wrote to Stephens regarding the 1864 Habeas Corpus Act, which allowed the administration to arrest arbitrarily anyone opposing the "cause," "I shall certainly give Mr. Davis an early opportunity to make me a victim by advising resistance, resistance to the death, to his law." One congressional Davis-hater, Henry S. Foote, went so far as to attempt to make a separate peace with the Union. The president himself did little to make his program more palatable among legislators. On one occasion president pro tem of the Senate, R. M. T. Hunter of Virginia, visited the Executive Mansion on some specific business. Davis proceeded to subject the influential Virginian to an hour-and-a-half tirade against Virginia and Virginians. Hunter left in a rage without ever discussing his business. Stephens, Wigfall, Toombs, Foote, and Hunter were conspicuous examples of the anti-Davis group within the government. The strength and vehemence of this opposition was a significant commentary on the depth of the political revolution wrought by the Davis government. Despite the disillusion and obstruction of state righters, the Confederacy became a national state.

The press, too, divided sharply on the conduct of Confederate statecraft. Davis, unlike Lincoln, never closed down opposition newspapers. He had ample opportunity, however. In his own capital, two of five dailies were hostile. The Richmond *Examiner* attacked the president from both ends of the political spectrum. In the anxiety of McClellan's campaign against Richmond, the *Examiner* thundered, "The Government must do all these things [for defense of Richmond] by military order, and without consulting anybody. . . . To the dogs with Constitutional questions and moderation! What we want is an effectual resistance." Later the *Examiner* had changed its tune. "God forbid that our fair and beloved land should be ruined by our own mal-administration, or that our people should lack the proper energy and independence to teach their Executive that he is their servant, not their master—their instrument, not their dictator." These two sentiments, usually more of the latter, found expression in newspapers throughout the South. Notable in its state-rightist opposition to Confederate policy was the Charleston *Mercury,* edited by former fire-eater Robert Barnwell Rhett.

The most vigorous Confederate state righters naturally operated at the state level. Their tactics have become legendary. In response to the first conscription law, which exempted officers of the states' militia forces, Governor Joseph E. Brown of Georgia commissioned 10,000 second lieutenants in the Georgia militia. North Carolina's Governor Zebulon Vance reportedly had over 90,000 new uniforms stored away for North Carolina troops when Lee's tattered army surrendered at Appomattox. Nevertheless, as one scholar has asserted, "The President did not beat the States, but they did not beat him." The Confederacy and its internal revolution went forward. And the strength of the state righters only accentuated the greater strength of Confederate nationalism. . . .

We need not here harangue on the merits of Jefferson Davis. We do need to respond to Davis' critics on some points, however. The Davis administration did reject state rights as [Clifford] Dowdey contends. In the face of strong, vocal opposition the Confederate government mobilized the South's human and material resources to the limit of its ability. In so doing the Richmond government imposed an arbitrary rule upon an individualistic people. The ultimate proof of the Confederacy's supreme effort came in 1865. When defeat came, it came not because the government had failed to mobilize the South's resources—defeat came because there was virtually nothing left to mobilize. The plain fact was that Davis and company revolutionized Southern politics to fight total war, and that when the Confederacy had shot its bolt, "as usual, God was on the side of the heaviest battalions." In this light much of the critique of the Davis government has all the rationality of the frustrated Confederate colonel who threatened to "march on Richmond, establish a military dictatorship, and let the people rule."

We need not render value judgments on the Confederate political metamorphosis. A revolution in politics which produces a political police force is not a transformation from darkness into light. The change in Confederate polity from state rights to nationalism came of course in response to wartime emergencies. No one originally willed or planned the transformation. Nor were the wartime political exigencies necessarily supposed to extend into peacetime. Thus it may be argued that the Confederate political revolution was neither so surprising nor, hypothetically at least, permanent. Yet such an argument is beside the point here. The point is, value judgments and hypotheses aside, that the political revolution happened. However much the Confederates wanted to alter their political doctrine or however much they were forced to do so by circumstances, the alteration occurred. It occurred within a nation supposedly fighting to defend the doctrine of state rights, and thus the political transformation was part of the internal revolution in the wartime South. Goaded by the demands of "modern," total war, the Confederate government abandoned the political system it was called into being to defend. The Confederacy raised a national army, conscripted troops, employed martial rule, managed the economy, and even interfered with Southern stills. The state and local governments expanded their powers in like measure. And all the while the bodies of Jefferson and Calhoun whirled in their graves.

Southern Yeomen and the Confederacy

PAUL D. ESCOTT

Nonslaveholding yeomen farmers had an anomalous position in the antebellum South. They were the dominant group in terms of numbers but not in political power or social influence. In these areas the slaveholding elite generally held sway. The potential for conflict between yeomen and planters had always been present, but secession raised the issue with special acuteness. Could a new southern nation—one which was based on slavery but dependent upon the support of nonslaveholders—win the support of the yeomen?

For years common social and economic patterns had drawn southerners together, and sectionalism promoted a sense of southern identity which seemed ready to ripen into nationalism. But something happened to arrest this process. In 1863, for example, when a Confederate impressment agent asked one farmer for supplies, he met with a bitter refusal to cooperate. "The sooner this damned Government [falls] to pieces," said the farmer, "the better it [will] be for us." Many southerners shared this attitude, and historians long have recognized that serious disunity plagued the Confederacy's effort to establish its independence. But not enough has been said about the major role of class resentments in weakening southern nationalism.

The farmer's ire at his "damned Government" illustrates the thesis of this essay—that the latent conflict between yeomen and planters became real during the Civil War and that a vital, positive commitment to the southern government failed to develop among the yeomen. Instead, poverty tested their willingness to sacrifice for a southern nation, and insensitive government policies provoked their anger. Strong class resentments developed which robbed the Confederacy of the support of many nonslaveholders. As will be shown, the yeomen were reluctant to secede. When fighting broke out, they gave their loyalty to their region, but soon this support faded. Very few yeomen took up arms against the South, and many fought to the end against hated Yankees. But large numbers of yeomen simply withdrew from the conflict and refused to work for a government which they felt was neglecting their needs and favoring the rich.

Signs of faltering commitment among the yeomen class appeared at the birth of the Confederacy. Shortly after the presidential election of 1860 there was an important shift in the voting pattern of nonslaveholding areas throughout the South. These areas broke away from a consensus which the planters had struggled to build. Southern leaders who were aware that

Paul Escott, "Southern Yeomen and the Confederacy," in *South Atlantic Quarterly,* Volume 77, Number 2, 1978, pp. 146–158. Reprinted with permission of Duke University Press.

the loyalty of the yeomen class might be a problem had always stressed the argument that enslavement of blacks guaranteed the status of the humblest white. In the presidential election of 1860 this tactic seemed to work: nonslaveholding southerners remained loyal to the southern Democratic party and voted for Breckinridge. In the balloting on secession, however, interclass unity broke down, and a different pattern emerged. Nonslaveholding areas swung from southern rights to compromise and sent delegates to the state conventions who pledged themselves to oppose secession or to work with other southern states for a settlement.

This shift emerged most clearly in Alabama, where the nonslaveholding northern part of the state had joined the southern counties in giving Breckinridge a strong majority. In the selection of a state convention, however, the two sections split sharply. Almost 75 percent of the vote in south Alabama was secessionist, while north Alabama gave more than 57 percent of its vote to cooperationist candidates. The predominantly white counties in Georgia also opposed secession, and in Louisiana there was a cleavage between "hillfarmer and planter," with the hillfarmers shifting away from secession. One study of seven southern states—Virginia, North Carolina, Tennessee, Georgia, Alabama, Mississippi, and Louisiana—found that of the counties with many slaves, 72 percent elected delegates who favored secession, while cooperationist or Unionist delegates won election in 63 percent of the counties with few slaves. Nonslaveholding small farmers were markedly less eager to risk the dangers of secession than black-belt planters, and this split along class lines indicated a potential fault in the structure of southern nationalism.

In the early days of the Confederacy this rift did not open. One reason for this fact was that Jefferson Davis skillfully minimized class differences. As a moderate who had supported secession reluctantly, he seemed to sense the potential divisions in the South and reached out for themes which would unite all southerners. He avoided mentioning slavery, which was relatively easy to do as long as Lincoln also skirted this issue. Instead Davis worked continually to identify the Confederacy with the founding fathers of 1787. Defining the new nation in terms which would appeal to those who still had some love for the old Union, Davis argued that the Confederacy did not destroy the American system but preserved it and guarded the founders' legacy. The North had departed from true principles, he said, but "the Constitution framed by our fathers is that of these Confederate States." Doubtful southerners did not have to surrender their feelings of affection for the Union but could merely transfer them to their true object, the southern government.

While Davis was facilitating a transfer of loyalties, hard facts compelled southerners to stand together. Fighting broke out, and Lincoln called for troops. With invasion likely, southerners had to choose, and their regional identity prevailed. The upper South promptly seceded, and a general outpouring of support took place. With the long season of tension and uncertainty finally broken, southern men and boys of all classes rushed to defend their homes. By July, 1861, the Confederate government had turned away 200,000 volunteers whom it could not arm. Sectional loyalty, the instinct of self-defense, and sensitive leadership had created a moment of impressive unity.

But the state of southern nationalism remained uncertain, for outward circumstances rather than inner convictions had brought about the change. Doubts and potential class divisions remained. Even in South Carolina in May, 1861, when enthusiasm ran high, former Senator James Chesnut, Jr., worried because small farmers were saying that this was a rich man's war. Opposition quickly developed among mountaineers in eastern Tennessee, North Carolina, and Virginia. Alabama Unionists unfurled Old Glory and opposed volunteering, while a peace society was organized in north-central Arkansas. In north Georgia one citizen publicly asked, "Is it right that the poor man should be taxed for the support of the war, when the war was brought about on the slave question, and the slave at home accumulating for the benefit of his master, and the poor man's farm left uncultivated, and a chance for his wife to be a widow, and his children orphans?" Florida's governor admitted that "in many parts" of his state "combinations existed to adhere to and maintain the United States Government. . . ." These problems were relatively minor in 1861, but they foreshadowed serious future difficulties. The editor of the Richmond *Examiner* solemnly warned: "Loyal as the great mass of our people are . . . , there is yet no doubt that the South is more rife with treason to her own independence and honour than any community that ever engaged before in a struggle with an adversary."

One can understand the editor's concern. If disaffection appeared so early, he probably wondered what would happen later in the war when living conditions would deteriorate, everyone's burdens would grow heavier, and the stress on interclass unity would intensify. Could unity persist? Let us examine the means southerners used to bind nonslaveholders to the planters and ask how well suited these were to the conditions of war.

Through the years southern leaders had told the yeoman farmer that slavery guaranteed his social status. Hundreds of politicians had echoed the words of Calhoun, who said, "With us, the two great divisions of society are not the rich and poor, but white and black; and all the former, the poor as well as the rich, belong to the upper classes, and are respected and treated as equals." This argument was largely successful. Combining racism with democratic values, it did bring whites together behind slavery.

But it also succeeded in convincing small farmers that they were the equals of aristocratic planters, and here lay significant consequences. The doctrine of equality among white men fed an already powerful tradition of individualism. Southern yeomen, who lived in proud rural independence, had an assertive sense of their rights and refused to accept discrimination. They believed that they were entitled to equal treatment from the planters. As David Donald has pointed out, this attitude quickly produced problems in the Confederate army. Notoriously lacking in discipline, southern troops scoffed at rigid obedience and insisted on electing their officers. Yeomen privates simply refused to abide a form of discipline which negated social equality among whites. Thus, the ideology which planters employed to protect slavery also had the potential of stimulating nonslaveholders to defend their interests. The nonslaveholders rarely rebelled before the war, but wartime conditions placed extraordinary strains on the mechanisms of interclass unity.

One basic change was the impoverishment of the yeoman class. For most nonslaveholders, the conditions of life deteriorated rapidly. One of the first indications of their plight was the flood of letters which poured into the War Department from rural communities throughout the South. Thousands of citizens complained that the rush of volunteering had deprived their areas of essential artisans. Tanners, millers, wheelrights, doctors, and other craftsmen were needed at home to keep the local economy going. Blacksmiths were especially important, for as one petition from Alabama declared, "Our Section of Country . . . [is] entirely Destitute of any man that is able to keep in order any kind of Farming Tules."

More serious in the long run was the rapid inflation of prices. Many items of everyday use rapidly became unattainable luxuries as the federal blockade aggravated shortages within the South and sent prices skyrocketing. Families boiled dirt from the smokehouse floor in order to have salt and did without coffee. Speculators bought up stocks of bacon, flour, leather, nails, and various manufactured goods. Many blamed greedy merchants and cold-hearted extortioners, and there was some evidence of organized profiteering. In several states the governor denounced speculators, and the Richmond *Examiner* declared that, "This disposition to speculate upon the yeomanry of the country . . . is the most mortifying feature of the war." The Atlanta *Daily Intelligencer* wrote that because of speculation, "want and starvation are staring thousands in the face."

The greatest cause of suffering was the loss of manpower on nonslaveholding farms. Thousands of southern families depended on one man: the husband, father, and breadwinner. While proslavery propagandists boasted that the war proved the value of slaves, who could work the fields while white men fought, the families of nonslaveholding yeomen confronted a severe shortage of labor. As the Edgefield, South Carolina, *Advertiser* observed, "The duties of war have called away from home the sole supports of many, many families. . . . Help must be given, or the poor will suffer." Soldiers' wives could not raise enough food and appealed in desperation to the Secretary of War. "I ask [you] in the name of humanity," read one letter, "to discharge my husband he is not able to do your government much good and he might do his children some good and thare is no use in keeping a man thare to kill him and leave widows and poore little orphen children to suffer while the rich has aplenty to work for them. . . ." State governors joined in these appeals and emphasized that the situation was grave. At one point Governor M. L. Bonham of South Carolina flatly predicted that if the Confederacy called up troops from a nonslaveholding area, "There will be great suffering next year, and . . . possible starvation."

As if to aggravate the serious conditions on many southern farms, the central government felt compelled to resort to a system of supplying its armies which Secretary of War James Seddon admitted was "a harsh, unequal, and odious mode of supply." Impressment fell most heavily on those who lived near major roads or railways or who happened to be near an army in the field. With no logic except convenience, troops often took from those who were nearby rather than from those who had a surplus to give. Officials in Richmond admitted that "the most scandalous outrages" took place and condemned the "lawless conduct of subaltern officers," but a steady st[r]eam of regulations had little effect. Confederate troops also destroyed much property as they moved through the country.

As a result of all these problems, harsh poverty gripped thousands of southern farms. The suffering was extremely widespread. An idea of its extent can be gained from the fact that in Alabama more than one-quarter of the state's white population was on relief at the end of the war. Hunger by itself was a strong test of the yeomen's devotion to southern nationalism, but other conditions aroused their anger at the Richmond government and encouraged them to support their families instead of the war.

Southern yeomen became convinced that they were receiving unequal treatment from their government. The first instance of discrimination arose in the midst of heavy volunteering in the spring of 1861. Blessed for once with more volunteers than it could arm, the Davis administration decided that it would accept and arm only those who volunteered for three years or the duration of the war. To increase the size of the forces, however, the government made an exception and allowed companies which could arm and equip their own men to enter the service for only twelve months. The effect of this provision was to make the price of patriotism three times higher for the poor man than for the rich man, since only the wealthy could afford to form the twelve-month units. Yeomen resented this discrimination. A senator from Mississippi warned President Davis that the rural masses opposed long enlistments, and William Brooks, who had presided at Alabama's secession convention, expressed dismay. He and other influential men had been working to change opinions in Perry County, Alabama, where the nonslaveholding majority had frequently declared that they would "fight for no rich man's slaves." Just as a small unit of volunteers was forming, the government announced its policy which favored the rich, and the consequences were disastrous.

Resentment increased after the Confederacy turned to conscription in April, 1862. The Confederate Congress adopted a system much like the twentieth-century's selective service and exempted men in various occupational categories. Perhaps the common people would have accepted this system if the government had administered it with rigid fairness, but examples of favoritism cropped up everywhere. Judge Robert S. Hudson advised Jefferson Davis that the incompetency and favoritism of conscription officers caused much of "the real and admitted disloyalty, discontent, and desertions" in Mississippi. A congressman from Virginia demanded "justice to the poor and uninfluential" and a citizen in Georgia summed up the common feeling when he wrote, "its [sic] a notorious fact if a man has influential friends—or a little money to spare he will never be enrolled."

President Davis himself expressed concern over the large number of men who managed to find "bombproof" jobs at depots and supply offices. Citizens complained of "wholesale conscription of the *poor* while the able-bodied & healthy men of property [are] all occupying *soft places*."

One of the worst outrages in conscription was the system of substitution. Those who had the money could hire substitutes to take their places in battle, and the provision of substitutes quickly became "a regular business." J. B. Jones, the War Department clerk and diarist, recorded the prices of substitutes as an index of inflation. Men of means paid $5,000 or $6,000 to stay out of the Army. According to a group of high-ranking officers in the Army of Tennessee, more than 150,000 wealthy southerners may have avoided service in this way, while the Assistant Adjutant General of the Confederacy placed a "moderate estimate" at 50,000. Not until the beginning of 1864 did the Confederacy abolish this system, but by then the damage to morale had been done.

Many observers felt that another category of exemption had even graver effects. Congress bowed to the protests of planters soon after conscription began and authorized the exemption of one white man for every twenty slaves under his control. This was the notorious "twenty nigger law," of which one congressman said, "never did a law meet with more universal odium. . . . Its influence upon the poor is most calamitous, and has awakened a spirit and elicited a discussion of which we may safely predict the most unfortunate results. . . ." The General Assembly of North Carolina formally protested the "unjust discrimination" of this law and other exemptions for the rich, but Congress enacted only mild measures to restrict the exemption of overseers. Planters gladly paid an additional tax on overseers, and the exemption remained to the end of the war.

Such favoritism was a predictable by-product of the southern social system with its muted but real privileges for the upper class. Although special treatment for wealthy individuals often harmed the war effort, the government's granting of considerations to "gentlemen" was a basic social pattern. J. B. Jones discovered to his amazement that in September, 1864, when the army was desperately short of horses and mules, the War Department was lending them to prominent citizens who had suffered relatively few of the calamities of war. About the same time, General Lee urged the War Department to look into charges that able-bodied men who should have gone to the field instead received details to serve in government bureaus. The harassed general also complained that rich young men sought election as magistrates and minor officials in order to avoid military service.

There were a few government officials who saw that bold action should be taken to relieve the suffering of the yeomen and win back their confidence. The strength of the outcry against the "twenty nigger law" deeply affected Secretary of War James Seddon, who realized that there was a shortage of labor on many nonslaveholders' farms. Admitting that if slaves deserved proper care during the war, nonslaveholding whites did also, Seddon recommended to President Davis that the Confederacy should exempt soldiers on whom several helpless dependents relied for food. The

Commissioner of Taxes, Thompson Allen, also became aware of the seriousness of the yeomen's plight as he read reports from local tax collectors. Allen decided that the entire structure of taxation needed to be changed. He advocated exempting small farmers from most taxes, including the tax-in-kind, and levying heavy progressive income taxes on the wealthy. Under his plan the government would take 50 percent of all incomes above $10,000. Earlier in the war a newspaper from the hill country of Georgia had articulated precisely the philosophy which underlay Allen's proposal: "*all classes of the community* MUST *do their share of the fighting, . . .* and those who have *the means* MUST *pay the expense,* as those who have not the means cannot pay."

However, Jefferson Davis ignored Seddon's proposal, and the Confederate Congress stopped far short of implementing Thompson Allen's plan. Wealthy slaveholders filled the Confederate Congress, and few if any privileged groups have ever attacked their own privileges in the manner which Allen recommended. Davis probably failed to act on Seddon's idea of exempting many nonslaveholders because it would have depleted the already thin ranks of the army. An atmosphere of military crisis usually enveloped the President's office in Richmond, and from 1862 to the end of the war the executive was preoccupied with augmenting the armies. The fear of states' rights opposition may also have held Davis back from bold actions to help the poor. Early in 1862 he had considered using the army to seize grain from distilleries, thus conserving food and driving down prices, but half of his cabinet opposed this step as a "dangerous and unauthorized use of power," and the idea was rejected. Overall, the Confederate government adopted many policies which injured the yeomen and few which relieved their suffering.

For all these reasons, the Confederacy never won the loyalty and enthusiasm of a large portion of the yeoman class. Hostility toward the government became very widespread, and hundreds of thousands of yeomen withdrew their support from the government and worked instead simply to care for their own needs during the war. The loss of yeoman support manifested itself in many ways, but the two most important were desertion and disaffection.

Men left the armies for many reasons, and undoubtedly some soldiers went home because they did not like army life or had a personal gripe. But for most men concern for their families was paramount. Mary Boykin Chesnut gave us a striking illustration of this when she told of a woman in a "cracker bonnet" who yelled to her husband as conscription officers dragged him off. "Desert agin, Jake!" the woman cried. "You desert agin, quick as you kin. Come back to your wife and children." State and Confederate officials realized that despairing letters from home played a catalytic role in inducing soldiers to desert, and class resentments strengthened many a soldier's resolution, if strengthening was needed. All authorities agree that most desertions came from the poorer classes of society.

In the words of Professor Ella Lonn, there was "an overwhelming amount of desertion in the Confederacy." Serious concern about the problem began in the summer of 1862, when, despite conscription, the number of men present in the ranks fell slightly. The adoption of stringent policing measures swelled the army to 360,000 men present out of a total of 498,000 on the rolls in April, 1863. From this point onward, however, the curve of army returns plunged downward while that of desertions rose steeply. By July, 1863, Assistant Secretary of War John A. Campbell wondered whether "so general a habit" as desertion should be considered a crime and estimated that 40,000 or 50,000 men were AWOL and that as many as 100,000 were evading duty in some manner. Despite liberal furloughs and proclamations of amnesty, the Secretary of War reported in November, 1863, that "the effective force of the Army is generally a little more than a half, never two-thirds, of the numbers in the ranks." One-third of the Army was absent without permission. The stream of desertion widened in 1863 and became a flood in 1864. At the end of the war, official Confederate returns showed only 150,000 soldiers present out of a total of 359,000.

Disaffection became so widespread that it effectively removed large portions of the South from the administrative reach of the Confederate government. An officer in the Bureau of Subsistence reported that, "in all the States impressments are evaded by every means which ingenuity can suggest, and in some openly resisted." Commissary agents found that southern farmers, when they would provide food for the government, refused to accept certificates of credit and government bonds as required by law. Tax collectors refused to enter some districts for fear of their lives, and conscription officers who came to localities to induct men increasingly discovered that no one was around to be drafted. In 1864 Senator Herschel Johnson advised Jefferson Davis that "the disposition to avoid military service is . . . general. . . ."

In state after state, yeoman discontent reached such proportions that certain districts welcomed deserters and fell under the dominant influence of those who wanted to withdraw from the war. Disaffection was particularly rife in the mountain areas of Georgia, North Carolina, Virginia, and Tennessee, but no state was immune. Alabama, Mississippi, Florida, and Arkansas also reported serious problems. Louisiana's governor warned Jefferson Davis in December, 1862, that unless the government sent Louisiana troops back to defend their state, the citizens might demand secession from the Confederacy. After planters in the Texas legislature blocked aid to soldiers' families, one prominent political leader confided to his diary that secession had been "the work of political leaders" without strong support from "the *mass of the people* without property."

Many elements contributed to the Confederacy's defeat, and it would be foolish to stress any one to the exclusion of the others. But it is clear that disaffection was extremely widespread among the southern yeomen, and that its effects were great. No historian could put the case more strongly than did John A. Campbell, the former Supreme Court Justice who became Assistant Secretary of War in the Confederacy. Commenting in 1863 on disaffection in part of the South, Campbell said, "the condition of things in the mountain districts of North Carolina, South Carolina, Georgia, and

Alabama menaces the existence of the Confederacy as fatally as either of the armies of the United States.''

The Road to Appomattox: The Problem of Morale in the Confederacy

KENNETH M. STAMPP

Some years ago one of America's best political commentators [Richard H. Rovere] made an observation about the problem of causation in history that every responsible historian would surely endorse:

> I hold a kind of Tolstoyan view of history and believe that it is hardly ever possible to determine the real truth about how we got from here to there. Since I find it extremely difficult to uncover my own motives, I hesitate to deal with those of other people, and I positively despair at the thought of ever being really sure about what has moved whole nations and whole generations of mankind. No explanation of the causes and origins of any war—of any large happening in history—can ever be for me much more than a plausible one, a reasonable hypothesis.

This is a position to which I fully subscribe, and I believe that it is as valid for explanations of why a war was won or lost as for explanations of why a war began.

With this cautionary statement in mind, I am going to suggest one of the conditions, among several, that may help to explain why the South lost the Civil War. I think there is reason to believe that many Southerners— how many I cannot say, but enough to affect the outcome of the war— who outwardly appeared to support the Confederate cause had inward doubts about its validity, and that, in all probability, some, perhaps unconsciously, welcomed its defeat. Like all historical explanations, my hypothesis is not subject to definitive proof; but I think it can be established as circumstantially plausible, because it is a reasonable explanation for a certain amount of empirical evidence. . . .

The problem of morale to which I am referring here should not be confused with another persistent but separate Confederate problem: that of disloyalty among southern Unionists. Nor should it be confused with the defeatism and demoralization that grew out of military reverses, shortages of civilian supplies, and financial collapse during the closing stages of the war. In the Confederacy, weak morale was not simply the ultimate consequence of war weariness, for the problem was present at its birth. It was the product of uncertainty about the South's identity, of the peculiar circumstances that led to secession and the attempt at independence, and of widespread doubts and apprehensions about the validity of the Confederate cause. The problem was obscured for a time by the semihysteria that swept the Deep South in the months after Lincoln's election. Historically, it has been obscured to some extent by early military successes and by the undoubted courage and tenacity of some of the Confederacy's fighting forces. But the morale of an army often may have little to do with devotion to a cause, and it is not necessarily an accurate gauge of the morale of the civilian population. Among civilians the morale problem was always there and soon began to make itself felt, for the South was ill-equipped for a long war not only physically but spiritually and ideologically as well.

That Confederate morale was not high enough and dedication to the cause fierce enough to offset its physical handicaps has sometimes been attributed to the failure of its leaders to perform their duties as propagandists and morale builders. Charles W. Ramsdell held the politicians responsible for failing to build an efficient propaganda organization or to portray some compelling issue for which the southern people would have made great sacrifices. Similarly, Bell I. Wiley blamed both Jefferson Davis and the Confederate Congress for not realizing "the necessity of winning the hearts and minds of the people." To [David M.] Potter the prime responsibility for the failure to dramatize the southern cause belonged to Davis. One of his major shortcomings was his inability to "communicate with the people of the Confederacy. He seemed to think in abstractions and to speak in platitudes."

If Davis had a penchant for abstract and platitudinous discourse, most other Confederate politicians and publicists, when upholding the Confederate cause, seemed to suffer from the same defect. Yet the South had more than its share of able speakers and editors, who exploited as best they could the available issues: the menace of a ruthless northern invader, the need to defend the constitutional principles of the Founding Fathers, and the threat to southern civilization posed by northern abolitionists and their doctrine of racial equality. Significantly, however, only occasionally did they identify the Confederacy with slavery. "Our new Government," Vice President Alexander H. Stephens once boldly proclaimed, "is founded upon . . . the great truth that the negro is not equal to the white man; that slavery, subordination to the superior race, is his natural and moral condition. This, our new Government, is the first, in the history of the world, based upon this great physical, philosophical and moral truth." In his message to the Confederate Congress, April 29, 1861, President Davis declared that "the labor of African slaves was and is indispensable" to the South's economic development. "With interests of such overwhelming magnitude imperiled, the people of the Southern States were driven by the conduct of the North to the adoption of some course of action to avert the danger with which they were openly menaced." This rhetoric was hardly inspiring, but more important, to a nineteenth-century audience neither was the cause it supported. Confederate propagandists apparently found the defense of slavery a poor tool with which to build southern morale, and they usually laid stress on other issues.

The reluctance of southern propagandists candidly to identify the Confederacy with slavery helps to explain their sterile rhetoric and their dismal failure; for, in my opinion, slavery was the key factor that gave the antebellum South its distinct identity, and the supposed northern threat to slavery (and the supremacy of the white race) was the basic cause of secession. To understand why southern propagandists failed, one must, in addition to evaluating their skill and techniques, compare the issues at their disposal with those at the disposal of their antagonists. Northern propagandists exploited all the historic traditions associated with the federal Union; reaffirmed America's mission and manifest destiny; proclaimed that democracy and self-government were on trial; above all, especially after the Emancipation Proclamation, identified their cause with the principles of the Declaration of Independence. These were the themes that Lincoln developed in the letters, speeches, and state papers which we remember more than a century later. It is of the utmost significance that no southern leader, even if he had had Lincoln's skill with words, could have claimed for the Confederacy a set of war aims that fired the nineteenth-century imagination as did those described in the Gettysburg Address. One wonders what Lincoln could have done with the issues available to him in the South, what even Jefferson Davis might have done with those that every northern politician had available to him.

When southern propagandists found it expedient, for reasons of domestic policy as well as foreign, to soft-pedal the very *cause* of the war, the Confederacy was at a considerable disadvantage as far as its moral position was concerned. This may help to explain why the Confederate Congress contained no group as fiercely dedicated to the southern cause as the Radical Republicans were to the northern cause. It illuminates Roy F. Nichols's impression that southern leaders were "beset by psychological handicaps." In short, it locates one of the fundamental reasons for the weakness of southern morale. The weakness was due not only to the failure of those who tried to uphold the cause, important as that may have been; but, viewing the cause as an appeal to the minds and emotions of nineteenth-century Americans, the weakness was due also to the inherent frailty of the cause itself.

At this point, keeping the southern morale problem in mind, I would like to introduce my hypothesis that many seemingly loyal Confederates lacked a deep commitment to the southern cause and that the behavior of some suggested that a Union victory was quite an acceptable result. Students of human behavior frequently encounter cases of persons involved in conflicts which outwardly they seem to be striving to win, when, for reasons of which they are hardly conscious, they are in fact inviting defeat. I believe that there is considerable circumstantial evidence indicating that an indeterminate but significant number of Southerners were behaving in this manner, and I would like to suggest two reasons why unconsciously they might have welcomed defeat, or at least declined to give that "last full measure" without which they could not have avoided it.

The first reason is related to the circumstances of southern secession. Fundamentally, this movement was not the product of genuine southern nationalism; indeed, except for the institution of slavery, the South had little to give it a clear national identity. It had no natural frontiers; its white

population came from the same stocks as the northern population; its political traditions and religious beliefs were not significantly different from
those of the North; it had no history of its own; and the notion of a distinct
southern culture was largely a figment of the romantic imaginations of a
handful of intellectuals and proslavery propagandists. Potter, though conceding that southern culture had its unique aspects, found that "the efforts
of historians to buttress their claim that the South had a wholly separate
culture self-consciously asserting itself . . . have led, on the whole, to paltry
results." The complaint of southern intellectuals "was not that the Union
inhibited a robust but repressed culture struggling to be born, but rather
that their cultural dependence upon the Yankees was humiliating." . . .

Historians of the South would be closer to reality if they accepted
Potter's admonition to give more emphasis to "the many cultural features
which Southerners shared with other nineteenth-century Americans: the
common language . . . ; the common religion of a people who were overwhelmingly evangelical and Protestant as well as Christian; the common
political commitment to democratic institutions; the common system of
values which exalted progress, material success, individual self-reliance,
and distrust of authority; and the bumptious Americanism which scorned
the 'decadent monarchies' of the Old World." Even after a generation of
intense sectional conflict over slavery, the South was still bound to the
Union by a heritage of national ideals and traditions. Nothing was more
common in southern political rhetoric than boasts of the South's manifold
contributions to the building of the nation and of the national heroes it had
produced. Southerners knew that the American dream was to have its
fulfillment not in a regional Confederacy but in the federal Union. Few
could resist the appeal of American nationalism; few found a viable substitute in that most flimsy and ephemeral of dreams: southern nationalism.

This is not to say that the people of the Deep South were dragged out
of the Union against their will. In all probability secession had the approval
of the overwhelming majority, but most of them were driven to secession
not by some mystical southern nationalism but by fear and anger, feeling
that secession was not so much a positive good as a painful last resort.
Potter's study of the secession movement left him with the impression "that
the South did not want a separate destiny so much as it wanted recognition
of the merits of southern society and security for the slave system, and
that all the cultural ingredients of southern nationalism would have had
very little weight if that recognition and that security had been forthcoming." At his inauguration as provisional President, Jefferson Davis spoke
of the "sincerity" with which Southerners had "labored to preserve the
government of our fathers" and explained that they had turned finally to
secession as "a necessity not a choice." A New Orleans editor believed
that many left the Union "with feelings akin to those they would experience
at witnessing some crushing national calamity." In January 1861, Mrs. Mary
Jones of Georgia wrote that "An indescribable sadness weighs down my
soul as I think of our once glorious but now dissolved Union! Our children's
children—what will constitute their national pride and glory?" Yet, she

added, "*We* have no alternative"—hardly a cry of exultation. In fact, nearly all the public celebrations in the seceded states during the dismal winter of 1860–61 had about them a quality of forced gaiety, and much of the flamboyant oratory had a slightly hollow sound. Whatever was to be gained from independence, Southerners knew that some priceless things would inevitably be lost. They could hate the Yankees, but that was not quite the same as hating the Union.

They hated the Yankees for questioning their fidelity to American traditions and for denying them a share of the American dream; and they held the Yankees responsible for driving them out of the Union. As they departed, Southerners announced their determination to cherish more than Northerners the sacred heritage of the Founding Fathers. "They separated from the Union," wrote Hans Kohn, "not because they wished to assert themselves as un-American but because they believed themselves the better Americans, more faithful to the original idea." In the Confederate Constitution, said Alexander H. Stephens, "all the essentials of the old Constitution, which have endeared it to the hearts of the American people, have been preserved and perpetuated." By 1861 it was too late for Southerners to escape this heritage, and rather than seeking to escape it they claimed it as their own. But in doing so they confessed rather pathetically the speciousness of southern nationalism.

This being the case, it may well be that for many Southerners secession was not in fact the ultimate goal. Roy F. Nichols suggested that even among the active secessionists "it may be doubted if all had the same final objective—namely, an independent republic, a confederacy of slave states." Nichols believed that some southern politicians were looking for a device that would enable them to negotiate for a better and stronger position in the old Union and that they thought of secession in these terms. "The real motive and object of many . . . was the creation of the Confederacy as a bargaining agency more effective than a minority group negotiating within the Union. As Thomas R. R. Cobb expressed it, better terms could be secured out of the Union than in it." John Bell of Tennessee described the secession movement as a stratagem to alarm the North, force it to "make such concessions as would be satisfactory and therefore the seceding states would return to the fold of the Union." Robert M. T. Hunter of Virginia hoped that a union of the southern states would be the first step toward a new union of all the states, "with such guarantees of principle and such a new distribution of power as will make it as permanent as any system of government can be." . . .

Southerners who went out of the Union in anguish hoping for negotiations and peaceful reunion were bitterly disappointed by events. The Union did not negotiate with the Confederacy, and two months after its birth the Confederacy was involved in a war for which it was poorly equipped both physically and morally. Those who had expected reunion through negotiation found themselves trapped in a war they had not anticipated, fighting for an independence they had never sought; and in spite of their indignation at northern "aggression," they may well have turned now unconsciously to reunion through defeat. The game had to be played out, the war had to be fought—and the men who served in the Confederate armies displayed their share of gallantry—but a contestant suffering from a lack of national identity and a serious morale problem, as well as from inferior resources, was involved in a lost cause from the start. Defeat restored to Southerners their traditions, their long-held aspirations, and, as part of the federal Union, the only national identity they ever had. It is instructive to contrast the myth of a special southern national identity with the reality of, say, Polish nationalism, which survived more than a century of occupation, partition, and repression. After Appomattox the myth of southern nationalism died remarkably soon. Commenting on the "swift restoration of American nationalism in the South" after 1865, Potter contended that "the readiness with which the South returned to the Union will defy explanation unless it is recognized that Southern loyalties to the Union were never really obliterated but rather were eclipsed by other loyalties with which, for a time, they conflicted."

Defeat gave white Southerners another reward: a way to rid themselves of the moral burden of slavery. This is the second reason why I think that some of them, once they found themselves locked in combat with the North, failed to give the Confederacy their unqualified and wholehearted support. To suggest as I do that slavery gave the South such identity as it had, caused secession and war, and at the same time gave some Southerners, at least unconsciously, a reason for accepting defeat will, I admit, take some explaining.

Let me begin with what I believe to be a fact, namely, that a large number of white Southerners, however much they tried, could not persuade themselves that slavery was a positive good, defensible on Christian and ethical principles. In spite of their defense of the kind of slavery that existed among them and denial of its abuses, many of them, as their unpublished records eloquently testify, knew that their critics were essentially right. In saying this, I do not think I am judging nineteenth-century men and women by twentieth-century standards, for among the romanticists of the nineteenth century there was no greater moral good than individual liberty. Hence, the dimensions of the South's moral problem cannot be appreciated unless one understands that slavery was, by the South's own values, an abomination. The problem would not have been nearly as serious for many Southerners if abolitionist criticism, strident and abrasive though it often was, had not been a mere echo of their own consciences.

In 1860, Robert M. T. Hunter observed that Southerners "no longer occupy a deprecatory attitude upon the question of negro slavery. . . . Whilst they by no means pretend that slavery is a good condition of things under any circumstances and in all countries, they do maintain that, under the relations that the two [races] stand to each other here, it is best for both that the inferior should be subjected to the superior." Hunter's statement was representative of the form that the southern defense of slavery usually took. Based primarily on race, it did not ordinarily endorse the general principle of slavery, only the principle of *black* slavery. But even this limited defense created moral problems and internal doubts, because all southern churches long ago had recognized the humanity of black people. However inferior in talents they might have been, they were acknowledged to be the sons and daughters of Adam, with immortal souls, equal to whites in the sight of God. How flimsy, then, was the foundation on which the proslavery argument was built! To defend the South's peculiar institution in this limited way and under these compromising circumstances was to leave room for a great deal of moral anxiety and self-doubt. . . .

I do not mean to suggest that every slaveholder was guilt-ridden because of slavery. The private papers of many of them give no sign of such a moral crisis—only a nagging fear of slave insurrections and bitter resentment at outside meddling in the South's affairs. Countless slaveholders, in spite of the position of the churches on the Negro's humanity, looked upon him as subhuman, or at least so far inferior to whites as to be suited only for bondage, and some showed little sensitivity to the ugly aspects of slavery. On the other hand, many slaveholders were more or less tormented by the dilemma they were in. They could not, of their own volition, give up the advantages of slavery—a profitable labor system in which they had a $2 billion capital investment. They dreaded the adjustments they would have to make if they were to live in the same region with four million free Negroes, for their racial attitudes were much like those of other white Americans, North and South. Yet they knew that slavery betrayed the American tradition of individual liberty and natural rights and that the attack on it was in the main valid.

In their extremity sensitive Southerners joined their less sensitive neighbors in angry attacks on their tormentors, until, finally, driven by their inner tensions, they were ready to seek an escape from their problems by breaking up the Union, or at least by threatening to do so. [Charles G. Sellers, Jr.] argued persuasively that this moral crisis eventually converted Southerners into an "aggressive slavocracy." "The almost pathological violence of their reaction to northern criticism indicated that their misgivings about their moral position on slavery had become literally intolerable under the mounting abolitionist attack." Slavery was doomed, Sellers concluded, but Southerners were so caught in its contradictions "that they could neither deal with it rationally nor longer endure the tensions and anxieties it generated. Under these circumstances the Civil War or something very like it was unavoidable."

Indeed, I believe that under these circumstances not only the Civil War but the outcome as we know it was, if not unavoidable, at least highly likely. Southerners, many of whom were unsure of their goals and tormented by guilt about slavery, having founded a nation upon nothing more substantial than anger and fear, were in no position to overcome the North's physical advantages. Moreover, at least some of them must have been troubled, at some conscious or unconscious level, by the question of what precisely was to be gained from winning the war—whether more in fact might be gained from losing it. For it soon became evident that, in addition to restoring the South to the Union, defeat would spell the doom of slavery.

Thus President Lincoln and the Union Congress would do for the slave-holders what even the more sensitive among them seemed unable to do for themselves—resolve once and for all the conflict between their deeply held values and their peculiar and archaic institution. "The Southern Confederacy was bound to fall," William P. Trent argued long ago, "because it was founded, precisely as Alexander H. Stephens had claimed, upon slavery as its cornerstone."

What circumstantial evidence is there to suggest that Southerners lost the Civil War in part because a significant number of them unconsciously felt that they had less to gain by winning than by losing? There is, first of all, the poor performance of some of the South's talented and experienced political leaders; the aggressive assertion of state rights even though it was a sure road to defeat; and the internal bickering and lack of individual commitment that would have made possible the discipline essential to victory. Thomas B. Alexander and Richard E. Beringer, in their study of the Confederate Congress, found little evidence of passionate dedication to the southern cause; from the uninspiring record and "helter-skelter operations" of that Congress they concluded that, "in 1861, a country was created on paper before it was a reality in the hearts of a sufficient number of its would-be citizens."

Equally significant was the behavior of Confederate civilians in areas occupied by Union military forces. One must be cautious in the use of historical analogies, but it is worth recalling the problems that plagued the German Nazis in the countries they occupied during the Second World War. Everywhere they met resistance from an organized underground that supplied information to Germany's enemies, committed acts of sabotage, and made life precarious for collaborators and German military personnel. At the same time, bands of partisans gathered in remote places to continue the war against the Nazis. The French had a similar experience in Algeria after the Second World War. The Algerian nationalists struggled with fanatical devotion to their cause; every village was a center of resistance, and no Frenchman was safe away from the protection of the French army. The country simply could not be pacified, and France, in spite of its great physical superiority, had to withdraw.

In the Confederate South, apart from border-state bushwhacking, there was only one example of underground resistance even remotely comparable to that demonstrated in Nazi-occupied Europe or French-occupied Algeria. This example was provided not by southern nationalists but by East Tennessee Unionists against the Confederacy itself. The counties of East Tennessee had been strongly opposed to secession, and so great was the disaffection that by the fall of 1861 some 11,000 Confederate infantry, cavalry, and artillery had occupied them. In response some 2000 Union partisans fled to Kentucky to begin training as an army of liberation, while others drilled in mountain fastnesses in preparation for the arrival of federal forces. Still other East Tennesseans organized an underground and engaged in such activities as cutting telegraph wires and burning bridges. The most strenuous

Confederate efforts at pacification failed to suppress these dedicated Unionists, and East Tennessee remained a cancer in the vitals of the Confederacy.

Nowhere in the South was there impressive resistance to the federal occupation, even making allowance for the fact that most able-bodied men of military age were serving in the Confederate armies. In 1862 Middle Tennessee, West Tennessee, part of northern Mississippi, and New Orleans fell under federal military occupation, but no significant underground developed. In 1864 General Sherman marched through Georgia and maintained long lines of communication without the semblance of a partisan resistance to trouble him. In commenting on this remarkable phenomenon, Governor Zebulon Vance of North Carolina wrote: "With a base line of communication of 500 miles in Sherman's rear, through our own country, not a bridge has been burnt, a car thrown from its track, nor a man shot by our people whose country has been desolated! They seem everywhere to submit. . . . It shows what I have always believed, that the great *popular heart is not now and never has been in this war!*" The absence of civilian resistance was quite as remarkable when, early in 1865, Sherman's army turned northward from Savannah into South Carolina. In the spring, when the Confederate armies surrendered, there were no partisans to take refuge in the mountains for a last desperate defense of southern nationalism. The Confederate States of America expired quietly, and throughout the South most people were reconciled to its death with relative ease. Though Edmund Ruffin preferred death to surrender, soon after Appomattox his fellow-Virginians, George Fitzhugh and Edward A. Pollard, both ardent champions of the cause of southern cultural nationalism, had become equally ardent American patriots. We hear much of unreconstructed southern rebels, but the number of them was not very large; the great majority of Southerners made haste to swear allegiance to the Union. Even the postwar cult of the Lost Cause was always more of a literary than an action group, and the Cause was one to be cherished within the safe confines of the restored Union.

Finally, and to me most significant of all, was the readiness, if not always good grace, with which most Southerners accepted the abolition of slavery—a readiness that I do not think is explained entirely by the circumstances of defeat. Probably historians have given too much emphasis to the cases of recalcitrance on this matter in the months after Appomattox, when, actually, slavery collapsed with remarkably little resistance. Just a few years earlier it had been impossible publicly to oppose slavery in all but the border slave states, and southern politicians and publicists had aggressively asserted that black slavery was a positive good. Yet, soon after the Confederate surrender no Southerner except an occasional eccentric would publicly affirm the validity of the proslavery argument. Indeed, I believe that as early as the spring of 1866, if Southerners had been permitted to vote for or against the re-establishment of slavery, not one southern state would have mustered a favorable majority.

In 1862, while the war was still in progress, Herschel V. Johnson of

Georgia expressed his belief that the days of slavery were numbered. "The first gun at Sumter tolled its funeral dirge. I have a sort of undefined notion that God . . . is permitting us by our own folly to work out the emancipation of our slaves." Two years later Fred A. Porcher of South Carolina asked privately: "Are we not fighting against the moral sense of the world? Can we hope to succeed in such a struggle?" Only two weeks after Appomattox, when a group of South Carolina aristocrats looked to the years ahead, though one of them could see only "poverty, no future, no hope," another found solace in the fact that at least there would be "no slaves, thank God!" In July another South Carolinian said more crudely: "It's a great relief to get rid of the horrid negroes." "Always I felt the moral guilt of it," recalled a Louisiana woman, "felt how impossible it must be for an owner of slaves to win his way into Heaven."

Very soon, as a matter of fact, white Southerners were publicly expressing their satisfaction that the institution had been abolished and asserting that the whites, though perhaps not the blacks, were better off without it. Many were ready now to give voice to the private doubts they had felt before the war. They denied that slavery had anything to do with the Confederate cause, thus decontaminating it and turning it into something they could cherish. After Appomattox, Jefferson Davis claimed that slavery "was in no wise the cause of the conflict," and Alexander H. Stephens argued that the war "was not a contest between the advocates or opponents of that Peculiar Institution." The speed with which white Southerners dissociated themselves from the cause of slavery is striking evidence of how great a burden it had been to them.

The acceptance of emancipation, of course, did not commit Southerners to a policy of racial equality. Rather, they assumed that the free Negroes would be an inferior caste, exposed to legal discrimination, denied political rights, and subjected to social segregation. They had every reason to assume this, because these, by and large, were the policies of most of the northern states toward their free Negro populations, and because the racial attitudes of the great majority of Northerners were not much different from their own. White Southerners were understandably shocked, therefore, when Radical Republicans, during the Reconstruction years, tried to impose a different relationship between the races in the South—to give Negroes legal equality, political rights, and, here and there, even social equality. At that point [the Virginian Edward A.] Pollard suddenly discovered that the basic issue of the Civil War had not been slavery but white supremacy. Now for the first time white Southerners organized a powerful partisan movement and resisted Republican race policy more fiercely than the civilian population had ever resisted the invading Union armies during the war. The difference, I think, was that in rejecting innovations in race relations they felt surer of their moral position, for they were convinced that Northerners were perpetrating an outrage that Northerners themselves would not have endured. As a result, the morale problem shifted to the other side; and the North, in spite of its greater physical power, lacked the will to prevail. Unlike slavery, racial discrimination did not disturb many nineteenth-century white Americans, North or South. Accordingly, in a relatively short time, chiefly because of the unrelenting opposition of white Southerners, Radical Reconstruction collapsed.

The outcome of Reconstruction is significant: it shows what a people can do against overwhelming odds when their morale is high, when they believe in their cause, and when they are convinced that defeat means catastrophe. Historian Lawrence H. Gipson once asked: "How differently would the south have been answered in its appeal for help had the northern radicals . . . been able in 1860 to carry a constitutional amendment providing not only for the freedom of the slaves but also for their enfranchisement? Would not every man in the south have sprung to arms determined to fight to the bitter end? . . . Would there not have been created within the new government a degree of zeal that would have made the south literally unconquerable? But there was no such issue." The fatal weakness of the Confederacy was that not enough of its people really thought that defeat would be a catastrophe; and, moreover, I believe that many of them unconsciously felt that the fruits of defeat would be less bitter than those of success.

ᔥ *F U R T H E R   R E A D I N G*

John A. Brumgardt, "The Confederate Career of Alexander H. Stephens," *Civil War History* 27 (1981), 64–81

David Donald, "Died of Democracy," in Donald, ed., *Why the North Won the Civil War* (1960), 79–90

Robert F. Durden, *The Gray and the Black: The Confederate Debate on Emancipation* (1972)

Clement Eaton, *A History of the Southern Confederacy* (1954)

Paul D. Escott, *After Secession: Jefferson Davis and the Failure of Southern Nationalism* (1978)

George M. Fredrickson, "Blue Over Gray: Sources of Success and Failure in the Civil War," in Fredrickson, ed., *A Nation Divided* (1975)

Mark W. Kruman, "Dissent in the Confederacy: The North Carolina Experience," *Civil War History* 27 (1981), 293–313

Harry P. Owens, and James J. Clarke, eds., *The Old South in the Crucible of War* (1983)

Frank L. Owsley, *States Rights in the Confederacy* (1925)

———, and Harriet Owsley, *King Cotton Diplomacy: Foreign Relations of the Confederate States of America* (1959)

Charles W. Ramsdell, *Behind the Lines in the Southern Confederacy* (1944)

Georgia Lee Tatum, *Disloyalty in the Confederacy* (1972)

Emory Thomas, *The Confederate Nation, 1861–1865* (1979)

Bell I. Wiley, *The Plain People of the Confederacy* (1943)

W. Buck Yearns, *The Confederate Governors* (1984)

CHAPTER
9

The Home Front:

Women and the War

⤵

Not surprisingly, interest in the Civil War has generally focused on military matters and the battlefield. But of course, wars also involve the people back home, and successful prosecution of wars requires the support and aid of non-combatants. In recent years, historians have begun to examine more fully the ways in which the Civil War affected those who remained behind. What was life like for them? How did the war and its demands impose hardship and suffering on civilians? And did it bring about significant social changes, as wars so often do? In fact, the American Civil War is widely referred to as the first modern war because it was not confined to the battlefield, but rather mobilized and affected the entire population on both sides. In that case, its impact would have to be felt among the civilian population, and no doubt to a considerable degree. Thus the war was fought on two fronts, and the home front made a contribution of great significance.

The home front was peopled and run primarily by women. Their encouragement of their husbands and sons to enlist, and then to stay in the army and fight valiantly, was crucial to the war effort. Also vital was their ability to assume new and burdensome roles as breadwinners and heads of household, even taking on the responsibility of managing family farms and plantations. When women did this—and millions did, on both sides—they were stepping outside the ''womanly sphere'' to which nineteenth-century men had restricted them. Others broke out of this confining status in a more public fashion. Some, for example, became involved in the local activities of the U.S. Sanitary Commission, which held fairs and raised funds to provide food and clothing for Federal soldiers. At the same time, others volunteered to serve as nurses in the army hospitals.

Nursing was a phenomenon worth examining in Civil War America. On the one hand, it was consistent with the nurturing, domestic role to which women of that era were assigned. But on the other, it required these women not only to leave home but also to enter a world of men and be exposed to scenes that were both gruesome and indelicate. Furthermore, the doctors and surgeons often resented their presence, and so the women had to fight them to *carry out their tasks. Although American women were not the first to work as army nurses—Florence Nightingale and her aides had served in the Crimea a few years earlier—their action was nevertheless so unusual that it sparked controversy about gender roles. Since women on both sides became nurses, this topic also yields insight about sectional differences.*

☙ D O C U M E N T S

Women who worked as nurses were frequently so conscious of the novelty and significance of what they were doing that they wrote diaries and memoirs about their experiences. In the first document, Hannah Ropes confides to her diary in October 1862 her frustration at how things were run and how she was treated at Union Hospital in Washington, D.C. Clara Barton, perhaps the most famous Civil War nurse because she later founded the American Red Cross, is the author of the second extract, wherein she relates her first encounter with the wounded at the battle of Chantilly in Virginia, September 1862. The third selection consists of two brief accounts by a black woman, Susie King Taylor, of her role in camp with the 33rd U.S. Colored Troops on the Sea Islands off South Carolina during 1864. Another famous nurse was Walt Whitman. In the fourth selection, he offers some views about nursing and hospitals in "Female Nurses for Soldiers" and "The Real War Will Never Get in the Books," both of which were published in a collection of his musings entitled *Specimen Days*.

The Confederate story can also be illustrated in documents of the era. In the fifth extract, a journal entry of September 3, 1863, Kate Cumming expresses her frustration that southern women were so unwilling to volunteer to serve as nurses like herself. By contrast, the sixth document shows Phoebe Yates Pember, a nurse in Richmond, Virginia, congratulating southern women on their service to the cause as nurses. Finally, James Cooper Nisbet, a Confederate soldier, commends the women of the South who served by staying at home and thereby encouraged and supported the men who had to go away to war.

A Northern Nurse Expresses Her Frustration, October 1862

October [1–9], 1862.

New days bring new trials to combat; and, while we are cheered with the prospective recovery of most of those brought in after the battles in which General Pope's command was engaged, we turn away with saddened eyes from the long list of those whose last sleep has fallen upon them in this hospital. Fifteen have died within the month just ended, some of them so worn out with fatigue and fasting as to be wholly unable to rally, others kept along with wounded limbs until too exhausted to bear amputation, and thus died. It would be folly to say they all might have lived with more prompt attention; it is also unjust to a true conviction not to say they have lost their only chance through a lack of earnest interest in the superior surgeon. Apothecary and medicine chest might be dispensed with if an equal amount of genuine sympathy could be brought home to our stricken men and the rations be converted into more delicate food. Not more than eight cents per day is the cost actually dealt out by the steward! Our men have been saved only by the best of nurses and the kind and constant help from friends at home; and to those good people we turn our eyes, as the fainting mariner throws his glance across the dreary distance of ocean towards some approaching sail.

This steward I think will prove the climax of unfaithful servants. Indeed they are a strange race of mortals, so far as I have watched them; and, as we have had four during our hospital life of three months, perhaps I am as well prepared to judge them as others. Our first was a *Jew*—round faced, beady eyes, black hair and short of stature. He would talk so sweet to me, and rob me of a bottle of wine, a shirt or pretty pocket handkerchief at the very moment I was looking at him to reply! It was the kind will of providence that this spawn of the reptile species should be sent to the Peninsula, after ushering into his place a gentle, well disposed Pennsylvanian, who knew about as much of the world and society as his neighboring Dutch farmers, of the present President. He soon grew tired of the annoyances of his position and was transferred. Number 3 was from Virginia, young, compact, becoming his uniform remarkably well; but his features all turned up and his manner suggested to me the nature of a porcupine.

He thrust his quills at everybody and the waters of our earnest but harmonious life were terribly troubled. I kept out of his way till he came to my premises. Then we had a pitched battle over the rights of the soldiers, lasting a good hour. At the close, he hauled down his colors, took a cup of hot tea from my hand, and we laid some plans for bettering the diet of the patients.

In a few days he was transferred to another hospital. When he came to tell me I told him I was *really sorry,* for I had become reconciled to him, and took him to be honest at heart, and not to blame for being born under the influence of slavery. We parted friends, and in kindness. Our next and last, a French Canadian, came in with the doubtful, dreary sphere of a raven or a bat. Dressed in his dark blue suit of pants and close fitting jacket, with a wide, bright green stripe down the side, and making a cuff to the sleeve above the elbow, a stiff linen collar up under his ears, and both hands thrust down into his pockets, we felt that this man was the opener of a new epoch.

The head surgeon was also a new man, tall, stiff, thin, light hair, whity blue eyes, and whity yellow complexion, glasses on eyes, and a way of looking out at the end of his glasses at you, surreptitiously, if I may use so big a word. He was young and I took to him. He was ignorant of hospital routine; ignorant of life outside of the practice in a country town, in an interior state, a weak man with good intentions, but puffed up with the gilding on his shoulder straps. If he had not been weak, and it had been my style to make a joke at the expense of others, there was a fine chance here; but he was safe at my hands, for he *was* weak, and I am strong in the knowledge at least which comes with age. And it is likely that in some way even this man, made giddy with an epaulette, will learn that God has made the private and officer of one equality, so far as the moral treatment of each other is concerned.

Clara Barton Intervenes to Alleviate Suffering, September 1862

. . . "Will they take away the wounded?" he asked. "Yes," I replied, "the first train for Washington is nearly ready now." "I must go," he said quickly. "Are you able?" I asked. "I must go if I die on the way. I'll tell you why; I am poor mother's only son, and when she consented that I go to the war, I promised her faithfully that if I were not killed outright, but wounded, I would try every means in my power to be taken home to her dead or alive. If I die on the train, they will not throw me off, and if I were buried in Washington, she can get me. But out here in the Virginia woods in the hands of the enemy, never. I *must* go!"

I sent for the surgeon in charge of the train and requested that my boy be taken.

"Oh, impossible, madam, he is mortally wounded and will never reach the hospital! We must take those who have a hope of life." "But you must take him." "I cannot"—"Can you, Doctor, guarantee the lives of all you have on that train?" "I wish I could," said he sadly. "They are the worst cases; nearly fifty per cent must die eventually of their wounds and hardships."

"Then give this lad a chance with them. He can only die, and he has given good and sufficient reasons why he must go—and a woman's word for it, Doctor. You take him. Send your men for him." Whether yielding to argument or entreaty, I neither knew nor cared so long as he did yield nobly and kindly. And they gathered up the fragments of the poor, torn boy and laid him carefully on a blanket on the crowded train and with stimulants and food and a kind-hearted attendant, pledged to take him alive or dead to Armory Square Hospital and tell them he was Hugh Johnson, of New York, and to mark his grave.

Although three hours of my time had been devoted to one sufferer among thousands, it must not be inferred that our general work had been suspended or that my assistants had been equally inefficient. They had seen how I was engaged and nobly redoubled their exertions to make amends for my deficiencies.

Probably not a man was laid upon those cars who did not receive some personal attention at their hands, some little kindness, if it were only to help lift him more tenderly.

This finds us shortly after daylight Monday morning. Train after train of cars was rushing on for the wounded, and hundreds of wagons were bringing them in from the field still held by the enemy, where some poor sufferers had lain three days with no visible means of sustenance. If immediately placed upon the trains and not detained, at least twenty-four hours must elapse before they could be in the hospital and properly nourished. They were already famishing, weak and sinking from loss of blood,

and they could ill afford a further fast of twenty-four hours. I felt confident
that, unless nourished at once, all the weaker portion must be past recovery
before reaching the hospitals of Washington. If once taken from the wagons
and laid with those already cared for, they would be overlooked and perish
on the way. Something must be done to meet this fearful emergency. I
sought the various officers on the grounds, explained the case to them, and
asked permission to feed all the men as they arrived before they should
be taken from the wagons. It was well for the poor sufferers of that field
that it was controlled by noble-hearted, generous officers, quick to feel and
prompt to act.

They at once saw the propriety of my request and gave orders that all
wagons should be stayed at a certain point and only moved on when every
one had been seen and fed. This point secured, I commenced my day's
work of climbing from the wheel to the brake of every wagon and speaking
to and feeding with my own hands each soldier until he expressed himself
satisfied. . . .

A Black Woman Describes Her Role in Camp, 1864

. . . I taught a great many of the comrades in Company E to read and
write, when they were off duty. Nearly all were anxious to learn. My
husband taught some also when it was convenient for him. I was very
happy to know my efforts were successful in camp, and also felt grateful
for the appreciation of my services. I gave my services willingly for four
years and three months without receiving a dollar. I was glad, however,
to be allowed to go with the regiment, to care for the sick and afflicted
comrades.

. . . About four o'clock, July 2, [1864], the charge was made [on Fort
Gregg, James Island, S.C.]. The firing could be plainly heard in camp. I
hastened down to the landing and remained there until eight o'clock that
morning. When the wounded arrived, or rather began to arrive, the first
one brought in was Samuel Anderson of our company. He was badly
wounded. Then others of our boys, some with their legs off, arm gone,
foot off, and wounds of all kinds imaginable. They had to wade through
creeks and marshes, as they were discovered by the enemy and shelled
very badly. A number of the men were lost, some got fastened in the mud
and had to cut off the legs of their pants, to free themselves. The 103d
New York suffered the most, as their men were very badly wounded.

My work now began. I gave my assistance to try to alleviate their
sufferings. I asked the doctor at the hospital what I could get for them to
eat. They wanted soup, but that I could not get; but I had a few cans of
condensed milk and some turtle eggs, so I thought I would try to make
some custard. I had doubts as to my success, for cooking with turtle eggs
was something new to me, but the adage has it, "Nothing ventured, nothing
done," so I made a venture and the result was a very delicious custard.
This I carried to the men, who enjoyed it very much. My services were

given at all times for the comfort of these men. I was on hand to assist whenever needed. I was enrolled as company laundress, but I did very little of it, because I was always busy doing other things through camp, and was employed all the time doing something for the officers and comrades.

Walt Whitman Comments on Nurses and Hospitals, (Undated)

I. Female Nurses for Soldiers

There are many women in one position or another, among the hospitals, mostly as nurses here in Washington, and among the military stations; quite a number of them young ladies acting as volunteers. They are a help in certain ways, and deserve to be mention'd with respect. Then it remains to be distinctly said that few or no young ladies, under the irresistible conventions of society, answer the practical requirements of nurses for soldiers. Middle-aged or healthy and good condition'd elderly women, mothers of children, are always best. Many of the wounded must be handled. A hundred things which cannot be gainsay'd must occur and must be done. The presence of a good middle-aged or elderly woman, the magnetic touch of hands, the expressive features of the mother, the silent soothing of her presence, her words, her knowledge and privileges arrived at only through having had children, are precious and final qualifications. It is a natural faculty that is required; it is not merely having a genteel young woman at a table in a ward. One of the finest nurses I met was a red-faced illiterate old Irish woman; I have seen her take the poor wasted naked boys so tenderly up in her arms. There are plenty of excellent clean old black women that would make tip-top nurses.

II. The Real War Will Never Get in the Books

And so good-by to the war. I know not how it may have been, or may be, to others—to me the main interest I found, (and still, on recollection, find,) in the rank and file of the armies, both sides, and in those specimens amid the hospitals, and even the dead on the field. To me the points illustrating the latent personal character and eligibilities of these States, in the two or three millions of American young and middle-aged men, North and South, embodied in those armies—and especially the one-third or one-fourth of their number, stricken by wounds or disease at some time in the course of the contest—were of more significance even than the political interests involved. (As so much of a race depends on how it faces death, and how it stands personal anguish and sickness. As, in the glints of emotions under

Walt Whitman text from *Specimen Days* from *The Viking Portable Library: Walt Whitman*, Mark Van Doren, ed., 1945, pp. 557, 587–588.

emergencies, and the indirect trait and asides in Plutarch, we get far profounder clues to the antique world than all its more formal history.)

Future years will never know the seething hell and the black infernal background of countless minor scenes and interiors, (not the official surface-courteousness of the Generals, not the few great battles) of the Secession War; and it is best they should not—the real war will never get in the books. In the mushy influences of current times, too, the fervid atmosphere and typical events of those years are in danger of being totally forgotten. I have at night watch'd by the side of a sick man in the hospital, one who could not live many hours. I have seen his eyes flash and burn as he raised himself and recurr'd to the cruelties on his surrender'd brother, and mutilations of the corpse afterward. (See, in the preceding pages, the incident at Upperville—the seventeen kill'd as in the description, were left there on the ground. After they dropt dead, no one touch'd them—all were made sure of, however. The carcasses were left for the citizens to bury or not, as they chose.)

Such was the war. It was not a quadrille in a ballroom. Its interior history will not only never be written—its practicality, minutiæ of deeds and passions will never be even suggested. The actual soldier of 1862–'65, North and South, with all his ways, his incredible dauntlessness, habits, practices, tastes, language, his fierce friendship, his appetite, rankness, his superb strength and animality, lawless gait, and a hundred unnamed lights and shades of camp, I say, will never be written—perhaps must not and should not be.

The preceding notes may furnish a few stray glimpses into that life, and into those lurid interiors, never to be fully convey'd to the future. The hospital part of the drama from '61 to '65, deserves indeed to be recorded. Of that many-threaded drama, with its sudden and strange surprises, its confounding of prophecies, its moments of despair, the dread of foreign interference, the interminable campaigns, the bloody battles, the mighty and cumbrous and green armies, the drafts and bounties—the immense money expenditure, like a heavy-pouring constant rain—with, over the whole land, the last three years of the struggle an unending, universal mourning-wail of women, parents, orphans—the marrow of the tragedy concentrated in those army hospitals—(it seem'd sometimes as if the whole interest of the land, North and South, was one vast central hospital, and all the rest of the affair but flanges—those forming the untold and unwritten history of the war—infinitely greater (like life's) than the few scraps and distortions that are ever told or written. Think how much, and of importance, will be—how much, civic and military, has already been—buried in the grave in eternal darkness.

A Southern Nurse Criticizes Southern Women,
September 1863

. . . There is one very important item which I have left out in this "Alabama woman's" letter. She says, let the women go into the hospitals. Now she comes to what is woman's true sphere: in war, the men to fight, and the women to nurse the wounded and sick, are words I have already quoted. I have no patience with women whom I hear telling what wonders they would do if they were only men, when I see so much of their own legitimate work left undone. Ladies can be of service in the hospitals, and of great service. I have heard more than one surgeon say, if he could get the right kind, he would have them in almost every department. I could name many things they could do, without ever once going into a ward.

All have not the gift of nursing, but they can do the housekeeping, and there is much of that in a hospital.

I know many will say the surgeons will not have them, nor can I blame the surgeons if the stories are true which I have heard about the ladies interfering with them. I have been nearly two years in the hospital service, and I have never spent one day without seeing women's work left undone, and I have had no time to do the surgeons'.

The sick in a hospital are as much under the care of the surgeon and assistant surgeons as men in the field are under the control of their officers. And would we not think a woman out of her senses were she to say that because she had made the clothes the soldiers wore, and attended to their wants otherwise, she had a right to command them; or that she would do nothing for them because that right was not given her, even if she had a better knowledge of Hardee's tactics than some of our officers. The surgeons are alone responsible for the sick under their control, and have the right to direct what should be done for them.

Are the women of the South going into the hospitals? I am afraid candor will compel me to say they are not! It is not respectable, and requires too constant attention, and a hospital has none of the comforts of home! About the first excuse I have already said much; but will here add, from my experience since last writing on that subject, that a lady's respectability must be at a low ebb when it can be endangered by going into a hospital.

I have attended to the soldiers of our army in hospitals and out of them, and in all sincerity I can say that, so far as their bearing toward ladies is concerned, I have never heard one word spoken or seen one act at which the most fastidious and refined woman could take exception.

This was more than I looked for; I knew that our army was composed of the lowest as well as the highest, and I did expect to find some among them void of delicacy.

I can not tell whether our army is an exception to the rule or not; but about it I can say that, as regards real native refinement, that which all the Chesterfields in the world can not give, a more perfect army of gentlemen could not be than they are. I do not know what they are in camp, but speak of what I have seen in other places.

To the next two excuses—that is, to constant work, and hospitals not being like home—I wonder if soldier's work is just such as they wish, and if the camp is any thing like home?—I think there is no need of giving the answers; they are obvious. . . .

A Southern Nurse Commends Southern Women, (Undated)

. . . The women of the South had been openly and violently rebellious from the moment they thought their states' rights touched. They incited the men to struggle in support of their views, and whether right or wrong, sustained them nobly to the end. They were the first to rebel—the last to succumb. Taking an active part in all that came within their sphere, and often compelled to go beyond this when the field demanded as many soldiers as could be raised; feeling a passion of interest in every man in the gray uniform of the Confederate service; they were doubly anxious to give comfort and assistance to the sick and wounded. In the course of a long and harassing war, with ports blockaded and harvests burnt, rail tracks constantly torn up, so that supplies of food were cut off, and sold always at exorbitant prices, no appeal was ever made to the women of the South, individually or collectively, that did not meet with a ready response. There was no parade of generosity; no published lists of donations, inspected by public eyes. What was contributed was given unostentatiously, whether a barrel of coffee or the only half bottle of wine in the giver's possession.

About this time one of these large hospitals was to be opened, and the wife of George W. Randolph, Secretary of War, offered me the superintendence—rather a startling proposition to a woman used to all the comforts of luxurious life. Foremost among the Virginia women, she had given her resources of mind and means to the sick, and her graphic and earnest representations of the benefit a good and determined woman's rule could effect in such a position settled the result in my mind. The natural idea that such a life would be injurious to the delicacy and refinement of a lady— that her nature would become deteriorated and her sensibilities blunted, was rather appalling. But the first step only costs, and that was soon taken.

A preliminary interview with the surgeon-in-chief gave necessary confidence. He was energetic—capable—skillful. A man with ready oil to pour upon troubled waters. Difficulties melted away beneath the warmth of his ready interest, and mountains sank into mole-hills when his quick comprehension had surmounted and leveled them. However troublesome daily increasing annoyances became, if they could not be removed, his few and ready words sent applicants and grumblers home satisfied to do the best they could. Wisely he decided to have an educated and efficient woman at the head of his hospital, and having succeeded, never allowed himself to forget that fact.

The day after my decision was made found me at "headquarters," the only two-story building on hospital ground, then occupied by the chief surgeon and his clerks. He had not yet made his appearance that morning, and while awaiting him, many of his corps, who had expected in horror the advent of female supervision, walked in and out, evidently inspecting me. There was at that time a general ignorance on all sides, except among the hospital officials, of the decided objection on the part of the latter to the carrying out of a law which they prognosticated would entail "petticoat government"; but there was no mistaking the stage-whisper which reached my ears from the open door of the office that morning, as the little contract surgeon passed out and informed a friend he met, in a tone of ill-concealed disgust, that *"one of them had come."*

A Confederate Soldier Applauds
Southern Womanhood, (Undated)

. . . Lieutenant Colonel Hamilton was granted a furlough and went down to his home in Jones County, Georgia, to see his good wife, who was managing their plantation, the "Bowen Place." It is wonderful how the Southern women managed those big plantations in the heart of the cotton belt, surrounded by hordes of black slaves, with nearly every able bodied white man absent in the army. It is eloquent of our women, and a good record of our Negroes.

It was upon the women that the greatest burden of this horrid war fell. Woman has always been a greater sufferer from war than man. She has borne that *silent anguish of the spirit* which is ten-fold more terrible to bear than the anguish of the body. While the men were carried away with the drunkenness of the war she dwelt in the stillness of her desolated home and "waited for the letter that never came," or perhaps came to tell her she was a widow or childless. May the movement to erect monuments in every Southern state to our heroic Southern women carve in marble a memorial to her cross and passion.

Napoleon declared to Madame De Stael that "the greatest woman in France is the woman who has given the most soldiers to my army."

Napoleon would have laurelled the Confederate mother! . . .

↘ *E S S A Y S*

The role of women nurses and the social repercussions of their initiative are discussed in these two essays. The first, by Ann Douglas of Columbia University, deals with the experience and impact of women who became nurses in the North. In the second essay, George C. Rable of Anderson College discusses northern nurses' southern counterparts as well as those women who found themselves running businesses and plantations in the South while their men were absent. The nature and extent of the impact that these new experiences had on the women, and also the men, of each section is likely to be revealing about the differences between the sexes in mid-nineteenth-century America as well as about the differences between the sections.

The War Within a War: Women Nurses
in the Union Army

ANN DOUGLAS

Dr. A. Curtis, president of the Botanico-Medical College of Ohio and author of *Lectures on Midwifery* published in 1836, lamented the passing of women midwives, and the take-over of their occupation by men. "The destruction of scores of modern women and infants, and the miserable condition of multitudes that escape immediate death" testified all too clearly, he believed, that the change was "not made for the better." For better or worse, the change was very real. In 1646, as Gerda Lerner tells us, a man had been prosecuted in Maine for practicing as a midwife. One hundred and thirty years later, Dr. William Shippen started to lecture on midwifery in Philadelphia. In the next half century, medical schools proliferated, and state after state legislated that a physician had to be licensed to practice. Professionalization served to drive women from medicine as it automatically excluded them from formal training, licenses, and hence practice. As Victor Robinson, the historian of nursing in America, sums it up, "in the change from colonial to national medicine, the casualty was woman: woman was not ignored, she was expelled." This expulsion was hardly an unforeseen result of professionalization; rather, it was a desired and sought-after end. One Boston doctor boasted in 1820:

> It was one of the first and happiest fruits of improved medical education in America that females were excluded from practice, and this has only been effected by the united and persevering efforts of some of the most distinguished individuals of the profession.

Women continued to play a role in the healing process, but it was a totally unprofessional one. Any sister, daughter or mother was expected to be able to nurse the sick of her household: indeed, she was idealized and glorified as a bedside watcher. Catharine Beecher's comparison of woman's role as healer to that of Jesus Christ was a commonplace. Woman's silent, long-suffering ministry was the subject of countless poems and tales, but it was to hold sway principally in the home, usually her own, and never in any circumstances to come into competition with the professional doctor's role. William A. Alcott, a Boston physician and author of many books on women's health, proposed that all women should be trained to care for the sick at home. Women needed a little occupation to save them from "ennui," "disgust," and even "suicide," and they were by nature better qualified as nurses than men: self-sacrificing and self-forgetful, "they are formed for days and nights and months and years of watchfulness." Not only capable of such marathons of selflessness, women also "more readily anticipate our wants." Naturally, given such altruistic na-

Ann Douglas Wood, "The War Within a War: Women Nurses in the Union Army," *Civil War History*, Volume 18, Number 3, September 1972, pp. 197–212. Reprinted with permission of The Kent State University Press.

tures, the women nurses who are to be employed officially outside of their homes, "can be employed much cheaper" than men. The essence of professionalism in nineteenth-century America was competition, and competition should clearly be anathema to the womanly watcher Alcott paints.

A rough bargain was being struck here as in so many other occupational fields at the turn of the nineteenth century. Women were exchanging some kind of professional expertise and official recognition for a domesticated version of the occupation in question, a version fed by official veneration but sapped by its distance from technological, scientific advance and its closeness to the hearth. In other words, women, told that they had been third-rate professional doctors, were promised that they could be first-rate amateur nurses. They could no longer be midwives, but they could be madonnas. One can even speculate that the sentimental adulation granted the mother watching at the sickbed was a kind of guilty, if unconscious compensation for the hostility which drove the female doctor from her paying patient. Be that as it may, it is clear that in the mid-nineteenth century, American women were to use this new mystique as an important weapon in an attack against the very professionalism which had exiled them to a domestic shrine, and as the basis for a renewed claim on their own part to active professional life.

Lerner and other historians who have treated the subject agree that the American Revolution hastened the professionalization of medicine by vastly increasing the need for medical skill and providing a battlefield on which to gain it. Hence, the Revolution was the death-knell of the woman physician. The Civil War, almost a hundred years later, also dramatically changed the medical picture. The study of gun-shot wounds led to important discoveries, anesthetics were developed, and the basic principles of sanitation slowly became apparent if only because they were so terribly violated. But as important as any of these was the opportunity this war offered women to return to the medical ranks from which they had been ejected at the time of the Revolution.

Wartime nursing, newly elevated and glamorized in the 1850s by the work of Florence Nightingale in the Crimea, not only provided wider outlets for feminine skills, but afforded women a way to debunk the officialdom which had been their enemy. In coming on to the battlefield, they brought with them the myth of the bedside Madonna, still resplendent with her healing maternal power, and pitted its potency against masculine authority. As northerners, the nurses who followed the Union Army reckoned the Confederacy to be the enemy, but in daily practice their battles were more often with the ponderous war machine of their own menfolk and with the bureaucratic professionals—military and medical—who struggled to maintain it.

Of course, the majority of American women, as contemporary feminine observers delighted to stress, stayed home during the war and suffered. Mary Livermore, a leader in the Sanitary Commission, pointed out rather proudly that the pain of men in battle, inspired by martial enthusiasm or at least distracted by military necessities, was as nothing next to the agony that women feel sending forth their loved ones to war, "knowing full well the risks they run—this involves exquisite suffering, and calls for another kind of heroism." Elizabeth Stuart Phelps, author of the best-selling novel *Gates Ajar,* designed to comfort the thousands of mourning women left in the war's wake, almost seemed to see the war as an act of hostility committed by men against the all-too-delicate sensibilities of their women-folk. She never worried greatly about the men who lost loved ones in the war, for the war, she implied, was their choice, their doing. It was rather "the women,—the helpless, outnumbering, unconsulted women; they whom war trampled down, without a choice at protest" who were her concern. These anxious, grieving women were very much performing their madonna-function, the selfless sickbed watchers, taking all the suffering of their ill husbands and brothers on their slender shoulders.

But the efforts of the women at home to aid their men were not all so passive. They formed some ten thousand Soldier's Aid Societies, they made countless bandages, they held huge Sanitary Fairs that together netted three million dollars. And not all of them confined their labors to the home-front. George A. Sale, a British journalist, wrote with some wonder that no conflict in history was so much "a woman's war" as the Civil War. These ladies would not let go. Mary Livermore proudly advertised their indomitability as they "refused to release their hold upon the men of their households although the government had taken them out of the home and organized them into an army." Waging their own war on military professionalism and on the masculine establishment that tried to exclude them, they simply refused to let this be the old kind of war, fought by men, with the wounded tended by men. They came along in a multitude, some on a single trip to care for a wounded or dying son or husband, but thousands "enlisted for the war" as volunteer nurses.

Their backgrounds ranged from blue-blood society to poor white communities, but they all had one thing in common. Whether they worked under Dorothea Dix, appointed by the government as Superintendent of Nurses, or later for the Sanitary Commission, or appeared, as many did, sent by themselves and God, they were all without formal training. No schools for nurses opened until after the Civil War, and so these volunteers had no experience beyond caring for the sick at home. Their ideal was, consequently, not the hospital, and certainly not the barracks, but the home. Indeed, many of them apparently were determined to turn the army camp with its masculine military code into the home, dominated by the maternal creed. This was a way of keeping their hold on the men who had just left the fireside for the campfire, but it was also a dramatic claim for greatly extended power. Woman's "influence," the genteel word favored by *Godey's Lady's Book,* was recognized as supreme within the sacred realm of home and family: not surprising, then, that these women seemed bent, with Clara Barton, in making the "mother earth" of the battlefield into their "kitchen hearth" and the soldiers into their sons. If the world was a home, where would their "influence" end? This subtle, yet sweeping question was posed by the actions of a minority. Most northern women, as we have seen, suffered patiently at home, sending only prayers, letters or bandages to wounded soldiers; but some moved to participate more directly in the Union effort, refusing to let sympathetic healing be outdistanced by destructive conflict. The progression from feminine self-abnegation to competitive involvement is clear, and it was all done under the maternal banner and the flags of the home fireside.

Many of the boys in blue were just that—boys, and they missed their homes and sang their songs not about their sweethearts, but about their mothers. The women who came to nurse them kept voicing a sense, however, that *all* these men, young and old, playing at war with such terrible earnestness, were just children, children, moreover, who had not quite known what they were doing when they put themselves so far from home. Sophronia Bucklin, a talented volunteer nurse explained sagely:

> Woman's help had not been counted upon, when, in the first tremultuous [*sic*] rush of excited feeling, the citizen enlisted to serve under the banner of the soldier. And when her hand with its softer touch pressed on the aching forehead, and bathed the fevered face, words failed in the attempt to express the gratitude of a full heart.

Miss Bucklin clearly had a sense that these men, whose "universal childishness" she stressed, were like little boys who had run away from home, heedless of the consequences, and were only too grateful when mother appeared. There is pity, but there is an undernote of I-told-you-so in the tone of these nurses when they describe, as Mary Livermore did, mutilated men, deliriously screaming, " 'Mother! Mother!' " Intent on rescuing such orphans, Clara Barton called the soldiers her "boys," and Emily E. Parsons, a handicapped but courageous nurse, wrote about the patients in her ward as her "forty-five children."

Re-establishing the rule of mother on the battlefield meant fighting loose military morals with hometown ethics. As Mary Elizabeth Massey has noted, "stories of drinking, gambling, and immorality in camp spread like wildfire," and they were not without foundation. E. W. Locke, the popular song-writer and temperance reformer who was constantly with the Union troops, devoted his chapter on "Women in the Army" in his war memoirs not just to the mothers and nurses, but also to "the Delilahs and Magdalenes" who followed the soldiers everywhere. When duty called, the nurses could act like fierce watchdogs for the domestic virtues. " 'What, my boy, playing checkers on Sunday?' " one nurse reproved a wounded patient, offering him a New Testament. But the real guardian was the legendary Dorothea Dix herself, pioneer in insane asylum and prison reform, now official Superintendent of Nurses, and determined to clean up the army as she had cleaned up the jails and asylums. Backed by her troops of nurses (by her own absolute requirement "plain-looking women," over thirty, dressed in black or brown, "with no bows, no curls, no jewelry, and no hoop-skirts"), she was a vigilance committee in herself. She did not take one day off in the entire course of the war.

Opening a branch of the American Home at the front was not the only way these women found to extend their power. Coupled with their maternal lust to care for the soldier was a desire to compete with him, even to outdo him. Historians now estimate that approximately four hundred women joined the ranks disguised as men. One, unmasked before Annie Wittenmeyer, a temperance leader prominent in the Sanitary Commission, when asked why she had done it, replied succinctly, " 'I thought I'd like camplife, and I did.' " The adventures of Pauline Cushman, actress and Federal spy, who disguised herself as a man, became the subject of two popular biographies. These pretenders to masculinity occasionally came rather frighteningly close to the real thing. Emma Edmonds, another spy and male impersonator, who wrote up her wartime adventures under the catchy title of *The Female Spy of the Union Army,* narrated with relish shooting a southern woman, and then, Achilles-like, dragging her prey behind her horse. Even some of the women at home waxed warrior-like, and one member of the fair sex complained that "the gentle-hearted ladies [were] admiring swords, guns, and pistols."

The actual Amazons were few, but many of the volunteer nurses showed sparks of the same martial fire. Katharine Wormeley, a nurse working for the Sanitary Commission, wrote a letter on board a hospital ship describing the chaos and confusion and activity around her and closed it, "Good-bye! *This is life.*" These women were getting a taste of a larger life; they were entering the masculine world of hard work and struggle, and many of them loved it. "I am in the army just as Chauncey [her brother] is, and I must be held to work just as he is," Emily Parsons explained proudly to her anxious parents. For the first time in her sheltered life, she senses she has become a participant in American history:

> I feel now as if I had really entered into the inner spirit of the times,—
> the feeling which counts danger as nothing, but works straight on as our
> Puritan forefathers worked before us.

Even though she knows her parents will worry, she cannot refrain from telling them how hard her bed is, how she is rained on at night, how poor the food is: these hardships are her badge of honor.

Many of the women leaders in the war were fighters from birth. A contemporary described Dix as "a general on a battlefield" long before the Civil War, and she herself knew that "the tonic I need is the tonic of opposition." But her best battles had already been fought elsewhere. Not so with Clara Barton. Forty when the war began, after two decades of teaching and civil service work, she was inwardly restless and deeply melancholy. Raised by a "soldier-father" as she loved to call him, she had grown up riding fast horses and listening "breathlessly to his war stories." When Fort Sumter was fired on, she went out to a rifle-range and shot at a target, "putting nine balls successively within the space of six inches at a distance of fifty feet." She obtained her father's blessing, and then promptly went to war. Only Dr. Mary Walker, surgeon and suffragist, outdid her: she joined the ranks in pants—but *not* disguised as a man—shot at the first soldier who was insolent with her, and retired from action dressed in an officer's uniform.

Such strongly aggressive, not to say belligerent gestures, conspicuous in the careers of not a few of the most famous nurses during the war, seem to unmask the element of competitive attack in their volunteer crusade. They said they wanted to take care of the men: but did not they also want to take them over? Onlookers may have wondered. This unspoken anxiety perhaps accounts for the ambivalent feelings expressed by American men about the invasion within an invasion taking place before their eyes. Despite popular tributes from the troops, the nurses received little monetary compensation and less government recognition. Compilations of laudatory sketches like Frank Moore's *Women of the War: Their Heroism and Sacrifice* (1866) sold immensely, but unpublished criticism of the women nurses was also current. Dr. Samuel Howe, although himself one of the original leaders of the Sanitary Commission, forbade his restless and patriotic wife, Julia Ward Howe, to be a nurse during the war. "If he had been engaged to Florence Nightingale," he explained, "and had loved her ever so dearly, he would have given her up as soon as she commenced her career as a public woman." No wonder that women like Mary Livermore felt compelled to stress how reluctant they were to leave cherished home duties even for the pressing obligations that wartime presented.

The hostility towards the female ranks was strongest, however, not at home, but in the army and at the front. Effort after effort was made by various officials to drive women out of the army, and even the most powerful of the nurses had to deal with constant challenges to their presence and their authority. Once, when Clara Barton was in the midst of heroic labors after a terrible battle, an officer remarked to her, " 'Miss Barton, this is a rough and unseemly position for you, a woman, to occupy.' " She quickly and unanswerably retorted, " 'Is it not as rough and unseemly for these pain-racked men?' " But she did not always come off as easily. In 1863, she was rudely ousted from her post by the officials, and spent the winter in depressed inactivity before she was again allowed to return to the troops. At the same time Dorothea Dix, originally given complete control over the appointment of nurses, was gently pushed aside, and her authority became permanently subordinate to that of the Surgeon General's.

This resistance to the women volunteers was apparently not shared by the men in the ranks, as the nurses typically got plenty of unofficial appreciation. The problem centered on their official professional status, and their opponents were principally, and predictably, the army officials and doctors. In Nurse Bucklin's opinion, these two groups were "determined by a systemmatic course of ill-treatment . . . to drive women from the service." Of course, some of the women volunteers were undoubtedly incompetent, ineffectual, and even harmful, but the skillful ones, as we have seen, had almost equal trouble establishing their position. They aroused official hostility precisely because they were challenging the male authorities directing the war, calling for credentials from men who thought they had left such tests decades of professional life behind, and then implicitly comparing the worth of such testimonies with that of the sources of their own vaunted authority as women and as mothers. Naturally the military officials were antagonized and threatened by this challenge, but the medical officials, directly dealing with these nurses in the wards, and supposedly having double authority over them as officers and as doctors, were especially threatened. And contemporary evidence suggests that they were especially antagonistic.

Indeed, many of these doctors apparently took an attitude of no-holds-barred in their resistance. Mary Phinney von Olnhausen, a protégé of Dorothea Dix's, summed up her impression of her male colleagues simply if sharply: surgeons were "the most brutal men I ever saw." Another nurse, Georgeanna Woolsey, bore eloquent witness to the sufferings inflicted by doctors on nurses. Explaining that the surgeons "determined to make their [the nurses'] lives so unbearable that they should be forced in self-defense to leave," she elaborates:

> [no-one knows] how much opposition, how much ill-will, how much un-feeling want of thought these women nurses endured. Hardly a surgeon of whom I can think, received or treated them with even common courtesy. . . . I have known women, delicately cared for at home, half fed in hospitals, hard worked day and night, and given, when sleep must be had, a . . . closet, just large enough for a camp bed to stand in.

Only the knowledge that they were "pioneers," blazing a trail for those to come, sustained the first volunteers.

Perhaps the doctors so fiercely defended their position because it was a particularly vulnerable one. The Medical Department of the Army consisted of the Surgeon General, an Assistant Surgeon General, and a number of short-term "contract surgeons." It was this latter group who received most criticism. They deserved it, but it is hardly surprising that they should have done a bad job. One of their more sympathetic critics, Jane Woolsey, a war-time nurse, explained their dilemma:

> Contract surgeons were more or less victims of a system which made them an anomalous civil element in a military establishment, with but little military restrictions, and no military incentive in the shape of promotion. They had no position, small pay, and mere nominal rank. They were a temporary expedient in the first place. . . . They served their little term, made their little experiments, and disappeared. The class was bad; it was under no obligations to be anything else.

As a result of this incentive problem, the men who became surgeons in the army were either talented physicians, patriotically donating their talents to the war effort at considerable loss to themselves, or men who had failed in their home practice, "to whose care," as one commentator ruefully noted, "we would not be willing to intrust a sick or disabled horse." Not surprisingly, *medical*—not war—casualties were such that one historian has calculated that a soldier's safety was more imperiled if he had to undergo medical treatment in an army hospital for an injury than if he fought all three days at Gettysburg.

Of this rather mixed crew of doctors, moreover, complicated demands were made. As E. W. Locke remarked, their medical knowledge, while absolutely necessary, was not all-sufficient as it might be in peacetime. In an age when few people, no matter how sick, went to hospitals, the doctor customarily drew for his nursing help chiefly on the amateur feminine nurses in his patients' homes. Now on the front, dealing with wounded or sick men who were far from their homes, he was asked to supply not only his professional skill, but this almost familial care as well. He must, in Locke's words, "stand in the place of parent, wife, or sister." As a result, Locke concludes, the best doctors were those with "heart-power," which goes far "deeper" than medicine, and they were "almost like mothers." Maternity had nearly become a professional requirement.

Locke's analysis, backed up by the motherly role a man like Walt Whitman chose to assume at the bedside of the wounded, casts the doctors and volunteer nurses in a competitive double contest for maternal and medical pre-eminence, a contest whose potential the women were quick to grasp. They were not officials of any kind. Poorly paid volunteers attached to various military hospitals, they had no regular professional status. But they *were* mothers or potential ones, and this apparently could now provide the basis for a professional claim. Not surprisingly, they proceeded to attack the errors and false professionalism of the surgeons and of the military authorities who backed them up with all the dignity and force lent them by their consecrated maternal natures.

Basic to these women's complicated urge to make the front truly a home-front, to replace the captain with the mother, the doctor with the nurse, and even to out-soldier the soldiers, was their sense that they were being kept out, of medicine, of war, of *life itself,* by a complicated professional code that simply boiled down to men's unwillingness to let anyone— including themselves—know what a mess they had made. And the first thing the volunteers wanted to reveal was the mess in all its enormity. Eliza Howland, an energetic nurse, wrote her husband about her herculean labors in a veritable Augean stable of a hospital. She and her fellow nurses cleaned the floors, covered with dust, nails, and shavings, taking up the "rubbish" with shovels and putting it in barrels. But the plight of the patients, "crowded in upon us" was less easily rectified: they were "soaked with malignant malarial fever, from exposure night after night, to drenching rain." She could only damn the prevalent "murderous, blundering want of prevision and provision" which caused their plight.

These women had little hesitation in calling a spade a spade and in marshalling their forces against the (in their view) heedless men in local positions of command. Annie Wittenmeyer was shocked to find an acting medical director of a military hospital on the job "reeling drunk." No wonder he ordered such a right-minded and astute woman off the premises, drunkenly insisting, " 'I'm boss here.' " Calmly but grimly thinking, " 'One or the other of us must certainly leave that hospital,' " she arranged for his dismissal. When she found another surgeon putting logwood in the coffee intended for the wounded, a "righteous indignation" burned in her heart, and another head rolled. Dorothea Dix, astonished by the laxities and lapses perhaps inevitable in the early stages of an unforeseen war, irritated military authorities by being in a perpetual state of "breathless excitement," as one exasperated official called it. Cynically, George Templeton Strong, a Sanitary Commissioner, could seize on the absurd and hysterical aspects of her over-concern:

> She is disgusted with us because we do not leave everything else and rush off the instant she tells us of something that needs attention. The last time we were in Washington she came upon us in breathless excitement to say that a cow in the Smithsonian grounds was dying of sunstroke, and she took it very ill that we did not adjourn instantly to look after the case.

What Strong understandably failed to note was that her anxiety, like Annie Wittenmeyer's strong-minded indignation, rose from her horror, here focused on a petty detail, that all these *men,* not just professing Christians (women were that, after all), but wage-earners and professionally trained, might be incompetent—incompetent despite the reassuring tokens of self-confidence, responsibility, training, in sum, of masculinity, which she and all her world were accustomed to accept as some kind of seal of approval. After she had opened the first door of her first state-run jail and seen the enormities of neglect and maltreatment there, she *doubted.* She enjoyed the doubts, because they implied that if men were apparently not helped, were even *disabled* by their training for the task of running the world right, the burden fell on her, and her apparent (and feminine) lack of qualifications became a positive asset for the task. Yet the intense reactions and distorted, but oppressive sense of responsibility which resulted from her frightening conclusion that she was the only wakeful passenger on a ship headed for certain wreck, were real too. When the Civil War came, thousands of other American women put themselves in a position to open the same door (or raise the equivalent tent-flap), and they saw similar sights and felt the same complex mingling of hysterical fear and righteous elation.

If this nightmare of untended men, dirty wards, overworked and sometimes incompetent doctors was military professional medicine, there was only one resource for these ladies: opposition. The necessary force and authority came from many different sources, as did the women volunteers themselves; some had or made friends in power, some had the backing of Dix's organization, some were acting for the increasingly powerful Sanitary Commission, some used personal charm. In the more belligerent line, Dix, who demanded no professional training of her nurses (she had seen enough to know what good *that* did!), simply told them to disregard the surgeons and obey her. In a different fashion, young and delicate Mary Safford, finding all "surgeons and authorities everywhere" opposed to her presence, disarmed the opposition by "her sweetness and grace and beauty." Hailed like Clara Barton as an "angel," she was also "the most indomitable little creature living." According to a contemporary report, "*She did just what she pleased.*"

And what these women wanted to do was to cut through the "red tape,''—a phrase they used over and over again to signify what they were fighting against. They wanted to destroy the professionalism, the bureaucracy that was keeping them out and keeping the wounded uncared for, and they hoped to replace it by the new and better professionalism at their command. Georgeanna Woolsey, in a witty mood, characterized ''that sublime, unfathomed mystery—'Professional Etiquette' '' as an ''absolute Bogie,'' a Bogie ''which puts its cold paw on private benevolence . . . which kept shirts from ragged men, and broth from hungry ones.''

The past-mistress of the art of defying and outwitting this omnipresent Bogie was a little-educated but superbly shrewd Illinois woman in her forties named Mary Ann Bickerdyke. She was soon called ''Mother'' Bickerdyke by the troops, and became the heroine of women like Annie Wittenmeyer and Mary Livermore. Both devote more space to her in their war memoirs than to any other single person, and their adoration is extremely significant. Leaders in the male-dominated, highly organized Sanitary Commission with its quickly developing professional code, Wittenmeyer and Livermore showed their true colors in their adulation of such a maverick as Bickerdyke. Totally unprofessional by any conventional standard, she made a profession of the calling both these women also exploited: motherhood. Wittenmeyer, who set up special sanitary diet kitchens in military hospitals, was cooking for a vastly extended family. ''Mother'' Bickerdyke, who had practiced before the war informally as a botanic doctor, was doing home nursing on an equally vast scale. The fact that all three women left families behind them to join the war effort indicates that they went to war not so much to satisfy their maternal urges as to use their maternal status as the basis for a play for a professional one. But the profession (nursing) they evolved was intended to share none of the weaknesses of its masculine rival. ''Mother'' Bickerdyke's work in the war represents the clearest example of this effort on the part of the volunteer nurses to put to shame the male bureaucratic professional organization behind the military hospitals by the shining example of a militant motherhood, which outdid its rival in efficiency but showed the heart its competitor so conspicuously lacked.

Bickerdyke's husband, whom, she privately stated, would have lived twenty years longer ''had he not worn himself into the grave trying to boss her,'' was dead when she agreed in 1861 to accompany medical supplies for the boys to Cairo, Illinois. Her words on that occasion were a battle cry:

> I'll go to Cairo, and I'll clean things up there [she promised]. You don't need to worry about that, neither. Them generals and all ain't going to stop me. This is the Lord's work you're calling me to do.

She kept her pledge. The Lord's was the only authority she ever did accept, and He generally sounded a good deal like Mother Bickerdyke. Even General Sherman toed her line. An admirer of Bickerdyke's, he told one furious officer that he could not help him against this formidable foe: '' 'She ranks me,' '' he explained. She brought in countless supplies, she nursed thousands, and, as Annie Wittenmeyer said, she ''cut red tape.'' She explained to one of many irate doctors as she calmly sidestepped medical protocol in her customary fashion: " 'It's of no use for you to try to tie me up with your red tape. There's too much to be done down here to stop for that.' " The underlying reproach to the dangerously silly men in command around her, unwilling to stop playing the games they have been trained to play even when life and death are at stake, is clear. Men can be allowed to play at authority in peacetime, she implies, but when a war comes, it's time to obey the women. In such a crisis, Mother Bickerdyke, an Admirable Crichton in the Union army, simply must assume her natural place of leadership. Bringing the primitive justice of the frontier and the ready kindness of what her biographers liked to call her "great maternal heart" to the front, she moved always to the point. When she discovered that an officer was stealing clothes reserved for sick soldiers, she stripped him publicly, "leaving him nude save his pantaloons."

Clara Barton too had a way of kicking over regulations to get to the men and their needs. Working alone, outside the Sanitary Commission and Dix's organization, she was the first woman, and one of very few, to take the actual front as her territory, turning up during battles with medical supplies and her own considerable nursing skill before any organized help could arrive. This was the absolute essence of her tactics: not to cut through red tape so much as to anticipate, and hence to forestall it, to appear at the actual moment of crisis when officialdom is always irrelevant. Many of the most prominent nurses saw their role in similar terms and loved to tell stories of how they provided some desperate or dying soldier, not with the standard treatment, so little susceptible of being bent to individual needs, but with precisely that thing which they, with lightning quick feminine intuition, knew he needed most.

Clara Barton's mission was to bring this instinct to a kind of perfection on the battlefield itself. She knew when to obey the doctors, but she had feuds with certain military medics and distrusted medicine to the point of being a near Christian Scientist in later life. At the core of her being was a profound suspicion of all organizations, and it seems significant that the great organization she helped to found, the Red Cross, was in key ways an anti-institution, at least as she ran it. Like the special kitchens run by Wittenmeyer, it was an effort which drew complex and double strength from implicitly attacking existing professional efforts in the same field even while endowing its own anti-institutional unprofessionalism with the forces of a profession—money, publicity and organized labor. The Red Cross was, in other words, an extension of the principles behind Barton's and Bickerdyke's work in the Civil War. As she explained it, its purpose was to deal with the damage wrecked by the forces "that red tape is not strong enough to hold . . . in check." It was "unlike any other organization in the country" because, in her words,

> It is an organization of physical action, of instantaneous action, at the spur
> of the moment; it cannot await the ordinary deliberations of organized
> bodies if it would be of any use to suffering humanity; . . . it has by its
> nature a field of its own.

The Red Cross as it began in America was organized feminine intuition, anti-professional and anti-institutional in nature, the logical culmination of the spirit of woman's efforts in the Civil War.

Clara Barton, with Mother Bickerdyke and many others, felt that she had the right to break through official medical protocol because she had the healing touch. Her thinking, like that of Dorothea Dix, in many ways paralleled that of Mary Baker Eddy. Dix had tremendous faith in what her first biographer called "the renovating power over bodily infirmity of a great purpose": it was this which gave her her fabled "divine magnetism," as Horace Mann reverently called it. In her work with the insane, she was given to rather expansive, not to say Messianic, statements about her power. Considering herself "the Hope" of all "poor, crazed beings" and "the Revelation" to them, she promised, "I shall see their chains off, I shall take them into the green fields . . . and a little child shall lead them." One of Barton's early biographers felt compelled to make similar claims for her: she had "magnetic power," the "magnetism of mercy." It is not far from here to the primitive healing power, originally allied to "animal magnetism," which Mary Baker Eddy advertised as her own.

At the start of the twentieth century, Robert Herrick would write a novel called *The Healer* (1911) about a brilliant young doctor who possessed this almost magical gift, but could keep it only if he disavowed totally the corrupt professionalism of modern medicine. The women nurses of the Civil War were believers in this creed: *because* they had been excluded from the ranks of the official medical world, they had found the healing power which their male colleagues had perhaps forever lost. Time after time, the diaries, letters and biographies of wartime nurses assert that what the wounded men need is not just medicine and food (which the nurses of course bring), but the *presence* of a woman, the touch of her hand. They seem to insinuate that if manhood brought on a war, womanhood was in itself healing. E. H. Locke makes clear the tremendous regenerating effect the simple appearance of two women actually had on a group of sick men in an army hospital: "Their very few words were woman's words, but they had a power man's do not." Unwilling or unable to explain this effect, Locke can only say that they seemed like beings from "another sphere," "representative" of all the women "at home." The magical perfume they exude is clearly the aura of home, and this aura was the secret weapon all the volunteer nurses possessed, a weapon both powerful in its effects and safe for its user.

Women had been told that the precincts of home were sacred and assured by men desirous of keeping them there that *they* were sacred because they stayed at home. Barred from professional medical ranks, they were encouraged to believe they could be healers by the hearth. Who could argue, then, when, at the imperious call of a land battling with itself, of a country engaged in *family* strife, some women charitably shared with the nation the precious powers they had lavished on their kin—the maternal gifts of protection and healing? And in doing so, they accomplished a great deal. Their work in improving sanitary conditions in Civil War hospitals has never been questioned, but they did more. In bringing home virtues to witness against "professional" methods, they did not so much make the world a home, as they helped to make themselves at home *in the world*. Nursing the troops in the Civil War had not only offered them a chance to criticize the imprisoning professional code of the military medical corps from the perspective of their maternal natures; it had also given them the opportunity to make a profession, and a competitive one, out of their maternity. Significantly, after the war accredited schools for nurses opened their doors and women doctors began to appear in small but increasing numbers. The wartime nurses, it seems, had joined a bigger army than they knew.

The New Women of the Confederacy

GEORGE C. RABLE

"The times are making strong women," reflected Kate Burruss early in 1864. "If they will be sure to stop at the right point, and not border on the masculine, it will be very well. I hope we are not to have our courage and sense put to such tests, but we have now much reason to fear that it will be so." Female courage and sense had of course been more than tested by this time, though Mary Chesnut doubted that the war would bring anything more than suffering to her sex: "I think *these* times make all women feel their humiliation in the affairs of the world. With *men* it is on to the field—'glory, honour, praise, &c, power.' Women can only stay at home—& every paper reminds us that women are to be *violated*—ravished & all manner of humiliation. How are the daughters of Eve punished."

In several ways, both of these apparently contradictory statements ring true. Many lives would change dramatically during the war as women temporarily divided their attention between familiar domestic tasks and other, less conventional work on plantations, in hospitals, in businesses, in schoolrooms, in offices, and even in munitions factories. Yet contemporaries hardly expected such changes to have long-lasting consequences; women might step outside their sphere, but only out of necessity. Few people at the time saw the effects of the war on women as an issue worth much consideration one way or the other. Men and women alike seem to have assumed that wartime arrangements would be temporary, that women still performed largely *auxiliary* tasks in the economy, and that peace would return women to the domestic circle. In both theory and practice, an essential conservatism prevailed, and Southerners had little trouble adjusting to seeing women in unfamiliar roles because they assumed that such arrangements would hardly change what modern historians call "gender ideology." Confederates did not see themselves as revolutionaries, despite attempts to identify with the Revolutionary fathers of 1776. Especially in domestic relations, they saw no need for a revolution that would create a

George C. Rable, "The New Women of the Confederacy," in George C. Rable, *Civil Wars: Women and the Crisis of Southern Nationalism,* 1989, pp. 112–128, 134–135. Reprinted with permission of University of Illinois Press.

"new" Confederate woman, and they would not have been very good revolutionaries anyway. Kate Burruss need not have worried; her sisters stopped at the "right point."

I.

At the beginning, wartime necessity seemed to shake up the comfortable antebellum assumptions of a tranquil and well-ordered agrarian society. Of course planters' wives had always worked hard, organizing households and supervising slaves; more rarely, they had managed plantations on their own. As the men went off to fight, such exceptional circumstances became commonplace, throwing many women into the breach with little training or experience, pushing them to perform new tasks and make more decisions on their own.

In the first year of the war, plantation mistresses remained dependent on their absent men for advice on everything from butchering hogs to disciplining slaves. So long as they deferred to male judgment, the traditional sexual division of labor remained safely intact. Leaving a decision about buying boots to her husband, Sarah Hamilton Yancey wanted to make sure he would "not think I am assuming too much in managing all our business." Reemphasizing the point, she added, "I shall be very glad when I can turn over the management to you." Were such women sincerely expressing doubts about their ability or merely soothing male egos? Probably a bit of each, because their new responsibilities thrust them into a situation filled with both peril and opportunity.

Most plantation mistresses went through periods of hesitation and uncertainty but could ill afford to be immobilized by doubt. Decisions on planting, cultivating, and marketing crops would not wait, and previous practice offered little guidance. Women played an important part in the transition from raising cotton and other staples to producing food—a complex process that left little time for worrying about what a husband, father, or son might think or for pondering questions of feminine propriety. Struck by the many changes in her life, Lizzie Simons listed the "unladylike" chores she had recently performed: unharnessing a horse from a buggy, rolling the buggy into the buggy house, reassembling a tub after the bottom had fallen out, leading a stray calf back home. Later on, this all seemed natural enough, but at the time, the adaptation to new roles and expectations was often incomplete. Catherine Edmondston sat one day in her storeroom watching the slaves at work while perusing a book on medieval history. As her bondsmen labored and she read, half her mind rested in a more leisurely past and the other half dwelt in a tiresome present.

Housewives who had never examined a ledger suddenly had to keep the plantation books. Fearful that merchants and factors might try to take advantage of their inexperience by overcharging, they worked by candlelight to straighten out their accounts. In early 1863, Mary Jones spent the day counting cattle, hogs, and sheep. That night she could not get to sleep, overwhelmed by the sudden strain of managing her late husband's three plantations. Though obviously proud of what she had accomplished so far, she worried about preparing the tax returns. The war made such calculations more difficult and at the same time more critical because the margin between profit and loss steadily narrowed.

Some plantation mistresses depended on overseers either to reconfirm or correct their decisions but often felt inadequate to the demands of their new responsibilities. Challenged by slaves who sensed the absence of experienced authority and by overseers who questioned their judgment, they simply floundered. In October 1861, Amelia Montgomery had run out of pork, molasses, slave shoes, and patience. The overseer had ruined the crop by letting the hogs run wild in the fields while he dallied with black women. Fearing her quarters would soon be "filled with mulattos," she whipped an old slave for suggesting the same possibility. Yet this obvious displacement of anger hardly dispelled it. In great perplexity after only two months of managing the plantation, she wrote to her husband detailing her problems and asking advice, apparently feeling she had failed to fill his place.

But for every woman whose nerve faltered or finances collapsed, another gained experience and confidence. The reliance on male advice and instructions, so characteristic of the war's first year, steadily diminished. Women soon became more familiar than their menfolk with a plantation's day-to-day operations. When her overseer did not begin slaughtering the hogs after a cold snap, Eliza Prince told him either to follow her instructions or leave. Willing to rely more and more on her own judgment, she decided to get along without him during the next planting season. Such assertiveness undoubtedly surprised her overseer and perhaps herself.

In many ways, Amelia Montgomery and Eliza Prince represented the extremes not only of failure and success but also of despair and confidence. More typically, competence and self-assurance evolved slowly. Running her family's place in central Louisiana, Mary Pugh at first seemed uncertain and vacillating. When the slaves worked indifferently, she could only threaten them with unspecified consequences on their master's return, which she prayed would be soon. But after a month on the job, her outlook had changed remarkably. Although by this time a refugee in Rusk, Texas, she did not even complain when the overseer left. Instead, she went out each morning to direct the day's work with a new air of authority. "I never saw the negroes both better or happier and have no fear of any trouble with them," she proudly reported to her husband, Richard, and admitted getting on "much better playing overseer than I expected." Mary Pugh did not see herself as a new Southern woman moving into a male bastion; necessity had forced her into taking charge, and she looked forward to ending the experiment.

Yet even the efficient and confident mistresses could hardly become too ambitious. After all they began directing plantation operations during the greatest crisis in the history of the Southern ruling class. All their other problems—whether with crops, livestock, or overseers—paled in comparison to dealing with the decay and eventual death of slavery.

Caught in this sea change, plantation mistresses tried to hold back the swirling tide by clinging to the familiar anchors of the ancien régime, most notably paternalism. Catherine Edmondston carefully weighed out the rations each day, apportioning them to the men, women, and children with the dignity and solemnity of a queen bestowing favors on humble subjects. Others visited the quarters each Sunday for Bible reading and religious instruction. Those who could still afford the extravagance of slave weddings presided over these affairs in the grand old manner.

But this patina of tradition was just that: a thin veneer covering up unmistakable evidence of imminent collapse. Whatever pleasure they derived from displays of beneficence, mistresses eventually had to recognize that their world was about to come crashing down around them. Walking about her estate as she prepared to flee from Sherman's advancing troops, a South Carolinian recalled her "quiet home where I was always welcomed by . . . loyal vassals." Although women claimed to be sick with worry about how their slaves would fare without their kindly protection, they also wondered how they would get along without them. Mistaking self-interest for sympathy merely added to the delusion of slaveholders who had long pictured themselves as the true friends of the black race.

The more women held onto the past, the more their actions revealed this other, harsher side of paternalism. The cliché "killing with kindness" well described the smothering affection of many women for their slaves, a cloying solicitude that still sought to govern the most intimate details of life in the quarters. For "da good mistis," like "da good massa," had more on her mind than Christian charity: behind her smile lay an obsession with control. Viewing blacks as pathetic and dependent children who little understood the tumult around them, mistresses bemoaned their loss of influence even as they welcomed any signs of its survival. When her old slave Rachel paid a visit only a few days before Robert E. Lee's surrender, Emma Holmes rejoiced to see her wearing the "respectable and becoming handkerchief turban" and frankly stated her preference for plain clothing in the "working class." The very casualness of this remark revealed the unthinking way in which mistresses had imposed their will on "their people." Habits of command and expectations of obedience survived long after slavery itself had disappeared.

Always virtuosos of self-deception, slaveholders of both sexes highly valued any displays of faithfulness, hoping that somehow the institution— or at least its spirit—might survive. Former slaves later recounted how they had crowded around the mistress to listen to letters from the master or had tried to comfort her when trouble came or had even brought food to "their white family" after Yankee bummers raided the plantation. "I cannot see that the war has made them [the slaves] a bit different," wrote Susan Bradford in a fit of wishful thinking, "unless it has made them more particular to do their work well. I believe we can trust our servants for if they had any unkind feelings they would certainly show it now." But would they? Could women believe their eyes and ears?

White mistresses' claims of expertise on the so-called Negro character rang ever more hollow. Mary Chesnut applied her acute powers of observation to slaves as she did to everyone else but wisely hedged her bets. "Not one word or look can we detect any change in the demeanor of these negro servants," she commented at the beginning of the war. Yet she was too smart to be taken in: "They [the slaves] carry it too far. . . . And people talk before them as if they were chairs and tables. And they make no sign. Are they stolidly stupid or wiser than we are, silent and strong, biding their time?" She could not answer this question but soon noticed subtle changes in the demeanor of certain house servants. Her mother's butler, Dick, performed his duties as efficiently as ever but seemed more aloof and no longer paused for friendly chitchat. "He looks over my head— he scents freedom in the air," she suspected. As for the others, "they go about in their black masks, not a ripple or an emotion showing—and yet on all other subjects except the war they are the most excitable of all races. Now, Dick might make a very respectable Egyptian sphinx, so inscrutably silent is he." How to interpret such silence became the question of the hour. Nervous mistresses watched their "servants" more closely but with little understanding and less confidence.

Their insecurity exposed the contradiction at the core of proslavery ideology. Despite common assumptions about the essential passivity and contentment of the slaves, nightmares of insurrection had often haunted the antebellum South, and the war exacerbated these fears. Proof of slavery's impending collapse appeared everywhere. Although whites had always complained about the inefficiency of black labor—even as they had exploited it—the war turned intermittent grumbling into a steady chorus of execration. In 1863 some Mississippi slaves went on a four-week vacation, refusing even to milk the cows. Expecting the worst, their mistress was "always thankful, when morning comes, that the house has not been fired during the night." The words *impudence* and *independence* cropped up time and again in descriptions of black behavior. Although Confederate memorialists later praised the "faithful darkies" who stood by their mistresses, contemporaries knew better. Slaves sullenly refused to do daily chores or performed their tasks with careless indifference. Yet most mistresses could not grasp or refused to see that black people might have their own goals and aspirations, that they might be using the wartime disruption, especially the discomfiture of their owners, to ease their own lot or even strike a blow for freedom. This failure of vision added to white women's exasperation. Lucy Muse Fletcher wished "the Yankees would take the whole race—they are so insufferably lazy & puffed up with their own importance." Baffled, disappointed, and disillusioned, mistresses soon realized that each grudgingly completed task signified their own loss of power.

Just as women had begun to master the skills required for running a farm or plantation, their authority over their slaves steadily evaporated. If blacks could feel the shackles of bondage loosening, so too did whites. Giving orders that were not obeyed, losing one's temper, and then trying to maintain some semblance of discipline became a daily challenge. Susanna Clay felt sorry for the blacks because they did not know any better, but her slaves apparently knew a great deal, at least about avoiding work and behaving with a new sense of independence. "I try by 'moral suasion' to get them to do their duty and it sometimes succeeds," she commented ruefully. Two months later, her approach was yet more oblique: "I make no point except in the mildest language with ours." By the fall of 1863 she had lost command completely: "We cannot exert any authority. I beg ours to do what little is done." For exasperated housewives, it often became easier simply to do the chores themselves. Cajolery, threats of punishment, and tactful requests: whatever approach was taken, none seemed to make the slaves more obedient. Disgusted mistresses soon arrived at the point where they did not care whether their slaves did anything at all. "I shall say nothing," a Texas woman sighed, "and if they [the slaves] stop work entirely I will try to feel thankful if they let me alone."

For the first time, white women discovered just how few blacks had really embraced the paternalistic ethos and how easily the supposedly secure bond between mistress and slave could be broken. The breach of trust was especially painful for mistresses who had long congratulated themselves on having elevated their slaves from a state of barbarism by caring for them like children. *Betrayed* was the only word that could describe their feelings. When supposedly spoiled dependents left without saying good-bye, often in the middle of the night, white women lashed out at the ingrates. The shock of favorite house servants deserting to the Yankees reverberated across the plantation South. Emotionally wounded mistresses feigned indifference, claiming that they were tired of bothering with the slaves anyway or even that abolition might best serve the interests of the ruling class. But such rationalizations could hardly ease the pain of watching a world and its comfortable assumptions fall apart.

Forced to revise their view of their slaves and themselves, some women honestly welcomed emancipation as a release from the burdens of slave management. Yet for most, the rejoicing was short lived. When the household servants left, women who had never before cleaned a room or cooked a meal quickly had to learn. Plantation belles, who had always prided themselves on having delicate hands, now skinned their knuckles and chapped their skin washing clothes. Even women who had worked hard before now tried their hand at unfamiliar tasks, such as milking cows.

Whether they labored cheerfully or not, they marveled at the sudden change in their lives and, lying in bed at night exhausted, assessed the extent of the domestic revolution. Churning butter, making medicines, cleaning closets—all became part of a day's work. Sarah Morgan was astonished that she "could empty a dirty hearth, dust, move heavy weights, make myself generally useful and dirty, and all this thanks to the Yankees!" Such experiences showed how managing a household on one's own or even working for wages outside the home did not necessarily foster a new sense of independence. Nor is this surprising given the persistent assumptions that despite all the changes wrought by the war women still needed the protection of a man. Too tired to enjoy her sudden "independence," the confident mistress simply lived from one uncertain day to the next. Black emancipation did not liberate the white mistress but instead further exposed her vulnerability to social and economic upheaval. The physical and psychological costs of this pseudoliberation seemed far too high.

For even the pride women took in surviving on their own never quite overcame their sense that the times remained out of joint. Grimy and discouraged, harried housekeepers still looked for better days. "I did not have a cake for times were so hard," Carrie Berry wrote in her diary, "so I celebrated with ironing. I hope by next birthday we will have peace in our land so that I can have a nice dinner." Some women would have defined a good meal as anything cooked by someone else. For despite the grit and humor that runs through these accounts, most plantation mistresses missed their slaves and would have readily welcomed them back.

But they would only have done so on their own terms because as slavery disintegrated, racism intensified. To many mistresses, including those few who felt ethical qualms about slaveholding, the blacks' wartime behavior reflected inherent racial characteristics: loyal slaves proved how little blacks valued freedom; runaways showed how most Negroes were ungrateful brutes. Although a few women understood the moral drama taking place, most had only pity or contempt for their fleeing chattels. "The characteristic of the negro is laziness," Grace Elmore noted, "few will work even for bread if not compelled to do so, and their greatest idea of freedom is not to work but plunder." Once free, she speculated, they would inevitably disappear in a ruthless competition with superior whites. Other mistresses took a less callous attitude toward their former slaves but only managed to nurse a different set of illusions. Mary Jones, paternalist ne plus ultra, was sure that the "scourge" of freedom would fall with "peculiar weight" upon the unsuspecting Negroes. To her, the barbarism of Africa, the horrible consequences of emancipation in the Caribbean and the degradation of free blacks in New England made Southern slavery, whatever its imperfections and cruelties, seem a progressively humane institution.

Indeed the threat of emancipation buttressed some white women's faith in slavery as an institution. Imaginations could no longer wander in the never-never land of lush plantations, kindly masters, and cheerful slaves, but the shock of black freedom showed once again how most white mistresses had been and remained committed to a proslavery world view. "Their [the blacks'] mission in America is accomplished," Harriet Moore argued, "The country is cleared for the white man and they will be colonized in some new country." Enjoying whatever solace these fantasies provided, many women turned to the catechism of white supremacy—their sole surviving bulwark against the revolutionary forces unleashed by the war. In words echoing those of Alexander H. Stephens in his cornerstone speech, Kate Mason Rowland intoned the litany of Southern orthodoxy: "We are indeed the most fortunate in the world, we peoples of the Confederate States, America. For we alone recognize & have founded society on the great principle of the inequality of races, & are thus far in advance of the age we live in. When this great truth & the system of servitude it entails shall be recognized by Europe, we will expand & be great & prosperous outwardly as one now fortunate & contented internally.''

Nearly drowned in a tide of sudden, radical, and wrenching social and economic change, many plantation mistresses searched for some sense of continuity as the foundations of their lives crumbled. The war had given upper-class women the chance to manage plantations, yet intractable problems on everything from crops to labor hardly made this opportunity a golden one. Less dependent on advice and directions from men, they ran their farms and plantations as well as could have been expected under trying circumstances, but their authority over their slaves steadily eroded. What power the war had given them, it soon took away. In the midst of seeming chaos, many women turned instinctively to the security provided by their culture's time-tested pieties, grasping at the remnants of family, class, and racial pride.

II.

In the popular imagination, the war created few new images of Southern womanhood. Charity, tenderness, mercy remained peculiarly feminine virtues. Indeed the calls for women to engage in wartime benevolence stressed the moral superiority of females and made such work outside the home seem more acceptable and more respectable. When women nursed sick, wounded, and dying soldiers, they also nurtured conventional ideas about their own place and character.

The emphasis on voluntarism meant that women working in the hospitals would only do so temporarily and would not neglect their domestic duties. The first Confederate nurses simply opened up their homes to feed the convalescent and console the hopeless cases. Before the government could establish a medical department, they raised money, set up hospitals near the camps, and opened wayside hospitals at railroad depots for sick and wounded men on their way home. The wealthy often paid for food and supplies out of their own pockets. These efforts showed how dependent the Confederacy was on contributions from private citizens, but the aid associations lacked the resources and organization to handle the thousands of men who required more extensive and professional care.

For the duration of the war, the army hospitals also maintained a mixed character: they were staffed by paid physicians and nurses along with volunteers and occasional visitors, and sustained by public funds and private contributions. For women who worked in what generally amounted to makeshift facilities, the distinction between the volunteer and employee was never quite clear. Nursing was not yet an established profession—though the Civil War would begin the process—and volunteers complemented the work of doctors and ward matrons by gathering extra food, reading to the patients, writing letters, or simply listening and offering words of comfort. Arranging their visits on a more regular basis, women brought order to this normally haphazard benevolence. In turn, hospital aid associations gathered supplies and assigned helpers.

Improved organization, however, did not mean that female visitors were always welcomed by either doctors, ward matrons, or the patients. These women had great potential for improving conditions but also could disrupt routines if not actually harm the men. Every ward had its quota of busybodies who claimed vast medical knowledge. Fannie Beers recalled two notorious cases: a seventeen-year-old girl who had killed a dysentary patient by giving him apple turnovers and a woman who loosened an amputee's bandages, causing him to bleed to death. Surgeons and matrons had to watch constantly for women smuggling in contraband food that the men craved but could not eat. Although many of these volunteers obviously served the soldiers well, the insensitive and foolish gave the entire group a bad reputation.

Much of this activity remained both private and haphazard because the hospitals employed so few regular nurses—according to one estimate no more than thirty-two hundred in both the Union and Confederacy. Yet applications for positions poured into the War Department. Women who could not find jobs at home traveled to Virginia or wherever the armies were fighting; the impoverished wives and mothers of Confederate soldiers competed with refugees for the available openings. In hiring nurses, hospitals followed no regular application or appointment procedures, and such administrative sloppiness further reflected the lowly status of Confederate nurses.

These women worked hard and long but did not earn enough money to be considered professionals. In the fall of 1862, Congress finally defined duties and set salaries. Each hospital was to have two chief matrons (forty dollars per month) to supervise the soldiers' diet; two assistant matrons (thirty-five dollars per month) to supervise the laundry; and two matrons in each ward (thirty dollars per month) to care for the bedding, feed the soldiers, and administer medicine. Additional nurses and cooks earned twenty-five dollars a month. Although convalescing patients and soldiers detailed to the hospitals also served as nurses, most matrons preferred women, as did Congress, which specified that females be used wherever possible. But the hospitals could not find enough suitable applicants. Even though many chief matrons were wealthy widows or spinsters who donated their services, such paragons were hard to find, and complaints against matrons for inefficiency, callousness, and even carousing appear in the records.

Whatever their qualifications and abilities, nurses could barely live on their salaries. One ward matron asked for permission to buy food at official government prices because her husband's army pay, combined with her own meager earnings, could not feed their four children. The class tensions that had developed in other areas of Confederate life also entered the hospitals. The contrast in dress, motive, and attitude between well-to-do volunteers and poorer women who did the menial jobs occasionally erupted into nasty quarrels. Phoebe Pember contemptuously described the "many inefficient and uneducated women, hardly above the laboring classes" who worked in Confederate hospitals. Kate Cumming agreed that not enough "ladies" applied for these positions. She thought the laundresses far too fussy about their quarters and delighted in repeating gossip about these women's dancing with black men. The mixture of benevolence, professionalism, and necessity made it difficult for women of such widely varying backgrounds to work together harmoniously. Indeed, the familiar stories of altruistic angels of mercy reveal little about the complex lives of Confederate nurses, especially the refugee women and soldiers' wives whose primary motive for working in the hospitals may well have been money.

Economic necessity inevitably clashed with expectations of disinterested benevolence. The high-minded volunteers exalting their own example of self-sacrifice could not understand how anyone could ignore the sacred call of patriotism. Kate Cumming advised young girls to "do what, in all ages, has been the special duty of woman—to relieve suffering." After serving in Mississippi and Tennessee hospitals for a year, she lashed out at the "rich, refined, intellectual, and will I say Christian" women who shirked their public responsibility. Seizing the high moral ground, hospital matrons condemned selfishness without acknowledging their own mixed motives.

In the tradition of antebellum ladies bountiful and paternalistic plantation mistresses, some volunteers and nurses viewed hospital work as poor relief, a part of their customary obligation to uplift the downtrodden. Constance Cary Harrison described Richmond ladies "flitting about the streets," their slaves in tow carrying "silver trays with dishes of fine porcelain under napkins of thick white damask, containing soups, creams, jellies, thin biscuit, eggs *á la creme* [sic], boiled chicken, etc., surmounted by clusters of freshly gathered flowers." When her mother offered one of these delicacies to a backwoods Carolinian, the man looked at her quizzically and stated a decided preference for greens and bacon. Despite the humor in this anecdote, some women treated ordinary soldiers with ill-concealed disdain. To yeomen and poor whites, one matron condescendingly sniffed, "gratitude is an exotic plant in a refined atmosphere. . . . Common natures look only with astonishment at great sacrifices, and cunningly avail themselves of them, and give nothing in return, not even the satisfaction of allowing one to suppose that the care exerted has been beneficial,—*that* would entail compensation of some kind, and in their ignorance they fear the nature of the equivalent which might be demanded." Yet these men had reason to avoid dependence on the wealthy, especially wealthy ladies. Southern notions of masculine honor made it difficult for proud soldiers to accept charity, even when they were lying flat on their backs in a hospital. Women who would serve only officers or soldiers from their own state reinforced the men's suspicions. Although most nurses and volunteers treated patients without regard to rank or class, social prejudice sometimes intruded.

And so did sexual tension. Flirtation in the hospitals seemed innocent enough, but for chief matrons, nurses, and patients alike, it sometimes became a serious problem. Sally Tomkins advised a volunteer to leave her "beauty at the door and bring in your goodness." When women innocently asked soldiers what they needed, many archly grinned and said, "A kiss." Some nurses thought most of the trouble came from rough and ragged poor whites, but even those who seemed to be gentlemen would make a pass at a likely-looking female. And sexual attraction ran in both directions. Kate Cumming overheard a pretty widow telling the doctors how much she enjoyed helping in the hospital because she had found a good candidate for a second husband. Her frank avowal shocked everyone, but she had simply stated what others were loath to admit. If some soldiers saw women as little more than sexual objects, some women obviously accepted such an evaluation of their worth and behaved accordingly. Both class prejudices and sexual stereotypes limited the ability of Confederate nurses to perform their tasks, acquire self-confidence, and establish professional credentials.

The drudgery of daily work in the wards, however, soon took most of the romance out of hospital service. Besides cooking, changing linen, and dressing wounds, nurses scrubbed floors, wrote letters, and listened to the inevitable complaints. Mary Chesnut helped feed hominy, rice, and gravy to badly wounded men who had lost parts of their jaws, teeth, or tongues. Although new patients arrived and problems changed, the days fell into a depressing pattern of madly dashing about with too little time for too many men—and everywhere death.

Women who had led sheltered lives suddenly confronted suffering and tragedy at every turn. Quietly reading from the Bible or singing hymns, they helped the mortally wounded accept their fate. Such experiences transformed squeamish girls. Closing dead men's eyes and cataloguing their personal effects made Phoebe Pember wonder whether she had "any feeling and sensibility left." At night she could hear the coughing and groaning of typhoid and pneumonia patients, although she had to save her strength for the more critically ill. Wearied by long hours, poor food, and cramped quarters, she and her comrades often became debilitated from contagious diseases; not everyone had the necessary physical or emotional stamina. After less than two months in a Virginia hospital, Ada Bacot could no longer stand the men: "Oh my to think of getting up early in the morning and going among them. I am so sick of the sight of them." The daily horrors of the wards naturally sapped morale, but as the war dragged on, conditions only worsened.

The flood of sick and wounded men overwhelmed the resources of most hospitals; shortages and high prices turned nurses into scavengers. Like everyone else, these women had little good to say about the supply system in military hospitals. When food was available, matrons sometimes saved the choicest items for their families or favorite patients—assuming the omnivorous rats did not devour it first. By 1864, nurses at the Chimborazo hospital near Richmond gave the men dry pieces of corn bread and stretched their meager supply of flour to make tiny rolls so that each patient received something.

Hospital societies took up some of the slack, but after 1862 their donations fell off rapidly, forcing even more reliance on individual charity.

Several poor women sent corn bread and beans to a Newman, Georgia, hospital though they probably could ill afford such generosity. Nurses bought food for the soldiers with their own money or asked their friends to cook favorite dishes. But wrangling valuable provisions out of tight-fisted civilians required the negotiating skills of a Talleyrand. Fannie Beers scoured the Georgia countryside, visiting the homes of parsimonious and suspicious farm women. She praised their weed-filled gardens, admired their ugly children, and then casually mentioned the hospitals' need for food. Her persistence and tact paid off, but such efforts were stopgaps at best.

As matrons, nurses, and volunteers wrestled with these problems, they assumed ever greater authority. Becoming more efficient, self-confident, and impatient with routine and bureaucracy, they inevitably clashed with the physicians in the hospitals. The most conscientious nurses often received little cooperation from doctors who had little use for women in the wards. At the Chimborazo hospital, the chief surgeon and his skeptical clerks carefully eyed Phoebe Pember, apparently fearing that her arrival marked the beginning of "petticoat government." She overheard a doctor remark to a colleague "in a tone of ill-concealed disgust, that '*one of them had come*'." Some administrators would not allow women to visit the wards. Even those who kept their opinions to themselves offered gallant excuses about the hospitals' being no place for ladies. To Kate Cumming, the issue was justice: "The war is certainly ours as well as that of the men. We cannot fight, so must take care of those who do." By asserting their right to do their job and receive due respect, nurses in effect acknowledged and accepted the limitations placed on their sex. With experience they became more assertive in dealing with surgeons, and eventually their competence and indispensability won them grudging acceptance.

Yet women too sometimes felt out of place in the hospitals. Kate Cumming scorned the fastidious who were hypersensitive about their reputations. "A lady's respectability must be at a low ebb when it can be endangered by going into a hospital," she remarked caustically. In claiming never to have heard a vulgar or indelicate remark from any of the soldiers, she surely exaggerated. But she rightly blamed "false notions of propriety" for making women of ability and strong character hesitant to defy popular prejudice. Fathers and brothers seemed especially protective of adolescent girls. Of course some women used these arguments as convenient excuses to avoid an unpleasant duty.

Many first-time visitors found hospital conditions so appalling that they never returned. Seeing badly wounded men or witnessing amputations, some fainted. Shortly after she began working in a Chattanooga hospital, Kate Cumming saw a stream of blood running off an operating table into a tub, which also held the patient's recently severed arm. On her way to the kitchen—just below the operating room—she frequently noticed blood oozing down the steps. And even if eyes adjusted, noses might not. The air in most wards was foul. "I dont like so much mess and so affluent odors," Lucy Bryan wrote in disgust. "It makes me sick to smell soldiers anyway." Some young women with the best of intentions never got used to such conditions and decided they could serve better by sewing or raising money for the hospitals.

Although few mentioned it, many delicately bred young ladies dreaded affronts to their modesty. When applying for a job as a nurse, an Alabama woman discreetly inquired whether she would have to dress "stomach" wounds. In her first hospital job, Phoebe Pember learned how a "lively imagination" could easily conjure up embarrassing situations. Bringing chicken soup to her first patient, she feared he would express his thanks by rising out of bed in his skimpy hospital gown. After more experience she concluded that "little unpleasant exposure" normally took place and that no women should let "one material thought lessen her efficiency" but instead "*must* soar beyond the conventional modesty considered correct under different circumstances."

Patriotism might overcome prudery, but complex ideas and emotions tugged would-be nurses in several directions at once, often making them deeply ambivalent about hospital work. Women were supposed to be brave and strong but at the same time remain loving and refined; endurance and perseverance were to characterize the actions of young girls who had been traditionally seen as weak and frivolous. Such contradictory and shifting expectations naturally confused women and made them uncertain about their proper roles and place. Were they stoically to endure the sights, sounds, and odors? Should they retreat to the safety of the domestic circle?

Although a few women went home unnerved from their first experience and had nightmares about the wounded and dying, most recovered from the initial shock, somehow learned to cope, and performed useful service. More important, they pressured doctors and army officers into improving procedures. In a report to Vice-President Alexander H. Stephens that was reminiscent of Florence Nightingale's scathing critiques of British medical practices during the Crimean War, Mary Johnstone dismissed most surgeons as drunken political appointees unfit to run hospitals. She suggested a more careful classification of patients, the creation of receiving wards, and the installation of screens to shield convalescing soldiers from scenes of suffering and death. Other nurses told of wounded men who slept on straw in clothes that had not been changed since their arrival.

In dealing with stubborn bureaucrats, arrogant surgeons, and cantankerous patients, women acquired informal political skills. Female administrators, such as Sally Tomkins and Juliet Opie Hopkins, wielded an authority that impressed and sometimes frightened their male colleagues. Like army officers and civilian leaders, they learned important lessons in organization. In their zeal for initiating reforms, women brought to the work previously untapped skills. The South's few female physicians either had to serve as matrons or as ordinary nurses. Ella Cooper, for example, had completed the curriculum at the Medical College of Cincinnati, but the faculty had not allowed her to graduate. "I am a woman and have been so trained to feel that a woman can not walk out of a certain routine, even to do good," she admitted. Though qualified as a surgeon, she was willing to serve as a nurse or even a cook. She thought the doctors were a "little astonished when they see me, to find that a woman can do something, [but] I presume it will not diminish their zeal or prove detrimental to the Confederacy.'' This well-directed sarcasm might have amused other women, who, though not as thoroughly trained as Ella Cooper, ran laundries, kitchens, and dispensaries with cool efficiency.

For once the official reports do not exaggerate: the accomplishments of Confederate nurses were impressive. Most matrons managed their wards as skillfully as the private hospital associations claimed, and their efforts markedly improved Confederate medicine where it counted most, in reducing the mortality rate. In hospitals run by men, the mortality rate was about 10 percent; in those run by women, less than 5 percent of the patients died. Contemporaries attributed this difference to superior cleanliness, but better food preparation and organization also helped.

As it turned out, such achievements would mean little in the postwar South. Hospital work had for a time offered women a challenging new profession, which—despite low salaries—had bolstered their self-confidence and had given their lives new meaning and importance. But such benefits proved to be fleeting, and few men or women assumed that nursing had been anything more than a temporary job in crisis times for women who would ultimately resume their places as wives and mothers. Former nurses found few opportunities to apply their administrative skills outside the home and instead returned to domestic life. Although a few later became the subject of syrupy obituaries, most died in obscurity.

III.

. . . In defeat, these new Confederate women—who had served their country outside their accustomed sphere, faced psychological, social, and, most of all, economic crises. Plantation mistresses lost their slaves [and] the nurses no longer had patients. . . . The war had opened doors for these women but had closed them just as quickly, and traditional notions about femininity survived more or less intact. Most Southerners saw the changes in sex roles between 1861 and 1865 as an aberration, an experiment launched out of necessity that would not be soon repeated. The Confederates had not promised a domestic revolution, and none occurred.

F U R T H E R   R E A D I N G

William E. Barton, *The Life of Clara Barton*, 2 vols. (1922)

Michael Chesson, ''Harlots or Heroines? A New Look at the Richmond Bread Riot,'' *Virginia Magazine of History and Biography* 92 (1984), 131–175

Catherine Clinton, *The Plantation Mistress: Woman's World in the Old South* (1982)

——, *The Other Civil War: American Women in the 19th Century* (1984)

Ellen DuBois, *Feminism and Suffrage: The Emergence of an Independent Women's Movement in America, 1848–1869* (1978)

Jacqueline Jones, *Labor of Love, Labor of Sorrow: Black Women, Work and the Family from Slavery to the Present* (1985)

Suzanne Lebsock, *The Free Women of Petersburg: Status and Culture in a Southern Town, 1784–1860* (1984)

Mary Elizabeth Massey, *Bonnet Brigades: American Women and the Civil War* (1966)

Phillip S. Paludan, *"A People's Contest": The Union and Civil War, 1861–1865* (1988)

Elizabeth B. Pryor, *Clara Barton: Professional Angel* (1987)

Ruth Scarborough, *Belle Boyd: Siren of the South* (1983)

Bell I. Wiley, *Confederate Women* (1975)

C. Vann Woodward, ed., *Mary Chesnut's Civil War* (1981)

CHAPTER
10

Emancipation and Its
Aftermath

❧

As the war began, Frederick Douglass lamented that, since the North was anti-slavery but opposed to abolition, the outcome of the contest was of little concern to the slaves themselves. Whichever side won, they would still remain in slavery. Nevertheless, pressure to widen the scope of the conflict to include abolition as a war aim was constantly brought to bear on the Lincoln administration by the abolitionists and their political allies, the radical wing of the Republican party.

The president resisted these demands, however. He feared that any advocacy of emancipation would stiffen Confederate resistance and, quite likely, scare slaveholders in Union areas like Missouri and Kentucky into carrying their states over to the Confederacy. Besides giving comfort to the enemy, sympathy for abolition would certainly frighten northern whites, who widely feared the consequence of slave liberation and would hesitate to support or fight in a war to free millions of blacks.

By midsummer 1862, after the border states had rejected his offer of financial compensation in return for gradual abolition, President Lincoln was compelled to move against slavery more forcefully. In September he announced his intention of proclaiming emancipation on January 1, 1863. This was a courageous and radical step. It made the destruction of slavery a certain consequence of northern victory, while it also confronted the nation with the eventual yet disturbing prospect of assimilating a vast population of black people. In the meantime, slaves within the Union lines could be conscripted into the Federal army and, with guns in their hands, fight to secure their freedom. Other aspects of Lincoln's initiative were less bold, however. The proclamation applied only to the slaves currently located inside the Confederacy, so in practice it freed no slaves at all. Moreover, emancipation would not be officially achieved until 1865, when the Thirteenth Amendment was ratified. Also, the tenor of Lincoln's announcement was rather grudging. He did not grandly proclaim liberation. Rather, he indicated that he was embarking upon it primarily out of military necessity.

The revolutionary implications of the decision for emancipation were, in effect, tempered by the cautious manner of its execution. Similarly mixed was the *experience of emancipation by the slaves themselves. After the exhilaration of the first months of liberation, the former slaves soon discovered that their freedom was to be severely limited. Gains were made, but frequently they turned out to be more fleeting and insubstantial than had been hoped. The freedmen must therefore have wondered, as have historians ever since, how radical and transforming emancipation really was.*

⤴ D O C U M E N T S

Emancipation was both a question of policy at the highest levels of the Federal government and a matter of practical experience for the liberated slaves on the lowest rungs of southern society. The documents reflect both aspects of this episode.

The first document is President Lincoln's much-quoted reply of August 22, 1862, to Horace Greeley, the antislavery editor of the *New York Tribune,* explaining to him that saving the Union was his "paramount object." A short time later, Lincoln decided that emancipation had become a necessary means to that end, and he defended his action in the second selection, a long letter of August 26, 1863 to James C. Conkling and other Illinois Republicans who had called a mass meeting in Springfield, and invited Lincoln to attend. The third extract is from the preliminary report of the American Freedmen's Inquiry Commission, issued on June 30, 1863, and it reveals the way that sympathetic members of a government commission initially approached the question of the free blacks' future status in society. In the fourth document, Frederick Douglass, the most influential African-American spokesman at the time, gives an impatient answer in April 1865 to the very same inquiry about the social status of the former slaves.

As for the freedmen themselves, the fifth selection provides some information, since it is a report of August 23, 1863, from Adjutant-General Lorenzo Thomas, the official responsible for those slaves in the Mississippi Delta who had fled to the Union lines from nearby plantations. An affidavit sworn by a black soldier named Joseph Miller, recounting his and his family's grim experiences after he enlisted in the Union army, is the sixth selection. His testimony was given to a Freedmen's Bureau agent on November 26, 1864. The seventh and final document is a long extract from a perceptive official report submitted on November 14, 1867, by a Freedmen's Bureau agent, Charles Raushenberg, who was stationed at Cuthbert in southern Georgia. His report focuses on how the freedmen were faring as laborers within his rural jurisdiction.

President Lincoln Discusses War Aims, August 1862

Executive Mansion,
Washington, August 22, 1862.

Hon. Horace Greely [*sic*]:

Dear Sir

I have just read yours of the 19th. addressed to myself through the New-York Tribune. If there be in it any statements, or assumptions of fact, which I may know to be erroneous, I do not, now and here, controvert them. If there be in it any inferences which I may believe to be falsely drawn, I do not now and here, argue against them. If there be perceptable [*sic*] in it an impatient and dictatorial tone, I waive it in deference to an old friend, whose heart I have always supposed to be right.

As to the policy I "seem to be pursuing" as you say, I have not meant to leave any one in doubt.

I would save the Union. I would save it the shortest way under the Constitution. The sooner the national authority can be restored; the nearer the Union will be "the Union as it was." If there be those who would not save the Union, unless they could at the same time *save* slavery, I do not agree with them. If there be those who would not save the Union unless they could at the same time *destroy* slavery, I do not agree with them. My paramount object in this struggle *is* to save the Union, and is *not* either to save or to destroy slavery. If I could save the Union without freeing *any* slave I would do it, and if I could save it by freeing *all* the slaves I would do it; and if I could save it by freeing some and leaving others alone I would also do that. What I do about slavery, and the colored race, I do because I believe it helps to save the Union; and what I forbear, I forbear because I do *not* believe it would help to save the Union. I shall do *less* whenever I shall believe what I am doing hurts the cause, and I shall do *more* whenever I shall believe doing more will help the cause. I shall try to correct errors when shown to be errors; and I shall adopt new views so fast as they shall appear to be true views.

I have here stated my purpose according to my view of *official* duty; and I intend no modification of my oft-expressed *personal* wish that all men every where could be free. Yours,

A. Lincoln

President Lincoln Defends Emancipation, August 1863

Executive Mansion,
Washington, August 26, 1863.

Hon. James C. Conkling

My Dear Sir:

. . . To be plain, you are dissatisfied with me about the negro. Quite likely there is a difference of opinion between you and myself upon that subject. I certainly wish that all men could be free, while I suppose you do not. Yet I have neither adopted, nor proposed any measure, which is not consistent with even your view, provided you are for the Union. I suggested compensated emancipation; to which you replied you wished not to be taxed to buy negroes. But I had not asked you to be taxed to buy negroes, except in such way, as to save you from greater taxation to save the Union exclusively by other means.

You dislike the emancipation proclamation; and, perhaps, would have it retracted. You say it is unconstitutional—I think differently. I think the constitution invests its commander-in-chief, with the law of war, in time of war. The most that can be said, if so much, is, that slaves are property. Is there—has there ever been—any question that by the law of war, property, both of enemies and friends, may be taken when needed? And is it not needed whenever taking it, helps us, or hurts the enemy? Armies, the world over, destroy enemies' property when they cannot use it; and even destroy their own to keep it from the enemy. Civilized belligerents do all in their power to help themselves, or hurt the enemy, except a few things regarded as barbarous or cruel. Among the exceptions are the massacre of vanquished foes, and non-combatants, male and female.

But the proclamation, as law, either is valid, or is not valid. If it is not valid, it needs no retraction. If it is valid, it cannot be retracted, any more than the dead can be brought to life. Some of you profess to think its retraction would operate favorably for the Union. Why better *after* the retraction, than *before* the issue? There was more than a year and a half of trial to suppress the rebellion before the proclamation issued, the last one hundred days of which passed under an explicit notice that it was coming, unless averted by those in revolt, returning to their allegiance. The war has certainly progressed as favorably for us, since the issue of the proclamation as before. I know as fully as one can know the opinions of others, that some of the commanders of our armies in the field who have given us our most important successes, believe the emancipation policy, and the use of colored troops, constitute the heaviest blow yet dealt to the rebellion; and that, at least one of those important successes, could not have been achieved when it was, but for the aid of black soldiers. Among the commanders holding these views are some who have never had any affinity with what is called abolitionism, or with republican party politics; but who hold them purely as military opinions. I submit these opinions as being entitled to some weight against the objections, often urged, that emancipation, and arming the blacks, are unwise as military measures, and were not adopted, as such, in good faith.

You say you will not fight to free negroes. Some of them seem willing to fight for you; but, no matter. Fight you, then, exclusively to save the Union. I issued the proclamation on purpose to aid you in saving the Union. Whenever you shall have conquered all resistance to the Union, if I shall urge you to continue fighting, it will be an apt time, then, for you to declare you will not fight to free negroes.

I thought that in your struggle for the Union, to whatever extent the negroes should cease helping the enemy, to that extent it weakened the enemy in his resistance to you. Do you think differently? I thought that whatever negroes can be got to do as soldiers, leaves just so much less for white soldiers to do, in saving the Union. Does it appear otherwise to you? But negroes, like other people, act upon motives. Why should they do any thing for us, if we will do nothing for them? If they stake their lives for us, they must be prompted by the strongest motive—even the promise of freedom. And the promise being made, must be kept. . . .

Peace does not appear so distant as it did. I hope it will come soon, and come to stay; and so come as to be worth the keeping in all future time. It will then have been proved that, among free men, there can be no successful appeal from the ballot to the bullet; and that they who take such appeal are sure to lose their case, and pay the cost. And then, there will be some black men who can remember that, with silent tongue, and clenched teeth, and steady eye, and well-poised bayonet, they have helped mankind on to this great consummation; while, I fear, there will be some white ones, unable to forget that, with malignant heart, and deceitful speech, they have strove to hinder it.

Still let us not be over-sanguine of a speedy final triumph. Let us be quite sober. Let us diligently apply the means, never doubting that a just God, in his own good time, will give us the rightful result. Yours very truly,

A. Lincoln

A Federal Commission Considers Policy Toward the Ex-Slaves, June 1863

. . . The commission here desire to record their profound conviction, that upon the judicious selection of department superintendents and of super-intendent general of freedmen will mainly depend the successful practical workings of the . . . plan of organization. The African race, accustomed to shield itself by cunning and evasion, and by shirking of work, whenever it can be safely shirked, against the oppression which has been its lot for generations, is yet of genial nature, alive to gratitude, open to impressions of kindness, and more readily influenced and led by those who treat it well and gain its confidence than our race, or perhaps than any other. The wishes and recommendations of government, if they are not harshly en-forced, but quietly communicated by those who understand and sympathize with the African nature, will be received and obeyed as commands in almost every instance. It is highly important, therefore, that those who have in charge the interests of these freedmen shall be men not only of adminis-trative ability, but also of comprehensive benevolence and humanitarian views.

On the other hand, it is equally desirable that these refugees, as readily spoiled as children, should not be treated with weak and injurious indulg-ence. Evenhanded justice, not special favor, is what they need. Mild firm-ness is the proper spirit in which to control them. They should find them-selves treated, not as children of preference, fostered by charity, dependent for a living on government or on benevolent associations, but as men from whom, in their new character of freedmen, self-reliance and self-support are demanded. . . .

Frederick Douglass States the Freedmen's Demands, April 1865

. . . I have had but one idea for the last three years to present to the American people, and the phraseology in which I clothe it is the old abolition phraseology. I am for the "immediate, unconditional, and universal" enfranchisement of the black man, in every State in the Union. Without this, his liberty is a mockery; without this, you might as well almost retain the old name of slavery for his condition; for in fact, if he is not the slave of the individual master, he is the slave of society, and holds his liberty as a privilege, not as a right. He is at the mercy of the mob, and has no means of protecting himself.

It may be objected, however, that this pressing of the Negro's right to suffrage is premature. Let us have slavery abolished, it may be said, let us have labor organized, and then, in the natural course of events, the right of suffrage will be extended to the Negro. I do not agree with this. The constitution of the human mind is such, that if it once disregards the conviction forced upon it by a revelation of truth, it requires the exercise of a higher power to produce the same conviction afterwards. The American people are now in tears. The Shenandoah has run blood—the best blood of the North. All around Richmond, the blood of New England and of the North has been shed—of your sons, your brothers and your fathers. We all feel, in the existence of this Rebellion, that judgments terrible, widespread, far-reaching, overwhelming, are abroad in the land; and we feel, in view of these judgments, just now, a disposition to learn righteousness. This is the hour. Our streets are in mourning, tears are falling at every fireside, and under the chastisement of this Rebellion we have almost come up to the point of conceding this great, this all-important right of suffrage. I fear that if we fail to do it now, if abolitionists fail to press it now, we may not see, for centuries to come, the same disposition that exists at this moment. Hence, I say, now is the time to press this right.

It may be asked, "Why do you want it. Some men have got along very well without it. Women have not this right." Shall we justify one wrong by another? This is a sufficient answer. Shall we at this moment justify the deprivation of the Negro of the right to vote, because some one else is deprived of that privilege? I hold that women, as well as men, have the right to vote, and my heart and my voice go with the movement to extend suffrage to women; but that question rests upon another basis than that on which our right rests. We may be asked, I say, why we want it. I will tell you why we want it. We want it because it is our *right*, first of all. No class of men can, without insulting their own nature, be content with any deprivation of their rights. We want it again, as a means for educating our race. Men are so constituted that they derive their conviction of their own possibilities largely from the estimate formed of them by others. If nothing is expected of a people, that people will find it difficult to contradict that expectation. By depriving us of suffrage, you affirm our incapacity to form an intelligent judgment respecting public men and public measures; you declare before the world that we are unfit to exercise the elective franchise, and by this means lead us to undervalue ourselves, to put a low estimate upon ourselves, and to feel that we have no possibilities like other men. Again, I want the elective franchise, for one, as a colored man, because ours is a peculiar government, based upon a peculiar idea, and that idea is universal suffrage. If I were in a monarchial government, or an autocratic or aristocratic government, where the few bore rule and the many were subject, there would be no special stigma resting upon me, because I did not exercise the elective franchise. It would do me no great violence. Mingling with the mass I should partake of the strength of the mass; I should be supported by the mass, and I should have the same incentives to endeavor with the mass of my fellow-men; it would be no particular burden, no particular deprivation; but here where universal suffrage is the rule, where that is the fundamental idea of the Government, to rule us out is to make us an exception, to brand us with the stigma of inferiority, and to invite to our heads the missiles of those about us; therefore, I want the franchise for the black man. . . .

I ask my friends who are apologizing for not insisting upon this right, where can the black man look, in this country, for the assertion of his right, if he may not look to the Massachusetts Anti-Slavery Society? [Douglass was addressing a meeting of this society.] Where under the whole heavens can he look for sympathy, in asserting this right, if he may not look to this platform? Have you lifted us up to a certain height to see that we are men, and then are any disposed to leave us there, without seeing that we are put in possession of all our rights? We look naturally to this platform for the assertion of all our rights, and for this one especially. I understand the anti-slavery societies of this country to be based on two principles,—first, the freedom of the blacks of this country; and, second, the elevation of them. Let me not be misunderstood here. I am not asking for sympathy at the hands of abolitionists, sympathy at the hands of any. I think the American people are disposed often to be generous rather than just. I look over this country at the present time, and I see Educational Societies, Sanitary Commissions, Freedmen's Associations, and the like,—all very good: but in regard to the colored people there is always more that is benevolent, I perceive, than just, manifested towards us. What I ask for the Negro is not benevolence, not pity, not sympathy, but simply *justice*. The American people have always been anxious to know what they shall do with us. Gen. Banks [the federal commander in Louisiana, 1863–1864] was distressed with solicitude as to what he should do with the Negro. Everybody has asked the question, and they learned to ask it early of the abolitionists, "What shall we do with the Negro?" I have had but one answer from the beginning. Do nothing with us! Your doing with us has already played the mischief with us. Do nothing with us! If the apples will not remain on the tree of their own strength, if they are wormeaten at the core, if they are early ripe and disposed to fall, let them fall! I am not for tying or fastening them on the tree in any way, except by nature's plan, and if they will not stay there, let them fall. And if the Negro cannot stand on his own legs, let him fall also. All I ask is, give him a chance to stand on his own legs! Let him alone! If you see him on his way to school, let him alone, don't disturb him! If you see him going to the dinner-table at a hotel, let him go! If you see him going to the ballot-box, let him alone, don't disturb him! If you see him going into a work-shop, just let him alone,—your interference is doing him a positive injury. . . .

The U.S. Adjutant General Describes the Condition of Fleeing Slaves, August 1863

Adjutant General of the Army to the Secretary of War

Cairo, Illinois, Augt 23. 1863.

Sir, I arrived at this place this morning with General Grant, and shall return with him to-day or tomorrow to Vicksburg.

I have delayed making a report of the condition of affairs until I visited the several positions on the river. I was disappointed at finding but few negroes at Vicksburg, as they had been either absorbed by the several Departments as laborers, or taken to fill up the regiments previously organized. Of these regiments I get good accounts and some of them are in a high state of discipline. I visited Natchez, which at the present time is the best place for obtaining negroes, and gave orders for the immediate organization of two regiments, one as heavy Artillery to garrison Vicksburg, and also a Cavalry regiment to be mounted on mules. These animals can be obtained in great abundance.

I was fortunate in arriving at Memphis before General Steele left Helena for the interior of Arkansas as I was enabled to have him instructed to bring back all the blacks he could possibly gather, and sent recruiting officers with him. This expedition must give me a large number of men. A force also goes up Red River, and another from Goodrich's Landing back to bayou Macon, and their commanders are also instructed to collect the able bodied men, and in future such will be the standing orders. All the surplus blacks employed by the troops, or hovering round the Camps will be gathered up, General Grant having at my request issued such an order. He gives me every assistance in my work.

On arriving at Lake Providence on my way to Vicksburg, I found upwards of a thousand negroes, nearly all women and children, on the banks of the river, in a most helpless condition, who had left the plantations in consequence of the withdrawal of the troops on account of sickness. They had successfully sustained one attack of guerillas, aided by a gun-boat, but expected another attack. I took them all to Goodrich's Landing where there is a garrison of negro troops. The number of this helpless class in the various camps is very large and daily increasing, and altho' everything is done for their well being, I find that sickness prevails to an alarming extent, and the bills of mortality are very high. This results from their change of life and habits, from daily work to comparative idleness, and also from being congregated in large numbers in camps, which is a matter of necessity. Besides, they will not take care of themselves much less of those who are sick. I have therefore after much reflection and consultation with officers, come to the conclusion that the old men, women and children should be advised to remain on the plantations, especially on those within our lines where we can have an oversight of them. Besides, it is important that the crops on the plantations within our lines should be gathered. A number of those now in our camps express a desire to return to their old homes, and indeed many have already done so. All such will be encouraged to do so, in cases where we are satisfied their former masters will not run them off or sell them. I have conversed with a number of planters, several strong union men at Natchez especially, and they all express the opinion that slavery has received its death blow, and cannot again exist in regions passed over by our armies. They are perfectly willing to hire the negroes and adopt any policy the Government may dictate. Many citizens of Mississippi, Louisiana and Arkansas are desirous that their States should resume their position in the Union with laws providing for the emancipation of slaves in a limited number of years. This feeling is constantly increasing, even among those who were strong advocates of secession. They now see it is vain to resist our arms, and only see utter ruin to themselves as the war goes on.

It is important that woodyards should be established on the river, and General Grant is encouraging the measure. I will permit persons duly authorized to cut wood for steamboats, to hire wood-choppers from those who are unfit for military service, including the women. It will be far more for their benefit to support themselves than to sit in idleness in camps depending on the Government for subsistence.

I have issued an order for general distribution in the armies of Generals Grant and Rosencrans [*sic*] setting forth some of the above points, a copy of which is enclosed—special Order No 45.—

I should be pleased to receive your instructions if my action is in any respect not in accordance with your views. The subject is now assuming vast proportions, and while I will do every thing in my power to carry out the policy of the administration and support the Government, I feel that my responsibilities are great and need the advice of my superiors. . . .

L. Thomas

A Black Union Soldier Protests His Mistreatment, November 1864

Camp Nelson   Ky   November 26, 1864

Personally appered before me E. B. W. Restieaux Capt. and Asst. Quartermaster Joseph Miller a man of color who being duly sworn upon oath says

I was a slave of George Miller of Lincoln County Ky. I have always resided in Kentucky and am now a Soldier in the service of the United

States. I belong to Company I 124 U.S.C. Inft now Stationed at Camp Nelson Ky. When I came to Camp for the purpose of enlisting about the middle of October 1864 my wife and children came with me because my master said that if I enlisted he would not maintain them and I knew they would be abused by him when I left. I had then four children ages respectively ten nine seven and four years. On my presenting myself as a recruit I was told by the Lieut. in command to take my family into a tent within the limits of the Camp. My wife and family occupied this tent by the express permission of the aforementioned Officer and never received any notice to leave until Tuesday November 22 when a mounted guard gave my wife notice that she and her children must leave Camp before early morning. This was about six O'clock at night. My little boy about seven years of age had been very sick and was slowly recovering My wife had no place to go and so remained until morning. About eight Oclock Wednesday morning November 23 a mounted guard came to my tent and ordered my wife and children out of Camp The morning was bitter cold. It was freezing hard. I was certain that it would kill my sick child to take him out in the cold. I told the man in charge of the guard that it would be the death of my boy I told him that my wife and children had no place to go and I told him that I was a soldier of the United States. He told me that it did not make any difference. he had orders to take all out of Camp. He told my wife and family that if they did not get up into the wagon which he had he would shoot the last one of them. On being thus threatened my wife and children went into the wagon My wife carried her sick child in her arms. When they left the tent the wind was blowing hard and cold and having had to leave much of our clothing when we left our master, my wife with her little one was poorly clad. I followed them as far as the lines. I had no Knowledge where they were taking them. At night I went in search of my family. I found them at Nicholasville about six miles from Camp. They were in an old meeting house belonging to the colored people. The building was very cold having only one fire. My wife and children could not get near the fire, because of the number of colored people huddled together by the soldiers. I found my wife and children shivering with cold and famished with hunger They had not recieved a morsel of food during the whole day. My boy was dead. He died directly after getting down from the wagon. I Know he was Killed by exposure to the inclement weather I had to return to camp that night so I left my family in the meeting house and walked back. I had walked there. I travelled in all twelve miles Next morning I walked to Nicholasville. I dug a grave myself and buried my own child. I left my family in the Meeting house—where they still remain And further this deponent saith not

his

(Signed) Joseph   Miller

mark

A Freedmen's Bureau Agent Discusses
Labor Relations, November 1867

Office Agent Bur. R. F. A. Lds.
Division of Cuthbert
Cuthbert, Ga. Novbr. 14, 1867.

Lieut O. H. Howard,
Sub. Asst Commnr Bur R. F. A. Lds
Albany, Ga.

Sir,

In obedience to the instructions received from you I have the honor to submit this Report on the General Condition of Affairs in my division.

When I entered upon my duties as Agent in this Division the Bureau of R. F. A. Lds [Bureau of Refugees, Freedmen and Abandoned Lands] seemed to be generally considered by the community, a substitute for overseers and drivers and to take up and return run away laborers and to punish them for real or imaginary violations of contract by fines, imprisonment and some times by corporeal punishment seemed to be the principal occupation of its agents.

The idea that a planter or employer of any kind should in case of dissatisfaction with his freedmen, instead of driving him [off] often without paying him his wages, first establish a complaint before the Bureau and let that tribunal decide wether a sufficient violation of contract existed to justify the discharge of the laborer or not, was then considered quite unreasonable; while every employer thought it perfectly proper that a Bureau agent, when notified of a freedmans leaving his employment should immediately issue an order for the arrest of the same and have him brought back—in chains if possible. The fairness of the principle that either party must submit its complaints to the Bureau for adjustment and that the white man can not decide the case a priori and only use the agent of the bureau as his executive organ and that employer as well as employee must submit to its decision wether the laborer ought to be discharged or ought to remain is just beginning to gain ground amongst both races and the negroes have ceased to a great extent to leave their employers as they used to do and employers are not as apt to run them off at will as they used to do. The common bulk of the population is just beginning to suspect that nothing else but what is justice and equity to a white man under certain circumstances would be justice and equity to a negro under the same circumstances and while they begin to feel the truth of this fact their moral courage and conscientiousness is generally not sufficient to overcome their prejudices and passions to a sufficient extent to give life and practical execution to this principle in their conduct towards and treatment of the negro in every day life.

The number of complaints made at this office is very large and increasing continually as the time of settlements is drawing nearer. The white man complains generally that the freedman is lazy, impudent and unreliable, that he will not fulfill his contract any further than it suits his convenience, that he claims the right to loose as much time as he pleases and when he pleases but wants full rations all the time, that he owes for goods and provisions more than his wages or his part of the crop amount to and that he wants to quit his employment on account of it; the freedman on the other hand generally complains that the white man has made him sign a contract, which he does not understand to mean what the white man says it does mean, that the white man wants him to do work which he did not contract to do, that the employer does not want to furnish him rations; that he charges him [too] much for lost time, that he curses him, threatens to whip him or has really struck him or shot at him. This is about the usual purport of the complaints of the two races and these complaints are frequently well established by each party and inevitably lead to the conclusion that a great deal of bad material exists in both races and that both in reality have much cause to complain of each other.

The freedpeople generally have worked better this year than last year and have adhered more faithfully to their contracts by staying out their time and a large number certainly at least one half of them have got along with their employers without serious dissatisfaction and trouble.

The majority of complaints that have been made at this Office by both races have found their origin in contracts, where freedmen received as compensation for their labor a certain share in the crop. The majority of the plantations in my division were worked under such contracts. The freedman claims under such contracts frequently that he has no other work to do but to cultivate and gather the crop, that being a partner in the concern he ought to be allowed to exercise his own judgement in the management of the plantation, that he ought to be permitted to loose time, when it suits his convenience to do so and when according to his judgement his labor is not needed in the field, that he ought to have a voice in the manner of gathering and dividing the corn and cotton and in the ginning, packing and selling of the latter product—while the employer claims that the labor of the employee belongs to him for the whole year, that he must labor for him six days during the week and do all kinds of work required of him wether directly connected with the crop or not, that he must have the sole and exclusive management of the plantation and that the freedman must obey his orders and do all work required as if he was receiving money wages, the part of the crop standing in the place of money, that the laborer must suffer deduction for lost time, that if he does not work all the time for him, he is not bound to furnish him provisions all the time, that the crop must be gathered, divided and housed to suit the convenience and judgement of the employer and that the share of the employee must be held responsible for what he has received in goods & provisions during the year. Taking in consideration that often quite a number of freedmen are employed on one plantation under such contracts, who frequently not only become discontented with the employer but with each other, accusing each other of loosing [sic] time unnecessarily and of not working well enough to be entitled to an equal share in the crop, it is easily understood to what amount of implicated difficulties and vexations questions these contracts furnish the material. . . .

The present aspect of the two races in their relations to each other therefore warrants no just expectation that they will get along amically with each other for any length of time but insures the belief that after the removal of the military authority the freedmen when allowed to exercise all the rights & privileges of citizens with their want of knowledge and experience in business and law, will generally fail to obtain justice from the hands of the white race in the daily relations of life as well as in the courts. They would generally come out the loosers, factors liens and mortgages being pushed in before their claims, frequently before they even suspected a danger of any loss, would yearly take away thousands of Dollars of their wages, all kinds of frauds would be practiced on them in making contracts, all kinds of impediments and obstacles would be put in the way of their complaints even reaching the courts and when there they would often fail to receive the necessary attention as the ignorance of the freedmen would often furnish opportunities to take advantage of them and to let them go by default or have them nol' pros.'d etc. This all would exasperate the freedmen more and more he would feel the wrong and still not be able to mend the matter and so, many outbreaks and at least local troubles would certainly take place. . . .

Charles Raushenberg

↘ *E S S A Y S*

Like the documents, the essays reflect the national as well as the local and individual aspects of emancipation. In the first selection, C. Vann Woodward of Yale University places the abolition of slavery in the southern United States within the larger context of emancipation throughout the New World (the Americas and the Caribbean) in the nineteenth century. The second essay is by Clarence L. Mohr of Tulane University, who shows how slaves in Georgia were, in effect, liberating themselves well in advance of the arrival of Sherman's armies. The third selection, by Leon F. Litwack of the University of California at Berkeley, describes the former slaves' initial encounter with freedom in the world of work, where they began to discover its limits and constraints.

The International Context of Emancipation

C. VANN WOODWARD

Comparisons are essential to all historical understanding. American understanding of freedom and of the price the nation paid for it has suffered from lack of comparative reference. In proposing such an approach to the

C. Vann Woodward, "The Price of Freedom," from *What Was Freedom's Price?*, David Sansing, ed., pp. 93–113 passim. Reprinted by permission of the University Press of Mississippi. Copyright © 1978 University Press of Mississippi.

study of emancipation and Reconstruction history, I am of course conscious of the recent outburst of interest in the comparative history of slavery and the light it has shed on an American institution that was thereby rendered less peculiar and more understandable. Comparative studies might also help understand what followed slavery. But, though the literature on comparative slavery has reached impressive proportions, very little has been written so far on the comparative history of emancipations and reconstructions. Yet there have been as many emancipations as there have been slavery systems, and we might presume that as much light could be shed upon the American experience by the comparative study of the one as of the other.

The nineteenth century was preeminently the century of emancipations, the period, as Victor Hugo said, of an idea whose time had come. Its time came relatively late in the defeated Confederate States of America, for on the world stage more emancipation dramas had been enacted before than after that of 1865. The great age of emancipations was the half-century from 1833, when the British opened it, to 1888, when Brazil (and two years earlier Cuba) belatedly closed it. Earlier small-scale abolitions in the newly independent northern states of British North America were somewhat similar to those of the newly independent states of Spanish South America in that they involved relatively few slaves and in that slavery was comparatively unimportant to their economies. The abolitions and reconstructions of the great age of emancipations were primarily those of plantation America, scattered southward from Virginia to southern Brazil and spread eastward from Texas along the Gulf and through the Caribbean to Barbados. I shall confine this paper to that scope, omitting other areas. This vast area of maritime and continental provinces and nations possessed enough common features and similarities, together with enough differences and cultural variables, to make plantation America, as Charles Wagley says, "a magnificent laboratory for the comparative approach." To explore the opportunities of comparative analysis would require a book. All I can attempt here is to suggest some possibilities and outline the framework of comparison.

Among the common features of the plantation America to which the American South belonged were a one-crop agriculture under the plantation system, a climate suitable for such a system, a background of slavery, a multiracial society, and a large population of African origin. Much more numerous than the common characteristics were the differences that distinguished the component parts. Six imperial powers controlled or had possessed parts of the area—the Spanish, Portuguese, English, French, Dutch, and Danish—not to mention the independent emancipating republics of Haiti, Brazil, and the United States. These powers were broadly divided in religious traditions between Catholics and Protestants, and their colonies and provinces differed among themselves in the crops they grew, the health and stage of development in their economies, in man-land ratios, and in racial, cultural, and political variables of bewildering complexity. Each of the many emancipations and readjustments involved was a unique historical event, and any valid comparative study will scrupulously respect the integrity of each and avoid facile generalizations. The most natural opportunity for comparison with the experience of the United States, and the one that will most often recur, is that presented by the British West Indies. Most of these colonies shared with the older slave states of the eastern seaboard a history of seventeenth- and eighteenth-century British rule and of populations with similar origins on the black and white sides, together with a common language and many common institutions. Yet, profound differences existed between the society of the island colonies and that of the continental states. Not only that, but probably as many differences existed among the fifteen island colonies that stretched from Jamaica to Trinidad as existed among the fifteen slave states that stretched from Delaware to Texas. The old sugar culture in Barbados, like the old tobacco culture in Virginia, went back to seventeenth-century origins, and, though Guiana and Trinidad were not so new and booming as Louisiana and Mississippi at the time of emancipation, they presented sharp contrasts to the older colonies within the empire. All these differences must be kept in mind when comparisons are ventured.

Since the experience of the United States is central to our concern and its illumination the main purpose of these comparisons, it is well to define first the unique character of its history. In all, some six million slaves were manumitted by the various abolitions of slavery in plantation America between 1834 and 1888. The slave states of the South accounted for four million of them, or about two-thirds of the total. The number liberated in the South was about five times that on the slave rolls of all the British West Indies in 1834 and eight times that of Brazil in 1888 at the time of abolition. In all the Latin American societies, of course, much liberation preceded abolition. Outside the South the slaves of the British West Indies and Brazil made up the two largest single liberated populations. The emancipation experience of the South therefore dwarfs all others in scale and magnitude.

Another unique feature of the southern experience was the high ratio of whites to blacks. In spite of the enormous number of slaves involved, the white population of the South outnumbered the black two to one. It is true that in two states the freedmen were in the majority and in one approached numerical equality, but nowhere save in isolated spots like the South Carolina Sea Islands did blacks reach such overwhelming preponderance as they did in the Caribbean islands, where ratios reached ten to one, though varying greatly. Three-quarters of the southern whites in 1860 did not belong to slaveholding families, and in them the freedmen faced competition and resistance to their aspirations that they faced nowhere else in plantation America. In all other parts of that great area save Brazil (with many uniquenesses of its own), the dominant cultural tradition was that of a small white minority wielding power over the vast black majority; in the South (and even more in the United States as a whole), the culturally dominant tradition was that of the overwhelming white majority.

Of comparable importance is a third circumstance (among many others) that added vastly to the uniqueness of the South's experience. This was the terrible war that brought about the end of slavery. Wars were not without influence on the weakening of the institution elsewhere, for example in Haiti, Cuba, and Brazil. But nowhere else did a slave society wage a life-and-death struggle for its existence with abolition at stake. And no other war in the western world between those of Napoleon and the two world wars compares with the Civil War in bloodshed—one life for every six slaves freed and almost as many lives sacrificed in America as there were slaves liberated in the British West Indies without any bloodshed. The end of slavery in the South can be described as the death of a society, though elsewhere it could more reasonably be characterized as the liquidation of an investment. Of the numerous peculiarities that set apart the South's experience with abolition, then, these three claim special consideration: the magnitude of emancipation, the preponderance of whites, and the association with a terrible war.

Neither in Brazil nor in Cuba is the phenomenon of emancipation related to formal abolition in the way emancipation and abolition are related in the colonies of north European powers—much less in the American South. In the latter areas the slave population generally increased in absolute numbers and usually in proportion to the free population right up to the time of abolition. Then, after periods of "apprenticeship" or semislavery (except in the South), all were simultaneously and legally freed. The situation was strikingly different in Cuba and Brazil. The slave population in Cuba reached its peak forty-five years, and in Brazil thirty-eight years, before formal abolition. The number as well as the proportion of slaves in the total population had been declining in Cuba since 1841, when there were 421,649 slaves, or a third of the total population. During the 1880s they dwindled from some 200,000 to fewer than 30,000 before abolition. The slave population of Brazil reached its peak in 1850, when 2,500,000 constituted about 30 percent of the total population, and before abolition in 1888 the number had declined to 500,000 and the percentage to less than 3.

It is clear that Cuba and Brazil present special problems for the comparative study of emancipations and reconstructions. The most elementary and baffling one is to locate these phenomena in time. It is not a simple choice such as that between 1834 and 1838 as in the case of British emancipation, or between 1863 and 1865 as in the United States. Slavery began to decline in both Cuba and Brazil before the period of abolition laws began, and emancipation had largely run its course before slavery was abolished. In the history of neither of these countries was there any phenomenon like the total emancipation of four millions coinciding with the abolition of slavery that occurred in the American South. Or even the smaller and more gradual process that occurred in the West Indies.

One instance of emancipation remains to be accounted for—one that is an exception to all the others and preceded all the others—that of Haiti, which became the first Negro republic in Western history and the second independent state in the New World. Both emancipation and independence were the products of slave rebellion during the French Revolution, the most successful and the bloodiest slave revolt of modern history. After massacring or driving out all whites, the rulers imposed a tight military control over black labor, dividing all men into laborers or soldiers, making all women laborers, and using the soldiers to impose an iron discipline on workers. With no commitment to tradition and no obligation to foreign white powers, the rulers held a carte blanche for the creation of a new black society and economy. And this is what they created. Emancipation and reconstruction in Haiti involved so many unique circumstances as to make comparisons with its experience of doubtful value.

Statistics on the Atlantic slave trade by Philip D. Curtin illuminate and enrich the comparative study of emancipations and reconstructions. During the whole period of the Atlantic slave trade, legal and illegal, British North America (including Louisiana) received 427,000 or only 4.5 percent of the total imports. This is compared with 4,040,000 or 42.2 percent imported in the Caribbean islands and 3,647,000 or 38.1 percent imported by Brazil. The disparities in imports, especially in view of later slave and Negro populations of the United States and elsewhere, are quite startling. The period of importation is as important for the comparative study of emancipations as the numbers and proportions. For British and North American territory, the legal slave trade ended in 1808. The last years of the trade were the heaviest for many islands, Jamaica importing 63,000 in the last seven years. Illegal trade continued to the United States but added only about 51,000 slaves after 1808. On the other hand, Cuba imported 570,000 between 1808 and 1865. That was 143,000 more than British North America had imported between 1619 and 1860, and it was 80 percent of the total Cuba had imported since the time of Columbus. From 1811 to 1860, Brazil took in 1,145,400 slaves, or nearly a third of its total importation since the sixteenth century and more than three times the number imported by the United States before the legal trade ended in 1808.

Curtin's statistics add a neglected set of variables to the comparative equation and point up additional aspects of uniqueness in the American experience. The 4,000,000 manumitted American slaves of 1865, as well as the 500,000 free blacks, were descendants of 427,000 Africans. The great majority of them were descended from seventeenth- and eighteenth-century stock (mainly the latter), as are their 20,000,000 or so descendants who are our contemporaries. All but a few were at least two generations removed from their African origins at the time of emancipation, and most of them were more than two generations. They were therefore further removed than any other emancipated population of the New World, and they had been through a longer period of adjustment, accommodation, and acculturation to America and to slavery than any other slave population at the time of abolition. It is true that abolition came a generation later in Cuba and Brazil and that slavery began earlier and lasted longer in both countries. But Cuba imported more than four-fifths of its total in the nineteenth century and, according to Fernando Ortiz, continued to import them up to six years before final abolition. For all of the 3,647,000 slaves landed in Brazil over the centuries, the maximum number of 2,500,000 on the slave rolls at any time was reached in 1850 and declined steadily thereafter. Yet nearly half the latter number were purchased after 1810, and only 500,000 remained on the rolls in 1888.

Of all the numerous components of plantation America, therefore, the American South seems to have had a slave population at the time of abolition that was unique in many respects. Not only was it by far the largest population, but it was derived from the smallest imports in proportion to the number emancipated or to the total black population; it was the furthest removed from African origins; and it had the longest exposure to slave discipline in large numbers. It is difficult to imagine any other slave powers, given the origins and circumstances of their slaves, attempting a simultaneous and total emancipation of their slave populations without periods of apprenticeship or other gradualist devices. At any rate, none of them made the attempt. This is not to suggest that the United States itself was prepared for the bold experiment or that the experiment was a success, but merely that this country was the only one that tried and that, though badly prepared, it was still better prepared in at least some respects than were older countries and colonies.

One of the most distinguished minds ever addressed to the problem of the transition from slavery to freedom was that of Alexis de Tocqueville. In July, 1839, he published a report he made to the French Chamber of Deputies on the abolition of slavery in the French colonies. Tocqueville proposed "an intermediate and transitory state between slavery and liberty," which would serve as "a time of trial, during which the Negroes, already possessing many of the privileges of free men, are still compelled to labor." The transition period he thought to be "indispensable to accustom the planters to the effects of emancipation" and "not less necessary to advance the education of the black population, and to prepare them for liberty." This was, he thought, "the most favorable moment to found that empire over the minds and the habits of the black population." Since Tocqueville believed that "only experience of liberty, liberty long possessed," could prepare a man to be "a citizen of a free country," he thought of the basic issue of reconstruction as a cruel dilemma. In words with universal application for our problem, he wrote "The period which follows the abolition of slavery has therefore always been a time of uneasiness and social difficulty. This is an inevitable evil; we must resolve to meet it, or make slavery eternal." Tocqueville resolved his dilemma with a classic paradox: we must, he declared, "if necessary, compel the laborious and manly habits of liberty." Compelling people to be free raised the ancient problem of reconciling force with freedom, its opposite, and that paradox lay at the heart of the problem of emancipations and reconstructions everywhere in the world.

One precedent for our comparative study is a monograph by a Dutch scholar, Wilhelmina Kloosterboer. In *Involuntary Servitude Since the Abolition of Slavery,* she extends her survey beyond plantation America, to which we are mainly limited, and takes in Africa, Asia, and Oceania. She concludes that some system of involuntary or forced labor almost invariably replaced slavery after abolition in all parts of the world. "Where slavery had been widespread," she writes, "emancipation was followed by the imposition of drastic measures to retain a labour force. Apart from other stipulations there was almost in all cases a decree against 'vagrancy' (Jamaica, Mauritius, South Africa, the United States, the Portuguese Colonies, etc.) which in effect always amounted to compulsory labour when strictly applied." The experience of remote and exotic countries will have a familiar ring to those who know the history of Reconstruction in the South. "The harshness of the measures taken in many countries directly after abolition is not surprising since . . . where the use of Negro slaves was widespread and almost essential for the economy, the direct result of abolition was chaos. The Negroes wanted to get away from their old work on the plantation, for to their minds it was slavery under any name; and the climate in most areas concerned was such as to make it possible for them, at least for a while, to live without having to work at all." Freedmen, under whatever flag and of whatever color, resisted signing labor contracts and sought land for themselves. Forceable measures all had the same purpose: to get the freedmen back to the fields—cotton fields, tobacco fields, sugar fields, coffee fields, all kinds of fields—and mines as well. Whether political control was in the hands of an imperial government or a federal government, it is remarkable how little restraint such authority actually exerted in protecting the lives, civil rights, and human rights of the exploited.

One purpose of this study is to test the validity of this thesis and of Tocqueville's speculations and to see what light they throw on the American experience. When Tocqueville made his report to the Chamber of Deputies in 1839, he had foremost in mind, as he said, "the events which are happening in the British colonies surrounding our own." The previous year the British West Indies had prematurely ended their unhappy experiment with apprenticeship as a sequel to abolition. It had displeased all parties—planters, apprentices, and abolitionists. For all the indulgence, which was beyond the wildest dreams of South Carolina and Mississippi planters who formed the black codes of 1865, the West Indian masters behaved remarkably like their continental cousins thirty years later. Like them the islanders complained when their servants retained the work ethic they had learned as slaves: lying, stealing, malingering, laziness, gross carelessness, and wastefulness. Masters alone knew the Negro character, they declared, and looked back to the old regime for models and techniques of discipline. Given the deferred promise of freedom, great tact was required to get freedmen back to work, but tact was not a part of the average overseer's training. He had been schooled, as the governor of Jamaica remarked, in "the diplomacy of the lash," not in the arts of persuasion.

Colonial legislatures framed black codes that put the later southern state legislatures to shame. Jamaican lawmakers made an undefined crime of "insubordination" punishable by thirty-nine lashes or two weeks on the chain gang and defined "vagrancy" as "threatening" to run away from one's family. A police officer could break up any meeting that he had "reasonable cause" to think would stir up insubordination. On that island an apprentice who absented himself from work for two days in a fortnight was subject to a week on the chain gang or twenty lashes. In legislative initiative and defiance, Jamaica was the Mississippi of the Caribbean on matters concerning Negroes, and other islands often followed its example as closely as they dared. The island legislatures displayed all the ingenuity and determination, for which their southern counterparts later became famous, in subverting the purposes of the abolitionists and recapturing their old powers. In this game of defying the Colonial Office of the home government, the colonial governors were thrust into the unhappy role played by the military governors and carpetbag administrators of the southern states. Complaints of the "sullen intractableness" of West Indian assemblies filed with the Colonial Office would have seemed quite familiar in the Washington, D.C., of the 1860s.

Four years of experience with the apprenticeship system brought it into disrepute in many quarters. Dissatisfaction varied from colony to colony, but it was generally argued that relations between labor and planter had deteriorated and that the system had generated bitter new frictions. Negroes complained endlessly about hours of work, mistreatment, and punishment. Their friends reiterated again and again that apprenticeship was only a modified slavery. About the only modification visible in most instances was the removal of the whip, legally at least, from the hands of the overseer— though that did not put an end to flogging. The special magistrates intervened to order flogging done in the workhouses, which was often done with excesses of brutality and bloodiness that were shocking even in a time when corporal punishment was still widely used. A series of books exposing such atrocities appeared in 1837, arousing special horror over the flogging and torture of women on treadmills. British humanitarians convinced people at home that they had been cheated and swindled into paying compensation for slaves who continued under a more brutal slavery. As a training for freedom, apprenticeship had consigned the freedman to compulsory labor that provided no experience of freedom. Returning to the battle, English abolitionists and humanitarians marshaled their forces to put an end to apprenticeship and declare full freedom, which was done in 1838. . . .

The failure of these efforts at full labor control in some islands, such as Jamaica and especially Trinidad and Guiana, was associated with two interrelated conditions: the decline in production and prosperity of the sugar plantations and an abundance of uncultivated land. The first demand of emancipated slaves was always for land. It was so among those of the southern states in 1865, but there the solution more nearly approximated that of Antigua, Barbados, and the Lesser Antilles. In islands with no extra land, the freedmen had little choice but to return to work for the white man. There was extra land in the South, but that which was most available was quickly snatched from their grasp by the frustration of the Freedmen's Bureau plans for distributing abandoned lands, and the less available land was beyond their reach for lack of capital. In Jamaica little more than a third of the arable land was under cultivation at the time of emancipation, and the number of uncultivated acres was annually increased by bankruptcies and the abandonment of plantations. Freedmen could not be kept off these lands, either by law or private agreement. Over the years a substantial independent black peasantry of small landholders developed. The same thing occurred in Trinidad and British Guiana, where even more land was available. All these movements diminished planter control over the blacks. . . .

Much has been made of benevolent Iberian slavery and race relations during slavery as a superior preparation for freedom. Whatever restraint Spain had exerted over Cuban labor policy to protect the blacks came to an end twelve years after abolition, when Cuba won its independence. In effect Cuba won home rule, not so quickly as Jamaica but at precisely the interval after abolition as South Carolina and Louisiana. Home rule in Cuba meant much the same as home rule in Jamaica and Mississippi: the rule of the whites and the exclusion of the blacks. At least the two dominant political parties of independent Cuba proclaimed that to be their purpose. Both came out squarely for white supremacy and agreed that Negroes "constitute a depraved and inferior race which must be kept in its proper place in a white man's society."

Brazilians are especially noted for their claims of racial felicity and patriarchal benevolence. One Brazilian historian maintains that "there was nothing [in Brazil] which can be compared with the period of Reconstruction in the United States." Certainly there were differences, but anyone acquainted with Reconstruction in the South will find in postabolition Brazil much that is comparable. The familiar "mass exodus from the plantations" occurred on schedule. There were the standard days of jubilation and the usual pictures of former slaves "wandering in groups along the roads with no destination," changing plantations, seeking lost relatives and of the old and decrepit, to whom freedom "brought hunger and death" and abandonment by their masters. In the early days the freedmen appeared "disoriented, not knowing what to do with their freedom," many of them "dazed by the rapidity of the transformation." Where possible, planters clung to the old plantation routine. A rumor spread among freedmen that a small plot of land was to be granted each former slave, but nothing came of it. Like southern planters, Brazilians complained that freedmen confused freedom with laziness. Like them too, Brazilian planters avoided creating a black peasantry by refusing to sell them land. Like southerners, they tried the wage system, gave it up, and turned their labor force into sharecroppers under the lien system while planters became supply merchants—the Brazilian-southern escape by compromise from the classic problem of "converting slaves into free laborers." Few know what went on in the backcountry, the depressed sugar country of the northeast, Brazil's counterpart of the American South. A modern writer asks whether slaves there were "really emancipated or merely freed from the name of slave? The fact is that whether he was slave or serf, farmhand, sharecropper or leaseholder, the Brazilian peasant, at least in the Northeast, has always been accustomed to forced labor, hunger, and misery." The long legacy of slavery was much the same here as elsewhere.

There is no space here for comparative analysis of the political ad-

justment to freedom, but it would be more a study of contrast than similarity. For nowhere in plantation America during the nineteenth century
did the white man share with black freedmen the range of political power
and office that the southern whites were forced to share briefly with their
freedmen. Not even in the British West Indies, with their overwhelming
preponderance of blacks, was there anything that could be described as
"Black Reconstruction." In effect the blacks, though nominally emancipated, were quickly eliminated from politics. It is true that a class of
"browns" or "coloreds" did gain a share of office and political power, but
that is another story.

This introduces the infinitely complicated subject of comparative race
relations. To do it justice would require a whole book, but some notice of
it is essential and I shall have to oversimplify. In general, I believe race
prejudice and discrimination were universal in plantation America. I find
very helpful a distinction that a Brazilian scholar, Oracy Nogueira, has
drawn between two models of prejudice, "prejudice of mark" and "prejudice of origin." The latter type, prejudice of origin, in its pure form is
peculiar to the United States. It is directed at anyone, regardless of physical
appearance or personal attribute, known to be in any degree of African
origin. This peculiar white myth of what constitutes a "black" is so universal in the United States as to be accepted by so-called black nationalists.
Elsewhere, particularly in Latin America, prejudice varies according to
"mark," physical or otherwise, and discriminates fastidiously among all
the infinite varieties, as well as personal attributes and attainments, that
amalgamations between Africans and other races can produce. In that sense,
prejudice of mark is literally more discriminating than prejudice of origin,
though the pure black appears to suffer as much exclusion from the one
as from the other type.

The British West Indies fall somewhere between the two models in
their recognition of a separate caste of "coloreds" or "browns" between
whites and blacks, sharing some of the privileges of the former and some
of the penalties of the latter. During the thirty years after abolition, whites
and blacks drifted farther and farther apart into separate cultures, economies, and religions. The coloreds were no help in mediating between races,
for their relations with blacks were worse than those between whites and
blacks. The browns renounced their black heritage and identified with the
whites. The early 1860s were a time of social tension, economic depression,
and natural disasters in Jamaica. The contrast between their former glory
and wealth and their current poverty and misery sent whites in search of
scapegoats. In this search white Jamaicans anticipated the whole demon-
ology of Reconstruction among southern whites, with their own varieties
of carpetbagger, scalawag, missionary, Radical, Freedmen's Bureau, and
most of all the Negro—the lazy good-for-nothing Quashee of the classic
stereotype, to which Thomas Carlyle lent his famous name. The old paternalistic ambivalence of slavery days toward blacks, half genial, half
contemptuous, gave way to feelings of insecurity, fear, and withdrawal.
One source of this was a steady decline in the number of whites, both

absolutely and relatively. By 1861 whites had dropped to 14,000 out of 441,000, only 3.1 percent, and the blacks were rapidly increasing. "In Jamaica," writes Philip Curtin, "the race question was often hidden behind other issues, while in the American South other issues tended to hide behind racial conflict." The blacks of Jamaica seemed stronger and more suspicious in the mid-sixties. A weird religious revival seized them, mixed with economic discontent and protest.

There had been other local riots, bloodshed, and lootings since abolition, but the Morant Bay riot of October, 1865, came in a time of great distress and social tension. It sprang from no revolutionary ideology and was over in two days of sporadic violence that took the lives of 22 and left 34 wounded, some shops looted, and 5 buildings burned—nearly all confined to one parish. But a hysterical governor declared it islandwide, conspiratorial, and insurrectionary and released uninstructed soldiers and colored maroons upon the people. In all they killed 439, many with excessive brutality; flogged 600 men and women with fifty to a hundred lashes, often with cruelly wired whips; and burned 1,000 huts, cottages, and buildings, most of them belonging to the poorest blacks. And then in the ensuing panic the whites voted to abandon what they had held for thirty years essential to their very existence—home rule and self-government—and the Colonial Office, swayed by stories of Negro fiendishness, approved the end of representative government and took over from the frightened planters.

Southerners were destined to repeat many of the errors of Jamaica, but not in their wildest excesses, not even those of New Orleans and Memphis in 1866, did they come near approximating the bloodbath of Morant Bay. The garbled and exaggerated account of the Jamaican tragedy that southern whites read in their newspapers opened an appalling vision of the future. In October, 1865, the whites of the crushed and defeated Confederacy faced with anxiety most of the uncertainties and terrors of their own ordeal of free labor and Negro equality. Would freedmen work without compulsion? Were they prepared for freedom and self-government? Was race war inevitable? For thirty years they had debated with American abolitionists the success of emancipation in the West Indies. The abolitionists felt they had the better of the old argument. But the news from Jamaica in the fall of 1865 seemed to southerners the final word in the old debate, the confirmation of their views: freedom was a failure in the West Indies.

And so it was, in a manner of speaking. And so would the southerners' own more gigantic experiment with freedom fail. And they might have gone further and pointed out its failure throughout plantation America. But failure, like most human experience, is relative. It depends on expectations and promises, on commitments and capabilities. One man's failure is another man's success. And in a way the American failure was the greatest of all. For in 1865 the democratic colossus of the New World stood triumphant, flushed with the terrible victories at Gettysburg, Vicksburg, and Appomattox. Its crusade for freedom had vindicated the blood shed by its sons, and in the full flush of power and victory and righteousness its leaders solemnly pledged the nation to fulfill its promises, not only of freedom but also the full measure of democracy and racial equality. The powers of fulfillment, sealed by the sacrifices of a victorious war, were seemingly unlimited, though of course they were not. At least the federal government was no remote transatlantic metropolitan parliament on the banks of the Thames or the Seine. It sat on the Potomac, with General Robert E. Lee's Arlington mansion in full view of the White House windows across the river, and its armies garrisoned the defeated states.

Yet we know that, although the North won its four-year war against a fully armed, mobilized, and determined South when the issue was slavery, it very quickly lost its crusade against a disarmed, defeated, and impoverished South when the issue was equality. For on this issue the South was united as it had not been on slavery. And the North was even more divided on the issue of equality than it had been on slavery. In fact, when the chips were down, the overwhelmingly preponderant views of the North on that issue were in no important respect different from those of the South—and never had been.

Before Sherman: Georgia Blacks and the Union War Effort, 1861–1864

CLARENCE L. MOHR

The collapse of slavery in Georgia has traditionally been identified with General William Tecumseh Sherman's devastating march from Atlanta to the sea during the autumn of 1864. According to some estimates as many as nineteen thousand bondsmen fled to freedom behind Sherman's advancing columns, thereby inflicting a crippling blow upon Georgia slavery if not on southern independence itself. In reality, however, Sherman's march to the sea represented the end rather than the beginning of black defections from Confederate Georgia. The most revealing escapes occurred earlier in the war and involved black people on or near the Georgia seaboard. Unlike the thousands of Negroes who followed Sherman's conquering army to Savannah, blacks reaching Union lines earlier in the war were usually the instruments of their own deliverance. The timing and method of their escape efforts were matters of conscious choice, and their decision to strike out for liberty meant risking recapture, punishment, and even death in case of failure. By looking for patterns in these early escapes and by examining the statements and actions of successful fugitives one can learn much about the culture, values, and aspirations of black Georgians on the eve of emancipation.

Escape from the seaboard became possible early in 1862 when northern naval and military forces bloodlessly captured Georgia's deserted Sea Islands. Ignoring an intense campaign of anti-Yankee atrocity stories, local

Clarence L. Mohr, "Before Sherman: Georgia Blacks and the Union War Effort, 1861–1864" from *Journal of Southern History* 3 (August 1979), pp. 331–352. Copyright 1979 by the Southern Historical Association. Reprinted by permission of the Managing Editor.

blacks immediately began making their way to Union-held territory. Hard-pressed sailors in the South Atlantic Blockading Squadron gave the refugees protection and assistance but recorded their arrival rather haphazardly. Consequently, only a small fraction (perhaps 25 percent) of the slaves and free Negroes who fled Georgia during this early period were mentioned in official documents.

The disparity between actual and reported incidents of escape is illustrated by population data from a settlement of black refugees on St. Simons Island near the mouth of the Altamaha River. Established by the Union navy in March 1862, the St. Simons settlement (officially designated a "colony") was only one of several locations to which escaped slaves from Georgia were taken. In the space of some nine months the island's black population grew from none to nearly 600, but during this same period the total number of black escapees reported by military and naval commanders on station off the Georgia coast was only 144, or about a fourth of the black population of St. Simons alone. By the most conservative estimates, then, commanders of individual blockading vessels failed to record some 70 to 80 percent of the Georgia fugitives who passed through their hands.

Whether or not this ratio remained constant throughout the thirty months preceding Sherman's invasion is uncertain. If it did and if three out of four black escapees went unreported, then the 561 Georgia slaves and free Negroes known to have reached Union lines from December 1861 through October 1864 would represent a total of 2,000 to 2,500 actual escapees. If one assumes, on the other hand, that the volume of escapes declined and the efficiency of reporting increased markedly after 1862, an estimate of 1,000 black refugees for the entire period would still be well within reason.

Whatever the precise number of refugees may have been, enough escapes were reported to reveal clear trends in several key areas. For purposes of analysis, escape efforts may, at the outset, be separated into two basic categories: (1) those conceived and initiated by blacks without initial Union assistance (hereafter designated "black initiated" escapes) and (2) those occurring during Union coastal or river raids (hereafter designated "rescues"). Out of a total of fifty-six reported escape incidents some forty-two fall within the first category. These "black-initiated" efforts involved 290 individuals, or roughly 45 percent of the 650 known Georgia fugitives. The volume and frequency of black-initiated escape efforts varied considerably over time. Whereas "rescue" incidents simply mirrored the pace of Union military operations along Georgia's coast, black-initiated efforts were concentrated most heavily during the first nine to twelve months after the arrival of Federal blockading vessels. The number of such incidents declined slowly throughout 1863 and dwindled to almost nothing after the first three months of 1864.

This pattern suggests that logistical factors were of central importance in determining the rate of black escapes. There was, for example, no perceptible increase in escape attempts following the issuance of the final Emancipation Proclamation in January 1863. To most black Georgians freedom was a condition rather than a theory, and in Georgia, as in neighboring South Carolina, Negroes who reached the Sea Islands were virtually free from the moment of their arrival. What varied in Georgia was not the desire of black people for liberty but their physical opportunity to obtain it. Black-initiated escapes were most numerous in 1862 because the number of blacks near the Georgia seaboard was larger then than at any subsequent period of the war. By 1863 nearly all coastal planters had moved their slaves well inland to areas where escape was difficult if not impossible. The impressment of 1,500 black laborers to work on Savannah's defenses in the summer of 1862 further increased the pool of potential escapees, while the Union navy's black settlement on St. Simons Island offered tangible proof of northern willingness to grant fugitives a sanctuary.

The size and composition of escape groups were even more revealing than their frequency. In antebellum days the typical runaway episode involved a young, healthy male traveling northward alone. The fugitive's major physical obstacle was distance, and the most crippling psychological barrier he faced was the pain of abandoning home, friends, and family. This picture changed drastically, however, when Union blockading forces reached Georgia's coast in 1862. With freedom then as close as the Union-controlled Sea Islands, escaping ceased to be a solitary endeavor. Adult men continued to lead or participate in most defections, but statistics reveal a clear trend toward collective escape efforts involving family groups or, occasionally, plantation communities.

Relevant information is available for a total of forty-two separate black-initiated escape incidents involving some 290 people. Thirty-two of the escapees fled Georgia alone or in company with one other person; 249 of the remaining 258 black fugitives (some 86 percent of the total) reached or attempted to reach the Sea Islands in groups of three or more. Although the specific age and sexual makeup of these groups was seldom recorded, surviving evidence suggests that most of the large parties included women and children as well as men. In 1862, for example, the black refugee population on St. Simons Island grew from 26 men, 6 women, and 9 children in late March to 60 men, 16 women, and 13 children by mid-April. When abolitionist clergyman Mansfield French visited the island in July a total of 52 black children were presented for baptism during one afternoon service. Susie King Taylor, an ex-slave from Savannah, recalled that by the time she left St. Simons in October a majority of its 600 inhabitants were women and children.

Strict policing made mass escapes more difficult in 1863, but black families continued to flee. In July "two or three families" of free Negroes from Darien, Georgia, reached Union lines together with "four slaves whom they owned." Nineteen blacks from Samuel N. Papot's plantation near Savannah were less successful in October, when their boat was captured by Confederate pickets. Approximately one-third of the would-be escapees in this group were men, the rest women and children. In late December 1863 thirteen black fugitives from McIntosh County, Georgia, were taken aboard the U.S.S. *Fernandina* in St. Catherines Sound. The leader of the party was a twenty-seven-year-old slave named Cain, who, like most of the escapees, had formerly belonged to William King. Accompanying Cain was the twenty-two-year-old woman Bella and her six-year-old son Romeo, the twenty-five-year-old woman Lizzie and her four children (Joseph, Sam, Eve, and Martha, aged twelve years, four years, two years, and five months, respectively), and finally the thirty-two-year-old woman Sallie with her four children (Fannie, Joseph, Emma, and Ben, who ranged in age from eleven years to seven months). Early in 1864 Cain left the *Fernandina* to rescue his relatives from the vicinity of Sunbury, Georgia. He returned on January 7, along with ex-slave Sam, bringing the forty-five-year-old woman Grace, her five children (Judy, Elizabeth, Phoebe, Victoria, and James), her son-in-law Charley, and her grandchildren (Arphee, Virginia, Clarissa, and Edward).

Under the best of circumstances black-initiated escape efforts were risky, a fact graphically illustrated by the failure of some eighty-nine Georgia fugitives to reach Union lines. From a purely pragmatic standpoint the lone young black man probably continued to stand the best chance of escape throughout most of the war. By including women, children, or old people in escape parties, therefore, black Georgians repeatedly showed their willingness to place family and group loyalty above individual self-interest. A typical episode occurred in September 1862 following the successful escape of twenty-three slaves from plantations on both sides of the Savannah River. The main party paddled their way to freedom in a large canoe, but two men, one woman, and a child failed to reach the boat on time and were left behind to face pursuers. A Georgia planter reported the grim outcome in a private letter. Overtaken while fording a creek, the group refused to stop, whereupon "Bob, who was leading, was shot in the leg and immediately taken. Peter was also fired at and fell" but fled deeper into the marshes in a "wounded condition." After a "pursuit of 3 or 4 miles" the woman and child "became exhausted" and surrendered but refused to reveal the hiding place of their wounded companion.

More successful escapes also underscored the importance of family ties among Georgia's black refugees. An abolitionist officer from Massachusetts recalled three or four brothers in a black family named Wilson who planned a daring escape from the interior of Georgia. Leaving their youngest brother behind to look after an aged mother, the other men, in company with their sister and her children, fled downriver in a log dugout. Before reaching the coast the boat came under heavy fire from Confederate pickets, who wounded every male occupant of the open craft. Despite their injuries the men eventually completed the voyage and reached the safety of Federal gunboats. Even more striking was the case of a seventy-year-old Georgia black woman, who, after failing in one escape attempt, assembled her twenty-two children and grandchildren on an abandoned flatboat and drifted forty miles down the Savannah River to freedom. When rescued by a Union vessel "the grandmother rose to her full height, with her youngest grandchild in her arms, and said only, 'My God! are we free?' "

If family commitments shaped the pattern of wartime escape efforts they also influenced the nature and scope of black support for the Union cause. Nowhere was the importance of family ties more evident than in the realm of actual military service. Northern recruiters discovered early that the prospect of securing the freedom of friends and relatives was a powerful inducement for blacks to join Union ranks. Or, taking the opposite viewpoint, blacks soon discovered that the Union army offered an effective vehicle for rescuing family members still held in bondage. Thomas Wentworth Higginson, who commanded numerous black Georgians in the famous First South Carolina Volunteers, candidly admitted that his soldiers "had more to fight for than [did] the whites. Besides the flag and the Union, they had home and wife and child." A northern official who spent the summer and fall of 1862 with Georgia blacks on St. Simons Island fully confirmed this judgment. In early October he attended a Negro "war meeting" at St. Helena village, where several speakers including one black man addressed an assembly of ex-slaves:

> They were asked to enlist for pay, rations and uniform, to fight for their country, for freedom and so forth, but not a man stirred. But when it was asked them to fight for themselves, to enlist to protect their wives and children from being sold away from them, and told of the little homes which they might secure to themselves and their families in after years, they all rose to their feet, the men came forward and said "I'll go," the women shouted, and the old men said "Amen."

Family considerations were clearly uppermost in the minds of many black Georgians as they embarked on their first combat mission in November 1862. At the staging area on St. Catherines Island the former bondsmen "needed no 'driver's lash' . . . for they were preparing to go up Sapelo River, along whose banks on the beautiful plantations, were their fathers, mothers, brothers, sisters, wives and children. Weeks and months before some of the men had left those loved ones, with a promise to return . . ." if the way were opened. A white observer who accompanied the expedition up river found it "very affecting" to see the soldiers gaze "intensely [at] the colored forms on land," frequently calling out such things as "Oh, masir, my wife and chillen lib dere" or "dere, dere my brodder." When the ships were unable to take away slaves from certain plantations the disappointment of relatives on board was acute and virtually "inexpressible (except by sighs)."

Some black Georgians were unwilling to risk such disappointments and took the business of rescuing friends and relatives into their own hands. One of the first to adopt this self-help philosophy was ex-slave March Haynes, who functioned unofficially within the military command structure of the Department of the South. Described as "a pure, shrewd, brave efficient man," Haynes was literate and had worked as a stevedore and river pilot in antebellum Savannah. "Comprehending the spirit and scope of the war," Haynes began smuggling Georgia fugitives into Union lines shortly after the fall of Fort Pulaski in April 1862. When white suspicions against him became too great, he fled Savannah with his wife but continued his rescue efforts from the Sea Islands. Although the term "commando" did not exist in the military vocabulary of the 1860s, Haynes's activities fit neatly under this modern rubric. General Quincy Adams Gillmore of the Tenth Army Corps recognized the value of Haynes's services and "furnished him with whatever he needed in his perilous missions," including a "staunch, swift boat, painted a drab color, like the hue of the Savannah River." Allowed to "select such negroes to assist him as he thought proper," Haynes landed repeatedly "in the marshes below Savannah" and entered the city under cover of darkness. Sheltered and supplied by local blacks, he sometimes remained for several days collecting "exact and valuable information" on the strength and location of Confederate defenses. He also made night reconnaissances "up the creeks along the Savannah, gathering information and bringing away boat-loads of negroes." On one expedition Haynes was shot in the leg by Confederate pickets and in April 1863 was apparently arrested and temporarily jailed by Savannah authorities.

Liberating friends and relatives was only one of many motives for black enlistment in Union ranks. Nearly all Negro soldiers shared a basic hatred of bondage and a desire to strike out directly at the slave system. Undoubtedly, some ex-slaves viewed military service as an opportunity both to demonstrate personal courage and to consummate the process of self-emancipation by meeting white southerners in battle. Yet even the most dedicated abolitionists admitted that black attitudes toward former masters were ambivalent and complex. Upon reaching the Sea Islands in 1862, for instance, Colonel Higginson "expected to find a good deal of the patriarchal feeling" among local Negroes but discovered instead a very different and more discriminating attitude. Many former slaves did indeed claim "to have had kind owners and some expressed great gratitude to them for particular favors received" during slavery. To these same black people, however, the central fact of being owned was "a wrong which no special kindness could right." Thus, whatever their feelings toward individual whites, they looked upon the mass of slaveholders as their "natural enemies." Confederate observers like Mrs. James Sanchez of Florida confirmed the existence of a generalized hostility toward slaveholders among black escapees. In early 1863, while traveling to Georgia under a flag of truce, Mrs. Sanchez was detained briefly at Union-occupied Fort Pulaski. "The negroes there were far more insolent than the [white] soldiers," she reported. The blacks "took great pleasure in insulting the whites; cursing the 'd—n rebel secesh women and men' and laughing in their faces."

Such racial antagonisms often went hand in hand with personal grievances against former owners. Higginson mentions several black Georgians who seethed with anger over slave experiences and whose desire for revenge steeled their courage on the battlefield. For some bondsmen the war was quite literally an extension of earlier rebellious activities. The theory that black defection to Federal lines acted as a "safety valve" against slave uprisings within the Confederacy finds at least partial confirmation in the career of a militant black runaway named Nat. Owned by a planter in Glynn

County, Georgia, Nat left his master some time in 1860 and remained at large for the next four years. By the summer of 1862 he had reached St. Simons Island, where he engaged in operations somewhat similar to those of March Haynes. Described by white Savannahians as a "notorious runaway . . . and rascal," Nat was ultimately accused of killing one white civilian and two Confederate soldiers. In his most daring wartime exploit he led six other black men some thirty miles up the Altamaha River to rescue their wives and children from bondage. In the course of the expedition he fought off white attackers twice and exchanged gunfire with a Confederate river patrol. Even after most black refugees had been moved to Port Royal, Nat remained on St. Simons and soon joined forces with another slave rebel named Harvey. Denounced on the mainland as "spies, murderers, incendiaries and thieves," the pair survived until June 1864, when both fell victim to a shotgun-wielding southern soldier. At the time of Nat's death Georgia whites held him responsible for the escape of from seventy to a hundred slaves from the coastal counties.

Whether or not they were rebels before the war, Georgia's black soldiers were ready to redress past wrongs if the opportunity arose. During the 1862 Sapelo River expedition, for example, black troops singled out the plantation of Captain William Brailsford for a special retaliatory attack. Brailsford, a wealthy cotton planter, known for his flamboyance and fiery temper, had succeeded Georgia slave trader Charles Augustus Lafayette Lamar as captain of the Savannah Mounted Rifles in 1861. By July of the following year he was actively engaged in a campaign to recapture slaves from the Georgia Sea Islands. After Union officers refused his request to return black fugitives from St. Simons, Brailsford descended on St. Catherines Island with thirty armed men in October 1862, killing two black refugees and capturing four others.

The memory of this attack was still fresh in the minds of black soldiers as they ascended the Sapelo early the next month. Even without the St. Catherines raid Brailsford would probably still have been a marked man, for on board the Union gunboats were several of Brailsford's former slaves, including Sam Miller, who had been whipped severely by the hot-tempered planter for refusing to betray another escapee. Since Brailsford's plantation was also a major Confederate picket station Union officers agreed after "full consultation" to destroy the place during their retreat. Landing after sunset the black troops routed a strong force of defenders and pushed inland nearly half a mile, burning cabins, outbuildings, and finally the Brailsford mansion itself. When interviewed immediately after the attack, morale among the black soldiers was high. Some spoke of having "grown three inches," while Sam Miller said simply, "I feel a heap more of a man."

If the alliance between Georgia blacks and the Union military was cemented with blood, it was also constructed upon the shifting foundation of pragmatic self-interest. Throughout most of the war the aims and goals of northern commanders corresponded neatly with individual priorities and racial or group loyalties of black refugees. So long as this community of interest existed black allegiance to the Stars and Stripes remained strong.

When Federal policies ceased to be mutually beneficial, however, black cooperation and white benevolence declined proportionately. The process was visible on St. Simons Island during the spring and summer of 1862 when naval authorities set out to make the black colony self-supporting. Shortly after the first blacks were landed on St. Simons in March Commander Sylvanus W. Godon decided they should "procure their own living from the land . . ." and ordered them also "to plant cotton and thus . . . become of use to themselves." By mid-April some eighty acres of corn plus additional fields of potatoes and beans were under cultivation, and in late May Godon reported triumphantly that "Thus far the Government has not spent a dollar on these people. . . ." Actually, the government probably did more than just break even, for by late July St. Simons's black residents had planted three hundred acres of food crops and picked 25,000 pounds of valuable Sea Island cotton.

The navy's agricultural achievement fell considerably short of being a genuine cooperative effort. Godon quickly discovered that black refugees showed "a great dislike to do the work they have been accustomed to . . ." under slavery. Toiling daily in the abandoned plantation fields seemed "to make their condition the same as before," and appointing an ex-slave to direct the work accomplished little because even the black foreman needed "pushing" and "indulges his men too much away from the care of fields . . . ." Ultimately, Godon's solution to the problem was simple and direct. "Where work is neglected my rule has been to stop off the ration of beef or something else," he wrote in late June; adding "and I have also placed men in irons for punishment."

If Godon's heavy-handed methods produced results, they did little to build black trust in the motives of the Federal officials. Confidence was further eroded by the navy's inability to shield the St. Simons settlement from Confederate attack. Naval officers did their best to protect the island, but black refugees seemed more impressed by the flintlock muskets they received for self-defense than by the navy's good intentions. In May 1862 a large Confederate force actually landed on St. Simons but was repulsed at the last moment by fire from a newly arrived Union gunboat. The island's black residents took the lesson to heart, and when a second rebel attack occurred in August the ex-slaves seized the initiative.

Ironically, the second Confederate landing on St. Simons coincided almost exactly with the arrival of some thirty-eight black soldiers from Port Royal, who were all that remained of General David Hunter's recently disbanded Negro regiment. Still lacking any official military status, the troops and their white commander Charles T. Trowbridge were eager for a chance to prove themselves in battle. Grabbing their knapsacks and cartridge boxes "with alacrity," the men came ashore only to discover that twenty-five local blacks were already armed and in pursuit of the invaders. According to one writer the action was "entirely a spontaneous thing." No white man accompanied the local defenders, who were commanded, instead, by two of their own number, John Brown and Edward Gould. Overtaking the invaders in a swamp, the ex-slaves fought a brief engagement and suffered several casualties including their leader John Brown, who was killed.

The August encounter was not the end of local defense efforts on St. Simons. When Captain Trowbridge's company left the island in early November, shortly before being mustered into Union service, the seventy or so black men who remained behind took further precautions against attack. "Immediately they organized a guard on each plantation, appointed their own sergeant or leader, and guarded the island day and night" until its evacuation five weeks later. The men met for drill each afternoon at Thomas Butler King's plantation, where assignments for night guard duty were also made. Even during this final period the defenders did not rely on government support and received neither clothing, pay, nor rations. . . .

Despite [its] unattractive pay rates the Union army . . . received its full share of Georgia recruits. Particularly valuable were the services of Abraham [or Abram] Murchison, a literate slave preacher from Savannah, who helped initiate the first recruiting efforts among black refugees on Hilton Head Island, South Carolina, in early 1862. After a private interview with General David Hunter, Murchison called a meeting of all black males on April 7, where the prospect of military service was first broached to the former bondsmen. Murchison addressed this meeting, explaining with "clearness and force . . . the obligations and interests" which should induce blacks to take up arms for the Union. A New York *Times* correspondent reported that Murchison's language on occasion "rose to eloquence . . ." as he described "the labors, hardships and dangers, as well as the advantages of soldier life . . . ." At the conclusion of his address 105 recruits were enrolled, and within a week the number of volunteers had reached 150.

Perhaps because of age, Murchison did not join the army himself but remained on Hilton Head throughout the war, serving as the religious and secular leader of local blacks. A Baptist during slavery, Murchison was formally ordained by Union army chaplains and reportedly baptized more than a thousand freedmen in Port Royal harbor during the war. By 1864 he had also become a pivotal figure in the self-governing black village of Mitchelville, where under army auspices he exercised the powers of magistrate. At night the village was off limits to all whites, and the black soldiers of the provost guard were placed under Murchison's control to make arrests for disorderly conduct. When Mitchelville residents held their first election in 1865 two black Georgians headed the ticket. March Haynes, the daring spy and commando, was elected marshal, while Abraham Murchison assumed the duties of recorder.

The men Murchison had helped recruit in April 1862 formed the nucleus of General Hunter's ill-fated black regiment which, as mentioned earlier, survived only in the form of a thirty-eight-man company sent to St. Simons Island. In November 1862 this hardy remnant, augmented by thirty to forty Georgia recruits from St. Simons, was mustered into service as Company A of the First South Carolina Volunteers. Company E was also composed largely of refugees from St. Simons, and black Georgians were scattered throughout the rest of the regiment. The mandatory conscription of Sea Island Negroes begun in 1863 ensured that Georgia bondsmen would ultimately find their way into all the black regiments raised in the Department of the South. Recruiting for Colonel James Montgomery's Second South Carolina regiment occurred mostly in Florida, but during June 1863 a special draft for the Third South Carolina Volunteers was conducted at Ossabaw Island and Fort Pulaski, Georgia, as well as at Fernandina, Florida, near Georgia's southern border. This regiment, which was soon consolidated with the embryonic Fourth and Fifth South Carolina Volunteers to form the Twenty-first United States Colored Troops, numbered slightly over three hundred men until December 1864, when its ranks were filled by black Georgians who had followed General Sherman to Savannah.

In addition to purely military training the army provided some blacks with valuable leadership experience and allowed many others to begin or expand their formal education. Much of the educational work was carried on by literate ex-slaves like Sergeant Edward King of Darien, Georgia, and his young wife Susie, who also served the regiment as nurse and laundress [see Susie King Taylor document in Chapter 9]. Although involved in no decisive military campaigns, the "First South" nonetheless acquitted itself well in numerous raids and partisan expeditions from the Edisto River to the St. Johns. Perhaps most important, the black troops' solid performance under close public scrutiny paved the way for slave enlistments throughout the South.

Students of both slavery and Reconstruction can gain valuable insights from the wartime behavior of Georgia's black refugees. Viewed from an antebellum perspective the escape and subsequent military service of many black Georgians underscore the importance of slave family ties and simultaneously cast doubt on the depth of black commitment to the paternalist ethic. On the pivotal questions of how southern bondsmen viewed the nature of the war and the meaning of emancipation the Georgia experience is particularly revealing. Some black fugitives may, as Joel R. Williamson argues, have "fled not so much to freedom as away from slavery," but the weight of surviving evidence suggests that most participants in well-planned and deliberately executed efforts to escape had a far more definite concept of liberty. From the outset blacks on the Sea Islands adopted a pragmatic stance which defined freedom in terms of immediate and tangible realities; family stability, physical security, freedom of movement, the right to determine one's own work and living arrangements, and the opportunity for education were apparently central concerns for numerous Georgia escapees.

To recognize that newly freed blacks had a clear sense of priorities is not necessarily to argue that their view of postemancipation life was sophisticated or fully defined. In certain realms black behavior was little more than an extension of familiar slave survival strategies altered or reshaped in the crucible of wartime chaos and uncertainty. There can be little doubt, however, that for the thousands of freedmen who took possession of Georgia's coastal and Sea Island region under the auspices of General Sherman's famous Field Order 15 much more was ultimately at stake than the simple issue of landownership. At its most elemental level the Georgia freedmen's ill-fated struggle for political power and economic independence can probably best be understood as a quest for collective autonomy, tempered by a largely defensive impulse toward racial separatism. In this broad objective, as well as in regard to more specific goals, the freedmen of 1865 shared much in common with those black Georgians who seized their liberty before the coming of Sherman.

Back to Work: The New Dependency

LEON F. LITWACK

The transition to free labor [was] seldom . . . smooth . . . . Not only was the situation without any clear precedent but the sharp divisions of race and class, exacerbated by the heritage of slavery and wartime memories, were bound to complicate the new relationship of white employer and black laborer. "I do not like the negro as well free as I did as a slave," a Virginian conceded, "for the reason that there is now between us an antagonism of interest to some extent, while, before, his interest and mine were identical. Then, I was always thinking of how I could fix him comfortably. Now, I find myself driving a hard bargain with him for wages; and I find that sort of feeling suggested directly by motives of interest coming in between the employer and the employed." When the former master came around to compensated labor, he would have to calculate precisely how much his ex-slaves were worth to him as free workers. That created some obvious conflicts, with employers and laborers entertaining different notions of value and both determined to stand by their estimates. "They have what seem to me to be extravagant ideas as to what they ought to receive," a North Carolinian observed, and scores of planters would register the same complaint. But surely, some freedmen suggested, they should not be worth any less now than the price for which their masters had occasionally hired them out as slaves. If the planter pleaded financial difficulties, as so many did, the freedmen had only to look out into the fields and calculate the value of the expected crops. "Massa fust said he find all de famly food and house for our work," a Virginia black remarked; "den I think that, as him grow 4,000 bushels corn, near 10,000 lbs. clover, and odder tings 'sides, he can 'ford to pay me better dan dat, so I no go with him. Me tell him me worth more, and p'raps he give me some of crop."

Accustomed to holding the upper hand in all dealings with blacks, the former slaveholder preferred to make his own decision about compensation rather than suffer the audaciousness of freedmen who confronted him with demands or ultimatums. In his region, a Florida farmer and physician revealed, the planters usually refused to pay "any who demand it" but several had promised to supply their freedmen with provisions at the end of the year if they worked faithfully. Even relationships of long standing, which had survived the war and the first years of emancipation, could fall apart when the ex-slave raised the question of additional pay. Within that tightly knit Jones clan of Georgia, for example, Kate had remained "faithful" to Mary Jones's daughter while many others defected. Not until late in 1867 did she assert herself on the wage question: "I wish to tell you if you will give me twelve dollars per month [an increase of three dollars] I will stay with you; but if not, I have had good offers and I will find another place." Despite the years of loyal, unpaid labor this servant had rendered, the mistress of the household turned down her request for a raise. When Kate then left her, the mistress noted that she did so "with a very impertinent air."

The sheer novelty of free black labor introduced complexities and nuances into the issues that traditionally separated employers and workers. The proposed compensation mattered less to some freedmen than what form it would take (crop shares or cash), when it would be paid (monthly or after completion of the crop), and the often arbitrary nature of the employer's deductions (for the provisions he supplied and the fines he levied for negligent work). Of equally vital concern to the freedman might be the kinds of crops he could now grow (the old staples or food), the quality of the provisions he received, the availability of schools for his children, the right to unrestricted travel, and freedom from verbal and physical abuse. Inseparable from all these considerations, and for many the most crucial, was the degree of personal autonomy he could now enjoy. The only way to keep the ex-slaves on the plantations without compromising their freedom, the *New Orleans Tribune* boldly suggested, was not simply to compensate them but to make them full partners in the management and in the crop yields; freedom implied the abolition of both "slaves" and "masters," the "democratization" of the plantations, and the opportunity for blacks to control their own crops, lands, and lives. Unless "the necessary step" was taken to free the workingman, the newspaper concluded, emancipation would remain "a mockery and a sham." By "the necessary step," the editor envisioned the free colored community of New Orleans investing their money in land and managing that land in partnership with the former slaves, who would perform the labor.

Early in the postwar period, at least, that ultimate question of who controlled the crops and the lands remained unresolved in the minds of many freedmen. After noting that planters now intended to pay their ex-slaves with crop shares, Henry M. Turner, the outspoken black clergyman, refused to applaud their action; instead, he dismissed the proposal as an "ingenious trickery . . . designed to keep the old master fat doing nothing, making the Yankees believe 'dis old nigga no wants to leave massa', and for the purpose of fizzling them out of all their claims upon the real estate." Rather than settle for compensation in wages or shares, the freedmen in some areas were already insisting that the crops they had planted in 1865, if not the land itself, rightfully belonged to them. "Some of them," wrote the police chief in Duplin County, North Carolina, "are declaring they intend to have lands, even if they shed blood to obtain them. Some of them are demanding all of the crop they have raised on the former master's lands, and in some cases, so obstinate are they in these demands, that I have had to arrest them before they would come to terms."

With emancipation, many former slaves obviously sensed a new power and evinced a determination to test it. The mere offer of compensation would not assure the employers of a stable and contented labor force. To pay them for their labor, after all, did not resolve all fundamental questions about authority, autonomy, and control of the land. Whether provoked by a wage dispute or some other grievance, freedmen continued to leave the old places, sometimes en masse. Still more remained and worked indifferently, reserving any enthusiasm they might have for their own individual garden plots. Looking at those small gardens, which they had tended and cherished as slaves, many freedmen had heard enough to imagine them expanded into forty-acre farms. That remained the most exciting prospect of all, exceeding in importance and in emotional investment any question of wages.

Shortly after the fall of Richmond, the scene acted out on the nearby Rosewood plantation posed the problem a number of landowners would have to face soon enough. After having promised to remain and work, a freedman named Cyrus absented himself from the fields. When Emma Mordecai, the plantation mistress, questioned him about his conduct, he replied by advancing his own perception of how matters stood between them.

> Seems lak we'uns do all the wuck and gits a part. Der ain't goin' ter be no more Master and Mistress, Miss Emma. All is equal. I done hear it from de cotehouse steps. . . . All de land belongs to de Yankees now, and dey gwine to divide it out 'mong de colored people. Besides, de kitchen ob de big house is my share. I help built hit.

Even as they toiled in the same fields, performed the familiar tasks, and returned at dusk to the same cabins, scores of freedmen refused to resign themselves to the permanent status of a landless agricultural working-class. Like most Americans, they aspired to something better and yearned for economic independence and self-employment. Without that independence, their freedom seemed incomplete, even precarious. "Every colored man will be a slave, & feel himself a slave," a black soldier insisted, "until he can raise him own bale of cotton & put him own mark upon it & say dis is mine!" Although often expressed vaguely, as if to talk about it openly might be unwise, the expectation many ex-slaves shared in the aftermath of the war was that "something extraordinary" would soon intervene to reshape the course of their lives. In the Jubilee they envisioned, the government provided them with forty-acre lots and thereby emancipated them from dependency on their former masters. "This was no slight error, no trifling idea," a Freedmen's Bureau officer reported from Mississippi in 1865, "but a fixed and earnest conviction as strong as any belief a man can ever have." The feeling was sufficiently pervasive, in fact, to prompt thousands of freedmen in late 1865 to hold back on any commitment of their labor until the question of land had been firmly resolved.

The only real question among some blacks was not whether the lands belonging to the former slaveholders would be divided and distributed, but when and how. Freedmen in South Carolina heard that the large plantations along the coast were to be distributed. Equally persistent reports suggested that the lands on which the ex-slaves were working would be divided among them. Few blacks in Mississippi, a Bureau officer reported in November 1865, expressed any interest in hiring themselves out for the next year. "Nearly all of them have heard, that at Christmas, Government is going to take the planters' lands and other property from *them,* and give it to the colored people, and that, in this way they are going to begin to farm on their own account." In a Virginia community, the freedmen had reportedly deposited their savings with "responsible" persons so as to be in the most advantageous position to purchase lots of "de confiscated land, as soon as de Gov'ment ready to sell it." And in Georgia a black laborer was so certain that he "coolly" offered to sell to his former master the share of the plantation he expected to receive "after the division."

Although confident of retaining their lands, planters expressed growing concern over the extent to which the freedmen's aspirations interfered with the normalization of agricultural operations. It proved difficult to raise crops when laborers went about "stuffed with the idea of proprietorship" and the anticipation of soon becoming their own employers. "You cannot beat into their thick skulls that the land & every thing else does not belong to them," a South Carolina planter wrote his daughter. Since many whites refused to believe their blacks capable of formulating perceptions of freedom, they blamed the land mania on "fanatical abolitionists," incendiary preachers, and the Yankee invaders. But those who had overheard the "curious" wartime discussions in which the blacks apportioned the lands among themselves knew better, as did the victims of black expropriation. Where planters had fled, abandoning their properties, the freed slaves had in numerous instances seized control and they gave little indication after the war of yielding their authority to the returning owners. Along the Savannah River, blacks under the leadership of Abalod Shigg seized two major plantations on the assumption that they were entitled to "forty acres and a mule." Federal troops had to be called in to dislodge them. Elsewhere, similar seizures revealed the intensity of black feelings about the land and created a volatile situation that many native whites and Federal officials feared might erupt into armed confrontations.

As if to confirm black land aspirations, the Federal government adopted an ambitious settlement program in direct response to the thousands of unwanted and burdensome freed slaves who had attached themselves to the Union Army in the wake of General Sherman's march to the sea. On January 12, 1865, Sherman and Secretary of War Stanton conferred with twenty black ministers and church officers in Savannah to ascertain what could be done about these people. The delegation suggested that land was the key to black freedom. "We want to be placed on land until we are able to buy it, and make it our own," the spokesmen for the group declared. Several days later, Sherman issued Special Field Order No. 15, a far-reaching document that set aside for the exclusive use of the freedmen a strip of coastal land abandoned by Confederate owners between Charleston, South Carolina, and Jacksonville, Florida, granting black settlers "possessory titles" to forty-acre lots. Although intended only to deal with a specific military and refugee problem, the order encouraged the growing impression among the freedmen that their Yankee liberators intended to provide them with an essential undergirding for their emancipation. That impression gained still further credence when Congress made the newly established Freedmen's Bureau the custodian of all abandoned and confiscated land (largely the lands seized for nonpayment of the direct Federal tax or belonging to disloyal planters who had fled); ex-slaves and loyal Unionists could pre-empt forty-acre lots, rent them at nominal rates for three years, and purchase them within that period at a fair price (about sixteen times the annual rent). If the Bureau had implemented this provision, and if blacks had been able to accumulate the necessary funds, some 20,000 black families would have been provided with the means for becoming self-sustaining farmers.

To apportion the large landed estates among those who worked them and who had already expended years of uncompensated toil made such eminent sense to the ex-slave that he could not easily dismiss this aspiration as but another "exaggerated" or "absurd" view of freedom. "My master has had me ever since I was seven years old, and never give me nothing," observed a twenty-one-year-old laborer in Richmond. "I worked for him twelve years, and I think something is due me." Expecting nothing from his old master, he now trusted the government to do "something for us." The day a South Carolina rice planter anticipated trouble was when one of his field hands told him that "the land ought to belong to the man who (alone) *could work it,*" not to those who "sit in the house" and profit by the labor of others. Such sentiments easily translated into the most American of aspirations. "All I wants is to git to own fo' or five acres ob land, dat I can build me a little house on and call my home," a Mississippi black explained. With the acquisition of land, the ex-slave viewed himself entering the mainstream of American life, cultivating his own farm and raising the crops with which to sustain himself and his family. That was the way to respectability in an agricultural society, and the freedman insisted that a plot of land was all he required to lift himself up: "Gib us our own land and we take care ourselves; but widout land, de ole massas can hire us or starve us, as dey please." And what better way to confirm their emancipation than to own the very land on which they had been working and which they had made productive and valuable by their own labor. . . .

Within the first two years after the war, freedmen who embraced and acted upon the expectation of "forty acres and a mule" learned soon enough to face up to the possibility of disappointment. When some former Alabama slaves staked off the land they had been working and claimed it as their own, the owner quickly set matters straight: "Listen, niggers, what's mine is mine, and what's yours is yours. You are just as free as I and the missus, but don't go foolin' around my land.'' Of course, planters derived considerable comfort from the knowledge that Federal officials were prepared to confirm their property rights. Until the blacks acknowledged the futility of land expectations, the Freedmen's Bureau recognized how difficult it would be to stabilize agricultural operations. With that sense of priorities, the Bureau instructed its agents to do everything in their power to disabuse the ex-slaves of any lingering illusions about taking over their masters' lands. ''This was the first difficulty that the Officers of the Bureau had to contend with,'' a Mississippi officer wrote, ''and nothing but their efforts and explanations, kept off the storm. Even now, it is but a temporary settlement.'' If the blacks refused to believe their old masters, Bureau agents were quite prepared to visit the plantations in person and impart the necessary confirmation: ''The government owns no lands in this State. It therefore can give away none. Freedmen can obtain farms with the money which they have earned by their labor. Every one, therefore, shall work diligently, and carefully save his wages, till he may be able to buy land and possess his own home.'' The blacks he encountered held so tenaciously to their illusions, a Bureau officer in Alabama observed, that ''unless they see me and hear me refute the story, they persist in the belief.'' Still other officers reported that the freedmen refused to believe them, too, or thought the question of land might be negotiable. After being told of the government's policy, a Virginia freedman offered to lower his expectations to a single acre of land—''ef you make it de acre dat Marsa's house sets on.''

As an alternative to confiscation, Freedmen's Bureau officers and northern white missionaries and teachers advanced the classic mid-nineteenth-century self-help ideology and implored the newly freed slaves to heed its lessons. Rather than entertain notions of government bounties, they should cultivate habits of frugality, temperance, honesty, and hard work; if they did so, they might not only accumulate the savings to purchase land but would derive greater personal satisfaction from having earned it in this manner. Almost identical advice permeated the editorials of black newspapers, the speeches of black leaders, and the resolutions adopted by black meetings. ''Let us go to work faithfully for whoever pays fairly, until we ourselves shall become employers and planters,'' the *Black Republican*, a New Orleans newspaper, editorialized in its first issue. With an even finer grasp of American values, a black Charlestonian thought economic success capable of overriding the remaining vestiges of racial slavery. ''This is the panacea which will heal all the maladies of a Negrophobia type. Let colored men simply do as anybody else in business does, be self-reliant, industrious, producers of the staples for market and merchandise, and he will have no more trouble on account of his complexion, than the white men have about the color of their hair or beards.''

To provide proper models for their people, black newspapers featured examples of self-made freedmen who had managed to accumulate land and were forming the nucleus of a propertied and entrepreneurial class in the South. Actually, a number of blacks had done precisely that, some of them fortunate enough to have purchased tax lands and still others who had taken advantage of the Homestead Act or who had made enough money to purchase a plot in their old neighborhoods. But the number of propertied blacks remained small, and some of these found they had been defrauded by whites who had an equal appreciation of the self-help philosophy and made the most of it. Even the blacks who obtained legitimate title to lands soon discovered the elusive quality of economic success. The land often turned out to be of an inferior quality, the freedman usually lacked the capital and credit to develop it properly, and he might consequently find himself enmeshed in the very web of indebtedness and dependency he had sought to escape. By the acquisition of land, he hardly avoided the same problems plaguing so many white farmers.

No matter what the freedmen were told or what precepts they were admonished to follow, the belief in some form of land redistribution demonstrated a remarkable vitality. The wartime precedents and promises were apt to speak louder in some regions than the insistent postwar denials. Thousands of ex-slaves had been placed on forty-acre tracts under Sherman's program, the earlier experiments at Davis Bend and on the Sea Islands persisted into 1865, and the stories of individual and collective success by the black settlers who worked these lands would seem to have assured the continuation and expansion of such projects. But even if few blacks elsewhere in the South knew of them, even if still fewer were aware of the congressional debate on Thaddeus Stevens' ambitious land confiscation program or of the immense generosity of the Federal government in awarding millions of acres to railroad corporations, the idea of "forty acres and a mule" simply made too much sense and had become too firmly entrenched in the minds of too many freedmen for it to be given up at the first words of a Bureau underling. Nor could the thousands of ex-slaves on abandoned and confiscated lands in 1865 understand that the Federal policies which made their settlement possible had not been long-term commitments but rather temporary military expedients, designed to keep them working on the plantations and away from the cities and the Union Army camps.

Resilient though they were, the hopes of the freedmen could withstand only so many shocks. When the governor of Florida told them, "The President will not give you one foot of land, nor a mule, nor a hog, nor a cow, nor even a knife or fork or spoon," he could be dismissed as a mouthpiece of planters who stood to lose the most from a confiscation scheme. When a Bureau officer told some Georgia blacks essentially the same thing, one disbelieving freedman remarked, "Dat's no Yank; dat just some reb dey dressed in blue clothes and brought him here to lie to us." But the denials began to assume a substance that could no longer be ignored. On May 29, 1865, President Andrew Johnson announced his Proclamation of Amnesty, whereby most former Confederates were to be pardoned and recover any of their lands which might have been confiscated or occupied. That had to be taken seriously—as seriously as the Federal officers who now prepared to implement the order. In some communities, the news coincided with a rumor, said to have been circulated by planters, that the President had revoked the Emancipation Proclamation. To many freedmen, contemplating what would happen to the lands they had worked and expected to own, that was no rumor at all. "Amnesty for the persons, no amnesty for the property," the *New Orleans Tribune* cried. "It is enough for the republic to spare the life of the rebels—without restoring to them their plantations and palaces." Under Johnson's magnanimous pardoning policy, any faint hope of a land division collapsed, along with the promising wartime precedents. Rather than confirm the settlers in possession of the land they had cultivated and on which they had erected their homes, the government now proposed to return the plantations to those for whom they had previously labored as slaves. Not satisfied with having their lands returned, some of the owners displayed their own brands of "insolence" and "ingratitude" by claiming damages for any alterations made by the black settlers and by suing them for "back rents" for the use of the land. . . .

Where substantial numbers of freedmen had settled on abandoned lands, as in the Sea Islands, the disappointment was bound to be felt most keenly. Appreciating that fact, General O. O. Howard, who headed the Freedmen's Bureau and may have been second only to Lincoln in the esteem of the ex-slaves, decided to pay a personal visit to Edisto Island to inform the settlers that they must give up the lands they had been cultivating as their own. Perhaps only Howard could possibly make them believe it. As if to prepare the assemblage for the ordeal ahead, he thought it might be appropriate for them to begin the meeting with a song. Suddenly an old woman on the edge of the crowd began to sing, "Nobody knows the trouble I've seen," and the entire throng of more than two thousand soon joined in a resounding chorus. Whether it was the song, the look of dismay on their faces, or the shouts of "No! No!" that greeted his announcement, Howard found himself so flustered that he could barely finish his speech. But he had nevertheless articulated the government's position. They should lay aside any bitter feelings they harbored for their former masters and contract to work for them. By working for wages or shares, he assured them, they would be achieving the same ends as possession of the soil would have given them. If the freedmen found Howard's advice incomprehensible, that was only because they understood him all too clearly.

The hope Bureau officials held out for the freedmen was largely a cruel delusion. The same men who had been disabusing the minds of the ex-slaves of their land expectations now urged them to bind themselves to the white man's land. That was another way of saying they should give up the struggle altogether. Not all of them were willing to do so, at least not at the outset. What the freedmen on Edisto Island found most offensive in Howard's speech, apart from having to give up their claims to the land, was the suggestion that they should now work for their former masters. In the petition they addressed to the President, the Edisto blacks argued that no man who had only recently faced his master on the field of battle should now be expected to submit to him for the necessities of life. He was more than willing to forgive his old master, another freedman remarked, but to have to submit to his rule again demanded too much. "He had lived all his life with a basket over his head, and now that it had been taken off and air and sunlight had come to him, he could not consent to have the basket over him again." Rather than face that eventuality, the blacks on several islands near Edisto rowed themselves to Savannah, leaving behind their household goods and the crops they had made. But some of the freedmen had worked too long and too hard on these lands to give them up so easily, and they resolved to remain and fight. . . .

Along the South Carolina coast, blacks barricaded themselves on the plantations, destroyed the bridges leading to them, and shot at owners seeking to repossess them. On several of the Sea Islands, they organized along military lines to hold their lands and treated any claimants as tres-passers. "They use threatening language, when the former residents of the Islands are spoken of in any manner," a Bureau officer reported, "and say openly, that none of them, will be permitted to live upon the Islands. They are not willing to be reasoned with on this subject." On Johns Island, the blacks in early 1866 persisted in refusing to contract, insisted they would work only for themselves, and refused to surrender ownership of the land— in theory or in fact. When "a party of Northern Gentlemen" proposed to look over real estate prospects on the island, they were made "prisoners" the moment they landed, disarmed, and advised never to return. With similar vigilance, the blacks on James Island repelled the first landing party of planters who had come to recover their lands. The battle over restoration of the lands soon resembled a series of mopping-up operations, with the Freedmen's Bureau and Federal troops always ready to guarantee the safety and property of the returning owners, and the blacks able to hold out only for so long against the dictates of the law and the force of an army.

If blacks could not acquire land by government action, neither would they find it easy to obtain it by any other means, even if they adopted the self-help precepts and accumulated the necessary funds. Appreciating the threat black proprietorship posed to a dependent, stable, and contented work force, and the feelings of "impudence and independence" it might generate, many planters refused to sell or to rent any land to blacks. Such a policy was in accordance with "the general good," a South Carolina rice planter insisted, for once lands were leased to freedmen, "it will be hard ever to recover the privileges that have been yielded." When whites tried to restrict landownership in the Black Codes or in combinations among themselves, the Federal government revoked their actions. But community pressures often achieved the same results. "I understand Dr. Harris and Mr. Varnedoe will rent their lands to the Negroes!" a much-scandalized Mary Jones wrote her daughter. "The conduct of some of the citizens has been very injurious to the best interest of the community." If whites per-sisted in such behavior, they faced social ostracism or violence to their property. Any white man found selling land in his parish, a Louisiana plantation manager observed, would "soon be dangling from some trees." Of course, restrictions on the sale and rental of land to blacks could not always be applied with the rigidity some whites desired, particularly when landowners found that leasing might be the only way to keep their land in productive use.

Within a year of the war's end, the planter class had virtually completed the recovery of its property. But repossession would be of limited value without a productive and regulated black laboring force to work the lands. Few stated the problem more candidly than Allen S. Izard, a Georgia planter. Now that the "game of confiscation" had been settled, his fellow planters needed most urgently to consolidate their triumph.

> Our place is to work; take hold & persevere; get labour of some kind; get possession of the places; stick to it; oust the negroes; and their ideas of proprietorship; secure armed protection close at hand on our exposed River, present a united and determined front; and make as much rice as we can. . . . Our plantations will have to be assimilated to the industrial establishment of other parts of the world, where the owner is protected by labour tallies, time tables, checks of all kinds, & constant watchfulness. Every operator will steal time and anything else.

The terms he chose to describe the challenge facing planters in the postwar South suggested the need to adopt modern industrial techniques to ensure their continued mastery over a class of workers who had only recently broken the chains of bondage. That the ideal binding force should have been introduced by Northerners would seem, therefore, to have been less ironic than logical. Like the planters, Federal authorities appreciated full well the need to guarantee and compel black labor. When the officers of the Freedmen's Bureau enlightened the ex-slaves in the fall of 1865 on the futility of their land expectations, they supplied at the same time the forms that the new dependency would assume.

When the postwar southern legislatures adopted measures to compel blacks to contract with an employer or face arrest as vagrants, they had merely written into law what the Union Army and the Freedmen's Bureau had already demanded of the freed slaves. Despite the virtual abrogation of the Black Codes, the contract system remained very much intact. In South Carolina, for example, the Union commander voided the Codes but simultaneously ordered freedmen to contract in the next ten days or leave the plantations on which they lived. The Codes had contained clauses which offended northern standards of justice and fairness. The contract, on the other hand, was a much-venerated instrument of law which enjoyed high standing both in the North and in the South. Embodying as it did a voluntary agreement between two parties, in which the terms and conditions were spelled out, the contract suggested what the Codes had not—impartiality, equality before the law, and the traditional American virtues of give-and-take and compromise.

Federal authorities introduced the contract into wartime labor relations in the South as a way of protecting the newly freed slaves, easing the transition from slave to free labor, and compelling former owners to recognize emancipation and compensate their workers. Drawn up initially by Union Army officers and Freedmen's Bureau agents, the contract also came to be accepted as the most expedient way to get the blacks back to the fields, to regulate the quality of their labor, and to ensure a stable working force for the highly seasonal agriculture of the South. With often the noblest of intentions, then, the Freedmen's Bureau, from the moment of its inception, urged the ex-slaves to sign contracts, assured them they would be treated fairly, and warned them of the consequences of noncompliance. "Your contracts were explained to you, and their sacredness impressed upon you, again and again," the Bureau commissioner for Mississippi told the freedmen. "If you do not have some occupation you will be treated as vagrants, and made to labor on public works."

The planters were in such perfect agreement about what they expected of their freed black laborers that they often used the same language in the contracts. By affixing his signature to the agreement, the freedman invariably promised to render "perfect obedience," to be "prompt and faithful" in the performance of his duties, and to maintain a proper demeanor. On the Heyward plantations in South Carolina, the laborers not only recognized the "lawful authority" of the employer and his agents but agreed to conduct themselves "in such manner as to gain the good will of those to whom we must always look for protection." Few employers went so far as the South Carolina planter who bound his blacks to be "strictly as my slaves" in obeying his instructions. Nor did many think it necessary to adopt the proviso which another planter insisted upon—that the freedmen always address him as "master." But few would have dissented from the spirit that had inspired such stipulations. It made little difference to H. A. Moore, a South Carolina planter, if his freedmen addressed him and his wife as "Mr. & Mrs. Moore" or simply as "Massa Maurice & Miss Bettie," but they were always to "speak politely to us."

Lest the freedman be in any way tempted to compromise his "perfect obedience," most contracts barred him from possessing "deadly weapons" or "ardent spirits," and the employer reserved the right to enter the freedman's cabin at any time. During working hours, moreover, the laborer agreed to have no visitors and to obtain his employer's permission before leaving the plantation for any reason (numerous contracts required such permission at all times). In some regions, the freedmen agreed to submit to punishment for contract violations—"our employer being the judge whether we are to be punished or turned off." But most contracts could not provide corporal punishment for violations, if only because a Bureau official might disallow the entire agreement; however, employers did specify fines for any absenteeism, negligence in work, or breakdowns in expected demeanor. For the more serious offenses, like insubordination or desertion, the laborer could be dismissed, thereby forfeiting all or a portion of his wages and crop shares for the year. In some rare instances, as on one South Carolina plantation, the employer agreed to submit cases of misconduct and conflicts between himself and the freedmen to a jury of his own laborers, whose judgments would be binding on both parties. The "model" contract drawn up by Martin Delany in South Carolina stipulated that the panel adjudging such disputes include the employer, a freedman, and a third party acceptable to both of them. But if the offense warranted dismissal or a forfeiture of pay, an officer of the Freedmen's Bureau would preside and make the final decision. . . .

If the constraints imposed by contracts upon the movements and behavior of black laborers assumed a near uniformity, the amount and the method of compensation tended to vary considerably, even within the same region. "I furnish everything but clothes, and give my freedmen one third of the crop they make," an Arkansas planter declared, but "on twenty plantations around me, there are ten different styles of contracts." The compensation offered a freedman reflected the scarcity of labor in the district, the planter's ability to pay, agricultural prospects, how successfully the laborers pressed their demands, and how effectively planters were able to decide among themselves on maximum rates. Despite variations within regions, the wage rates and crop shares tended to be higher in the lower than in the upper South: a first-class male field hand could generally expect to make no more than $5–$10 a month in Virginia, North Carolina, and Tennessee; $8–$12 in South Carolina and Georgia; $10–$18 in Mississippi, Alabama, Florida, and Louisiana; and $15–$25 in Arkansas and Texas. On the same plantation, however, wage scales fluctuated according to how the employer classified his laborers; on a Mississippi plantation, for example, the employer paid first-class male laborers $15 a month, first-class women $10, and drivers $40, while the average hand netted about $10.

The value of these wages obviously depended upon the degree to which the employer maintained his laborers—that is, whether he furnished the lodgings, food, clothing, and medical care or deducted those items from wages. On a plantation in Louisiana, for example, field hands earned $25 a month but they had to purchase their food, clothing, and other provisions, and each hand paid a tax to ensure regular visits by a doctor; most of the wage, they testified, went for food, they could ill afford a contemplated tax for schools, and it was "pretty tight living." The method and time of payment reflected an employer's dim view of black character. The alleged propensity of blacks to spend their wages quickly and foolishly induced employers to insert clauses in contracts whereby they would provide certain necessities "at the current prices" and deduct the expense from the freedmen's pay. And to ensure compliance with the contract, they preferred to pay the laborer half of his earnings on a quarterly or monthly basis, withholding the rest until the end of the year; in many cases, they withheld all payments until the crop had been completed, although advancing money or provisions against the final settlement. If a laborer worked for a portion of the crop rather than wages, his share usually ranged from one fifth (with board) to one half (less the deductions made for provisions). Since the agreed-upon share would be divided among all the laborers on the plantation, individuals received amounts commensurate with the work they performed and their position and sex. . . .

Although designed to protect the interests of planters and freedmen alike, the contract in practice gave employers what they had wanted all along—the crucial element of control by which they could bind the ex-slaves for at least a year and compel them to work and maintain proper behavior. Nor did the presence of a Freedmen's Bureau officer necessarily make the contracts any less oppressive; after all, one agent conceded, the objective of the contract was to prevent black laborers from deserting their employers "at a critical time" in the making of the crop. Whatever the initial intent, the contract system embodied that universally accepted dictum that only compulsion and discipline could induce free blacks to work. Unlike the northern worker who entered into a verbal contract with an employer, the black laborer in the postwar South was bound by a legal instrument which not only stipulated objective terms of service (compensation, hours, and duties) but imposed conditions of demeanor and attitude on the laborer and not on the employer. That feature in itself made the question of compliance or noncompliance necessarily arbitrary and revealed the contract as something less than a bilateral agreement between equals. In so many ways, in fact, the new arrangements simply institutionalized the old discipline under the guise of easing the ex-slave's transition to freedom. After comparing the regulations under slavery with those which now controlled free labor, the *New Orleans Tribune* found but few differences: "All the important prohibitions imposed upon the slave, are also enforced against the freedman. . . . It is true that the law calls him a freeman; but any white man, subjected to such restrictive and humiliating prohibitions, will certainly call himself a slave."

By hedging the freedman's newly acquired rights, by narrowing his room for maneuverability, by robbing him of his principal bargaining strengths, by seeking to control both his social behavior and his labor, the contract between a former master and his former slaves reminded one observer of a "patent rat-trap." No one, he noted, could have devised a surer instrument to compel black labor. "Rats couldn't possibly get out of it. The only difficulty was that they declined to go in."

❧ *F U R T H E R   R E A D I N G*

Herman Belz, *A New Birth of Freedom: The Republican Party and Freedmen's Rights, 1861–1866* (1976)
George R. Bentley, *A History of the Freedmen's Bureau* (1965)
Ira Berlin, et al., eds., *Freedom: A Documentary History of Emancipation*, 2 vols., 1984–1985
Dudley T. Cornish, *The Sable Arm: Negro Troops in the Union Army* (1956)
LaWanda Cox, *Lincoln and Black Freedom* (1981)
Eric Foner, *Nothing but Freedom: Emancipation and Its Legacy* (1983)
John Hope Franklin, *The Emancipation Proclamation* (1963)
Louis S. Gerteis, *From Contraband to Freedman: Federal Policy Toward Southern Blacks, 1861–1865* (1973)
———, "Salmon P. Chase, Radicalism and the Politics of Emancipation, 1861–1864," *Journal of American History* 60 (1973), 42–62
Thomas Holt, " 'An Empire over the Mind': Emancipation, Race and Ideology in

the British West Indies and the American South," in Morgan Kousser and James M. McPherson, eds., *Region, Race, and Reconstruction* (1982), 283–314

Clarence L. Mohr, *On the Threshold of Freedom: Masters and Slaves in Civil War Georgia* (1986)

Donald G. Nieman, *To Set the Law in Motion: The Freedmen's Bureau and Legal Rights for Blacks, 1865–1869* (1979)

Benjamin Quarles, *The Negro in the Civil War* (1953)

Roger Ransom, and Richard Sutch, *One Kind of Freedom: The Economic Consequences of Emancipation* (1977)

James L. Roark, *Masters Without Slaves: Southern Planters in the Civil War and Reconstruction* (1977)

Willie Lee Rose, *Rehearsal for Reconstruction: The Port Royal Experiment* (1964)

V. Jacque Voegeli, *Free But Not Equal: The Midwest and the Negro During the Civil War* (1967)

Bell I. Wiley, *Southern Negroes, 1861–1865* (1938)

Forrest Wood, *Black Scare: The Racist Response to the Civil War and Reconstruction* (1968)

CHAPTER
11

The Republican Party
and Reconstruction Policy

❧

Reconstruction was, in a real sense, what the war was all about. After putting down the southerners' attempted secession and liberating their slaves in the process, the Federal government now had to decide what kind of society should emerge in the South. Simply ending slavery and terminating hostilities were not enough. The freed slaves now had to be protected and given the opportunity to enjoy and develop their new status. This meant guaranteeing their legal rights and economic security, perhaps even giving them access to the vote or to land. At the same time, the leaders of the rebellion had to be punished and their political influence curbed, if not eliminated altogether. Since most of these men were also slaveholders, their economic power might be reduced, especially if some of their land was to be made available to the former slaves. All of these possibilities had to be considered as part of a final settlement of the issues and problems raised by the sectional conflict and the war that had ensued.

In the seven months between Andrew Johnson's sudden accession to the presidency in April 1865 and December of that year, when the new Thirty-ninth Congress convened, the president's approach to Reconstruction was to impose minimal demands on the South. He required the former Confederates to make only minor concessions before being allowed to resume their political rights and retain their lands. As for the freedmen, he seemed to think that they needed no further protection beyond the fact of their emancipation. The Republican-dominated Congress disagreed, however. The terms for southern readmission were, in its view, to be determined by the legislative branch—a position that had already brought Congress into a confrontation with Lincoln over the Wade-Davis bill and its veto in 1864. The Republican majority in Congress also rejected the specifics of Johnson's terms as far too conciliatory.

But exactly what alternative did the party have in mind? Some Republicans recognized that the former Confederates needed firmer restrictions and the freedmen greater protection, but they were concerned about causing further disruption in southern society and politics and about involving the Federal government in the internal affairs of states now that the war was over. Other Republicans, however, saw the moment of southern defeat as a vital opportunity to reorganize the region's politics and economy, and move it in a new, more democratic and egalitarian direction.

From early 1866 until March 1867, the congressional Republicans struggled to establish a policy to replace that of the president. After their first proposal, the Fourteenth Amendment, met with resistance from both Johnson, who vetoed it, and the South, which rejected it, the Republicans proposed a plan to reorganize the southern state governments and enfranchise the freedmen. This measure was called the Reconstruction Act, *and its terms were mandatory.*

This lengthy and difficult struggle revealed the dimensions of Republican thought on the problem of reunion and Reconstruction. What was the general thrust of the party's thinking and policymaking? Was the party radical and innovative in its approach, or was it, in reality, rather cautious? Historians have debated this question almost as vigorously as the Republicans debated Reconstruction policy.

D O C U M E N T S

The testimony about the Republican party's Reconstruction policy in the documents that follow comes from congressmen involved in the formulation and passage of the legislation or from others who were affiliated with the party. The first selection is the angry manifesto drawn up on August 5, 1864, by the two authors of the Wade-Davis bill, Senator Benjamin F. Wade and Representative Henry Winter Davis, after Lincoln had pocket-vetoed their proposed measure. The second document contains extracts from the "Grasp of War" speech given in Boston on June 21, 1865, by Richard Henry Dana, Jr., a prominent Republican lawyer, in which he outlined an important constitutional theory about Reconstruction—a theory that is later discussed in the two essays of this chapter. In the third selection, Senator Lyman Trumbull's view of the scope of his Civil Rights bill is presented. His remarks are from two speeches in the Senate—the first on January 29, 1866, when the bill was initially introduced, and the second on April 4, 1866, when the Senate was about to override President Johnson's veto of it.

The remaining documents relate to the Reconstruction Act of 1867, which embodied the Republican-dominated Congress's final terms for southern readmission. The fourth selection is from a speech of January 3, 1867, by Representative Thaddeus Stevens on an early version of the bill in which he stated his radical views about Reconstruction. The specifics of a radical approach to Reconstruction are enumerated in the fifth extract, which is from a speech of January 28, 1867, called "Regeneration Before Reconstruction" by George W. Julian, a radical Republican Congressman from Indiana. The position of a more conservative Republican is presented in the sixth document—Senator John Sherman of Ohio raises objections to some of the proscriptive terms of the bill in a Senate speech on February 19, 1867. The seventh selection contains text from the Reconstruction Act of March 2, 1867 as well as the Fourteenth Amendment that the South had already rejected in the fall of 1866 but which was now part of the terms required for readmission under the Reconstruction Act. The eighth and last selection is from the 1879 novel *A Fool's Errand*, by Albion W. Tourgee, an Ohioan who had been a leading figure in the Republican party of North Carolina during Reconstruction but who regarded the provisions of the Reconstruction Act as quite inadequate for the task at hand.

The Wade-Davis Manifesto Denounces Lincoln's Reconstruction Policy, August 1864

. . . [T]he President persists in recognizing those shadows of governments in Arkansas and Louisiana [formed under Lincoln's presidential Proclamation of Amnesty and Reconstruction, December 8, 1863] which Congress formally declared should not be recognized—whose representatives and senators were repelled by formal votes of both Houses of Congress—which it was declared formally should have no electoral vote for President and Vice-President.

They are mere creatures of his will. They are mere oligarchies, imposed on the people by military orders under the form of election, at which generals, provost marshals, soldiers and camp-followers were the chief actors, assisted by a handful of resident citizens, and urged on to premature action by private letters from the President. . . .

Mark the contrast! The bill requires a majority, the [president's Reconstruction] proclamation is satisfied with one-tenth; the bill requires one oath, the proclamation another; the bill ascertains voters by registering, the proclamation by guess; the bill exacts adherence to existing territorial limits, the proclamation admits of others; the bill governs the rebel States *by law,* equalizing all before it, the proclamation commits them to the lawless discretion of Military Governors and Provost Marshals; the bill forbids electors for President, the proclamation and defeat of the bill threaten us with civil war for the admission or exclusion of such votes; the bill exacted exclusion of dangerous enemies from power and the relief of the nation from the rebel debt, and the prohibition of slavery forever, so that the suppression of the rebellion will double our resources to bear or pay the national debt, free the masses from the old domination of the rebel leaders, and eradicate the cause of the war; the proclamation secures neither of these guaranties.

It is silent respecting the rebel debt and the political exclusion of rebel leaders; leaving slavery exactly where it was by law at the outbreak of the rebellion, and adds no guaranty even of the freedom of the slaves he undertook to manumit.

It is summed up in an illegal oath, without sanction, and therefore void.

The oath is to support all proclamations of the President, during the rebellion, having reference to slaves.

Any government is to be accepted at the hands of one-tenth of the people not contravening that oath.

Now that oath neither secures the abolition of slavery, nor adds any security to the freedom of the slaves the President declared free.

It does not secure the abolition of slavery; for the proclamation of freedom merely professed to free certain slaves while it recognized the institution.

Every constitution of the rebel States at the outbreak of the rebellion may be adopted without the change of a letter: for none of them contravene that proclamation; none of them establish slavery.

It adds no security to the freedom of the slaves; for their title is the proclamation of freedom.

If it be unconstitutional, an oath to support it is void. Whether constitutional or not, the oath is without authority of law, and therefore void.

If it be valid and observed, it exacts no enactment by the State, either in law or constitution, to add a State guaranty to the proclamation title; and the right of a slave to freedom is an open question before the State courts on the relative authority of the State law and the proclamation.

If the oath binds the one-tenth who take it, it is not exacted of the other nine-tenths who succeed to the control of the State government, so that it is annulled instantly by the act of recognition.

What the State courts would say of the proclamation, who can doubt?

But the master would not go into court—he would seize his slaves.

What the Supreme Court would say, who can tell?

When and how is the question to get there?

No *habeas corpus* lies for him in a United States Court; and the President defeated with this bill the extension of that writ to his case.

Such are the fruits of this rash and fatal act of the President—a blow at the friends of his Administration, at the rights of humanity, and at the principles of Republican Government.

The President has greatly presumed on the forbearance which the supporters of his Administration have so long practised, in view of the arduous conflict in which we are engaged, and the reckless ferocity of our political opponents.

But he must understand that our support is of a cause and not of a man; that the authority of Congress is paramount and must be respected; that the whole body of the Union men of Congress will not submit to be impeached by him of rash and unconstitutional legislation; and if he wishes our support, he must confine himself to his Executive duties—to obey and execute, not make the laws—to suppress by arms armed rebellion, and leave political reorganization to Congress.

If the supporters of the Government fail to insist on this, they become responsible for the usurpations which they fail to rebuke, and are justly liable to the indignation of the people whose rights and security, committed to their keeping, they sacrifice.

Let them consider the remedy of these usurpations, and, having found it, fearlessly execute it.

> B. F. Wade,
> Chairman Senate Committee.
>
> H. Winter Davis,
> Chairman Committee
> House of Representatives
> on the Rebellious States.

Republican Richard H. Dana, Jr., Presents His "Grasp of War" Theory, June 1865

. . . A war is over when its purpose is secured. It is a fatal mistake to hold that this war is over, because the fighting has ceased. [Applause.] This war is not over. We are in the attitude and in the *status* of war to-day. There is the solution of this question. Why, suppose a man has attacked your life, my friend, in the highway, at night, armed, and after a death-struggle, you get him down—what then? When he says he has done fighting, are you obliged to release him? Can you not hold him until you have got some security against his weapons? [Applause.] Can you not hold him until you have searched him, and taken his weapons from him? Are you obliged to let him up to begin a new fight for your life? The same principle governs war between nations. When one nation has conquered another, in a war, the victorious nation does not retreat from the country and give up possession of it, because the fighting has ceased. No; it holds the conquered enemy in the grasp of war until it has secured whatever it has a right to require. [Applause.] I put that proposition fearlessly—*The conquering party may hold the other in the grasp of war until it has secured whatever it has a right to require.*

But what have we a right to require? We have no right to require our conquered foe to adopt all our notions, our opinions, our systems, however much we may be attached to them, however good we may think them; but we have a right to require whatever the public safety and public faith make necessary. [Applause.] That is the proposition. Then, we come to this: *We have a right to hold the rebels in the grasp of war until we have obtained whatever the public safety and the public faith require.* [Applause, and cries of "good."] Is not that a solid foundation to stand upon? Will it not bear examination? and are we not upon it to-day?

. . . Now, we have got to choose between two results. With these four millions of negroes, either you must have four millions of disfranchised, disarmed, untaught, landless, thriftless, non-producing, non-consuming, degraded men, or else you must have four millions of land-holding, industrious, arms-bearing, and voting population. [Loud applause.] Choose between these two! Which will you have? It has got to be decided pretty soon which you will have. The corner-stone of those institutions will not be slavery, in name, but their institutions will be built upon the mud-sills of a debased negro population. Is that public safety? Is it public faith? Are those republican ideas or republican institutions? Some of these negros have shed their blood for us upon the public faith. Ah! there are negro parents whose children have fallen in battle; there are children who lost fathers, and wives who lost hubands, in our cause. Our covenant with the freedman is sealed in blood! It bears the image and superscription of the republic! Their freedom is a tribute which we must pay, not only to Cæsar, but to God! [Applause.]

We have a right to require, my friends, that the freedmen of the South shall have the right to hold land. [Applause.] Have we not? We have a right to require that they shall be allowed to testify in the state courts. [Applause.] Have we not? We have a right to demand that they shall bear arms as soldiers in the militia. [Applause.] Have we not? We have a right to demand that there shall be an impartial ballot. [Great applause.]. . .

One step further. Suppose the states do not do what we require—what then? I have not heard that question answered yet. Suppose President Johnson's experiment in North Carolina and Mississippi fails, and the white men are determined to keep the black men down—what then? Mr. President, I hope we shall never be called upon to answer, practically, that question. It remits us to an ultimate, and, you may say, a fearful proposition. But if we come to it, though I desire to consider myself the humblest of the persons here, I, for one, am prepared with an answer. I believe that if you come to the ultimate right of the thing, the ultimate law of the case, it is this: that this war—no, not the war, *the victory in the war*—places, not the person, not the life, not the private property of the rebels—they are governed by other considerations and rules—I do not speak of them— *but the political systems of the rebel states, at the discretion of the republic.* [Great applause.] Secession does not do this. Treason does not do this. The existence of civil war does not do this. It is the necessary result of conquest, with military occupation, in a war of such dimensions, such a character, and such consequences as this. . . .

When a man accepts a challenge to a duel, what does he put at stake? He puts his life at stake, does he not? And is it not childish, after the fatal shot is fired, to exclaim, "Oh, death and widowhood and orphanage are fearful things!" They were all involved in that accepted challenge. When a nation allows itself to be at war, or when a people make war, they put at stake their national existence. [Applause.] That result seldom follows, because the nation that is getting the worst of the contest makes its peace in time; because the conquering nation does not always desire to incorporate hostile subjects in its dominions; because neutral nations intervene. The conqueror must choose between two courses—to permit the political institutions, the body politic, to go on, and treat with it, or obliterate it. We have destroyed and obliterated their central government. Its existence was treason. As to their states, we mean to adhere to the first course. We mean to say the states shall remain, with new constitutions, new systems. We do not mean to exercise sovereign civil jurisdiction over them in our Congress. Fellow citizens, it is not merely out of tenderness to them; it would be the most dangerous possible course for us. Our system is a planetary system; each planet revolving round its orbit, and all round a common sun. This system is held together by a balance of powers—centripetal and centrifugal forces. We have established a wise balance of forces. Let not that balance be destroyed. If we should undertake to exercise sovereign civil jurisdiction over those states, it would be as great a peril to our system as it would be a hardship upon them. We must not, we will not undertake it, except as the last resort of the thinking and the good—as the ultimate final remedy, when all others have failed.

I know, fellow citizens, it is much more popular to stir up the feelings of a public audience by violent language than it is to repress them; but on this subject we must think wisely. We have never been willing to try the experiment of a consolidated democratic republic. Our system is a system of states, with central power; and in that system is our safety. [Applause.] State rights, I maintain; State sovereignty we have destroyed. [Applause.] Therefore, although I say that, if we are driven to the last resort, we may adopt this final remedy; yet wisdom, humanity, regard for democratic principles, common discretion, require that we should follow the course we are now following. Let the states make their own constitutions, but the constitutions must be satisfactory to the Republic [applause], and—ending as I began—by a power which I think is beyond question, the Republic holds them in the grasp of war until they have made such constitutions. [Loud applause.]

Senator Lyman Trumbull of Illinois Explains His Civil Rights Bill, January and April 1866

I. January 29, 1866

. . . With this bill passed into a law and efficiently executed we shall have secured freedom in fact and equality in civil rights to all persons in the United States. There will be no objection to this bill that it undertakes to confer judicial powers upon some other authority than the courts. It may be assailed as drawing to the Federal Government powers that properly belong to "States"; but I apprehend, rightly considered, it is not obnoxious to that objection. It will have no operation in any State where the laws are equal, where all persons have the same civil rights without regard to color or race. It will have no operation in the State of Kentucky when her slave code and all her laws discriminating between persons on account of race or color shall be abolished. . . .

II. April 4, 1866

. . . This bill in no manner interferes with the municipal regulations of any State which protects all alike in their rights of person and property. It could have no operation in Massachusetts, New York, Illinois, or most of the States of the Union. How preposterous, then, to charge that unless some State can have and exercise the right to punish somebody, or to deny somebody a civil right on account of his color, its rights as a State will be destroyed. It is manifest that unless this bill can be passed, nothing can be done to protect the freedmen in their liberty and their rights.

Whatever may have been the opinion of the President at one time as to "good faith requiring the security of the freedmen in their liberty and their property" it is now manifest from the character of his objections to this bill that he will approve no measure that will accomplish the object. That the second clause of the constitutional amendment [the Thirteenth, abolishing slavery] gives this power there can be no question. Some have contended that it gives the power even to confer the right of suffrage. I have not thought so, because I have never thought suffrage any more necessary to the liberty of a freedman than of a non-voting white, whether child or female. But his liberty under the Constitution he is entitled to, and whatever is necessary to secure it to him he is entitled to have, be it the ballot or the bayonet. If the bill now before us, and which goes no further than to secure civil rights to the freedman, cannot be passed, then the constitutional amendment proclaiming freedom to all the inhabitants of the land is a cheat and a delusion. . . .

Representative Thaddeus Stevens of Pennsylvania Sets out His Terms, January 1867

. . . It is to be regretted that inconsiderate and incautious Republicans should ever have supposed that the slight amendments [embodied in the pending Fourteenth Amendment] already proposed to the Constitution, even when incorporated into that instrument, would satisfy the reforms necessary for the security of the Government. Unless the rebel States, before admission, should be made republican in spirit, and placed under the guardianship of loyal men, all our blood and treasure will have been spent in vain. I waive now the question of punishment which, if we are wise, will still be inflicted by moderate confiscations, both as a reproof and example. Having these States, as we all agree, entirely within the power of Congress, it is our duty to take care that no injustice shall remain in their organic laws. Holding them "like clay in the hands of the potter," we must see that no vessel is made for destruction. Having now no governments, they must have enabling acts. The law of last session with regard to Territories settled the principles of such acts. Impartial suffrage, both in electing the delegates and ratifying their proceedings, is now the fixed rule. There is more reason why colored voters should be admitted in the rebel States than in the Territories. In the States they form the great mass of the loyal men. Possibly with their aid loyal governments may be established in most of those States. Without it all are sure to be ruled by traitors; and loyal men, black and white, will be oppressed, exiled, or murdered. There are several good reasons for the passage of this bill. In the first place, it is just. I am now confining my argument to negro suffrage in the rebel States. Have not loyal blacks quite as good a right to choose rulers and make laws as rebel whites? In the second place, it is a necessity in order to protect the loyal white men in the seceded States. The white Union men are in a great minority in each of those States. With them the blacks would act in a body; and it is believed that in each of said States, except one, the two united would form a majority, control the States, and protect themselves. Now they are the victims of daily murder. They must suffer constant persecution or be exiled. The convention of southern loyalists, lately held in Philadelphia, almost unanimously agreed to such a bill as an absolute necessity.

Another good reason is, it would insure the ascendency of the Union party. Do you avow the party purpose? exclaims some horror-stricken demagogue. I do. For I believe, on my conscience, that on the continued ascendency of that party depends the safety of this great nation. If impartial suffrage is excluded in rebel States then every one of them is sure to send a solid rebel representative delegation to Congress, and cast a solid rebel electoral vote. They, with their kindred Copperheads of the North, would always elect the President and control Congress. While slavery sat upon her defiant throne, and insulted and intimidated the trembling North, the South frequently divided on questions of policy between Whigs and Democrats, and gave victory alternately to the sections. Now, you must divide them between loyalists, without regard to color, and disloyalists, or you will be the perpetual vassals of the free-trade, irritated, revengeful South. For these, among other reasons, I am for negro suffrage in every rebel State. If it be just, it should not be denied; if it be necessary, it should be adopted; if it be a punishment to traitors, they deserve it.

But it will be said, as it has been said, "This is negro equality!" What is negro equality, about which so much is said by knaves, and some of which is believed by men who are not fools? It means, as understood by honest Republicans, just this much, and no more: every man, no matter what his race or color; every earthly being who has an immortal soul, has an equal right to justice, honesty, and fair play with every other man; and the law should secure him those rights. The same law which condemns or acquits an African should condemn or acquit a white man. The same law which gives a verdict in a white man's favor should give a verdict in a black man's favor on the same state of facts. Such is the law of God and such ought to be the law of man. This doctrine does not mean that a negro shall sit on the same seat or eat at the same table with a white man. That is a matter of taste which every man must decide for himself. The law has nothing to do with it. . . .

Representative George W. Julian of Indiana Outlines the Scope of Reconstruction, January 1867

. . . Mr. Speaker, I further object to the measure [the proposed Reconstruction bill] before us that it is a mere enabling act, looking to the early restoration of the rebellious districts to their former places in the Union, instead of a well-considered frame of government contemplating such restoration at some indefinite future time, and designed to fit them to receive it. They are not ready for reconstruction as independent States, on any terms or conditions which Congress might impose; and I believe the time has come for us to say so. We owe this much to their misguided people, whose false and feverish hopes have been kept alive by the course of the Executive and the hesitating policy of Congress. I think I am safe in saying that if these districts were to-day admitted as States, with the precise political and social elements which we know to exist in them, even with their rebel population disfranchised and the ballot placed in the hands of radical Union men only, irrespective of color, the experiment would be ruinous to the best interests of their loyal people and calamitous to the nation. The withdrawal of federal intervention and the unchecked operation of local supremacy would as fatally hedge up the way of justice and equality as the rebel ascendency which now prevails. Why? Simply because no theory of government, no forms of administration, can be trusted, unless adequately supported by public opinion. The power of the great landed aristocracy in these regions, if unrestrained by power from without, would inevitably assert itself. Its political chemistry, obeying its own laws, would very soon crystallize itself into the same forms of treason and lawlessness which to-day hold their undisturbed empire over the existing loyal element. What these regions need, above all things, is not an easy and quick return to their forfeited rights in the Union, but *government,* the strong arm of power, outstretched from the central authority here in Washington, making it safe for the freedmen of the South, safe for her loyal white men, safe for emigrants from the Old World and from the Northern States to go and dwell there; safe for Northern capital and labor, Northern energy and enterprise, and Northern ideas to set up their habitation in peace, and thus found a Christian civilization and a living democracy amid the ruins of the past. That, sir, is what the country demands and the rebel power needs. To talk about suddenly building up independent States where the material for such structures is fatally wanting, is nonsense. States must *grow,* and to that end their growth must be fostered and protected. The political and social regeneration of the country made desolate by treason is the prime necessity of the hour, and is preliminary to any reconstruction of States. Years of careful pupilage under the authority of the nation may be found necessary, and Congress alone must decide when and upon what conditions the tie rudely broken by treason shall be restored. Congress, moreover, is as solemnly bound to deny to disloyal communities admission into our great sisterhood of States as it is to deny the rights of citizenship to those who have forfeited such rights by treason. . . .

Senator John Sherman of Ohio Urges Caution and Moderation, February 1867

. . . We sweep from our legislation all tests for voting except such as each State may prescribe. We build reconstruction upon the broadest humanity and invite all men to take part in the work. So far as voting is concerned we proclaim universal amnesty in exchange for universal suffrage, and yet the Senator [Sumner] is not satisfied. What more did he ask a year ago? Nothing. If we exclude from voting the rebels of the South, who compose nearly all the former voting population, what becomes of the republican doctrine that all governments must be founded on the consent of the governed? I invoke constitutional liberty against such a proposition. Beware, sir, lest in guarding against rebels you destroy the foundation of republican institutions. I like rebels no better than the Senator from Massachusetts; but, sir, I will not supersede one form of oligarchy in which the blacks were slaves by another in which the whites are disfranchised outcasts. Let us introduce no such horrid deformity into the American Union. Our path has been toward enfranchisement and liberty. Let us not turn backward in our course, but after providing all necessary safeguards for white and black, let us reconstruct society in the rebel States upon the broad basis of universal suffrage.

This bill does not proclaim universal amnesty except as to voting. On the contrary, it requires these States to adopt a constitutional amendment [the Fourteenth] by which the leading men disable themselves from holding office. Six thousand or perhaps ten thousand of the leading men of the South are embraced in the restriction of the constitutional amendment, and are forever excluded from holding office until two thirds of both Houses of Congress relieve them from that restriction. Is not that enough? Is it not enough that they are humiliated, conquered, their pride broken, their property lost, hundreds and thousands of their best and bravest buried under their soil, their institutions gone, they themselves deprived of the right to hold office, and placed in political power on the same footing with their former slaves? Is not that enough? I say it is, and a generous people will not demand more.

But, sir, when the attempt is made to defeat a measure of this kind, which yields all that the Senator has ever openly demanded in the Senate, all that has ever been demanded by any popular community in this great country, all that has been demanded by any Legislature, more than we claimed at the last election, I have the right to characterize this opposition as unusual and unnatural. Sir, let us issue this call to the people of the southern States. We have given here our deliberate judgment on a legal proposition: we say that the State governments organized by the President of the United States were without authority of law, because they were without the sanction of Congress. We therefore sweep them away, not for all purposes, but for all State purposes. We deny their validity as State governments. They only have the same force and effect as the local Mexican law had in California after we conquered California, the same effect that the local law of Maryland would have if the British should overrun the whole of Maryland; no more, no less. The State communities are swept out of existence, and the people are required to proceed in their own way to form State governments. What objection can there be to this? . . .

Congress's Terms for Readmission and Reconstruction, June 1866 and March 1867

I. 14th Constitutional Amendment

Joint Resolution proposing an Amendment to the Constitution of the United States.

Be it resolved by the Senate and House of Representatives of the United States of America, in Congress assembled, (two-thirds of both Houses concurring,) That the following article be proposed to the Legislatures of the several States as an amendment to the Constitution of the United States, which, when ratified by three-fourths of said Legislatures, shall be valid as part of the Constitution, namely:

Article XIV.

Section 1.   All persons born or naturalized in the United States, and subject to the jurisdiction thereof, are citizens of the United States and of the State wherein they reside. No State shall make or enforce any law which shall abridge the privileges or immunities of citizens of the United States; nor shall any State deprive any person of life, liberty, or property, without due process of law, nor deny to any person within its jurisdiction the equal protection of the laws.

Sec. 2.   Representatives shall be apportioned among the several States according to their respective numbers, counting the whole number of persons in each State, excluding Indians not taxed. But when the right to vote at any election for the choice of electors for President and Vice President of the United States, representatives in Congress, the executive and judicial officers of a State, or the members of the Legislature thereof, is denied to any of the male inhabitants of such State, being twenty-one years of age, and citizens of the United States, or in any way abridged, except for participation in rebellion or other crime, the basis of representation therein shall be reduced in the proportion which the number of such male citizens shall bear to the whole number of male citizens twenty-one years of age in such State.

Sec. 3.   No person shall be a Senator or Representative in Congress, or elector of President and Vice President, or hold any office, civil or military, under the United States, or under any State, who, having previously taken an oath as a member of Congress, or as an officer of the United States, or as a member of any State Legislature, or as an executive or judicial officer of any State, to support the Constitution of the United States, shall have engaged in insurrection or rebellion against the same, or given aid or comfort to the enemies thereof. But Congress may, by a vote of two thirds of each House, remove such disability.

Sec. 4.   The validity of the public debt of the United States, authorized by law, including debts incurred for payment of pensions and bounties for services in suppressing insurrection or rebellion, shall not be questioned. But neither the United States nor any State shall assume or pay any debt or obligation incurred in aid of insurrection or rebellion against the United States, or any claim for the loss or emancipation of any slave; but all such debts, obligations, and claims shall be held illegal and void.

Sec. 5. That Congress shall have power to enforce, by appropriate legislation, the provisions of this article.

Passed June 13, 1866.

II. Reconstruction Act of Thirty-Ninth Congress

An act to provide for the more efficient government of the rebel States.

Whereas no legal State governments or adequate protection for life or property now exists in the rebel States of Virginia, North Carolina, South Carolina, Georgia, Mississippi, Alabama, Louisiana, Florida, Texas, and Arkansas; and whereas it is necessary that peace and good order should be enforced in said States until loyal and republican State governments can be legally established: Therefore

Be it enacted, &c., That said rebel States shall be divided into military districts and made subject to the military authority of the United States, as hereinafter prescribed, and for that purpose Virginia shall constitute the first district; North Carolina and South Carolina the second district; Georgia, Alabama, and Florida the third district; Mississippi and Arkansas the fourth district; and Louisiana and Texas the fifth district.

Sec. 2. That it shall be the duty of the President to assign to the command of each of said districts an officer of the army, not below the rank of brigadier general, and to detail a sufficient military force to enable such officer to perform his duties and enforce his authority within the district to which he is assigned.

Sec. 3. That it shall be the duty of each officer assigned as aforesaid to protect all persons in their rights of person and property, to suppress insurrection, disorder, and violence, and to punish, or cause to be punished, all disturbers of the public peace and criminals, and to this end he may allow local civil tribunals to take jurisdiction of and to try offenders, or, when in his judgment it may be necessary for the trial of offenders, he shall have power to organize military commissions or tribunals for that purpose; and all interference under color of State authority with the exercise of military authority under this act shall be null and void.

Sec. 4. That all persons put under military arrest by virtue of this act shall be tried without unnecessary delay, and no cruel or unusual punishment shall be inflicted; and no sentence of any military commission or tribunal hereby authorized, affecting the life or liberty of any person, shall be executed until it is approved by the officer in command of the district, and the laws and regulations for the government of the army shall not be affected by this act, except in so far as they conflict with its provisions: *Provided,* That no sentence of death under the provisions of this act shall be carried into effect without the approval of the President.

Sec. 5.   That when the people of any one of said rebel States shall have formed a constitution of government in conformity with the Constitution of the United States in all respects, framed by a convention of delegates elected by the male citizens of said State twenty-one years old and upward, of whatever race, color, or previous condition, who have been resident in said State for one year previous to the day of such election, except such as may be disfranchised for participation in the rebellion, or for felony at common law, and when such constitution shall provide that the elective franchise shall be enjoyed by all such persons as have the qualifications herein stated for electors of delegates, and when such constitution shall be ratified by a majority of the persons voting on the question of ratification who are qualified as electors for delegates, and when such constitution shall have been submitted to Congress for examination and approval, and Congress shall have approved the same, and when said State, by a vote of its legislature elected under said constitution, shall have adopted the amendment to the Constitution of the United States, proposed by the Thirty-ninth Congress, and known as article fourteen, and when said article shall have become a part of the Constitution of the United States, said State shall be declared entitled to representation in Congress, and Senators and Representatives shall be admitted therefrom on their taking the oaths prescribed by law, and then and thereafter the preceding sections of this act shall be inoperative in said State: *Provided,* That no person excluded from the privilege of holding office by said proposed amendment to the Constitution of the United States shall be eligible to election as a member of the convention to frame a constitution for any of said rebel States, nor shall any such person vote for members of such convention.

Sec. 6.   That until the people of said rebel States shall be by law admitted to representation in the Congress of the United States, any civil governments which may exist therein shall be deemed provisional only, and in all respects subject to the paramount authority of the United States at any time to abolish, modify, control, or supersede the same; and in all elections to any office under such provisional governments all persons shall be entitled to vote, and none others, who are entitled to vote under the provisions of the fifth section of this act; and no person shall be eligible to any office under any such provisional governments who would be disqualified from holding office under the provisions of the third article of said constitutional amendment.

Passed March 2, 1867.

A Southern Republican Later Condemns
Congress's Reconstruction Policy, 1879

So it must have been well understood by the wise men who devised this short-sighted plan of electing a President beyond a peradventure of defeat, that they were giving the power of the re-organized, subordinate republics, into the hands of a race unskilled in public affairs, poor to a degree hardly to be matched in the civilized world, and so ignorant that not five out of a hundred of its voters could read their own ballots, joined with such Adullamites among the native whites as might be willing to face a proscription which would shut the house of God in the face of their families, together with the few men of Northern birth, resident in that section since the close of the war,—either knaves or fools, or partaking of the nature of both,—who might elect to become permanent citizens, and join in the movement.

Against them was to be pitted the wealth, the intelligence, the organizing skill, the pride, and the hate of a people whom it had taken four years to conquer in open fight when their enemies outnumbered them three to one, who were animated chiefly by the apprehension of what seemed now about to be forced upon them by this miscalled measure of "Reconstruction"; to wit, the equality of the negro race.

It was done, too, in the face of the fact that within the preceding twelvemonth the white people of the South, by their representatives in the various Legislatures of the Johnsonian period, had absolutely refused to recognize this equality, even in the slightest matters, by *refusing to allow the colored people to testify in courts of justice* against white men, or to protect their rights of person and property in any manner from the avarice, lust, or brutality of their white neighbors. It was done in the very face of the "Black Codes," which were the first enactments of Provisional Legislatures, and which would have established a serfdom more complete than that of the Russian steppes before the *ukase* of Alexander.

And the men who devised this plan called themselves honest and wise statesmen. More than one of them has since then hugged himself in gratulation under the belief, that, by his co-operation therein, he had cheaply achieved an immortality of praise from the liberty-lovers of the earth! After having forced a proud people to yield what they had for more than two centuries considered a right,—the right to hold the African race in bondage,—they proceeded to outrage a feeling as deep and fervent as the zeal of Islam or the exclusiveness of Hindoo caste, by giving to the ignorant, unskilled, and dependent race—a race who could not have lived a week without the support or charity of the dominant one—equality of political right! Not content with this, they went farther, and, by erecting the rebellious territory into self-regulating and sovereign States, they abandoned these parties like cocks in a pit, to fight out the question of predominance without the possibility of national interference. They said to the colored man, in the language of one of the pseudo-philosophers of that day, "Root, hog, or die!"

It was cheap patriotism, cheap philanthropy, cheap success!

⤴ *E S S A Y S*

These two essays concern the question of whether or not the Republican party's approach to Reconstruction should be considered radical. In the first, M. Les Benedict of Ohio State University claims that Republican policy was in fact far from radical, but was instead quite conciliatory and conservative in thrust. According to Peyton McCrary of the University of South Alabama, on the other hand, the Republicans were radical and saw themselves as instruments of revolutionary change.

The Conservative Basis of Radical Reconstruction

M. LES BENEDICT

. . . [The purpose of this article is to] help explain why Reconstruction failed to achieve its goals and why so many Republicans appeared so quickly to abandon the struggle after 1869. [Indeed] historians may be mistaken when they refer to a retreat from Reconstruction [because t]he distaste of many Republicans for federal intervention in the South was manifest in the Reconstruction program itself. Although they insisted on guarantees for the security of loyal whites and blacks in the South and passed laws and constitutional amendments which appeared to delegate power to the national government to secure citizens' rights, most Republicans never desired a broad, permanent extension of national legislative power. Republicans framed the most limited, conservative Reconstruction possible, adhering until 1868 to the position that their legislation was merely a temporary aberration in the federal system. When continued violence in the South after 1868 forced many Republicans to endorse some permanent broadening of national power—a constitutional position which was truly radical—most Republicans tried to limit the degree of the expansion, and many others refused to make this new departure at all. Nor is it accurate to charge that the courts in interpreting Reconstruction legislation betrayed the principles and purposes of the Republicans who had framed it; rather they carried over to the judicial arena Republicans' reluctance to alter fundamentally the federal system.

Even as the exigencies of war forced the national government to exert broad, new powers, most Republican legalists justified wartime measures in such a way as to preserve the old balance of the Constitution. Rather than admitting that the war had precipitated a fundamental alteration in the federal system, they argued it merely had forced a suspension of peacetime constitutional provisions. Unionists reached this conclusion by different routes. Francis Lieber, the leading student of government in mid-nineteenth-century America, espoused the first interpretation: "The whole Rebellion is beyond the Constitution," he insisted. "The Constitution was not made for such a state of things. . . . [T]he life of a nation is the first substantial thing and far above the formulas [for government] which . . . have been adopted." The Constitution had been intended to serve a nation forged by a common heritage and experience before and during the War for Independence. That nation had to be preserved even if the Constitution was violated. A second school argued that the Constitution itself incorporated

Michael Les Benedict, "Preserving the Constitution: The Conservative Basis of Radical Reconstruction," *Journal of American History* 61 (June 1974), pp. 67–90. Reprinted with permission of the publisher.

virtually unlimited war powers through the clause vesting in Congress the power to prosecute war (Art. 1, sec. 8). These powers were as much a part of the Constitution as its peacetime provisions, but in a state of war the war powers naturally became more prominent while other provisions receded into the background.

By justifying the massive wartime expansion of the national government's power in this way, Republicans believed they had preserved the Constitution from contamination. With war's end, the occasion for using the war powers—whether under the Constitution's authority or outside it—would cease. The limitations of the peacetime fundamental law would regain their sway.

The desire to preserve the federal system's prewar balance weighed heavily on the minds of leading Republicans. As early as 1861, a worried Republican Senator James W. Grimes wrote fellow Senator Lyman Trumbull: "We are gradually surrendering all the rights of the states & functions & shall soon be incapable of resuming them." Five years later, as one of the respected members of the prestigious Joint Committee of Fifteen on Reconstruction, Grimes was insisting that "During the prevalence of the war we drew to ourselves here as the Federal Government authority which had been considered doubtful by all and denied by many of the statesmen of this country. That time, it seems to me, has ceased and ought to cease. Let us go back to the original condition of things, and allow the States to take care of themselves as they have been in the habit of taking care of themselves."

This kind of constitutional conservatism left Republicans ill prepared to cope with the complex problems of Reconstruction, which so clearly called at minimum for long-term national protection of citizens' rights. By 1865, Republicans had become so committed to the proposition that the national government's power would shrink to prewar dimensions at war's end that an immediate recognition of continued southern statehood upon the surrender of the rebel armies would have restored prewar state rights virtually intact, rendering the national government powerless to secure any guarantees of loyalty from the South. Because Republicans had refused during the war to acquiesce in a permanent expansion of national power at the expense of the states, they were in 1865 and 1866 forced to deny that the southern political organizations were as yet entitled to the rights of states. Therefore, the great constitutional controversy between President Andrew Johnson and his supporters and the Republican party centered on the constitutional issue of the status of the former southern states. . . .

Students of Reconstruction history are familiar with the theories of Reconstruction outlined by [William A.] Dunning, [John W.] Burgess, and other historians and recapitulated in most textbooks—the "southern," "presidential," "conquered provinces," "state suicide," and "forfeit rights" theories. Each of these was designed to fix the status of the former southern states and the degree of national power over them. All but the southern theory maintained that the southern states were either out of the Union *de facto* or had ceased to exist at all. Only if southern state organizations remained out of normal federal relations would the Republicans' claim of power for the national government over the South in Reconstruction be consistent with their wartime constitutional conservatism. Thus, Republicans clearly acknowledged that once the government recognized the restoration of the southern states they would enjoy the same relations with the national government as existed before the war. . . .

Having defined the status of the rebel states in a way that denied them immediate restoration to prewar rights, Republicans turned to three sources of national power over them. Thaddeus Stevens enunciated one alternative suggesting that, "as there are no symptoms that the people of these provinces will be prepared to participate in constitutional government for some years, I know of no arrangement so proper for them as territorial governments." [Then,] "They would be held in a territorial condition until they are fit to form State Constitutions, republican in fact not in form only, and ask admission into the Union as new States." In a certain sense, Congress' power over the South would indeed expand if Stevens' scheme were adopted. Congress had absolute control over territorial property of the United States subject only to the few general prohibitions the Constitution imposed on congressional power. In the 1860s Congress generally allowed territories to govern themselves through territorial legislatures, but their powers were derived from and subject directly to that of Congress. And territorial governors were appointed by the President with the advice and consent of the Senate. But this power over the South would not be permanent; it would cease with statehood. In fact, it was precisely because Congress lost its power once the "territories" were readmitted as states that special care had to be taken to see that they had learned their lessons: "If Congress approve their Constitutions, and think they have done works meet for repentance they would be admitted as new states," suggested Stevens. "If their Constitutions are not approved of, they would be sent back, until they have become wise enough so to purge their old laws as to eradicate every despotic and revolutionary principle. . . ." Nor could Congress force permanent changes on an unwilling people. The sole hope for a permanent rearrangement of the southern political, economic, and social order lay in southerners themselves voluntarily agreeing to such changes in return for statehood. "If they are to be admitted as new States they must form their own constitutions; and no enabling act could dictate its terms," Stevens insisted.

Although many Radicals preferred Stevens' territorial policy to establish congressional control over the South, his program met with such a negative response from non-Radical Republicans that when he presented a Reconstruction bill to the House in 1867 it bore no resemblance to his earlier suggestion.

Republicans discerned a second source of congressional power over Reconstruction in Congress' war powers. Building consciously on the legal-constitutional justifications for expanded national power developed during the war, these Republicans suggested that, although peace would indeed restore the sway of peacetime constitutional limitations on the national government, it was up to the government to decide precisely when peace had arrived. In that case the government might demand that the rebel states meet certain conditions in return for recognition that peace was restored. This view was popularized by the conservative Richard Henry Dana in a speech delivered in Faneuil Hall on June 21, 1865: *"The conquering party may hold the other in the grasp of war until it has secured whatever it has a right to acquire,"* he maintained. This theory was received with favor in Boston. Ohio's new governor, Jacob D. Cox, House speaker Schuyler Colfax, Senator Fessenden, Representative George S. Boutwell, also named to the Reconstruction Committee, Representative William Lawrence of the House Judiciary Committee, and Carl Schurz all expressed views similar to Dana's.

Like the theory of temporarily expanded national power in time of war from which it sprang, the grasp of war doctrine was designed to protect the federal system from fundamental, permanent change as a result of crisis. The federal system, Dana warned, "is held together by a balance of powers—centripetal and centrifugal forces. Let not their balance be destroyed." By simply continuing military occupation this danger could be avoided. "If we should undertake to exercise sovereign civil jurisdiction over those States, it would be as great a peril to our system as it would be a hardship upon them."

So like Stevens' territorial scheme, the grasp of war policy gave no permanent power to Congress. Dana had proposed a consciously conservative program. As he wrote to Charles Francis Adams, Jr., immediately after his speech, "It would be an irreparable mischief for Congress to assume civil and political authority in state matters, but it is not an irreparable mischief for the general government to continue the exercise of such war powers as are necessary until the people of those States do what we in conscience think necessary for the reasonable security of the republic. . . ."

Not only did Congress gain no power under Dana's doctrine, but even while the South remained in the "grasp of war," Congress' prerogatives were strictly limited. The people of the southern states themselves were "voluntarily" to give guarantees of security through their own legislation. This might be done under the pressure of continued exclusion from the Union, but the guarantees were to be achieved through state rather than national legislation. Thus, both Stevens' and Dana's proposals not only left ultimate power to protect citizens' rights with the states, but even during the period of Reconstruction maintained a fiction of voluntarism around state action in meeting conditions for a restoration of peace and normal relations. Even during the crisis Congress could not presume to dictate state action.

Republicans found a third source of congressional power in the duty the Constitution imposed on the national government to guarantee to the states republican forms of government. Republicans who argued that the southern states had ceased to exist during the war particularly favored this theory. If there were no state governments at all in the South, then "manifestly, the first step after the war ended was for someone to establish a local government there." And this duty the guarantee clause placed on the national government.

This was the only constitutional basis for Reconstruction which could promise the national government permanent power, even after the rebel states were restored to normal relations. Some Republicans felt it assumed a standard of republicanism and gave the national government power to enforce that standard whenever a state—any state—fell short of it. But few Republicans endorsed such a radical expansion of national power. In 1867 the House of Representatives agreed to a resolution instructing the Judiciary Committee to investigate "whether the States of Kentucky, Maryland, and Delaware now have State governments republican in form." Such resolutions normally passed without Republican opposition as they embodied no actual legislation, but on this occasion twenty-two Republicans joined Democrats in opposition. The committee took testimony and evidence but let the matter die. Several Republicans proposed bills based on the guarantee clause in efforts to extend universal male suffrage and protect its exercise throughout the Union, but none passed or even won endorsement by a committee.

Although Republicans regularly pointed in campaign speeches to the guarantee clause as somehow sanctioning their Reconstruction policy, they were reluctant to base their actual legislation on it. Instead they used it as a vague guide in setting the conditions that southern states had to meet before Congress would recognize them as entitled to normal state rights. Most Republicans relied on the grasp of war doctrine to justify their Reconstruction legislation, and in so doing they employed the narrowest, most conservative theory of the three available—the one which virtually sanctified "the federal system as it was."

Republicans twice formulated conditions for the southern states to meet before Congress would recognize their restoration. Each time they conditioned restoration on the voluntary passage of state legislation, stolidly preserving the states as the primary authors of legislation, firmly refusing to force compliance through exercise of national power. And southern reaction demonstrated that this "voluntarism" was more than illusory.

The first set of conditions were the propositions embraced in the Fourteenth Amendment to the Constitution, framed in 1866. Holding that "the conquered rebels were at the mercy of the conquerors," the Joint Committee on Reconstruction offered the amendment under "a most perfect right to exact indemnity for injuries done and security against the recurrence of such outrages in the future." Written by Fessenden, the committee's report closely paralleled Dana's views. The report emphasized the temporary nature of the exclusion of the southern states and conceded the "distracting and demoralizing" tendency of such a state of affairs. The dangerous situation would end, the committee implied, when the southern states signified their agreement to the conditions embodied in the Fourteenth Amendment by ratifying it.

More than the mere method of proposing the Fourteenth Amendment manifested Republicans' fundamental constitutional conservatism. By the very terms of the Fourteenth Amendment, Republicans once again demonstrated their overriding desire to preserve for the states the primary responsibility for the protection of citizens' rights. The initial section, which for the first time defined American citizenship and guaranteed citizens' rights, did not itself expand the national government's jurisdiction in areas traditionally left to the states. Its language recognized implicitly that states continued to be the primary source of the legislation which regulated citizens' rights and duties. The amendment limited states' alternatives in framing and possibly administering laws involving these rights; it did not transfer to the national government the power to frame all laws touching on them. No longer could states pass laws which denied or abridged the privileges and immunities of United States citizens, or which deprived any person of life, liberty, or property without due process of law, or which denied equality before the law. Possibly, states could not informally administer laws unequally. But this interpretation trod upon the farthest limit of the amendment. So long as the states did none of these things, the national government had no more power in areas of traditional state jurisdiction than it had before the war. "The political system of this Republic rests upon the right of the people to control their local concerns in their several states . . . ," affirmed Carl Schurz in a speech defending the Amendment. "This system was not to be changed in the work of reconstruction."

Republicans understood the dangers inherent in their first, conservative Reconstruction plan. Many of them feared that, without political power, blacks might be victimized by restored governments in the hands of former rebels. Given the political situation in spring 1866, however, Republicans felt they could not retain power if they presented more extreme conditions for restoration. In an effort to minimize the danger, they passed two bills which appeared to mark radical changes in the relations between the states and the national government.

The Freedmen's Bureau bill and the Civil Rights bill both seemed to place the rights of the newly freed slaves under the protection of the national government. Yet, even with the prospect of restored, white, former rebel-dominated state governments facing them, Republicans refused to offer blacks the permanent protection they realized was needed. Offered by the conservative constitutionalist Lyman Trumbull, the Freedmen's Bureau bill was avowedly a temporary measure, based primarily on Congress' war powers, a measure the authority for which would cease soon after the southern states were restored to the Union, the very time the freedmen would need its protection most. Despite this conservatism, Republican Senate leader Fessenden barely could bring himself to support the measure, acquiescing in its passage only after personal discussions with Trumbull.

The Civil Rights bill promised to stir even more doubts. It was manifestly a peacetime measure, to be passed by virtue of Congress' power under the second section of the Thirteenth Amendment to enforce emancipation by appropriate legislation. As originally presented, the bill declared the inhabitants of every state and territory entitled to certain fundamental rights without regard to color or previous status and made it a crime for anyone to deny these rights under the cover of law. All violations of the bill were to be tried in United States district courts. Most important, any person who could not secure the rights guaranteed under the bill in state or local courts could transfer his case to the United States district or circuit courts in his locality. Other sections of the bill outlined enforcement procedures. Later Trumbull added a provision conferring citizenship on all persons of African descent born in the United States.

On its face the Civil Rights bill radically expanded national power. For the first time the national government accepted the responsibility for protecting the rights of its citizens. Under the bill national courts might try cases of every description, civil and criminal, wherever state and local courts did not grant all citizens equal protection in the rights guaranteed by the bill. This broad, apparently radical bill was patently inconsistent with Trumbull's political conservatism on Reconstruction matters and his constitutional conservatism generally. But in fact Trumbull had found a way to preserve rather than alter the old federal system.

Although theoretically Trumbull's bill vastly expanded the duties of the national government, in fact these new duties would not be permanent. The bill was to provide the threat of national assumption of jurisdiction over civil rights in order to force states to fulfill that role themselves. Court jurisdiction was the key to the bill's real purpose. Jurisdiction would be taken from the state courts only so long as they enforced state laws or court procedures which discriminated in the rights guaranteed to all inhabitants by the first section of the Civil Rights bill. Once the states enforced these rights equally, there could be no removal of jurisdiction from state to national courts. Thus there would be great pressure on states to change their laws in order to regain their old spheres of jurisdiction. There would be no point in resisting. Retain unequal law or procedures and blacks would simply take their cases into the federal courts.

Trumbull had found a way to force the states themselves to alter their discriminatory laws. Once they did, they would regain jurisdiction over all their citizens, and the balance of power between the state and national governments would remain unchanged. Trumbull emphasized this in his defense of the measure:

> [The bill] may be assailed as drawing to the Federal Government powers that properly belong to "States"; but I apprehend, rightly considered, it is not obnoxious to that objection. It will have no operation in any State where the laws are equal, where all persons have the same civil rights without regard to color or race.

The goal of the first Republican program of Reconstruction was to protect freedmen's rights in the South with the minimum possible coercion of white southerners and least possible alteration of the traditional boundaries of state and federal jurisdiction. Despite its manifest conservatism, southerners rejected this first offer of conditions precedent to restoration; only Tennessee chose to ratify the proposed constitutional amendment, and

Republicans quickly responded by recognizing the state's return to normal rights and privileges in the Union.

Faced with southern intransigence and growing public impatience, Republicans framed a second plan of Reconstruction in February 1867. In 1866 the Reconstruction Committee had been willing to restore the rebel-dominated state organizations erected under the guidance of President Johnson in return for ratification of the constitutional amendment. In the Military Government bill, which the committee reported to Congress in 1867, the Johnson governments were expressly disavowed and the southern people remanded to the direct control of the military authorities (who could utilize civil tribunals and officers if they wished, however). The plan seemed to justify Stevens' conquered province theory of southern status, but in fact it was proposed by two conservative Republicans, Senator George H. Williams and Representative Roscoe Conkling. Stevens fought for this bill so tenaciously that possibly he saw it as an opening wedge for his views on "territorialization," but other Republicans believed, with Representative Augustus Brandegee, that it simply "holds those revolted communities in the grasp of war until the rebellion shall have laid down its spirit, as two years ago it formally laid down its arms," until, in John A. Bingham's words, "those people return to their loyalty and fealty in such a manner as shall satisfy the people of the United States, . . . represented in Congress, of their fitness to be restored to their full constitutional relations."

Fearing the Military Government bill might lead to a long period of exclusion, conservative Republicans in the House, led by Bingham and James G. Blaine, offered an amendment "to notify [southern whites] in the most solemn form . . . that . . . all they have to do, in order to get rid of military rule and military government, is to present to the Congress of the United States a constitutional form of State government in accord with the letter and spirit of the Constitution and laws of the United States, together with a ratification of the pending constitutional amendment." Defeated in the House, the so-called "Blaine amendment" succeeded in the Senate where it was offered by the conservative Republican Senator John Sherman. The bill as finally passed promised restoration on four conditions: the people of each southern state had to frame a new constitution at a convention elected by universal male suffrage; the constitution had to be ratified in a second election; the new constitution had to provide for equal male suffrage; and the state legislature elected under the new constitution had to ratify the Fourteenth Amendment.

Dana happily recognized in this bill the vindication of his doctrine of Reconstruction. "[I]t is on the principle which I had the honor to be the first to lay down in my Faneuil Hall speech of June, 1865,—what my flattering friends call my 'Grasp-of-war Speech'," he wrote proudly. "Not that my speech had any agency in the result, but that the result justifies it." Hardly a constitutional defense of the bill was made that did not justify it on these grounds.

Like the first Reconstruction plan, the Reconstruction Act called for voluntary state action under the threat of continued exclusion and military government if the state refused. As [Representative James A.] Garfield put it, "Congress shall place civil Governments before these people of the rebel States, and a cordon of bayonets behind them."

The major conditions Congress demanded the southern states meet before being released from "the grasp of war" were the ratification of the Fourteenth Amendment and the enfranchisement of their male black citizens. Because the Reconstruction Act required black suffrage historians have generally viewed it as a true embodiment of radical principles. By imposing Negro suffrage on recalcitrant southerners, historians have believed, Radical Republicans demonstrated their willingness to disregard traditional lines of state and national authority. But in fact by 1867 the argument for black suffrage was distinctly conservative. Republicans were unwilling to leave black Americans at the mercy of former rebels; they were equally unwilling permanently to extend the power of the national government to protect them. As Edwin L. Godkin, editor of the *Nation,* explained, "our Government owes to those who can get it no other way that one thing for which all governments exist . . .—security for person and property. This . . . we can supply either by the provision of a good police or by the admission of the blacks to such a share in the management of state affairs that they can provide a police for themselves. The former of these courses is not strictly in accordance with the spirit of our institutions; the latter is."

The enfranchisement of black men in the southern states, then, was the one measure which would provide security for the Union and its loyal southern supporters and yet allow Reconstruction to continue on a conservative constitutional basis. "Far from desiring centralization repulsive to the genius of this country, it is in the distinct interest of local self-government and legitimate State rights that we urge these propositions," wrote Schurz, "and nothing can be more certain than that this is the only way in which a dangerous centralization of power in the hands of our general government can be prevented." As the *Nation* pointed out, Negro suffrage "though brought forward as a radical remedy . . . is anything but radical."

Only as the Reconstruction process neared completion did many Republicans finally realize its essential weakness. As southerners met Congress' conditions and pressed for restoration in 1868, Republicans suspected that their compliance with the Reconstruction acts was more apparent than real. "You are hastening back States where rebelism is pervading them from end to end," complained an outspoken Radical. The grasp of war theory had worked too well, perhaps. In many states southerners had met the conditions set forth in the Reconstruction acts not out of reawakened loyalty or new devotion to racial justice but out of a simple desire to be rid of the national presence. Radicals who recognized the weakness of the loyal forces in the South urged delay in restoration. In reality, "there are not ten men in this Senate who believe it is a safe thing to do at this time," Timothy Otis Howe charged. Other Radicals agreed, but political necessities required readmission.

Realizing the futility of trying to delay restoration, many Republicans finally decided on an effort to guarantee permanence to the new political order in the South. As a new "fundamental condition" for readmission, Republicans insisted southern states agree never to alter the basis of suffrage in their new constitutions. For the first time Republicans were trying to gain a measure of permanent power for the national government to protect the rights of its citizens in the South. In doing so, they were forced to abandon the grasp of war theory under which they had thus far proceeded. Some, like the respected constitutionalist, Senator George F. Edmunds, turned at last to the guarantee clause. The power to guarantee republican forms of government to states, he argued, was "plenary and absolute," and therefore Congress clearly had the power "to put that government in such a form that it shall 'stay put'. . . . " But the guarantee clause justification implied a sweeping alteration in national-state relations. Radical Illinois Senator Richard Yates brought this home to his colleagues in his defense of the guarantee clause:

> When the question arises whether a constitution is republican in form, who decides it? Congress. May not Congress say that no constitution is republican in form which excludes any large class of people from voting . . . ?
> If New York excludes any portion of her citizens who bear arms and pay taxes from the right of suffrage, hers is not, according to our republican theory, a government republican in form. Congress, not the States, decide that question.

But most Republicans who favored the imposition of new fundamental conditions preferred a more restrained justification. Led by William M. Stewart, the second-ranking Republican on the Senate Judiciary Committee, they drew a parallel between the restoration of the southern states and the admission of new states, insisting that Congress had regularly exacted concessions from petitioning territories in return for grants of statehood. Although these unhappy Republicans perceived that their new theory inevitably implied expansion of national power, they intended to keep that expansion to the absolute minimum. Republicans did not include any provisions for enforcing the conditions if violated, hoping they would be self-enforcing. Even Stewart finally conceded that "I do not pretend to say that the insertion of this declaration in the bill [to restore the southern states] will alter either the constitution of the State or of the General Government." It was merely "a declaration of principle, which has generally been respected."

This hesitant, timorous attempt to provide permanent national power to protect rights precipitated the first of the series of intra-Republican confrontations on constitutional questions which would mark Reconstruction legislation of the post-1868 era. Conservative constitutionalists in the Republican party, including the very architects of congressional Reconstruction—Fessenden, Trumbull, and Conkling—were unprepared to cooperate in this new attempt to limit state prerogatives. "[T]he States have the right to alter or amend their Constitutions at pleasure . . . ,'' they insisted. Once restored to the Union, a southern state ''will have the same power to regulate the question of suffrage that the State of New York has, unquestionably.'' A motion to eliminate the ''fundamental conditions'' from the resolution restoring Arkansas to the Union failed by only one vote in the Senate, despite the overwhelming Republican majority there. . . .

Republicans never shook off their state-centeredness. In passing the Force Act of 1871—constitutionally far more radical than previous legislation—they progressed to the position that Congress could step in to protect citizens' rights when states failed to do so as well as when states positively discriminated, but Republicans would not agree to the proposition that Congress had acquired direct, permanent jurisdiction over citizens' rights through the Fourteenth Amendment. Republicans were circumscribed not only by their continuing reluctance to alter the balance of federalism but by their past conservatism as well. They remembered how carefully they had limited the scope of the constitutional amendments, how tender their concern had been to preserve old areas of state jurisdiction. When Bingham was finally driven to new ground by southern intransigence and argued for the broadest interpretation of congressional powers under the Fourteenth Amendment, James A. Garfield gently reminded him, ''My colleague can make but not unmake history.'' The limits on congressional power had been set by Republicans' earlier conservatism. Those limits could not be undone. Even Radical Charles Sumner, struggling to pass his new, broad Civil Rights bill from 1870 until his death in 1874, had to argue that the discrimination he sought to eliminate in inns, theaters, carriers, and cemeteries was somehow sanctioned by state law. Given this continuing conservatism, it appears that historians might characterize Republicans' final decision in 1877 to cease attempting to protect citizens' rights in the South through national power more aptly as a consequence than a betrayal of their principles of 1865–1868.

The disastrous consequences of Republican conservatism in Reconstruction legislation are readily apparent. Congress withdrew its protection of southern citizens in 1877, unwilling any longer to exercise powers Republicans had so purposefully tried to avoid before 1868. The federal courts followed suit. Judges and justices, most of whom as Republicans remembered well the circumstances surrounding the passage and ratification of the constitutional amendments, carefully preserved the state jurisdiction upon which Republicans had been so unwilling to encroach. Accepting the Republican position that the national government could protect citizens whose rights to equal protection of the laws were deprived either through state action or failure to act, lower federal courts and ultimately the Supreme Court rigorously scrutinized congressional legislation to make certain it stayed within those boundaries. And when the loosely worded Force Act of 1871 and Civil Rights Act of 1875 came before them, the perhaps overly cautious courts found both to exceed the constitutional limits with which their framers had intended to comply. Even today, it is only with the utmost reluctance that our national government will intervene to protect citizens' rights within states. After 100 years, the constitutional conservatism which prevented Republicans from protecting adequately the rights of citizens remains a part of American political character.

The Radicalism of the Northern Republicans

PEYTON McCRARY

The ideology of the Republican party in the 1860s is among the enduring subjects of historiographical debate. According to one school of thought, the Republican ideology was essentially moderate. The party's adherence to laissez-faire principles of political economy and its constitutional conservatism placed severe constraints in the path of social change. Just as clearly, the conservative racial views most Republicans shared with other Americans doomed reconstruction from the start. Perhaps the most extreme statement of this interpretation belongs to George M. Fredrickson. Many Republican intellectuals believed that "the American Revolution was over and that revolutionary ideology had no further application to American society," he asserts bluntly. Indeed, for some conservatives "the war had permanently discredited the ideology of the Declaration of Independence and its latter-day apologists, the abolitionists."

A second school of thought treats the ideology of the Republican party as quite radical. These historians contend that Lincoln and his party perceived the war as a struggle to perfect the Union of their fathers by extending the democratic principles of 1776 to include emancipation and civil equality for blacks. Far from discrediting the abolitionist movement, argues James M. McPherson, the war made it more influential than ever. During the four years of bloody conflict, according to C. Vann Woodward, the Union government "moved from hesitant support of a limited war with essentially negative aims toward a total war with positive and revolutionary aims."

To the ongoing debate over the nature of the Republican ideology, this essay offers a modest contribution. In an earlier study of Reconstruction in Louisiana, I found that Republicans in that state regularly characterized their organization as a party of revolution, engaged in cataclysmic struggles with the slaveholding oligarchy of the South. Many of them argued that the usual rules of political negotiation and compromise did not apply in such a revolutionary situation, and they urged that federal military and political power be used to implement a program of radical change in the former Confederate states. Radicals and moderates within the party engaged in bitter arguments over political strategy, but shared a basic commitment to social and political change that marked them all as unacceptably radical in the eyes of conservative Democrats. In this essay, I explore the possibility that the Louisianans' image of the Republican organization as a

Peyton McCrary, "Republican Ideas About Politics and Social Change," *Civil War History* Volume 30, Number 4, December 1984, pp. 330–350. Reprinted with permission of The Kent State University Press.

"party of revolution" was widely shared in Northern states further from the scene of battle.

A logical source for understanding the image a political party seeks to place before the electorate is the campaign literature it offers to the public. Political pamphlets played an integral role in the electoral process of the 1860s. During election campaigns, politicians had long distributed copies of speeches delivered to mass rallies or on the floors of Congress. The war added to this traditional medium a tremendous infusion of intellectual energy, as Republican laymen organized publication boards to rally opinion behind the Union cause. In New York, prominent business and professional men formed the Loyal Publication Society to combat the pamphlet barrage laid down by the Democratic Party's ingenuously entitled Society for the Diffusion of Political Knowledge. The Republican organization circulated 900,000 copies of its 89 pamphlets to Union army units, charitable associations, and newspaper editors. The Philadelphia Union League issued an additional 4.5 million copies of 145 pamphlets and 44 broadsides on behalf of the party between 1863 and 1868. The editors of general magazines such as the *Atlantic Monthly* or the *North American Review* served on the executive committees of the publication societies, and as a result, essays appearing in their journals often circulated as pamphlets. After the war Massachusetts businessman George L. Stearns began an ad hoc publication society at his own expense, in order to disseminate pamphlets about reconstruction. The ideas expressed in this pamphlet literature constitute the basic concern of this essay.

Many themes find expression in this pamphlet literature. The most common element among radicals and conservatives alike was nationalism: commitment to the Union and to the expansion of national power drew no factional lines. For some conservative Republicans the limited goal of preserving the nation—with as little change as possible in its social, political, and constitutional fabric—was the primary goal throughout the war. They vented much of their anger, however, not at more radical Republicans but at the Democrats. That party spent most of its energies trying to convince the voters that the Lincoln administration was a tyrannical regime because it jailed advocates of disloyalty and suspended the writ of habeas corpus in the border states. To combat this view, Republican pamphlet writers vigorously defended the suppression of dissent in time of war, noting that the dissenters in question sympathized with the South's attempt to subvert the Constitution whose protection these "copperheads" now claimed.

The most widely circulated expression of this conservative viewpoint was Charles J. Stillé's elegant essay in comparative history, *How a Free People Conduct a Long War*. The Loyal Publication Society, the Philadelphia Union League, and the U.S. Sanitary Commission distributed a half-million copies of the pamphlet. Stillé draws an analogy between the Union army's struggle against the Confederacy and the British general Lord Wellington's "peninsula campaign" in Spain against Napoleon. In both cases disloyal criticism—"that hideous moral leprosy"—threatened the government's capacity to carry on the war. "The base spirit of faction" led the opposition party in England to criticize the slow progress of Wellington's armies, just as the Democrats now wrung their hands at "the impossibility of conquering or subjugating the South." Stillé believed ardently that the current war could be won, but he implies that the appropriate model for the Union government to follow is that of England's constitutional monarchy.

A quite different model—embodying a radical image of the Union government as a revolutionary regime—played a prominent role in the Republican pamphlet literature of the war years. A growing number of party spokesmen compared the American Civil War with the French Revolution of the 1790s and with a larger European revolutionary tradition culminating in the upheavals of 1848. Republicans saw this European tradition as an outgrowth of the American Revolution and insisted that they, not the Southern secessionists, were the true heirs of the principles of 1776. This image of the party of Lincoln as a party of revolution is sufficiently novel to require careful documentation.

Among the earliest pamphlets expounding the revolutionary model was that of B. Gratz Brown, reprinting a speech to the radical wing of the Missouri Republican movement. "We are the revolution," declared Brown. "The seceded states began this conflict," he emphasized, not to promote the cause of liberty but to preserve slavery and "a social system reposing exclusively upon caste. "To compare" their unprincipled revolt to the revolutionary struggle of their fathers," agreed his radical colleague, Charles D. Drake, was absurd. The Declaration of Independence defended the right of revolution only against tyranny, not against a democratic form of government. The war initiated by the slaveholders for reactionary purposes had, however, created the conditions for what Brown called "a great historic revolution," and he compared the Civil War with the French upheaval of 1789. Just as the French had taken "the axe to the root of the feudal system" and then adopted a "stern and vigorous policy of subjugation" against the counterrevolution in the Vendée, the Union government must now employ "the fierce surgery of revolution" to abolish slavery. Because the planter class had dominated the South's political system, moreover, the success of reconstruction would depend upon the willingness of the victorious North "to establish by force the supremacy of the new order."

In Missouri, the upheavals of the war made the image of Brown and his colleagues as a party of revolution plausible. The state's prewar governor and a minority of the legislature had sided with the Confederacy and moderate Unionists under the leadership of Hamilton Gamble and had established a provisional government. The moderates tried to preserve slavery but the initiative passed to more radical Unionists, who succeeded in winning immediate abolition before the end of the war. Eventually both Brown and Drake sat in the U.S. Senate, while their conservative opponents, Frank and Montgomery Blair, denounced them as "Jacobins."

The abolition of slavery was, in the eyes of many Americans, a revolutionary act. Democrats reiterated throughout the war the old proslavery claim that blacks would not, or could not, work efficiently without the compulsion of their white masters; some conservative Republicans feared this might be true. Yet whenever federal troops occupied Southern territory, they attracted large numbers of fugitive slaves and set up wage labor systems to get the local economy moving again. The South Carolina sea islands in particular became a laboratory for demonstrating to a skeptical Northern public that freedom would work. Comparative history was brought into the fray once again, as Republican intellectuals published articles, pamphlets, and books about the abolition of slavery in the West Indies. Immediate emancipation had worked better than the "apprenticeship system" by which the British had tried gradually to phase slavery out of existence on some of the islands, agreed all these accounts, and the local economies had flourished everywhere that the freedmen were able to obtain small plots of land. The abolition of serfdom in Russia also aroused interest. If Alexander II could impose emancipation on the Russian nobility, argued one pamphleteer, then the Lincoln administration could legitimately confiscate the slaves of Southern planters who were, unlike the Russian aristocracy, rebelling against their own government.

Throughout 1862, the Democrats made political capital from the charge that the administration was waging an abolitionist war, and tried to persuade midwestern voters that freed slaves would pour across the Ohio River to compete for their jobs. Republicans countered that such a migration would be more likely if slavery continued in the South. If they were instead freed from bondage, blacks would have every incentive to remain where they were. Lincoln and other Republicans toyed with the idea of colonizing the freedmen in Africa, the Carribean, or perhaps western territories, and for a time, the president promoted a gradual program of compensated emancipation for the border states. It is of some significance that the pamphlets circulated by the publication societies virtually ignored each of these conservative alternatives. Instead, they highlighted the more radical policy Lincoln ultimately proclaimed on January 1, 1863.

The Republican commitment to emancipation as a war aim—and to the idea that the Civil War was a revolutionary experience—finds eloquent expression in a volume of speeches delivered at a mass rally commemorating the second anniversary of the attack on Fort Sumter. An audience estimated by newsmen at thirty thousand, including representatives from twenty different loyal leagues along the east coast, gathered before six different speakers' platforms in Union Square, New York City, on April 11, 1863. Each platform had a half dozen speakers; two of the stands allowed them to address German-speaking audiences and another focused largely on War Democrats. Despite the effort to cast the rally as a nonpartisan event, the *New York Herald* noted that the only buildings in the area not flying the American flag were "the two headquarters of the democracy—Tammany Hall and Mozart Hall."

Republicans of every faction identified the Northern cause with the liberal tradition in nineteenth-century Europe. Postmaster General Montgomery Blair, considered one of the most conservative men in Lincoln's cabinet, declared that "this is a battle for common people throughout the world" who hoped to establish in their own lands "the great idea underlying our political fabric." The aristocracy of England and the continent sympathized instead, said Blair, with "the feudal lords who hold the slaves in bondage." New York Congressman Roscoe Conkling expressed a similar thought: "the struggle now raging in America is only the old battle for human rights transplanted from the Old World to the New." Texas Unionist Andrew J. Hamilton called it "the old struggle of liberty on the one hand, and despotism on the other." A German speaker told his countrymen at one platform that "many of you have already fought the same combat before"—presumably in 1848. This war was part of "the revolution which for the last seventy years has been going the rounds of Europe . . . the combat of free labor against the large landed property system." General Franz Sigel located the origins of this European revolutionary tradition in "the spirit of 1776," and emphasized that "it is in this country where the last blow should be struck." Francis W. Pierpont, Virginia's Unionist provisional governor, asked the Germans: "haven't you seen enough of aristocracy in the Old World?" Peace would not be possible, Pierpont insisted, unless the power of the Southern elite were destroyed. "Are you going to subjugate the master and return to him his property?" (The crowd yelled, "No, never.")

In describing the Civil War as a revolution, the Republicans emphasized the irreconcilability of slavery and freedom, and the impossibility of compromise with the South or with Peace Democrats. At each of the six stands the theme was ideological polarization. "There is no middle ground," declared both Congressman George W. Julian and S. B. Chittenden in identical words. "You who are not unconditionally for the war are against it," asserted Chittenden. "Since slavery has the nation by the throat," said Julian, the government was "at last ready to smite it," adding that if he commanded the invading armies, he would "lay waste their plantations; I would free and arm their negroes; I would write desolation and death on the very soil."

The rhetoric of the War Democrats at the rally was just as bloodthirsty. "There can be no compromise," said Daniel Dickinson bluntly. "I am for the olive branch myself, but I want it to be a stout tree, and about eight feet from the ground and have a good strong rope hanging at the end of it." Peace, urged the old New York Democrat, must be "anchored upon a sure foundation stone." Without emancipation no postwar settlement would be secure. "I object to this institution of slavery," said Dickinson, "as I would to a powder-house in the city of New York." James A. Brigg, another War Democrat, declared that "when Charleston is captured it should be razed to the earth and the ground on which it now stands should be ploughed over." Briggs added that, although "not long ago most men were afraid to be called emancipationists," but after two years of war "to call a man an abolitionist now does not stir his blood unpleasantly at all."

Theodore Tilton, editor of the powerful religious magazine *The Independent,* had long been an abolitionist but his view of Charleston's future was less bellicose. "That fort of Charleston's harbor was built upon a foundation of New England granite," he observed. "That state of South Carolina is to be rebuilt upon a foundation of New England ideas!" Tilton insisted that "there shall be no end of the war between North and South until freedom shall reign, and therefore peace. Justice is the only calmer of revolutionary storms."

The views expressed at the Sumter anniversary were acceptable to the mainstream of the Republican party in 1863; this was not a meeting of oldline abolitionists but a patriotic gathering designed to increase public support of the war effort. Yet not all of the speakers who used the rhetoric of revolution were equally committed. For example, within two years, George W. Julian would be pushing for the confiscation and redistribution of Southern plantations, and Montgomery Blair would defect to his old party, the Democrats. What can be said with confidence is that at this stage the speakers did not see it as a political liability to describe their party as revolutionary, to compare the abolition of slavery with the freeing of the European peasantry, or to demand the destruction of the economic power of the planter class.

To the Republicans of 1863, the elimination of slavery would alter the basic fabric of Southern society and liberate white farmers as well as black slaves. In a pamphlet that appeared in several editions, Columbia University political scientist Francis Lieber offered the thesis that the "small and respectable freeholder is indispensable to the cohesion and permanency of our country. Slavery is incompatible with such yeomanry." Lieber cited a recent study of English rural society that documented an unhealthy pattern of increasing land concentration in the hands of the elite. "Between these British landowners and the vast ignorant, immoral, pauperized, and dangerous peasantry, there is nothing but an impassable gulf," he asserted, adding that precisely the same trend had been at work in the antebellum South. He also compared the planter's domination of Southern rural society with the growth of latifundia in the agricultural system of ancient Rome. "Gracchus saw that the latifundia-holders were gradually substituting slaves, imported from Greece and Asia, for the free farmer," according to Lieber. "Gracchus did not desire to uproot Roman society by his agrarian laws," just to protect "the independent Roman farmer" from extinction. The Union government should follow his example of agrarian reform, thought Lieber, beginning with the abolition of slavery.

The next logical step in the argument was the confiscation of landed as well as human property, coupled with a program of assisting white-Unionists and freedmen to acquire farms. Radicals in the abolitionist movement had advocated such a policy since the beginning of the war, and gradually the idea of land reform began to acquire a grudging respectability. One influential advocate of land reform was James M. McKaye, whose pamphlet, *The Mastership and Its Fruits,* focused on the contract labor system in Louisiana. In the lower Mississippi valley the sweep of war left "the emancipated slave face to face with his old master . . . in the presence of the great revolution," wrote McKaye. He described in critical detail the halfway house between slavery and freedom erected by federal commander Nathaniel P. Banks; the army required blacks to sign annual wage contracts with plantation operators and to obtain military passes when leaving the plantations. Yet the freedmen also received wages for the first time, protection from corporal punishment or the separation of families, and in some areas, education for their children. As a temporary measure Banks's system had its merits, as McKaye saw it, but it would quickly be necessary to insist upon equality before the law. He also urged that the government grant the freedmen "the right to the elective franchise" in order to protect their interests in the postwar political system. The final step should be "the ultimate division of the great plantations into moderate sized farms, to be held and cultivated by the labor of their owners." McKaye's support for land redistribution grew out of the same theory of society expressed by Lieber, that "no such thing as free, democratic society can exist in any country where all the lands are owned by one class of men and are cultivated by another."

McKaye's views received official sanction because he was a member of the American Freedmen's Inquiry Commission, appointed by the Lincoln administration to investigate the condition of Southern blacks. In their published reports, the three commissioners urged the creation of a special federal bureau to facilitate the transition from slavery to freedom along the lines spelled out in McKaye's pamphlet. The establishment of the Freedmen's Bureau in March 1865 represented in one sense no more than a logical extension of the role already performed by the army of occupation in certain areas of the South. Yet to have a federal agency supervising the negotiation of labor contracts, setting up public schools for blacks, and undertaking a program of land reform—however limited in scope—was a remarkable intrusion into social and economic affairs for the nineteenth century.

All questions concerning the status of the freedmen depended, however, on the nature of the civil governments to be established in the former Confederate states. Inevitably the issue of reconstruction was embroiled in partisan politics, for every method of reorganizing government had implications for the balance of power between the parties. Sometimes the debate over reconstruction also became entangled in abstract constitutional issues, to the bemusement of English and European observers.

If Americans seemed preoccupied with "the wise inhibitions of the constitution," rationalized spokesmen of the Loyal National League in a public letter to French supporters of the Union cause, it was only because of the special nature of this war. "In all the revolutionary movements of modern Europe, the insurgents have usually represented liberty, nationality, and progress," the Americans pointed out, while the incumbent regimes were conservative defenders of autocracy. In the American case, however, "exactly the reverse is true." Here the rebels advocated slavery and repudiated "all ideas of liberty and progress, while the national government, founded upon the principles of the Declaration of Independence . . . wars only to preserve the institutions in which these rights are embodied." The cause of revolutionary change depended, in short, on the exercise of power by the existing regime through constitutionally accepted channels.

Perhaps the most familiar of these abstract questions was the argument over whether the rebel states were in or outside the Union, which Senator Charles Sumner described in a widely circulated pamphlet as "a topic fit for the old schoolmen or a modern debating society." Earlier, Sumner had contributed the theory of "state suicide" to this debate, but now he declared: "I discard all theory, whether it be of state suicide or state forfeiture or state abdication, on the one side, or of state rights, immortal and unimpeachable, on the other side." Each of the theories offered by Republicans led to the same conclusion, he pointed out: Congress had ample constitutional authority to establish guidelines for reorganizing civil governments in the occupied South. Sumner expressed preference for the moderate argument which most Republicans now accepted as the proper basis for congressional action: the clause of the Constitution providing that "the United States shall guarantee to every state in this union a Republican form of government."

Maryland Congressman Henry Winter Davis also dramatized the significance of this clause in a speech delivered at Concert Hall in Philadelphia which the city's Union League printed as a pamphlet. "Whatever Congress may think . . . necessary to restore and guarantee republican forms of government in the rebel states," Davis asserted, "Congress may pass." Sumner's interpretation was equally expansive: "the whole broad Rebel region is *tabula rasa,* or a 'clean slate', where Congress, under the Constitution . . . may write the laws." The dominant method of reorganizing government had been by military authority, although in Missouri and West Virginia local Unionists had taken the initiative. Lincoln simply had the army of occupation order elections, justifying his action by the same broad interpretation of the war powers of the presidency that sanctioned the denial of habeas corpus. Radicals conceded this presidential power, but only as a temporary expedient. In fact, Sumner described the creation of new state governments by military commanders as a "revolutionary proceeding," by which he meant in this instance that it was extraconstitutional.

Despite these reservations, Sumner and Davis joined other radicals in approving Lincoln's "ten per cent plan" of reconstruction. Although it continued to rely on military commanders to initiate elections, the president's proclamation required that all voters take an oath of loyalty to the Union and stipulated that emancipation was a prerequisite for federal recognition of new state governments. Within a few months, however, their initial suspicion of military authority was renewed. General Banks intervened in the reconstruction process in Louisiana by throwing his support to conservative Unionists after the local radicals came out in favor of limited Negro suffrage. The Louisiana radicals carried their complaint to Congress, where Davis and Sumner lent a willing ear. In the summer of 1864 the Congress passed the Wade-Davis Bill in large part to obviate recognition of Banks's Louisiana regime and to institute congressional supervision over reconstruction. Lincoln's pocket veto of the bill aroused the fury of congressional radicals and launched a lively little pamphlet war. Yet, on the whole, the debate between the president and Congress over the best means of reorganizing state governments in the South—a debate of surpassing importance on Capitol Hill—received little attention in the vast pamphlet literature circulated by the loyal publication societies.

In the midst of a presidential election year, understandably, the focus of most Republicans was on the threat of a Democratic victory. The aspiration of radical Salmon P. Chase to secure the Republican nomination never drew much support among the publicists of the patriotic associations, who generally favored a second term for Lincoln. After the Democrats nominated George B. McClellan on a platform advocating a negotiated peace with the South, allowing the return of the Confederate states with slavery intact, the partisan cast of the publication societies became more clear than ever. A flood of pamphlets poured from the presses, denouncing "the coward's convention" and picturing the contest between Lincoln and McClellan as an ideological choice between freedom and slavery.

After his triumphant reelection, the president pressed successfully for congressional passage of the Thirteenth Amendment abolishing slavery. He also threw his weight behind an effort to secure congressional recognition of the new Louisiana state government, in exchange for signing a reconstruction bill which at one point included a provision for limited Negro suffrage. Neither Louisiana recognition nor the proposed bill secured the necessary votes. The debates produced a widely circulated pamphlet, however, reprinting a memorable address on behalf of racial equality by Philadelphia Congressman William D. Kelley. He justified congressional reconstruction on the basis of the guarantee clause, but defined a "republican" form of government as one in which the abolition of slavery was accompanied by equal suffrage. Such a guarantee was both just in principle and necessary in practice, Kelley argued. Without the ballot, Negroes could not protect themselves from the establishment of apprenticeship or serfdom by the planter class, nor would white Unionists be secure from reprisals at the hands of returning Confederates. In his last public address, Lincoln conceded that his approach had not produced large Republican constituencies in the South, and as a result, the president openly endorsed limited Negro suffrage for the first time.

The assassination of Lincoln altered the political situation dramatically, for his successor Andrew Johnson pursued the sort of reconstruction policy favored by the Democrats. The failure to enfranchise blacks meant that Confederate veterans overwhelmed the white Unionists at the polls, contrary to the wartime situation under Lincoln. Johnson also ordered the Freedmen's Bureau to restore the land of all pardoned rebels and to grant newly organized civilian courts jurisdiction over the freedmen. Because Congress was not in session during the first eight months of peace, the president was able to implement an essentially counterrevolutionary program that defied every tenet of the Republican ideology.

The ideas about reconstruction that dominated Republican speeches and pamphlets in 1865 followed logically from the party's wartime commitments, adjusted in some respects in a more radical direction. Perhaps the most influential formulation was the "grasp of war" theory propounded by moderate Richard Henry Dana, Jr., in a speech at Boston's Faneuil Hall. "It is a fatal mistake to hold that this war is over, because the fighting has ceased," declared the scholarly attorney and literary figure. The victor "holds the conquered enemy in the grasp of war until it has secured whatever it has a right to require." The nation's security required that the former Confederate states meet certain conditions before restoration, Dana argued, using the guarantee clause as his justification. Despite his affiliation with the anti-Sumner wing of the state party, Dana's list of preconditions was more radical than many Republicans had demanded. "Four millions of disfranchised, disarmed, untaught landless, thriftless, non-producing, non-consuming, degraded men" are a poor foundation for "republican ideas and institutions," he observed: "a complete and perfect freedom" for Southern blacks would mean "four millions of landholding, industrious, arms-bearing, and voting population."

"To introduce the free negroes to the voting franchise is a revolution," Dana admitted. "If we do not secure that now, in the time of revolution, it can never be secured, except by new revolution," he added (to "loud applause," we are told). Surprisingly for a man who was critical of Sumner's radicalism, Dana stipulated that "we have a right to require . . . that the freedmen of the South shall have the right to hold land." He was also quite candid in defending the coercion of states by the central government. "Do you say this is coercion? Certainly it is. War is coercion, and this is war."

The grasp of war doctrine won immediate approval from a wide range of Republicans, including Indiana Governor Oliver P. Morton. In an influential pamphlet Morton refused to endorse the enfranchisement of Southern freedmen as a prerequisite for restoration, however, on the grounds that they were not yet prepared for full citizenship and that it was hypocritical of Republicans in a state like Indiana—which still deprived blacks of the ballot—to demand higher standards of the South. Morton was among those party leaders trying to remain on good terms with Johnson in the fall of 1865, despite reservations about the political effects of the president's policy. He compared Johnson favorably with Lincoln, stressing the continuity in constitutional procedures and ignoring the return to power of the Southern planter class under Johnson's policy of restoration. In discussing Lincoln's last public address, for example, Morton did not mention the martyred president's open support for black suffrage.

Republicans who favored black voting rights, on the other hand, publicized both Lincoln's endorsement in his last speech and his private letter to Louisiana Governor Michael Hahn in March 1864, urging the enfranchisement of Negroes at least on a limited basis. "We know now, from the record exposed since his death," asserted George S. Boutwell in a July 4th speech, "that it was one of the objects which he had near his heart, to secure to the negro population the right of suffrage." Advocates of political equality stressed that throughout the war Lincoln had continually shifted to the left. "If true to Mr. Lincoln, we shall see that the work of emancipation is made sure,'' said Joseph P. Thompson, pastor of the Broadway Tabernacle Church in New York, "by going beyond his own position as the logic of events shall lead us forward.''

Once it became clear that Johnson would lead the nation backward rather than forward, open conflict between the Republican Congress and the president was inevitable. By the time the Thirty-ninth Congress assembled in December 1865, a growing number of Republicans were prepared to believe Carl Schurz's report that Johnson's policy promoted the growth of frankly counterrevolutionary regimes. The same view dominated the books and articles by journalists who traveled South after Appomattox, and the letters from Northern veterans who decided to settle below the Mason-Dixon line: the returning Confederates enacted "black codes" to reduce the freedmen to a state of virtual peonage, and frequently reacted with personal violence to the open expression of Republican ideas.

The creation of these Democratic regimes headed by the nation's wartime enemies—enemies who had, after all, lost the war—angered Southern Unionists as well as Northern veterans. The practical necessity for enfranchising the freedmen quickly became apparent, and Louisiana once again led the way. The large Unionist movement formed the Friends of Universal Suffrage, changing the name of the organization in September 1865 to the Louisiana Republican party with some reluctance on the grounds that "the Republican Party in the North was not unequivocally committed to the cause of universal suffrage." Southern Unionists applauded when Congress refused to seat representatives and senators from the former Confederate states, passed the Civil Rights Act over the president's veto, and sent the Fourteenth Amendment to the states for ratification. Yet from their perspective, no reconstruction plan could work if it allowed the existing state governments to remain in power.

This theme dominated the proceedings of the Southern Loyalists' Convention which met in Philadelphia in September 1866 (proceedings were published as a pamphlet and circulated widely during the fall congressional campaign). All agreed that congressional intervention in the reconstruction process was essential, but there were differences on the shape a congressional program should assume. Delegates from the deep South advocated universal suffrage as the only hope of building viable Republican regimes. Texas Unionist Andrew J. Hamilton argued that the freedmen "have earned, sir, by their blood, upon a hundred historical battlefields, their right to participate in the obligations and privileges of government." Albion W. Tourgée, an Ohio veteran now living in North Carolina, saw this as preferable to the alternative favored by some Republicans: refusal to allow former rebels to vote. "The disfranchisement of all rebels," he declared, would produce an initial Republican victory but in the long run would "establish a banditti more dangerous than that of Corsica." Thus, the optimal course was "the enfranchisement of all loyal men."

Delegates from Tennessee and the border states—where disfranchisement of whites was more popular—tried to prevent the loyalist convention from endorsing universal male suffrage by pushing for resolutions praising the Fourteenth Amendment as a basis for reconstruction. Moderate Republicans preferred this compromise, rather than wage the fall elections on a platform favoring the ballot for Southern freedmen. Republicans from the lower South bluntly rejected the moderate plan. The Democrats who controlled the South "claim to rule over us . . . to degrade, debase, and proscribe us," said Louisiana's Henry Clay Warmouth angrily: "there can be no middle ground." The delegates from the "unreconstructed" states therefore adopted resolutions in favor of universal suffrage and campaigned throughout the North on behalf of their radical program.

Not only in the South was there "no middle ground." The rupture between president and Congress was complete by the fall of 1866. Johnson characterized Congress as a "rump parliament" and implied that its actions were unconstitutional. Republicans described him as a "usurper"—an invidious comparison with the martyred Lincoln—and denounced "the President and his accomplices" as a threat to the nation. In an influential pamphlet, Sherman M. Booth of Wisconsin compared Johnson's defiance of Congress with Bismarck's contemptuous handling of the Prussian Landtag in the country's recent constitutional crisis. "Congress has so far yielded power to the President," Booth added disdainfully, "as to withhold political power from its friends, who saved the nation from dismemberment, and confer it upon its enemies." Together the freedmen and white Unionists "constitute a majority in every Southern state," he observed, and thus, universal suffrage, even without large-scale rebel disfranchisement, would place the former Confederate states in trustworthy Republican hands. "The alternatives are virtual enslavement, or partial protection by Federal bayonets."

Johnson was no Bismarck, however, and Congress was more independent than the Prussian parliament. The elections of 1866, which according to the normal pattern of off-year campaigns should have increased the number of Democratic seats, resulted instead in a greater Republican majority. Congress returned and passed a series of military reconstruction bills, removing the existing provisional governments from power, enfranchising Southern freedmen, and protecting law and order during the conduct of the first elections under the new dispensation. Recent historians emphasize that the most radical Republicans on Capitol Hill were not primarily responsible for the passage of these reconstruction bills. Yet the actual content of the congressional program, at least in political and constitutional terms, was genuinely radical.

Many Republicans seem to have agreed with Carl Schurz that the initiation of this program represented the culmination of "a great political and social revolution." The abolition of slavery and the emergence of a free labor system was in itself "a great social revolution," he argued, but "this mere negative step was far from completing the transformation of a community consisting of masters and bondsmen into a community of citizens equal before the law." Such a transformation could, theoretically, have been imposed by a powerful central government, Schurz continued. "The Czar of Russia, when emancipating the serfs . . . held the whole development of the great reform in his powerful hand.'' In a democratic system like the United States, however, ''the emancipated class must be endowed with political rights sufficient to enable it to protect itself,'' he believed, ''and to cooperate in the control of the revolutionary results.''

For the preceding five years, many Republicans had characterized themselves in speeches and pamphlets as members of a revolutionary party. This point of view may be summarized as follows. They understood the term revolution to mean a political upheaval in which the two sides fought for antithetical ideologies. They identified the Northern cause with the liberal principles of the Declaration of Independence and the free labor system. They saw the Confederacy as a reactionary effort to defend the class interests of a slaveholding oligarchy, and they regarded Northern Democrats as ideological allies of the rebels. Despite the fact that the South initiated the war, Republicans insisted that their party was the true inheritor of the revolutionary legacy of 1776, 1789, and 1848. Their preoccupation with respecting constitutional principles, they confessed, might seem inconsistent with the idea of revolution. They were defending an existing national government, however, and the structure of that government was radically democratic by European standards. The political achievements of 1867—equality before the law and universal male suffrage—were radical by anyone's standards, Republicans felt, and these changes could only have been achieved by the bayonets of the Union army.

Most Republicans also saw the results of the Civil War as a social revolution in the South. The abolition of slavery was, in their eyes, a revolutionary confiscation of the capital of the planter elite and a far-reaching transformation of the slave's economic situation. Indeed, the most recent econometric research suggests that they were correct. During the war, some Republicans actively pursued the prospect of agrarian reform as a logical extension of emancipation. Had Andrew Johnson not restricted the rental and sale of land by the Freedmen's Bureau after the war, more might have come of this promise of land for the freedmen.

In addition, Republicans often expressed the view that emancipation would lead inevitably to a middle class society, in which small farmers of both races would control the bulk of the land in the rural South. This did not happen, of course; the assumption was, no doubt, naive. Even had the Republicans attempted to carry out an ambitious program of land reform, the economic conditions in the postwar South were hardly conducive to the achievement of the yeoman ideal, even for whites. Some historians see the failure of the Republican Party to implement massive land redistribution as evidence that their ideology was not revolutionary. Such a judgment imposes a particular twentieth-century definition of revolution on the analysis of nineteenth-century revolution.

What do we make of this image of the Republicans as the party of revolution? It was not employed by all Republicans; Abraham Lincoln, for example, avoided the rhetoric of revolution which many supporters used to describe his policies. The Democrats tried to gain political mileage by denouncing the president and his party as dangerous revolutionaries, however. The odd thing about the war years is that such charges did not cause Republicans—even Lincoln—to move cautiously back toward the center. The term "revolution" may have been used with greater frequency by Republicans who were considered radicals, but as we have seen, it also sprang to the lips of many moderates as well. Talk is cheap, we are tempted to say, and some of those who boasted of the revolutionary achievements of the war may have voted a conservative line on Capitol Hill or back home in Indiana. Yet talk is not cheap for a politician whose constituents may turn him out of office because he sounds too radical. Therein lies the significance of the pamphlet literature, which reflects the image the Republican party wanted to put before the electorate. And that image was, quite often, radical.

The Civil War radicalized Republican opinion because political and military necessity required the Lincoln administration to take actions no one would have dreamed possible a few years earlier. In perceiving the war as a revolution, Republicans were able to rationalize these actions as falling within a sanctified revolutionary tradition that justified the use of force to achieve rapid social and political change. By accepting the moral legitimacy of revolution, they were also able to take more seriously the radical implications of their own Declaration of Independence. The principles of 1776 had long been a centerpiece of the Republican ideology, even for moderates like Lincoln, but only the war made possible the extension of the idea that "all men are created equal" to include the Afro-American population.

From the perspective of the freedmen, certainly, emancipation was itself a revolutionary change. For a few brief years after 1867, it seemed that the ideal of civil and political rights for blacks might also become a reality in the South, even though the prospect of economic democracy had all but vanished. The mechanism for implementing this ideal—congressional reconstruction—had required major adjustments in constitutional theory as well as a transformation in racial attitudes. Yet the adjustments were made. The success of the party's program in the South demanded no more new ideas, but it did require fidelity to the ideology by which Republicans had justified reconstruction in the first place. The collapse of their program in the face of overwhelming white hostility stemmed less from the intellectual limitations of the party's ideology than from an ultimate failure of will.

ᴥ *F U R T H E R   R E A D I N G*

Richard H. Abbott, *The Republican Party and the South, 1855–1877* (1986)
Herman Belz, *Reconstructing the Union: Theory and Policy During the Civil War* (1969)
———, *Emancipation and Equal Rights: Politics and Constitutionalism in the Civil War Era* (1978)
M. Les Benedict, "The Rout of Radicalism: Republicans in the Election of 1867," *Civil War History* 18 (1972), 334–344

———*Compromise of Principle: Congressional Republicans and Reconstruction* (1974)

W. R. Brock, *An American Crisis: Congress and Reconstruction 1865–1867* (1963)

Dan T. Carter, *When the War Was Over: Self-Reconstruction in the South, 1865–1867* (1985)

Stanley Coben, "Northeastern Business and Radical Reconstruction," *Mississippi Valley Historical Review* 46 (1959) 67–90

LaWanda Cox and John Cox, *Politics, Principle and Prejudice, 1865–1866* (1963)

David Donald, *Charles Sumner and the Rights of Man* (1970)

Eric Foner, "Thaddeus Stevens, Confiscation and Reconstruction," in *Politics and Ideology in the Age of the Civil War* (1980), 128–149

Harold M. Hyman, *A More Perfect Union: The Impact of the Civil War and Reconstruction on the Constitution* (1973)

Peyton McCrary, *Abraham Lincoln and Reconstruction: The Louisiana Experiment* (1978)

Eric L. McKitrick, *Andrew Johnson and Reconstruction* (1960)

Michael Perman, *Reunion Without Compromise: The South and Reconstruction, 1865–1868* (1973)

———, *Emancipation and Reconstruction, 1862–1879* (1979)

James E. Sefton, *Andrew Johnson and the Uses of Constitutional Power* (1980)

Hans Trefousse, *The Radical Republicans: Lincoln's Vanguard for Racial Justice* (1969)

C. Vann Woodward, "Seeds of Failure in Radical Race Policy," in *American Counterpoint: Slavery and Racism in the North-South Dialogue* (1971), 163–183

CHAPTER
12

Reconstructing the South

↙

By June 1868, all of the former Confederate states—except Virginia, Mississippi, and Texas, where the process took a little longer—had been reconstructed and readmitted to the Union. This had been accomplished under the terms of the Reconstruction Act of March 1867. These terms required, first, that all adult male African-Americans be entitled to vote and that leading Confederates be disfranchised as well as disqualified from holding office. Second, the transformed electorate in each state was then to ensure that new governments were elected and new constitutions written. When each state met these conditions, that state was readmitted.

Naturally enough, these reorganized state governments were to be controlled by loyal elements that supported Reconstruction and were Republican in party affiliation. To keep the South out of disloyal as well as Democratic hands had, after all, been essential to an effective Federal policy for the defeated section. But electing and installing these governments was just the beginning. If Reconstruction was to endure and thereby introduce much needed economic, political, and even social changes in the South, these Republican administrations had to be sustained and remain in power. Yet most citizens viewed them as alien and illegitimate, and even those who voted for them and held office under them gained little respect. Moreover, the kinds of reforms and innovations that the Reconstruction governments had to introduce were certain to provoke vigorous, even violent, opposition from the planter class and its allies, who currently dominated southern society. Intense opposition was likely because the mandatory agenda included such goals as a broadening of political participation, the passage of civil-rights legislation, the creation of a free and independent labor force, and the development of railroads and industry.

The newly created and inexperienced party was therefore confronted with more than just the daunting task of political and economic change; it also faced a terrible dilemma. If these reform measures were not undertaken, Reconstruction would be stillborn. If, on the other hand, they were embarked upon, then they would arouse such opposition that Reconstruction would be resisted and probably thwarted. Consequently, either of the two courses could be disastrous.

Historians have all too often criticized and blamed the southern Republicans for Reconstruction's failure. But before rushing to judgment, it is only fair to try to understand the nature and extent of the difficulties that the party encountered.

✑ D O C U M E N T S

When the Republicans assumed power between 1868–1869 and began to govern the southern states, they were confronted with an acute political dilemma, as the first three documents illustrate. One horn of the dilemma is presented in the first selection, by Joseph E. Brown, who was affiliated with the Republican party and had just been appointed chief justice of his state of Georgia. In a letter to the new governor, Rufus B. Bullock, of December 3, 1868, Brown urged the party to conciliate its Democratic opponents by splitting off their more moderate wing. The other alternative is evident from the second document, in which Senator Morgan Hamilton, a leading Texas Republican, warns of the dangers of conciliation in a letter of August 10, 1870, to James P. Newcomb, another influential Republican from Texas. The third selection was written during a later stage in southern Reconstruction; Governor Daniel H. Chamberlain of South Carolina, in a letter of January 13, 1876, to U.S. Senator Oliver P. Morton of Indiana, defends his effort to reform his party and the state government in order to win the respect and cooperation of the more moderate Democrats.

The chapter's remaining documents highlight some of the achievements of the Republican party in the South. The fourth selection is from a speech on March 13, 1868, by Thomas J. Mackey, president of the South Carolina constitutional convention of 1868, adjourning the assembly and congratulating it on its accomplishments. And the fifth document is Albert T. Morgan's positive evaluation of his own work as sheriff of Yazoo County, Mississippi, from his memoir of his grim experiences during Reconstruction entitled *Yazoo; Or, On the Picket Line of Freedom in the South* (1884).

Georgia Chief Justice Joseph E. Brown Urges Republicans to Be Conciliatory, December 1868

Atlanta [Georgia],
Dec. 3rd, 1868.

His Excellency R. B. Bullock.

Dear Governor,

I regretted, as you no doubt did, to hear of the defeat of our friend Blodgett for mayor. This is the loss of the last stronghold of the Republican party in the State. The result of the late elections prove very clearly that the negro vote will not do to rely upon unless there is a white party in the locality of the election strong enough to give them the necessary moral support. As I have often said to Republicans North and South, so soon as the Democrats admit the right of the freedmen to vote, and make no farther issue upon it, they will carry a large proportion of them in every election. Indeed they did so in the Presidential election, while the mass of the party denied their right to vote, or at least avowed their object to do all in their power to take away the right as soon as possible.

It seems to me this should teach us as Republicans that it is impossible to maintain the party in this State, or indeed in the South, without a division of the white vote. We must divide the present Democratic party and unite with a strong wing of them who, if properly managed, will support Ge[nera]l Grant's administration, or it is utterly hopeless to attempt to contend with them. They possess most of the intelligence and wealth of the State which will always control tenants and laborers. This is so in every State and Georgia will not be an exception. You may ask if it is possible to divide them. I answer it can be done easily if properly managed. They are now divided into two wings with nothing in common except the name. The leaders of the two wings hate each other and will never act together for any length of time unless by our blunders we enable the leaders of the crazy wing to apply the party lash so strongly, by appeals to prejudice, as to hold them together. My opinion is that we should make terms with the moderate wing and that the new administration should treat them with such consideration as to gratify them. If this is done, we can easily unite and carry the State in the next elections. Let the Ben Hill and [Robert] Toombs wing go. We have no terms to offer them and no wish to coalesce with them. . . .

As you know, I have taken an active part in the politics of the State for over ten years and have studied this question carefully and feel fully satisfied I am not mistaken as to the effect. I repeat, our only chance is "divide and conquer." We must conciliate the moderate wing, or this is not possible.

Excuse the plainness and frankness with which I have written you the deliberate conclusions to which my mind has arrived on this vexed question.

Very truly your friend,

Joseph E. Brown

A Texas Republican Laments His Party's Leniency, August 1870

Glen Haven N.Y.
10 August 1870

Hon. J. P. Newcomb
Austin, Texas

My dear Sir

. . . I may be mistaken, but I think we are now passing through the same ordeal in Texas which most if not all the southern states have experienced, and shall find the same result i.e. bankruptcy and general disgust from our want of brains, patriotism and integrity.

If the *passage,* simply, of the Militia and Police bills shall bring quiet to the country then I shall be rejoiced to find myself mistaken—that is all I shall say on this point.

I shall be equally glad to have my gloomy prognostications falsified by the returns of the next election. Your confident assertion that that occasion "will prove that we can spare some of the new converts who are now trimming" satisfies me more than ever that the party is already hopelessly broken down. It has recruited too many already, and the more it takes in, the worse for the cause of Republicanism. All the southern states have been increasing the strength of the Republican party in the same way, and most of them have realized at the first election under their respective constitutions a signal defeat so far as elections have been holden. North Carolina has just passed into the hands of the Democracy, and she contained the most numerous and most reliable material for permanent Republican government of any state in the south. If the party has been unable to hold that state, it will be folly to think of keeping the control of any other southern state. They will all go, and you may as well make up your mind to that. Indeed, it would seem that the members of the Legislature of Texas are, most of them, of this mind; for there is no indication of an adjournment, though the body has been in session since the admission of the state. It seems probable that they will after a short recess for vacation, continue the session until the end of their term. They appear to think that they are entitled to and are determined to have their eight dollars a day. Clearly they never expect to be returned again. No party can hold power long when it is so scandalously abused. . . .

Yours very truly,

M[organ] C. Hamilton

Governor Daniel H. Chamberlain of South Carolina Defends Conciliation and Reform, January 1876

13 January 1876

To Hon. Oliver P. Morton:

Dear Sir—I have to-day received a letter from a friend who has recently conversed with you, in which he writes: "Mr. Morton looks on your (my) attitude as in practical identification with the Democrats, and already gives up the State (South Carolina) to the opposition."

I am sure you would not willingly reach either of the above conclusions, and therefore I am forced to think that you are greatly misinformed in regard to the posture of political affairs in this State. I am aware, too, that you are greatly and sincerely interested in the fortunes of Southern Republicans, and I therefore conclude that you will listen to statements which may be laid before you, though they may not agree with the conclusions which you have already reached. I beg your indulgence while, as briefly as possible, I give you my views of the situation here.

Ex-Governor F. J. Moses, Jr., was my predecessor in office. During his term of office the conduct of public affairs by him and his followers was such that a vast majority of the Republican party became convinced that a thorough reform, or the promise of it, was the only way in which the success of the party could be secured in 1874. For some reason I was selected as the candidate for Governor of those who held such views. I had been Attorney General of the State from 1868 to 1872, and on account of my connection with public affairs here during that period I was distrusted by many Republicans, and my nomination was hotly contested, on the sole ground that I was not likely to carry out the promised reforms of our party. Upon my nomination, though I had pledged myself in every form to immediate and rigid reform, a bolt took place, embracing many of our best and most devoted Republicans, who refused to support me because I could not, in their judgment, be trusted to carry out practical reform. My election was fiercely contested by those Republicans on that ground alone, while my friends and I stoutly asserted, by our platform and speeches everywhere, that if I was elected thorough and complete reform should take place. I was elected by a majority of 11,000 votes, against a majority of 35,000 for Moses two years previous, and 40,000 for Scott four years previous, this reduced majority being solely due to the distrust of me and my supporters by a considerable wing of our party on the single issue of reform.

I took my seat as Governor, December 1, 1874, and I addressed myself earnestly to the work of keeping the pledges I had made and the pledges made for me by all my friends and by our platform in the campaign. I soon found that many of those who had supported me in the campaign and had talked reform did not want reform; but I persevered, determined, as a matter of right and of good policy, to adhere to my party platform and pledges. Of course those who disliked practical reform cried out: "He is going over to the Democrats!" "He wants social recognition from the rebels!" and all the rest of those senseless cries such as you now hear about me. Still I persevered; and when our Legislature met in November last there was apparent harmony between me and my party, and a complete acquiescence in the wisdom of the policy of reform as carried out by me. The result was that at that time the Democracy of this State was disarmed and had no hope, apparently, of even nominating a separate State ticket in opposition to the Republican party. Neither under the guise of "tax unions" or the "Conservative" party could they or did they maintain even an organization worthy [of] the name. The leaders could not persuade the masses of the white people that they could secure any better government than they were enjoying under my Administration.

Now what had I done up to that time? I challenge contradiction from any source when I solemnly affirm that I had done nothing; not one thing which was not pledged by me on every stump in the State when I was a candidate; nothing which our party platform did not demand; nothing but what every man who now opposes me declared in that campaign to be indispensable; nothing which you or any other honest Republican would not say was right and Republican. This is a broad statement, but I defy proof of any sort in contradiction of it in any particular. Suppose you talk with some one in Washington who is now denouncing me—and it certainly cannot be difficult, judging from what I hear, to find such. Ask him what Governor Chamberlain had done before these recent judicial elections, that indicated any infidelity to the Republican party? Ask him if I had appointed Democrats to office? If he tells you the truth, he will say no, for the fact is that never since 1868 were there so few Democrats in office in this State as since my Administration. I know whereof I affirm, and will prove it to you if you find it denied. Ask him further if I advocated or approved any measures of legislation which were in any possible sense un-Republican or opposed to the interests of the Republican party. He cannot name one, for there is not one. Ask him if I proclaimed any doctrines which were not held by the Republican party. He will not be able to point out one. Ask him if I ever in any way affiliated politically with the Democracy or had any thing to do with them politically, nearly or remotely. He will not be able to point out any such action or tendency of any kind or degree. What, then, is the matter with me? Why was I disliked or denounced by some members of my own party? Simply for this, I insisted on reasonable taxes, competent officers, honest expenditures, fair legislation, and no stealing, and the Democrats praised me for it.

The last two things are my offence. I did not sanction schemes of public plunder—such as our "printing ring," for instance, but the cost of public printing per year was cut down from $180,000 to $50,000, and contingent funds from $80,000 to $27,000, and, I repeat, the Democrats praised me. . . .

A South Carolina Republican Applauds His State's New Constitution, March 1868

. . . The work which we were sent here to do was most momentous to the Commonwealth which we represent, and the members of this Convention are, I think, worthy of much commendation for the improvements they have made in the organic law, when their labors are compared with those of their predecessors. We here present to our constituents a Constitution in which, for the first time in the political history of the State, the great doctrine of manhood suffrage is distinctly recognized, and all the rights are secured to every citizen to which nature and nature's God have entitled him. Here, have we stricken every vestige of serfdom from our institutions, and that too in so emphatic and unambiguous a way, that no doubt can be entertained of our determination that this relic of barbarism shall never again, in any form, pollute our soil. Here we have made every needful arrangement for the free education of our people, so that if future legislators shall carry out in good faith the provisions which we have ordained on this vital subject, in a few years the stain of ignorance which now pollutes our history will be forever obliterated, and the happy period will have arrived when no son or daughter of South Carolina will be unable to read and write. Thus have we broadly sown the seeds of public education, and thus shall we, in no distant time, reap the rich harvest of public virtue. Crime and ignorance are inseparable companions. We have stricken a heavy blow at both, and may look for the natural and inevitable result in the elevation of all our people to a social, political and religious eminence, to which, under the former Constitution and laws of the State, they had never attained.

Here, too, we have obliterated from our political system that most pernicious heresy of State sovereignty—a heresy which, for nearly half a century, taught by our leaders, had, like an *ignis fatuis* [*sic*], led the people of South Carolina, on more than one occasion, to the brink of rebellion, until there arose at length, as a necessary result of this doctrine, one of the most fratracidal wars that the world ever saw. The theory of a divided allegiance, and of a sovereignty within a sovereignty, alike incongruous with all the principles of political science and with the system of national power established by our fathers, has received from you a death blow. No longer, if the Constitution you have adopted should be ratified by the people, will there be any danger of a future rebellion, in which the glorious flag of our common country—a flag which has often "braved the battle and the breeze"—shall be treated by a portion of the nation with insult, and for it an ensign to be substituted, consecrated by no national traditions, and simply the novel insignia of a disrupted Confederacy. In establishing this principle of a paramount allegiance to the national Government you have thrown a protection around the national life for the future, and you have justified the acts of those Union men who, in the midst of a wide-spread and threatening rebellion, nobly stood by this doctrine you have announced, and would not acknowledge that the State, however much they loved it as their home, could supplant, in their affections, the nation from which they received protection.

I speak not of these, as parts of the results of our labors, in any spirit of acrimony toward those who have heretofore neglected these great duties of legislators—for I would desire to bury the past in that oblivion which best befits it, or to hold it only as a beacon light to warn us from its follies and its perils in the future—but because as stewards of a great trust we have a right to show to our constituents how we have discharged the duties of the stewardship in which they had confided to us.

To the people of South Carolina, we submit the Constitution which we were instructed to frame, in the confident expectation that its manifest superiority over all other Constitutions by which this Commonwealth has hitherto been governed, will secure for it a triumphant ratification. We do not claim for ourselves a pre-eminence of wisdom or virtue, but we do claim that we have followed in the progressive advancement of the age; that we have been bold and honest enough and wise enough to trample obsolete and unworthy prejudices under foot, and thus have been enabled, with impartial legislation, to provide for the civil and political interests of all men of every rank, station or race, within the borders of our beloved State.

But the painful moment of separation has arrived, and that word which friends always dread to hear has to be pronounced. Associates, I bid you an affectionate farewell, and wishing you all a safe and happy return to your respective homes, I now, in accordance with the resolution of the house, declare the Constitutional Convention of South Carolina to be adjourned *sine die*.

The Convention then adjourned *sine die*.

A Mississippi Sheriff Recalls His Achievements During Reconstruction, 1884

The reader has already seen what was accomplished by "the enemy" during the years of its control prior to the war, and in the four years which followed that event, in the way of county public improvements. In this chapter I shall endeavor to faithfully set down what was accomplished by "we all radicals," in the six years of my "dictatorship." By the beginning of the year 1875, the requisite repairs upon the county highways and bridges had been completed, and new bridges built, so that in that respect the county had never before enjoyed equal facilities. Improvements upon the poor-farm buildings had been made, the farm put in cultivation, system and order enforced in its management and among its inmates, and the institution had become nearly self-sustaining.

The capacity and security of the jail had been enlarged by the addition of safe, iron cells.

A new court-house, costing quite seventy thousand dollars, had been erected and paid for as the work progressed, and had been "accepted" by a committee of the oldest and best members of our Yazoo bar association. Everybody said it was a credit to the county.

The county indebtedness had at no time exceeded the annual levy for current expenses. The finances had been managed in such a way that within the first year of our control, county warrants went up to par, and remained there during the entire period, with only short exceptional occasions. At the close of 1873 there were outstanding obligations amounting to quite thirty thousand dollars, but nearly if not quite the entire sum would be absorbed by the tax-levy of that year, the collection of which had been interfered with by the "insurrection."

Yazoo City was an incorporated town, its government was under the control of the Republicans, who were in a majority. As in the county so it was here; extensive improvements had been wrought; new side-walks, pavements, and gutters, had been made, and, above all, perhaps, a new steam fire-engine had been provided. Our Yankee postmaster, aided by a few public-spirited fellow-citizens, was foremost in all these good works.

We had failed, it is true, to get a railroad to our town, but that was by no fault of "we all Yankees." Three lines had been chartered, and at one time the prospect was very bright indeed that we would have one. But the great panic spreading throughout the North had interfered with our plans. Mississippi hardly felt the great shock, it is true, but as we were depending largely upon Northern capital for our road, and as the panic wrecked for a season all such prospects, our proposed railroad withered and shrank so far away that it had not yet reached Yazoo City, nor even Mississippi.

On all these improvements our party leaders had been practically a unit, and the great body of the freed people had stood squarely by us. I am sorry to say that there was not the same harmony among "we all Republicans" upon the school question. . . .

At the outset the free-school idea met the determined hostility of the irreconcilables, the faint acquiescence of the conservatives in the ranks of the enemy, the lukewarm adherence of the Unionists, the sympathy and active co-operation of the Northerners and the unanimous and greedy support of the "freedmen, free negroes and mulattoes."

But in spite of all the obstacles in the way of its growth, in 1875 the system in Yazoo was a complete success, a fact acknowledged by all except possibly a handful of the most violent of the irreconcilables.

It had become so popular that old and wealthy planters often came personally to the superintendent or members of the board, and pleaded for a school on their own plantations, declaring that they not only wished it as a means of improving the freed people, but also, because they had observed that the laborers on other plantations where schools were, or who were in the neighborhood of schools, were more contented and worked better.

It was found impossible to supply the demand. To have done so at once would have so greatly increased the taxes that it would have been burdensome to the government.

It is with a feeling of no little pride and gratification that I am able to add here, at the close of this account of my stewardship, that the tax-levy at no time during the entire period exceeded two and one-half per cent, and in 1875, was but two and one-fifth per cent for all purposes.

⤳ E S S A Y S

The essays that follow present two approaches to understanding the problems involved in reconstructing the South. The obstacles and dilemmas facing the southern Republicans are the concerns of the first selection by Ted Tunnell of Virginia Commonwealth University. Although this essay deals entirely with Louisiana, the author's observations also apply to the rest of the reconstructed states. In the second selection, Eric Foner of Columbia University focuses on the question of how labor was to be organized in the post-emancipation South, and he explains why the idea and practice of "free labor" proved so difficult to establish. At the same time, he assesses the position of the Republican party in the region's political economy.

The Contradictions of Power

TED TUNNELL

. . . Unlike most Northern migrants of the war era, [the future Reconstruction governor of Louisiana, Henry C.] Warmoth pursued a political career from the start. Active in the organization of the state Republican party, he went to Washington in late 1865 as Louisiana's unofficial "territorial" delegate. Though his public speeches from this early period were quite ordinary (he stood for universal suffrage, loyal government, the return of General Butler, and the ex-soldier), his contemporaries marked him as a comer. Louisiana abounded with ex-brigadiers and major generals: yet the former lieutenant colonel emerged as the leader of the Grand Army of the Republic. Warmoth easily formed friendships with influential older men of widely varying views and backgrounds: Thomas J. Durant, the Reverend John P. Newman, General McClernand, George S. Denison, his law partner John F. Deane, William L. McMillen, and later Henry S. McComb. A tall, strikingly handsome man, Warmoth's appearance was one of his strongest political assets. Like Banks, [Benjamin F. Butler's successor as federal military commander in Louisiana], he looked the part of the statesman. In fact, Mrs. Banks had informed him at a wartime ball that he spoke and acted like young General Banks. Warmoth blushed and danced with the lady. Several days later, Banks offered him the judgeship of the provost court.

In his autobiography Warmoth described the condition of Louisiana in July 1868, when he took over as governor. New Orleans and the state government were bankrupt. The value of assessed property had fallen from $470 million in 1860 to only $250 million. Taxes were in arrears for every year since 1859. The state's agriculture had been ravaged by war, flood, and infestation. The longest piece of railroad track stretched a mere sixty miles; the only canal extended six miles from New Orleans to Lake Pontchartrain. The levees of the Mississippi and other waterways remained in a deplorable state. Almost no extractive or manufacturing industries marred the landscape. The public roads were little more than mud trails. Epidemics of yellow fever and malaria visited the state yearly. Of New Orleans, whatever romantic images it usually evokes, Warmoth recorded that it had only four paved streets, and "the slaughter-houses were so located that all of their offal and filth were poured into the Mississippi River, just above the mains that supplied the people with their drinking water." Overrun with gamblers, prostitutes, and thugs; ruled by corrupt and ignorant officials; the Crescent City was "a dirty, impoverished, and hopeless place." In sum, the state foundered in a veritable sea of troubles, but the paramount concern of the new regime was survival.

The response of the white South to the onset of Radical Reconstruction has been aptly described as "Counter Reconstruction." Rejecting the le-

From *Crucible of Reconstruction 1862–1877* by Ted Tunnell, 1984, pp. 152–172. Reprinted by permission of Louisiana State University Press. Copyright © 1984 by Louisiana State University Press.

gitimacy of Republican governments based on Negro suffrage, white Southerners organized secretly and massively to destroy them. By the fall of 1868 there existed in Louisiana, as in other Southern states, a vast shadowland of secret paramilitary political clubs and societies: Knights of the White Camellia, Swamp Fox Rangers, Innocents, Seymour Knights, Hancock Guards, and the seldom seen but widely rumored Ku Klux Klan. The Knights of the White Camellia ranked as the largest and most important of these. Led by the "best" citizens and organized statewide, in many parishes its membership claimed half or more of the white males. The veil of secrecy shrouding these organizations concealed a fantasy world, where respectable citizens, like the heroes of a Thomas Dixon novel, guarded the "nest of the White Eagle" against the "black Vulture." In this paranoid realm, Negro uprisings were always imminent, and the carpetbagger and scalawag stereotypes of Reconstruction legend took on a sinister reality. The need to restore white rule justified every means, every sadistic impulse, every enormity.

A few instances of intimidation and fraud marred the April elections of 1868. On the upper Red River and a few other places, whites kept Negroes from the polls, destroyed Republican tickets, and tampered with the returns. None of this, though, prepared the new regime for the terrible ordeal of the presidential election. Starting in May and continuing through November, gangs of armed whites rode by day and night, spreading terror across the state. Among the first casualties was William R. Meadows, the literate ex-slave who had represented Claiborne Parish in the constitutional convention. Assassins murdered him in his yard. In a neighboring parish whites pulled a black leader from his home, shot him, and cut off his head. In St. Mary Parish disguised whites entered a hotel in the town of Franklin and publicly murdered the sheriff and judge with knives and pistols. A white Republican warned a colleague that unless the "almost daily" murders of Union men in north-central Louisiana could be stopped and stopped soon, "the Republican Party is at an end." Unprecedented murders and outrages in Franklin Parish convinced local Unionists that their enemies intended to drive them out of the country or exterminate them. In an unsuccessful appeal to President Johnson for more Federal troops, Warmoth estimated on August 1 that 150 persons had been killed in Louisiana since the middle of June. Two weeks later an investigator informed him that his estimate erred by half and that "authentic evidence" indicated "double the number of Murders stated by you in your letter to the President."

The violence crested in the fall in a series of bloody massacres. In the Crescent City the first serious clash occurred on September 22 when white Democrats attacked a Republican procession. The last week in October New Orleans resembled a major European city in the throes of violent revolution. By day and night white mobs roamed the city and its suburbs, robbing, beating, and killing Negroes; breaking up Republican clubs and processions; and ambushing and so intimidating the police that patrolmen feared to leave their station houses. The violence spread to neighboring St. Bernard Parish where a series of clashes over four days left many people dead. Throughout the strife hundreds of Federal troops stood by passively, unable or unwilling to act. Estimates of deaths vary widely; clearly, however, at least sixty people, mostly black Republicans, died violent deaths between September 22 and election day in St. Bernard, Jefferson, and Orleans parishes. . . .

State officials reported that the terrorists of 1868 killed 784 people and wounded or mistreated 450 more. A subsequent federal report estimated the dead alone at over a thousand. Election day revealed the full political effect of the violence. Warmoth had received 65,000 votes in April; in November Grant obtained only 33,000. In twenty-four parishes the Republican tally declined by over 27,000; in seven parishes Grant received not a single vote; in nine others he obtained a total of nineteen.

Had the voters that November chosen a state government, Radical Reconstruction in Louisiana would have ended almost before it started. The lesson was not lost on Warmoth and his party. Over the next three years they adopted an extraordinary legislative program. Like Republicans in other Southern states, they organized a state militia. They feared, however, that a militia made up largely of blacks would prove inadequate; the massacres of 1868 had demonstrated all too vividly that nothing inflamed whites more than Negroes with guns. The regime badly needed dependable law officers in those parishes where the sheriffs were unreliable. Hence, they set up a constabulary force in the rural parishes directly under the governor. The constables and their deputies would guard the voting precincts on election day and arrest people who committed violent crimes. In time of trouble, the constabulary could be expanded indefinitely. In subsequent years Republican constables proved extremely effective in solidly Republican parishes, but much less so in Democratic or contested areas.

The Republican organization had taken a severe beating at the local level in 1868. All over the state party leaders had fled to New Orleans, perhaps 200 from St. Landry Parish alone. To break the Democratic hold over the countryside and reestablish their own position, the Republicans created eight new parishes, securing at least temporary dominance through the simple expedient of letting Warmoth appoint the new officials who then served until the next general election. This plan proved extremely effective in places. In Red River, for example, Marshall Harvey Twitchell built up such a base that it took the massed power of the White League in the Coushatta Massacre [of 1873] to tear it down. A ninth parish, Lincoln, organized in 1873 under Kellogg [Warmoth's successor as governor], emerged as the bailiwick of the Unionist Allen Greene and his family. Overall, however, parish reorganization did not significantly alter the balance of power in the countryside.

New Orleans ranked high on the Republican agenda. Nearly half the white males in the city belonged to the Knights of the White Camellia and other secret societies. The preelection riots there and in the adjacent parishes of Jefferson and St. Bernard not only cost the Republicans nearly 16,000 votes, they paralyzed the seat of government and mocked the authority of the new regime. The crux of the problem lay with the immense white majority in the Crescent City. Even in an honest election, the Republicans could rarely hope to elect the city government. They could, however, reorganize it, or transfer its powers to the state. In 1869–1870 the legislature gave New Orleans a new charter, joined part of Jefferson Parish to Orleans, and combined the cities of New Orleans and Jefferson. Under this reorganization, Warmoth temporarily appointed the city government. Thus, from 1870 until the 1872 election, for the only time during Reconstruction, the top officials of New Orleans were Republicans. Even more important, the legislature combined Orleans, Jefferson, and St. Bernard parishes into the Metropolitan Police District, administered by a board of commissioners appointed by the governor. It also made the mayor of New Orleans and the sheriffs of all three parishes strictly subservient to the Metropolitan Police in matters of law enforcement. Although normally fixed at 500 patrolmen, the governor could expand the force indefinitely in special circumstances. Much more so than the state militia or the constabulary, the Metropolitan Police served as the military arm of both Governor Warmoth and Governor [William P.] Kellogg throughout Reconstruction.

Finally, in the election law of 1870, the legislature gave the governor broad authority over the conduct of elections and, most important, created the state Returning Board. The Returning Board compiled the official results of every election; the law empowered it to discard the polls of any precinct in which violence or intimidation occurred; and the governor, lieutenant governor, and secretary of state served as ex officio members. In the political wars that followed, the Returning Board proved the most feared weapon in the Radical arsenal. The Returning Board cheated the Democrats in 1872, lamented one disgruntled member of that party, and robbed them a second time in 1874, "and we all believed that we would be cheated again in 1876 if the returning board dared to do it."

Considering the provocation, the Republican response was entirely logical. Nonetheless, it entrapped Warmoth and his party in the first of a series of fateful contradictions. The Republicans set out, as they believed, to democratize a land corrupted by the tyranny of slavery and, in fact, created the most democratic government the state had ever seen or would see again for a hundred years. But to protect themselves from those who would destroy them with violence, they constructed a police and election apparatus the internal logic of which subverted democratic government as surely as the tactics of their opponents. What leaders in American history could be trusted with a Returning Board legally authorized to alter election returns at will? Whether they fully realized it or not, the Republicans had created the instruments of one-party rule for the simple, compelling reason that the new implements of power could never be permitted to fall into the hands of the opposition. To lose one election, after all, meant surrendering the police and the Returning Board to Democratic control. Forced to use these powerful tools to remain in power, the Republicans employed them for that purpose in every election after 1870. They then found themselves caught in still another contradiction. Dependent on support from Washington, each time they employed their election apparatus to stave off the Democrats, they lost support in the nation's capital. Weary of the whole

Reconstruction question, influential Northerners listened with renewed interest to Southern talk of home rule and the evils of carpetbag government.

At the start, though, all this lay in the future, and Warmoth never attempted to rule by such means alone. His strategy for consolidating Republican strength was twofold: Side by side with the policy of force, he pursued a policy of peace, a conciliatory approach intended to soften white resistance to Republican rule and win white converts to the Republican party. He used his patronage liberally, appointing prominent white conservatives to the bench and other state and local offices. His chief state engineer was a former Confederate general; as adjutant general of the state militia, he chose James A. Longstreet, distinguished corps commander of the Army of Northern Virginia, and he chose Penn Mason, a former officer on Robert E. Lee's staff, as major general. He divided the 5,000-man militia force equally between whites, who were mostly ex-Rebel soldiers, and blacks. Depicting himself as a fiscal conservative, Warmoth obtained a constitutional amendment limiting the state debt to $25,000,000. He vetoed thirty-nine bills, many of them pork barrel projects favored by Republican politicos. The governor also obtained the repeal of Article 99, the disfranchisement clause of the Radical constitution. Campaigning at Shreveport in 1870, the Illinoian boasted that his great-grandfather was a Virginian, his father a Tennessean, and that "every drop" of his own blood was Southern. He claimed that he and President Grant "wanted every old 'Rebel' and every young 'Rebel' to come in and join the Republican Party." He also stressed his efforts to hold down the public debt and promised a railroad to connect the former Confederate capital with New Orleans and Houston; afterwards the band played "Dixie."

Although they were opportunistic, these actions were not steeped in hypocrisy. Unlike many carpetbaggers, Warmoth, who was a prewar Democrat, remained comparatively free of sectional prejudice. Although outraged by Southern atrocities, he expressed his anger against specific acts committed by specific people. He never concluded, as Ephraim S. Stoddard did, that the South was a "political fungus upon the body politic." Nor does one find him, like Marshall Harvey Twitchell, describing Southern chivalry as a savage and barbaric "remnant of the dark ages." Stoddard and Twitchell, of course, were New Englanders, whereas Warmoth came from southern Illinois and boasted of his Southern blood, probably with genuine pride. The young governor was plainly uncomfortable as the head of a mostly Negro party; whitening the party would have increased his personal self-esteem. Above all he held fast to the hope that expanding the Republican party's support among white voters would gain the respectability and acceptance that would make a repetition of the 1868 terror unthinkable.

Warmoth's policy achieved its most notable success among the state's foreign population. By the 1870 census, 113,486 of Louisiana's 726,915 people had either been born abroad or came from families in which both parents were foreign born. Eighty-two percent of this predominantly German and Irish population was strategically located in New Orleans. The employment rolls of the federal bureaucracy show that the Republicans recruited for members heavily among these people: Of 393 jobholders in 1875 whose nativity is listed, 108 were foreign born. Many other federal employees almost certainly came from immigrant families. If the Republicans could combine enough immigrant votes with black votes, they might challenge Democratic control of the Crescent City. . . .

Beyond the foreign population, the interim elections of 1870 revealed the Warmoth administration attempting to embrace a broad spectrum of white Louisianians. In the Florida parishes, a predominantly small farming region, the governor asserted that staple of Republican doctrine that held slavery had oppressed "the poor white man" almost as much as the Negro. The Republican party, he therefore concluded, had done as much for Southern whites as for blacks. Too often in the past, he said, yeoman whites had spurned the party of emancipation, but all that had [now] changed; every day brought new recruits as white Southerners saw the truth. The "old line Whigs" represented another recruitment target; they "are abandoning the ranks of the Democracy and joining the Republican clubs all through the northern portion of the State," asserted the *Republican*. The newspaper also predicted that "scores of the best citizens" in Shreveport and "leading Democratic merchants" in New Orleans intended to vote Republican. The official journal even placed faith in "that large and intelligent class of citizens who vote for the best men without regard to politics." Indeed, wherever the *Republican* looked it discovered unhappy whites deserting the Democratic standard.

The 1870 returns, moreover, seemed to justify optimism. In the freest election of the decade, the Republicans won their most sweeping victory, cementing their hold on the legislature, controlling New Orleans, and sending five carpetbaggers to Congress. In the statewide races for auditor and treasurer, an Irishman, James Graham, and a free man of color, Antoine Dubuclet, rolled up 24,000-vote majorities, sweeping the Crescent City with a 6,000-vote edge, carrying the white-dominated rural parishes, Sabine, Cameron, Tangipahoa, Catahoula and finishing close in others. Warmoth's goal of a Republican party "in which the conservative and honest white people of the State should have a share," appeared on the verge of reality. But the appearance was deceptive. Graham and Dubuclet received only about 300 more votes than Warmoth had obtained in 1868. In other words, Louisiana whites, instead of converting to Radicalism, simply failed to vote.

Despite victory, the Republicans were a troubled party. Many Radicals failed to share the governor's vision of their future; more fundamentally, the policy of peace, like the policy of force, entrapped Warmoth and his party in damaging contradictions. There was, to begin with, the patronage dilemma. In a patronage-hungry party, every job the governor gave a Democrat took a job away from a Republican, arousing resentment in the Radical party. One disgruntled man asked state superintendent of education Thomas W. Conway, if Warmoth "is the staunch Republican you take him to be, why is it, that he invariably appoints the most ultra democrats to offices of trust & emolument?" In East Feliciana Parish, the man claimed, Warmoth appointed a Confederate colonel who tried "to have me snobbed" by the "leading rebel families." Among those most alarmed was Lieutenant Governor Oscar J. Dunn, who, before his death in November 1871, was among the most influential Negro leaders in the South. Pointing to War- moth's Democratic appointments, he warned a black leader in Opelousas that "an effort is being made to sell us out to the Democrats . . . and we must nip it right in the bud." In a widely published letter to Horace Greeley, Dunn charged that Warmoth "has shown an itching desire . . . to secure the personal support of the Democracy at the expense of his own party, and an equally manifest craving to obtain a cheap and ignoble white re- spectability by the sacrifice of . . . the masses of that race who elected him." Warmoth, Dunn alleged, was "the first Ku Klux Governor" of the Republican party. . . .

To blacks, conciliation was not simply a matter of jobs; jobs involved race, and race emerged as the central contradiction in Warmoth's policy. Few words revealed the conflict more fully than those the *German Gazette* wrote about the new editor of the New Orleans *Republican,* Michael Hahn, in 1869. Under Hahn, a German and a Southerner, the *Gazette* observed approvingly, the *Republican* had abandoned its ultra-Radical, anti-Southern bias. Most important, the new editor was not addicted to the "nigger- question." He believed that the Negro had received his due, and the country should now turn to other matters; nothing would be gained by abasing white Southerners for the benefit of Africa.

Warmoth and the official press strove to subordinate the race issue in the 1870 election. At Shreveport the governor stressed that he had not pressed the Negro question on white Louisiana. The party supported the political equality of all men, said the *Republican,* but "we have denounced social equality, for that is neither beneficent nor practical." The official journal looked forward to the day when "the grave of caste and color will be sealed up irrevocably, and our only issues will be as to good men and correct principles." A parish newspaper argued that the Republican party "has got to rise superior to a white man's party or a black man's party." The Negro, it claimed, had to resist being "the tool of men who would make him . . . vote as a black man and not as a Republican." Another rural Republican paper asserted that promoting individuals to public office merely because they were black "is not the principle of the Republican party." Intelligence and integrity, it argued, ought to be the qualifications for office, regardless of color.

The conflicts in Warmoth's policy showed up most clearly in the long controversy over civil rights in Louisiana Reconstruction. As set forth in the Radical constitution, the legal and political equality of all men was the keystone of the new order, Warmoth asserted in his inaugural address. Yet he recognized that a significant portion of the population, "not wanting in intelligence and virtue," resisted this doctrine. "Let our course," then, "while resolute and manly, be also moderate and discreet." Better, he added, that our laws should lag behind popular opinion than outrun it. Two months later the legislature gave him a chance to demonstrate this manly discretion; it adopted a bill to enforce Article 13 of the constitution, making it a criminal offense for steamboats, railroads, and places of public resort to discriminate against Negroes. Warmoth resolutely vetoed it. Public opinion, he maintained, was not ready for such measures, and "we cannot hope by legislation to control questions of personal association." He also observed that the eve of the 1868 election was notably bad timing for "what is practically class legislation." The bill's author, Robert H. Isabelle, a free man of color, and other black legislators fumed.

When the legislature convened again a few months later, P. B. S. Pinchback sponsored a second bill to enforce Article 13. The election was past, and Pinchback, after Dunn, ranked as the most powerful black leader in the state. During his entire governorship Warmoth worked to keep him on his side. In 1871, for example, the New Orleans, Mobile and Chattanooga Railroad denied Pinchback sleeping car accommodations, resulting in a $25,000 lawsuit by the Negro senator. Behind the scenes, Warmoth tried to get the railroad's policy reversed. "Just tell your ticket agents," he advised Henry S. McComb, "to give tickets to those who apply without regard to color and it will be soon forgotten entirely that whites and negroes had not been sleeping together always (as indeed they have in this country)." When Dunn died, Warmoth secured Pinchback's election in his place, or, probably more accurately, Pinchback, controlling the balance of power in the senate between rival factions of the Republican party and the Democrats, secured his own election. Pinchback the realist perceived what Dunn never did: that Negroes would not attain their rights to any greater degree under Kellogg and Packard than under Warmoth. In any event, Warmoth signed the civil rights act of 1869.

Under the new law segregation in Louisiana remained virtually unchanged. The Negro sheriff of Orleans Parish won a lawsuit against a tavern owner, but apart from that race relations continued as they had before. When Senator William Butler demanded equal accommodations on the steamer *Bannock City,* white passengers clubbed him with an iron bar and threw him out of his cabin onto the deck. It was a measure of black frustration that in 1870 the legislature adopted yet a third bill "forbidding unjust discrimination" in places of public accommodation "on account of race or color." It was passed in the last five days of the session, and under Louisiana law Warmoth had until the next legislature met to sign or reject it. It was an election year, and Warmoth waited, his delay coinciding exactly with his turnabout in the Casey controversy. When the annual state convention of the Republican party met in August, a coalition of indignant carpetbaggers and blacks skillfully ambushed him. The convention first nominated both Warmoth and Dunn for president, and then humiliated Warmoth by choosing his lieutenant governor. His enemies then stacked the central executive committee against him and started a heated debate over the unsigned civil rights bill. Packard and Charles W. Lowell denounced Warmoth as "the great stumbling-block" to Negro rights in the state. Despite the uproar, the governor vetoed the held-over civil rights bill early in 1871. . . .

The debacle of the Warmoth years resulted from a failure to resolve a crisis of legitimacy. Louisiana Republicans, as did their counterparts elsewhere in the South, confronted enemies who challenged not only Radical policies but the very existence of the Radical regime, enemies who held Warmoth and all his party to be criminal usurpers. The Warmoth administration met the threat with a twofold strategy: the policy of force and the policy of peace. The strategy failed. The policy of force helped protect the regime, but at an unacceptable cost. The Republican election apparatus was so patently undemocratic that it made Northern voters as well as Southerners question the legitimacy of the Republican government. By the end of 1872 the crisis of legitimacy was fast emerging as a national, not just a regional, problem. The policy of peace, on the other hand, not only failed, on any significant scale, to conciliate white Louisianians, it destroyed the Republican party from within. The Warmoth strategies were in fact mutually contradictory; they negated each other and demolished his government.

Reconstruction and the Crisis of Free Labor

ERIC FONER

. . . At the center of Reconstruction, North and South, stood a transformation of labor relations and the emergence of widespread tension between capital and labor as the principal economic and political problem of the period. The change was more subtle in the North: it involved not the overthrow of an earlier system of labor, but the spread of new forms of industrial organization and labor discipline, and a crisis of the free labor ideology inherited from the pre-war years and based upon the idea of harmony between diverse economic groups. In the South, the abolition of slavery posed the question of labor in a starker form. There, the crucial problem became the one which, over forty years ago, W. E. B. Du Bois identified as the key to Reconstruction: the new status of black labor in the aftermath of emancipation. As William H. Trescot, an unusually far-sighted South Carolina planter, explained to his state's governor late in 1865, "You will find that this question of the control of labor underlies every other question of state interest."

That the transition from slave to free labor involved a revolution in social and racial relations in the South, few contemporaries doubted. "Society has been completely changed by the war," observed former Confederate General Richard Taylor. "The revolution of [1789] did not produce a greater change in the 'Ancien Regime' than has this in our social life." A striking example of the pervasive experience of revolutionary change is afforded in the account of a visit by the great rice planter Louis Manigault to his Savannah River plantation in 1867:

I imagined myself, for the moment a Planter once more, followed by Overseer and Driver. . . . These were only passing momentary thoughts . . . soon dispelled by the sad reality of affairs. . . . In my conversation with these Negroes, now free, and in beholding them my thoughts turned to other Countries, and I almost imagined myself with Chinese, Malays, or even the Indians in the interior of the Philippine islands. That mutual and pleasant feeling of Master toward Slave and vice versa is now as a dream of the past.

Manigault, of course, may have been entirely mistaken as to how extensively that "mutual and pleasant feeling" had been shared by his slaves. But it is clear that he perceived himself to be living in a new and alien world.

The confused early years of Reconstruction become more comprehensible when we consider the difficulty planters had in adjusting to their new status as employers, and freedmen in becoming free laborers. "The former relation has to be unlearnt by both parties," was how a South Carolina planter put it. For many planters, the unlearning process was a painful one. The normal give and take of employer and employee was difficult to accept; "it seems humiliating," wrote one Georgian, "to be compelled to bargain and haggle with our servants about wages." One North Carolina farmer employed a freedman in the spring of 1865, promising to give him "whatever was right" when the crop was gathered. Another said he would pay wages "where I thought them earned, but this must be left to me." Behavior completely normal in the North, such as a freedman informing a Georgia farmer he was leaving because "he thought he could do better," provoked cries of outrage and charges of ingratitude.

Among white southerners, the all-absorbing question of 1865 and 1866 was, "Will the free Negro work?" For it was an article of faith among white southerners that the freedmen were inherently indolent and would work only under supervision and coercion by whites. The papers of planters, as well as newspapers and magazines, were filled with complaints of black labor having become "disorganized and repugnant to work or direction." As one group of Mississippi blacks observed, "Our faults are daily published by the editors, not a statement will you ever see in our favor. There is surely some among us that is honest, truthful and industrious." But to whites, the problem was clear-cut: as a member of South Carolina's Middleton family put it, "there is no power to make the negroes work and we know that without that they will not work."

In the years following the Civil War, a complex triangular debate was played out among freedmen, northern whites, and southern planters, over the nature of the South's new free labor system. For northerners, the meaning of "free labor" derived from the anti-slavery crusade, at the heart of which stood a critique of slavery dating back at least as far as Adam Smith. Slavery, Smith had insisted (more as an ideological article of faith than on the basis of empirical investigation) was the least efficient, most expensive method of making people work. The reason lay in unalterable facts of human nature. Labor was distasteful, and the only reason men worked productively was to acquire property and satisfy their material wants. Since the slave had no vested interest in the results of his labor, he worked as little as possible. Smith's message had been hammered home by the anti-slavery movement in the years before the Civil War: slavery was costly, inefficient, and unproductive; freedom meant prosperity, efficiency, and material progress.

An elaborate ideology defending the northern system of "free labor" had developed in the two decades before the Civil War. To men like Abraham Lincoln the salient quality of northern society was the ability of the laborer to escape the status of wage earner and rise to petty entrepreneurship and economic independence. Speaking within a republican tradition which defined freedom as resting on ownership of productive property, Lincoln used the term "free-labor" to embrace small farmers and petty producers as well as wage laborers. But within this definition a question persisted: why should the independent artisan or farmer work at all, except to satisfy his immediate wants? The answer, once again, derived from the classical paradigm of Adam Smith, as elaborated by his American descendants Henry Carey, E. Pershine Smith, and others. The ever-increasing variety of human wants, desires, and ambitions was, for these writers, the greatest spur to economic progress. It was these "wants" which led northern farmers to produce for the market; indeed, from the northern point of view, participation in the marketplace honed those very qualities that distinguished northern labor from that of the slave—efficiency, productivity, industriousness.

Thus, there was no contradiction, in northern eyes, between the freedom of the laborer and unrelenting personal effort in the marketplace. As General O. O. Howard, head of the Freedmen's Bureau, told a group of blacks in 1865, "he would promise them nothing but their freedom, and freedom means work." Such statements, as well as the coercive labor policies adopted by the Bureau in many localities, have convinced recent scholars that an identity of interests existed between the Bureau and southern planters. Certainly, many Bureau practices seemed designed to serve the needs of the planters, especially the stringent orders of 1865 restricting blacks' freedom of movement and requiring them to sign labor contracts, while withholding relief rations from those who refused. On the other hand, it is difficult to reconcile this recent view of the Bureau with the unrelenting hostility of southern whites to its presence in the South.

The Freedmen's Bureau was not, in reality, the agent of the planters, nor was it precisely the agent of the former slaves. It can best be understood as the agent of the northern free labor ideology itself; its main concern was to put into operation a viable free labor system in the South. To the extent that this meant putting freedmen back to work on plantations, the Bureau's interests coincided with those of the planters. To the extent that the Bureau demanded for the freedmen the rights to which northern laborers were accustomed, it meant an alliance with the blacks. The issue was how the freedmen should be induced to work. Northerners looked to the market itself to provide the incentive, for it was participation in the marketplace which would make self-disciplined free laborers of the blacks, as well as generating a harmony of interests between capital and labor and allowing for social mobility, as, ostensibly, existed in the North. The northern preference for a system in which skilled and educated men worked voluntarily to satisfy ever-expanding wants, generating an endless spiral of prosperity for both capital and labor, was strikingly articulated by the Maine-born Georgia Bureau agent, John E. Bryant:

> Formerly, you were obliged to work or submit to punishment, now you must be induced to work, not compelled to do it. . . . You will be better laborers if educated. Men do not naturally love work, they are induced to work from necessity or interest. That man who has the most wants will usually labor with the greatest industry unless those wants are supplied without labor. The more intelligent men are the more wants they have, hence it is for the interest of all that the laborers shall be educated.

Although Bryant, like so many other Army and Bureau agents in 1865, issued stringent regulations against black "idleness and vagrancy," he essentially viewed the problem of southern economic readjustment through the lens of labor, rather than race. The same psychology that governed white labor, applied to blacks: "*No* man loves work naturally. . . . Why does the *white man* labor? That he may acquire property and the means of purchasing the comforts and luxuries of life. The *colored man* will labor for the same reason."

Spokesmen for the free labor ideology like Bryant viewed the contract system inaugurated by the Freedmen's Bureau in 1865 not as a permanent framework for the southern economy, but as a transitional arrangement, a way of reestablishing agricultural production until cash became readily available and a bona fide free labor system could emerge. General Robert K. Scott, head of the Bureau in South Carolina, explained rather cavalierly to Governor James L. Orr that the state could not hope to escape "the fixed principles which govern [free labor] all over the world." "To the establishment of these principles," he added, "the Bureau is committed." Even Wager Swayne, considered one of the most pro-planter state Bureau chiefs, believed the contract system was "only excusable as a transient." Eventually, as in the North, the natural internal mechanisms of the labor market would regulate employment: "This is more and better than all laws."

Men like Swayne and Scott, however, quickly became convinced that the planters did not comprehend the first principles of free labor. Scott found in 1866 that their idea of a contract was one "that would give the land owner an absolute control over the freedman as though he was his slave." Northern visitors to the South reached the same conclusion. Whitelaw Reid found planters "have no sort of conception of free labor. They do not comprehend any law for controlling laborers, save the law of force." Carl Schurz, one of the most articulate spokesmen for the free labor ideology before the war, concluded that white southerners were unable to accept the cardinal principles that "the only incentive to faithful labor is self-interest," and that a labor contract must be "a free transaction in which neither coercion nor protection is necessary."

Northern and southern perceptions of "free labor" did indeed differ. Planters did not believe that freedmen could ever achieve the internal self-discipline necessary for self-directed labor. The free labor ideology, they insisted, ignored "the characteristic indolence of the negro, which will ever be manifested and indulged in a condition of freedom." It was pointless, therefore, to speak of white and black labor in the same breath: the black was "*sui generis*, and you must argue for him upon his own characteristics." Only legal and physical compulsion could maintain the discipline and availability of plantation labor, in the face of the collapse of the planters' authority and the "indolence" of the laborers. "Our little sovereignties and Feudal arrangements are all levelled to the ground," bemoaned one South Carolina planter. As a result, planters turned to the state to provide the labor discipline which they could no longer command as individuals. "A new labor system," declared a New Orleans newspaper in 1865, must be "prescribed and enforced by the state." Hence, the southern legislatures of 1865–66 enacted a series of vagrancy laws, apprenticeship systems, criminal penalties for breach of contract, and all the other coercive measures of the Black Codes, in an effort to control the black labor force. As one Georgian explained, despite the general conviction that "the negro will not work. . . . we can control by wise laws." . . .

. . . The central premise of the free labor ideology—the opportunity for social mobility for the laborer—was anathema to planters, who could not conceive of either a plantation economy or their own social privileges surviving if freedmen were able to move up the social scale. "You must begin at the bottom of the ladder and climb up," General Howard informed a black New Orleans audience in 1865, but at least he offered the opportunity to climb. A Natchez newspaper at the same time was informing its readers, "the true station of the negro is that of a servant. The wants and state of our country demand that he should remain a servant." A delegate to the Texas Constitutional Convention of 1866 agreed: the freedmen must remain "hewers of wood and drawers of water." As for white labor, there was a concerted, though unsuccessful effort to attract immigrants to the South during Reconstruction. Pamphlets appeared singing the praises of "the thrifty German, the versatile Italian, the sober Englishman, the sturdy sons of Erin," in contrast to blacks who did not understand "the moral obligations of a contract." Yet others noted that such immigrants might bring with them unwanted ideas. "Servants of this description may please some tastes," said a southern newspaper in 1867, "but the majority of our people would probably prefer the sort we have, who neither feel nor profess equality with their employer."

Nor could white southerners accept the other half of the free labor equation—market-oriented rationality on the part of their laborers. In the recent work of "cliometricians" investigating post-bellum southern history, the freedmen emerge from slavery as, to use their terminology, rational, market-oriented profit-maximizers. It is difficult, however, to accept the idea that slavery produced workers socialized to the discipline of capitalist wage labor. The slave's standard of consumption, and his experience with the marketplace, was, of necessity, very limited. The logic of ever-greater effort to meet ever-expanding needs (what capitalist society calls "ambition") had no meaning for him. As one planter complained, freedmen did not respond to the marketplace incentives to steady labor: "released from the discipline of slavery, unappreciative of the value of money, and but little desirous of comfort, his efforts are capricious."

Here, indeed, lies the ultimate meaning of the innumerable complaints about the freedman's work habits—so reminiscent, it might be noted, of labor "problems" in the Third World today. Why did so many whites constantly claim that blacks were lazy and idle? The tendency of historians has been to deny the accuracy of such complaints, attributing them to simple racism. Doubtless, there is justification for this response, but it does not go to the heart of the matter. Consider two examples of such complaints. The first is from a Maryland newspaper in 1864, just after emancipation in that state: "The ambition of the negro, as a race, when left to his own volition, does not rise above the meagre necessaries of life. . . . One fruitful source of idleness has been the ability to possess themselves of a hut and a few acres of land, thereby enabling them to preserve the semblance of a means of living." The second is a remark by the North Carolina planter and political leader Kemp P. Battle in 1866: "Want of ambition will be the devil of the race, I think. Some of my most sensible men say they have no other desire than to cultivate their own land in grain and raise bacon."

On the face of it, a desire to cultivate one's own land in food crops does not appear to warrant the charge of "want of ambition." The term "indolence," it appears, encompassed not simply blacks unwilling to work at all, but those who preferred to work for themselves. The same plantation blacks arraigned for idleness spent considerable time and effort on their own garden plots and, as is well known, it was the universal desire of the freedmen to own their own plots of land. What one Mississippi white called the freedman's "wild notions of right and freedom" were actually very traditional in republican America. Blacks believed, according to another Mississippi planter, "that if they are hirelings they will still be slaves." Whether in withdrawing from churches dominated by whites, refusing to work under drivers and overseers, or in their ubiquitous desire for forty acres and a mule, blacks made clear that, for them, freedom meant independence from white control. "Their great desire," wrote a Georgia planter, "seems to be to get away from all overseers, to hire or purchase land, and work for themselves." From the freedmen's point of view, an Alabama Bureau agent reported, this would "complete their emancipation."

The vast majority of freedmen, of course, were compelled by necessity to labor on the plantations, but they too appeared to respond only imperfectly to the incentives and demands of the marketplace. Many freedmen did seek the highest wages available, whether this meant moving to states like Texas and Arkansas where labor was scarce and wages high, or seeking employment in railroad construction crews, turpentine mills, and lumber companies. Others, however, seemed to value things like freedom of movement off the plantations and personal autonomy more than pecuniary rewards. "Let any man offer them some little thing of no real benefit to them, but which looks like a little more freedom," Georgia's Howell Cobb observed, "and they catch at it with alacrity." And a Mississippi Bureau agent reported, "many have said to me they cared not for the pay if they were only treated with kindness and not over worked."

Instead of working harder than they had as slaves, as Adam Smith would have predicted, the freedmen desired to work less, and black women sought to withdraw from field labor altogether. "The women say that they never mean to do any more outdoor work," said a report from Alabama. "White men support their wives and they mean that their husbands shall support them." Those women who did remain in the fields were sometimes even more "undisciplined" than the men. One rice plantation worker told her employer in 1866 on being ordered to complete a task, "she did not know if she would . . . and could 'not work herself to death before her time came.' "

Most distressing of all, many freedmen evinced a strong resistance to growing the "slave crop" cotton. As one Georgia freedman said, "If ole massa want to grow cotton, let him plant it himself." On the Sea Islands, they refused to repair broken cotton gins and displayed more interest in subsisting on garden plots, fishing, and hunting than producing a crop for the marketplace. Freedom, for Sea Island blacks, seemed to mean "no more driver, no more cotton." The South Carolina planter Edward B. Heyward noted the irony of the situation:

> It seems the belief among planters, that negroes *will not plant cotton* but are interested only in *food*. Wouldn't it be curious if by the voluntary act of the emancipated blacks, the New England manufacturers should fail. . . . They are going to worry somebody, and I think it will be their friends the Yankees. They say we can't *eat cotton* and there they stop.

As Heyward suggested, on the question of cotton a community of interest did indeed exist between northern and southern whites interested in the revitalization of the plantation economy. Their great fear was that the freedmen might retreat into self-sufficiency. "The products of these islands are absolutely necessary to supply the wants of the commercial world," wrote a northern investor from St. Helena, South Carolina, in 1865. Two years later another northerner with an eye to southern investments commented on the absolute necessity of reviving an export cotton crop to "pay our debts and get the balance of trade in our favor." To such men, and many others who looked to the post-war South for the investment of war-generated surplus capital, the idea of granting subsistence plots to the freedmen was disastrous. As Willie Lee Rose has shown, the arguments between land reform and cotton production were articulated during the war itself, in the conflict on the Sea Islands between the freedmen and moral reformers like Laura Towne on the one hand, and representatives of northeastern business like Edward Atkinson and Edward Philbrick, who envisioned a post-war economy in which blacks worked cotton plantations for reasonable wages. . . .

The experience of labor in other post-emancipation situations was hardly reassuring to such men [as Atkinson and Philbrick]. Southerners were well aware of the aftermath of emancipation in the West Indies, which appeared to demonstrate that the end of slavery spelled the end of plantation agriculture. Plantations could not be maintained with free labor, wrote a prominent Charlestonian, "the experiments made in Hayti and Jamaica settled that question long ago." On those islands the freedmen had been able to drift off the plantations and take up small farming, and the result had been a catastrophic decline in sugar production. "See what ruin emancipation brought on that paradise of the tropics," observed one southern writer. Comparative studies of emancipation in the West Indies and South America reveal that nearly every plantation society enacted vagrancy, contract, and debt peonage laws in an attempt to keep freedmen on the plantations. But only where land was not available—or another source of unfree labor was—did the plantation survive. Trinidad, with little free land, was a success: "land . . . is owned by the white man and the negro is unable to get possession of a foot of it." So was Guyana, where imported East Indian coolies replaced the blacks on sugar plantations. But not Jamaica, where uninhabited land was available for the freedmen. . . .

In the end, if the plantations were to continue, it would have to be with black labor. This was why white southerners absolutely insisted that blacks not be allowed access to land. Unlike the West Indies, the "availability" of land in the South was a political issue, not a matter determined by geography, for there was an abundance of uncultivated land. Less than a tenth of Louisiana's thirty million acres, for example, were being tilled at the end of Reconstruction. The fear that access to land for blacks would lead to the disintegration of staple production was graphically expressed by an Alabama newspaper, commenting on the Southern Homestead Act of 1866, which offered public land to black farmers:

> The negroes will become possessed of a small freehold, will raise their corn, squashes, pigs and chickens, and will work no more in the cotton, rice and sugar fields. In other words, their labor will become unavailable for those products which the world especially needs. . . . The title of this law ought to have been, "A bill to get rid of the laboring class of the South and make Cuffee a self-supporting nuisance."

Even if relatively few independent black farmers succeeded economically, the result would be disastrous. As a Mississippi planter put it, in that case, "all the others will be dissatisfied with their wages no matter how good they may be and thus our whole labor system is bound to be upset."

Thus, the problem of adjustment from slave to free labor was compounded by racial and class assumptions, ideas about the nature of labor itself, which dictated to white southerners that blacks not be allowed to escape the plantations, and led many northerners to agree that the road to black landownership should lie through patient wage labor—while market values and responses were learned—rather than a sudden "gift" of land. To complicate matters further, the transition to a free labor system took place within the context of an economic transformation which profoundly affected the status of white farmers in the South as well as blacks.

As is well known, the southern states emerged from the war into a pattern of economic underdevelopment and dependency. Whether one views the ante-bellum South as capitalist (Fogel and Engerman), pre-capitalist (Genovese), or capitalist but not bourgeois—whatever that means—(Barrington Moore), it is certain that the Civil War unleashed an expansion of market relations, reflected in both the emancipation of the slaves and the transformation of the status of the white farmer. The extension of transportation into the predominantly white upcountry, the increased use of commercial fertilizer, and the spread of country stores made possible the absorption of the previously subsistence-oriented upcountry into the Cotton Kingdom during and after Reconstruction. A recent article by Grady McWhiney delineates the change in Alabama from a relatively self-sufficient late ante-bellum society in which 70 per cent of white farmers owned their own land, to a colonial economy, forced into a one-crop mould, and a region that could not feed itself. The most significant aspects of the transformation were first, the fastening of endemic poverty upon the entire South and second, the loss of what McWhiney describes as an independent and leisured, if not indeed "lazy" way of life, based on the free ranging of livestock in the ante-bellum years. The debate over fencing laws in the South after the Civil War reflects the controversy engendered by the change from an almost communal view of land, in which all unenclosed property was deemed open to neighbors' livestock, to a more capitalist and individualist conception. Certainly, economic changes were rapidly undermining the traditional idea that ownership of land was a guarantee of personal autonomy.

The transformation of the status of the white farmer provides an indispensable angle of vision on one of the least understood aspects of Reconstruction, southern white Republicanism. For a time, scalawags, as they were called, controlled the politics of Tennessee, Missouri, Arkansas, North Carolina, and to a lesser degree, Georgia and Alabama. Studies of individual states in recent years have moved beyond earlier debates over whether scalawags were pre-war Democrats or Whigs, to an emphasis on ante-bellum hostility to the planter regime, and Unionist disaffection during the Civil War, as the roots of white Republicanism, especially in the mountain areas stretching from West Virginia down into northern Georgia, Alabama, and Mississippi.

But second only to Unionism as an issue in these areas was the question of debt, the vehicle by which thousands of white farmers were trapped into the cycle of tenancy and cotton production in the post-war decades. The mountain and piedmont areas of Mississippi, Alabama, Georgia, and other states had been devastated by a civil war within the Civil War. Property, tools, and livestock had been destroyed, and the result was severe destitution in 1865–67. "Scenes of the Irish famine" were reported in northern Alabama. As small farmers went bankrupt, large numbers fell into tenancy and lost their lands. Others were forced to grow cotton to obtain needed credit. Governor James L. Alcorn reported in 1871 that tenant farming among Mississippi whites had doubled in the previous decade, and by 1880 one-third of the white farmers in the cotton states were tenants.

The issue of debtor relief pervades the early years of Reconstruction; debates over stay laws and homestead exemptions were as intense as those concerning civil rights for blacks. One correspondent of the North Carolina railroad promoter and banker George Swepson reported in 1867, "everything is so demoralized that men have lost all sight of paying debts," adding that the people would surely "defeat the constitution if repudiation is not in." In Georgia, the homestead and debtor relief provisions of the Constitution of 1868 were the "strong card" of the Republican party, "the most serious obstacle" to Democratic attempts to unite the white vote against Reconstruction. In our preoccupation with the racial politics of Reconstruction we may have overlooked the first stirring of class politics within the white community, a politics as yet inchoate and inhibited by racial divisions, but which foreshadowed the great agrarian upheaval [of Populism] two decades later.

Like the Black Codes of 1865–66, the issue of debtor relief illustrates how economics and politics were intertwined during Reconstruction. For blacks, having lost the struggle for land distribution immediately after the Civil War, the political arena offered an opportunity to compensate for their economic weakness. In many respects, of course, the Reconstruction governments betrayed black dreams. Except in South Carolina, and to a lesser extent, Mississippi, Republican regimes did little to fulfill the shattered dream of forty acres and a mule. In less dramatic ways, however, blacks and their white allies used political power to provide a modicum of protection for black laborers. From the beginning of Radical rule, black legislators pressed for laws granting agricultural laborers a first lien on crops, and such measures were enacted by most of the southern states during Reconstruction. . . .

Perhaps even more significant was the emergence during Reconstruction of local officials, black and white, who actively sympathized with the economic plight of the black laborer. A recent study criticizes South Carolina's black legislators for not using their power "for the social and economic advancement of the black masses." At the local level, however, that was precisely what many Republican officials tried to do. Contract disputes, during Reconstruction, were heard by locally elected trial justices, and planters were bitter in their complaints over the partiality of these officials toward their black constituents. One leading rice planter observed in 1869, "the planter must have entire control of the crop," but that this was impossible in a situation where "the negro magistrate or majesty as they call him tells them that no rice is to be shipped until it is all got out and divided 'according to law.' " Another Carolinian informed Governor Daniel

H. Chamberlain that the state's game laws "would be of great benefit . . . but with such trial justices as we now have, they are not enforced," enabling blacks to hunt on white-owned land. . . .

An understanding of the class constituency of the southern Republican party not only helps us appreciate the intense opposition it generated, but to reconsider the whole question of the "extravagant" taxation and state expenditures during Reconstruction. That there was corruption and misappropriation of funds is undeniable. But, as Howard K. Beale observed forty years ago, "was not a part of the offense of the Radical leaders that they sought to serve the interests of *poor* men?" As Beale suggested, it was not simply the amount of state expenditure, but that it was "money lavishly spent by men who pay no taxes"—as a Mississippi Democrat put it—which aroused hostility. Property-holders blamed the increasing tax burden on the fact that blacks had no vested interest in government economy, since "nine-tenths of the members of the Legislature own no property and pay no taxes." But there was more here than simply a desire of the propertyless to despoil the propertied. State expenditures during Reconstruction reflected an activism common enough in the North in these years, and should perhaps be viewed as a kind of unarticulated Keynesianism, in which deficit spending financed the promotion of economic growth and the creation of an economic and social infrastructure (railroads and schools) while tax policy promoted a modest redistribution of wealth.

"The Republican party is emphatically the poor man's party of the State," declared a black political leader in South Carolina in 1870. "We favor laws to foster and elevate labor . . . we denounce all attempts of capital to control labor by legislation," a Georgia Republican meeting echoed. In terms of its constituency, the Republicans were indeed "the poor man's party" of the South, but in policy, the situation was more ambiguous. The dominant theme in the policies of state Republican leadership was not precisely the elevation of the poor, but economic modernization. A subsidiary theme, articulated primarily by black leaders (although by no means all of them) looked to a more class-conscious program of economic redistribution. The division was analogous to the Civil War debate on the Sea Islands between humanitarian reformers favoring land distribution and northern investors like Atkinson and Philbrick who feared such a policy would prevent the revitalization of staple agriculture. It had also surfaced in the debates in 1867 over whether southern Republicans should endorse the idea of the confiscation of planter lands.

At stake were competing visions of the role of the state in the post–Civil War South. The "modernizers" saw the task of the Radical governments as moving the South as quickly as possible along the economic road marked out by the North, through aid to railroads, industry, and agricultural diversification. They were willing to protect the essential political and economic rights of southern laborers, and harass the planters with heavy taxation, but would generally go no further, although the assumption of their free labor outlook was that their policies would produce a prosperity in which blacks would share. The "redistributionists" were not opposed to economic diversification, but had little interest in grandiose schemes of economic development. Their aim was to use the power of the state to promote land distribution and in other ways directly assist the black and white poor. Generally, party discipline led most Republicans to support such modernizing programs as aid to railroad development, but there were exceptions. The South Carolina Labor Convention of 1869, headed by the state's most prominent black politicians, urged the legislature to withhold the state's credit from railroads, using the money instead to secure land for agricultural laborers. There were also disputes over the exemption of manufacturing corporations from taxation and the repeal of usury laws, measures modernizers believed necessary to attract outside investment, but which others feared would simply raise the tax bill and credit prices for the poor. As for fence laws, demanded by those seeking a more diversified and modern agricultural system, it was widely assumed that "the negroes will defeat any measures" for such legislation, which would deprive landless blacks of the right to graze their livestock on the land of others.

Control of the state, therefore, played a critical role in labor relations during Reconstruction. The point is not that Reconstruction revolutionized the southern economic order—recent research has demonstrated convincingly that it did not. But in seeking seismic changes, historians may have overlooked ones more subtle but significant nonetheless. In some areas, Reconstruction did serve as a shield, protecting black labor from the most exploitive implications of economic relationships, and preventing planters from using the state to bolster their own position. The class conflict between planters and freedmen in this period should be viewed as an anomalous struggle between two weak economic classes, each of which sought to use political power to obtain economic objectives. The result was a stalemate, in which neither side obtained what it wanted. "Capital is powerless and labor demoralized," complained the South Carolina agricultural reformer D. Wyatt Aiken in 1871. What he meant was that, in the absence of Black Codes and vagrancy laws, blacks, though generally landless, were able to utilize the "labor shortage" to improve their economic standing. Like the land question, the labor shortage was a question not simply of numbers, but of power. Labor was scarce, Aiken explained, not primarily because there were fewer workers, but because those who did work were unmanageable: "Though abundant, this labor is virtually scarce because not available, and almost wholly unreliable." "The power to control [black labor]," the *Southern Argus* agreed, "is gone." . . .

Obviously, the economic gains achieved by blacks during Reconstruction were more modest than their striking advances in political and civil rights and education. The failure of land distribution ensured that this would be the case. Moreover, another signal failing of the Reconstruction governments, their inability to protect blacks against violence, often had disastrous economic consequences. While Klan violence was most commonly intended to intimidate Republican local leaders and voters, it had economic motivations and consequences as well. Victims were often those blacks who had succeeded economically, or simply resisted white control of their labor. In Demopolis, Alabama, the Klan acted to prevent black renters from gathering their crops. In Georgia, according to a black legislator, "whenever a colored man acquires property and becomes in a measure independent, they take it from him." In South Carolina, a "posse" illegally harassed a plantation, "because it is rented by colored men, and their desire is that such a thing ought not to be." . . .

In his classic study *Black Reconstruction,* W. E. B. Du Bois referred to the Reconstruction regimes as the rule of the "black proletariat." The terminology is exaggerated, but Du Bois did have a point, for this was how these governments were viewed by their Conservative opponents. Despite all the complaints about corruption, it was the disjunction between property-holding and political power which most alarmed them. The situation in the South, claimed one "Tax-Payers Convention," was entirely "anomalous; it is perhaps without a parallel in the history of civilized communities." The problem, put simply, was the inability of the upper class to exert its traditional influence on state and local government. Reconstruction, this address continued, presented "the unprecedented spectacle of a state in which the Government is arrayed against property." . . .

In South Carolina, where black political power was most pronounced, so too was the assertion by the white upper class that men of property had a right to rule, and willingness to threaten economic reprisals against those who disagreed. Thus, a Democratic address to black citizens, written by Civil War General James Conner, put the issue with admirable candor:

> We have the capital and give employment. We own the lands and require labor to make them productive. . . . You desire to be employed. . . . We know we can do without you. We think you will find it very difficult to do without us. . . . We have the wealth. The houses in which you live are ours; the lands upon which you must labor or starve are ours.

This address, the wife of a planter observed, was "clear and to the point." The problem was that blacks did not respond to such threats. Unexpectedly, perhaps, while the freedmen did not achieve economic autonomy, they did exhibit a remarkable political independence. As Trescot complained, the result of the Civil War and Reconstruction was to destroy utterly "the natural influence of capital on labor, of employer on employee," with the result that "negroes who will trust their white employers in all their personal affairs . . . are entirely beyond advice on all political issues." (Trescot's interchangeable use of the terminology of race and class was not uncommon during Reconstruction—an Alabama opponent of that state's 1867 Constitution asked, "Shall the white man be subordinated to the negro? Shall the property classes be robbed by the no property herd?") It was the remarkable tenacity of black voters in loyalty to the Republican party, despite economic intimidation, which led Democrats increasingly to resort to violence to destroy their political rights. But whatever the method, "the first thing to be done," as Georgia's Democratic leader Benjamin H. Hill explained, "is to secure Home Government for Home Affairs. . . . We must get control of our own labor." . . .

In 1875, as the struggle over Reconstruction entered its final years, John E. Bryant penned an article for the New York *Times,* explaining political alignments in Georgia and the South. After his retirement from the Freedmen's Bureau, Bryant had enjoyed a prominent political career, although he had alienated many Georgia Republicans by aligning himself on occasion with the state's Democrats. But in 1875, his analysis was fully within the free labor tradition. The actions of Georgia's Redeemers [Democrats who overthrew Reconstruction] Bryant argued, demonstrated that at the heart of Reconstruction lay the same issue which had caused the Civil War—the struggle between "two systems of labor," one slave and one free. Northerners believed "that the laboring man should be as independent as the capitalist." Southern whites still, in their heart of hearts, felt workers "ought to be slaves."

Although perhaps overstated, Bryant's analysis did underscore once again the centrality of the labor question to the politics of Reconstruction. But on one point, he was out of date. Was it still an article of faith in the North that the laborer should be "as independent as the capitalist?" As one of Bryant's northern friends informed him, while the *Times* article "shows clearly the views of the old ruling class at the South with regard to the labor question," there was "reason to fear that their general view of society and government was substantially shared by a large class in the North."

From his southern vantage point, Bryant was perhaps unaware of the decline of the Radical impulse in the northern Republican party, its shift, as a recent student has noted, toward "a more distinctly antilabor and procorporate stance." Here, in the increasingly divergent social and ideological bases of northern and southern Republicanism, lay a crucial weakness of the Reconstruction governments. They depended for their existence on the support of the federal government and northern public opinion, but their northern allies were now emerging as the party of respectability, the Union, and business. And northern businessmen, especially those interested in investment in the South had, even in the late 1860s, concluded that the policies of Reconstruction governments were inimical to business enterprise. "No one," a New Yorker wrote Governor Orr, "will invest or emigrate, so long as . . . stay laws are made to prevent the collection of debts." Others insisted that so long as ignorant blacks had a dominant voice in southern public affairs, capital would boycott the South. The conclusion was heightened by the effects of the Panic of 1873, for, as Bryant's northern correspondent informed him, "there is a pretty general impression in the country that the financial crisis of 1873 was owing in great part to the paralysis of the South."

But there was more to the erosion of support for Reconstruction than a simple matter of dollars and cents, more, too, than the racism which remained so pervasive in northern life. The change in northern attitudes reflected a crisis of the free labor ideology itself. The rapid expansion of industrial capitalism in the post-war years, reflected in the spread of factory production, the beginnings of modern managerial institutions, the expansion of the mining and farming frontiers, the emergence of a powerful trade unionism, and the devastating depression of the 1870s, posed issues which that ideology, with its emphasis on a harmony of interests between capital and labor, proved unable to answer. For one thing, it seemed increasingly difficult to contend that wage labor was simply a temporary stopping point on the road to economic independence. During Reconstruction the coalition which had fought the Civil War dissolved into its component elements, and strands of the free labor ideology were adopted by contending social classes, each for its own purposes. For the middle class, free labor became a stolid liberal orthodoxy, in which individualism, laissez-faire, the defense of private property, and the rule of the "Best Men" defined good government. At the same time, the labor movement, especially after 1873, adopted the free labor outlook as an affirmation of the primacy of the producing classes and a critique of the emerging capitalist order, rather than as a testament to the harmony of all interests in society.

The irony here is indeed striking. With emancipation, the South came face to face with the problem [of] how to preserve social order in the face of a large, propertyless class of laborers. Yet at the same time, the North was also having to face up to this question. After all, 1877 was not only the year of the end of Reconstruction, but of the great railroad strike, the first national strike in American history, and the first to be suppressed by the massive intervention of federal troops. The same administration which withdrew the last federal troops from the South, within a few months sent them against strikers in the North, while the city of Baltimore, which had rioted against the entrance of federal troops on their way to Washington early in 1861, frantically requested the army to restrain the strikers in 1877. "The Southern question," a Charleston newspaper declared, was "dead"— the railroad strike had propelled to the forefront of politics "the question of labor and capital, work and wages."

Sometimes, historical coincidences are revealing, and 1877 is one of those occasions. For if the Civil War proved that America was not unique politically—that it could not always solve its problems by reasoned disputation—the railroad strike shattered an even greater myth, that Americans could have industrialization without the dark satanic mills of Europe and a permanent wage-earning class, could have capitalism without class conflict. So, in the end, Reconstruction came full circle. It began with southerners trying to adjust to the northern system of free labor. It ended with northerners having to accept the reality of conflict between capital and labor—a reality that southerners, white and black alike, had understood all along.

❧ *F U R T H E R   R E A D I N G*

Richard N. Current, "Carpetbaggers Reconsidered," in Kenneth M. Stampp and Leon Litwack, eds., *Reconstruction: An Anthology of Revisionist Writings* (1969), 223–240

———, *Those Terrible Carpetbaggers: A Reinterpretation* (1988)

Eric Foner, "Politics and Ideology in the Shaping of Reconstruction: The Constitutional Conventions of 1867–1869," Numan V. Bartley, ed., *The Evolution of Southern Culture* (1988) 28–46

Steven Hahn, *The Roots of Southern Populism: Yeoman Farmers and the Transformation of the Georgia Upcountry, 1850–1890* (1983)

William C. Harris, *The Day of the Carpetbagger: Republican Reconstruction in Mississippi* (1979)

Carl H. Moneyhon, *Republicanism in Reconstruction Texas* (1980)

Elizabeth Studley Nathans, *Losing the Peace: Georgia Republicans and Reconstruction, 1865–1871* (1968)

Otto H. Olsen, "Reconsidering the Scalawags," *Civil War History* 12 (1966), 301–320

———, ed., *Reconstruction and Redemption in the South* (1980)

Michael Perman, *The Road to Redemption: Southern Politics, 1869–1879* (1984)

Armstead L. Robinson, "Beyond the Realm of Social Consensus: New Meanings of Reconstruction for American History," *Journal of American History* 68 (1981), 276–297

Kenneth M. Stampp, *The Era of Reconstruction, 1865–1877* (1965)

Mark W. Summers, *Railroads, Reconstruction and the Gospel of Prosperity: Aid Under the Radical Republicans, 1865–1877* (1984)

CHAPTER
13

The African-American Experience
in the Reconstruction South

↙

The promise of emancipation to the slaves and the enlistment of 180,000 blacks
in the United States armed forces had helped the Union win the war and, in
the process, guaranteed the demise of slavery. The contribution of southern
blacks was also crucial to the success of Reconstruction, since the Republican governments in the South relied on the support of the newly enfranchised black voters to gain power as well as keep it. For the African-Americans themselves, the
triumph of Reconstruction was, needless to say, an outcome they devoutly wished
for, just like victory in the war. And this convergence of aims simply confirmed
how dependent upon each other the Federal government and southern blacks
were in their parallel struggles against the slaveholders and their allies.

African-Americans' needs and demands lay at the center of the contest over
Reconstruction. From the beginning, blacks insisted on equal rights before the
law, military protection, economic security, and even the vote, which they made
known through petitions to the Federal government and the state conventions
and legislatures. Once some of these goals were obtained, they then kept up the
pressure for their enforcement. Meanwhile, African-Americans voted Republican
and began to hold office in increasingly large numbers at all levels of government. And this occurred despite the unrelenting vilification and violence that
was employed to deter black voters and officials.

The status of African-Americans as laborers was also a major question during Reconstruction. Landownership was the overriding objective of the liberated
slaves because it would give them autonomy from white control as well as a
stake in the economy. When they were denied land, however, the freedmen refused to work as laborers in gangs under supervision, as in slavery, and demanded instead to rent land and work it independently as tenants. A number of
blacks did manage to pool their resources and buy land, and some even formed
self-governing and self-sufficient communities. Meanwhile, they established their
own churches and self-help and benevolent societies. Also, black children went to
school for the first time when volunteer teachers and the Freedmen's Bureau set
up schools after the war, and later when systems of public education were intro-

duced by the Reconstruction governments. Finally, black women ceased working in the fields and began to assume new roles at work and in the family.

With the end of Reconstruction in the mid-1870s, however, these changes and gains were in jeopardy. Some even claimed that they had been ephemeral and pretty insignificant all along. Later on, historians wondered how much blacks had gained during Reconstruction—was it a period of achievement or an opportunity denied? They have also questioned whether Reconstruction collapsed because Federal policy was tied so closely to black interests and advancement or whether it would have failed in any case.

↘ *D O C U M E N T S*

These documents illuminate the diversity of the African-American role and contribution in the Reconstruction of the South. In the first selection, John W. De-Forest, a Freedmen's Bureau agent who later became a well-known novelist, reveals how prejudiced even educated and sympathetic northern officials could be. The comments are from his reminiscences that first appeared in *Harper's, Atlantic Monthly,* and *Putnam's Magazine* in 1868 and 1869, and were later published as *A Union Officer in the Reconstruction* (1949). The second document, a petition to Congress of the Colored People's Convention of South Carolina on November 24, 1865, shows that from the outset African-Americans were calling public meetings to present demands. In the third selection, Richard H. Cain, an African-American who would later be elected to Congress, tries to convince the Constitutional Convention of South Carolina to endorse his petition to Congress for a loan of $1 million to purchase land for the freedmen. His forceful speech of February 17, 1868, was, however, unsuccessful. In the same convention, Francis L. Cardozo, a black soon to become state treasurer, wrestled with the question of mixed schools on March 4, 1868; the fourth document presents his conclusions.

The fifth selection features a speech by Representative Robert B. Elliott of South Carolina on January 6, 1874, in which he demands that the House pass the Civil Rights bill that was finally enacted the following year. In the sixth extract a freed slave, Mattie Curtis, recalls how she fared in the post-emancipation years. Finally, the seventh document contains a report by an African-American observer named Henry Adams on black women's response to working in the fields after they were freed.

A Freedmen's Bureau Agent Predicts a Grim Future for the Freed Slaves, 1868–1869

. . . What is to become of the African in our country as a race? Will he commingle with the Caucasian, and so disappear? It is true that there are a few marriages, and a few cases of illegal cohabitation, between Negro men and the lowest class of white women. For example, a full-blooded black walked twenty miles to ask me if he could have a white wife, assuring me that there was a girl down in his "settlement" who was "a-teasin'" every day about it."

He had opened his business with hesitation, and he talked of it in a tremulous undertone, glancing around for fear of listeners. I might have told him that, as it was not leap year, the woman had no right to propose to him; but I treated the matter seriously. Bearing in mind that she must be a disreputable creature, who would make him a wretched helpmeet, I first informed him that the marriage would be legal and that the civil and military authorities would be bound to protect him in it, and then advised him against it, on the ground that it would expose him to a series of underhanded persecutions which could not easily be prevented. He went away evidently but half convinced, and I presume that his Delilah had her will with him, although I heard no more of this odd love affair.

Miscegenation between white men and Negresses diminished under the new order of things. Emancipation broke up the close family contact in which slavery held the two races, and, moreover, young gentlemen did not want mulatto children sworn to them at a cost of three hundred dollars apiece. In short, the new relations of the two stocks tended to separation rather than to fusion. There will be no amalgamation, no merging and disappearance of the black in the white, except at a period so distant that it is not worth while now to speculate upon it. So far as we and our children and grandchildren are concerned, the Negro will remain a Negro and must be prophesied about as a Negro.

But will he remain a Negro, and not rather become a ghost? It is almost ludicrous to find the "woman question" intruding itself into the future of a being whom we have been accustomed to hear of as a "nigger," and whom a ponderous wise man of the East [the British writer Thomas Carlyle] always persisted in abusing as "Quashee." There was a growing disinclination to marriage among the young freedmen, because the girls were learning to shirk out-of-door work, to demand nice dresses and furniture, and, in short, to be fine ladies. The youths had, of course, no objection to the adornment itself; indeed, they were, like white beaux, disposed to follow the game which wears the finest feathers; but they were getting clever enough to know that such game is expensive and to content themselves with looking at it. Where the prettiest colored girls in Greenville were to find husbands was more than I could imagine.

There are other reasons why the blacks may not increase as rapidly as before the emancipation. The young men have more amusements and a more varied life than formerly. Instead of being shut up on the plantation, they can spend the nights in frolicking about the streets or at drinking-places; instead of the monotony of a single neighborhood, they can wander from village to village and from South Carolina to Texas. The master is no longer there to urge matrimony and perhaps other methods of increasing population. Negroes, as well as whites, can now be forced by law to support their illegitimate offspring and are consequently more cautious than formerly how they have such offspring.

In short, the higher civilization of the Caucasian is gripping the race in many ways and bringing it to sharp trial before its time. This new, varied, costly life of freedom, this struggle to be at once like a race which has passed through a two-thousand-years' growth in civilization, will probably diminish the productiveness of the Negro and will terribly test his vitality.

It is doubtless well for his chances of existence that his color keeps him a plebeian, so that, like the European peasant held down by caste, he is less tempted to destroy himself in the struggle to become a patrician.

What judgment shall we pass upon abrupt emancipation, considered merely with reference to the Negro? It was a mighty experiment, fraught with as much menace as hope.

To the white race alone it was a certain and precious boon.

South Carolina Blacks Assert Their Demands, November 1865

Memorial to the Senate and House of Representatives of the United States in Congress Assembled

Gentlemen:

We, the colored people of the State of South Carolina, in Convention assembled, respectfully present for your attention some prominent facts in relation to our present condition, and make a modest yet earnest appeal to your considerate judgment.

We, your memorialists, with profound gratitude to almighty God, recognize the great boon of freedom conferred upon us by the instrumentality of our late President, Abraham Lincoln, and the armies of the United States.

"The fixed decree, which not all Heaven can move,
Thou, Fate, fulfill it; and, ye Powers, approve."

We also recognize with liveliest gratitude the vast services of the Freedmen's Bureau together with the efforts of the good and wise throughout the land to raise up an oppressed and deeply injured people in the scale of civilized being, during the throbbings of a mighty revolution which must affect the future destiny of the world.

Conscious of the difficulties that surround our position, we would ask for no rights or privileges but such as rest upon the strong basis of justice and expediency, in view of the best interests of our entire country.

We ask first, that the strong arm of law and order be placed alike over the entire people of this State; that life and property be secured, and the laborer free to sell his labor as the merchant his goods.

We ask that a fair and impartial instruction be given to the pledges of the government to us concerning the land question.

We ask that the three great agents of civilized society—the school, the pulpit, the press—be as secure in South Carolina as in Massachusetts or Vermont.

We ask that equal suffrage be conferred upon us, in common with the white men of this State.

This we ask, because "all free governments derive their just powers from the consent of the governed"; and we are largely in the majority in this State, bearing for a long period the burden of onerous taxation, without a just representation. We ask for equal suffrage as a protection for the hostility evoked by our known faithfulness to our country and flag under all circumstances.

We ask that colored men shall not in every instance be tried by white men; and that neither by custom nor enactment shall we be excluded from the jury box.

We ask that, inasmuch as the Constitution of the United States explicitly declares that the right to keep and bear arms shall not be infringed and the Constitution is the Supreme law of the land—that the late efforts of the Legislature of this State to pass an act to deprive us of arms be forbidden, as a plain violation of the Constitution, and unjust to many of us in the highest degree, who have been soldiers, and purchased our muskets from the United States Government when mustered out of service.

We protest against any code of black laws the Legislature of this State may enact, and pray to be governed by the same laws that control other men. The right to assemble in peaceful convention, to discuss the political questions of the day; the right to enter upon all the avenues of agriculture, commerce, trade; to amass wealth by thrift and industry; the right to develop our whole being by all the appliances that belong to civilized society, cannot be questioned by any class of intelligent legislators.

We solemnly affirm and desire to live orderly and peacefully with all the people of this State; and commending this memorial to your considerate judgment.

Thus we ever pray.

Charleston, S. C., November 24, 1865
Zion Presbyterian Church.

Richard H. Cain of South Carolina Stresses the Importance of Land, February 1868

. . . *Mr. R. H. Cain.* I may be mistaken, but I watched very closely the arguments made by the gentleman last Saturday, and I distinctly understood him to say he was in favor of taxing the lands so as to compel the sale of them, and throw them into the market. The poor would then have a chance to buy. I am unqualifiedly opposed to any measure of taxation for the simple purpose of compelling the owners to sell their lands. I believe the best measure to be adopted is to bring capital to the State, and instead of causing revenge and unpleasantness, I am for even-handed justice. I am for allowing the parties who own lands to bring them into the market and sell them upon such terms as will be satisfactory to both sides. I believe a measure of this kind has a double effect: first, it brings capital, what the people want; second, it puts the people to work; it gives homesteads, what we need; it relieves the Government and takes away its responsibility of feeding the people; it inspires every man with a noble manfulness, and by the thought that he is the possessor of something in the State; it adds also to the revenue of the country. By these means men become interested in the country as they never were before. It was said that five and one-seventh acres were not enough to live on. If South Carolina, in its sovereign power, can devise any plan for the purchase of the large plantations in this State now lying idle, divide and sell them out at a reasonable price, it will give so many people work. I will guarantee to find persons to work every five acres. I will also guarantee that after one year's time, the Freedman's Bureau will not have to give any man having one acre of land anything to eat. This country has a genial clime, rich soil, and can be worked to advantage. The man who can not earn a living on five acres, will not do so on twenty-five. I regret that another position taken by gentlemen in the opposition, is that they do not believe that we will get what we ask for. I believe that the party now in power in the Congress of the United States, will do whatever they can for the welfare of the people of this State and of the South. I believe that the noble men who have maintained the rights of the freedmen before and since their liberation, will continue to do everything possible to forward these great interests. I am exceedingly anxious, if possible, to allay all unpleasant feeling—I would not have any unpleasant feeling among ourselves.

I would not have any unpleasant feelings between the races. If we give each family in the State an opportunity of purchasing a home, I think they will all be better satisfied.

But it is also said that it will disturb all the agricultural operations in the State. I do not believe if the Congress of the United States shall advance one million of dollars to make purchase of lands, the laborers will abandon their engagement and run off. I have more confidence in the people I represent. I believe all who have made contracts will fulfill those contracts, and when their contracts have expired, they will go on their own lands, as all freemen ought to go. I claim it would do no harm. It would be a wonderful concatenation of circumstances indeed, to find that because the Government had appropriated one million of dollars for the purchase of lands, to see all of four hundred thousand people, rushing pell mell down to Charleston to get a homestead. I know the ignorance of the people with whom I am identified is great. I know that four hundred years of bondage has degraded them, but I have more confidence in humanity than to believe the people will leave their homes and their families to come to Charleston just to get five acres of land.

If I understood the speaker in the opposition this morning, he offered it because he said it was simply a scheme for colored men. I wish to state this question right. If there was one thing on which I thought I had been specific, it was on that point. The clock had struck two and I had dashed down my pen when the thought struck me it might be misunderstood. I retraced my steps and so shaped the petition as simply to state the poor of any class. I bore in mind the poor whites of the upper districts. I saw, not long ago, a poor white woman walk eighteen miles barefooted to receive a bag of corn and four pounds of meat, resting all night on the roadside, eating one-half and then go away, living on roots afterwards and half starved. I desire that class of people to have homes as well as the black man. I have lost long since that hateful idea that the complexion of a man makes any difference as far as rights are concerned. The true principle of progress and civilization is to recognize the great brotherhood of man, and a man's wants, whatever he may be, or whatever clime he comes from, are as sacred to me as any other class of men. I believe this measure will advance the interests of all classes.

Francis L. Cardozo of South Carolina Discusses Mixed Schooling, March 1868

. . . Before I proceed to discuss the question, I want to divest it of all false issues, of the imaginary consequences that some gentlemen have illogically thought will result from the adoption of this section with the word compulsory. They affirm that it compels the attendance of both white and colored children in the same schools. There is nothing of the kind in the section. It means nothing of the kind, and no such construction can be legitimately placed upon it. It simply says all the children shall be educated; but how is left with the parents to decide. It is left to the parent to say whether the child shall be sent to a public or private school. The eleventh section has been referred to as bearing upon this section. I will ask attention to this fact. The eleventh section does not say, nor does the report in any part say there shall not be separate schools. There can be separate schools for white and colored. It is simply left so that if any colored child wishes to go to a white school, it shall have the privilege to do so. I have no doubt, in most localities, colored people would prefer separate schools, particularly until some of the present prejudice against their race is removed.

We have not provided that there shall be separate schools; but I do not consider these issues as properly belonging to the question. I shall, therefore, confine myself to the more important matter connected with this subject.

My friend yesterday referred to Prussia and Massachusetts as examples that we should imitate, and I was much surprised to hear some of the members who have spoken, ridicule that argument. It was equivalent to saying we do not want the teachings of history, or the examples of any of those countries foremost in civilization.

It was said that the condition of affairs in Prussia and Massachusetts was entirely different. But they are highly civilized countries, with liberty-loving, industrious citizens, and the highest social order exists there. I want South Carolina to imitate those countries, which require the compulsory attendance of all children of certain ages for fixed periods, at some school. If you deem a certain end worthy of being attained, it must be accompanied by precisely the same means those countries have attained it. . . .

Another argument was that this matter had better be left to the Legislature. I have been charged with appealing to the prejudices and feelings of the colored delegates to this Convention. It is true to a certain extent. I do direct their attention to matters concerning their peculiar interests, but if it is meant to charge me with appealing to their passions as against the white people, I respectfully deny the charge, and stamp the assertion as gratuitous. But I do desire we shall use the opportunities we now have to our best advantage, as we may not ever have a more propitious time. We know when the old aristocracy and ruling power of this State get into power, as they undoubtedly will, because intelligence and wealth will win in the long run, they will never pass such a law as this. Why? Because their power is built on and sustained by ignorance. They will take precious good care that the colored people shall never be enlightened. . . .

Representative Robert B. Elliott of South Carolina Demands Federal Civil Rights, January 1874

. . . Sir, it is scarcely twelve years since that gentleman [Alexander H. Stephens of Georgia] shocked the civilized world by announcing the birth of a government which rested on human slavery as its corner-stone. The progress of events has swept away that *pseudo*-government which rested on greed, pride, and tyranny; and the race whom he then ruthlessly spurned and trampled on are here to meet him in debate, and to demand that the rights which are enjoyed by their former oppressors—who vainly sought to overthrow a Government which they could not prostitute to the base uses of slavery—shall be accorded to those who even in the darkness of slavery kept their allegiance true to freedom and the Union. Sir, the gentleman from Georgia has learned much since 1861; but he is still a laggard. Let him put away entirely the false and fatal theories which have so greatly marred an otherwise enviable record. Let him accept, in its fullness and beneficence, the great doctrine that American citizenship carries with it every civil and political right which manhood can confer. Let him lend his influence, with all his masterly ability, to complete the proud structure of legislation which makes this nation worthy of the great declaration which heralded its birth, and he will have done that which will most nearly redeem his reputation in the eyes of the world, and best vindicate the wisdom of that policy which has permitted him to regain his seat upon this floor.

To the diatribe of the gentleman from Virginia, [Mr. Harris,] who spoke on yesterday, and who so far transcended the limits of decency and propriety as to announce upon this floor that his remarks were addressed to white men alone, I shall have no word of reply. Let him feel that a negro was not only too magnanimous to smite him in his weakness, but was even charitable enough to grant him the mercy of his silence. [Laughter and applause on the floor and in the galleries.] I shall, sir, leave to others less charitable the unenviable and fatiguing task of sifting out of that mass of chaff the few grains of sense that may, perchance, deserve notice. Assuring the gentleman that the negro in this country aims at a higher degree of intellect than that exhibited by him in this debate, I cheerfully commend him to the commiseration of all intelligent men the world over—black men as well as white men.

Sir, equality before the law is now the broad, universal, glorious rule and mandate of the Republic. No State can violate that. Kentucky and Georgia may crowd their statute-books with retrograde and barbarous legislation; they may rejoice in the odious eminence of their consistent hostility to all the great steps of human progress which have marked our national history since slavery tore down the stars and stripes on Fort Sumter; but, if Congress shall do its duty, if Congress shall enforce the great guarantees which the Supreme Court has declared to be the one pervading purpose of all the recent amendments, then their unwise and unenlightened conduct will fall with the same weight upon the gentlemen from those States who now lend their influence to defeat this bill, as upon the poorest slave who once had no rights which the honorable gentlemen were bound to respect.

But, sir, not only does the decision in the Slaughter-house cases [a Supreme Court decision of 1873 limiting federal jurisdiction over the citizens of individual states] contain nothing which suggests a doubt of the power of Congress to pass the pending bill, but it contains an express recognition and affirmance of such power. I quote now from page 81 of the volume:

> "Nor shall any State deny to any person within its jurisdiction the equal protection of the laws."
>
> In the light of the history of these amendments, and the pervading purpose of them, which we have already discussed, it is not difficult to give a meaning to this clause. The existence of laws in the States where the newly emancipated negroes resided, which discriminated with gross injustice and hardship against them as a class, was the evil to be remedied by this clause, and by it such laws are forbidden.
>
> If, however, the States did not conform their laws to its requirements, then, by the fifth section of the [fourteenth] article of amendment, Congress was authorized to enforce it by suitable legislation. We doubt very much whether any action of a State not directed by way of discrimination against the negroes as a class, or on account of their race, will ever be held to come within the purview of this provision. It is so clearly a provision for that race and that emergency, that a strong case would be necessary for its application to any other. But as it is a State that is to be dealt with, and not alone the validity of its laws, we may safely leave that matter until Congress shall have exercised its power, or some case of State oppression, by denial of equal justice in its courts shall, have claimed a decision at our hands.

No language could convey a more complete assertion of the power of Congress over the subject embraced in the present bill than is here expressed. If the States do not conform to the requirements of this clause, if they continue to deny to any person within their jurisdiction the equal protection of the laws, or as the Supreme Court had said, "deny equal justice in its courts," then Congress is here said to have power to enforce the constitutional guarantee by appropriate legislation. That is the power which this bill now seeks to put in exercise. It proposes to enforce the constitutional guarantee against inequality and discrimination by appropriate legislation. It does not seek to confer new rights, nor to place rights conferred by State citizenship under the protection of the United States, but simply to prevent and forbid inequality and discrimination on account of race, color, or previous condition of servitude. Never was there a bill more completely within the constitutional power of Congress. Never was there a bill which appealed for support more strongly to that sense of justice and fair-play which has been said, and in the main with justice, to be a characteristic of the Anglo-Saxon race. The Constitution warrants it; the Supreme Court sanctions it; justice demands it.

Sir, I have replied to the extent of my ability to the arguments which have been presented by the opponents of this measure. I have replied also to some of the legal propositions advanced by gentlemen on the other side; and now that I am about to conclude, I am deeply sensible of the imperfect manner in which I have performed the task. Technically, this bill is to decide upon the civil status of the colored American citizen; a point disputed at the very formation of our present Government, when by a short-sighted policy, a policy repugnant to true republican government, one negro counted as three-fifths of a man. The logical result of this mistake of the framers of the Constitution strengthened the cancer of slavery, which finally spread its poisonous tentacles over the southern portion of the body-politic. To arrest its growth and save the nation we have passed through the harrowing operation of intestine war, dreaded at all times, resorted to at the last extremity, like the surgeon's knife, but absolutely necessary to extirpate the disease which threatened with the life of the nation the overthrow of civil and political liberty on this continent. In that dire extremity the members of the race which I have the honor in part to represent—the race which pleads for justice at your hands to-day, forgetful of their inhuman and brutalizing servitude at the South, their degradation and ostracism at the North—flew willingly and gallantly to the support of the national Government. Their sufferings, assistance, privations, and trials in the swamps and in the rice-fields, their valor on the land and on the sea, is a part of the ever-glorious record which makes up the history of a nation preserved, and might, should I urge the claim, incline you to respect and guarantee their rights and privileges as citizens of our common Republic. But I remember that valor, devotion, and loyalty are not always rewarded according to their just deserts, and that after the battle some who have borne the brunt of the fray may, through neglect or contempt, be assigned to a subordinate place, while the enemies in war may be preferred to the sufferers.

The results of the war, as seen in reconstruction, have settled forever the political status of my race. The passage of this bill will determine the civil status, not only of the negro, but of any other class of citizens who may feel themselves discriminated against. It will form the cap-stone of that temple of liberty, begun on this continent under discouraging circumstances, carried on in spite of the sneers of monarchists and the cavils of pretended friends of freedom, until at last it stands in all its beautiful symmetry and proportions, a building the grandest which the world has ever seen, realizing the most sanguine expectations and the highest hopes of those who, in the name of equal, impartial, and universal liberty, laid the foundation stones. . . .

A Freed Slave Remembers Her Struggle After Emancipation, (Undated)

I got married before de war to Joshua Curtis. I always had craved a home an' plenty to eat, but freedom ain't give us notin' but pickled hoss meat an' dirty crackers an' not half enough of dat. Josh ain't really care 'bout no home but through dis land corporation I buyed dese fifteen acres on time. I cut down de big trees dat wus all over dese fields an' I hauled out de wood an sold hit, den I plowed up de fields an' planted dem. Josh did help to build de house an' he worked out some. All of dis time I had nineteen chilluns an' Josh died, but I kep' on.

I'll never fergit my first bale of cotton an' how I got hit sold. I was some proud of dat bale of cotton, an' atter I had hit ginned I set out wid hit on my steercart for Raleigh. De white folks hated de nigger den, 'specially de nigger what was makin' something so I dasen't ax nobody whar de market wus. I rid all day an' had to take my cotton home wid me dat night 'case I can't find no place to sell hit at. But dat night I think hit over an' de next day I axes a policeman 'bout de market.

I done a heap of work at night too, all of my sewin' and such and de piece of lan' near de house over dar ain't never got no work cept at night. I finally paid for de land.

A Black Observer Reports on Women and Fieldwork, 1867

I seen on some plantations on Red River where the white men would drive colored women out in the fields to work, when the husbands would be absent from their home, and would tell colored men that their wives and children could not live on their places unless they work in the fields. The colored men would tell them they wanted their children to attend school; and whenever they wanted their wives to work they would tell them themselves; and if he could not rule his own domestic affairs on that place he would leave it and go somewhere else. So the white people would tell them if he expected for his wife and children to live on their places without working in the field they would have to pay house rent or leave it; and if the colored people would go to leave, they would take everything they had, chickens, hogs, horses, cows, mules, crops, and everything and tell them it was for what his damn family had to eat, doing nothing but sitting up and acting the grand lady and their daughters acting the same way, for I will be damn if niggers ain't got to work on my place or leave it.

↳ *E S S A Y S*

Three facets of the black experience during Reconstruction are represented in the following essays. In the first selection, Thomas C. Holt of the University of Chicago identifies the African-Americans who served in the South Carolina legislature during Reconstruction and assesses their record as legislators. The second essay, by Jacqueline Jones of Wellesley College, provides an analysis of the economic role of black women and families in the immediate post-abolition years. The third and final piece, by the sociologist Elizabeth Rauh Bethel of Lander College, describes a small African-American community that was formed in South Carolina during Reconstruction.

Black State Legislators in South Carolina During Reconstruction

THOMAS C. HOLT

Reconstruction was "a frightful experiment which never could have given a real statesman who learned or knew the facts the smallest hope of success." Daniel H. Chamberlain, the last Republican governor of South Carolina, wrote this post-mortem a quarter of a century after he had been driven from office by a violent and fraudulent campaign to restore native whites to power in the fall and winter of 1876–77. Undoubtedly his view was colored by the social milieu of America at the turn of the century, when racism of the most virulent type had become the intellectual orthodoxy. On the other hand, these later reflections do not differ much from his assessment just two months after he had been forced to relinquish his office. In June 1877 he explained to [the famous abolitionist] William Lloyd Garrison that "defeat was inevitable under the circumstances of time and place which surrounded me. I mean here exactly that the uneducated negro was too weak, no matter what his numbers, to cope with the whites." In later years he described that weakness more explicitly: blacks were "an aggregation of ignorance and inexperience and incapacity." . . .

But it is difficult to reconcile . . . these views with events in South Carolina during Reconstruction. Certainly the cause of its failure cannot be laid to the political incapacity and inexperience of the black masses. They were uneducated. They were inexperienced. But they overcame these obstacles to forge a formidable political majority in the state that had led the South into secession. During the Reconstruction era 60 percent of South Carolina's population was black. This popular majority was turned into a functioning political majority as soon as Reconstruction legislation was put into effect with the registration for the constitutional convention in 1867. Despite violence and economic intimidation, the black electorate grew rather than declined between 1868 and 1876. The only effective political opposition before the election of 1876 came from so-called reform tickets,

---

Thomas C. Holt, "Negro State Legislators in South Carolina During Reconstruction," from *Southern Black Leaders of the Reconstruction Era*, Howard N. Rabinowitz, ed., 1982, pp. 223–244. Reprinted with permission of University of Illinois Press.

especially in 1870 and 1874. On these occasions, black and white Republican dissidents fused with Democrats to challenge the regular Republican party. But the strength of these challenges was generally confined to the predominantly white up-country counties and Charleston with its large white plurality and freeborn Negro bourgeoisie. Indeed, many observers condemned the unflinching, "blind" allegiance of black Republicans as evidence of their lack of political sophistication. But given the political alternatives and the records of so-called reform and fusion candidates, the black electorate could just as easily be credited with a high degree of political savvy. For South Carolina certainly, Frederick Douglass was right: the Republican party—despite its weaknesses and inadequacies—was the deck, all else the sea.

In an era when primaries were almost unknown and the nomination of party candidates was subject to manipulation by various intraparty factions, the voters had little leverage on the selection of their political leadership beyond the general election. It is difficult, therefore, to discern the political thinking and preferences of the masses of voters in any systematic fashion. However, one revealing report from an army chaplain just after the first election of Reconstruction offers some clues to the newly formed political mind of the ex-slaves. Chaplain F. K. Noble's literacy class for enlisted men of the 128th United States Colored Troop in Beaufort was polled on the advisability of immediate suffrage for illerates. While "the more intelligent" favored a literacy qualification for voters, he observed, "those who learned less easily were in favor of immediate suffrage."

> One of the speakers—a black thick-lipped orator—commenced his speech as follows: "De chaplain say we can learn to read in short time. Now dat may be so with dem who are mo'heady. God hasn't made all of us alike. P'raps some *will* get an eddication in a little while. *I knows de next generation will*. But we'se a downtrodden people. We hasn't had no chance at all. De most uf us are slow and dull. We has bin kept down a *hundred years* and I tink it will take a *hundred years to get us back agin*. Dere fo' Mr. Chaplain, I tink we better not wait for eddication."

Despite efforts by some of their elected leaders to include literacy and poll-tax qualifications for suffrage in the new constitution, the 1868 Constitutional Convention vindicated the views of Chaplain Noble's class by bestowing the right to vote on all male citizens of the state.

Activities other than partisan politics also demonstrate the freedmen's capacity for collective political action. For example, in the lowland rice-growing areas, cash-poor planters instituted a system wherein their workers were paid in scrip rather than currency. The scrip or "checks" could be redeemed only at designated stores in exchange for goods priced significantly above normal retail items. Although the legislature made some attempts in 1872 and again in 1875 to reform and control the system, its essential features remained unchanged: the workers exchanged low-paid labor for high-priced goods. Since their political representatives appeared to be unable to correct this problem, in July 1876 the workers took matters into their own hands. They struck. The strike was widespread and involved considerable violence against nonstrikers. Governor Chamberlain sent in the militia and had the strike leaders jailed. He also sent Negro Congressman Robert Smalls to convince the strikers to renounce violence and concede scabs their right to work. Smalls reported to the governor that he had succeeded in his mission, but subsequent reports of continued violence suggest that the right-to-work principle was attended more in the breach than in the observance. Eventually the planters capitulated and abolished the scrips system.

There had been earlier efforts to organize black laborers. In 1869 South Carolina workers organized to send delegates to the National Colored Labor Convention in Washington, D.C., and to pressure the state's General Assembly for changes favorable to workers' rights in agriculture and the trades. However, in this instance, it is less clear to what extent the freeborn bourgeoisie, rather than ex-slaves, and politicians, rather than workers, initiated and controlled the agitation.

Thus it is difficult to see how freeborn whites could have utilized the political system to fulfill their aspirations and to satisfy their needs—given its inherent limitations—any more effectively than did the black ex-slaves. They identified and articulated their needs quite clearly and forcefully: they wanted land, economic justice, and education. They shrewdly discerned the organized political force most favorable to their objectives, the regular Republican party. They supported that party faithfully, despite the constant threat and reality of violence and economic reprisals. Whatever lessons their paternalistic masters had tried to instill did not paralyze them politically nor rob them of collective will. The black ex-slaves of South Carolina were, and acted as, political men.

Ultimately the failures of South Carolina Republicans must be laid not to their black ex-slave constituents but to the party leadership. . . . Surely there were venal men. Clearly corruption was rife. But there were corrupt Democrats before, during, and after Reconstruction, including the architects of the Democratic campaign of 1876, Martin W. Gary and M. C. Butler. Republican corruption merely offered a propagandistic advantage in the Democratic efforts to discredit the Radical regime. With the possible exception of the land-commission frauds, corruption was secondary to the major failures of that regime while in office and to its ability to sustain office. Very likely native whites viewed the fact that blacks wielded political power as itself a form of corruption of governmental process.

South Carolina was unique among American state governments in that blacks enjoyed control over the legislature and many other political entities. Of the 487 men elected to various state and federal offices between 1867 and 1876, 255 were black. While it is true that they never succeeded in elevating any of their number to the U.S. Senate, they did fill nine of the state's fifteen congressional terms between 1870 and 1876, including four of the five seats available from 1870 to 1874. J. J. Wright was elected to one of the three positions on the state supreme court in 1870, which he held until 1877. However, no black was ever even nominated for the governorship, and all of the circuit judges, comptrollers general, attorneys general, and superintendents of education during this period were white. Only a handful of blacks served in the important county offices of sheriff, auditor, treasurer, probate judge, and clerk of court. More commonly blacks were elected to such local offices as school commissioner and trial justice; but even among these they were not a majority.

Clearly blacks enjoyed their greatest power in the General Assembly. Their membership averaged from just over one-third during the first five sessions of the Senate to about one-half during the last five; but in the House of Representatives they were never less than 56 percent of the membership. More important than their membership was their growing control of key committees and leadership posts in both branches of the General Assembly. Samuel J. Lee became the first black Speaker of the House in 1872; he was succeeded by Robert B. Elliott from 1874 to 1876. The president pro tem of the Senate was a black after 1872, as was the lieutenant governor, who presided over that body. Better than two-thirds of the respective committee chairmanships were held by blacks in the House after 1870 and in the Senate after 1872. Furthermore, in both houses the key committees—those controlling money bills or the flow of major legislation—generally had black chairmen.

Little wonder then that former slaveholders viewed the new order with alarm. Indeed, the displaced local whites often became hysterical in their denunciations of the new order. For example, when William J. Whipper was elected to a judgeship in the important Charleston circuit, the *News and Courier* ran a banner headline declaring its "Civilization In Peril." As a deliberate Republican policy, the judicial system had been kept inviolately white and conservative. The election of a black radical to fill one of the most important of these posts was the first step toward the creation of "an African dominion," indeed "a new Liberia." Here, as elsewhere in the South, to involve blacks in the political process was "to Africanize" the social system.

The biographical profile of the Negro leadership justifies neither the fears of white contemporaries nor the charges of many historians of that era. While the overwhelming majority of their constituents were black, illiterate, and propertyless ex-slave farmworkers, most of the political leadership was literate, a significant number had been free before the Civil War, many were owners of property, and most were employed in skilled or professional occupations after the war. At least one in four of the 255 Negroes elected to state and federal offices between 1868 and 1876 were of free origins. Indeed, counting only those for whom information is available, one finds that almost 40 percent had been free before the Civil War. Of those whose educational attainments are known, 87 percent were literate, and the 25 identifiable illiterates approximately matched the number who had college or professional training. Information on property ownership is available for little more than half the legislators. Seventy-six percent of these men possessed either real or taxable personal property, and 27 percent of them were worth $1,000 or more. Indeed, one in four held over $1,000 in real property alone.

Among both ex-slaves and legislators of free origin whose prewar occupations can be identified, artisans were the most numerous group. The numbers of common laborers, fieldhands, and domestics were far fewer than among the Negro population as a whole. After the war the largest proportion took up professional occupations, mostly teaching and preaching. Farmworkers composed the second largest group, but 60 percent of these owned their farms. Better than 1 in 5 remained in skilled trades, especially carpentry and tailoring. However, there were significant occupational discontinuities between legislators of free origin and those who were formerly slaves. About 70 percent of the former were employed in professions, most of them as teachers, as compared with only 24 percent of the ex-slaves, who were mostly preachers. Only 9 of the 64 leaders of free origin whose occupations are known were farmers, and just 2 were tenants. Thirty-eight percent of the 90 ex-slaves worked on farms, 12 of them as tenants. About equal proportions of both groups (21 and 24 percent) were skilled tradesmen.

These occupational differences reflect other variations in the antebellum backgrounds of ex-slaves and those who had been free before the war. Despite various legal regulations and economic harassment during the antebellum period, many free Negroes had been able to acquire impressive educations and property. Only 3 percent of the freeborn legislators were illiterate and 29 percent had acquired education or training beyond the common-school level; at least 14 percent of the ex-slaves were illiterate and only 4 percent had gotten better than a grade-school education. Legislators of free origin were more likely to own property (76 percent versus 53 percent) or to come from propertied families. William McKinlay, who represented Charleston in the 1868 Constitutional Convention and in the House of Representatives from 1868 to 1870, was probably the wealthiest of the Negro politicians with $15,320 in taxable real estate in 1860. The McKinlay family—which included McKinlay's son and fellow representative William J.—paid taxes on real property worth $40,000 during the 1870s. Other freeborn legislators had more modest holdings. Henry Jacobs of Fairfield owned $1,200 in real property and personal items worth $2,500 in 1860. Although Thaddeus K. Sasportas and Florian Henry Frost, who were still in their twenties when elected to the House, owned little property, they were both scions of property-holding families. Joseph Sasportas owned $6,700 in real property in 1860, and Henry Maine and Lydia Frost left their son an estate worth $2,000 in the mid-1870s. While these sums were not particularly impressive to South Carolina's white ruling class, they mark a considerable gap between the ex-slaves and their freeborn colleagues. The median financial worth was $1,100 for the 45 legislators of free origins, but only $300 for the 75 ex-slaves.

Nevertheless, the freedmen moved very aggressively to close the gap between themselves and their freeborn colleagues. Several of them took advantage of schools established by missionary societies, the Freedmen's Bureau, and the army after the war. Others may have emulated Robert Smalls, who hired a tutor. They also seized various opportunities for enterprise in the postwar period. Hastings Gantt, a plantation slave in Beaufort before the war and its state representative after the war, had acquired an 84-acre farm worth $900 by 1870. He was elected president of the St. Helena Planters Society in 1871. William R. Jervay owned only the shirt on his back when he fled his owner to join the Union army; by the mid 1870s he owned a 275-acre plantation and a lucrative construction business. William Beverly Nash, a hotel porter during slavery, acquired a brick manufacturing plant after the war. It should be noted, however, that those legislators who had been employed as artisans or house servants during slavery appear to have been most successful in acquiring property after the war. In some way, then, though slaves, their occupational profiles are similar to the successful freeborn legislators.

Thus, while there were differences in their respective social and economic backgrounds, neither the freeborn nor ex-slave legislators conform to the traditional stereotype of ignorant, pennyless sharecroppers rising from cotton fields to despoil the legislature and plunder the state. In truth, most of the freeborn and many of the slaveborn were a "middle" class of artisans, small farmers, and shopkeepers located on the social spectrum somewhere between the vast majority of Negro sharecroppers and the white middle and upper classes. Indeed, because of their education, class position, and general aspirations, they were more likely to embrace than reject the petty bourgeois values of their society.

But while their political opponents have distorted the social and economic backgrounds of the Negro leadership, charges that they were politically inexperienced can scarcely be denied. Northern as well as southern blacks had few if any opportunities to gain experience in partisan politics during the antebellum period. Most could not vote in the state in which they resided, and they were unlikely to hold office in any state. In various ways, employees of the missionary societies and churches, the army, and the Freedmen's Bureau gained experience in public life and in serving and mobilizing constituents. Between 1865 and 1868 about one-fourth of the black elected officials had been affiliated with one or more of these institutions, as also had more than 37 percent of those who served in the first Republican government in 1868. But, of course, while these affiliations could help prepare men for public service, they were no substitute for direct legislative and partisan political experience.

The black legislator's lack of prior political experience was further exacerbated by the likelihood of an abbreviated service for most of their number. The high turnover in the House of Representatives suggests the volatility of that body. Only two black members, William M. Thomas of Colleton and Joseph D. Boston of Newberry, served the entire four terms of the Reconstruction period. Eight other men served three terms; but 61 percent of the 212 blacks elected to the House between 1868 and 1876 were one-term members. Only 15 of these advanced to higher elective offices in the state senate or executive branch or at the federal level. Clearly, for most of its sessions, the House of Representatives was composed of a disproportionate number of freshmen legislators.

It is difficult to evaluate the political impact of this rather high turnover in membership. Generally, a low turnover rate is evidence of significant institutionalization in a legislature that is reflected in strong party leadership and discipline. Conversely the relatively weak party discipline of the South Carolina Republican party would appear to be congruent with the high turnover of its members. Certainly the evidence of intraparty dissension and weak leadership among Republican legislators is formidable by almost any standard. The index of relative cohesion developed by sociologist Stuart Rice in the 1920s provides one way of measuring unity or conflict within a party or subgroup. On the Rice scale a score of 100 indicates unanimity of the group, while a score of 0 indicates a perfect split, half of the members voting for a measure and half against it. Throughout the Reconstruction era, Democrats voted together more consistently than did Republicans. While the Democrats' average score was never less than 68, the Republicans never exceeded 50.

Although the Rice index is a useful indicator of the overall performance of a political party or subgroup, it does not identify the sources of that disunity or unity. An alternative way to examine legislative voting behavior is to count how often specific pairs of legislators agreed with each other on roll-call votes. These agreement scores are superior to Rice cohesion indices to the extent that individual performances can be highlighted as well as the aggregate performances of the party or various subgroups. It is conceivable, for instance, that a small group of maverick party members would vote consistently against their party and thereby lower the aggregate cohesion score of the whole group. Thus there might be solidarity in the party as a whole which a small bloc of dissident members might obscure. Was the Republican weakness relative to the Democrats caused by a weak link within its ranks? Were the politically inexperienced freedmen that link?

Apparently they were not. A comparison of the agreement scores of the two parties in the 1876 session of the House of Representatives not only confirms the same overall pattern of Republican disunity and Democratic solidarity shown by the Rice index, but shows that pattern to be pervasive and continuous among all Republican members. The 1876 legislative session was particularly significant because it occurred in a period of clear and present danger for Republicans when the necessity for unity was self-evident. When the legislature convened in December 1875, South Carolina was one of only three southern states still under Republican control. There was every reason to expect that the violent crusade Mississippi Democrats had launched to "redeem" their state would be extended to South Carolina during the fall. If Republicans were ever to be united, the time was at hand.

Despite the obvious incentives for party unity, on "critical" roll calls the 89 Republican legislators voted with each other an average of 43.2 percent of the time as compared with 56.8 percent for the Democrats.

Furthermore, the party's relative weakness does not appear to have been caused by any consistent bloc of dissidents. An examination of individual pairings of legislators reveals a lack of cohesion throughout the membership; there were hardly any strong pairs among Republicans comparable to pairings among Democrats. Twenty-eight percent of all possible Democratic pairs voted together on more than 80 percent of the roll calls, while only 3.9 percent of the Republican pairs scored as high. Furthermore, only 2 pairs of Republican members (0.06 percent) agreed on 90 percent or more of the roll calls, while there were 33 such pairs (6.6 percent) among Democrats. It is unlikely that the high turnover among the Republican membership is responsible for the difference between their political performance and that of the Democratic membership. The proportion of Democratic freshmen in the 1876 legislature was even greater than that of inexperienced Republicans, and veteran Republicans appear to have broken party ranks as frequently as did freshmen. The question remains then: Why were Republicans so fractious, especially when faced with the challenge of a reviving Democratic party?

Although no single bloc or segment of the Republican party was solely responsible for its weakness, there were political differences within the party that diminished its strength. Evidence suggests that the lack of party solidarity revealed on legislative roll calls reflected differences in aspirations and ideological orientations of various subgroups within the party. From the beginning of Reconstruction there had been conflict between white and Negro Republicans and between Negroes with roots in the freeborn mulatto bourgeoisie and the black ex-slaves. During the early meetings between 1865 and 1868, Negro aspirations for greater representation and power clashed with white efforts to maintain political control, and the demands for universal manhood suffrage and land reform articulated by black ex-slaves did not always resonate with the policy objectives and ideological orientation of their freeborn colleagues. At the end of the Reconstruction era, such differences in interests, perceptions, and orientation still undermined party unity. The cohesion indices for all ten legislative sessions and the agreement scores for the 1876 session generally reflect these conflicts. For instance, by calculating the average number of times a given subgroup voted with other Republicans, one can uncover the breaks in the party's ranks. In 1876 the average agreement score for white Republicans was 37.3 as compared with 44.6 for Negroes. Similarly, black former slaves scored 46.9 as compared with 38.7 for mulattoes of free origin. Clearly, what little political stability Republicans could lay claim to was provided not by the better educated and more experienced whites or by the brown bourgeoisie, but by the blacks of slave origin.

Internal conflict plagued Republicans outside the legislature as well. John Morris, an agent of the Republican National Committee visiting South Carolina on the eve of its first Reconstruction election, was dismayed by its vehemence. Any other state party would be doomed by the internecine warfare, he observed; only South Carolina's overwhelming black electoral majority insured a Republican victory. Even at the party's founding convention in 1867, Francis Cardozo found it necessary to warn his colleagues:

> From the unhappy state of things which has existed here in the enjoyment of this new privilege the colored find themselves divided and disunited by a variety of sentiments and feelings. Whatever may be a man's social status, whatever may be his religious views, whatever may be the state of his knowledge, if he will come with you and vote for this platform, unite with him, if it be Satan himself. (Cheers.) Let no cause of dissension, no feeling of animosity, no objection to social condition, prevent you from securing to yourselves and your children the liberty that has been committed to you.

Much of the intraparty conflict to which Morris and Cardozo referred was idiosyncratic, caused by personal competition of politically ambitious men. But some of the more important disagreements reflected overtones of racial and class antagonism. This was true certainly of the rather consistent deviation in the voting behavior of white and Negro Republicans. On critical roll calls a majority of the white Republicans opposed a majority of Negroes on at least one of every three votes. From 1872 to 1874 they opposed each other on an astounding 60 percent of the critical votes. Since white legislators constituted about a fifth to a third of the Republican legislative majority, such general and continuous defections could prove devastating to the party's fortunes.

It is not surprising that white Republican legislators did not see eye to eye with their black colleagues; there was ample evidence of distrust and animosity between these segments of the party. During the early years of Reconstruction, whites actively discouraged blacks from seeking their appropriate share of offices and power. On several occasions during the first two years of Republican rule, whites tried to exclude blacks from major state executive offices, congressional seats, judgeships, and even key party leadership posts. During the 1870 campaign Negroes rebelled against this policy and demanded their fair share of state and party offices. Nevertheless, during the final year of Republican rule, the party again would be split badly by the governor's effort to deny an important judicial post to William J. Whipper, a northern black lawyer.

Such conflicts cannot be traced solely to racial animosities, but there is evidence that racism was a contributing factor. For example, in 1868 Franklin J. Moses, Jr., Speaker of the House and governor of the state from 1872 to 1874, advised Governor Robert K. Scott to appoint only native whites to state judicial posts. In 1871 State Representative T. N. Talbert was even more explicit. "My policy," he wrote the governor, "is to get as many of the native whites of the state to unite with us as we can and try and induce Northern men to come and settle among us. There is not enough virtue and intelligence among the Blacks to conduct the government in such a way as will promote peace and prosperity."

Given the nation's racial climate it is not surprising, perhaps, that tensions would develop between Negro and white Republicans or that they would often perceive policy issues differently; but there was no reason to expect that Negro legislators would be so much less cohesive among themselves than their Democratic rivals. For much of the Reconstruction period a unified Negro leadership could have dominated the legislature. Their overwhelming majority in the House together with a consistently large plurality in the Senate should have enabled Negroes, given inevitable absenteeism and defections among white Republicans and Democrats, to attain most of their major legislative objectives. But in fact Negro leaders were often at odds on legislative objectives, political policies, and ideology. Furthermore, the nature of their disunity followed a consistent pattern from the earliest political meetings and is best explained by reference to differences in their socioeconomic status and antebellum experience.

The most visible, though not necessarily most significant, divisions were between the black ex-slaves and those mulattoes who had been free before the war [Blacks who were free represented 6.2 percent of the total African-American population of South Carolina in 1860]. The number of freeborn brown officeholders was far out of proportion to their share of the state's population, especially in the early conventions and legislative sessions, and their control of leadership positions was even more striking. In the 1868–70 House of Representatives, for example, half the committee chairmanships held by Negroes were filled by freeborn mulattoes. Between 1868 and 1876, over half the Negro state senators were drawn from this class and their average term of service was longer than that of black freedmen. Five of the seven Negroes elected to the state executive branch were freeborn brown men as well as four of the state's seven Negro congressmen.

Obviously, free brown men successfully offered themselves as prominent leaders of a predominantly black ex-slave electorate, but their very success aroused jealousy and political divisiveness within the party. In 1871 black leader Martin R. Delany complained to Frederick Douglass about mulatto dominance of patronage positions. In 1870 William H. Jones, Jr., black representative from Georgetown, publicly ridiculed Joseph H. Rainey, his mulatto rival for the state Senate, because of his extremely light complexion. State Senator William B. Nash, a black ex-slave, once referred to his mulatto colleagues as "simply mongrels."

It is misleading, however, to consider these intraracial tensions as merely a consequence of differences in skin color and antebellum origins. The fact is that among South Carolina Negroes a light complexion and free origins correlated very strongly with other indicators of bourgeois class status; mulattoes and those who had been free before the war were more likely to own property and thus to enjoy higher status than black ex-slaves, who were more likely to be propertyless. These general patterns were reflected in the General Assembly, where legislators of free origins were generally better educated than the freedmen, more likely to own property, and more likely to be employed as artisans or in a profession rather than as farmworkers. These objective differences, as minor as they might have appeared to whites, generated not only consciousness of class differences but social institutions that confirmed and reinforced those differences. The Brown Fellowship Society was one such institution. Founded in 1790, the society limited its membership to free brown men, providing them with a variety of financial services as well as social connections. At least three legislators belonged to the Brown Fellowship Society, and several others were members of social clubs with a similar orientation though less prestige. Church affiliation was another indicator of status aspirations if not class position. Thomas W. Cardozo, brother of Francis L. Cardozo and a representative of the American Missionary Association in 1865, complained to his superiors that he could not "worship intelligently with the colored people [meaning black freedmen]" and urged the formation of a separate missionary church for himself and his teachers. The pattern of religious affiliation among Negro legislators suggests that Cardozo's prejudices were not uncommon. Of the legislators whose religious affiliations can be identified, all but one of the freeborn were Catholic, Presbyterian, or Episcopalian, while 70 percent of the former slaves were either Methodist or Baptist.

It appears that these differences in social background and status produced differing perspectives on public policy. During the 1868 Constitutional Convention, for example, black ex-slave delegates voted with other Negro delegates an average of 72 percent of the time, while freeborn mulatto delegates averaged 67.9 percent. The differences in voting behavior were more dramatic when sensitive issues of land reform and confiscation were debated. Robert C. De Large's resolution to halt the disfranchisement of ex-Confederates and the confiscation of their property was one early test of radical and conservative tendencies in the convention. Although De Large's motion was opposed by a majority of the Negro delegates, it drew its heaviest support from mulatto delegates who had been free before the war, about 40 percent of whom supported the resolution, and its heaviest opposition from those blacks who had been slaves, about 75 percent of whom opposed it. Debates on whether to impose literacy and poll-tax requirements for voting reveal similar divisions. Delegates from the antebellum free class argued strenuously, though unsuccessfully, that illiterates and persons failing to pay a poll tax should not be allowed to vote.

The biographical profile of Negro delegates is far too incomplete to construct a composite index of class status for all ten legislative sessions; nevertheless, a variety of indicators reveal a consistent tendency over several sessions: the higher a member's social status the more likely was he to support conservative positions. In 1876, for example, Governor Chamberlain sponsored a series of conservative measures designed to placate and attract the support of Democrats for his gubernatorial bid. He wanted to cut funds for education, place the local school commissions in the hands of planters, eliminate the scholarship program at the state university, and reinstitute convict lease. When Chamberlain's measures came to a vote in the House, his main supporters were white Democrats and Negro legislators of high social status. Negro planters of moderate means like John Westberry, Jacob C. Allman, and Thomas Hamilton and merchants like William

J. Andrews supported the governor and the Democrats on most of these measures. . . .

For most Negro leaders, however, the differences probably resulted less from specific class interests than general differences in consciousness and modes of perception. Negro and white Republicans shared generalized, though not clearly articulated, "progressive" values and orientations. Negroes were unanimous in their support for civil rights and free public education, for example. There was also general support for expanded social services, such as mental asylums and almshouses, and for state-sponsored economic developments, such as railroad construction and phosphate mining. But as we have seen, measures to regulate the new farm-labor system and to reform land ownership, both of which were critical issues for the majority of their constituents, produced no unified positions and no effective programs from the legislators. . . .

The 1876 legislative session was the last opportunity Republicans had to ensure economic justice for their constituents. Elected by a very close margin in 1874, Governor David Chamberlain moved openly to build a political coalition of conservative Republicans and Democrats. His "reform" policies won general approval among Democrats. Chamberlain sought to cut government spending by reducing social services and education programs. He removed Republicans from important local offices and replaced them with Democrats. These policies won Democratic support but alienated and demoralized Republicans. J. W. Rice's despondent letter to Chamberlain protesting the appointment of several Democrats to Laurens County offices formerly held by Republicans was typical of the governor's correspondence during this period: "I am at last discouraged and thinking about resigning." Generally, the party morale declined and dissension increased. During the spring of 1876, Democrats watched gleefully as Republican conventions often tottered on the brink of physical violence. As A. P. Aldrich told a cheering audience, the Democrats planned "to keep Chamberlain and some of the carpetbaggers fighting, till they eat each other up all but the tails, and that he would keep the tails jumping at each other, until Southern raised gentlemen slide into office and take the reins of government." . . .

The failure of South Carolina's Reconstruction then was not caused by a weak and ignorant electorate. Despite the economic threats and physical terrors of the 1876 campaign, black freedmen turned out in force and delivered a record vote to Republican candidates. True, there was "political paralysis," an absence of "stern collective discipline," and a failure of will; but these were shortcomings of the Republican leadership, not of the masses of black voters. Divisions among the leaders—between white and black and among Negroes themselves—diminished the power these voters had entrusted to them and betrayed the aspirations they had clearly articulated. The freedmen made an amazing transformation after the Civil War; slaves became political men acting forcefully to crush the most cherished illusions of their former masters. The tragedy of Reconstruction is that they received so much less than they gave.

The Political Economy of the Black Family During Reconstruction

JACQUELINE JONES

The northerners' hope that black workers would be able to pursue their interests as individuals did not take into account the strong family ties that bound black households tightly together. More specifically, although black women constituted a sizable proportion of the region's labor force, their obligations to their husbands and children and kin took priority over any form of personal self-seeking. For most black women, then, freedom had very little to do with individual opportunity or independence in the modern sense. Rather, freedom had meaning primarily in a family context. The institution of slavery had posed a constant threat to the stability of family relationships; after emancipation these relationships became solidified, though the sanctity of family life continued to come under pressure from the larger white society. Freedwomen derived emotional fulfillment and a newfound sense of pride from their roles as wives and mothers. Only at home could they exercise considerable control over their own lives and those of their husbands and children and impose a semblance of order on the physical world.

As soon as they were free, blacks set their own work pace and conspired to protect one another from the white man's (and woman's) wrath. Plantation managers charged that freed people, hired to work like slaves, were "loafering around" and "lummoxing about." More than one postwar overseer, his "patience worn plum out," railed against "grunting" blacks (those "pretending to be sick") and others who sauntered out into the fields late in the day, left early to go fishing, or stayed home altogether; "damd sorry work" was the result. Modern economic historians confirm contemporary estimates that by the 1870s the amount of black labor in the fields had dropped to one-quarter or one-third preemancipation levels.

The withdrawal of black females from wage-labor—a major theme in both contemporary and secondary accounts of Reconstruction—occurred primarily among the wives and daughters of able-bodied men. (Women who served as the sole support for their children or other family members had to take work wherever they could find it.) According to a South Carolina newspaper writer in 1871, this development necessitated a "radical change in the management of [white] households as well as plantations" and proved to be a source of "absolute torment" for former masters and mistresses. The female field hand who plowed, hoed, and picked cotton under the ever-watchful eye of an overseer came to symbolize the old order.

Employers made little effort to hide their contempt for freedwomen who "played the lady" and refused to join workers in the fields. To apply the term ladylike to a black woman was apparently the height of sarcasm; by socially prescribed definition, black women could never become "ladies," though they might display pretensions in that direction. The term itself had predictable racial and class connotations. White ladies remained cloistered at home, fulfilling their marriage vows of motherhood and genteel domesticity. But black housewives appeared "most lazy"; they stayed "out of the fields, doing nothing," demanding that their husbands "support them in idleness." At the heart of the issue lay the whites' notion of productive labor; black women who eschewed work under the direct supervision of former masters did not really "work" at all, regardless of their family household responsibilities.

In their haste to declare "free labor" a success, even northerners and foreign visitors to the South ridiculed "lazy" freedwomen working within the confines of their own homes. Hypocritically—almost perversely—these whites questioned the "manhood" of husbands whom they charged were cowed by domineering female relatives. South Carolina Freedmen's Bureau agent John De Forest, for example, wrote that "myriads of women who once earned their own living now have aspirations to be like white ladies and, instead of using the hoe, pass the days in dawdling over their trivial housework, or gossiping among their neighbors." He disdained the "hopeless" look given him by men told "they must make their wives and daughters work." George Campbell, a Scotsman touring the South in 1878, declared, "I do not sympathize with negro ladies who make their husbands work while they enjoy the sweets of emancipation."

Most southern and northern whites assumed that the freed people were engaged in a misguided attempt to imitate middle-class white norms as they applied to women's roles. Even recent historians have suggested that the refusal of married women to work in the fields signified "conformity to dominant white values." In fact, however, the situation was a good deal more complicated. First, the reorganization of female labor resulted from choices made by *both* men and women. Second, it is inaccurate to speak of the "removal" of women from the agricultural work force. Many were no longer working for a white overseer, but they continued to pick cotton, laboring according to the needs and priorities established by their own families.

An Alabama planter suggested in 1868 that it was "a matter of pride with the men, to allow all exemption from labor to their wives." He told only part of the story. Accounts provided by disgruntled whites suggest that husbands did often take full responsibility for deciding which members of the family would work, and for whom: "Gilbert will stay on his old terms, but withdraws Fanny and puts Harry and Little Abram in her place and puts his son Gilbert out to a trade," reported a Georgia plantation mistress in January 1867. However, there is good reason to suspect that wives willingly devoted more time to childcare and other domestic matters, rather than merely acquiescing in their husbands' demands. A married freedwoman, the mother of eleven children, reminded a northern journalist that she had had "to nus' my chil'n four times a day and pick two hundred pounds cotton besides" under slavery. She expressed at least relative satisfaction with her current situation: "I've a heap better time now'n I had when I was in bondage."

The humiliations of slavery remained fresh in the minds of black women who continued to suffer physical abuse at the hands of white employers and in the minds of freedmen who witnessed or heard about such acts. . . . [I]t is important to note only that freedmen attempted to protect their womenfolk from rape and other forms of assault; as individuals, some intervened directly, while others went to local Freedmen's Bureau agents with accounts of beatings inflicted on their wives, sisters, and daughters. Bureau records include the case of a Tennessee planter who "made several base attempts" upon the daughter of the freedman Sam Neal (his entire family had been hired by the white man for the 1865 season). When Neal protested the situation, he was deprived of his wages, threatened with death, and then beaten badly by the white man and an accomplice. As a group, men sought to minimize chances for white male–black female contact by removing their female kin from work environments supervised closely by whites.

At first, cotton growers persisted in their belief that gangs afforded the most efficient means of labor organization because they had been used with relative success under slavery and facilitated centralization of control. Blacks only had to be forced to work steadily. However, Charles P. Ware, a Yankee cotton agent with [Edward] Philbrick on the Sea Islands, noted as early as 1862, "one thing the people are universally opposed to. They all swear that they will not work in a gang, i.e., all working the whole, and all sharing alike." Blacks preferred to organize themselves into kin groups, as evidenced by the "squad" system, an intermediary phase between gang labor and family sharecropping. A postwar observer defined the squad as "a strong family group, who can attach other labour, and bring odd hands to work at proper seasons"; this structure represented "a choice, if not always attainable, nucleus of a 'squad.' "

Described by one scholar as a "non-bureaucratic, self-regulating, and self-selecting worker peer group," the squad usually numbered less than a dozen people (seven was average), and performed its tasks under the direction of one of its own members. In this way kinship patterns established under slavery coalesced into work relationships after the war. Still, blacks resented an arrangement under which they continued to live together in old slave quarters grouped near the landowner's house and lacked complete control over the work they performed in the field.

In the late 1860s this tug of economic and psychological warfare between planters determined to grow more cotton and blacks determined to resist the old slave ways culminated in what historians have called a "compromise"—the sharecropping system. It met the minimal demands of each party—a relatively reliable source of labor for white landowners, and, for freed people (more specifically, for families), a measure of independence in terms of agricultural decision making. Sharecroppers moved out of the old cabins and into small houses scattered about the plantation. Contracts were renegotiated around the end of each calendar year; families not in debt to their employers for equipment and fertilizer often seized the opportunity to move in search of a better situation. By 1870 the "fifty-fifty" share arrangement under which planters parceled out to tenants small plots of land and provided rations and supplies in return for one-half the crop predominated throughout the Cotton South.

According to historians and econometricians who have documented the evolution of sharecropping, the system helped to reshape southern race and class relations even as it preserved the "stagnant" postbellum economy. The linking of personal financial credit to crop liens and the rise of debt peonage enforced by criminal statutes guaranteed a large, relatively immobile labor force at the expense of economic and social justice. In increasing numbers, poor whites would come under the same financial constraints that ensnared black people. But, for the purposes of this discussion, the significance of this "almost unprecedented form of labor organization" lies in its implications for black family life.

Although 1870 data present only a static profile of black rural households in the Cotton South, it is possible to make some generalizations (based on additional forms of evidence) about the status of freedwomen five years after the war. The vast majority (91 percent) lived in rural areas. Illiterate and very poor (even compared to their poor white neighbors), they nonetheless were not alone, and shared the mixed joys of work and family life with their husbands, children, and nearby kin. Fertility rates declined very slowly from 1830 to 1880; the average mother in 1870 had about six or seven children. The lives of these women were severely circumscribed, as were those of other family members. Most of the children never had an opportunity to attend school—or at least not with any regularity—and began to work in the fields or in the home of a white employer around the age of ten or twelve. Young women found it possible to leave their parents' home earlier than did the men they married. As a group, black women were distinguished from their white neighbors primarily by their lower socioeconomic status and by the greater reliance of their families on the work they did outside the realm of traditional domestic responsibilities.

Within the limited public arena open to blacks, the husband represented the entire family, a cultural preference reinforced by demographic and economic factors. In 1870, 80 percent of black households in the Cotton Belt included a male head and his wife (a proportion identical to that in the neighboring white population). In addition, most of the husbands were older than their wives—in more than half the cases, four years older; in one out of five cases, at least ten years older. Thus these men exercised authority by virtue of their age as well as their sex.

Landowners, merchants, and Freedmen's Bureau agents acknowledged the role of the black husband as the head of his family at the same time they encouraged his wife to work outside the home. He took "more or less land according to the number of his family" and placed "his X mark" on a labor agreement with a landowner. Kin relationships were often recognized in the text of the contract itself. Indeed, just as slaveholders had opportunistically dealt with the slave family—encouraging or ignoring it according to their own perceived interests—so postbellum planters seemed to have had little difficulty adjusting to the fact that freedmen's families were structured "traditionally" with the husband serving as the major source of authority. Patrick Broggan, an employer in Greenville, Alabama, agreed to supply food and other provisions for wives and children—"those who do not work on the farm"—"at the expense of their husbands and Fathers," men who promised "to work from Monday morning until Saturday night, faithfully and lose no time. . . ."

The Freedmen's Bureau's wage guidelines mandated that black women and men receive unequal compensation based on their sex rather than their productive abilities or efficiency. Agents also at times doled out less land to families with female (as opposed to male) household heads. Moreover, the bureau tried to hold men responsible for their wives' unwillingness to labor according to a contractual agreement. For example, the Cuthbert, Georgia, bureau official made one black man promise "to work faithfully and keep his wife in subjection" after the woman refused to work and "damned the Bureau" saying that "all the Bureaus out cant make her work."

A black husband usually purchased the bulk of the family's supplies (either in town or from a rural local merchant) and arranged to borrow or lease any stock animals that might be needed in plowing. He received direct payment in return for the labor of a son or daughter who had been "hired out." (It is uncertain whether a single mother who operated a farm delegated these responsibilities to her oldest son or another male kin relation, or took care of them herself.) Finally, complaints and criminal charges lodged by black men against whites often expressed the grievances of an entire household.

Thus the sexual division of labor that had existed within the black family under slavery became more sharply focused after emancipation. Wives and mothers and husbands and fathers perceived domestic duties to be a woman's major obligation, in contrast to the slave master's view that a female was first and foremost a field or house worker and only incidentally the member of a family. Women also worked in the fields when their labor was needed. At planting and especially harvest time they joined their husbands and children outside. During the late summer and early fall some would hire out to white planters in the vicinity to pick cotton for a daily wage. In areas where black men could find additional work during the year—on rice plantations or in phosphate mines or sugar mills, for example—they left their "women and children to hoe and look after the crops. . . ." Thus women's agricultural labor partook of a more seasonal character than that of their husbands.

The fact that black families depended heavily upon the field work of women and children is reflected in the great disparity between the proportion of working wives in Cotton Belt white and black households; in 1870 more than four out of ten black married women listed jobs, almost all as field laborers. By contrast, fully 98.4 percent of white wives told the census taker they were "keeping house" and had no gainful occupation. Moreover, about one-quarter (24.3 percent) of black households, in contrast to 13.8 percent of the white, included at least one working child under sixteen years of age. The figures related to black female and child labor are probably quite low, since census takers were inconsistent in specifying occupations for members of sharecropping families. In any case, they indicate that freedmen's families occupied the lowest rung of the southern economic ladder; almost three-fourths of all black household heads (compared to 10 percent of their white counterparts) worked as unskilled agricultural laborers. By the mid-1870s no more than 4 to 8 percent of all freed families in the South owned their own farms.

The rural *paterfamilias* tradition exemplified by the structure of black family relationships after the Civil War did not challenge the value and competence of freedwomen as field workers. Rather, a distinct set of priorities determined how wives and mothers used their time in terms of housework, field labor, and tasks that produced supplements to the family income. Thus it is difficult to separate a freedwoman's "work" from her family-based obligations; productive labor had no meaning outside the family context. These aspects of a woman's life blended together in the seamless fabric of rural life.

Since husbands and wives had different sets of duties, they needed each other to form a complete economic unit. As one Georgia black man explained to George Campbell in the late 1870s, "The able-bodied men cultivate, the women raise chickens and take in washing; and one way and another they manage to get along." When both partners were engaged in the same kind of work, it was usually the wife who had stepped over into her husband's "sphere." For instance, Fanny Hodges and her husband wed the year after they were freed. She remembered, "We had to work mighty hard. Sometimes I plowed in de fiel' all day; sometimes I washed an' den I cooked. . . . " Cotton growing was labor-intensive in a way that gardening and housework were not, and a family's ability to obtain financial credit from one year to the next depended upon the size of past harvests and the promise of future ones. Consequently the crop sometimes took precedence over other chores in terms of the allocation of a woman's energies.

Age was also a crucial determinant of the division of labor in sharecropping families. Participation in household affairs could be exhilarating for a child aware of her own strength and value as a field worker during these years of turmoil. Betty Powers was only eight years old in 1865, but she long remembered days of feverish activity for the whole family after her father bought a small piece of land in Texas: "De land ain't clear, so we 'uns all pitches in and clears it and builds de cabin. Was we 'uns proud? There 'twas, our place to do as we pleases, after bein' slaves. Dat sho' am de good feelin'. We works like beavers puttin' de crop in. . . . " Sylvia Watkins recalled that her father gathered all his children together after the war. She was twenty years old at the time and appreciated the special significance of a family able to work together: "We wuked in de fiel' wid mah daddy, en I know how ter do eberting dere ez to do in a fiel' 'cept plow. . . . ''

But at least some children resented the restrictions imposed by their father who "raised crops en made us wuk in de fiel." The interests of the family superseded individual desires. Fathers had the last word in deciding which children went to the fields, when, and for how long. As a result some black women looked back on their years spent at home as a time of personal opportunities missed or delayed. The Federal Writers Project slave narrative collection contains specific examples of fathers who prevented daughters from putting their own wishes before the family's welfare during the postbellum period. Ann Matthews told a federal interviewer, "I didn't go ter schul, mah daddy wouldin' let me. Said he needed me in de fiel wors den I needed schul." Here were two competing "needs," and the family had to come first.

The status of black women after the war cannot be separated from their roles as wives and mothers within a wider setting of kinship obligations. Herbert Gutman has argued that these obligations probably assumed greater significance in nineteenth-century Afro-American life than in immigrant or poor white communities because blacks possessed "a distinctive low economic status, a condition that denied them the advantages of an extensive associational life beyond the kin group and the advantages and disadvantages resulting from mobility opportunities." Indeed, more than one-third of all black households in the Cotton Belt lived in the immediate vicinity of people with the identical (paternal) surname, providing a rather crude— and conservative—index of local kinship clusters. As the persons responsible for child nurture and social welfare, freedwomen cared not only for members of their nuclear families, but also for dependent relatives and others in need. This postemancipation cooperative impulse constituted but one example of a historical "ethos of mutuality" developed under slavery.

The former slaves' attempts to provide for each other's needs appear to have been a logical and humane response to widespread hardship during the 1860s and 1870s. But whites spared from physical suffering, including southern elites and representatives of the northern professional class, often expressed misgivings about this form of benevolence. They believed that any able-bodied black person deserved a "living" only to the extent that he or she contributed to the southern commercial economy. Blacks should reap according to the cottonseed they sowed.

Soon after she returned to her family's Sea Island estate in 1866, Frances Leigh thought there was nothing else "to become of the negroes who cannot work except to die." In this way she masked her grief over the death of slavery with professed concern for ill, young, and elderly freed people. But within a few months she declared with evident irritation, " . . . it is a well-known fact that you can't starve a negro." Noting that about a dozen people on Butler's Island did not work (in the cotton fields) at all and so received no clothes or food supplies, the white woman admitted that she saw "no difference whatever in their condition and those who get twelve dollars a month and full rations." Somehow the field workers and nonworkers alike managed to take care of themselves and each other by growing vegetables, catching fish, and trapping game. Consequently they relied less on wages paid by their employer. The threat of starvation proved to be a poor taskmaster in compelling these freed people to toil for Frances Leigh.

Too many blacks, according to bureau agent John De Forest, felt obliged to look after "a horde of lazy relatives" and neighbors, thus losing a precious opportunity to get ahead on their own. This tendency posed a serious threat to the South's new economic order, founded as it was, in De Forest's view, on individual effort and ambition. He pointed to the case of Aunt Judy, a black laundress who barely eked out a living for herself and her small children. Yet she had "benevolently taken in, and was nursing, a sick woman of her own race. . . . The thoughtless charity of this penniless Negress in receiving another poverty-stricken creature under her roof was characteristic of the freedmen. However selfish, and even dishonest, they might be, they were extravagant in giving." By calling the willingness to share a "thoughtless" act, De Forest implied that a "rational" economic being would labor only to enhance her own material welfare.

The racial self-consciousness demonstrated by black women and men within their own kin networks found formal, explicit expression in the political arena during Reconstruction. As Vincent Harding and others have shown, freedmen actively participated in postwar Republican politics, and leaders of their own race came to constitute a new and influential class within black communities (though rivalries among members of this group could at times be intense). Class relationships that had prevailed before the war shifted, opening up possibilities of cooperation between the former slaves and nonelite whites. The two groups met at a historical point characterized by landlessness and economic dependence, but they were on two different trajectories—the freed people on their way up (no matter how slightly) from slavery, the poor whites on their way down from self-sufficiency. Nevertheless, the vitality of the political process, tainted though it was by virulent racial prejudice and violence, provided black men with a public forum distinct from the private sphere inhabited by their womenfolk.

Black men predominated in this arena because, like other groups in nineteenth-century America, they believed that males alone were responsible for—and capable of—the serious business of politicking. This notion was reinforced by laws that barred female suffrage. However, black husbands and fathers, unlike their white counterparts, perceived the preservation and physical welfare of their families (including protection from terrorists) to be distinct political issues, along with predictable measures like land reform and debt relief. In political activity, freedmen extended their role as family protector outside the boundaries of the household. One searches in vain for any mention of women delegates in accounts of formal black political conventions held during this period—local and state gatherings during which men formulated and articulated their vision of a just postwar society. Freedwomen sometimes spoke up forcefully at meetings devoted to specific community issues, but they remained outside the formal political process. (In this respect white women occupied a similarly inferior position.) The sight of black wives patiently tilling the soil while their husbands attended political conventions, at times for days on end, convinced at least one white teacher that freedwomen deserved to participate more actively in the community's public life. Elizabeth Botume wrote in 1869:

> We could not help wishing that since so much of the work was done by the colored women,—raising the provisions for their families, besides making and selling their own cotton, they might also hold some of the offices held by the men. I am confident they would despatch [*sic*] business if allowed to go to the polls; instead of listening and hanging around all day, discussing matters of which they knew so little, they would exclaim,—
> "Let me vote and go; I've got work to do."

In praising black women and their potential for political leadership, Botume denigrated black men. Like so many northerners, she could hardly express positive sentiments toward one sex without belittling the other.

It is true that freedmen monopolized formal positions of power within their own communities during Reconstruction. But that did not necessarily mean that women quietly deferred to them in all matters outside the home. For example, in some rural areas two sources of religious authority—one dominated by men, the other by women—coexisted uneasily. At times formal role designations only partly reflected the "influence" wielded by individuals outside their own households. In the process of institutionalizing clandestine religious practices formed during slavery and separating them from white congregations, freed people reserved church leadership positions for men. In other ways, individual congregations fashioned a distinctly inferior role for women; some even turned women out of the sanctuary "before the men began to talk" about matters of church policy. On the Sea Islands, whites reported the public censure of freedwomen who had committed marital transgressions by showing a lack of proper respect for their husbands' authority. The biblical injunction "Wives submit yourselves to your husbands" provided preachers with a succinct justification for church-based decisions that seemed arbitrary or unfair to the women involved.

These examples must be contrasted with equally dramatic cases of women who exercised considerable influence over their neighbors' spiritual lives, but outside of formal religious bodies and, indeed, of Protestant denominationalism altogether. Elderly women in the long line of African and Afro-American conjurers and herb doctors were often eagerly consulted by persons of both sexes. They included the African-born Maum Katie, "a great 'spiritual mother', a fortune-teller, or rather prophetess, and a woman of tremendous influence over her children," as well as other women whose pronouncements and incantations were believed to be divinely inspired. Rural communities had two (in all probability competing) sources of spiritual and secular guidance—one a male, and formal, the other female, and informal—and this pattern magnified the sex-role differentiation within individual households.

In rejecting the forced pace of the slave regimen and embracing a family-based system of labor organization, freed people exhibited a preference for work patterns typical of a "traditional" rural society in which religious, regional, and kinship loyalties are the dominant values, as opposed to personal ambition or the nationalistic goal of social and economic "progress." Indeed, very soon after emancipation emerged black households—set within larger networks of kin and community—that closely conformed to the "premodern" family model. In this case the terms traditional and premodern are misleading, however, because the sharecropping family that lived and worked together actually represented an adaptation, or response, to postwar conditions rather than a clinging to old ways. This development, initiated so boldly by blacks, was particularly significant because it contrasted sharply with trends characteristic of late nineteenth-century northern society, in which making a living was increasingly carried on by individuals, apart from family life.

A Black Settlement in South Carolina, 1870–1880

ELIZABETH RAUH BETHEL

For Sale: The homestead, grist mill, and 2742 acres of farmland from the estate of Samuel Marshall, six miles from Abbeville. Contact estate executors, S. S. Marshall and J. W. W. Marshall.
                          Abbeville, South Carolina *Press*
                          12 November 1869

Dr. Marshall's Farm

Promised Land was from the outset an artifact of Reconstruction politics. Its origins, as well, lie in the hopes, the dreams, and the struggles of four million Negroes, for the meaning of freedom was early defined in terms of land for most emancipated Negroes. In South Carolina, perhaps more intensely than any of the other southern states, the thirst for land was acute. It was a possibility sparked first by General William T. Sherman's military actions along the Sea Islands, then dashed as quickly as it was born in the distant arena of Washington politics. Still, the desire for land remained a goal not readily abandoned by the state's freedpeople, and they implemented a plan to achieve that goal at the first opportunity. Their chance came at the 1868 South Carolina Constitutional Convention.

South Carolina was among the southern states which refused to ratify the Fourteenth Amendment to the Constitution, the amendment which established the citizenship of the freedmen. Like her recalcitrant neighbors,

Elizabeth Rauh Bethel, "Settlement, 1870–1880," in *Promiseland: A Century of Life in a Negro Community*, pp. 17–40. Copyright © 1981 by Temple University. Reprinted by permission of Temple University Press.

the state was then placed under military government, as outlined by the Military Reconstruction Act of 1867. Among the mandates of that federal legislation was a requirement that each of the states in question draft a new state constitution which incorporated the principles of the Fourteenth Amendment. Only after such new constitutions were completed and implemented were the separate states of the defeated Confederacy eligible for readmission to the Union.

The representatives to these constitutional conventions were selected by a revolutionary electorate, one which included all adult male Negroes. Registration for the elections was handled by the Army with some informal assistance by "that God-forsaken institution, the Freedmen's Bureau." Only South Carolina among the ten states of the former Confederacy elected a Negro majority to its convention. The instrument those representatives drafted called for four major social and political reforms in state government: a statewide system of free common schools; universal manhood suffrage; a jury law which included the Negro electorate in county pools of qualified jurors; and a land redistribution system designed to benefit the state's landless population, primarily the freedmen.

White response to the new constitution and the social reforms which it outlined was predictably vitriolic. It was condemned by one white newspaper as "the work of sixty-odd Negroes, many of them ignorant and depraved." The authors were publicly ridiculed as representing "the maddest, most unscrupulous, and infamous revolution in history." Despite this and similar vilification, the constitution was ratified in the 1868 referendum, an election boycotted by many white voters and dominated by South Carolina's 81,000 newly enfranchised Negroes, who cast their votes overwhelmingly with the Republicans and for the new constitution.

That same election selected representatives to the state legislature charged with implementing the constitutional reforms. That body, like the constitutional convention, was constituted with a Negro majority; and it moved immediately to establish a common school system and land redistribution program. The freedmen were already registered, and the new jury pools remained the prerogative of the individual counties. The 1868 election also was notable for the numerous attacks and "outrages" which occurred against the more politically active freedmen. Among those Negroes assaulted, beaten, shot, and lynched during the pre-election campaign months were four men who subsequently bought small farms from the Land Commission and settled at Promised Land. Like other freedmen in South Carolina, their open involvement in the state's Republican political machinery led to personal violence.

Wilson Nash was the first of the future Promised Land residents to encounter white brutality and retaliation for his political activities. Nash was nominated by the Republicans as their candidate for Abbeville County's seat in the state legislature at the August 1868 county convention. In October of that year, less than two weeks before the general election, Nash was attacked and shot in the leg by two unidentified white assailants. The "outrage" took place in the barn on his rented farm, not far from Dr.

Marshall's farm on Curltail Creek. Wilson Nash was thirty-three years old in 1868, married, and the father of three small children. He had moved from "up around Cokesbury" within Abbeville County, shortly after emancipation to the rented land further west. Within months after the Nash family was settled on their farm, Wilson Nash joined the many Negroes who affiliated with the Republicans, an alliance probably instigated and encouraged by Republican promises of land to the freedmen. The extent of Nash's involvement with local politics was apparent in his nomination for public office; and this same nomination brought him to the forefront of county Negro leadership and to the attention of local whites.

After the attack Nash sent his wife and young children to a neighbor's home, where he probably believed they would be safe. He then mounted his mule and fled his farm, leaving behind thirty bushels of recently harvested corn. Whether Nash also left behind a cotton crop is unknown. It was the unprotected corn crop that worried him as much as his concern for his own safety. He rode his mule into Abbeville and there sought refuge at the local Freedmen's Bureau office where he reported the attack to the local bureau agent and requested military protection for his family and his corn crop. Captain W. F. DeKnight was sympathetic to Nash's plight but was powerless to assist or protect him. DeKnight had no authority in civil matters such as this, and the men who held that power generally ignored such assaults on Negroes. The Nash incident was typical and followed a familiar pattern. The assailants remained unidentified, unapprehended, and unpunished. The attack achieved the desired end, however, for Nash withdrew his name from the slate of legislative candidates. For him there were other considerations which took priority over politics.

Violence against the freedmen of Abbeville County, as elsewhere in the state, continued that fall and escalated as the 1868 election day neared. The victims had in common an involvement with the Republicans, and there was little distinction made between direct and indirect partisan activity. Politically visible Negroes were open targets. Shortly after the Nash shooting young Willis Smith was assaulted, yet another victim of Reconstruction violence. Smith was still a teenager and too young to vote in the elections, but his age afforded him no immunity. He was a known member of the Union League, the most radical and secret of the political organizations which attracted freedmen. While attending a dance one evening, Smith and four other League members were dragged outside the dance hall and brutally beaten by four white men whose identities were hidden by hoods. This attack, too, was an act of political vengeance. It was, as well, one of the earliest Ku Klux Klan appearances in Abbeville. Like other crimes committed against politically active Negroes, this one remained unsolved.

On election day freedmen Washington Green and Allen Goode were precinct managers at the White Hall polling place, near the southern edge of the Marshall land. Their position was a political appointment of some prestige, their reward for affiliation with and loyalty to the Republican cause. The appointment brought them, like Wilson Nash and Willis Smith, to the attention of local whites. On election day the voting proceeded without incident until midday, when two white men attempted to block Negroes from entering the polling site. A scuffle ensued as Green and Goode, acting in their capacity as voting officials, tried to bring the matter to a halt and were shot by the white men. One freedman was killed, two others injured, in the incident which also went unsolved. In none of the attacks were the assailants ever apprehended. Within twenty-four months all four men—Wilson Nash, Willis Smith, Washington Green, and Allen Goode—bought farms at Promised Land.

Despite the violence which surrounded the 1868 elections, the Republicans carried the whole of the state. White Democrats refused to support an election they deemed illegal, and they intimidated the newly enfranchised Negro electorate at every opportunity. The freedmen, nevertheless, flocked to the polls in an unprecedented exercise of their new franchise and sent a body of legislative representatives to the state capitol of Columbia who were wholly committed to the mandates and reforms of the new constitution. Among the first legislative acts was one which formalized the land redistribution program through the creation of the South Carolina Land Commission.

The Land Commission program, as designed by the legislature, was financed through the public sale of state bonds. The capital generated from the bond sales was used to purchase privately owned plantation tracts which were then subdivided and resold to freedmen through long-term (ten years), low-interest (7 percent per annum) loans. The bulk of the commission's transactions occurred along the coastal areas of the state where land was readily available. The labor and financial problems of the rice planters of the low-country were generally more acute than those of the up-country cotton planters. As a result, they were more eager to dispose of a portion of the landholdings at a reasonable price, and their motives for their dealings with the Land Commission were primarily pecuniary.

Piedmont planters were not so motivated. Many were able to salvage their production by negotiating sharecropping and tenant arrangements. Most operated on a smaller scale than the low-country planters and were less dependent on gang labor arrangements. As a consequence, few were as financially pressed as their low-country counterparts, and land was less available for purchase by the Land Commission in the Piedmont region. With only 9 percent of the commission purchases lying in the up-country, the Marshall lands were the exception rather than the rule.

The Marshall sons first advertised the land for sale in 1865. These lands, like others at the eastern edge of the Cotton Belt, were exhausted from generations of cultivation and attendant soil erosion; and for such worn out land the price was greatly inflated. Additionally, two successive years of crop failures, low cotton prices, and a general lack of capital discouraged serious planters from purchasing the lands. The sons then advertised the tract for rent, but the land stood idle. The family wanted to dispose of the land in a single transaction rather than subdivide it, and Dr. Marshall's farm was no competition for the less expensive and more fertile land to the west that was opened for settlement after the war. In 1869 the two sons once again advertised the land for sale, but conditions in Abbeville County were not improved for farmers, and no private buyer came forth.

Having exhausted the possibilities for negotiating a private sale, the family considered alternative prospects for the disposition of a farm that was of little use to them. James L. Orr, a moderate Democrat, former governor (1865 to 1868), and family son-in-law, served as negotiator when the tract was offered to the Land Commission at the grossly inflated price of ten dollars an acre. Equivalent land in Abbeville County was selling for as little as two dollars an acre, and the commission rejected the offer. Political promises took precedence over financial considerations when the commission's regional agent wrote the Land Commission's Advisory Board that "if the land is not bought the (Republican) party is lost in this district." Upon receipt of his advice the commission immediately met the Marshall family's ten dollar an acre price. By January 1870 the land was subdivided into fifty small farms, averaging slightly less than fifty acres each, which were publicly offered for sale to Negro as well as white buyers.

The Marshall Tract was located in the central sector of old Abbeville County and was easily accessible to most of the freedmen who were to make the lands their home. Situated in the western portion of the state, the tract was approximately sixty miles northwest of Augusta, Georgia, one hundred and fifty miles northeast of Atlanta, and the same distance northwest of Charleston. It would attract few freedmen from the urban areas. Two roads intersected within the lands. One, running north to south, linked those who soon settled there with the county seat of Abbeville to the north and the Phoenix community, a tiny settlement composed primarily of white small-scale farmers approximately eighteen miles to the south. Called New Cut Road, Five Notch Road, and later White Hall Road, the dirt wagon route was used primarily for travel to Abbeville. The east-west road, which would much later be converted to a state highway, was the more heavily traveled of the two and linked the cluster of farms to the village of Greenwood, six miles to the east, and the small settlement of Verdery, three miles to the west. Beyond Verdery, which served for a time as a stagecoach stop on the long trip between Greenville and Augusta, lay the Savannah River. The road was used regularly by a variety of peddlers and salesmen who included the Negro farmers on their routes as soon as families began to move onto the farms. Despite the decidedly rural setting, the families who bought land there were not isolated. A regular stream of travelers brought them news of events from well beyond their limited geography and helped them maintain touch with a broader scope of activities and ideas than their environment might have predicted.

The Marshall Tract had only one natural boundary to delineate the perimeter of Negro-owned farms, Curltail Creek on the north. Other less distinctive markers were devised as the farms were settled, to distinguish the area from surrounding white-owned lands. Extending south from White Hall Road, "below the cemetery, south of the railroad about a mile" a small lane intersected the larger road. This was Rabbit Track Road, and it marked the southern edge of Negro-owned lands. To the east the boundary was marked by another dirt lane called Lorenzo Road, little more than a trail which led to the Seaboard Railroad flag stop. Between the crossroads and Verdery to the west, "the edge of the old Darraugh place" established the western perimeter. In all, the tract encompassed slightly more than four square miles of earth.

The farms on the Marshall Tract were no bargain for the Negroes who bought them. The land was only partially cleared and ready for cultivation, and that which was free of pine trees and underbrush was badly eroded. There was little to recommend the land to cotton farming. Crop failures in 1868 and 1869 severely limited the local economy, which further reduced the possibilities for small farmers working on badly depleted soil. There was little credit available to Abbeville farmers, white or black; and farming lacked not only an unqualified promise of financial gain but even the possibility of breaking even at harvest. Still, it was not the fertility of the soil or the possibility of economic profit that attracted the freedmen to those farms. The single opportunity for landownership, a status which for most Negroes in 1870 symbolized the essence of their freedom, was the prime attraction for the freedmen who bought farms from the subdivided Marshall Tract.

Most of the Negroes who settled the farms knew the area and local conditions well. Many were native to Abbeville County. In addition to Wilson Nash, the Moragne family and their in-laws, the Turners, the Pinckneys, the Letmans, and the Williamses were also natives of Abbeville, from "down over by Bordeaux" in the southwestern rim of the county which borders Georgia. Others came to their new farms from "Dark Corner, over by McCormick," and another nearby Negro settlement, Pettigrew Station—both in Abbeville County. The Redd family lived in Newberry, South Carolina, before they bought their farm; and James and Hannah Fields came to Promised Land from the state capitol, Columbia, eighty miles to the east.

Many of the settlers from Abbeville County shared their names with prominent white families—Moragne, Burt, Marshall, Pressley, Frazier, and Pinckney. Their claims to heritage were diverse. One recalled "my grandaddy was a white man from England," and others remembered slavery times to their children in terms of white fathers who "didn't allow nobody to mess with the colored boys of his." Others dismissed the past and told their grandchildren that "some things is best forgot." A few were so fair skinned that "they could have passed for white if they wanted to," while others who bought farms from the Land Commission "was so black there wasn't no doubt about who their daddy was."

After emancipation many of these former bondsmen stayed in their old neighborhoods, farming in much the same way as they had during slavery times. Some "worked for the marsters at daytime and for theyselves at night" in an early Piedmont version of sharecropping. Old Samuel Marshall was one former slave owner who retained many of his bondsmen as laborers by assuring them that they would receive some land of their own—promising them that "if you clean two acres you get two acres; if you clean ten acres you get ten acres" of farmland. It was this promise which kept some freedmen on the Marshall land until it was sold to the Land Commission. They cut and cleared part of the tract of the native pines and readied it for planting in anticipation of ownership. But the promise proved empty, and Marshall's death and the subsequent sale of his lands to the state deprived many of those who labored day and night on the land of the free farms they hoped would be theirs. "After they had cleaned it up they still had to pay for it." Other freedmen in the county "moved off after slavery ended but couldn't get no place" of their own to farm. Unable to negotiate labor or lease arrangements, they faced a time of homelessness with few resources and limited options until the farms became available to them. A few entered into labor contracts supervised by the Freedmen's Bureau or settled on rented farms in the county for a time.

The details of the various postemancipation economic arrangements made by the freedmen who settled on the small tracts at Dr. Marshall's farm, whatever the form they assumed, were dominated by three conscious choices all had in common. The first was their decision to stay in Abbeville County following emancipation. For most of the people who eventually settled in Promised Land, Abbeville was their home as well as the site of their enslavement. There they were surrounded by friends, family and a familiar environment. The second choice this group of freedmen shared was occupational. They had been Piedmont farmers throughout their enslavement, and they chose to remain farmers in their freedom.

Local Negroes made a third conscious decision that for many had long-range importance in their lives and those of their descendants. Through the influence of the Union League, the Freedmen's Bureau, the African Methodist Church, and each other, many of the Negroes in Abbeville aligned politically with the Republicans between 1865 and 1870. In Abbeville as elsewhere in the state, this alliance was established enthusiastically. The Republicans promised land as well as suffrage to those who supported them. If their political activities became public knowledge, the freedmen "were safe nowhere"; and men like Wilson Nash, Willis Smith, Washington Green, and Allen Goode who were highly visible Negro politicians took great risks in this exercise of freedom. Those risks were not without justification. It was probably not a coincidence that loyalty to the Republican cause was followed by a chance to own land.

Land for Sale to the Colored People

I have 700 acres of land to sell in lots of from 50 to 100 acres or more situated six miles from Abbeville. Terms: *A liberal cash payment; balance to be made in three annual payments from date of purchase.*
J. Hollinshead, Agent
(Advertisement placed by the Land Commission
in Abbeville *Press,* 2 July 1873)

The Land Commission first advertised the farms on the Marshall Tract in January and February 1870. Eleven freedmen and their families established conditional ownership of their farms before spring planting that year. They were among a vanguard of some 14,000 Negro families who acquired small farms in South Carolina through the Land Commission program between 1868 and 1879. With a ten-dollar down payment they acquired the right to settle on and till the thin soil. They were also obliged to place at least half of their land under cultivation within three years and to pay all taxes due annually in order to retain their ownership rights.

Among the earliest settlers to the newly created farms was Allen Goode, the precinct manager at White Hall, who bought land in January 1870, almost immediately after it was put on the market. Two brothers-in-law, J. H. Turner and Primus Letman, also bought farms in the early spring that year. Turner was married to LeAnna Moragne and Letman to LeAnna's sister Frances. Elias Harris, a widower with six young children to raise, also came to his lands that spring, as did George Hearst, his son Robert, and their families. Another father-son partnership, Carson and Will Donnelly, settled on adjacent tracts. Willis Smith's father Daniel also bought a farm in 1870.

Allen Goode was the wealthiest of these early settlers. He owned a horse, two oxen, four milk cows, and six hogs. For the other families, both material resources and farm production were modest. Few of the homesteaders produced more than a single bale of cotton on their new farms that first year; but all, like Wilson Nash two years earlier, had respectable corn harvests, a crop essential to "both us and the animals." Most households also had sizable pea, bean, and sweet potato crops and produced their own butter. All but the cotton crops were destined for household consumption, as these earliest settlers established a pattern of subsistence farming that would prevail as a community economic strategy in the coming decades.

This decision by the Promised Land farmers to intensify food production and minimize cotton cultivation, whether intentional or the result of other conditions, was an important initial step toward their attainment of economic self-sufficiency. Small scale cotton farmers in the Black Belt were rarely free agents. Most were quickly trapped in a web of chronic indebtedness and marketing restrictions. Diversification of cash crops was inhibited during the 1870s and 1880s not only by custom and these economic entanglements but also by an absence of local markets, adequate roads, and methods of transportation to move crops other than cotton to larger markets. The Promised Land farmers, generally unwilling to incur debts with the local lien men if they could avoid it, turned to a modified form of subsistence farming as their only realistic land-use option. Through this strategy many of them avoided the "economic nightmare" which fixed the status of other small-scale cotton growers at a level of permanent peonage well into the twentieth century.

The following year, 1871, twenty-five more families scratched up their ten-dollar down payment; and upon presenting it to Hollinshead obtained conditional titles to farms on the Marshall Tract. The Williams family, Amanda and her four adult sons—William, Henry, James, and Moses—

purchased farms together that year, probably withdrawing their money from their accounts at the Freedmen's Savings and Trust Company Augusta Branch for their separate down payments. Three of the Moragne brothers— Eli, Calvin, and Moses—joined the Turners and the Letmans, their sisters and brothers-in-law, making five households in that corner of the tract soon designated "Moragne Town." John Valentine, whose family was involved in A.M.E. organizational work in Abbeville County, also obtained a conditional title to a farm, although he did not settle there permanently. Henry Redd, like the Williamses, withdrew his savings from the Freedmen's Bank and moved to his farm from Newberry, a small town about thirty miles to the east. Moses Wideman, Wells Gray, Frank Hutchison, Samuel Bulow, and Samuel Burt also settled on their farms before spring planting.

As the cluster of Negro-owned farms grew more densely populated, it gradually assumed a unique identity; and this identity, in turn, gave rise to a name, Promised Land. Some remember their grandparents telling them that "the Governor in Columbia [South Carolina] named this place when he sold it to the Negroes." Others contend that the governor had no part in the naming. They argue that these earliest settlers derived the name Promised Land from the conditions of their purchase. "They only promised to pay for it, but they never did!" Indeed, there is some truth in that statement. For, although the initial buyers agreed to pay between nine and ten dollars per acre for their land in the original promissory notes, few fulfilled the conditions of those contracts. Final purchase prices were greatly reduced, from ten dollars to $3.25 per acre, a price more in line with prevailing land prices in the Piedmont.

By the end of 1873 forty-four of the fifty farms on the Marshall Tract had been sold. The remaining land, less than seven hundred acres, was the poorest in the tract, badly eroded and at the perimeter of the community. Some of those farms remained unsold until the early 1880s, but even so the land did not go unused. Families too poor to consider buying the farms lived on the state-owned property throughout the 1870s. They were squatters, living there illegally and rent-free, perhaps working a small cotton patch, always a garden. Their condition contrasted sharply with that of the landowners who, like other Negroes who purchased farmland during the 1870s, were considered the most prosperous of the rural freedmen. The freeholders in the community were among the pioneers in a movement to acquire land, a movement that stretched across geographical and temporal limits. Even in the absence of state or federal assistance in other regions, and despite the difficulties Negroes faced in negotiating land purchases directly from white landowners during Reconstruction, by 1875 Negroes across the South owned five million acres of farmland. The promises of emancipation were fulfilled for a few, among them the families at Promised Land.

Settlement of the community coincided with the establishment of a public school, another of the revolutionary social reforms mandated by the 1868 constitution. It was the first of several public facilities to serve community residents and was built on land still described officially as "Dr.

Marshall's farm." J. H. Turner, Larkin Reynolds, Iverson Reynolds, and Hutson Lomax, all Negroes, were the first school trustees. The families established on their new farms sent more than ninety children to the one-room school. Everyone who could be spared from the fields was in the classroom for the short 1870 school term. Although few of the children in the landless families attended school regularly, the landowning families early established a tradition of school attendance for their children consonant with their new status. With limited resources the school began the task of educating local children.

The violence and terror experienced by some of the men of Promised Land during 1868 recurred three years later when Eli and Wade Moragne were attacked and viciously beaten with a wagon whip by a band of Klansmen. Wade was twenty-three that year, Eli two years older. Both were married and had small children. It was rumored that the Moragne brothers were among the most prominent and influential of the Negro Republicans in Abbeville County. Their political activity, compounded by an unusual degree of self-assurance, pride, and dignity, infuriated local whites. Like Wilson Nash, Willis Smith, Washington Green, and Allen Goode, the Moragne brothers were victims of insidious political reprisals. Involvement in Reconstruction politics for Negroes was a dangerous enterprise and one which addressed the past as well as the future. It was an activity suited to young men and those who faced the future bravely. It was not for the timid.

The Republican influence on the freedmen at Promised Land was unmistakable, and there was no evidence that the "outrages" and terrorizations against them slowed their participation in local partisan activities. In addition to the risks, there were benefits to be accrued from their alliance with the Republicans. They enjoyed appointments as precinct managers and school trustees. As candidates for various public offices, they experienced a degree of prestige and public recognition which offset the element of danger they faced. These men, born slaves, rose to positions of prominence as landowners, as political figures, and as makers of a community. Few probably had dared to dream of such possibilities a decade earlier.

During the violent years of Reconstruction there was at least one official attempt to end the anarchy in Abbeville County. The representative to the state legislature, J. Hollinshead—the former regional agent for the Land Commission—stated publicly what many local Negroes already knew privately, that "numerous outrages occur in the county and the laws cannot be enforced by civil authorities." From the floor of the General Assembly of South Carolina Hollinshead called for martial law in Abbeville, a request which did not pass unnoticed locally. The editor of the *Press* commented on Hollinshead's request for martial law by declaring that such outrages against the freedmen "exist only in the imagination of the legislator." His response was probably typical of the cavalier attitude of southern whites toward the problems of their former bondsmen. Indeed, there were no further reports of violence and attacks against freedmen carried by the *Press,* which failed to note the murder of County Commissioner Henry

Nash in February 1871. Like other victims of white terrorists, Nash was a Negro.

While settlement of Dr. Marshall's Farm by the freedmen proceeded, three community residents were arrested for the theft of "some oxen from Dr. H. Drennan who lives near the 'Promiseland.' " Authorities found the heads, tails, and feet of the slaughtered animals near the homes of Ezekiel and Moses Williams and Colbert Jordan. The circumstantial evidence against them seemed convincing; and the three were arrested and then released without bond, pending trial. Colonel Cothran, a former Confederate officer and respected barrister in Abbeville, represented the trio at their trial. Although freedmen in Abbeville courts were generally convicted of whatever crime they were charged with, the Williamses and Jordan were acquitted. Justice for Negroes was always a tenuous affair; but it was especially so before black, as well as white, qualified electors were included in the jury pool. The trial of the Williams brothers and Jordan signaled a temporary truce in the racial war, a truce which at least applied to those Negroes settling the farms at Promised Land.

In 1872, the third year of settlement, Promised Land gained nine more households as families moved to land that they "bought for a dollar an acre." There they "plow old oxen, build log cabin houses" as they settled the land they bought "from the Governor in Columbia." Colbert Jordan and Ezekiel Williams, cleared of the oxen stealing charges, both purchased farms that year. Family and kinship ties drew some of the new migrants to the community. Joshuway Wilson, married to Moses Wideman's sister Delphia, bought a farm near his brother-in-law. Two more Moragne brothers, William and Wade, settled near the other family members in "Moragne Town." Whitfield Hutchison, a jack-leg preacher, bought the farm adjacent to his brother Frank. "Old Whit Hutchison could sing about let's go down to the water and be baptized. He didn't have no education, and he didn't know exactly how to put his words, but when he got to singing he could make your hair rise up. He was a number one preacher." Hutchison was not the only preacher among those first settlers. Isaac Y. Moragne, who moved to Promised Land the following year, and several men in the Turner family all combined preaching and farming.

Not all of the settlers came to their new farms as members of such extensive kinship networks as the Moragnes, who counted nine brothers, four sisters, and an assortment of spouses and children among the first Promised Land residents. Even those who joined the community in relative isolation, however, were seldom long in establishing kinship alliances with their neighbors. One such couple was James and Hannah Fields who lived in Columbia before emancipation. While still a slave, James Fields owned property in the state capitol, which was held in trust for him by his master. After emancipation Fields worked for a time as a porter on the Columbia and Greenville Railroad and heard about the up-country land for sale to Negroes as he carried carpet bags and listened to political gossip on the train. Fields went to Abbeville County to inspect the land before he purchased a farm there. While he was visiting, he "run up on Mr. Nathan

Redd," old Henry Redd's son. The Fieldses' granddaughter Emily and Nathan were about the same age, and Fields proposed a match to young Redd. "You marry my granddaughter, and I'll will all this land to you and her." The marriage was arranged before the farm was purchased, and eventually the land was transferred to the young couple.

By the conclusion of 1872 forty-eight families were settled on farms in Promised Land. Most of the land was under cultivation, as required by law; but the farmers were also busy with other activities. In addition to the houses and barns which had to be raised as each new family arrived with their few possessions, the men continued their political activities. Iverson Reynolds, J. H. Turner, John and Elias Tolbert, Judson Reynolds, Oscar Pressley, and Washington Green, all community residents, were delegates to the county Republican convention in August 1872. Three of the group were landowners. Their political activities were still not received with much enthusiasm by local whites, but reaction to Negro involvement in politics was lessening in hostility. The *Press* mildly observed that the fall cotton crop was being gathered with good speed and "the farmers have generally been making good use of their time." Cotton picking and politics were both seasonal, and the newspaper chided local Negroes for their priorities. "The blacks have been indulging a little too much in politics but are getting right again." Iverson Reynolds and Washington Green, always among the community's Republican leadership during the 1870s, served as local election managers again for the 1872 fall elections. The men from Promised Land voted without incident that year.

Civic participation among the Promised Land residents extended beyond partisan politics when the county implemented the new jury law in 1872. There had been no Negro jurors for the trial of the Williams brothers and Colbert Jordan the previous year. Although the inclusion of Negroes in the jury pools was a reform mandated in 1868, four years passed before Abbeville authorities drew up new jury lists from the revised voter registration rolls. The jury law was as repugnant to the whites as Negro suffrage, termed "a wretched attempt at legislation, which surpasses anything which has yet been achieved by the Salons in Columbia." When the new lists were finally completed in 1872 the *Press,* ever the reflection of local white public opinion, predicted that "many of [the freedmen] probably have moved away; and the chances are that not many of them will be forthcoming" in the call to jury duty. Neither the initial condemnation of the law nor the optimistic undertones of the *Press* prediction stopped Pope Moragne and Iverson Reynolds from responding to their notices from the Abbeville Courthouse. Both landowners rode their mules up Five Notch Road from Promised Land to Abbeville and served on the county's first integrated jury in the fall of 1872. Moragne and Reynolds were soon followed by others from the community—Allen Goode, Robert Wideman, William Moragne, James Richie, and Luther (Shack) Moragne. By 1874, less than five years after settlement of Dr. Marshall's farm by the new Negro landowners began, the residents of Promised Land remained actively involved in Abbeville County politics. They were undaunted by the *Press* warning that "just so soon as the colored people lose the confidence and support of the North their doom is fixed. The fate of the red man will be theirs." They were voters, jurors, taxpayers, and trustees of the school their children attended. Their collective identity as an exclusively Negro community was well established.

Only Colored Down in This Old Promised Land

Abbeville County, South Carolina
Mr. John Lomax passed through the Promised Land yesterday, and he thinks the crops there almost a failure. The corn will not average two bushels to the acre, and the cotton about 300 pounds [less than one bale] to the acre. A large quantity of sorghum cane was planted. It was almost worthless. The land appeared as if it had been very well cultivated.

Abbeville *Press*
30 September 1874

The forty-eight men and women who established conditional ownership of the farms at Promised Land between 1870 and 1872 were required by law to place at least half of their land under cultivation within three years of their purchase. There was, however, no requirement about the crops to be planted. The men who established that cultivation standard probably assumed that cotton would be the major cash crop, as it was throughout the Piedmont. At Promised Land cotton was indeed planted on every one of the farms, but not in overwhelming amounts. The relatively small cotton fields were overshadowed by fields of corn, peas, and sorghum cane; and the sense of permanence among the settlers was clearly evident when "they planted peach trees and pear trees and had grape vines all over" the land, which only a few years before was either uncleared of native pine forests or part of the up-country plantation system. Cotton, the antebellum crop of the slaves, became the cash crop of freedom. It would never dominate the lives of the farmers at Promised Land.

The 1870s were economically critical years for the new landowners. They had mortgage payments to meet and taxes to pay, but they also had families to feed. In 1870, when the price of cotton reached twenty-two cents a pound, all this was possible. In the following years, however, cotton prices declined dramatically. This, combined with generally low cotton yields, resulted in economic hardship for many of the farmers. Poverty was their constant neighbor, and their struggle for survival drew them into a cycle of indebtedness to white "lien men."

In those depression years there was little credit in the Piedmont. "The poor people wasn't able to buy their fertilize. That's what makes your cotton." Storekeepers and merchants reserved their resources for the local white planters, and the Negro farmers were forced to find credit from other sources. They turned to their white landowning neighbors and in some cases their former masters, the Devlin family in Verdery; the Tuck family, nearby farmers; and the Hendersons, Verdery merchants. To them the

Promised Land farmers paid usurious interest rates for the fertilizer they needed "to make a bale of cotton" and the other supplies and foodstuffs they required to survive the growing season.

It was during this decade that the community farmers learned to maintain a skillful balance between a small cotton cash crop and their subsistence fields. Careful in the management of debt, most landowners probably used their cotton crop to meet their mortgage payment to the Land Commission and their tax bill to the county. There was never any surplus on the small farms, and a crop failure had immediate and personal consequences. At best a family would go hungry. At worst they would lose their farm.

Times were hard; and, despite generally shrewd land and debt management, twenty of the original settlers lost title to their land during the early 1870s. All migrated from Promised Land before the 1875 growing season. An advertisement in the *Press* attracted some new purchasers to the vacated farms, but most buyers learned of the land through friends and relatives. New families once again moved onto the land. Wilson Nash bought the farm originally purchased by John Valentine; both men were church leaders and probably discussed the transaction in some detail before the agreement was finalized.

Allen Goode, Wells Gray, and James Fields added to their holdings, buying additional farms from discouraged families who were leaving. Moses Wideman's younger brothers, William and Richmond, together bought an eighty-five–acre farm and then divided it, creating two more homesteads in the community. J. H. Turner, who secured a teaching position in an Edgefield County public school, sold his farm to his brother-in-law Isaac Y. Moragne. Each of the landowners had a brother, a cousin, or a friend who was eager to assume the financial burden of landownership; and none of the twenty vacated farms remained unoccupied for long. Promised Land quickly regained its population. The new arrivals strengthened and expanded the kinship bonds, which already crisscrossed and united individual households in the community.

Marriage provided the most common alliance between kinship groups. The Wilson and Wideman families and the Fields and Redds were both so related. The use of land as dowry, first employed by James Fields to arrange his granddaughter's marriage to Nathan Redd, provided a convenient and viable bargaining tool. When Iverson Reynolds bought his thirty-acre farm he also purchased a second, twenty-acre tract in his daughter's name, looking forward to the time of her marriage. "When Oscar Pressley married Iverson Reynolds' daughter, Janie, Iverson Reynolds give [sic] him that land or sold it to him. But he got that farm from old Iverson Reynolds when he got married." The Moragnes, Turners, Pinckneys, and Letmans were also united through land-based dowry arrangements. "The Moragne women is [sic] the ones that had the land. All them, the Turners, the Pinckneys, and the Letmans—all them got into the Moragnes when the women married these men."

Marriage did not always accompany kinship bonds, for at Promised Land, like every place else, "some folks have childrens when they not married. Things get all mixed up sometimes.'' Still, the community was a small and intimate place, woven together as early as the 1880s by a complex and interlocking series of kin ties, which were supplemented by many other kinds of personal relationships. The separation of public and private spheres blurred; and, married or not, ''when the gals get a baby'' everyone was aware of the heritage and family ties of new babies. ''Andrew Moragne supposed to been his daddy, but his momma was a Bradley so he took the name Bradley.'' Even so, promiscuity and illegitimacy were not casually accepted facts of life. Both were sinful and disgraceful not just to the couple but to their families as well. For women a pregnancy without marriage was particularly painful. ''Some might be mean to you then,'' and many refused to even speak publicly to an unmarried woman who became pregnant. ''All that stop when the baby is born. Don't want to punish an innocent baby.'' Legitimate or not, babies were welcomed into families and the community, and the sins of the parents were set aside. Ultimately, the bonds of kinship proved more powerful than collective morality, and these bonds left few residents of the community excluded from an encompassing network of cousins, aunts, uncles, and half-brothers and sisters.

As the landowning population of Promised Land stabilized, local resources emerged to meet day-to-day needs. A molasses mill, where the farmers had their sorghum cane ground into molasses by Joshuway Wilson's oldest son Fortune, opened in the community. Two corn and wheat grist mills opened on Curltail Creek. One, the old Marshall Mill, was operated by Harrison Cole, a Negro who subsequently purchased a vacant farm in the community. The other, the former Donalds Mill, was owned and operated by James Evans, an Irish immigrant whose thirst for land equaled that of his Negro neighbors. North Carter, the youngest son of landowner Marion Carter, opened a small general store at the east-west crossroads, where he sold candy, kerosene, salt, and other staples to his neighbors, extending credit when necessary, knowing that they would pay when they could. Long before the final land purchase was completed, the freedmen at Promised Land had established a framework for economic and social self-sufficiency.

The farms, through hard work, decent weather, and an eight-month growing season, soon yielded food for the households. A pattern of subsistence agriculture provided each Promised Land family a degree of independence and self-reliance unknown to most other Negro families in the area. Cows produced milk and butter for the tables, and chickens eggs and fresh poultry. Draft animals and cash money were both scarce commodities, but ''in them days nobody ever went hungry.'' Hogs provided the major source of meat in the community's subsistence economy. ''My mother and them used to kill hogs and put them down in salt in wood boxes and cover them so flies couldn't get to them for about five or six weeks. Take it out and wash it, put on red pepper and such, hang it up to dry, and that meat be *good*.'' The absence of an abundant cotton crop was not a sign of lack of industry. Prosperity, as well as productivity, was measured against hunger; and, in the never-ending farm cycle, fields were planted according to the number of people in each household, the number of mouths to be fed.

Community and household autonomy were firmly grounded in the economic independence of the land. Both were strengthened with the establishment of a church in Promised Land. In 1875, fully a decade before the final farms were settled, James Fields sold one acre of his land to the Trustees of Mt. Zion A.M.E. Church. It was a sign of the times. At Promised Land, as elsewhere in the South, freedmen withdrew from white churches as quickly as possible. Membership in the Baptist and Methodist denominations increased tenfold between 1860–1870 as the new Negro churches in the South took form. Mt. Zion was relatively late in emerging as a part of that movement for independence from white domination, but the residents of Promised Land were preoccupied for a time with more basic concerns. The fields had to be established as productive before community residents turned their energies to other aspects of community development.

The Fields' land, located squarely in the geographical center of Promised Land, was within a two-mile walk of all the houses in the community. On this thinly wooded tract the men carved out a brush arbor, a remnant of slavery days; and Isaac Y. Moragne led everybody in the young settlement in prayers and songs. From the beginning of their emancipation schools and churches were central components of Negro social life; and at Promised Land religion, like education, was established as a permanent part of community life while the land was still being cleared.

Newcomers and Community Growth

Most families survived those first settlement years, the droughts and crop failures, Ku Klux Klan attacks, and the violent years of Reconstruction. They met their mortgage payments and their taxes, and the years after 1875 were relatively prosperous ones. Promised Land was well established before the Compromise of 1877, the withdrawal of federal troops from the state, and the election of Wade Hampton as governor. The political squabbles among the white Democrats during the years after Hampton's redemption of South Carolina touched the folks at Promised Land only indirectly. The community was, for the most part, preoccupied with internal events.

By 1880 the community had expanded from forty-nine to eighty-nine households, an average growth of four new families each year for the previous decade. Fifty of those families were landless, attracted to Promised Land for a combination of reasons. Probably at least some of them hoped to acquire land there. Promised Land was the only place in the area where Negroes had even minimal hope of buying land after 1877. Local farmers and planters, never eager to sell land to Negroes, now grew even more recalcitrant as Democratic white rule was re-established. Sharecropping dominated farming arrangements between whites and Negroes throughout the Cotton Belt. The landowners at Promised Land, "well, they was wheels. They *owned* their farms." And the respect and prestige they commanded within the county's landless Negro population were another kind of attraction for landless families.

The violence of Reconstruction was moderated only slightly, and a concern for personal safety was surely another reason Negroes moved to Promised Land. Few of the early settlers, those who came before the mid-1880s, could have escaped that violence, even if their contact was indirect. Wilson Nash, Willis Smith, Allen Goode, Washington Green, Wade and Eli Moragne all headed landowning households. For any who might forget, those men were constant reminders of the dangers which lay just beyond the community's perimeter.

The men at Promised Land still exercised their franchise, fully aware of both the dangers and the benefits which they knew accompanied political activity. Together they walked the three miles to Verdery and collectively cast their ballots at the post office "where Locket Frazier held the box for the niggers and Red Tolbert for the whites." Perhaps they walked together as a symbolic expression of their solidarity, but much more likely it was because of a practical concern for their own safety. They were less vulnerable to attack in a group. As it had in the past, however, this simple exercise of citizenship enraged the local whites; and, once again, in the early 1880s the men at Promised Land faced the threat of violence for their partisan political activities.

> Them old Phoenix rats, the Ku Klux, come up here to beat up the niggers 'cause they went to Verdery and voted. Them old dogs from Phoenix put on red shirts and come up here to beat the poor niggers up. Old George Foster, the white man, he told them "Don't go down in that Promiseland. Josh Wilson and Colbert Jordan and them got some boys up there, and they got shotguns and Winchesters and old guns. Any white man come in to Promiseland to beat the niggers up, some body going to die. They'll fight 'til hell freezes over. You Phoenix rats go back to Phoenix." So they went on down to Verdery, and they told them the same thing.

Their reputation, their readiness, and their willingness to defend their land were clearly well-known facts about the people at Promised Land. The "Red Shirts" heeded the warning, and white terrorists never again attempted to violate Promised Land. This, too, must have been a part of the community's attraction to landless families who moved there.

Promised Land in 1880 was a community which teemed with activity. Most of the newcomers joined in the brush arbor worship services and sent their children to the community schools. Liberty Hill School and the white schoolmaster were replaced by "schools scattered all around the woods" taught by Negro men and women who lived at Promised Land. Abbeville County maintained a public school. Crossroads School for Colored was taught by H. L. Latimer. The Mill School, maintained by the extensive Moragne family for their children, was held in James Evans' mill on Curltail Creek and was taught by J. H. Turner, Moragne brother-in-law. The Hester School, located near the southern edge of the community, was so named because it met in the Hester family's home. All three private schools supplemented the meager public support of education for Negro children; and all were filled to capacity, because "folks had big families then—ten and twelve childrens—and them schools was crowded."

The representatives to the 1868 South Carolina Constitutional Convention who formulated the state's land redistribution hoped to establish an economically independent Negro yeomanry in South Carolina. The Land Commission intended the purchase and resale of Dr. Marshall's farm to solidify the interests of radical Republicanism in Abbeville County, at least for a time. Both of these designs were realized. A third and unintended consequence also resulted. The land fostered a socially autonomous, identifiable community. Drawing on resources and social structures well established within an extant Negro culture, the men and women who settled Promised Land established churches and schools and a viable economic system based on landownership. They maintained that economic autonomy by subsistence farming and supported many of their routine needs by patronizing the locally owned and operated grist mills and general store. The men were actively involved in Reconstruction politics as well as other aspects of civil life, serving regularly on county juries and paying their taxes. Attracted by the security and prestige Promised Land afforded and the possible hope of eventual landownership, fifty additional landless households moved into the community during the 1870s, expanding the 1880 population to almost twice its original size. Together the eighty-nine households laid claim to slightly more than four square miles of land, and within that small territory they "carved out their own little piece of the world."

FURTHER READING

Carol R. Bleser, *The Promised Land: The History of the South Carolina Land Commission* (1963)

LaWanda Cox and John Cox, "The Promise of Land for the Freedmen," *Mississippi Valley Historical Review* 45 (1958), 413–440

W. E. B. Du Bois, "Reconstruction and Its Benefits," *American Historical Review* 4 (1910), 781–799

———, *Black Reconstruction in America, 1860–1880* (1935)

Barbara J. Fields, *Slavery and Freedom on the Middle Ground: Maryland in the 19th Century* (1985)

Eric Foner, *Nothing but Freedom: Emancipation and Its Legacy* (1983)

———, *Reconstruction: America's Unfinished Revolution, 1863–1877* (1988)

John Hope Franklin, *Reconstruction: After the Civil War* (1961)

Janet Sharp Hermann, *The Pursuit of a Dream* (1981)

Thomas C. Holt, *Black over White: Negro Legislators in South Carolina During Reconstruction* (1977)

Gerald Jaynes, *Branches Without Roots: The Genesis of the Black Working Class in the American South, 1862–1882* (1986)

Peter Kolchin, *First Freedom: The Response of Alabama's Blacks to Emancipation and Reconstruction* (1972)

Betty Lamson, *The Glorious Failure: Black Congressman Robert Brown Elliott and the Reconstruction in South Carolina* (1973)

Leon Litwack, *Been in the Storm So Long: The Aftermath of Slavery* (1979)

Edward Magdol, *A Right to the Land: Essays on the Freedmen's Community* (1977)

Robert Morris, *Reading, 'Riting and Reconstruction: The Education of Freedmen in the South, 1861–1870* (1981)

Howard N. Rabinowitz, "From Exclusion to Segregation: Southern Race Relations, 1865–1890," *Journal of American History* 63 (1976), 325–350

———, ed., *Southern Black Leaders of the Reconstruction Era* (1982)

Dorothy Sterling, ed., *We Are Your Sisters: Black Women in the Nineteenth Century* (1984)

William P. Vaughn, *Schools for All: Blacks and Public Education in the South, 1865–1871* (1974)

Joel Williamson, *After Slavery: The Negro in South Carolina During Reconstruction, 1861–1877* (1965)

CHAPTER
14

The Collapse of Reconstruction

↻

By early 1877 the Republicans had lost control of every southern state. Some states, among them Georgia, North Carolina, Texas, and Virginia, had fallen to the Democrats a few years after being reconstructed. Others, such as South Carolina, Louisiana, and Florida, lasted until the disputed election of 1876–1877 when, in exchange for their presidential support, the Republican candidate Rutherford B. Hayes let the Democrats of those three states regain power. Southern Reconstruction, which had been started as a crusade to bring progress and democracy to the region, was therefore brought to a close in one of the most notorious political bargains in American history. What had happened?

Of course, it could be said that nothing much had happened at all, since the Reconstruction governments had been so vulnerable from the outset that their demise was only a matter of time. But if they had been provided with means that were predictably inadequate, what was the point of reconstructing the South in the first place? Surely Reconstruction was important enough that it would not have been undertaken with the expectation of certain failure.

Perhaps it can be assumed therefore that these Reconstruction governments had a good chance of success. After all, they had the political support and military protection of the Federal authority. Furthermore, the Republicans in each state did control the administrative and legal apparatus as well as the legislative branch of government. Besides, were there not thousands of white southerners who would be drawn to a party that could offer a new deal; that is, an agenda that would appeal to those who had been deprived and exploited by the plantation regime as well as to those who wanted the South to become modern and prosperous? Since these administrations still collapsed, it is reasonable to conclude that mistakes and shortcomings on the part of the Republicans themselves could have accounted for the collapse of Reconstruction.

There is, however, an alternative explanation. It can be argued that the opposition mounted by the former Confederates, who were now arrayed in the Democratic party, was so skillful or so relentless that only a far more firmly established political organization could have withstood the onslaught. In that case, the cause of Reconstruction's downfall is shifted away from the Republicans, in the South as well as in Congress, and onto the southern Democrats, often referred to as Redeemers because they redeemed the South.

Historians still debate this issue, and two questions seem to be the focus of the discussion. First, was Reconstruction doomed from the start, or did it have a *reasonable chance of success? Second, assuming that there was such a chance for success, what contributed more to its unattainability—Republican inadequacies or Democratic resistance?*

✤ D O C U M E N T S

The shortcomings of the southern Republicans, the attacks of their Democratic opponents, and a growing disenchantment in the North all contributed to Reconstruction's collapse. The following documents illustrate these features. In the first selection, Carl Schurz, a Missouri republican senator and a leader in the Liberal Republican movement of 1872, calls for amnesty and conciliation toward the South in a Senate speech of January 30, 1872. The second selection is a defense of northerners' activities in the southern Republican party offered in the House on February 4, 1875, by Representative Alexander White, himself a native southerner in the Alabama Republican party. By contrast, the third document is a critical report on the performance of the Republicans in Mississippi— and the Democrats to some extent—by the northern journalist Charles Nordhoff during a tour of the South in the spring and summer of 1875.

The Democrats' verbal and physical assault on the southern Republicans is the subject matter of the remaining documents. The fourth extract is from a June 8, 1874, speech in Congress, by Representative L. Q. C. Lamar of Mississippi, in which he appeals to his fellow congressmen to restore to the southern states the self-government that he claims has been denied them by Federal interference. In the fifth selection, Governor William P. Kellogg of Louisiana issues a proclamation on September 3, 1874, describing the assassination at Coushatta of Republican officials of Red River parish and offering a reward for information about their assailants. Further evidence of anti-Republican violence is revealed in the sixth selection, in which Governor Adelbert Ames of Mississippi tells his wife of the dire situation in the state on September 5, 1875. In the seventh and last document, dated July 26, 1876, President Grant gives a noncommittal response to the urgent plea of the South Carolina governor, Daniel H. Chamberlin, for federal military aid.

Senator Carl Schurz of Missouri Condemns
Reconstruction, January 1872

. . . But the stubborn fact remains that they [Southern black voters and officeholders] *were* ignorant and inexperienced; that the public business *was* an unknown world to them, and that in spite of the best intentions they *were* easily misled, not infrequently by the most reckless rascality which had found a way to their confidence. Thus their political rights and privileges were undoubtedly well calculated, and even necessary, to protect their rights as free laborers and citizens; but they were not well calculated to secure a successful administration of other public interests.

I do not blame the colored people for it; still less do I say that for this reason their political rights and privileges should have been denied them. Nay, sir, I deemed it necessary then, and I now reaffirm that opinion, that they should possess those rights and privileges for the permanent establishment of the logical and legitimate results of the war and the protection of their new position in society. But, while never losing sight of this necessity, I do say that the inevitable consequence of the admission of so large an uneducated and inexperienced class to political power, as to the probable mismanagement of the material interests of the social body, should at least have been mitigated by a counterbalancing policy. When ignorance and inexperience were admitted to so large an influence upon public affairs, intelligence ought no longer to so large an extent to have been excluded. In other words, when universal suffrage was granted to secure the equal rights of all, universal amnesty ought to have been granted to make all the resources of political intelligence and experience available for the promotion of the welfare of all.

But what did we do? To the uneducated and inexperienced classes— uneducated and inexperienced, I repeat, entirely without their fault—we opened the road to power; and, at the same time, we condemned a large proportion of the intelligence of those States, of the property-holding, the industrial, the professional, the tax-paying interest, to a worse than passive attitude. We made it, as it were, easy for rascals who had gone South in quest of profitable adventure to gain the control of masses so easily misled, by permitting them to appear as the exponents and representatives of the National power and of our policy; and at the same time we branded a large number of men of intelligence, and many of them of personal integrity, whose material interests were so largely involved in honest government, and many of whom would have cooperated in managing the public business with care and foresight—we branded them, I say, as outcasts, telling them that they ought not to be suffered to exercise any influence upon the management of the public business, and that it would be unwarrantable presumption in them to attempt it.

I ask you, sir, could such things fail to contribute to the results we read to-day in the political corruption and demoralization, and in the financial ruin of some of the Southern States? These results are now before us. The mistaken policy may have been pardonable when these consequences were still a matter of conjecture and speculation; but what excuse have we now for continuing it when those results are clear before our eyes, beyond the reach of contradiction? . . .

Representative Alexander White of Alabama Defends the Carpetbaggers, February 1875

. . . These white republicans are known by the contemptuous appellation of carpet-bagger and scalawag, names conferred upon them by the chivalry, in whose political interest prowl the bands of Ku-Klux and White League assassins in the South, and as such, especially the carpet-bagger, they have become a by-word and reproach. We of the South are not responsible for them; they are a northern growth, and unless going South expatriates them, they are still northern men, even as you are—bone of your bone, flesh of your flesh. But who are they? I can speak for my State, for I think I know nearly all in the State, and there are a good many of them. Most of them have titles, not empty titles complaisantly bestowed in piping times of peace, but titles worthily won by faithful and efficient service in the Federal armies, or plucked with strong right arm from war's rugged front upon the field of battle. Many of them bear upon their bodies scars of wounds received while fighting under your flag for the nation's life and the country's glory. These men either went South with the Union armies and at the close of the war remained there, or went there soon after, in the latter part of 1865 or early in 1866, to make cotton. The high price of cotton in 1865 and 1866, and the facility with which cheap labor could be obtained, induced many enterprising northern men, especially the officers in the Federal armies in the South who had seen and become familiar with the country, to go or remain there to make cotton. Many purchased large plantations and paid large sums of money for them; others rented plantations, in some instances two or three, and embarked with characteristic energy in planting. This, it should be remembered, was before the civil-rights bill or the reconstruction acts, before the colored people had any part in political matters, and two years before they ever proposed to vote or claimed to have the right to vote at any election in the Southern States.

When the political contests of 1868 came on in which the colored people first took a part in politics, as near all the native population in the large cotton-growing sections were opposed to negro suffrage and opposed to the republican party, they very naturally turned to these northern men for counsel and assistance in the performance of the new duties and exercise of their newly acquired political rights, and they as naturally gave them such counsel and became their leaders, and were intrusted with official power by them.

This brief summary will give you a correct idea of the manner in which, as I believe, nine-tenths of those who are called carpet-baggers became involved in political affairs [in the] South, and dispose of a very large part of the slanders which have been promulgated against them not only by their political enemies at the South, but by the treacherous northern knaves who, under the pretense of being republicans and as correspondents of so-called republican papers at the North, have gone down South prepared in advance to stab the cause of justice and of truth, of humanity and freedom, of the law and the Constitution, to the heart. Could these miserable miscreants have known with what ineffable contempt they were regarded by the very men whose credulous dupes they were, with what scathing scorn they regarded northern men who would lend themselves to traduce whole classes of northern men, who would allow themselves to be used as the tools to break down the political party to which they professed to belong, it would have diminished much the self-complacency with which their work was done. They could have realized that southern men, though bold and often reckless of the means by which they seek to attain political ends, that earnest and vehement, ardent and high-spirited, under the influence of one great ultimate aim to which all else is subordinated, they may reach politically to the parallel of the dogma which once prevailed in the religious world, "there is no faith to be kept with heretics," yet they can never be brought to descend to sympathy with or respect for such low-browed infamy as theirs.

These two classes, the carpet-baggers and scalawag[s], are the object of peculiar assault by the democracy, for they know that these constitute the bulwark of the republican party in the South. Without their co-operation and assistance the colored republicans could neither organize nor operate successfully in political contests, and without them the party would soon be extinguished in the Southern States. . . .

A Northern Correspondent Censures Mississippi Politicians, 1875

. . . Mississippi is, politically, in a melancholy condition. . . . [The state] has a colored majority in its voting population of probably fifteen thousand, and possibly twenty thousand. To these must be added about nine thousand or ten thousand white Republicans, of whom at least two-thirds are natives of the State. About five thousand negroes are counted on to vote the Democratic ticket.

The Ames faction in the Republican party contains but a small part of the white Republicans—a majority of the petty officeholders and the camp-followers; but it controls the colored vote. In the anti-Ames wing of the Republican party, I found a number of men, Northern and Southern, who have a substantial interest in the State; who are men of culture, upright, wise, and good citizens in the best sense of the phrase; such men as Judge Tarbell, of the Supreme Court; Judge Luke Lea; Mr. Musgrove, late State Auditor; General M'Kee, a member of Congress; Judge Hill, of the United States Circuit Court; G. W. Wells, United States District Attorney for the Northern District; and many others.

The large majority of the Democratic party also is composed of men of moderate and conservative views, who would prefer peace, harmony, and good government, but who are influenced to a large degree by a small but fierce band of fire-eaters whose head-quarters are at Vicksburg, and who control a number of presses in different parts of the State, and keep the people in a ferment by their violent language and their exaggerations of evils which are great enough in fact, but not nearly so great as they pretend, nor by any means entirely blamable upon the Republicans. Through the appeals of these persons the people of Mississippi have been led to believe themselves outraged and oppressed in some ways in which they are not; partisan bitterness has been maintained to a degree which leads the ignorant Democrat to unite in the same denunciation honest and dishonest Republicans; and so intense is the feeling kept up that the material interests of the State suffer by reason of it—confidence is shaken, values are depressed, and even industry is disturbed. Meantime these Democratic demagogues strive to lead the people away from the legitimate and natural means by which they could rid themselves of corrupt rulers and establish a sound government, based upon the union of the best men of both parties.

That there have been wastefulness and corruption in the government of Mississippi there is no doubt. I am so weary of official grand and petit larceny that I do not mean to go at any length into Mississippi finances. It is enough to say that the State debt is trifling; there have been no great railroad swindles; a constitutional provision wisely forbids the loan of the State credit. But there has been gross financial corruption in many counties; officers with high salaries have been needlessly multiplied; there have been notorious jobs, such as the State printing; and the ruling powers, the Ames Republicans, have unscrupulously used the ignorance and greed of the negroes to help them in their political schemes. Controlling the negro vote, and using it as a solid mass, they have put into such offices as county supervisors and treasurers, as well as into the Legislature, negroes who were often not only unable to read and write, but who were notoriously corrupt and corrupting demagogues. For instance, the late treasurer of Hinds County, in which the State capital lies, was a negro who could neither read nor write, and who was killed by another negro a few weeks ago for a disgraceful intrigue. In the last Legislature were several negroes who could neither read nor write. It has happened that the members of a grand jury were totally illiterate. A city government was to be elected last August in Vicksburg, and the Republicans nominated for mayor a white man at the time under indictment for twenty-three offenses, and for aldermen seven colored men, most of them of low character, and one white man who could neither read nor write, the keeper of a low groggery. This ticket was denounced by General M'Kee, Republican member of Congress, in a public speech, and, with the help of the Republicans, was beaten. Of the present supervisors of Warren County (Vicksburg), the president and two others cannot read. It is a notorious fact that Governor Ames has appointed to judicial places men ignorant of law, and that he has used his appointing power to shield criminals, who were his adherents, and to corrupt the judiciary of the State.

These are serious matters; but, on the other hand, it must be said that the Democratic demagogues have repeatedly urged the negroes to nominate only colored men for office. They say they "would rather have a Mississippi nigger than a carpet-bagger"; and, moreover, in the notable cases of corruption, both in State and counties, Democrats have in many cases shared the plunder, and in some have got up the scheme. Now, on this head the Democratic leaders are silent. They cry out that the State is ruined, which is not true; but they have themselves helped to rob it, and it is at least a doubtful question whether, if some of those who so loudly denounce corruption had power, they would make an honest government.

There is, for instance, a loud outcry about the enormous debt of Vicksburg; but of the money spent for street improvements, Democratic contractors got the most; and the money given to railroads was voted by Democrats and Republicans alike.

Such men as Barksdale, Wharton, Lamar, and hundreds of other prominent Democrats, have clean hands and are men of honor; but there is an undoubted propensity to corruption among some Democratic as well as among Republican leaders. For instance, Vicksburg has been, since August, under Democratic rule; but the expenses of the city government, I am told, have increased, and order is not as well maintained under Democratic rule as formerly.

Nor, if the Democratic leaders were fair, would they omit to tell their people that the expenses of State and county governments have necessarily increased, for the colored people being free give business to the courts and the officers and institutions of justice; they must have schools; and in other ways the cost of government is increased. That a very large balance of waste and theft and high taxation remains, is perfectly true, and of that all may rightfully complain, as well as of other and graver wrongs which I have mentioned above.

It is a complaint, also, of the Democrats that their opponents have, for corrupt purposes, maintained the color-line in politics. It is true that the Ames men cultivate the negro vote by corrupt means; but it is also true that the Democrats have helped them. In Arkansas and Louisiana, I do not remember having once heard of the negro except as a part of the body politic, ignorant, to be sure, but a good worker, and, as was often said to me by Democrats, "not to be blamed that he went wrong under bad advice." But in Mississippi the commonest topic of discussion is the "damned nigger." A dozen times, at least, prominent Democrats told me he was a peculiar being, not possessing the virtues of the Caucasian race, and not fitted by nature to vote, or to sit on jury, or to bear witness—a creature admirably fitted to make cotton, and so on. I have heard such discussions going on in the presence of colored men, who naturally listened with all the ears they had.

Now, the negro is not an idiot. He would be if he voted for and with men who habitually call him a "nigger," and often a "damned nigger," and who openly assert his incapacity by nature to perform the functions of a citizen. When the "most respectable citizen in Vicksburg" blustered about the postmaster appointing a "damned nigger," he was heard by at least twenty-five colored men and women. Yet, in that very town leading Democrats groan about the impossibility of breaking the color-line. One would have a contempt for such politicians were not their course a constant injury to the State in which they are so foolishly noisy, and in which the quiet, sensible, and orderly people seem to have almost entirely resigned the power and supremacy which belong to them.

The thing which was oftenest said to me in Mississippi by Democratic politicians was this: "Our only hope is in the Democratic success in the next Federal election. The Democratic successes last fall gave us our first gleam of light." But when I asked how a Democratic administration could help them, the reply was, "Because then we can disorganize the colored vote. They will not vote without white leaders to organize them." And when I asked one of the white leaders of the "white-line" movement, whose object is to draw the color-line strictly, how he could hope to get all the white people, with their strongly diverging views, into his movement, his reply was, "We'll make it too damned hot for them to stay out."

Now, to me this does not look like the American way of carrying an election. It is a method of bluster and bullying and force. The honest Republicans whom I asked whether the white-line movement could possibly draw in all the white voters, all replied in the affirmative. It would silence opposition at any rate, they said. . . .

Representative L. Q. C. Lamar of Mississippi Demands Self-Government for the South, June 1874

. . . There is but one principle by which the people who bear the burdens of taxation can keep themselves from being despoiled and ruined by those who impose and consume the taxes; that is the principle which will not permit taxes to be imposed except with the consent of the tax-payers—or, in other words, which makes the tax-consumers, the men who impose and receive the taxes, responsible to the men who pay them.

Such was the relation of these two classes of the South before the war. Men who imposed the taxes were responsible to the people who paid them. The consequence was, their governments were models of republican simplicity and prudential economy and virtue in the administration of affairs.

[Mr. Speaker], the events since the war have reversed these relations. When, in order to consummate your policy, you divided the southern country into military districts, your military commanders, distrusting the purposes of the southern people and knowing the negroes were incompetent to manage the affairs of government, called to their aid and installed into all the offices of the States, from the highest to the lowest, a set of men from the North who were strangers to our people, not possessing their confidence, not elected by them, not responsible to them, having no interest in common with them, and hostile to them to a certain extent in sentiment.

I am not going to characterize these men by any harshness of language. I am speaking of a state of things more controlling than ordinary personal characteristics. Even if it were true that they came to the South for no bad purposes, they were put in a position which has always engendered rapacity, cupidity corruption, grinding oppression, and taxation in its most devouring form. They were rulers without responsibility, in unchecked control of the material resources of a people with whom they had not a sentiment in sympathy or an interest in common, and whom they habitually regarded and treated as rebels who had forfeited their right to protection. These men, thus situated and thus animated, were the fisc of the South. They were the recipients of all the revenues, State and local. Not a dollar of taxes, State or local, but what went into their pockets. The suffering people on whom the taxes were laid could not exercise the slightest control, either as to the amount imposed or the basis upon which they were laid. The consequence was that in a few short years eight magnificent Commonwealths were laid in ruins. This condition of things still exists with unabated rigor in those Southern States. For when, by your reconstruction measures, you determined to provide civil governments for these States, the machinery by which these men carried their power over into those civil governments was simple and effectual. Under your policy generally—I repeat, my purpose to-day is not arraignment—under that policy you disfranchised a large portion of the white people of the Southern States. The registration laws and the election laws in the hands of these men kept a still larger proportion away.

But there was an agency more potent still.

By persistent misrepresentation a majority in Congress was made to believe that the presence of the United States Army would be necessary not merely to put these governments in force, but to keep them in operation and to keep them from being snatched away and worked to the oppression and ruin of the black race and the few loyal men who were there attempting to protect their rights. Thus was introduced into those so-called reconstructed civil governments the Federal military as an operative and predominant principle. Thus, with a quick, sudden, and violent hand, these men tore the two races asunder and hurled one in violent antagonism upon the other, and to this day the negro vote massed into an organization hostile to the whites is an instrument of absolute power in the hands of these men. These governments are in external form civil, but they are in their essential principle military. They are called local governments, but in reality they are Federal executive agencies. Not one of them emanates from the uncontrolled will of the people, white or black; not one which rests upon the elective principle in its purity. They have been aptly styled by a distinguished statesman and jurist in Mississippi, (Hon. W. P. Harris,) State governments without States, without popular constituencies. For they are as completely insulated from the traditions, the feelings, the interests, and the free suffrages of the people, white and black, as if they were outside the limits of those States. Where is the public sentiment which guides and enlightens those to whom confided the conduct of public affairs? Where is the moral judgment of a virtuous people to which they are amenable? Where is the moral indignation which falls like the scathing lightning upon the delinquent or guilty public officer? Sir, that class and race in which reside these great moral agencies are prostrated, their interests, their prosperity jeopardized, their protests unheeded, and every murmur of discontent and every effort to throw off their oppressions misrepresented here as originating in the spirit which inaugurated the rebellion. Sir, the statement that these southern governments have no popular constituencies is true, but they nevertheless have a constituency to whom they bear a responsibility inexorable as death. It is limited to the one point of keeping the State true and faithful to the Administration; all else is boundless license. That constituency is here in Washington; its heart pulsates in the White House. There is its intelligence and there is its iron will. I do not exaggerate when I say that every one of these governments depends, every moment of their existence, upon the will of the President. That will makes and unmakes them. A short proclamation backed by one company determines who is to be governor of Arkansas. A telegram settles the civil magistracy of Texas.

A brief order to a general in New Orleans wrests a State government from the people of Louisiana and vests its control in the creatures of the Administration. . . .

But the people of the United States cannot afford to have destroyed the principles of constitutional government and representative liberty. I need not waste your time nor my strength in eulogies upon our political system. What it was previous to the late war we all recognize and rejoice over. What it is to be we cannot tell, for we are in the midst of one of those great political transitions in which a people, deceived by the retention of the form, are in danger of losing the substance of free government. Because their rights and liberty have to be won by bloody and violent struggles, it is difficult for them to realize that those very rights and liberties may silently disappear through the subtle, insidious usurpations of the power and the unseen and covert attacks of political chicanery and fraud. Yet such has been the history of the failure of republican institutions in all ages. . . .

Governor William P. Kellogg of Louisiana Demands Punishment for the Coushatta Assassins, September 1874

Proclamation—The Assassination of Red River Parish Officers

State of Louisiana,
Executive Department,
New Orleans, September 3, 1874.

Whereas, during the morning of Sunday, August 30, 1874, at the McFarland plantation, in the parish of Bossier, about forty miles east of the Texas line, Homer J. Twitchell, Robert A. Dewees, Clark Holland, W. J. Howell, Frank S. Edgerton, and M. C. Willis, peaceful and law-abiding citizens of this State, were cruelly murdered in cold blood by a body of armed and mounted men, claiming to belong to an organization known as the White League of Louisiana:

Now, therefore, I, William Pitt Kellogg, governor of the State of Louisiana, with a view, if possible, of bringing the perpetrators of this great outrage to justice, and of preventing the repetition of such crimes in the future, do issue this my proclamation, offering a reward of $5,000 each for such evidence as shall lead to the arrest and conviction of the said murderers, or any of them.

Given under my hand and the seal of the State hereunto attached this 3d day of September, in the year of our Lord 1874, and of the Independence of the United States the ninety-ninth.

William P. Kellogg.

By the governor:

P. G. Deslonde, Secretary of State.

A Statement to the Public

Having felt it my duty to issue my proclamation offering a large reward for the apprehension and conviction of the murderers in the Coushatta outrage, and to the end that the law-abiding citizens of the State may fully comprehend the magnitude of the crime committed and be induced to render more active assistance to the officers of the law, I deem it proper to make the following statement.

These facts are gathered from reliable information received at the executive department:

On or about the 28th day of August, 1874, a body of persons belonging to a semi-military organization known as the White League of Louisiana assembled in the town of Coushatta, parish of Red River, in this State, for the purpose of compelling, by force of arms, the State officers of that parish to resign their positions.

These officers were men of good character, most of them largely interested in planting and mercantile pursuits. They held their positions with the full consent of an admittedly large majority of the legal voters of the parish, this being a largely republican parish, as admitted even by the fusion returning-boards.

The only known objection to them was that they were of republican principles. Frank S. Edgerton, the duly qualified sheriff of the parish, in strict compliance with the laws of this State and of the United States, summoned a *posse comitatus* of citizens, white and colored, to assist him in protecting the parish officers in the exercise of their undoubted rights and duties from the threatened unlawful violence of the White Leagues. His posse, consisting of sixty-five men, was overpowered by a superior force, assembled from the adjacent parishes, and finally, after several colored and white men had been killed, surrendered themselves prisoners, with the explicit guarantee that their lives would be spared if the more prominent republicans would agree to leave the parish, and those holding office would resign their positions.

These stipulations, though unlawfully exacted, were complied with on the part of the republican officials, who were then locked up in the jail for the night.

The following-named persons were among those so surrendering and resigning:

Homer J. Twitchell, planter and tax-collector of Red River, and deputy United States postmaster in charge of the post-office at Coushatta; Robert A. Dewees, supervisor of registration, De Soto Parish; Clark Holland, merchant and supervisor of registration, Red River Parish; W. J. Howell, parish attorney and United States commissioner; Frank S. Edgerton, sheriff of Red River Parish; M. C. Willis, merchant, and justice of the peace.

On the following morning, Sunday, the 30th day of August, these persons were bound and conducted by an armed guard to the McFarland plantation, just over the parish line of Red River, within the boundaries of Bossier Parish, about forty miles east of the Texas line. There they were set upon and deliberately murdered in cold blood. Their bodies were buried near where they fell, without inquest or any formality whatever.

On the night preceding the surrender, a body of forty members of the White League of Caddo Parish, mounted and armed, left the city of Shreveport, and were seen riding in the direction of the place where the murder was subsequently committed.

William P. Kellogg, Governor.

Governor Adelbert Ames Deplores the Violence in Mississippi, September 1875

Jackson, Miss., September 5, 1875

Dear Blanche: I had finished my letter to you yesterday and was looking for George to mail it when Capt. Fisher came to me out of breath and out of heart to tell me of a riot which had just taken place at Clinton (a village ten miles west of here) and from which he had just escaped, with his wife. He was speaking when the riot began. It was a premeditated riot on the part of the Democracy which resulted in the death of some four white men and about the same number of Negroes and quite a large number of Negroes wounded. There were present at a Republican barbecue about fifteen hundred colored people, men, women, and children. Seeking the opportunity white men, fully prepared, fired into this crowd. Two women were reported killed, also two children. As the firing continued, the women ran away with the men in many instances, leaving their children on the ground. Today there are some forty carriages, wagons and carts which were abandoned by the colored people in their flight. Last night, this morning and today squads of white men are scouring the county killing Negroes. Three were killed at Clinton this morning—one of whom was an old man, nearly one hundred years old—defenseless and helpless. Yesterday the Negroes, though unarmed and unprepared, fought bravely and killed four of the ringleaders, but had to flee before the muskets which were at once brought onto the field of battle. This is but in keeping with the programme of the Democracy at this time. They know we have a majority of some thirty thousand and to overcome it they are resorting to intimidation and murder. It is cold-blooded murder on the part of the "white liners"—but there are other cases exactly like this in other parts of the state. You ask what are we to do. That is a question I find it difficult to answer. I told you a day or two ago that the whole party has been opposed to organizing the militia and furthermore I have been unable to find anyone who was willing to take militia appointments.

The Mansion has been crowded all day long with Republican friends and Negroes from the field of battle. I have run off to the northwest chamber for my daily chat with you, leaving a crowd in the other rooms. There has also been a crowd at the front gate all day long. The town is full of Negroes from the country who come to escape harm. The whites here are afraid of the Negroes who have come in. A committee of white men have just waited on me and offer to keep the peace so far as may be in their power. The Sheriff has selected a number of them to act as a posse to go out into the country and arrest those who are murdering Negroes. This last step has caused a subsidence of the excitement felt by the whites as well as blacks.

I anticipate no further trouble here at this time. The "white liners" have gained their point—they have, by killing and wounding, so intimidated the poor Negroes that they can in all human probability prevail over them at the election. I shall at once try to get troops from the general government. Of course it will be a difficult thing to do.

I send a world of love.

Adelbert

President Grant Disclaims Responsibility, July 1876

Executive Mansion,
Washington, D.C., July 26th.

Dear Sir:—I am in receipt of your letter of the 22d of July, and all the inclosures enumerated therein, giving an account of the late barbarous massacre at the town of Hamburg, S. C. The views which you express as to the duty you owe to your oath of office and to citizens to secure to all their civil rights, including the right to vote according to the dictates of their own consciences, and the further duty of the Executive of the nation to give all needful aid, when properly called on to do so, to enable you to ensure this inalienable right, I fully concur in. The scene at Hamburg, as cruel, blood-thirsty, wanton, unprovoked, and uncalled for, as it was, is only a repetition of the course which has been pursued in other Southern States within the last few years, notably in Mississippi and Louisiana. Mississippi is governed to-day by officials chosen through fraud and violence, such as would scarcely be accredited to savages, much less to a civilized and Christian people. How long these things are to continue, or what is to be the final remedy, the Great Ruler of the universe only knows; but I have an abiding faith that the remedy will come, and come speedily, and I earnestly hope that it will come peacefully. There has never been a desire on the part of the North to humiliate the South. Nothing is claimed for one State that is not fully accorded to all others, unless it may be the right to kill negroes and Republicans without fear of punishment and without loss of caste or reputation. This has seemed to be a privilege claimed by a few States. I repeat again, that I fully agree with you as to the measure of your duties in the present emergency, and as to my duties. Go on—and let every Governor where the same dangers threaten the peace of his State go on—in the conscientious discharge of his duties to the humblest as well as the proudest citizen, and I will give every aid for which I can find law or constitutional power. A government that cannot give protection to life, property, and all guaranteed civil rights (in this country the greatest is an untrammelled ballot) to the citizen is, in so far, a failure, and every energy of the oppressed should be exerted, always within the law and by consti-

tutional means, to regain lost privileges and protection. Too long denial of
guaranteed rights is sure to lead to revolution—bloody revolution, where
suffering must fall upon the innocent as well as the guilty.

Expressing the hope that the better judgment and co-operation of citizens of the State over which you have presided so ably may enable you
to secure a fair trial and punishment of all offenders, without distinction
of race or color or previous condition of servitude, and without aid from
the Federal Government, but with the promise of such aid on the conditions
named in the foregoing, I subscribe myself, very respectfully, your obedient
servant,

U. S. Grant.

To the Hon. D. H. Chamberlain,
Governor of South Carolina.

↘ *E S S A Y S*

The downfall of the Reconstruction governments is approached from two different angles in the following essays. In the first, Lawrence N. Powell of Tulane
University examines the destabilizing role of northerners, or "carpetbaggers," in
the southern Republican party, and also points out how the new party was beset
by many major institutional problems. The second essay, by Michael Perman of
the University of Illinois at Chicago, describes and assesses the tactics employed
by the Democrats in attempting to topple their Republican opponents.

Carpetbaggers and the Problems of Republican Rule in the South

LAWRENCE N. POWELL

It is now beginning to dawn on historians of Reconstruction that Southern
Republicans during those years were inordinately addicted to factional quarrels. In fact, the infighting probably had more than a casual bearing on the
eventual collapse of Reconstruction, which makes it frankly bewildering
and hard to explain. Though the party was admittedly composed of wildly
disparate elements, Southern Republicans had more reason to hang together
than did any comparable group of politicians in American electoral history.
Their political opponents, known variously as Conservatives or Democrats
or Conservative-Democrats, were not a "loyal opposition" in any ordinary
sense. They favored a "rule or ruin" policy and did not scruple to employ
the methods of fraud, terror, and assassination in order to achieve their
ends. But Southern Republicans were sometimes slow to catch on. At the
very moment when their existence as a viable political party was at stake,

From *Region, Race, and Reconstruction: Essays in Honor of C. Vann Woodward,* edited by
J. Morgan Kousser and James M. McPherson. Copyright © 1982 by Oxford University Press,
Inc. Reprinted by permission.

they often seemed to devote less energy to fighting the opposition than to fighting one another. They appear to have been incapable of *"party discipline* and self control," to quote a typical complaint they made about themselves. What explains this puzzling failure of Republicans in the Reconstruction South to pull together in the face of common adversity? Why was the Southern wing of the party of emancipation unable "to create a political culture in which solidarity was a virtue?"

A look at the experience of carpetbaggers provides a partial answer. Over the past twenty-odd years we have been taught to view these Northern Republicans in the South more objectively and charitably, and we have learned in addition a great deal that is informative about their background, their political creed, their voting behavior, and their typical constituency. Yet few have taken the time to explore the question of why they entered and remained in Republican politics in the first place. The answer is revealing on several scores. Northern newcomers became Republican politicians in the South partly because they had to make a living that could not be easily earned at that time in the usual ways. That is to say, carpetbaggers in the Lower South, which for the purposes of this essay includes Alabama, Florida, Georgia, Louisiana, Mississippi, and South Carolina (where most of them were concentrated), were in a worse predicament than the ordinary American politician ever finds himself in. They relied on office not only for power and prestige but for economic survival. This dependence upon politics for their livelihood in turn greatly aggravated the factional weaknesses to which Southern Republicans were already prone.

No attempt is being made here to resurrect the Redeemer myth that the carpetbaggers were low-flung, penniless adventurers who came South originally for the purpose of living off of office. Every modern study of Reconstruction politics demonstrates conclusively that the carpetbaggers scarcely fit the caricature of them that used to pass for historical truth. They were, as a class, fairly well educated, a large proportion of them having attended college, and they came from backgrounds that were solidly middle class. They were not the jetsam and flotsam of Northern society. Nor did they come South strictly for the sake of office. The fact is, as Richard N. Current reminded us several years ago, the overwhelming majority of carpetbaggers arrived in the region well before congressional enactments in 1867 made Republican politics a live possibility and officeholding a thing to be pursued. The few Northern newcomers who did hunger after office during presidential Reconstruction soon learned that Andrew Johnson preferred Southern men for federal appointments, and that Southern men frowned on Northern men who meddled in local politics without an invitation. In short, most Northerners who later ended up as carpetbaggers did not anticipate this aspect of their careers at all. They came to the former Confederacy for reasons other than politics.

Of course, what mostly attracted Northerners to the South, or tempted them to remain or return there after their discharges from the military, were the manifold opportunities of a business nature that the region held forth in the years just preceding and following Appomattox. Land speculators and developers from the Old Northwest were sure that the former Confederacy would be the next frontier to roll into vision. Merchants and jobbers were just as positive that their special talents would find full scope in the consumer market that emancipation had recently enlarged. Lawyers for their part sensed that there might be "much litigation growing out of the Confiscation Act[s] of the U.S. Congress, [and] also out of the Sequestration Act of the late Confederate Congress and other matters connected with the war." In addition to all these types were those countless Northerners, numbering possibly in the tens of thousands, who believed that cotton growing at prices then prevailing was the quickest way imaginable to secure a financial "competency" of the sort that most men in nineteenth-century America envied and aspired to. In a word, economic, not political, motives impelled most carpetbaggers originally to move to the South. And it remains to say that the newcomers were scarcely impecunious when they first put in their appearance. They invested thousands of dollars in the Southern economy, and in all likelihood they brought more money into the former Confederacy than they took out.

If carpetbaggers originally came South for financial reasons, and if some of them abandoned whatever political ambitions they had not long after arrival, why then did they become involved in the Southern Republican party at the time they did? What were those "conditions which none of [them] could control" and which before long caused them to find themselves "up to [their] eyes in politics"? The answers that have been given by revisionist historians cannot be lightly dismissed. It is undoubtedly true that the enfranchisement of the former slaves in the spring and summer of 1867 brought with it not only "political opportunity" but "political responsibility" as well, and that more than a few carpetbaggers seized both the opportunity *and* the responsibility out of a sense of duty. In fact, some carpetbaggers had to be called to the colors, if not by the freedmen then by the native whites or, more common still, by the military commanders who were charged with putting the congressional plan of Reconstruction into motion. Union generals were often unable to find white Southern natives who could take the Ironclad Oath, so they simply selected many of their voting registrars and judicial officers from among "the late volunteer officers of our army when it [was] practicable. . . . " Though the summons to office caught a few by surprise, the newcomers usually overcame initial reservations about officeholding and concluded that it was their solemn duty to assist the government and the newly enfranchised in the grand experiment about to be launched. No explanation of the origins of carpetbaggers can do full justice to the subject if it disregards the feelings of public altruism and patriotic duty that were awakened in many Northerners by the birth of the Southern Republican Party.

Yet there was another motive that tended to draw many Northerners into Republican politics. It often had little to do with idealism and civic-mindedness, though it was by no means inconsistent with these virtues. This other motive was the practical one of how to earn a living. It figured rather large in the calculations of many soon-to-be carpetbaggers. For, although the majority of the carpetbaggers were anything but penniless at the time they arrived in the South, they were very nearly penniless at the time they became Republican politicians, which is more than partly why they chose that occupation when they did. They needed to secure a livelihood.

The truth is, the Southern Republican party was born in the midst of hard times, and the bitter circumstances of its birth profoundly affected the style of politics to which it would be prone. To understand why this was so we need only consider for a moment the experiences of Northern cotton planters. Practically all of them were financially strapped when Radical Reconstruction commenced in the South. Every year since 1864 they had been planning to make a fortune, and every year since that time they had been going broke, casualties of agricultural disasters that, like misfortune, never came singly. By the beginning of 1867 they were on the ropes; at the end of the year they were on the canvas, for the price of cotton had fallen to levels that did not cover the cost of cultivation. Individual losses commonly ran into the tens of thousands of dollars. Henry W. Warren, a Yankee planter who later became Republican speaker of the Mississippi House of Representatives, summed up cotton raising as "an occupation that proved disastrous." . . .

Yankee planters were certainly not alone among carpetbaggers in viewing Republican politics in the South as a source of livelihood. They were only more conspicuous in this regard, having been heavy losers in the crop failures of 1866–67. Yet everyone in the Lower South, at least, felt the reverberations of these cotton losses, and most everyone had to adjust his plans accordingly. As one Indiana native explained of a fellow Mississippi carpetbagger in distress, "Like nearly all of us northern men in the South, he is broken up financially. . . . " Individual instances of what he meant can be found in a variety of occupations. A Northern lawyer in Mobile, Alabama, for example, who counted several former Confederates among his personal friends, said his clients were so poor, "I can't make anything." He wanted to be appointed recorder of deeds and mortgages in New Orleans. Attorneys for the freedmen were in financial straits just as dire, if not more so. John Emory Bryant, a former Freedmen's Bureau agent in Georgia who had tried without success to make a living as a lawyer for the ex-slaves, saw in the Republican party a future that might bring him "position and money." Northern teachers in the South also had pecuniary motives for a change of occupation. "I am tired of the schoolroom," one of them wrote the commanding general in Alabama in 1867, "and I would like to have an appointment . . . which will pay me liberal wages." Northern-born editors of Republican sheets likewise found themselves in "financial distress" and in need of political assistance. They would continue to find themselves in this predicament throughout Radical Reconstruction, for it was nearly impossible to support a Republican journal in the South during these years except by means of state or federal printing contracts.

At a time when business in general was flat and decent prospects were lacking, the financial attractions of political positions in the South could not be taken for granted. The prosaic duty of registering voters under the military Reconstruction acts of 1867, for instance, paid a commission fee of thirteen to forty cents a voter and could bring in several thousand dollars in some districts. These were not low wages for the time, and several Northerners who actively sought out registrar appointments apparently sensed as much. Fees available to sheriffs and tax collectors, moreover, often added up to more than pocket change; salaries of $5,000 to $20,000 a year were not unheard of. State legislators were not paid so liberally, but ordinarily they could supplement their incomes with generous per diem and travel expenses, and in other ways. State officers, on the other hand, from the governor on down, were usually—though not always—well remunerated, and federal officeholders were everywhere handsomely rewarded. To name one case, registers in bankruptcy, a newly created federal position that did a brisk business in the Reconstruction South, earned annual incomes that ranged from $5,000 to $12,000. George E. Spencer, a future carpetbagger U.S. senator, landed one of these for Alabama's fourth congressional district. The position made him feel, as he put it, "that my duty is to remain here and help reconstruct this God forsaken and miserable country." . . .

That this style of politics lasted for as long as it did was owing in large measure to the stark reality of Southern poverty, on the one hand, and the unpleasant reality of pervasive ostracism, on the other. The two realities seem to have worked in tandem to reinforce the attitude that political patronage was indispensable to personal financial well-being. The poverty can scarcely be exaggerated. Never during Reconstruction—or for the remainder of the century, for that matter—did the former Confederacy enjoy anything like true prosperity. The years 1868–72 saw a return of commercial health and a quickening of business energies, but this was a prosperous period only in comparison with the economic desperation of the immediate past and future. When the panic of 1873 struck, triggering a depression that reversed such small gains as had been registered since the surrender, cotton prices had already commenced a long-term, though fluctuating, decline that before it ended would further impoverish white yeomen and black freedmen and leave the planters more land poor than ever. Added to these problems was the handicap the South faced in the form of inadequate banking capital and currency, which the National Banking Act [of 1863] and supplemental congressional legislation did much to create. . . .

Hardly less effective in reinforcing the same attitude [of political patronage as being indispensable for personal financial well-being] was the ostracism to which carpetbaggers were subjected. The proscription of Northern Republicans was as prevalent as it was relentless, and it ranged in intensity from the cold shoulder and the audible insult to the coarser techniques of terrorism, bullyism, and plain assassination, which was favored by the Ku Klux Klan and similar groups. Commercial ostracism was also popular, and sometimes went forward on an organized basis. A Democratic editor in Alabama recommended it as superior to violence. "STARVE

THEM OUT!'' was the advice he gave for bringing white Republicans to heel.
"Don't put your foot in the doors of their shops, offices, and stores. Purchase from true men and patronize those of known Southern sympathies.''
The effect was merely to add an extra weight to the burden of economic difficulties carpetbaggers were already shouldering in their efforts to make a living in the Reconstruction South, particularly if they were business and professional men or otherwise dependent on the goodwill of the surrounding community. Their only clientele, the freedmen, were the most poverty-stricken of all Southerners, which partly explains why one Northern physician in Florida found it necessary to moonlight as a clerk of court (the position paid $5,000 annually). . . .

Even the financial security of political office in the South was not always a safe gamble. The Radical governments may have offered good salaries, but in truth these regimes were as poor as the people they represented. Their securities seldom sold at face value, yet on occasion they had to float bonds in order to meet current operating expenses. Their treasuries were usually bare, yet officials drew pay in warrants they were expected to redeem for greenbacks the government almost never had on hand. Governor Harrison Reed of Florida, for example, who was paid in state scrip, realized only $1,000 from his $3,500 salary. This widespread indigence in both the private and public economy understandably tempted several carpetbaggers to supplement their incomes by less than honest means. Thus we find some newcomers participating in various Reconstruction bond and railroad rings, profiting from inside information on state finances, and using their connections to secure lucrative state contracts for their private internal-improvement companies. Thus, we discover still more Northerners padding expense accounts, liberalizing per diem allowances, mixing together public and private accounts, stealing school funds, and coming up with ingenious ways to speculate in warrants. If the official salary was not what it appeared to be, then one could always collect taxes or fees in greenbacks, settle accounts in depreciated scrip, and bank the difference. Several sheriffs and tax collectors used these methods to shore up their incomes, until state governments undercut them by making scrip acceptable in the payment of taxes. The motive of the speculators was probably financial need, though the means employed could stimulate financial greed as well. Unlike large spoilsmen in Washington and New York, the carpetbaggers as a class could at least plead the excuse of economic hardship for yielding to the easy morals of Gilded Age America. . . .

It is admittedly misleading, not to say unfair, to stress the pecuniary preoccupations of the carpetbaggers to the exclusion of other motives. The Southern Republican party had more than its share of Northerners who became carpetbaggers not because they loved money less, but humanity more. After all, Albert T. Morgan and his brother entered Republican politics not simply to secure to themselves a financial "restoration," but also to secure to the freedman "the right to life, liberty and pursuit of happiness." Who is to say which motive was the controlling one? In the case of Albert Morgan, who kept faith with his principles long after it was popular or safe to do so, it was probably the idealistic motive that was dominant. He once passed up an opportunity to be sheriff of Yazoo County, a position "worth in fees and commissions six to ten thousand per year," because he wished to remain in the state legislature, where he thought he would "be able to do more good." And what are we to make of the fact that Albion Tourgée ran for a seat in the North Carolina Constitutional Convention and later welcomed a state judgeship because his private business affairs were in disarray and he needed the money? Surely to say this about him is to leave a lot unsaid. To the list of high-minded carpetbaggers should be added the names of John Emory Bryant in Georgia, Reuben Tomlinson in South Carolina, Leonard G. Dennis in Florida, and that skillful nepotist himself, Marshall H. Twitchell in Louisiana. They and many like them were all committed to the proposition that racial and social justice were things worth dedicating one's life to. Their motives may have been complex, even contradictory at times, but this is no argument against either their integrity *or* their accomplishments, which were real and considerable. It is no part of wisdom to sneer at sincere purpose even when it is difficult to dissociate from economic motivation. . . .

Which brings us back to the subject of Southern Republican factionalism. A substantial amount of it appears to have originated in the financial weaknesses of the organizational leadership; otherwise there is no explaining why Southern Republicans fought about nothing so much as the loaves and fishes of office. By all accounts patronage was usually *the* issue over which the Reconstructionists quarreled the most. To be sure, a certain degree of internecine feuding was to be expected in a party composed of former slaves and former slaveholders, wealthy landlords and impoverished tenants, former Whigs and former Democrats, wartime Unionists and original secessionists, black-belt planters and hill-country yeomen, blacks and whites, and, not least, the victor and the vanquished. Once the Reconstructionists in the Deep South wrote into law their minimal reform agenda, these incongruent elements began to war among themselves over who should run the party and in whose interests. Did more need to be done in the way of racial integration and black economic uplift, or did wisdom dictate slighting the black vote in order to enlarge the white vote? If the latter was the case, which whites should be appealed to, the masses or the classes? And what of reform in general? Should it be in the direction of greater economic democracy or diversified economic development? Over the question of leadership the debate often became sulfurous. Many carpetbaggers, as we have seen, believed they had special claims to dominance. Several scalawags, as native white Republicans were called, replied that they were "opposed to newcomers occupying prominent positions either in the State or general government." They felt they deserved preeminence by virtue of their pre-war residence, wartime sufferings, or high antebellum status, as the case might be, or in recognition of the fact that they had sometimes been the first to come forward as party organizers in their respective states. Black Republicans also excelled at special pleading, especially in the latter phases of Reconstruction. Since they supplied the bulk of the votes, they reasoned they should receive a fair share of the offices. Especially hard words were exchanged between quondam Whigs and Democrats, and the recriminations that ex-Confederates and persistent Unionists hurled at one another could not always be repeated in polite company. Factionalism along these lines and over these issues was altogether natural, and when and where Southern Republicans enjoyed comfortable legislative and electoral majorities, it thrived nearly unchecked.

Yet, what gave these antipathies of race, class, section, and party an edge they might not otherwise have had was the financial indigence of so much of the rank-and-file Republican leadership. The simple truth is that carpetbaggers were by no means alone in their reliance upon political office for a livelihood. Numerous scalawags appear to have been in similar straits. Several pre-war officeholders in Mississippi, for instance, converted to Republicanism largely for economic purposes. "I am in need of employment which would give me some remuneration," one of them confessed. J. Madison Wells, the Johnsonian governor of Louisiana who later joined the Republican party, offered this explanation as to why his son should receive a federal appointment: "All things being equal, I think preference should be given to those 'of the manor born' and who have lost everything by the war." A desire to secure a steady income was admittedly not the only—or even the major—reason many scalawags identified with the party of black rights. Their motives for becoming Republicans were probably more mixed than were those of the carpetbaggers, ranging from reform to revenge and including opportunism of the broadest kind. But poverty and proscription worked upon native white Republicans with particular severity; in Alabama, at least, "scalawags were much more bitterly hated than carpetbaggers," and the financial effects of persecution caused many wartime Unionists to scurry for Republican appointments. Of course, no class of Republican politician was more financially needy than were black officeholders. As we now know, many were artisans and small tradesmen and thus singularly vulnerable to the economic reprisals the white community was especially prone to bring down upon maverick black citizens. W. McKee Evans explains their situation best: "Once a Negro acquired the reputation of being a politician, for better or for worse, he became dependent upon political jobs for a livelihood." Negro and native white Republicans also felt constrained to employ the various unethical means carpetbaggers relied on to supplement their incomes. Honest and dishonest graft were not a Northern import but generally selective adaptations for survival in the hostile Southern environment.

In short, here was a party that was financially hard pressed from head to toe and unusually wedded to political patronage for economic sustenance and well-being. Its leaders may not have pursued office entirely for financial reasons, but they soon discovered they had to stay in office largely for such reasons. The poverty of Southern life in these years made Republican offices peculiarly attractive; the commercial and social ostracism that most Republicans suffered made those same offices things that could not be gladly given up. Thus, Republican politicians intrigued and conspired, libeled and slandered and occasionally assassinated one another, and even bolted their party often for no loftier purpose than to get an office, hold on to an office, recover an office, or vent their anger at having lost an office. As one South Carolina Republican complained, "Anyone who is defeated swears, abuses all the rest, and bolts the action." The only wonder about the defections is that there were not more of them (which is another way of saying that the courage and commitment of Republicans should never be lost sight of). Since nearly every Republican had made great personal sacrifices on behalf of the party, nearly every single one of them had a compelling argument as to why he should be rewarded with patronage. And if a paying office was not forthcoming, what good reason was there to remain within the Republican fold and thus continue enduring the proscription that was a sure guarantee lean times were around the corner? The bolting was understandable, and so was the factionalism. It was as though the entire Southern Republican party was composed of so many newspaper editors who had to get up little quarrels with their competitors in order to obtain the public printing contracts that often meant the difference between survival and insolvency. The multiplication of offices beyond the requirements of even the modern state barely improved the situation. Nor was relief provided by granting to various governors appointive power over many local offices heretofore elective. The demand for office always exceeded the supply. The scalawag governor James L. Alcorn of Mississippi lamented early in his term that there were usually twenty applicants for every position at his disposal. At one time he controlled over one thousand appointments.

Indeed, as Reconstruction wore on, the quarreling that grew out of office seeking began increasingly to cut across the other fault lines that rent the Republican party. Factional distinctions based on race, section, and party broke down or blurred around the edges. Carpetbaggers joined hands with scalawags, blacks with whites, in shifting, almost kaleidoscopic patterns, ostensibly for no larger purpose than personal convenience and private gain. As Adelbert Ames, the Northern-born governor of Mississippi, later recalled, "If one's own kind could not or would not meet a demand for office, an alliance would be made with another kind." And so it went during most of Radical Reconstruction in the Deep South. Even ideological divisions showed great fluidity, or at least lost much meaning. Conservatives one day might become Radicals the next, and vice versa, as many of the internal struggles within the Republican party soon reduced themselves to naked struggles for spoils between the ins and the outs, the hopefuls and the disappointed. Everywhere it seemed the same. Jerrell Shofner's description of Republican politics in Florida gets at the heart of what was taking place elsewhere in the Lower South at the time: "There were many possible coalitions among the various groups in Florida, . . . but they were never clearly divided along racial lines and they were not static." Nor were they always ideologically clear-cut. As Joel Williamson remarks of South Carolina, "many political contests . . . were merely fights between Republican factions standing on the same program and principles, the real issue being personal." "Such politics also produced strange electoral bedfellows," Williamson goes on to observe. By the same token, they gave rise to a host of personal political machines on both the state and local levels, for ring politics usually flourish where patronage for its own sake assumes unusual importance. . . .

There was admittedly one group within the Southern Republican party that was not financially dependent upon officeholding, but it is the exception that proves the rule. These were the conservative Republicans, composed for the most part of former Whig planters and merchants and relatively well-to-do carpetbaggers. The latter usually resided in urban centers, in places like Jacksonville, Florida, and Vicksburg, Mississippi, but where they could be found in the rural districts they were almost always large landowners who were resentful of the high land taxes, frightened and annoyed by the labor instability caused by Reconstruction, and embarrassed by the corruption and factionalism that plagued their party. Conservative Northerners in the South especially craved respectability, which they believed their wealth entitled them to. In short, there was a rough correspondence between wealth and conservatism within Republican ranks, as seen in the extreme example of impecunious carpetbaggers who defected to the Democrats as soon as they accumulated some property. Whether in town or country, moreover, conservative Republicans were very eager to encourage economic development through an alliance between government and business, and they hoped to give their party respectability and strength by attracting to it Democrats and Southern conservatives of the better sort. That patronage would have to serve as the means of conversion posed no threat to conservative Republicans, since they did not have to rely on office for any considerable portion of their livelihood. Republican governors of conservative leanings were forever courting Southern Democrats with the zeal of a young suitor, and in the name of reform often pledged to make their party into something better than a mere spoils agency by distributing patronage on the basis of merit. It must be admitted that Southern Democrats were very adroit at encouraging Republican overtures merely for the purpose of fostering Republican dissension. Democrats played their hand with consummate skill. Conservative Republicans could not broaden the base of the party without robbing Peter to pay Paul, without depriving some needy loyal Republican of his job in order to give it to some flirtatious but insincere Democrat, and without therefore plunging their party into factional patronage quarrels that in many states made the Republicans peculiarly vulnerable to Redeemer [i.e. Democratic] assaults. The Republican rank and file were simply too financially indigent and dependent upon office to survive attempts by their leaders to build bridges to the political opposition.

In fact the party of emancipation could not even easily enact so-called good-government reforms, which conservative Republicans deemed essential to their strategy and which several Republican administrations late in Reconstruction found it necessary to press forward. Only at the risk of disrupting party unity could one correct even the most obvious abuses. When Governor Harrison Reed of Florida, for example, moved to put a stop to plural officeholding, he made himself the target of an impeachment effort engineered by the very carpetbag state senators against whom his reform was directed. The impeachers could afford to legislate a reduction in their state salaries, which they did do, but they could not sacrifice one of their county offices, which might have accounted for half of their income. In Mississippi, by contrast, after the panic of 1873 began to be felt, Republican lawmakers refused even to cut their salaries or reduce expenditures and printing contracts, despite loud demands from various taxpayers' conventions that they do so. It bears repeating that Republican politicians in the Deep South during Reconstruction were probably not more greedy than the average American politician, only more needy, and this fact doubtless explains in large measure the ruinous factionalism that plagued the Southern Republican party during the years of its ascendancy, and beyond as well.

In their motives for seeking office, in their reasons for holding on to office, and in their methods of living off of office, carpetbaggers in the Deep South illustrate a tragic truth about Republican Reconstruction that is unpleasant to acknowledge. If several carpetbaggers went into politics in order to secure a livelihood, if they grabbed for as many offices as they could in order to protect that livelihood, and if they tried by factionalist means to retain those offices because public and private poverty and economic and social ostracism made it necessary for them to do so, the Northern newcomers only throw into sharp relief the formidable handicaps that the Reconstructionists were up against. Those handicaps were the colonial economic status that the defeated Confederacy was sliding into, the weak social base of the party that the abandonment of land reform did nothing to strengthen, and the utter unwillingness of the conquered to concede legitimacy, not to mention fellowship, to the party of black rights. Between the poverty that resulted from the former two handicaps and the economic coercion that resulted from the latter, Southern Republicans could find little room to maneuver save by cannibalizing one another in patronage fights that they could ill afford. The experience of carpetbaggers in the Lower South makes the factionalism that brought the Republicans to grief a little more comprehensible.

Southern Democrats and the Overthrow of Reconstruction, 1873–1876

MICHAEL PERMAN

The election of 1872 was a major setback for the Democratic-Conservatives [as the party of the former Confederates was known at this point in Reconstruction]. It seemed that the Republicans were proving far less easy to dislodge than many had thought and that, as a result, the return of their own party to power was far from inevitable, but behind the election returns,

"The Forked Road to Redemption, 1873–1876," in Michael Perman, *The Road to Redemption: Southern Politics, 1869–1879,* pp. 149–177 © 1984 The University of North Carolina Press. Reprinted by permission.

grim though they were, there lurked an even more significant and disturbing reality. The Democratic-Conservatives had reached a political dead end. Their endorsement of [Horace] Greeley and their fusion with the Liberal-Republicans at the state level had been the culmination of the New Departure strategy [a maneuver by the party's moderate wing to undermine Republicans by acknowledging black suffrage and gaining black votes] that they had pursued for the four years since 1868. Yet it had failed miserably, leaving the party in a state of crisis. Its entire approach to electoral politics in the reconstructed South had now to be reassessed, and, perhaps, an alternative strategy found to replace it.

To many in the party, however, the potential for its revitalization had already become apparent. During the 1872 campaign, they had observed that the party's problem was not that it was failing to gain new adherents and broader support but simply that it was not capitalizing on the electoral assets it already possessed. Vast numbers of its supporters were just not being mobilized but, instead, were withdrawing and refusing to vote. . . . Yet the antidote was obvious. If the leadership could stimulate the interest of these apathetic voters and organize them to get out and vote, the party's chances of success would be increased considerably. As the party chairman in Arkansas perceived in the 1873 campaign, "A closer and more thorough organization of the party" might make the difference.

As the Democratic-Conservatives became increasingly aware of the latent internal strength of their party and thus of how little they needed to depend on attracting additional support from outside their own ranks, there soon emerged a more drastic and clear-cut version of this idea of partisan self-reliance. It was not a new formulation because, during the past four years, there had been a sizable contingent advocating it within each state. In the crisis confronting the party after the debacle of 1872, the strategy and its proponents began to grow in influence. This approach to electoral politics, which was earlier identified with the Bourbon wing of the party, was the exact antithesis of the New Departure. In contrast with the New Departure's emphasis on expanding the party's base through direct appeal to black voters or through fusion with dissident Republican factions, the alternative formula demanded that the party forego coalition and campaign with a separate and exclusive organization. Paralleling this change of direction towards organizing their party on what was called the "straight-out" basis, the Democratic-Conservatives were also to cease downplaying the differences between themselves and their opponents. Instead, they were to accentuate the contrasts and distinctions. This dramatic reorientation of the party's priorities and direction was to be given specificity, first, by throwing out its current mongrel sobriquet of Democratic-Conservative and unashamedly adopting instead the designation of Democratic. The second change was that the difference between the parties was to be defined by race, a distinction that was unmistakable and not open to challenge. In effect, the color line was to be politicized.

Adoption of the thoroughgoing straight-out, white-line formula was not necessary in a closely contested state like Texas. In the very next year,

1873, the Democratic-Conservatives gained control there simply by means of better electoral organization and closer attention to the party's loyal rank and file. But in the states of the lower South—Alabama, Louisiana, Mississippi, and South Carolina—where the party was confronted by an entrenched opposition, sustained by a majority or near-majority of dependable black voters, the alternative formula could be successful only if it were pursued with as much vigor and ruthlessness as possible. Even then, however, victory was far from certain because campaigns based on race were, on the face of it, unlikely to benefit the party identified with the white minority. In fact, many argued that the politicization of race would be suicidal for the Democratic-Conservatives in the black states. As the Charleston *Daily News* warned early in 1873, "Any policy which contemplates the arraying of whites against blacks at the polls, must fail, and will deserve to fail. Fortunately, there is little likelihood that so wild a project will be seriously submitted to the public." Nonetheless, despite these predictions of disaster from a straight-out, white-line strategy, pressure was building throughout the Deep South for a complete reversal of the party's electoral priorities. As a result, there occurred within what was by the mid-1870s the stronghold of Republicanism, a decisive confrontation over the course the Democratic-Conservatives should pursue, and, naturally, this struggle also involved a contest for dominance within the party.

Faced with the challenge to their ascendancy, the New Departurists dug in and refused to yield. On grounds of both expediency and principle their position seemed unassailable. They argued that, as a practical matter, it was unlikely that a party which had for years been unable to win power with the help of support from outside its ranks could now expect to succeed on its own. More important still, a policy based on partisan and racial exclusiveness was in itself thoroughly undesirable. What the New Departurists feared most of all was a division of the parties along racial lines and the setting of whites against blacks in a contest for political dominance. It had been for the very purpose of precluding such an outcome that they had, in the first place, embraced the biracial and accommodationist approach that the New Departure had embodied. The function of political parties in the South, they argued, was to mask and temper the existing racial cleavage within the society. Therefore, if the Democratic-Conservatives adopted race as the key symbol of party differentiation, they would be confirming this perilous division and thereby inflicting on their state and region a dangerously turbulent politics that they would live to regret.

In the postemancipation South, this racial distinction almost certainly would be further compounded by a division on the basis of wealth and class, and New Departurists constantly warned of the fearful dangers it involved. Albert G. Brown, who was Mississippi's leading opponent of the white-liners, was troubled because "the capital of the state is mainly on one side of a political line and the labor on the other." Rather than accepting this as reality, Brown and the New Departurists denounced it as something "abnormal [that] must not be allowed to continue." At the same time, James Chesnut, Brown's equivalent in South Carolina, was expressing concern that the "no property and no taxes" element was in one party aligned against the taxpaying property owners in the other. The situation was extremely dangerous, they believed, and, now more than ever before, it required the antidote that the New Departure had always offered.

The foolishness of adopting a white-line policy in a situation that was so precarious was heightened, so the New Departurists judged, by the risk of committing the party to an overt and close identification with the national Democratic party. In view of its utter rout in the 1872 elections, the cultivation of ties with the Democratic party was hardly the essence of political wisdom. In addition to the weakness of the Democrats nationally, there was also the consideration that, during the year or so since the Greeley upset, the nation's politics had become extremely fluid and uncertain. There was a growing sense that the parties were about to undergo a significant rearrangement. By 1874, this perception was becoming widespread. In June, the New York *Tribune* was commenting, "Party lines no longer certify anything but past prejudices," and, a few months earlier, the New York *Herald* had been convinced that "disintegration . . . appears to be inevitable," even for the Republican party since it had "no fixed policy—no principles of policy." New issues had to appear soon, it was believed, in order to breathe life into the political system. But, in the meantime, the *Arkansas Gazette* concluded, "The condition of all parties is now exceptional—they float upon uncertain waters . . . the disposition is and ought to be, rather to avoid trouble than to propagate opinions," and besides, the *Gazette* added, "In the past, national politics have occupied too great a share of [the South's] attention."

Nevertheless, electoral trends during 1873 and 1874 did seem to reveal a discernible shift against the Republicans which the party's southern opponents could not but take seriously. After scandal rocked the Grant administration during 1873 and the panic of that fall produced widespread economic distress, the reverses suffered by the Republicans in the eighteen state elections held during the twelve months since the canvass of 1872 were being considered by many political observers as nothing short of remarkable; some even went so far as to believe it the most dramatic electoral shift in the country's political history. All the same, the leading New Departure organ in South Carolina quickly warned that this was "a victory for the anti-administration party, not the Democracy pure and undefiled." A year later, when the Democrats captured the United States House of Representatives, Alexander Horn, a prominent straight-out editor in Mississippi, hailed it as conclusive evidence that "the Democratic party of the whole country is coming to our relief and we must be in strict alignment with it." Once again, the New Departure faction warned against jumping to conclusions concerning the strength of the national Democratic party that they were so eager to embrace. "The victories of last fall were not strictly Democratic victories," observed L. Q. C. Lamar, a leader of the Mississippi fusionists. "They were anti-administration victories." By discounting the significance of the political shift away from the Republicans, the New Departurists were attempting two simultaneous maneuvers. In the first place, they were trying to undercut their intraparty rivals by refuting claims that an identification with the Democrats through the adoption of straight-outism on the state level was politically wise and necessary. Their second purpose derived more from principle than expediency. From the outset, the New Departurists had based their strategy on the premise that a policy of accommodation would appease and relax northern opinion. Therefore, if sentiment outside the South was now moving in the Democratic-Conservatives' direction as, despite their own disclaimers, it seemed to be, this development was a vindication of the effectiveness of conciliation, not proof that it should be abandoned. However, if a politics of race and extremism were embraced in the South, it might provoke federal intervention, and it would undoubtedly, as the Jackson *Clarion* warned, "check the rising sentiment in our favor at the North."

Thus, armed with a quite different stance on the function of race and party in southern politics, the New Departure faction confronted its rivals in the struggle for party control in the Deep South. For the first year or so after the setback in 1872, the competing forces jostled for the advantage. . . .

Nevertheless, during the course of the following year, 1874, the outcome of the contest within the Democratic-Conservative party became clearer, for in two states, Alabama and Louisiana, the white-liners achieved ascendancy, leaving just Mississippi and South Carolina still contested. Alabama was the first state to defeat the Republicans with the politics of the color line. Interestingly, however, there was no need, at the same time, to reject fusion and adopt the straight-out formula because Alabama's Democratic-Conservatives had never previously employed fusion [the New Departure wing's electoral strategy of allying with dissident, breakaway Republicans] in statewide campaigns. When they had won in 1870, they had operated as a separate and distinct organization, just like North Carolina and Georgia that same year. Nevertheless, even though they had rejected fusion, the Alabamians had endorsed the politics of the New Departure and had campaigned actively for black votes. Three years later, in 1873, those who had earlier advised against even the New Departure began to demand that the party renounce that policy as well. Led by John Forsyth, the prewar Douglas Democrat and earlier a leading opponent of the New Departure, a campaign was mounted, beginning in the summer of 1873, to convince the party leadership that Alabama could be won if all attempts to woo blacks and reassure white Republicans were abandoned. Instead, a vigorous appeal was to be made to the white voters of southern Alabama where Forsyth himself was based and, more importantly, to the same element in north Alabama whose apathy in 1872 was thought to have been pivotal in allowing the state to return to Republican control.

Although Forsyth had for long been confident that a campaign based on race was capable of arousing the apathetic and thus ensuring victory, others were not so enthusiastic. A powerful opposition arose which was concentrated in the Black Belt [those areas with a concentrated black population]. The entire press of the area opposed the color line and one of these newspaper editors, Robert McKee of the Selma *Times and Argus,* was the chief spokesman and organizer. What they objected to was perhaps expressed most forcefully by Ben L. Herr of the Livingston *Journal.* He complained to McKee in August 1873 that "the aim of certain parties is to *coerce* acquiescence in what they may dictate. West Ala. is vitally interested and I am desirous of conferring with reference to her interests. A *race* alignment will involve serious consequences to the 'black' counties, and I trust they will not decide upon a line of action without counting the cost." Besides losing the state through a course "being forced on us by men not reknowned for statesmanship," Herr feared that a white-line campaign would absolutely guarantee that the black counties would go to the Republicans and their local governments would certainly be remanded to Republican control. So objectionable was this prospect that, as late as June 1874, the Demopolis *News* was urging the Black Belt counties to secede from the party if it adopted the white-line.

While much of the Black Belt opposition simply objected to race as the campaign issue, the group around McKee proposed a positive alternative instead. They wanted the contest with the Republicans to be based on an issue of substance and principle rather than the opportunistic and emotional rallying cry of race. As old-line Democrats who wanted the hybrid Democratic-Conservative organization with which they were currently affiliated to return to sound Democratic doctrine, renunciation of the public debt and of the state aid program that had been responsible for creating most of it was thought to be a far better issue. In Charles C. Langdon's view, the debt, not race, was "the great question of the day." Unlike everywhere else in the Deep South, black-belt opponents of the white-line in Alabama could not propose as a substitute the continuation of the party's fusion policies because they had never taken root. Instead, Bourbon Democrats, like McKee, Langdon, Burwell B. Lewis, and Rufus K. Boyd, seized the opportunity to push the party towards embracing those enduring Democratic doctrines of minimal government and laissez-faire. As Boyd told McKee, "You do not now see and read so often the sneering allusions to Bourbonism, etc. The tide is changing and we may well hope [for] success in the immediate future upon the basis of Democratic principles as understood in the olden time modified somewhat by the changed condition of the country." If this path were taken, then not only would the parties' distinctiveness become more apparent but so too would the differences among the Democratic-Conservatives themselves, and the Bourbons very much wanted to dramatize this cleavage.

Also objectionable to the McKee forces was the attempt by the white-liners headed by Forsyth and Walter Bragg, the party chairman, to place George S. Houston at the head of the ticket in 1874. A prewar congressman from north Alabama who had opposed secession, Houston was thought to be the ideal candidate to deliver the crucial, Unionist-inclined northern counties. Yet, to the McKee forces, he was anathema. It was not just that he was old and uninspiring when the party needed "some live strong man who has made his record during & since the war" to get out the vote, but, far more important, as Langdon insisted, Houston "is not with us on the bond question." As a result, a fierce anti-Houston protest arose which was to continue up until the party's state convention assembled. Ultimately, however, the campaign for Houston and white supremacy triumphed. Partly, this was because its proponents conducted a well-organized pre-convention strategy, but it was also attributable to the shortcomings of the debt issue. It was, first of all, less compelling and electrifying than race, but, in addition, once the specifics were broached, a wide range of divergence soon became apparent, even among its proponents. Questions about what parts of the debt were to be regarded as illegitimate and how much of it should be repudiated gave rise to unresolvable dispute. Nevertheless, the antidebt sentiment was so powerful that the convention inserted a plank in the party platform pledging drastic reduction. Despite this concession, however, the white-liners controlled the party in 1874, and their victory was facilitated by their not having to challenge an entrenched fusionist element or to create a party organization *de novo* since straight-outism was already party practice in Alabama. The issue, therefore, was merely whether the New Departure was an effective platform and, if not, whether race was the best alternative. All the same, it still precipitated a vigorous contest for hegemony.

Although its outcome was similar, the sequence of events in Louisiana was quite different. The triumph there of straight-out white supremacy was surprising because there had been a powerful fusionist element among the Democratic-Conservatives in Louisiana which had forged an alliance with Governor Henry C. Warmoth's bolting Republicans in 1872. In addition, the Unification Movement of 1873 had promised a continuance, and perhaps expansion, of this approach. Behind these auspicious signs, there was, however, a deeper political reality, for the party was in the process of detaching itself from fusion. Rather than indicating that the New Departure was flourishing, the appearance of the Reform party in 1872 and of the [Unification] initiative the following year, both of which had originated outside the Democratic-Conservative organization, were evidence that the party had rejected it. The party's attention in the year or so after 1872 was not so much on deciding its electoral strategy at the state level as on discovering how the victory, which it claimed the Democratic-Fusion ticket headed by John McEnery had won in 1872, could be secured in the face of the objections and intervention of the federal government. By the end of 1873, when negotiation and remonstrance had failed to resolve the contested election in the party's favor, forces outside politics, increasingly impatient at the ineffectualness of this approach, began to mobilize on their own to overthrow the "Kellogg usurpation."

During the spring and summer of 1874, the White League was organized throughout most of Louisiana's parishes. By means of public pressure and physical intimidation, it was to sap Republican morale in the local outposts of Governor William P. Kellogg's administration and force Republican officials to resign in Natchitoches, Avoyelles, Iberia, St. Martin, and many other parishes. This undermining of the Kellogg government was climaxed by two military confrontations in September 1874, at Coushatta in Red River Parish and at Liberty Place in New Orleans. So powerful had the league become that, during the summer, it threatened to take Democratic-Conservative politics into its own hands by preventing the party from holding its convention. To avert this disaster, the convention was moved from Alexandria, in the league's heartland, to Baton Rouge. This maneuver prompted E. John Ellis, a leader of the party in New Orleans and a high-ranking officer of the league, to comment knowingly, "I now feel the State is safe and that all opposition to the Democratic convention will be at once withdrawn."

With the league able to undermine the Republicans' grip on power, a hold that was only secured by the federal government's imposition of the Wheeler Adjustment in late 1874 guaranteeing Kellogg's tenure, the Democratic-Conservatives' concern thereafter was to make sure that the para-military organization was held in check and that no occasion was offered for more extensive federal intervention. Unless that were done, the chances of defeating the Republicans at the next state election in 1876 would be slim. Accordingly, the party in Louisiana, unlike everywhere else, was preoccupied not with the problem of how to arouse its constituents but rather with how best to restrain them. There was no need to debate whether to adopt a white-line strategy; that had already been decided by the actions of the White League. Instead, the party leadership had to devise a means to win the 1876 election without giving cause for federal interference and thereby firmly securing the redemption of the state which had been all but accomplished in 1874. To this end, they counselled their supporters to be patient and they developed a platform and ticket in the 1876 campaign which was unexceptionable, both to the federal government and to the party's accommodationist New Departure wing. Thus, the platform was conciliatory, with its endorsement of black suffrage and public education as well as its vague commitment to retrenchment and reform. Furthermore, the head of the ticket was Francis T. Nicholls, a planter from Ascension Parish, with "well-known moderate views upon the issues of the day." Nicholls had the additional asset of being a political neophyte, of whom it was said, "Neither Bourbon, nor Liberal, nor Reformer, nor Last Ditcher, nor White Leaguer can claim him as of their faction." Rather than becoming more extreme and strident as the crucial election approached, the party leaders in Louisiana were proceeding in the reverse direction. . . .

. . . The fight was, however, by no means over in Mississippi and South Carolina, where the opponents of the white-liners were so tenacious that they were able to present a clear-cut and well-organized alternative. Their stance in these states was less vulnerable because it was advocated and promoted by a group of politicians who wielded considerable influence within the party. Furthermore, fusion had been implemented in every state election since 1868 and thus was a well-established strategy. As the confrontation with the straight-outs grew in intensity, the advocates of fusion in South Carolina and Mississippi were able to consolidate their forces and entrench their position. The basis of their support was to be found in the black counties of both states. There, the practice of biracial and fusion politics had been essential to the survival of the party locally, while, conversely, statewide adoption of an electoral strategy based on racial exclusiveness would be disastrous. In South Carolina, the center of cooperationism, as fusion was called there, was located in the tidewater, especially Charleston and adjacent districts. At the head of this wing of the party were James Chesnut, James Kershaw, John L. Manning, James Connor, and not least, Francis W. Dawson, the English-born editor of the Charleston *News and Courier,* who was the faction's spokesman and leading wirepuller. Further evidence about the source of cooperationist support was offered by Dawson himself, for, on one occasion, he wrote, "The upcountry . . . must face the unpleasant truth, which is that, as long as radicalism preponderates in South Carolina, the middle and low country will rule the state. No combination among the white counties can prevent it." He remarked at another time how important a fusion policy was to Charleston because "straight-outism, with its threat and bluster, with its possible disturbances and certain turmoil, is the foe of mercantile security and commercial prosperity" and also, he might have added, of good labor relations on the plantations of the tidewater.

The fusionists' counterparts in Mississippi also derived their essential support from the Black Belt, particularly the western delta counties. They also had considerable strength in Hinds County where the "Jackson clique," headed by Ethelbert Barksdale and Albert G. Brown, was located. Associated with this group were John W. C. Watson, Amos Johnston, L. Q. C. Lamar, former Governor Charles Clark, and Robert Lowry, a future governor. These men had been the guiding force behind the party since at least the fusion campaign of Louis Dent in 1869 and their sway was being contested by a white-line faction whose most prominent and vociferous leaders were, for the most part, newspaper editors, such as William McCardle of Vicksburg, Arthur J. Frantz of Brandon, C. L. Worthington of Columbus, and Alexander Horn of Meridian. Former governors William L. Sharkey and Benjamin G. Humphreys were the leading politicians involved. Although the white-liners developed some support in the black counties, such as those containing Vicksburg and Meridian, their mainstay was in the northeastern and southern sections that were predominantly white.

Unlike their equivalents in Alabama and Louisiana, the fusionists in Mississippi and South Carolina were more firmly established within the party, and they were even able to develop a separate organizational apparatus with which they could wage their contest with the white-liners. This was the Taxpayers' Union, an institution that had appeared earlier in Reconstruction—in Texas and South Carolina during 1871 to be precise— but which, in the hands of the fusionists of 1874 and 1875, became the centerpiece of their effort to outflank the straight-outs. Through the Taxpayers' Union, they could harness the widespread discontent with the burden of taxation and thereby broaden and strengthen the base of their appeal. In the first place, the union provided the organizational structure that had

been so lacking under the New Departure that the Democratic-Conservatives had never run an independent statewide campaign. This intent was
made evident by the remarks of James B. Kershaw, a leading South Carolina
fusionist, who explained that "[James] Chesnut and his committee, at the
first, expected that our tax union would be the Conservative machinery for
political action."

The Taxpayers' Union scheme offered two other benefits to the fusionists. Because aggrieved taxpayers were overwhelmingly white, the tax
issue would appeal to white voters through their pocketbooks rather than
on the grounds of race. Thus, the fusionists could hope to cut into the
white support that the white-liners were trying to win over through the
newly formed rifle clubs and White Leagues. Moreover, because taxation
was a nonpartisan issue, discontented Republicans could be expected to
join and, indeed, the taxpayers' protest in Mississippi was graced by such
eminent Republicans as Henry Musgrove and Joshua Morris, who had been
state auditor and attorney-general, respectively, under Alcorn and Powers.
A final advantage provided by the Taxpayers' Union was that it enabled
the fusionists to present themselves as men who were above party, reformers interested in good government rather than mere partisans seeking
political gain. As Francis Dawson saw it, "The necessity of checking corruption and procuring honest officials is paramount to all questions of party
politics or affiliation." Consequently, "The only party needed in this state
is the taxpayers' party, arrayed in solid opposition to the horde of non-
taxpayers." This kind of approach also accorded with the New Departurists'
distaste for rigid partisanship and their fear about its impact on their state's
political life. Indeed, they often hoped that party might be eliminated, a
sentiment proclaimed publicly by the South Carolina Taxpayers' Convention of 1874 when it predicted that the movement would ultimately "sweep
away party lines and destroy the trade of hungry political adventurers."
In their critique of party, the southern fusionists were expressing attitudes
similar to the liberal reformers and mugwumps of the 1870s and 1880s in
the North.

The Taxpayers' Unions were therefore to operate both as a nonpartisan
pressure group demanding retrenchment and reduced taxation from the
incumbent Republicans and as the organizational structure for the fusionists'
campaign to keep their party from falling into the hands of the white-liners.
Despite the sophistication of the fusionists' approach, it nevertheless went
down to defeat. As in the Republican party, the center collapsed, eliminating
the possibility that a competitive two-party system might develop which
was unhampered by racial exclusiveness and partisan rigidity. For, while
the fusionists were holding taxpayers' conventions and encouraging the
reform Republicans, even negotiating with them, their intraparty opponents
were organizing with immense success at the grass-roots and demonstrating
how effective race was in arousing whites who were their party's essential
constituency. This was particularly true in Mississippi where the white-
liners' success in getting control of Warren County, with its black majority,
in 1874 enabled them to seize the initiative and even go so far as to usurp

the jurisdiction of the party's executive committee and call a state convention for January 1875. Thrown on the defensive, the fusionists tried to repulse this frontal attack by arguing that there was no need for a state convention in a year when there were no statewide elections. To outflank the white-liners, a committee of the party's legislators called a meeting in May to discuss the propriety of a state convention and, when it met, managed to defeat proposals to make race the issue of the canvass and to change the party's name to just Democratic. Nevertheless, with the defeat of Ames's efforts at retrenchment during the legislative session, the fusionists' strategy of reform and realignment was dealt a fatal blow. By August, the fusionist-controlled state executive committee had to capitulate and summon a convention, which their opponents would almost certainly control.

Although they failed to prevent a convention, the fusionists fought hard to restrain the white-liners once it met. They made sure that the platform was conciliatory, especially on suffrage, education, and civil rights, and they prevented the party from adopting the white-line as a mandatory statewide policy. Indeed, one of their most prominent leaders, Congressman L. Q. C. Lamar, claimed immediately afterwards that he had "just emerged from a struggle to keep our people from a race conflict," which would have resulted in "conflicts and race passions and collisions with the Federal power." But these remarks were either disingenuous or else an exaggeration of the fusionist influence. More accurate was Adelbert Ames's analysis, "The true sentiment of the assembly was 'color line' though the platform said nothing about it. The understanding evidently is that each locality can act as it chooses. But the state convention shall put out a platform for Northern consumption." Or, as the Republican Jackson *Pilot* described it most succinctly, "While the platform is peace, the canvass will be war."

The denouement of the fusionist endeavor in South Carolina followed a similar pattern. Nevertheless, until mid-December 1875, the collaboration between the cooperationists and Chamberlain was proceeding sufficiently smoothly that the straight-outs were kept at bay. Then, on 15 December, "Black Thursday" as it was to be called, the Republican leadership in the assembly deliberately broke with Chamberlain. The breach was made through the rejection of Chamberlain's nominees for trial justice and the selection instead of the notorious former governor, Frank Moses, and the equally controversial William Whipper.

Lamenting this "horrible disaster," Chamberlain predicted that the straight-outs would seize on the event as conclusive evidence that the Republican party was unreliable as an ally and incapable of reform. Dawson, too, was distressed: "Year after year we have argued and fought to prevent such an issue as this. We still hope and pray that extreme measures may not be necessary." To this end, the cooperationists focused on reorganizing and tightening the party's electoral machinery, while stopping short of making separate nominations. This goal was accomplished at the first state convention in May when it adjourned with a course of action mapped out but with no ticket selected. The second tactic was to delay the nominating convention until after the Republicans had held theirs and, with luck, had chosen Chamberlain. The Republican could then be presented as a ready-made moderate nominee whose endorsement by the Democratic-Conservatives would salvage fusion and cooperation.

The straight-outs, however, captured the new state executive committee, thus enabling its incoming chairman, Alexander C. Haskell, who was an exponent of the white-line strategy of M. C. Butler and Martin Gary, to call a convention. To compound his success, Haskell had it meet on 15 August before the Republican convention and in Columbia, which was located in the Piedmont where the straight-outs were strong, rather than in Charleston. Furthermore, a delegate count by the *News and Courier* indicated that 89 out of 158 favored straight-out Democratic nominations. But the cooperationists were still not daunted, and they hoped to force an adjournment without nominations. When that failed, however, they tried to defeat the straight-outs' gubernatorial choice, Wade Hampton, whom many regarded as insufficiently cautious and responsible. So vigorous was their opposition that the convention was compelled to meet in secret session and to forego a secret ballot to select him. Even then, the fusionists' resistance was not over, for, as in Mississippi, they required that the party's platform be conciliatory in tone and uphold the civil rights and suffrage protections introduced by Reconstruction.

All the same, these concessions did not gainsay the fact that the cooperationists had been defeated. One of them, Richardson Miles of Charleston, confirmed this estimation when he observed that "the minority have yielded their views to the majority." A cooperationist himself, Miles had "preferred the plan which altho slower, promised to be more certain and lasting." Nevertheless, he conceded the issue by deciding: "Any policy however wanting in wisdom, foresight and breadth of view—but which commends itself to the instincts and feelings of the people—and which will *unite* them—and enlist their enthusiasm and earnest effort; is better for us than the wisest policy which statesmanship can suggest, but which the people are unwilling to accept, or would be lukewarm in carrying out."

This change of direction meant that the party was now embarking upon a line of policy entirely at odds with the priorities it had espoused under the New Departure and fusion. As a result, the campaigns that ensued in South Carolina as well as in Mississippi and in Alabama were quite different from the kind of canvass that had been characteristic of the earlier phase. They were highly organized and carefully coordinated operations. The campaign was under the exclusive control of the party chairman (Walter Bragg in Alabama, James Z. George in Mississippi, and Alexander Haskell in South Carolina), while the rifle clubs and White Leagues were the instrumentalities for stirring up and organizing the voters at the grass roots. In this way, the party's previous inability to discipline and mobilize its supporters was substantially counteracted. Furthermore, to arouse their constituents from their apathy and inertia, race was introduced as the focal point, the essence, of the canvass. Not only was race the identifying characteristic and symbol of the Democratic party, but, with party approval, racial violence was unleashed to satisfy the frustrations of whites and to intimidate blacks. Whereas during the Klan phase, violence had, for the most part, been covert, sporadic and uncoordinated, in the white supremacy campaigns, it was systematic and focused. First, the rifle clubs organized torchlight parades through the country towns to overawe local blacks. In addition, a racial affray, culminating in a massacre of blacks such as occurred at Clinton, Mississippi, and at Hamburg, South Carolina, was instigated at the outset of the campaign to set its tone and reveal its terrible possibilities. Finally, terroristic violence was inflicted on several targeted counties in the black belt, notably Greene, Choctaw, and Sumter in Alabama and Yazoo and "all the large Republican counties" in Mississippi, so as to illustrate white determination and power in the strongholds of black voting.

By means of campaigns like these, the last bastions of Republican rule were eliminated from the Deep South. Their success can be explained by their ability to arouse and mobilize the party's electoral resources in a way that the New Departure had utterly failed to do. The appeal to voters on the basis of old party loyalties and racial identities had resonated so strongly that the gains from so risky a course far outweighed its dangers. The benefit to be won from the affirmation of partisan, racial, and even sectional exclusiveness rather than from its denial was the great discovery that the Democratic-Conservatives made between 1874 and 1876. What it meant was that a profound change in the way southern politics was conducted occurred in those years, as the straight-outs uncovered and then fanned into flames the pervasive and immutable elements of southern political culture.

Since this decisive change occurred in the process of a struggle for ascendency within the Democratic party, what were its implications for the party's future? Because they were observing this shift in their opponents' demeanor at close quarters, Republicans were quick to offer explanations of what was involved. Mississippi's leading Republican newspaper, the *Pilot,* noted, "The fiery element is again at work in the State—the same leaders are again on the stump! Look at Lamar—Singleton—Hooker—Featherston, and others with all the great host of great and small sensation editors. They duped the people before. Will they do it again?" From Alabama, "One Who Knows" answered that question resoundingly in the affirmative, claiming that the secessionists "have in truth, so far as the leadership of the party is concerned, usurped the banner of the old Democratic party. Like the parasite, they have smothered the old truth upon which it has grown." Because of this, George Houston, the well-known Unionist and Douglas Democrat from north Alabama, was really a foil behind which the secessionists were reinstalling themselves in control of the party. This analysis of the transfer of power within the Democratic party in Alabama was reiterated in the Republican party's official campaign address. Pointing to a meeting in Blount Springs on 27 August at which James L. Pugh, William E. Clarke, John T. Morgan, and John W. A. Sanford were featured speakers, the address noted that these men were "the ablest and most prominent advocates of secession in 1861," and they now "give tone and spirit, purpose and direction to the democratic party of Alabama in 1874, as essentially as they did in 1861. States rights and centralization is their rallying cry, just as it was at that period." The New York *Herald* drew a precise connection between the two campaigns, asserting that the straight-outs in South Carolina were the Rhett wing of the party. Governor Chamberlain's paper, the Columbia *Union-Herald,* concurred, observing that "men having a thorough knowledge of the masses" were at the head of the straight-out movement, for, after all, "They had played upon them before and they knew what they could do."

Although the parallels with the frenzied campaigns of the secession crisis often prompted observers to draw connections between the politicians involved in both, none went as far as Alexander White, the Republican congressman from Alabama's First District, in establishing the identity of the personnel involved on each occasion. In a speech to the U.S. House of Representatives on 4 February 1875, White provided specific instances showing an increasing secessionist influence in the state's Democratic party. In the organization of the victorious Democrats, he discovered that "of the executive committee of the Democratic party in Alabama, consisting of twenty-one members, there are none who were not active and conspicuous secessionists in 1861, several of them members of the secession convention; eight others equally pronounced as belonging to the extreme states-rights school but not old enough to have been conspicuous in 1861; while all over the State the old secession leaders entered into the canvass of last fall with a unanimity and ardor not approximated since the war, and not equaled by the fiery contest of 1860." The trend that Alex White was documenting was really not all that surprising. After all, the meaning of the change in strategy was that a conciliatory, northern orientation had given way to a state-centered approach, while the Democratic-Conservatives' unequivocal identification with the Democracy reestablished the credentials of the party of secession and the politicians whose careers had been closely linked with it. Accordingly, the reappearance on the political stage of men who had in the past been prominent Democrats and secessionists accompanied the introduction and successful implementation of the straight-out campaigns. . . .

An abrupt change in the direction of Democratic politics had been ushered in with the shift to straight-outism as an organizational device and to white supremacy as a partisan issue. Sharply dramatized by the presence of, as well as the approval accorded to, the previously overlooked secessionists, this cleavage was characterized by three distinct features. Of these, two had been noted by Alexander White in his speech in Congress on 4 February 1875. The first was the apparent resurgence of the secessionists. Yet, despite the attention that White and others gave to this development, its meaning and implication was not so obvious as it seemed. White had graphically charted the secessionists' rise, but that occurrence in itself had little political significance since secession was no longer under consideration in the mid-70s. Furthermore, it was not a position that currently differentiated the factions and elements in the Democratic party. In other words, secession was no longer a live issue. Instead, what the secessionist resurgence signified was a change of tone and policy in the party. In explaining the meaning behind the return of the secessionists, White noted, "Now, as in 1861, the violent and extreme lead the way, others follow in the whirl of excitement." Conciliation was being replaced with confrontation as, under the pressure of the insurgents, the Democracy was setting aside the priorities that had governed it under the New Departure. Consequently, politicians whose current inclinations and past record suggested they were moderate and not rigidly partisan were no longer so necessary or so prominent, and, of course, the use of racial violence as an organized political instrument in the Redemption campaigns could not but help to stimulate the elevation of extreme men.

A second tendency stressed by Alexander White was the reintroduction into political discourse of the traditional principles and basic tenets of the Democracy. Drawing their inspiration and force from the idea of local autonomy and the right of particular political and social entities to pursue their own course without restraint or hindrance, Democratic dogma was reactivated by the rhetorical appeal of the straight-outers for home rule and self-determination. This facet of the straight-out movement Alexander White noticed with a good deal of alarm. "The danger to our country," he argued, "is not in centralization, but in decentralization," and, he continued, "The illusion of State rights which has been so fatal to our country . . . is now raising itself under the euphonious title of 'home rule', in form more specious and dimensions more formidable than when it shook the nation to its center with the convulsions of war." White was worried by this development, but Democrats who had been lamenting the betrayal of principle and the departure from basic party doctrine which had taken place since the war rejoiced that a return to the living fundamentals of the party was now possible. In the editorial columns of the Mobile *Register,* John Forsyth, an old-line Democrat who had supported Douglas in 1860, began to proclaim the Democratic credo of "Home Rule, Free Trade, and Hard Money" and to accompany this with a demand for its implementation. Evaluating the meaning of the victory of 1874 in his state, Forsyth offered a classic restatement of Democratic doctrine: "That revolution is farther-reaching than mere disgust at local outrages. It reaches to the foundations of the political economy and of government itself. It means that the reserved rights of the States, the Constitutional rights of home rule, shall be more scrupulously guarded. It means that monopolies shall give way to the natural law of open harbors and free trade. It means that business shall revive and public confidence be restored by a return to a gold basis at the very earliest moment."

Although the hard money element in Forsyth's trinity of Democratic principles would not produce universal assent among the party's politicians in the 1870s, home rule and free trade did. Party policy therefore reflected this in its emphasis, first, on curbing government intervention in the private sector and attacking the monopolies it fostered and, second, on restricting the size and expense of government. Democratic doctrines permeated the party in the mid-70s, though few state organizations went as far as the Texas convention in 1875 which avowed that Jefferson's inaugural and Jackson's farewell address together comprised its articles of faith and its guide for political action. The decision to force the issue with the Republicans and abandon fusion and conciliation had resulted in an agreement to call the Democratic-Conservative party by its generic name of Democratic and it had also actually promoted and legitimized all the essential elements of the party's constituency, of its identity, and of its principles and beliefs. Since they referred to themselves as Democrats and strove to draw sharply the line between the two parties, the Democrats were reaching back beyond the eclectic trimming of latter days to the party's roots and essentials. It was there that they were discovering the slogans and philosophy that would shape their future approach to politics.

The third characteristic of the Democrats' change of direction was not referred to directly by White but it was obvious enough. The party had decided to call itself Democratic rather than Conservative partly, no doubt, because of pressure from former Democrats. But, once the breach had occurred, there was no reason why politicians whose past allegiance had been to the Democrats should feel constrained, either by pressure within the party or by their own political instincts, to remain in the shadows. The stigma of being an old-line Democrat or even a secessionist was no longer so intense. As a result, known Democrats, who previously had been denied preferment or nomination, reentered the party's affairs and ran successfully for office. A couple of examples will suffice to demonstrate this. In Alabama, the 1874 state convention produced a ticket that was so solidly Democratic that U.S. Senator Francis W. Sykes implored the gathering to make some provision for a Whig. If this were not done, he feared that Whig support would be lost to the party in the election. The result was that Robert S. Ligon, a well-known Whig, was nominated for lieutenant governor. Confirmation of this was provided by the *Alabama State Journal,* which observed: "We noticed among the delegates nearly, if not all, the old political hacks of the Democratic party, who have been kept in the background for some time by the younger and more tolerant members of the party; but the race issue has been a sweet morsel, which they have rolled under their tongues until they have again succeeded in being brought to the front." . . .

The repudiation by the Democrats of their policies of electoral fusion and the New Departure marked a turning point in postwar southern politics. When the Republicans had failed to secure control of the political center by substantially increasing their white vote, their opponents accordingly discarded the parallel approach they had been pursuing. The realignment and reorganization of the parties which had been so widely anticipated was evidently not going to occur. Instead, both parties regrouped and consolidated around their loyal constituents and their original identities, a development that, as it happened, was also under way in the rest of the nation in the mid-1870s. In the South, the reaffirmation of party identity resulted in the introduction of race as the primary characteristic distinguishing the

Democrats from the Republicans. This politicization of race offered further evidence of how decisive was the shift in the region's political life after about 1873. . . .

↘ *F U R T H E R   R E A D I N G*

M. Les Benedict, "Southern Democrats in the Crisis of 1876–1877," *Journal of Southern History* 46 (1980), 489–524

William Gillette, *Retreat from Reconstruction, 1869–1879* (1979)

Morton Keller, *Affairs of State: Public Life in Late Nineteenth-Century America* (1977)

William S. McFeely, *Grant: A Biography* (1981)

James T. Moore, "Redeemers Reconsidered: Change and Continuity in the Democratic South, 1877–1900," *Journal of Southern History* 64 (1978), 357–378

Otto H. Olsen, "The Ku Klux Klan: A Story of Reconstruction Politics and Propaganda," *North Carolina Historical Review* 39 (1962), 340–362

————, ed., *Reconstruction and Redemption in the South* (1980)

Michael Perman, *Emancipation and Reconstruction, 1862–1879* (1987)

George C. Rable, *But There Was No Peace: Violence and Reconstruction* (1984)

Terry L. Seip, *The South Returns to Congress: Men, Economic Measures, and Intersectional Relationships, 1868–1879* (1983)

J. Mills Thornton, III, "Fiscal Policy and the Failure of Reconstruction in the Lower South," in J. Morgan Kousser and James M. McPherson, eds., *Region, Race, and Reconstruction* (1982), 349–394

Allen W. Trelease, *White Terror: The Ku Klux Conspiracy and Reconstruction* (1971)

Jonathan Wiener, *Social Origins of the New South: Alabama, 1860–1885* (1978)

C. Vann Woodward, *Origins of the New South, 1877–1913* (1951)

————, *Reunion and Reaction: The Compromise of 1877 and the End of Reconstruction* (1951)

CHAPTER
15

Economic Developments
After the Civil War

What impact did the Civil War have on the nation's economic growth? At first
glance, the answer seems obvious. By removing slavery, which was widely assumed to have been an obstacle to economic growth in the South as well as the
nation as a whole, the Civil War had unclogged America's economic arteries.
And indeed, judging by the transformed American economy at the turn of the
century—about forty years later—the beneficial consequences appear overwhelming. But were those developments directly attributable to the war itself, or did
they emerge so much later that other explanations besides the Civil War have to
be considered? It has been argued that, even in the short run, the Civil War
may not have stimulated economic growth, since it diverted valuable capital and
resources into war production, consumed massive amounts of labor and assets,
and then laid waste to the entire southern economy. Rather than a stimulus, it
could be argued that the war had little effect upon economic expansion.

More recently, historians have focused on some rather different aspects of the
war's relation to economic change. One of these is government economic policy.
Because of the war, the role of government, especially at the federal level,
changed quite substantially. In mobilizing resources for the war effort, Washington created institutions and took initiatives that recast the economic environment.
Its activism in implementing a protective tariff, promoting railroad building, and
controlling the currency and banking were especially noticeable. Surprisingly,
however, this breakthrough was not developed and expanded. Instead, the postwar years witnessed a reduction of governmental intervention and an attempt to
return to the pre-war status quo.

Similarly mixed were the effects of the changes in the second area to which
historians have turned their attention—the southern economy after the abolition
of slavery. In many respects, emancipation marked a decisive transition in the
nature of labor and capital in the South. At the same time, however, the southern labor system remained coercive and backward as a result of the substitution
of sharecropping for slavery, while the region's economy as a whole was not so
transformed that the much-vaunted "New South" began to emerge.

Despite these qualifications, the southern economy and the economic role of *government were, in fact, different after the war. How different is the issue that warrants investigation.*

⳹ D O C U M E N T S

The documents that follow examine economic changes after the Civil War as well as attitudes toward those changes. The first selection consists of several statistical tables on the output of the American economy in the Civil War era. A speech by Representative William D. ("Pig Iron") Kelley of Pennsylvania, a leading protectionist, is reprinted as the second document. A staunch defense of the tariff, it was delivered on February 4, 1869, in response to the official report of David A. Wells, Special Commissioner of the Revenue and a prominent free-trader. The third selection is a brief observation about governmental activism from *The Science of Wealth: A Manual of Political Economy* (1869) by Amasa Walker, one of the most distinguished economists of the era and an uncompromising advocate of laissez-faire. The fourth selection, by another well-known free-trader and anti-interventionist, the sociologist William Graham Sumner, is drawn from his *Lectures on the History of Protectionism in the United States* (1886).

The fifth selection, taken from Edward King's book *The Great South* (1875), describes the labor system that King observed operating on the plantations in the Natchez District during his extensive tour of the South. The sixth document is the ecstatic "New South" speech given to the New England Society of New York on December 21, 1886, by Henry W. Grady, the Atlanta editor and leading propagandist for a transformed South. Finally, in the seventh document, D. Augustus Straker, a prominent African-American lawyer and activist in the 1880s, evaluates the "New South." Straker stresses the fatal flaws that offset the economic achievements of the postwar South. The extract is from his *The New South Investigated* (1888).

Statistics on the U.S. Economy After the War

Table 1 U.S. Commodity Output, Population, and Gainful Workers in Commodity Production, Quinquennial, 1839–1859 and 1869–1899

YEAR OR END OF DECADE	OUTPUT	POPULATION	OUTPUT PER CAPITA	GAINFUL WORKERS	OUTPUT PER WORKER
		ABSOLUTE FIGURES			
	(MILL.)	(THOUS.)		(THOUS.)	
1839	$ 1,094	17,120	$ 64	4,484	$244
1844	1,374	20,182	68		
1849	1,657	23,261	71	6,190	268
1854	2,317	27,386	85		
1859	2,686	31,513	85	8,140	330
1869	} 3,271	39,905	82	{ 9,695	337
1869				9,635	339
1874	} 4,297	45,073	95		
1879	5,304	50,262	105	12,850	413
1884	7,300	56,658	129		
1889	8,659	63,056	137	16,570	523
1894	10,258	69,580	147		
1899	11,751	76,094	154	19,512	602
	DECENNIAL RATES OF CHANGE (PERCENT)				
1849	52	36	11	38	10
1854	69	36	24		
1859	62	36	20	32	23
1869	23	27	−4	19	2
1874					
1879	62	26	29	33	22
1884	70	26	35		
1889	63	25	30	29	27
1894	41	23	15		
1899	36	21	13	18	15
Averages:					
1839–99	49	28	16	28	16
1839–59	57	36	16	35	16
1869–99	54	24	24	27	21

Source: Robert E. Gallman, "Commodity Output 1839–1899," *Trends in the American Economy in the Nineteenth Century*, p. 16.

Table 2 Industrial Production, 1850–1880

YEAR	PIG IRON (1,000 SHORT TONS)*	RAILS PRODUCED (1,000 LONG TONS)*	STEEL INGOTS AND CASTINGS (1,000 LONG TONS)	RAW COTTON CONSUMED (1,000 BALES)	SUGAR REFINED (MILLIONS OF LBS.)	WHEAT FLOUR MILLED (MILLIONS OF BBLS.)*
1850	631	—	—	—	—	—
1851	—	—	—	—	—	—
1852	560	—	—	—	—	—
1853	—	—	—	—	—	—
1854	736	—	—	—	—	—
1855	784	—	—	—	—	—
1856	883	—	—	—	—	—
1857	798	—	—	—	—	—
1858	705	—	—	—	—	—
1859	841	—	—	—	—	—
1860	920	183	—	845	788	39.8
1861	732	170	—	842	978	41.6
1862	788	191	—	369	590	42.4
1863	948	246	—	287	607	42.5
1864	1,136	299	—	220	565	42.4
1865	932	318	—	344	733	42.5
1866	1,350	385	—	615	886	42.8
1867	1,462	413	19.6	715	841	44.3
1868	1,603	452	26.8	844	1,149	44.9
1869	1,917	530	31.3	860	1,254	46.8
1870	1,865	554	68.8	797	1,196	47.9
1871	1,912	693	73.2	1,027	1,413	49.0
1872	2,855	893	143.0	1,147	1,454	49.2
1873	2,868	795	198.8	1,116	1,526	51.3
1874	2,689	651	215.7	1,213	1,638	53.6
1875	2,267	708	389.8	1,098	1,642	54.4
1876	2,093	785	533.2	1,256	1,583	56.1
1877	2,315	683	569.6	1,314	1,698	56.5
1878	2,577	788	732.0	1,459	1,778	59.8
1879	3,071	994	935.3	1,457	1,709	61.9
1880	4,295	1,305	1,247.3	1,501	1,988	64.3

Source: *Historical Statistics of the United States Colonial Times to 1957*, pp. 365–366, 415, 416–417

* 1 long ton = 2,240 pounds; 1 short ton = 2,000 pounds; bbls. = barrels

Table 3 Federal Expenditures for Rivers and Harbors: 1850–1880 Public Land Grants by the United States to Aid in the Construction of Railroads, Wagon Roads, Canals, 1823–1871

YEAR	FEDERAL EXPENDITURES FOR RIVERS, ETC. (THOUSANDS OF DOLLARS)	LAND GRANTS (IN THOUSANDS OF ACRES)			
		TOTAL	RAILROADS	WAGON ROADS	CANALS
1850	42	—	—	—	—
1851	70	3,752	3,752	—	—
1852	40	1,773	1,773	—	—
1853	489	3,379	2,629	—	750
1854	937	—	—	—	—
1855	791	—	—	—	—
1856	161	14,085	14,085	—	—
1857	268	6,689	6,689	—	—
1858	427	—	—	—	—
1859	290	—	—	—	—
1860	228	—	—	—	—
1861	172	—	—	—	—
1862	37	—	—	—	—
1863	65	31,401	30,877	524	—
1864	102	2,349	2,349	—	—
1865	305	42,794	41,452	941	401
1866	295	200	—	—	200
1867	1,217	25,173	23,535	1,538	100
1868	3,457	—	—	—	—
1869	3,545	105	—	105	—
1870	3,528	129	129	—	—
1871	4,421	3,253	3,253	—	—
1872	4,962	—	—	—	—
1873	6,312				
1874	5,704				
1875	6,434				
1876	5,736				
1877	4,655				
1878	3,791				
1879	8,267				
1880	8,080				

Note: Figures include only the area of lands for which title passed to the grantee states and corporations. For the series presented, the areas shown in the instruments of title which were issued for each grant over the years were totaled and shown as of the fiscal year in which the grant was originally enacted, even though in certain instances grants were revived at a later date after the expiration of statutory time limits, while others were enlarged by subsequent legislation.
Source: *Historical Statistics of the U.S. Colonial Times to 1957*, pp. 233, 239, 455.

Representative William D. "Pig Iron" Kelley of Pennsylvania Endorses the Wartime Tariff, February 1869

. . . In my judgment, the first duty of an American statesman is to watch and guard the rights of the laboring classes of the country. They produce its wealth, they fight its battles, and in their hands is its destiny; for at every election they cast a majority of the ballots, and upon their intelligence, integrity, and manly independence rest the welfare of the country. To make Republican government an enduring success, we must guard the productions of our laborers against competition with those of the ill-paid and oppressed laborers of Europe, so that each head of a family may by the wages he can earn maintain a home, and be able to support his children during the years required to give them the advantages of our common school system. If the Commissioner's report proves anything to those who are able to detect its fallacies, and test the fulness and accuracy of its comparative tables, it is that under the influence of the cheap and abundant currency we now have, and the system of protection which the war forced us to adopt, the American people are consuming more of the necessaries and comforts of life than they were ever before able to consume; are producing more of what they consume than ever before, and in spite of the taxes imposed by the national debt and other incidents of the war, are coming to be commercially independent of other nations. Yes, sir, under the influence of a tariff which, though it levies duties on raw materials and commodities which we do not and cannot produce, is still in a measure protective, and an adequate amount of currency, we are slowly emerging from our commercial dependence upon England, as is shown by the fact that our imports have steadily diminished since 1865. Thus in 1866, 1867, and 1868, respectively, the amounts of foreign merchandise imported into the country were as follows:

Year ending 30th of June, 1866	$423,470,646
Year ending 30th of June, 1867	374,943,502
Year ending 30th of June, 1868	344,873,433

Thus it appears that notwithstanding the facts that the increase of our wealth is unparalleled, and the natural increase of our population is very rapid, and that "from the 1st of July, 1865, to the 1st of December, 1868, about one million natives of foreign countries have sought a permanent home in the United States," our purchases of foreign commodities are steadily diminishing. The sapient deduction of the Special Commissioner of the Revenue from these facts is, that we are unable to trade with foreign nations, and that to stimulate foreign trade we must reduce the wages of our laborers, and diminish the amount of currency now profitably employed in the development of our productive power. His theory is that "all commerce is in the nature of barter or exchange," and his complaint is that:

> We have so raised the cost of all domestic products that exchange in kind with all foreign nations is almost impossible. The majority of what foreign nations have to sell us, as already shown, we must or will have. What foreign nations want and we produce, cotton and a few other articles excepted, they can buy elsewhere cheaper. We are, therefore, obliged to pay in no small part for such foreign productions as we need or will have, either in the precious metals or, what is worse, in unduly depreciated promises of national payment.

The Commissioner's exception of "cotton and a few other articles" leaves Hamlet out of the play, and surrenders his whole case, for we can raise enough of the articles he excepts, and of which we have a natural monopoly, to pay for every foreign product "we must or will have."

The beneficent results of free labor in the former slave States are an agreeable surprise to its most sanguine friends. The South is abundantly rich in mineral and agricultural resources, but she is suffering from the want of currency to develop them. Were she adequately supplied with currency, and the season should be a favorable one, her production of cotton, and the few other articles excepted by the Commissioner, would more than double that of 1868, and as other nations must have her cotton, tobacco, rice, and other semi-tropical productions which they cannot procure elsewhere, it seems to me that the true way to stop the flow of precious metals and Government bonds is to stimulate production by protecting the wages of labor and avoiding any contraction of the currency. In support of this view, let me call attention to the fact that we send from eighty to one hundred million dollars abroad annually for sugar. If capitalists will lend the planters of Florida, Louisiana, and Texas the means to cultivate their sugar-fields, they will produce crops that will save a large percentage of this vast sum to the country. . . .

Amasa Walker Denounces Wartime Governmental Intervention, 1874

. . . We have seen, that any expenditure by government, even for necessary purposes, is made at a disadvantage to itself, and is attended by many marked inconveniences and mischiefs to society; and that, so far as consistent, individual enterprise should be substituted. In how strong a light, then, do we see the folly of that scheme of national prosperity which looks to lavish outlay by government for any purpose, whether productive or destructive, of luxury or war! The share of some interested portion of the community may be larger, or come more easily; but the sum of wealth is diminished, and the healthful laws of distribution are disturbed.

Yet, in the recent gigantic warlike operations of the United States, it was a daily experience to hear the accepted teachers of political philosophy gravely pronounce the condition of the country to be most gratifying, loudly congratulating the public on the stimulus given to industry by the outlay of government. Trade was brisk, because the nation was running three thousand millions in debt, to be just so much poorer for centuries. We do not question that the occasion justified the expense; but this was none the less an unfortunate necessity, and the liveliness of business was the most melancholy feature of the national condition. . . .

William Graham Sumner Derides Protectionism, 1886

. . . The system was elaborated as a "temporary" system—as a war measure—like the paper money, and we have been living under it ever since. Too many people find their interest in sustaining it to let it fall without a struggle, on behalf of the great public which elects all the Congressmen, but finds few representatives. The internal taxes, which formed the excuse for a large part of the advance in duties have been gradually abolished, and the whole weight of destructive restraint is left to fall on the industries of the country. Evidently the whole policy was erroneous and false, even from the point of view adopted. In going into a great war, the nation wanted its powers free. It wanted cheapness and abundance then, if ever. It wanted the maximum of revenue according to the most approved methods of obtaining it. It was no time to re-undertake the task of encouraging industries, even if that ever was wise, and I believe that the historian, when he comes to criticise this period in our history, will say that the welfare of a great nation never was so recklessly sacrificed by ignorant empiricism in legislation, nor the patriotism of a great people ever so wantonly abused, as in the tariff legislation of our war. Our position then and since as to tariff and paper money always reminds me of one of the blessings of Jacob: "Issachar is a strong ass, bowed down between two burdens. And he saw that rest was good, and the land that it was pleasant, and bowed his shoulders to bear, and became a servant unto tribute." [quote from the Old Testament] . . .

Our exports have likewise been killed by the inevitable operation of the tariff. We no longer offer a market and cannot attract miscellaneous orders. We cannot export to countries whose products we do not take. We cannot trade directly with South America, the East Indies, or Australia, even for the exports in which we could doubtless compete in those markets, because we refuse to take their products. We cannot make round voyages because no one could tell what would be done with the tariff at home during the interval which must elapse. Our manufacturers having secured the home market, find that the home market becomes a restraint, not an advantage, and they move out of the country in order to get rid of the trammels of the tariff while working for export. Our own sewing machines are provided for foreign nations cheaper than we can get them ourselves. The system has been pushed so far, and its complicated developments have become so interlocked with each other that the protective system is to-day a dead weight on all the production of the country of every kind. Its complete overthrow would be a grand emancipation for manufactures as well as for everything else. . . .

A Northerner Assesses the South's Postwar Labor System, 1875

. . . The region [the Mississippi Delta] which finds its market and gets its supplies in Memphis, Vicksburg, and Natchez, is probably as fair a sample of the cotton-producing portion of the South as any other, and I found in it all the ills and all the advantages complained of or claimed elsewhere. Imagine a farming country which depends absolutely for its food on the West and North-west; where every barrel of flour which the farmer buys, the bacon which he seems to prefer to the beef and mutton which he might raise on his own lands, the clothes on his back, the shoes on his feet, the very vegetables which the poorest laborer in the Northern agricultural regions grows in his door-yard—everything, in fact,—has been brought hundreds of miles by steamer or by rail, and has passed through the hands of the shipper, the carrier, the wharfmen, the reshipper (if the planter live[s] in a remote section), and the local merchant!

Imagine a people possessed of superior facilities, who might live, as the vulgar saying has it, on the fat of the land, who are yet so dependent that a worm crawling over a few cotton leaves, or the rise of one or two streams, may reduce them to misery and indebtedness from which it will take years to recover! Men who consider themselves poorly paid and badly treated in Northern farming and manufacturing regions live better and have more than do the overseers of huge plantations in this cotton country. If you enter into conversation with people who fare thus poorly, they will tell you that, if they raise vegetables, the "niggers" will steal them; that if times were not so hard, and seasons were not so disastrous, the supply system would work very well; that they cannot organize their labor so as to secure a basis on which to calculate safely; and will finally end by declaring that the South is ruined forever.

These are the opinions of the elders mainly. Younger men, who see the necessity of change and new organization, believe that they must in [the] future cultivate other crops besides cotton; that they must do away with supply-merchants, and try at least to raise what is needed for sustenance. There are, of course, sections where the planter finds it cheapest to obtain his corn and flour from St. Louis; but these are small items. There are a hundred things which he requires, and which are grown as well South as North. Until the South has got capital enough together to localize manufactures, the same thing must be said of all manufactured articles; but why should a needless expenditure be encouraged by the very people whom it injures and endangers?

There are many plans of working large plantations now in vogue, and sometimes the various systems are all in operation on the same tract. The plan of "shares" prevails extensively, the planter taking out the expenses of the crop, and, when it is sold, dividing the net proceeds with the negroes who have produced it. In some cases in the vicinity of Natchez, land is leased to the freedmen on condition that they shall pay so many bales of cotton for the use of so many acres, furnishing their own supplies. Other planters lease the land in the same way, and agree to furnish the supplies also. Still others depend entirely upon the wages system, but of course have to furnish supplies at the outset, deducting the cost from the wages paid hands after the crop is raised. Sometimes the plantation is leased to "squads," as they are called, and the "squad leader" negotiates the advances, giving "liens" on the squad's share of the crop and on the mules and horses they may own. This plan has worked very well and is looked upon favorably.

Under the slave *régime,* the negroes working a large plantation were all quartered at night in a kind of central group of huts, known as the "quarters"; but it has been found an excellent idea to divide up the hundred or five hundred laborers among a number of these little villages, each located on the section of the plantation which they have leased. By this process, commonly known as "segregation of quarters," many desirable results have been accomplished; the negro has been encouraged to devote some attention to his home, and been hindered from the vices engendered by excessive crowding. On some plantations one may find a dozen squads, each working on a different plan, the planters, or land owners, hoping in this way to find out which system will be most advantageous to themselves and most binding on the negro. . . .

I took a ride one morning in this same Concordia parish [on the west bank of the Mississippi River] for the purpose of conversing with the planters, and getting testimony as to the actual condition of the laborers. Concordia was once the garden spot of Louisiana; its aspect was European; the fine roads were bordered with delicious hedges of Cherokee rose; grand trees, moss-hung and fantastic in foliage, grew along the green banks of a lovely lake; every few miles a picturesque grouping of coarsely thatched roofs marked negro "quarters," and near by gleamed the roof of some planter's mansion. In this parish there was no law and but little order— save such as the inhabitants chose to maintain. The negroes whom I met on the road were nearly all armed, most of them carrying a rifle over their shoulders, or balanced on the backs of the mules they were riding. Affrays among the negroes are very common throughout that region; but, unless the provocation has been very great, they rarely kill a white man.

In a trip of perhaps ten miles I passed through several once prosperous plantations, and made special inquiries as to their present condition. Upon one where six hundred bales of cotton were annually produced under slave culture, the average annual yield is now but two hundred and fifty; on another the yearly average had fallen from one thousand to three hundred bales; and on two others which together gave the market fifteen hundred bales every year, now barely six hundred are raised. The planters in this section thought that cotton production had fallen off fully two-thirds. The number of negroes at work on each of these plantations was generally much less than before the war. Then a bale to the acre was realized, now about one bale to three acres is the average. Much of this land is "leased" to the negro at the rate of a bale of cotton weighing four hundred and thirty pounds for each six acres.

The planters there raise a little corn, but are mainly supplied from the West. The inundation was upon them at the epoch of my visit, and they were in momentary expectation of seeing all their year's hopes destroyed. The infamous robberies, also, to which they had been subjected by the Legislature, and the overwhelming taxation, had left them bitterly discouraged. One plantation which I visited, having sixteen hundred acres of cleared land in it, and standing in one of the most fertile sections of the State, was originally valued at one hundred dollars per acre; now it could not be sold for ten dollars. In Madison parish recently a plantation of six hundred improved acres, which originally cost thirty thousand dollars, was offered to a neighboring planter for *seven hundred dollars*. . . .

While there is no doubt that an active, moneyed, and earnest immigration would do much toward building up the southern portion of the Mississippi valley, it is evident that so long as the negro remains in his present ignorance, and both he and the planter rely on other States for their sustenance, and on Providence never to send them rainy days, inundations, or caterpillars, the development of the section will be subject to too serious drawbacks to allow of any considerable progress. All the expedients, the tenant systems, and years of accidental success will not take the place of thorough and diversified culture, and intelligent, contented labor resulting from fair wages for fair work. Nothing but the education of the negro up to the point of ambition, foresight, and a desire to acquire a competence lawfully and laboriously, will ever thoroughly develop the Lower Mississippi valley. As the negro is certainly to inhabit it for many years at least, if not forever, how shall he learn the much-needed lesson?

On the other hand, the whites need to be converted to a sense of the dignity of labor, to learn to treat the laboring man with proper consideration, to create in him an intelligent ambition by giving him education. Something besides an introduction to political liberties and responsibilities is needed to make the negro a moral and worthy citizen. He is struggling slowly and not very surely out of a lax and barbarously immoral condition. The weight of nearly two centuries of slavery is upon his back. He needs more help and counsel. An old master will tell you that he can discover who of his employés has been a slave, "for the slave," he says, "cannot look you in the eye without flinching." . . .

Henry W. Grady Enthuses over the "New South," December 1886

. . . But have we kept faith with you? In the fullest sense, yes. When Lee surrendered—I don't say when Johnson [*sic*] surrendered, because I understand he still alludes to the time when he met General Sherman last as the time when he determined to abandon any further prosecution of the struggle—when Lee surrendered, I say, and Johnson [*sic*] quit, the South became, and has since been, loyal to this Union. We fought hard enough to know that we were whipped, and in perfect frankness accept as final the arbitrament of the sword to which we had appealed. The South found her jewel in the toad's head of defeat. The shackles that had held her in narrow limitations fell forever when the shackles of the negro slave were broken. Under the old régime the negroes were slaves to the South; the South was a slave to the system. The old plantation, with its simple police regulations and feudal habit, was the only type possible under slavery. Thus was gathered in the hands of a splendid and chivalric oligarchy the substance that should have been diffused among the people, as the rich blood, under certain artificial conditions, is gathered at the heart, filling that with affluent rapture but leaving the body chill and colorless.

The old South rested everything on slavery and agriculture, unconscious that these could neither give nor maintain healthy growth. The new South

presents a perfect democracy, the oligarchs leading in the popular movement—a social system compact and closely knitted, less splendid on the
surface, but stronger at the core—a hundred farms for every plantation,
fifty homes for every palace—and a diversified industry that meets the
complex need of this complex age.

The new South is enamored of her new work. Her soul is stirred with
the breath of a new life. The light of a grander day is falling fair on her
face. She is thrilling with the consciousness of growing power and prosperity. As she stands upright, full-statured and equal among the people of
the earth, breathing the keen air and looking out upon the expanded horizon,
she understands that her emancipation came because through the inscru-
table wisdom of God her honest purpose was crossed, and her brave armies
were beaten. . . .

A Leading African-American Unmasks the "New South," 1888

The New South

. . . The South today has, amid all its troubles, political and otherwise,
made great advancement in industry, education and commerce. Our land
owners are now ready and willing to utilize their lands and not let them
lie uncultivated. Our farmers no longer confine themselves to the growing
of cotton only, but are engaged in the more varied industry of planting
corn and rice. This latter article is cultivated in South Carolina to a degree
of almost perfection, as all those who visited the late Cotton Exposition,
held at New Orleans, can testify, if they saw it. Manufactories begin to
dot the South in all of its principal cities and towns. Who that has visited
the cities of Augusta, Atlanta, Savannah and Macon, in Georgia; Charleston, Greenville and Columbia, in South Carolina; Selena, Montgomery,
Birmingham and Anniston, in Alabama; the City of New Orleans; Jacksonville, in Florida; and other cities of the South, can fail to discover the
great advancement in the industry of the South in the past twenty years.
The hum of the spinning wheel, and the noise of the manufactories' whistles
are now heard in every principal city in the South today, and the ring of
the anvil follows the church bell. The spirit of industry has taken hold of
our water-power and our mineral resources, and has utilized them as far
as the capital of the South will admit. Along our canals are being built
numerous factories, and the cotton which we now grow is no longer entirely
sent to foreign parts for manufacture, but is manufactured on the spot at
Graniteville, Greenville, Columbia, Charleston, Atlanta, Savannah and Augusta. This shows the need for a protective tariff for the South. From the
bowels of the earth we now dig iron, coal, gold and other minerals. Our
industries are more varied than is generally known. We not only manufacture cotton, but we turn the cotton seed into oil. We have successfully
cultivated the tea plant. The tea farm is now reckoned among the industrial

pursuits of South Carolina. Our mills are numerous. We have the paper-mill, the saw-mill, the grist-mill, moulding our future alongside of other industries. Our railroads also show the advancement of the South. The old iron rail is now supplanted by the modern steel rail, and the dog-kennel depot is supplanted in many places by the beautiful artistic building of modern days. We have the improved air-brake; we run with greater speed. I remember when, not more than ten years ago, it took twelve hours from Charleston to Columbia, a distance of 130 miles. To-day it is reached by rail in five hours. We even *kill* more people on the railroad than we did before, and then, following in the march of progressive ideas, we have our railroad attorneys to plead as a defense, "contributory negligence or common hazard." . . .

The Social Problem

. . . Is it true that the progress of the South, which I have shown to have taken place, has improved the social condition of the South? Is it true that the Negro of the South, which is known as largely the laboring class, and, therefore, the producing class, has improved in *his* social condition compared with the white class, which is known as largely the capital or non-producing class? Why is it, in plainer terms, that the Negro who was poor at the close of the war when made free, is today yet poor when compared to the white man of the South? You may say that this is the result of the ignorance of the one and the knowledge of the other, but while I do not deny that ignorance and knowledge enter largely into the producing and non-producing quality of material advancement, it has not, and should not, have anything to do with the just relationship between capital and labor and the just wages paid as compensation for adequate labor.

None will deny that the labor in quality required for making cotton in the South is fully adequate to the need of producing the same, and this is seen in the fact that the cotton produced in the South since the war has greatly exceeded the amount produced before the war; and yet the producing power makes no material progress as compared with the non-producing power. I can see no other reason for this, than because capital has been, and still is, unjust to labor in the South as in a degree it is in the North, added to which there has been a greater degree of caste prejudice on account of color and former condition in the South, blocking the avenues to industry and progress. As I have said before, it is not only the political change in the administration which is daily causing thousands of colored farm hands, and even mechanics, to migrate from the South to the West, but it is also caused by unjust wages, wages which do not admit of a bare living, such as 15 cents a day, and $6 or $8 per month. These low wages is carrying out the plan, said to have been suggested by [John C.] Calhoun, for the purpose of "keeping the Negro down." And how is this done in the South? Not only by paying him poor wages and giving him poorer rations, but still further denying him the opportunity for material advancement. A colored man in the South cannot purchase land with the facility of his white brother, not only because of his poor wages as compensation for his services, but because of the general indisposition to sell him land. Since the war, thousands of colored people who have commenced to purchase lands have been unable to do so and have lost what they have already paid, not only because some were defaulters in payment, but because more were the victims of the white man's original design to defraud him by some clause in the mortgage or fee simple deed, which defeated his tenure just at the time when he thought most sure he was the absolute owner. . . .

This system of discrimination between labor and capital, as seen in unjust wages and no protection, is also to be found among the few mechanics who perform operative labor in the South. It is not an unusual thing to see a white and a black mechanic, who although doing the same work, yet receive different wages. Discrimination is introduced even into the precincts of the schoolhouse. A first-class colored teacher never receives the equal salary of a first-class white teacher, a practice which, upon its face, carries with it the purpose of seeking inferior teachers for one class and superior for another. The professional, on account of caste prejudice, is shut out from equal opportunity of securing an equal patronage with his white fellow, because of his color. But added to all this is the further obstruction to social progress, as seen in the closing of the doors of industry, few as they are in the South, to the colored brother because of his color, and shutting them against him in every vocation in life which is not strictly menial. How then can the social condition of the South be other than a dividing and a divergent one between the races? And the question here arises, is the present social condition of the South one of true progress—materially or socially? I unhesitatingly answer, no! The South's progress, socially, is only apparent and shadowy; it is not substantial; it cannot be with a divided and unequal people in condition and opportunity.

The present social condition of the South, as found in its white and black population, arises not so much from the habit of keeping separate these two classes on account of race or color, as by reason of the disparity in conditions and the hindrance to industrial pursuits set up by the same powerful whites against their weaker brethren—the blacks. You may say this is equally so with these two classes in the North, East and West, and yet the social condition is not the same. The principle is not different, but the facts are, and only serve to prove the truth of the principle. In the North, East and West, the largest number is the white class, and the result is in the order of the inverse ratio.

It cannot be denied that the social condition of the South in which it finds itself so far behind the other portions of our country in industry, is owing to the folly of keeping out from engaging in industrial pursuits the class of people largest in numbers in its midst. The folly of trades unions, or the spirit which denies colored persons admission to the workshops in the South, is the chief cause of Southern depression in trade, and despite the progress it has made, is the reason it has not made greater progress. It is evident that if the South could receive into its midst a large amount of capital, and would then open its avenues of industry for the large quantum of labor it possesses, in the large number of colored people in its midst, it would spring into a powerful, rich and more prosperous portion of our country, with magic and alacrity, and would be the garden spot of these United States. . . .

✍ E S S A Y S

The essays in Chapter 15 focus on postwar changes in the economic role of the Federal government and in the southern economy. In the first, Morton Keller of Brandeis University describes the unprecedented governmental activism of the war years and just after, and shows how this change was soon countered. By contrast, the economist Gavin Wright of Stanford University argues that changes in the South's system of land and labor that originally did not seem to be far-reaching were in fact quite decisive in their impact.

The Political Economy of Postwar America

MORTON KELLER

The Civil War left its mark on economic as well as social policymaking. Postwar northern economic policy had two distinctive features: a new readiness to call on government to assist economic development; and a perception of the economy (like the society at large) as a national fusion of harmonious, compatible interests.

But as in other areas of postwar public life, these assumptions were quickly overborne by opposing social realities. The respectability of laissez-faire economic theory, and a pervasive American individualism and localism, worked against any sustained state economic policy. And the underlying clash of interests—sectional, occupational, class, ideological—always present in American life was sharpened by the depression of the 1870s and the growth of American industrialism. By the mid-seventies the postwar hope that an active state might shape a more harmonious economic system was as chimerical as the hope that it might assure a more beneficent and egalitarian social order.

The Active State and the Harmony of Interests

The most influential pre–Civil War critic of laissez-faire was the Philadelphia economist Henry C. Carey, who vigorously championed a protective tariff and a "National school" of political economy. A high tariff, he argued, assured national prosperity and "harmony" among "the various portions of society." The *sauve qui peut* [i.e., laissez-faire] British system of Malthus and Ricardo led only to social conflict and lower class despair. A critic of

Reprinted by permission from *Affairs of State: Public Life in Late Nineteenth Century America,* by Morton Keller, pp. 162–171 and 181–188, Cambridge, Mass.: Harvard University Press, Copyright © 1977 by Morton Keller.

the time decried Carey's "more than German readiness to refer to the co-ordinating power of the state, as a specific for social or economic discords." But that readiness had a special appeal to the generation that fought and won the Civil War.

Philadelphia Republican Congressman William D. Kelley was Carey's leading postwar disciple. Kelley espoused a protective tariff (protective both of industry and wage scales), a mildly inflationary paper currency to stimulate economic growth, a federal eight-hour work law, and government-supported development of the Northwest. He rejected the "iron laws" of wages and labor prevalent in conventional economic thought: "The theory that labor . . . is merely a raw material, and that that nation which pays least for it is wisest and best governed, is inadmissible in a democracy." Kelley derived his views from experience, not theory: "it became apparent to me, not only that Political Economy was not a science, but that it was impossible to frame a system of abstract economic propositions which would be universally applicable and beneficent." Fortunately, "the intimate relations of many . . . students with the industries and people of the country render the scholasticisms of their teachers harmless."

Kelley's perspective was hardly a disinterested one. Like Carey he spoke for Philadelphia manufacturers (and workers) who welcomed tariff protection and the debt-easing power of paper money. But his views were widely shared in postwar America. Horace Greeley's *Political Economy* (1871) attacked free trade, defended government subsidies for internal improvements, and endorsed labor unions. California insurance executive Caspar T. Hopkins and *Alta California* editor John S. Hittell advocated similar policies.

The most important postwar spokesman for a political economy of state intervention and harmonious interests was Francis A. Walker. The son of Amasa Walker, a leading prewar laissez-faire economist, the younger Walker fought in the war and emerged a brigadier general. He entered the federal bureaucracy in 1865, serving as David Ames Wells's assistant in the Bureau of Internal Revenue, and then as chief of the Bureau of Statistics, superintendent of the 1870 and 1880 censuses, and (briefly) as commissioner of Indian affairs. His wartime and postwar experience led him to challenge the reigning economic orthodoxy.

Walker like Kelley took issue with the prevailing theory that locked wages into an iron-bound relationship to national wealth. This he called "a complete justification for the existing order of things respecting wages." He argued that unions and strikes were appropriate devices for workers who sought to attain a greater share of the wealth generated by their labor, especially as technological change increased productivity. Walker thought it proper, too, for the state to guarantee laborers freedom of movement, an education, and decent working conditions. With typical postwar optimism he looked forward to a national future in which entrepreneurs and workingmen shared an ever higher level of national prosperity.

This outlook—in part a continuation of prewar Whig-Republican ideas, in part a product of the special experience of the war—found fertile soil in the boom years after 1865. The economy of the late sixties and early seventies was dominated by "a rise of prices, great prosperity, large profits, high wages, and strikes for higher [wages]; large importations, a railway mania, expanded credits, over-trading, over-building, and high living." The postwar economic boom was sparked by government-supported railroad construction. Trackage more than doubled from 35,085 miles in 1865 to 74,096 miles in 1875. State aid to canal and railroad building had been common in the years after 1815; but corruption and extravagance led to its widespread prohibition before the Civil War. Now once again government fueled the expansion of the American transportation system.

Between 1862 and 1872 a hundred million acres of land from the public domain, and about the same number of dollars in federal bonds and loans, went to the support of railroad construction. The apex of this effort was the "great national enterprise" of the transcontinental lines. The pioneering Union and Central Pacific (chartered in 1862 and 1864), the Northern Pacific (1864), the Atlantic & Pacific (1866), and the Texas & Pacific (1871) sought and usually received federal aid on an unprecedented scale. The Union Pacific was a mixed enterprise, with a congressional charter and public as well as private directors. When in May 1869 the Union Pacific and the Central Pacific met at Promontory, Utah, the event unleashed a flood of rhetoric. It symbolized the reunified republic, it marked "a new chapter in American nationality, in American progress and in American power."

The federally aided transcontinental lines were only the most conspicuous examples of a massive postwar railroad expansion. Counties, cities, towns, and villages throughout the North lavishly subsidized lesser projects. Between 1866 and 1873, twenty-nine state legislatures approved over eight hundred proposals to grant local aid to railroad companies. The three leaders—New York, Illinois, and Missouri—authorized over $70 million worth of aid.

State legislatures (most of them constitutionally prohibited from granting direct subsidies) cooperated by passing local aid bills. Illinois in 1869 gave tax advantages to local units that issued railroad bonds. The euphoria transcended party lines. Democratic Governor Henry Haight of California strongly supported local aid in 1870, and Republican John W. Geary of Pennsylvania declared in his 1867 inaugural: "all public works, among these a liberal and properly restricted general railroad system, . . . should receive the fostering care and most liberal aid of the government."

Assistance most commonly took the form of stock subscriptions by municipalities, paid for through tax-secured bond issues. Company bonds also were underwritten, and at times local authorities made outright gifts to railroad developers. Promoters were quick to capitalize on this open-handedness. The New York & Oswego Railroad meandered over the upstate New York countryside in search of local aid, finally touching (in both senses of the word) some fifty communities with 250 labyrinthine miles of track. The line was finished in 1873, just in time for the financial crisis of that year, and promptly went into bankruptcy.

By 1873 about a thousand state court and twenty Supreme Court decisions upheld state and local railroad aid. Iowa's judiciary, which had attempted to block city railroad bonding during the Civil War and had been countermanded by the state Supreme Court, underwent a "radical change" in 1869 and thereafter freely approved local aid.

Government contributed in other ways to the railroad boom. The Hoosac Tunnel, penetrating the Berkshires to give Boston a direct rail link to the West, was a languishing prewar state project that gained new support after 1865. "The Great Bore"—a label earned both by its five mile length and the interminable public controversy that it generated—was completed in 1872.

Another venture of the time was the Cincinnati Southern Railroad, a wholly public enterprise. Ohio's constitution forbade either state or local aid to railroad companies. But Cincinnati had a compelling need to obtain a direct rail route to the upper South (and ultimately to New Orleans), lest it lose out to its great commercial competitor Louisville. The city's voters in 1868 overwhelmingly approved a proposal that Cincinnati build its own line. The municipality floated some $18 million worth of construction loans over the ensuing decade and built a road that was run by city-appointed trustees. In 1872 Ohio's Boesel Law authorized all minor civil divisions to build, lease, or operate their own railroads. Before the state Supreme Court found the law unconstitutional a year later, about ninety local governments voted bonds for the construction of such lines.

Contemporaries were increasingly concerned over the financial shakiness and political corruption that attended railroad subsidization. But there was more than jobbery and profiteering to the postwar railroad boom. The spreading web of trackage was a highly visible expression of a profound American desire to master space and distance—a desire fed by the postwar commitment to active government and a unified nation.

While railroads made the largest and most successful demands on government for aid, other interests turned to the state as well. Commercial and transportation conventions seeking government support flourished after the war. A number of such gatherings in 1869 called on the federal government to build canals across Michigan and Florida and to link the Mississippi and the Great Lakes so that ocean-going vessels might ply directly between the continental heartland and Europe, South America, and Asia.

Congress failed to respond to the more grandiose of these schemes. But it did vote substantial postwar rivers and harbors aid: a yearly average of $3,987,500 from 1866 to 1875, as compared to $370,100 from 1851 to 1860. And it assisted in the construction of telegraph lines and the establishment of steamship mail routes to Europe and the Far East. President Grant in 1871 asked Congress to set up a federal telegraph network operated by the Post Office Department, and Congressman James A. Garfield believed that the United States "must ultimately take control of the telegraph, or at least must have telegraph lines of its own."

States and municipalities also explored new economic roles. California in 1863 created a pioneering Board of Harbor Commissioners to own and operate a share of the city's port facilities. The Pennsylvania legislature of

1870 seriously considered assuming control of the state's telegraph system. Ben Butler observed of Massachusetts in 1871: "*our whole state government has gone into commission.*" He estimated that in the preceding decade over thirty new state boards and commissions had been created.

A new era in state data collection began in 1869 when Massachusetts created the first Bureau of Labor Statistics. Carroll Wright became the bureau's director in 1873, and made the gathering of information on the condition of workers a form of "practical sociology," designed to reveal social conditions that called for reform.

A number of states quickly followed Massachusetts's lead. At the same time, federal and state governments cooperated to establish agricultural experiment stations designed to increase the productivity of the nation's farmers. There was even an occasional glimmer of concern for the future of the country's natural resources. The 1867 Wisconsin legislature set up a commission to determine "whether the destruction of the forests of this state, now going on so rapidly, is likely to prove as disastrous to the future inhabitants . . . as is claimed by many."

Postwar economic policy was marked not only by more active government, but also by the assumption that there was an underlying harmony to the economic interests of the American people. Again, this was not a new idea, nor was it unique to the postwar years. But in the wake of a war that affirmed the strength of American nationalism and the ideal of social unity, that belief now had special appeal.

The assumption of harmonious economic interests underlay the most important postwar labor and agrarian organizations. Large numbers of American workingmen responded to the organizational lessons and the hope of social betterment that were part of the legacy of the Civil War. Major advances in unionization occurred between 1862 and 1875: more so than at any time since the Jacksonian years. The National Labor Union, the first national organization of workers, began in 1866 as a coalition of established trade unions. But it soon reached out to include unskilled as well as skilled workers, blacks as well as whites, antimonopoly associations, land and labor leagues, and the Marxist International Workingmen's Association. Charles Sumner, Wendell Phillips, and Horace Greeley were members of the NLU, and at its peak in the late sixties it claimed a membership of between 200,000 and 400,000.

The primary cause of the politically-minded NLU, and indeed of postwar organized labor in general, was the "all-absorbing subject of Eight Hours." Legislation enforcing a maximum number of hours in each workday was an issue well before the Civil War; but it peaked in appeal after 1865. Support was widespread and intense. In 1872 60,000 New York City workingmen marched to demonstrate their fealty to the cause. A shorter working day promised not only eased working conditions but also the leisure necessary for education and self-improvement. "Before this movement stops," said Wendell Phillips, "every child born in America must have an equal chance in life." Massachusetts governor Israel Washburn explained his support for a ten-hour bill for women and children in similar terms: "The assumption of our law is, that the highest intelligence of all is the highest goal of the entire people.'' The Greenback party argued in 1877 that shorter hours meant ''more leisure for mental improvement and saving from premature decay and death.'' Congress in 1868 passed a bill fixing an eight-hour day for the federal government's manual workers. Andrew Johnson's administration held that a proportionate reduction in wages was consistent with the bill's intent; but President Grant ruled otherwise in 1869.

There were other instances of heightened activity by and for labor in the postwar years. Small but active labor reform parties appeared in Massachusetts and other states. The 1872 Pennsylvania legislature repealed that state's Conspiracy Act, which impeded the organization of striking anthracite miners. A number of states passed laws regulating the hours and conditions of factory work. The first case involving a state law that limited the working hours of women and children came before the Massachusetts Supreme Judicial Court in 1876. The court readily concluded that the act was an appropriate application of the commonwealth's police power to protect public health.

Postwar publicists and intellectuals showed a new concern for the problems of labor. *Nation* editor E. L. Godkin (who later displayed a strong antilabor bias) dwelt on the community of interest that united labor and capital. He and others called for profit-sharing plans and the arbitration of disputes to modify a divisive and class-breeding wage system. Leisure, education, land ownership, profit-sharing, arbitration: these were the themes of a public discourse that assumed the inherent harmony of worker and employer.

Oliver H. Kelley, a clerk in the newly established Bureau of Agriculture, founded the National Grange of the Patrons of Husbandry in 1867. ''Everything is progressing. Why not the farmers?'' was his justification. The Grange combined a fraternal function—it was modeled on the Masons—with the goal of protecting its members ''against the numerous combinations by which their interests are injuriously affected.'' Its conception of eligible membership was as broad as that of the NLU. Besides farmers, the Grange included grain dealers and commission men, an urban, YMCA–like Pandowdy Club, and even a workingmen's affiliate, the Sovereigns of Industry. By 1874, the organization claimed 450,000 family memberships in over 20,000 local chapters, primarily in the Midwest and the South.

Many Granges were active in the movement for railroad regulation during the seventies. But the Patrons of Husbandry hardly were a society of the poor and the dispossessed. Henry George thought that the Grange attracted ''a class which . . . is the one least likely to accept radical ideas. It is warmly supported by men who hold five, twenty, fifty thousand acres of land.'' Just as organized labor drew on the higher ranks of skilled workingmen, so did the Grange consist of landed farmers rather than sharecroppers, tenants, or farm laborers. It is not surprising that the Grange, like its labor union counterparts, operated on the assumption that postwar America was a nation of harmoniously related producers, not of divided classes.

The Limits of Government

The political and economic atmosphere of postwar America changed in the 1870s, and with it the relationship of government to the economy. Just as the postwar ideal of social unity ran afoul of the realities of racial antipathy and group difference, so did the vision of an active state fostering an economy of harmonious elements succumb to the prevailing belief in laissez-faire economics and to powerful class, sectional, and individual clashes of interest.

An observer predicted in 1871: "from this time forward, it will be incumbent upon Congress to devote its time and thought chiefly to the material interests of the nation." Certainly the economy of the seventies posed new and difficult problems. Widespread unemployment, bankruptcy, and labor unrest followed the panic of 1873, but did not impede economic growth. One measure (using an 1899 productivity index of 100) is that output, which had gone from 13 in 1860 to 23 in 1870, continued to rise to 39 in 1880. A third more wage earners were in manufacturing in 1879 than a decade before; farm productivity spiraled upward. An increasingly mechanized agriculture supplying large urban and international markets; an expanding industrial plant dependent on ever more elaborate systems of transportation, marketing, and finance; growing problems of unemployment, falling crop prices, and maldistribution of wealth: this was the shape of the economy in the seventies.

It was a new and puzzling economic order. The most consequential attempt of the time to explain it, Henry George's *Progress and Poverty* (1879), perceptively focused on the paradox of want and depression in the midst of technological progress and material abundance. But George's stress on the rent that derived from land ownership as the central source of inequality ignored the complexities of industrial capitalism. And for all the boldness of his core reform—that through taxation the possession of land be vested in the community at large—his ultimate social vision was the Jeffersonian one of a small-unit, decentralized economy.

Most educated men of the time believed that natural laws controlled the market, the flow of money, and the cost of labor. New intellectual developments—social Darwinism, the rise of a statistical approach to economics—did not upset these assumptions. Simon Newcomb, an astronomer at the Naval Observatory in Washington and a pioneer in the application of mathematics to economic theory, warned that if government intervened too much in "the peculiar and limited field of political economy, nothing but harm will result." Legal tender, the protective tariff, laws limiting interest rates were instances of such improper meddling. "In the long run," Newcomb concluded, "each individual is a better judge of what is the most advantageous employment to his labor or his capital than any man or set of men can be." He was echoed by the government economist and statistician David Ames Wells, who warned against legislation that sought "the distribution of wealth by direct or indirect compulsion, or . . . diminishing the incentives for personal accumulation." William Graham Sumner, the great academic proponent of laissez-faire in the late nineteenth century, already was telling his students at Yale: "You need not think it necessary to have Washington exercise a political providence over the country. God has done that a great deal better by the laws of political economy."

The change in tone of Francis A. Walker's writings is a revealing measure of the degree to which the conventional economic thought of the nineteenth century overwhelmed the deviant views that followed the Civil War. Walker's postwar speculation as to the capacity of government and men to shape the economy was quickly subordinated to more conventional beliefs. He criticized "the weakening and distracting of the economical sense of the country, by the debasement and perversion of the national currency," and approved of those economic conditions that would "starve out the superfluous members, the poorest fruit" in the retail trades, "driving these to other more directly productive branches of industry."

Hostility to the active state went hand in hand with belief in a self-regulating economy. Politicians of the seventies were as much inclined that way as intellectuals and publicists. New York Republican leader Roscoe Conkling expressed a common attitude: "Legislation and administration will never create wealth, or pay debts or taxes. Statesmanship may do much, but all it can do is to clear the way of impediments and dangers, and leave every class and every individual free and safe in the exertions and pursuits of life. . . . Wealth can never be conjured out of the crucible of politics." James A. Garfield, who once believed that the government should operate the telegraph system, had second thoughts: to do so would be unwise, since it would increase government centralization and create an additional source of political corruption. Republican Senator Timothy Howe of Wisconsin had no use for attempts to conserve natural resources: "If a full-grown man with unimpaired intellect really thinks he needs to cut down and cut up a pine tree, and is willing to pay a fair price for it to the owner of the tree, why should he not have that privilege? What right have we to say that he shall not have it?"

This state of mind reinforced the tendency to draw back from or dismantle government intervention in the economy. The Supreme Court in 1879 found the 1870 Trade Mark Act to be unconstitutional. The 1867 Bankruptcy Act also fell victim to the pressure for federal disengagement. Its opponents concentrated on the high legal and receivership fees that came with a national system of bankruptcy, and on the fact that it exposed businessmen to the dangers of involuntary bankruptcy: a serious problem after the 1873 panic. Maine Democrats attacked the law for unduly interfering in private affairs. It was amended in 1874 to make involuntary bankruptcy more difficult, but state legislatures and business interests called for outright repeal. Though many merchants and boards of trade continued to support the 1867 law, Congress in 1878 overwhelmingly repealed it, thus leaving the bankruptcy process to the varied authorities of the states.

By the end of the seventies, general incorporation acts—which began to appear before the Civil War—had superseded individual corporation chartering in almost every state. Special interests sometimes fostered this change. In New Jersey, for example, the Pennsylvania Railroad supported general incorporation as a means of closing the door to special (and potentially more favorable) charters to new railroad lines. But the major thrust behind the general incorporation movement was the desire to rob the corporation charter of its privileged character. General incorporation did this by making chartering an almost purely administrative process, accessible to all who could meet a few undemanding requirements. New Jersey's comptroller of the treasury said of special chartering acts: "if the state is governed too much, as the world is said to be, this is one of the appliances by which the thing is done, the unnecessary multiplication of the laws." Special charters implied that the legislature had a specific regulatory authority. Near-mechanical general incorporation implied an authority so vague and diffuse as to be all but meaningless.

A policy that democratized incorporation, yet weakened the authority of government to check corporate abuses, nicely exemplified the ambiguities of political economy in the 1870s. Republicans no less than Democrats warned of corporate abuses. The Connecticut Republican platform of 1873 declared that it was the duty of the state "to be vigilant in the protection of the rights and interests of the people, against the encroachments of powerful corporations," and Garfield cautioned that corporations constituted an "Industrial Feudalism" that had to be contained. But a profound and not readily resolved tension existed between the fear of industrialism and corporate growth and the fear of government power strong enough to cope with the new economy.

The railroads were the great beneficiaries of postwar government aid; and they bore the brunt of the reaction against such aid in the 1870s. By the middle of the decade the roads were staggering beneath the weight of their breakneck postwar expansion. Fierce competition in the East and Midwest forced rates and earnings down. The overcapitalized lines, with high fixed costs, suffered also from the price deflation of the seventies. Widespread bankruptcy, reorganization, consolidation, rate discrimination, and price-fixing pools were among the consequences of these conditions. All had the effect of increasing antirailroad sentiment.

There was ample ground by the seventies for dissatisfaction with government's relationship to the railroads. That great venture in mixed enterprise the Union Pacific became a major source of grievance. The UP's troubles stemmed in large part from the fact that it was a "premature enterprise": its cost far outreached its earning capacity. There also were difficulties inherent in the federal role in the railroad's capitalization and direction. Congressmen bitterly protested the UP's inability (or disinclination) to meet its fiscal obligations to the government. But not until 1878 did the Supreme Court sustain the right of Congress to require that the UP and other transcontinental lines establish sinking funds to meet those debts. The directors and commissioners who were supposed to represent the public interest too often acquiesced in the company's policies. The Credit Mobilier scandal of 1872, in which stock in the construction company that built the UP was distributed to a number of highly placed politicians, epitomized the problems afflicting the venture: "What was labelled corruption was a result rather than a cause of the defects in the government, a mere symptom of a more pervasive flaw." The Pacific Railroad Commission finally concluded: "The sovereign should not be mated with the subject."

Railroad land grants were another fertile source of controversy. Altogether too much of this subsidy remained in undeveloped limbo, or passed into the hands of speculators: "The chief beneficiaries, of late, have been neither the government, the railroad companies, nor the settlers, but the capitalists and middle-men." The House unanimously resolved in 1870 that "the policy of granting subsidies in public lands to railroads and other corporations ought to be discontinued." The very principle of such aid now came under attack: "These grants . . . have been made on the theory that government is an organized benevolence, and not merely a compact for the negative function of repelling a public enemy or repressing disorders." During the late seventies and early eighties Congress recovered over 28 million acres because of the railroads' failure to live up to the terms of their grants.

Much of the public domain turned over to the states, and to individuals through the Homestead Act, also failed to serve its original purpose. A good deal of acreage was held off the market in hope of a future rise in value. Tenantry was on the increase (by 1880, one in five Nebraska settlers did not own the land he worked). An estimated 8 million acres in Illinois and 12 million acres in Iowa were held by speculators in 1866. The Morrill Land Grant College Act acreage moved with distressing ease into the hands of jobbers. One such, Gleason F. Lewis of Cleveland, acquired scrip from a number of northern and southern states for some 5 million acres of Morrill Act lands.

The consequences of state and local railroad aid were no less distressing. The New York educator-politician Andrew D. White's somber warning to Michigan jurist Thomas M. Cooley in 1867 came to be a widespread view: "So you [in Michigan] are at town-bonding. I don't know how you regard it, but I . . . am one of five in this body [the New York legislature] who have voted steadily against the whole batch of bonding bills last year and exemption bills this year, which last follow the first as sharks follow plague stricken ships." A substantially completed railroad network, debt-burdened towns and counties, and the hard times of the seventies squelched the postwar enthusiasm for subsidies. Governors John White Geary of Pennsylvania and John T. Hoffman of New York vetoed numbers of railroad aid bills as early as 1869; Henry H. Haight of California, under fire in 1871 for approving too many local subsidies, now condemned such aid. Most state legislatures in the 1870s limited or flatly prohibited local subsidies. The municipally owned Cincinnati Southern was leased to a private company in 1877.

The judiciary added its weight to the backlash against government subsidization. Its entering wedge was the distinction between public and private enterprise. Deciding just what constituted a public purpose bore "a far closer resemblance to the deduction of a politician than the application of a legal principle by a judge." It was a pair of policy-minded jurists, John F. Dillon and Thomas M. Cooley, who led the assault on railroad and other aid.

Dillon, who served on the Iowa Supreme Court and the Eighth Federal Circuit, condemned subsidies as "a coercive contribution in favor of private railway corporations" which violated "the general spirit of the Constitution as to the sacredness of private property." Railroads were "not organized for the purpose of developing the material prosperity of the State, but solely to make money for their stockholders." Cooley, a justice of the Michigan Supreme Court, objected to railroad subsidization on similar grounds, arguing that "a large portion of the most urgent needs of society are relegated exclusively to the law of demand and supply."

While this argument was not generally accepted with regard to railroad aid, it did serve to block other forms of subsidization. In Loan Association *v.* Topeka (1875) the Supreme Court in effect adopted the Dillon-Cooley view to void a Kansas law authorizing city aid for a prefabricated bridge factory. Justice Miller's majority opinion grudgingly conceded that railroads fell within the range of the public purpose rule. But he acidly observed: "Of the disastrous consequences which have followed its recognition by the courts and which were predicted when it was first established there can be no doubt." The Topeka attempt at government aid violated those limits "which grow out of the essential nature of all free governments," those "reservations of individual rights, without which the social compact could not exist." . . .

From Laborlords to Landlords: New Channels for Old Energies

GAVIN WRIGHT

. . . The economy that the slave South bequeathed to its successor was dispersed, agricultural, isolated from the outside world; it had a poor transportation system, few cities and towns, and undeveloped markets. The best proof that the antebellum economic structure was shaped by slavery is what happened after the war. Historians may debate "continuity" versus "discontinuity" interminably, because some things changed and some did not. But to an economic historian concerned with the *direction* of structural change, the break was dramatic. The new incentives associated with the change in property rights provide the thread that unifies a wide range of otherwise disparate economic pursuits. Formerly labor was wealth and wealth was chiefly labor; the location and investment decisions of slave owners served to augment the value of particular slaves, and the slave-owner politics served to keep the value of slave labor high in general. After

Adapted from *Old South, New South* by Gavin Wright, pp. 33–50. Copyright © 1986 by Basic Books, Inc. Reprinted by permission of Basic Books, Inc., Publishers, New York.

emancipation, the "masters without slaves" were *landlords,* whose concern was to raise the value of output per acre, treating labor as a variable cost. Since land is fixed in place, what occurred was a pronounced *localization* of economic life. Farmers now reoriented their investments and their politics toward raising land yields and land values in particular localities. Local coalitions of landowners began to push for markets, towns, railroads, and eventually factories. "Abounding resources" appeared on all sides, and publicists everywhere.

Land, Labor, and Crops

The phrase "King Cotton" dates from pre–Civil War political rhetoric, but, in fact, the South moved much more heavily into cotton growing *after* the war than before. The major symptom was the disappearance of self-sufficiency in basic foodstuffs, which had been characteristic of smaller farms as well as of slave plantations, and the initiation of large-scale imports of grains and meats from the Midwest. Table 1 shows the decline in southern corn and hog production, to little more than half of their 1860 levels.

The swing toward cotton is a familiar theme in southern history, but its nature is not so well known. There were many pressures and incentives toward specialization in cotton, but behind them all lies the fact that cotton was far more valuable *per acre* than were alternative uses of land. . . . My point here is not the net *profitability* of cotton, but the fact that cotton represents an *intensification of land use.* In other words, the higher levels of other inputs per acre is equally part of the process.

Another development that was part of the process was the *eastward* shift of the center of gravity of cotton production. Comparison of geographical patterns in 1859 and 1899 shows that the shift was not at all a

Table 1   Corn and Hogs Per Capita, Rural Population, 1860–1880

	CORN (BU.)		HOGS	
	1860	1880	1860	1880
Alabama	36.3	21.3	1.91	1.05
Arkansas	41.3	31.4	2.71	2.03
Florida	21.0	13.1	2.02	1.18
Georgia	31.3	16.6	2.07	1.05
Louisiana	32.2	14.1	1.21	0.90
Mississippi	37.7	19.5	1.99	1.05
North Carolina	31.1	20.8	1.95	1.08
South Carolina	23.0	12.8	1.47	0.68
Tennessee	49.0	44.0	2.21	1.51
Texas	28.6	20.1	2.37	1.35
Virginia	26.2	22.0	1.10	0.72
11 States	33.1	23.4	1.92	1.14
5 Deep South States	29.0	17.3	1.80	0.97

Sources: Donald B. Dodd and Wynelle S. Dodd, *Historical Statistics of the South* (University: University of Alabama Press, 1973); U.S. Census Office, *Compendium of the Tenth Census* (1880) (Washington, D.C.: Government Printing Office, 1883), 681.

continuation of prewar trends. Indeed, the phenomenon has no parallel in American agricultural history. Parts of the Piedmont that were among the oldest cotton-growing areas and had long been considered "exhausted," enjoyed a new revival in cotton growing. And formerly isolated, up-country areas that had been largely bypassed by the slave economy now found themselves pulled into cotton and its associated commercial relationships. There is no more vivid illustration of the impact of slavery on spatial patterns of economic activity. The highlight in the Southeast was the application of fertilizers, while in the plantation areas, it was the application of labor; the unifying element was the effort of landlords to raise the value of their land's product.

A major recent book by Roger L. Ransom and Richard Sutch, *One Kind of Freedom,* on the economic consequences of emancipation, emphasizes the withdrawal of black labor from field work, particularly the labor of females and children. This development was undoubtedly real and significant, but the Ransom-Sutch account conveys an impression that the increased scarcity of labor caused a rise in the ratio of land to labor. In reality the change was the opposite. In the plantation areas, per capita allotments of land to black families *declined* by more than 50 percent between 1860 and 1880, much more, in other words, than the estimated fall in labor force participation. This perspective, in turn, raises the question whether the observed labor force withdrawal was entirely voluntary. As economic historians Robert E. Gallman and Ralph V. Anderson suggest, "changes in the work proclivities of freed men may not have been altogether a product of their choice . . . [because] labor no longer had the character of fixed capital to the planter."

Because cotton requires more labor per acre than corn, the shift in crop is closely connected with the rise in the ratio of labor to land. They may be thought of as alternative ways of viewing the same phenomenon: in part, the move to cotton was a *reflection* of greater land intensity, in part it was a *cause.* The Civil War marked a fundamental break in the relative trends of farmland and farm labor in all the southern states except Texas (Table 2). It would complete the picture neatly if we could now record that the break reflected massive inflows of immigrant labor. Emancipation did, in fact, instantly transform the planters' attitude toward immigration; the former opponents became avid proponents and organizers. But these efforts were not generally successful over the long run, . . . and the bulk of the postwar population growth was natural increase. Black fertility was high both before and after emancipation, but only after the war did the South emerge as the nation's high-fertility region for the white population.

The Rise of Interior Towns and Railroads

Economists commonly explain the move into cash crops as a response to improvements in transportation and marketing facilities, and from the standpoint of the individual farmer, whose ability to influence his own market is small, this is perfectly correct. But from the perspective of the regional

Table 2   Improved Acres/Rural Population

	1850	1860	1870	1880	PERCENTAGE OF CHANGE, 1860–1880
Alabama	6.02	6.98	5.42	5.34	−23.5
Arkansas	3.72	4.59	3.94	4.67	1.7
Florida	3.99	4.86	4.27	3.91	−19.5
Georgia	7.35	8.21	6.30	5.87	−28.5
Louisiana	4.14	5.18	3.90	3.91	−24.5
Mississippi	5.78	6.57	5.30	4.76	−27.5
North Carolina	6.43	6.73	5.08	4.82	−28.4
South Carolina	6.57	6.98	4.67	4.49	−35.7
Tennessee	5.28	6.39	5.88	5.96	−6.7
Texas	3.14	4.59	3.88	8.75	90.6
Virginia	8.26[a]	8.31[a]	7.56	6.43	−22.6
11 States	6.22	6.72	5.61	5.68	−15.5
5 Deep South States	6.22	6.97	5.76	5.02	−28.0
10 States[b]	6.32	6.88	5.78	5.25	−23.7

Source: Donald B. Dodd and Wynelle S. Dodd, *Historical Statistics of the South 1790–1970* (University: University of Alabama Press, 1973).
[a] Excludes West Virginia.
[b] Excludes Texas.

economy, this amounts to explaining (as the economists would put it) one endogenous variable in terms of another endogenous variable. Both may be attributed more compactly and economically to the change in property rights and the new interest in land values. Despite all the problems of the cotton economy, the immediate postwar years saw a rush of entrepreneurship and new investment in interior towns and the transportation network.

In contrast to the antebellum experience, the South shared fully in the national railroad building boom of 1865–1875. Railroad historian John Stover wrote: "By 1866 Southern rail recovery was so complete that nearly every state had new railroad projects in mind and in some cases, work had actually begun." Of more importance than total mileage were the new locational patterns, the penetration of previously isolated counties and towns, and the creation of new trade centers at rail crossings. The use of a term like "penetration" should not, however, be taken to mean that these railroads were alien intrusions by large outside interests. In their origins, the new lines were local and regional. A survey of ten major lines and their presidents during the period 1865–1880 shows that virtually every one had strong local ties and investments in local enterprises. Railroad stock tended to be widely distributed among local holders, which often included the municipalities themselves.

The local railroads may be thought of as an early phase of the town-building activity that accelerated after the war (Figure 1). The older cotton factorage system was unable to reestablish itself because of the new competition from scores of rural merchants and country stores offering to ad-

Figure 1   Number of Urban Centers in the South, 1790–1950

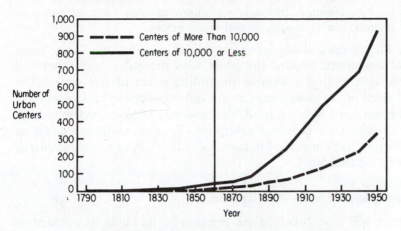

Note: Reprinted, by permission of the publisher, from Gavin Wright, "The Strange Career of the New Southern Economic History," *Reviews in American History* 10 (1982): 169.
Data from Kenneth Weiher, "The Cotton Industry and Southern Urbanization," *Explorations in Economic History* 14 (1977): 123.

vance credit, supply goods, and market cotton, at new and more accessible locations. The speed and discontinuity of this local blossoming suggests that it was in response to an equally discontinuous change, the new system of property rights.

The rise of small interior towns also refutes the notion that southern economic geography simply recorded the limited processing requirements of the staple crops. It may have looked that way before the war, but afterward many of these towns began to service the cotton crop as their main economic function. Increasingly after 1880, cotton pressing and cottonseed-oil milling came to be central activities for dozens of fast-growing cities in the cotton regions. There is no technological reason why services such as these could not have been dispersed much earlier. Their emergence after the war reflects on the one hand the channeling of entre-preneurship into location-specific activities and pursuits; on the other hand, it may be seen as a response to the new demands of local landowners for facilities that enhanced the value of their particular land holdings. Recent studies indicate that these developments had the support of landowning planters and farmers.

On this score the New South was doing no more than moving in the direction of the American mainstream. As the economist and social critic Thorstein Veblen put it:

> Habitually and with singular uniformity, the American farmers have aimed to acquire real estate at the same time that they have worked at their trade as husbandmen. . . . They have been cultivators of the main chance as well as the fertile soil.

The location of any given town has commonly been determined by collusion between "interested parties" with a view to speculation in real estate, and it continues through its life-history . . . to be managed as a real estate "proposition." Its municipal affairs, its civic pride, its community interest, converge upon its real estate values.

Crucial to the success of any such enterprise is publicity. Every small chamber of commerce flooded the mails with pamphlets and brochures boosting the local cotton market or promoting wares or real estate. The "booster" spirit of the newspapers was a reflection of the basic economic impulses behind town building itself, the tendency of townspeople to treat their communities as a common enterprise. To dismiss these editors as mere "publicists" is to miss the fundamental redirection of economic energy that followed emancipation.

Manufacturing and Resource Development

Many readers will have followed the argument thus far in its application to spatial patterns in agriculture and trade, and yet still wonder how the abolition of property rights in labor could directly stimulate mining and manufacturing, as the New South publicists claimed. Since slave labor was employed successfully in mining and even in factories, what basis could there be for the warning in the *Southern Recorder* that Northerners "will yet find out to their sorrow that the destruction of our negro property has laid the foundation for an independence that will strike fatal blows at their prosperity." The "fatal blows" were at least a half-century off, but it is a fact that the 1860s saw the largest percentage increase in southern manufacturing establishments of any decade in the nineteenth century, and after

Figure 2   Number of Manufacturing Establishments in All Southern States, 1850 to 1900

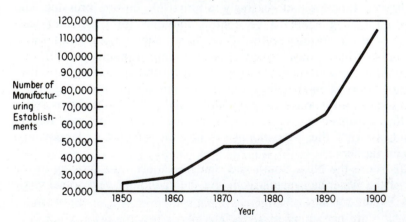

Note: Reprinted, by permission of the publisher, from Gavin Wright, "The Strange Career of the New Southern Economic History," *Reviews in American History* 10 (1982): 170.
Data from Donald B. Dodd and Wynelle S. Dodd, *Historical Statistics of the South, 1790–1970* (University: University of Alabama Press, 1973).

1880 this growth accelerated (Figure 2). There were direct links between these trends and the new localization of economic life, in at least three cases: cotton manufacturing, the fertilizer industry, and the emergence of the coal and iron region in Alabama and Tennessee.

Broadus Mitchell's 1921 classic, *The Rise of the Cotton Mills in the South,* portrayed the spread of cotton mills after 1880 as a public-spirited crusade in which philanthropic and altruistic motives predominated. Since C. Vann Woodward, no analyst (and certainly none of the many economists who have studied the rise of southern textiles) has had any good word to say for this interpretation: surely economic motives must have been foremost, and surely economic conditions must have been ripe. What these critics missed is that the early mill-building movement was an outgrowth of town building. The mills clustered around towns and transportation facilities. Their local supporters were merchants and landowners in the town and surrounding areas. Their rhetoric was boosterism, the town as a collective enterprise. And while the claimed moral/social benefits and philanthropic purposes were undoubtedly exaggerated, there was a sense in which the beneficiaries really could be seen as "the community": namely, the property holders who all stood to gain, either explicitly in the form of higher land values, or implicitly through the volume of commerce or improved local markets for cotton and farm produce.

What was most misleading about the cotton mill rhetoric was the implication that non-property-owning laborers and concern for their welfare played a major role. The enthusiasts certainly did not see *themselves* as potential mill workers, and the residents of the new mill villages quickly became objects of revulsion and fear on the part of town residents. It is also true that an industry needs more than local enthusiasm to become competitive in a national market, and the supply of cheap labor was the key to the continued growth of southern textiles over the subsequent half-century. . . . Though Mitchell may be rightly criticized for taking the rhetoric of boosterism literally, the point here is that this rhetoric was intimately linked to one of the genuine economic impulses behind the industry, and that this sprang from the abolition of slavery. This indirect connection is the element of truth in Mitchell's statement that the slave owners "shut out the average man from economic participation; but with the rise of the cotton mills, the poor whites were welcomed back into the service of the South."

The location of textile manufacturing has been historically sensitive to the cost of labor, but many other nineteenth-century industries required in close access to fuel and raw materials. An example is the manufacture of commercial fertilizers, which began in South Carolina in the 1870s in the wake of the development of large-scale phosphate mining in the lowland areas of that state beginning in 1867. The phosphate deposits which had previously been items of scientific curiosity now became objects of intense interest and mobilization. Rice planters began to engage in active prospecting and to consider offers from mining companies. One should not necessarily think of this search as a response to the new interest in fertilizers among southern farmers generally, because an active international trade in fertilizer had existed for decades prior to the war, with European markets in phosphate fertilizers from at least 1845. The new deposits were, however, rich enough to affect world and domestic fertilizer prices, so that a real economic symbiosis prevailed between the efforts of two sets of southern landowners to gain more revenue from their holdings. Though the South Carolina phosphate-fertilizer industry dwindled in the twentieth century, the fact that this occurred only confirms the mechanism at work, since it succumbed to the discovery of still richer deposits in Tennessee and Florida; both were the results of active searches.

An industrial development that combined mineral exploration and town building was the coal and iron complex in Alabama and Tennessee, which emerged as the Birmingham steel industry by the end of the century. Birmingham itself began as a real estate venture undertaken by a group of land speculators in association with officials of the Louisville and Nashville Railroad who were interested in freight. But Birmingham was only the most successful of the town-promotion schemes that dotted the northern Alabama countryside with blast furnaces, beginning almost immediately with the postbellum period. Virtually every industrial beginning may be traced to someone's attempt to make a capital gain on property in land. To be sure, much of this activity was unproductive: towns were promoted on "the merest hint of ore and coal deposits," and many of the blast furnaces were unprofitable. But the net result was that the hills were scoured for coal and iron, settlers and outside investors flowed in, and a major industrial complex emerged. It was a far cry from the economic geography of slavery, but essentially similar to the process by which the northern economy had operated all along.

Property Rights and Political Economy: Did the Planter Class Survive the War?

From the time of C. Vann Woodward's classic *Origins of the New South* (1951), historians have debated whether the old planter class was destroyed by the war, or whether they survived to continue their regional domination. Woodward's answer was that the planter class had not survived, but had given way to a new middle class of merchants, lawyers, and industrialists, and that those who did survive largely accepted the values of these new groups. The many critics of this position have made two main points: first, that the majority of large planters from before the war were able to retain their lands, and hence their positions of economic power, after the war; and second, that the conservative Redeemer governments that came to power in the 1870s were not wholeheartedly favorable to internal improvement, banks, corporations, and industrial development.

But what is the essence of the "planter class"? In the classical economic tradition handed down from Smith, Ricardo, and Marx, the concept of class is rooted in a factor of production, and class interest represents the interest of that factor. The term *planter class* applied to both slave owners and landlords obfuscates the economics of the matter; according to that standard they were all a "new class," because the interests associated with their property had changed. Whether the same individuals and families happen to be involved may be interesting sociologically, but it is really not an essential question from an economic standpoint. When writers argue that because the "old agrarian class . . . encouraged the New South" in North and South Carolina, "there was no real break in the character of the social support for the Old and New Souths," they are mixing incompatible concepts of class, much the way the New South spokesmen blended conflicting ideologies in their rhetoric. If after the revolution, the members of a class vigorously pursue goals they staunchly opposed before, in what economic sense has that class survived? Most planters may have held onto their land, but after the war, they had to deal with a nonslave labor market that was a completely new experience and that involved an "ideological capitulation" that took several years to complete. Before they were laborlords, now they were only landlords.

There is also no doubt that the political priorities of planters in economic matters changed direction after the war. A good example is the campaign to close the open range to grazing and other forms of trespassing. For generations the southern range had been open, and property rights in land given lower priority than the rights of small herdsmen and farmers to hunting, fishing, and foraging. After the war, landowners in state after state led campaigns for fence laws, stock laws, strict trespass laws, and enforcement. Often there were bitter protracted struggles between big landowners and small farmers or tenants, who regarded such measures as "calculated seriously to injure their rights and privileges." At the conclusion of one recent study, the author observes:

> The question remains as to why Alabama's range was in no way restricted until after the Civil War. There is a common belief that one of the results of America's bloodiest war was to break the grip of the great landowning class and democratize the South. It then seems odd that the planter class did not get what it had been seeking until *after* the war.

The puzzlement is resolved by the analysis of this chapter: the planters were a "great landowning class" only after the war; previously, they were laborlords more than landlords.

None of this discussion is meant to deny the force of the view, capably expressed by historian Carl Degler, that there were many threads of continuity in southern history over the whole century. The structural legacy of slavery took a long time to undo. For another three-quarters of a century, the state of world cotton demand remained the main determinant of prosperity or depression for the South. The color line remained firm long after slavery. The major continuity, however, was simply the fact of separateness. Even though the South moved toward the American mainstream in its economic behavior, it emerged in the 1870s as a low-wage region in a high-wage country, a consideration that shaped its economic future for another century.

⤸ *F U R T H E R   R E A D I N G*

Ralph Andreano, ed., *The Economic Impact of the Civil War* (1967)

Thomas C. Cochran, "Did the Civil War Retard Industrialization?" *Mississippi Valley Historical Review* 48 (1961), 191–210

Richard A. Easterlin, "Regional Income Trends, 1840–1950," in Seymour F. Harris, ed., *American Economic History* (1961), 525–547

Stanley L. Engerman, "The Economic Impact of the Civil War," *Explorations in Entrepreneurial History* 3 (Spring–Summer 1966), 176–199

Sidney Fine, *Laissez Faire and the General Welfare State: A Study of Conflict in American Thought, 1865–1901* (1956)

David T. Gilchrist, and W. David Lewis, eds., *Economic Change in the Civil War Era* (1965)

Walter T. K. Nugent, *The Money Question During Reconstruction* (1967)

Roger L. Ransom, *Conflict and Compromise: The Political Economy of Slavery, Emancipation and the American Civil War* (1989)

———and Richard Sutch, *One Kind of Freedom: The Economic Consequences of Emancipation* (1977)

Irwin Unger, *The Greenback Era: A Social and Political History of American Finance, 1865–1879* (1964)

Michael Wayne, *The Reshaping of Plantation Society: The Natchez District, 1860–1880* (1983)

Harold D. Woodman, *King Cotton and His Retainers: Financing and Marketing the Cotton Crop of the South, 1800–1925* (1968)

C. Vann Woodward, *Origins of the New South, 1877–1913* (1951)